SWEET DREAMS

also by Dylan Jones

The Wichita Lineman:
Searching in the Sun for the World's Greatest Unfinished Song

David Bowie:
A Life

Elvis Has Left the Building:
The Day the King Died

The Eighties:
One Day, One Decade

From the Ground Up:
The U2 360 Degrees Tour

When Ziggy Played Guitar:
David Bowie and Four Minutes That Shook the World

iPod Therefore I Am:
A Personal Journey Through Music

Meaty Beaty Big & Bouncy:
Classic Rock and Pop writing from Elvis to Oasis (Ed.)

Jim Morrison:
Dark Star

SWEET DREAMS

From Club Culture to Style Culture

THE STORY OF THE
NEW ROMANTICS

DYLAN JONES

faber

First published in 2020
by Faber & Faber Limited
Bloomsbury House
74–77 Great Russell Street
London WC1B 3DA

Published in the USA in 2020

Typeset by Paul Baillie-Lane
Printed and bound by CPI Group (UK) Ltd, Croydon, CR0 4YY

A CIP record for this book
is available from the British Library

ISBN 978–0–571–35343–9

2 4 6 8 10 9 7 5 3 1

For Fiona Dealey

'Sometimes, I feel the past and the future pressing so hard on either side that there's no room for the present at all.'

JULIA FLYTE, BRIDESHEAD REVISITED

CONTENTS

	Preface: Plato's Cave	1
	Introduction: *La Vie en Rose*	7
1975	Fed Up with Fandango	19
1976	Fireworks	67
1977	England's Screaming	95
1978	Transition	127
1979	The Blitz	175
1980	The Charms, Such as They Were	241
1981	Video Killed the Radio Star	311
1982	Wake Me Up Before You Whiskey-A-Go-Go	367
1983	The Cradle of Choruses	433
1984	The Pleasuredome	481
1985	Like Punk Never Happened	559
	Dramatis Personae	627
	Discography	639
	Acknowledgements	657
	Bibliography	661
	Index	663

PREFACE: PLATO'S CAVE

'Obviously I'm into myself, but I'm not walking around just saying, "Oh, everybody look at me." I wear make-up and dress this way because it makes me look better. I'm not doing it to get people to stare at me. If I wanted to do that, I could just put a pot on my head, wear a wedding dress and scream down the high street. It's easy just to get attention. People also think if you look like this, you're running away from something . . . I'm not hiding. It's a long way from hiding.'

BOY GEORGE

Who *were* all these people?

It was late March 1979, a Tuesday night, around ten thirty, and Covent Garden was dark, wet and ominously quiet. The street lights were off, there were no cars, no bodies. It was springtime, but still cold and empty, looking not unlike the set of some fifties spy movie – one of the austere black-and-white ones, before James Bond and Harry Palmer came bounding in with their smirks and their colourful ironic cool. The 'Winter of Discontent' may have just drawn to a close, with the dustmen finally going back to work, but the central London streets were still full of rotting rubbish, with food scraps spilling out of the sodden cardboard boxes, cracked plastic containers and torn black bin liners dumped by the neighbourhood restaurants. Five years ago, the famous fruit and vegetable market had moved south, over the Thames to Nine Elms, taking any hustle and bustle along with it, and the new shopping centre in the Covent Garden piazza was still over a year away (the new arcade development would have quaint, old-fashioned gas lamps at the request of the architect). So Covent Garden still felt very much like a postcode in limbo.

Tonight, though, at the eastern end of Great Queen Street, near Kingsway, a crowd of extravagantly attired night owls was gathering outside a small, nondescript wine bar, some of them clogging up the pavement in their shawls and funny-looking capes, their hairstyles making several appear far taller than they actually were, rivalling the unlit street lamps for attention in the moonlight. Their stilettos and brogues may have been wet from the puddles, but they all looked polished. There was someone who looked a little like a young Clark Gable, another wearing black leggings and a skirt under his black Lewis Leathers jacket. Others were sporting metallics and neon.

Squeezed next to a tiny secretarial agency, from the outside the Blitz looked completely unprepossessing, almost as though it was daring you to ignore it. A small sign inside asked you to keep the noise down as you left, out of respect to the local residents, although it was difficult to see where they might have lived.

To the uninitiated the place just looked like any other wine bar.

It was the people, though, who appeared to make the Blitz what it was. One by one, they slowly filed into the club, passing by the concertinaed metal grille across the front and nodding to the doorman, who appeared to be just as extravagantly dressed as they were. Actually, he seemed far more important than a doorman – often acknowledging someone he knew, and even occasionally asking someone to step aside, usually the least extravagantly dressed. Tonight, he was dressed in some weird leather jodhpurs and a massive German overcoat. 'I'm strict on the door because once people are inside I don't want them to feel they are in a goldfish bowl,' he would say, when asked by the papers. 'I want them to feel they are in their own place, amongst friends.'

And there were so-called friends everywhere. Covent Garden might have been desolate and badly lit, but then you walked into the club and it was suddenly, 'Ta-da!'

The reason they were all here was because Steve Strange – the abundantly attired doorman – and Rusty Egan – the DJ – had decided to move their regular Bowie night at Billy's – a club way over in Soho

– to a more hospitable venue. The Blitz's manager, Brendan Connolly, had apparently been struggling to fill the club towards the start of the week, and so took a gamble on the Billy's crowd. But they were all here tonight, as they were every week, as were the press, who had started to take notice too, calling them the Peacock Punks, the Cult with No Name or – worse – New Romantics.

Once inside, the Blitz actually looked a bit seedy, almost as though it hadn't been decorated since . . . well, since the Blitz. The Second World War-style austerity echoed the flatlining seventies: bare floorboards, gingham tablecloths, old film posters, a bit of wood panelling, an overhead fan, pendant lights with dusty enamel shades, and the obligatory framed pictures of Churchill. There was a small blackboard – 'All Blitz cocktails £1.95' – with a hastily drawn martini glass, complete with its own olive. There were even some old gas masks.

The people were glamorous, though. A lot of them – and there was almost no one over the age of twenty-five – looked like they'd come straight from Central Casting, extras in their very own movie. There was a girl over there with cascading copper-red hair, dressed up to look like Rita Hayworth – if Rita Hayworth had been wearing a silver spray-on cocktail dress and S&M stilettos, that is. Indeed, some of the girls were in such tight dresses they looked like egg timers. One had such defined cheekbones they appeared to be almost swollen.

Chatting over by the bar were Steve Dagger, the super-slick manager of Spandau Ballet (who would soon become the Blitz's in-house band); Robert Elms, who was the scene's most reliable Boswell; Fiona Dealey, a St Martin's fashion student and generally regarded as one of the queens of the Blitz; Chris Sullivan, soon to form a short-lived jazz–salsa band called Blue Rondo à la Turk; milliner Stephen Jones; fashion student Michele Clapton, who would one day become an Emmy-winning costume designer, working on *Game of Thrones*; and Cerith Wyn Evans, another St Martin's boy, who would go on to win the Hepworth Prize for Sculpture. So many people in this room would go on to become something or other, but for now they seemed content to pose about in their satin and tat.

Over in the corner was the society photographer Richard Young, who had descended into Covent Garden tonight, forsaking the bold-face names at Tramp, the Embassy and the Dorchester. For him, there were rich pickings here. Everyone was dressed up as though their lives depended on being photographed, swishing and pouting and looking almost like mobile sculptures. They smiled, they glowered, they knew they were in exactly the right place at the right time.

As you passed the cloakroom, you'd see a seventeen-year-old George O'Dowd, who in a few years would be known as Boy George. Ostensibly he was here to check coats, although there was always a suspicion he rifled through the pockets when everyone was on the dancefloor. He already had the razor-blade wit that would stand him in good stead when he was being besieged by the world's press in a few years' time: 'Doing that one to death, aren't you, darling?' he would say, if he thought you hadn't been adventurous enough with what you were wearing. People tried to avoid the cloakroom as much as possible.

Sitting in a huddle at one of the small, rickety, gingham-covered tables around the edge of the club were a couple of 'them', the small nucleus of London archy-farties who until the Blitz Kids arrived were the crowd who populated the paparazzi pages in *Ritz* magazine: Andrew Logan, Duggie Fields, Zandra Rhodes and Peter York, one of the greatest social chroniclers of our time, and someone who *loved* a new set of sparkling young wannabes. He liked nothing better than bending into a conversation – like George Sanders' Shere Khan – and asking one of the extravagantly dressed urchins some question or other about an arcane ecclesiastical reference, usually to the bewilderment of the recipient.

There was a real buzz about the Blitz – a word that in some circles was being said in inverted commas, almost as though its original meaning had been consigned to history – a buzz determined by 'faces'. This very poor jet set included the dancer Michael Clark, future global superstar

Sade and more St Martin's students than you could quite believe. The dancefloor was full of an intoxicatingly random mix of people: DIY futurists, make-believe nuns (the ones Peter York was talking to), rich boys trying to look poor and poor girls trying to look rich.

The Blitz was a creation myth, and those involved mostly believed it.

Tonight, it was all about divine decadence. Over by the back wall was a girl wearing a black beaded dress and a bandeau, clutching a long cigarette-holder and wielding a frown. Very *Cabaret*. A bit *Night Porter*. By the stairs, two boys were surreptitiously kissing; standing right next to them, two girls were doing the same, although rather more ostentatiously. One of them was Kim Bowen, a St Martin's student who had started to be photographed a lot with Steve Strange. Lazy journalists would one day say that Strange held a mirror up to people trying to enter the club, asking, 'Seriously? Would you let you in?' This would happen, but six years later, at Leigh Bowery's nightclub Taboo, when the notorious Mark Vaultier was on the door. Strange might have said, 'Sorry, you're not blonde enough . . .' but that was about it.

There were girls here with fire-engine-red lips, and boys with such pronounced eyeliner that it looked permanent. And as you moved back to the dancefloor, the music overwhelmed you: Yellow Magic Orchestra, Space, Ultravox, Eno, Fad Gadget, Sparks, Grace Jones, Thomas Leer, Cerrone, Psychedelic Furs and Bowie, obviously, lots of Bowie. On and on it went, a constant swirl of automated Germanic beats – hard-edged European disco, synth-led, bass-heavy . . . all very angular: Kraftwerk and Gina X, Giorgio Moroder and Donna Summer, and some early Roxy Music. Robotic sounds, anglepoise limbs and unmoving chins. In a room that tried to imagine the past, the music seemed to emanate from somewhere in the future, like some sort of benign sci-fi attendant. Sometimes there would be an ad hoc quadrille on the dancefloor, before one of the team fell about laughing.

There was a rather annoying girl called Rebecca, who liked to hold court over by the stairs – tonight talking to the young designer John Galliano. 'I'm like Rosemary,' she would say, meaning the character in

F. Scott Fitzgerald's *Tender Is the Night*. 'I'm detached!' Rebecca said something like this every week, and always cackled afterwards, throwing her head back, waiting for everyone around her to laugh. Behind her was Malcolm McLaren, his orange curls sitting uncomfortably underneath a massive oversized fedora; Midge Ure, with his pencil moustache and Oxfam film noir, and soon to take John Foxx's role in Ultravox; and Thin Lizzy's Phil Lynott, all bubble perm and leather trousers, and a throwback to when it was cool to look like a rock star, talking to a girl with a face so white she looked like she was in a silent film. 'We're the New Swells,' she screamed at a journalist from the *Daily Express*, who was actually writing this down in a notebook. Occasionally, there would be a commotion by the door, that mysterious sense that sweeps over a room when someone really famous walks in.

Outside it was all dark, but here in this tatty old wine bar the future – and the past – reigned supreme.

Did the Blitz already feel like a living museum? Completely. But the people inside were loving every second. They also seemed to be heeding the words of Dr Frank-N-Furter, the narcissistic transvestite in *The Rocky Horror Show*: 'Don't dream it, *be* it.'

INTRODUCTION: LA VIE EN ROSE

'This British future style is a dandy one – it's software rather than hardware. What they're setting up is the cellar club of the future rather than the next shuttle station. They're working on the great look, rather than the five-year plan.'

PETER YORK

As a pinch-point for the seventies, 1975 couldn't have come at a better time. Politically the UK was still in turmoil, economically the country was very much in the doldrums, and culturally we were still living in the sixties, albeit without any of the verve, and certainly none of the optimism. Defined by power cuts and the three-day week (with no television after 10 p.m.), endless public sector strikes, IRA bombings and apparent industrial collapse, the decade – which had also seen a diaspora of the underground community – appeared almost too busy to worry about culture. At home, after our evening meal we would be sent to bed in darkness, either to read by candlelight or listen to the radio (Radio Luxembourg, always). There was also double-digit inflation, which had reached 20 per cent, and the miserable economic climate was reflected by a country still littered with outside lavatories, derelict docklands and townscapes blighted by undeveloped bomb sites, thousands of wartime prefabs and the rapid emergence of new brutalist housing estates.

It wasn't exactly a dystopian nightmare – the extraordinary success of Queen's baroque epic 'Bohemian Rhapsody' yet again underscoring the British public's appetite for the absurd and the excessive – but in 1975, Britain was largely stagnant and dull.

This was the year forty-three people were killed in an underground train crash at Moorgate; the year Biba finally went out of business, closing its Kensington store. Like New York at the time, London was unsafe, economically undynamic and physically fraying, while provincial Britain, in the words of the poet Lavinia Greenlaw, 'was a place of boredom and violence, suspicious of difference, ambition and pleasure'.

Between the late forties and the mid-sixties, a cultural and lifestyle revolution had swept through Britain, fundamentally changing the social landscape. By 1975, however, that landscape was in stasis. The future prime minister, James Callaghan, then foreign secretary, wrote in his memoirs: 'Our place in the world is shrinking; our economic comparisons grow worse . . . sometimes when I go to bed at night I think if I were a young man I would emigrate.' In his 2009 book *When the Lights Go Out: Britain in the Seventies*, Andy Beckett said declinism 'darkened the work of artists, novelists, dramatists, film-makers and pop musicians. It soured foreign commentary on Britain . . . And it shifted in tone: from the anxious to the apocalyptic.'

By 1975, the country was not just heading for a very particular economic crisis, it was still a conflicted territory, as the collapse of the IRA's 1974–5 ceasefire had triggered a new wave of terrorist bombings. Nineteen seventy-five would also be the year the Conservatives would choose Margaret Thatcher as their first female leader, the year just over 67 per cent of the electorate supported the Labour government's campaign to stay in the Common Market, the year North Sea oil started to flow, and the year that saw the first episode of *Fawlty Towers*. This year there would also be radical new laws to end the battle of the sexes, with legislation introducing a woman's right to equal pay and status in the workplace. The Sex Discrimination and Equal Pay Act was designed to prevent women being paid less than their male counterparts, and was introduced to coincide with the end of International Women's Year. Sex discrimination by employers would now be illegal, unless they employed five people or fewer, as would any form of bias by landlords, finance companies, schools and restaurants. Elsewhere, Charlie Chaplin was knighted, Saigon surrendered, Arthur Ashe won the men's singles title at Wimbledon, Franco's thirty-six-year reign was brought to an end in Spain, and

Elizabeth Taylor and Richard Burton thought the time was right to remarry.

But it was the economic and cultural drought which seemed to define the UK, a country caught between a past that refused to die and a future that had stubbornly refused to arrive. So it was perhaps no surprise when some people decided to take matters into their own hands.

Decades usually take a good few years before their character starts to emerge, and this was certainly the case with the seventies, a decade which even by its midpoint was having trouble sustaining itself. Towards the end of 1975, however, things began to change. The first stirrings of what would eventually become punk started to emerge on the outskirts of Chelsea, as a malcontent shopkeeper called Malcolm McLaren busied himself with his Situationist game plan, thinking up ways he could draw attention to his King's Road clothes shop – principally by launching an insurrectionary version of the Bay City Rollers. On 6 November, McLaren's Sex Pistols (in his mind, a kind of sexed-up New York Dolls) played their first concert, at St Martin's School of Art, on the Charing Cross Road. At precisely the same time, disaffected soul boys (and girls) were starting to experiment with the way they dressed, keen to pursue slightly more esoteric worlds. Their heads had been turned by David Bowie and Bryan Ferry's Roxy Music, both of whom had started to experiment with dance music. Already adored by the rock fraternity, Bowie and Ferry became revered by the dancers who frequented the standout southern clubs (such as the Goldmine in Canvey Island, the Royalty in Southgate and the Lacy Lady in Ilford) when they both adopted the rigours of the dancefloor – Ferry with 'Love Is the Drug' and 'Both Ends Burning', from the 1975 Roxy Music album *Siren*, and Bowie with the 'plastic soul' of *Young Americans*. Long before such things became pejoratives, Bowie and Ferry were seen as arbiters of cool, *indicators*, men who understood the benefits of looking sharp in both a retro and a modern sense, and who had purposefully rejected the ideological orthodoxies of the world of rock. Neither Bowie nor Ferry wore denim.

Between them, the punks and the soul boys kick-started a continuum of rapidly morphing pop trends that would result in one of the most creative and combustible periods of post-war pop culture, a decade of genuine animated idealism. What happened between 1975 and 1985 – in terms of music, style, design and pop-cultural perspective – would have a lasting effect, and these ten years would be remembered for everything from gender-bending synth duos and the emancipation of gay pop to the globalisation of the entertainment industry, a publishing and design revolution, and widespread social upheaval.

This was a real pop-cultural epoch, one defined by urgency as much as variety; it was a very British one at that, as this rich seam of creativity was almost exclusively UK-based. Not since the sixties had Britain been so golden – not in terms of creativity, anyway. And at its heart, bathed in a soft tungsten glow, were the New Romantics, a small batch of young London-based creatives who, initially through the way they looked, and eventually by how they behaved and what they produced, soon became the toast of the town, both here and abroad.

How this came about warrants attention.

Punk. Soul. New Romantics. Synth pop. What worlds they were. *Sweet Dreams* is the story of how these worlds and narratives interlinked, and how they were all undeniably helixed together.

The original New Romantic scene revolved around self-expression, being a platform for identity. Today we are all encouraged to be who we are, feel who we are, show who we are and exaggerate who we are; this certainly wasn't the case in 1978, when this particular reinvention of teenage rebellion was considered by most to be simply a fashion play, all about dressing up and little else. However, over forty years since a couple of hundred people started dressing up in order to show off in a tacky theme bar in Covent Garden, the way we look is now intrinsic to who and how we are. We live in a bespoke world. In the tailor-made twenty-first century, we not only choose our own clothes, careers and narcotics, we can also choose what's between our legs. In the eighties, choice, the free market and rampant individualism were all vilified as the trappings of virulent capitalism, but they were an inevitable stepping stone to the fractious libertarian world we live in now.

Death confers dignity on the famous for only a short time, as within a year or so their reputations begin to dip. Then, as the wheel turns, so time reconfers dignity and importance, and the dead are rediscovered and reappraised, their legacies balanced out.

It's often the same with decades. 'The recent past always seems tawdry and passé in comparison to the more distant past, and this applies to the people who were celebrities in it,' wrote A. C. Grayling. 'Look at images of the people and fashions in the eighties and compare them to images from the fifties; the latter seem far more interesting because more remote and magical. The eighties just seem old hat. While the past moves through old hat to its magical stage, the personalities in it have to suffer the same fate.'

The eighties have changed, though, and the farther away they become, the more interesting, the more complex they appear. In Britain, the decade has been repeatedly rubbished, held responsible for the divisive economic and social policies of Margaret Thatcher and derided for its celebration of the trivial, the shallow and the expensively produced. But the farther away we get from it, the more the decade is reassessed, its legacies re-evaluated and regraded. The farther it disappears into the distance, the fonder we feel about it.

As Bob Stanley, the journalist and Saint Etienne member, says: 'Where the Clash had been terrified that *Top of the Pops* would contaminate them, singer Adam Ant recognised it could amplify his music and challenge his fans. As Malcolm McLaren had before him, Adam understood that the formats and possibilities of mainstream broadcasting, from *Top of the Pops* to *Smash Hits*, were not only available but wide open, and had huge and thrilling expressive potential. New pop took punk's self-determination and sense of urgency and married them to values that post-punk had spurned: flash, cash, high theatre, high chart positions, great image. Like French new wave cinema, it was born from a love of pop history: for Godard read Horn, for Antoine Doinel read George O'Dowd.'

Tom Wolfe may have identified the seventies as the Me Decade, but the idea really came to fruition in the eighties. The extraordinary transformation of lifestyles occasioned by the sixties confronted a generation with decisions they had never been asked to make before – decisions of taste. In the eighties, those decisions became even more fundamental as society became more market-driven, and choice became a lifestyle decision in itself.

The eighties is a much maligned decade, often referred to only in a pejorative way. It's the designer decade, the reductive decade of style over content, the decade of bad pop and terrible clothes, of shoulder pads and ra-ra skirts, of yuppies and Filofaxes, glass bricks and the matt black bachelor pad. The eighties is often painted as the divisive decade, a decade of no redeeming features.

Yes, but also no. During the eighties, the media went style crazy as London became a crucible of self-expression. Club culture produced a generation of show-offs, people as desperate to be photographed as the papers were desperate to feature them. Everyone wanted to buy into the dream, especially pop stars. Club culture was trendy, and there was no better photo opportunity than the bar at the right nightclub. It was also deemed cool to have more than a cursory idea of what was 'going on'. Towards the end of 1985, I wrote a long and rather overwrought piece in *i-D* about a silly Italian youth cult called the Paninari. In a style that now seems rather overexcited, I catalogued the Paninari obsession with casual sportswear, their predilection for riding little red motorbikes through the streets of Milan and hanging out in sandwich bars (hence the name: a *panino* is a bread roll), and, of course, their reactionary prepubescent machismo. Acting on disinformation, I also wrote that the Pet Shop Boys – who were apparently big fans of Paninari fashion – had even recorded their own paean to the cult, called, simply enough, 'Paninaro'. As the song eventually appeared a few months later, I thought nothing of it. Until about three years later, that is, when I read an interview with the Pet Shop Boys in *Rolling Stone* magazine. They had read my piece. 'We read that we'd recorded this song,' said Pet Shop Boy Chris Lowe (the laconic one). 'Of course we hadn't, but we thought it was such a good idea that we soon did.'

Style culture actually became the binding agent of *all* that was supposed to be cool. Catwalk models were no longer simply clothes horses and were rechristened 'supermodels'. Fashion designers were sanitised for everyday consumption, so they could appear on early-evening television shows. Pop stars were no longer considered to be council-house Neanderthals; they were suddenly elevated to front-page sex symbols whose every word was copied down, amplified and endlessly repeated in the gossip columns of the national press. It was a sartorial melting pot, a visual melange of crushed-velvet miniskirts, high heels and lipstick. It was almost as if there was a blueprint for the celebrity interface with the fashion industry, one that determined that the best place to be at any given time was propping up the bar in the Wag Club.

If the seventies in Britain had suggested that the country was a shrinking state on the verge of collapse – imagined as a vitrified landscape full of abandoned, broken machinery – in the eighties all anyone could talk about was growth. The nationalised industries may have been taking a pounding, unemployment may have been rising as quickly as the shiny new buildings in Canary Wharf and the poorer pockets of the country may have been starting to become disenfranchised as the disparity between rich and poor began to escalate, yet everywhere you looked things were getting bigger, grander, more expensive. As Alwyn W. Turner said so eloquently in *Rejoice! Rejoice! Britain in the 1980s*: 'Models mutated into supermodels, supermarkets into superstores, cinemas into multiplexes. Building societies became banks and humble record shops developed delusions of grandeur, turning themselves into megastores. High streets were eclipsed by out-of-town shopping centres, and the number of television channels, newspapers and magazines simply grew and grew. If something wasn't already big, then advertising – one of the great growth industries of the time – could make it seem so, or else the overblown price tag would suffice, as with the rise of nouvelle cuisine or the trend away from drinking in pubs towards bottled beers in bars.'

Gentrification had started in earnest, with London undergoing a kind of mass architectural disfigurement with postmodern steel and glass. Repositioning was everywhere. You only had to look at the 1982 advertising campaign for Stella Artois to understand how the eighties was starting to define itself. The 'Reassuringly Expensive' slogan was created by Frank Lowe, formerly of Collett Dickenson Pearce, who had worked on the Stella brand in the seventies, and who took the account with him when he left to form his own agency in 1981. Within a year, he had turned a considerable negative (the beer's high alcohol content made it more expensive due to greater duty) into a positive, convincing the consumer that because it was more expensive than its competitive set, it was better. This rationale would start to be applied to everything, from clothes and cars to apartments and holidays, from food and drink (the more expensive the cocktail, the more we wanted it) to art and design. Taste was suddenly an intangible it was acceptable to buy; so what if you didn't know anything about white leather Italian furniture or Scandinavian kitchens, you could simply buy the most expensive and be done with it.

Taste as a commodity became big business in the eighties, as it developed into a growth industry in the media. Magazines, newspapers and lifestyle television programmes aimed not just at teenagers hungry for culture, but also at avaricious adults who had enough money to buy into the good life. If, in the sixties, taste was something discovered by the few, in the seventies, it became something owned by the few; in the eighties, taste started to become not only something that most people wanted, but something a considerably larger number of people could afford.

At least, this was what we were told.

The illusion of affluence played an enormous part in the designer-lifestyle boom of the early-to-mid-eighties, creating a divisive culture in which the yuppie dream was allowed to thrive as though it were a religion. If you were on the right side of the fence, then the party went on all night.

Perhaps predictably, 'designer' became a pejorative almost as quickly as it became a prefix, while the consumers of anything 'designer' were brutally lampooned. It would become death by acronym, with yuppies the first urban tribe, Young Urban Professionals whose hobby was money, their aim self-fulfilment, surrounding themselves with the accoutrements and occupational hazards of the newly empowered: the waterfront conversion, the better-buffed personal trainer, the foreign domestic help and the Golf GTI convertible with the personalised number plate. If you didn't have a Barcelona chair, a Richard Sapper anglepoise or a Braun shaver, then there was really no point in turning up at the office. And, like *The Face* said, all was black, matt black, in the matt black dream home: this was the matt black dream conversion, with a black hi-fi on a black shelf and black clothes in the black wardrobe. Having parked your black BMW in the underground car park, you settled down on a black sofa (bought from Habitat, or maybe the Conran Shop), your sublime good taste confirmed, and then read with horror the red bank statement.

Of course, as you settled into your evening, perhaps reclining in a tubular steel and leather Breuer chair, you would be listening to a Sade CD. As a metaphor for the eighties, the CD is as good as any other. Like Madonna, the black Gucci loafer, MTV, privatisation, shoulder pads or Terry Farrell's truly dreadful postmodern architecture (such as MI6's headquarters in Vauxhall, for instance), the CD was the defining symbol of the age, an age when presentation wasn't just paramount, it was pretty much everything. The compact disc compartmentalised its contents, cleaned them up, washed behind their ears and then dressed them up for the market; it digitally improved them, shrunk them and then enshrined them in a transparent pocket-sized jewel case. Albums were messy things and didn't fit in with the ideas the decade had about itself. Albums were OK if you went back to a flat filled with grey metal shelving units, all the better for showing off your adolescent good taste. But having good taste in music didn't matter as much in the eighties as it had in the seventies; taste had changed anyway, drifting off to the borders and corners, diversifying in extraordinary ways. But even music that determinedly originated in the dark, on the edges of society, or was designed to appeal to those for whom music had become too commercial, too blemish-free, even this was codified, commodified. The CD made a commodity out of everything.

During the eighties, much like the seventies, you weren't allowed to be on the other side of the political divide. Being the most divisive prime minister in living memory made Thatcher the most visible manifestation of right-wing authority the so-called counter-culture had ever had, at least in Britain. To the British, she was that generation's Nixon, a wall on which to project all of society's evils. The country went through transformative changes, as Thatcher's belief that Britain's great nationalised industries could be replaced by service industries such as banking and insurance became a manifesto. What she will never be forgiven for was the brutal manner in which this was carried out.

The country was becoming a very different place under her leadership, and the way she rapidly took ownership of Britain's psyche was more than remarkable. And even by 1985, the country had changed dramatically since her arrival in Downing Street. However, as Alwyn W. Turner points out, it would be a mistake to conflate these two things, 'for it was by no means certain that the changes that Britain went through were in the direction she wished. Rather it was as though she had unlocked a Pandora's box and released forces into a society over which she had little or no control. She called for a return to thrift and good housekeeping, and presided over a massive increase in credit card and mortgage indebtedness; she sought to encourage the entrepreneurial spirit, and saw the City of London overrun by what detractors viewed as a generation of spivs and speculators; she wished to reverse the effects of sixties permissiveness and found herself in a country . . . where home video recorders and satellite television made pornography ever more available.'

For many, the eighties remains a binary decade, one that penalised those who weren't caught by society's buffers, and which celebrated success at all costs. 'I wouldn't wish the eighties on anyone,' declared the late Derek Jarman. 'It was a time when all that was rotten bubbled to the surface.'

As the period drew to a close, critics were quick to dismiss what had just been and gone, criticising style culture for its lack of intellectual nerve. Jon Savage once said that we would look back upon this time and say: 'They fiddled while the world was burning. Then they put the burning world into car adverts.'

However, from where we sit today, the eighties looks far more benign, a decade of cultural experimentation and sexual emancipation, and the start of a prolonged period of bohemianism, one that in many respects is still with us. It was a decade of cultural deregulation.

What do the people in *Sweet Dreams* mean in relation to their era? How important are they to the cultural mission creep of the period? I'd say they are vital, crucial, in part responsible for one of the most creative periods of post-war culture, helping frame a decade of wildly diverse accomplishment. Perhaps these years – these ten brimming years – were a series of happy accidents. Perhaps. Consequence, then, from inconsequence.

The alchemical relationship between this period and its custodians was not based exclusively on material success, in spite of what critics tend to say. There are so many people who were emancipated by the period and who thrived in other ways. What few appreciated was that the eighties were also a time of great experimentation, a time when people felt liberated enough to explore their own personal journeys by creating alternative communities (many of the principals involved with the Blitz club are still going strong today, clubbing in their fifties and sixties), operating very much on the margins of society or living in a pansexual environment that pre-dates the sexual fluidity that is so much a part of contemporary culture. Not everyone wanted to be a pop star, not everyone wanted to reach for the stars; some simply used the period to enliven and enrich their own lives, refusing to be anaesthetised by other people's. It was almost a moral obligation. The eighties weren't just about androgyny, and in a sense they embraced polymorphous perversity in a way it had never been embraced before, an exploration of self that hadn't been as intense since the sixties. This was a new type of bohemianism, one empowered by a certainty and an optimism that was only fleeting back in the so-called Swinging Sixties.

The ten years between 1975 and 1985 were one large invitation, an unregulated playpen that encouraged entrepreneurial freethinkers as well as unrelenting hedonists. Norman Mailer once defined democracy as a society in which you can head as far as you can into the distance and wait for somebody to stop you. For many, this was the eighties, a decade that actually started in 1975.

The New Romantic period, however loosely you define it, certainly produced a cavalcade of extremely singular artists, many of whom were keen exponents of what would briefly be known as 'white European dance music': Spandau Ballet, Duran Duran, Soft Cell, the Eurythmics, Depeche Mode, Ultravox, Simple Minds, the Normal, the Human League, Heaven 17, Visage, Orchestral Manoeuvres in the Dark, Tubeway Army (and then Gary Numan), Yazoo, Classix Nouveaux and Japan. As the eighties developed, the genre became even more splintered, resulting in groups such as Bow Wow Wow, ABC, Funkapolitan, Culture Club, Haysi Fantayzee, Blue Rondo à la Turk, Tears for Fears, Wham! and a regeared Adam and the Ants. Some happened as a direct consequence of the moment (Spandau, Duran, Culture Club), some morphed into more glittery versions of themselves (Simple Minds, Psychedelic Furs, Japan, etc.) and others were grouped together simply out of happenstance (including those involved with Daniel Miller's Mute Records, for instance).

For a while, Sweet Dreams were made of this.

1975
FED UP WITH FANDANGO

'What happened at the beginning of the seventies with guys like myself and Bryan Ferry and Brian Eno, we were all pretty excited about letting people know what went into our work, that we weren't all trying to be Chuck Berry. I know Ferry was a huge Dada fan, for instance. He even did an album called *The Bride Stripped Bare*. Eno and I went, "He shouldn't do that," thinking we should have done it first.'

DAVID BOWIE

Jason Cowley (*journalist*): It is hard now to recall just how drab and defeated Britain was in the seventies, that wretched decade of strikes and power cuts, of football violence and casual racism, of macho unionism and rampant inflation, of charmless class conformity and bad food. There was David Bowie and Roxy Music, and later in the decade, Kraftwerk from Germany began making strange and difficult 'electronic' music using the new technology of the synthesizer. But on the whole, before punk smashed the social consensus, there was not much to look forward to if you were young and born outside the metropolitan loop.

Steve Dagger (*manager*): I was brought up in Holborn, so the West End was my playground, but the early seventies were very much in the shadow of the sixties. I used to go to Carnaby Street to use the swimming pool in Marshall Street, so I was always in the area, thinking that the sixties were one great big party, but worried I'd missed it. I wasn't old enough to be part of the sixties – I was born in 1957 – and by the time I was a teenager, Swinging London had moved to LA or Rome, as those people certainly weren't in London. As a teenager, you were left looking around for some kind of attitude that you could cling on to, as culturally the decade was very confused. There were fashionable clothes, but there was no ideology. We had David Bowie and Roxy Music, and glam was quite interesting, but it wasn't the kind of thing you could buy into. Then there was southern soul, but soul was all about imported American music. I went everywhere looking for the next big thing. I went to rock gigs at the Rainbow and Hammersmith Odeon and thought that was pretty dull. I went to jazz-funk venues like Countdown in Wells Street and the Global Village in Charing Cross, but I didn't feel I was part of any one thing. I felt cheated, frustrated that there wasn't a UFO club or a Scene club, a summer of love or a mod explosion. There was nothing.

David Bowie (*icon*): At the time, Bryan Ferry was my only real rival.

For those who cared about such things, in the early seventies, David Bowie and Bryan Ferry were the only two British rock stars who seemed capable of connecting with their public in a forward-facing way. They had managed to co-opt the fringes of a generation who weren't content with the orthodoxies of the rock milieu, and would be cited as harbingers of change for the rest of the decade in one way or another. In 1975, they both adopted the doctrines of the disco: Bowie (who at the time tended to be slightly ahead of the curve) in February with his single 'Young Americans', and Ferry's Roxy Music with 'Love Is the Drug', from the Siren *album, in December (Nile Rodgers says that John Gustafson's bassline was a big influence on Chic's 'Good Times'). Bowie and Ferry were the lodestars of '75: the* Siren *tour featured Ferry and his two glamorous backing singers costumed in khaki GI chic, inspired by Elvis Presley and created by the fashion designer Antony Price; Bowie, meanwhile, adopted a hennaed wedge and plastic sandals. Both were mercilessly copied. 'Fans dressed for the concerts with meticulous attention to detail,' says the writer Michael Bracewell, 'creating a total look that mirrored the super-stylised spectrum of imagery that Roxy Music merged into a single artistic statement.' Their devotees were so attentive, so analytical in their dress, that in*

1973 the NME *ran a review of the audience at a Roxy gig, rather than the concert itself.*

Like Ferry, Bowie didn't do sequels. On the 1974 Diamond Dogs *tour of Canada and North America – which began in Montreal on 14 June – his fans went berserk. He hadn't appeared live in the country since the previous March, and in that time had become the kind of pop star who attracted limpet-like adoration. The concert-goers on the* Diamond Dogs *tour seemed obsessed. Having not toured the US for over a year, Bowie's followers were expecting him to turn up on stage wearing his Ziggy clothes; instead he appeared wearing baggy pleated trousers, braces, a white cotton shirt and black ballet pumps, with his hair slicked back. During the show's intermission – a convention borrowed from the theatre – the more heavily made-up audience members could be seen heading for the bathrooms, where they would wet down their spiky hair, rub off the lightning bolts from their faces and alter their clothing. The obsessives would stalk him at the hotels on the tour, hanging out in the lobby, forcing themselves into the elevators, stealing Bowie's hairs from the back seat of his limo parked outside and occasionally emptying his cigarette butts from the car's ashtray. If they couldn't sleep with him, other souvenirs would have to do.*

Marco Pirroni (*guitarist*): Roxy were more down to earth than Bowie in a strange sort of way because it all was based on fifties and sixties pop art and you could sort of hear or understand all the references. As a family we'd moved from Camden Town to Harrow, and Roxy seemed to speak to the suburbs more than anywhere else. We all wanted to escape into something that wasn't really there, so you kind of had to create it. I also loved the whole *American Graffiti* thing and Sha Na Na. I loved the look of the fifties. I wanted a pair of brothel creepers, and this small news item on TV mentioned a Teddy boy shop on the King's Road run by Malcolm McLaren. So that's where I went. I bought a pair of white pointy brothel72 creepers with the buckskin tops. This was 1973.

Robert Elms (*broadcaster*): I started going to clubs when I was fifteen, in 1975. I was living in Burnt Oak, on the outer fringes of the Northern Line, and started going to a local club called the Bandwagon in Kingsbury, sneaking in on a Friday night with my bigger mates. It was very suburban, but real hardcore funk – War, the Fatback Band, all that sort of stuff. I remember dressing exactly like Bryan Ferry, with the GI outfit and the tie tucked in, and a cap. I actually got sent home from school for wearing pale-blue pegs, a cap-sleeved T-shirt and a pair of plastic sandals. I think my pegs were a rip-off pair; they should have been from Lord John or Take Six, but mine were from Wembley market. The grammar school where I went was divided, as there was a little group of us who were into soul, and the other guys who were into greatcoats and prog rock. We were buying jazz-funk records on import at Contempo. This was around the time of *Young Americans*, when Bowie started to dress like us. It was an affirmation, if anything, as suddenly he had hair like us and was wearing clothes like us. I grew my hair in a nice symmetric wedge, along with some of the boys at the Bandwagon.

Neil Tennant (*pop star*): In 1975, I was finishing my time at North London Polytechnic, where I was studying history. About a week after doing my finals, I got a job as the production editor of Marvel Comics. Ever since I was a child I had wanted to write songs and be a pop singer, so every night I would go home and write singer-songwriter stuff and tape it on a little cassette recorder. I regarded that as a parallel career. I didn't go to many discos or concerts, but I could afford to buy LPs, as we called them. So, in 1975, I would've bought *Born to Run* and *Young Americans*. That's probably all I could afford to buy. I wasn't part of any tribe, but I was a Bowie fan and a Bryan Ferry fan.

Peter York (*cultural analyst*): Nineteen seventy-five was the cusp, wasn't it, the cusp of everything? In 1975, I had just signed up to *Harpers & Queen*, where I was about to start as their style editor, a new thing. My first piece was about the New Seriousness, but then I got going into the things I liked to do, like the funny people of New York and so on. And at the same time, I had a proper job as a licensed boy executive for my then wonderful management consultancy, SRU. At the time, I hadn't written any journalism, but I had a girlfriend who was a journalist who got swept up into *Harpers & Queen*, and because of that I met the editor Ann Barr and thought, 'I can do this job.' So she let me write about things the *Harpers & Queen* readership wasn't interested in, like Sloane Rangers and German disco music and eventually punk. That hadn't happened yet, but I loved Bowie and Roxy and the big black acts of the Earth, Wind and Fire variety. By 1974, I'd somehow met Bryan Ferry, who by this time had been sort of co-opted by the Notting Hill set, and I thought he was a completely wonderful person. You'd go to see Roxy Music and everyone would be dressed as Bryan, which was absolutely fascinating. And you could see that thing of people following as closely as they could their great heroes, and there was already that thing that Robert Elms described later as pale faces and white socks, which is a combination of art students and aspiring working-class kids of all kinds, from all sorts of regions. Fabulous audiences. My eyes were out on stalks for the audiences. There was a lot of home-grown ingeniousness, a lot of theatricality, a very art-school feeling. It was all about Bowie and Roxy and their worshippers worshipping them.

David Bowie: With *Young Americans*, I sunk myself back into the music that I considered the bedrock of all popular music: R&B and soul. I guess from the outside it seemed to be a pretty drastic move. I think I probably lost as many fans as I gained new ones.

Robert Elms: I saw my first real soul boy on a London District Line underground train in about 1975. This creature's clothes were shocking, the very antithesis of seventies excess, but it was his hair that really got you: it was both long and short at the same time, heavy on top and falling over one eye, but karate-chop short at the neck. It was like a lop-sided pudding basin but streaked as if this boy had spent some time in the sun.

The wedge had been invented by Trevor Sorbie, a hairdresser at one of Vidal Sassoon's London salons, in 1974. Originally created specifically for girls, it was quickly adopted by their boyfriends, who flaunted their newly acquired aerodynamic masterpieces in nightclubs from Ilford to Southend (along the A13, the backbone of British club culture). Co-opted by the soul fraternity as a tonsorial flag, the wedge became one of soul-boy culture's most durable emblems.

Quite unlike all those 'rock culture' haircuts (long, dank and dirty), the wedge was, says Peter York, 'the uniform for the southern English, club-going, working-class soul stylist'. As pop archivists are always keen to point out, the mid-seventies were clearly polarised, and in the cathedrals of dance along the A13, the wedge-wearing funkateers enjoyed the euphonious delights of imported American soul music; third-generation boogie and progressive pomp rock just didn't get a look-in. On the southern soul scene, your clothes were as important as the steps you traced on the dancefloor, but neither was as important as your wedge. York describes its construction in detail: 'When they first cut it and blow it dry, they keep brushing the sides flat, pushing them back underneath the long bits at the crown so the bob part of it is resting on the pushed-back horizontal part. The stylists' trick then is to let it go, so it springs out, the long bits bouncing out on top of the side, all that bouncing volume disappearing into razored flatness, with nothing hippie or impromptu around the neck.'

Graham Ball (*club entrepreneur*): I started clubbing when I was fourteen, going to see two DJs at the Park Hotel in Hanwell, Wild Walt Brown and Steve Maxstead. While one of them put a song on, the other would juggle knives over the decks. Everyone was drinking, and everyone was under sixteen, which shows you how dysfunctional things were at the time concerning licensing and young people. That was our youth club. We were all soul boys, and when Bowie got his wedge, it made us all want one.

Stephen Jones (*milliner*): In 1975, I was at High Wycombe School of Art doing a foundation course. I was seventeen and obsessed with David Bowie and Roxy Music. I had been heavily into glam rock, but I wore a lot of suits at the time. I was living in Maidenhead, in Berkshire, with my parents, and had just come down from the Wirral in Cheshire, where I was boarding at Liverpool College. Wycombe had a fantastic reputation because as well as doing foundation, the town was also the centre of the furniture and textiles businesses. When I arrived at the college, I realised there were lots of other people who were good, if not better than me, at art, at communicating. That was quite a wake-up call. So I really didn't know what I was going to do. I did two-week blocks of textiles and ceramics and interiors and car design and all those different things, and then, finally, fashion.

David Bowie: My Young American was plastic, deliberately so, and it worked in a way I hadn't really expected, inasmuch as it really made me a star in America, which is the most ironic, ridiculous part of the equation. Because while my invention was more plastic than anyone else's, it obviously had some resonance. Plastic soul for anyone who wants it.

Bryan Ferry (*icon*): You needed to visually carry the mood of the music. A couple of times we had grandiose-looking stage sets – trying to do something reasonably interesting within the quite strict confines of what you can do on a stage. We once had a huge eagle and a rather de Chirico open piazza. For *Country Life* [the album before *Siren*], there were banners, and I wore some military stuff which Antony [Price] designed: a black tie and a strap across the chest. The banners seemed to go with this fascistic look, which was tongue-in-cheek but quite good to look at, I thought. I can't remember spending very much time over it, to be honest, other than saying, 'Why don't we do it like this?' For a few years we were very popular, and there was a very strong following, not only in London, but also in the provinces and internationally. Maybe the fact I come from a provincial town [Washington, County Durham] also struck a chord with the northern industrial cities, where we always seemed to have a really strong following – with boys as well as girls. You did see people in the audience dressing up like us, and therefore each concert did have a sense of occasion. There were devotees. We didn't really dictate a style so much as favour certain styles. It was a way of playing around with style, rather than defining one. Generally, I would favour tailored clothes as a rule, thus ending up looking like a character from a movie or something. We were perhaps the most cinematic-looking band.

Bowie's influence on the punk generation, and on the Blitz Kids who came in their wake, is well documented. Bryan Ferry's influence at the time was no less important, although it has dimmed a little over the years. Ferry was the Tyneside proto-lounge lizard who, along with Bowie and Marc Bolan, helped invent the feel of the early seventies. Mixing the glamour of nostalgia with edgy modernity is nothing special now, but Ferry experimented with this long before most. When Roxy Music first appeared at the very start of the seventies, they were so different from their peers that they may as well have been from outer space. Roxy's music was certainly arresting – pop-art Americana mixed with searing R&B and avant-garde electronics – but it was their clothes that really turned heads. Leopard and snakeskin. Gold lamé. Pastel-pink leather. At a time when most pop groups thought long hair, cowboy boots and denim were the height of sartorial elegance, Ferry and his band walked into the world looking like renegade spacemen. The first Roxy Music album was like a whirlwind of playful decadence, a members-only nightclub, with Ferry as the quintessential playboy making a bumblebee exit, buzzing from table to table on his way out.

Roxy were a montage of hot music, giddy, drunken laughter, stoic, almost minatory posing and nightclub reverie. The music took the sweet old rock'n'roll melodies and twisted them like hairpins. This was a seemingly classless world full of bright lights and dark alleys, of loose women wearing tight dresses and bad men wearing good suits. A glamorous world etched with danger, a full-scale escape from reality, Roxy were its fulcrum, the very zenith of Style Centrale.

Much like the generation he inspired, as a boy Ferry had longed for escape. Having grown up in the north-east of England in a fairly impoverished mining village called Washington, near Durham, Ferry was desperate to travel south, to London, to metropolitan excess. He was helped in his cause by the legendary pop artist Richard Hamilton, who taught Ferry at Newcastle University. Hamilton not only inspired the Roxy Music cover-girl album covers, he also inspired the music itself, a mixture of sci-fi aspiration and fifties Americana. 'To go that route seemed the only option,' says Ferry. 'I mean, we could've had a picture of a band looking rather glum, which was normal, standing on a cobbled street or something. But I didn't fancy that. The pin-up was a great way to sell things traditionally, whether it was a Cadillac or a Coke bottle or a packet of cigarettes.'

Or even Roxy Music, come to that.

In 1957, Hamilton had come up with a definitive description of pop art, one that could easily apply to Roxy themselves, and one that Ferry took to heart: 'Popular (designed for a mass audience), transient (short-term solution), expendable (easily forgotten), low cost, mass produced, young (aimed at youth), sexy, gimmicky, glamorous, big business.' Throw in some fifties balladry, white noise and synthesizer treatments, plus some futuristic Teddy boys, and there you had Ferry's vision. Even their name was pop: 'We made a list of about twenty names for groups,' says Ferry. 'We thought it should be magical or mystical but not mean anything, like cinema names – Locarno, Gaumont, Rialto . . .' According to Andy Mackay, Roxy's bequiffed sax player, 'If Roxy Music had been like cooking, it would be like a dish in Marinetti's Futurist Cookbook,

Car Crash: a hemisphere of puréed dates and a hemisphere of puréed anchovies, which are then stuck together in a ball and served in a pool of raspberry juice. I mean, it's virtually inedible, but it can be done.' A fashion grenade rather than a fashion parade (Roxy were roughly analogous to a Gucci or a Chanel, only with a yard of fake leopard skin and a sachet of sequins thrown in for good measure), Roxy transmitted aspiration, travel, power . . . sex. It was a modern-day love letter to an anglicised America, a seventies idea of fifties space nobility. They were conquering the new frontier. In silver jump suits! Playing guitars! In front of girls!

Although they didn't know it at the time, Ferryphiles were part of the first postmodern generation, while Roxy Music were the first postmodern pop group. Ferry courted the art-school crowd and paid lip service to the fashion industry, while never forgetting the ossified denim-clad punters who paid his wages. Essentially, Ferry discovered his own identity via the assumption of false ones, in a bid, perhaps, to spend the rest of his life in a world full of Roxy Music album covers. Using a little bit of Billy Fury, a little bit of Biba and a soupçon of good old-fashioned music hall, Ferry reinvented himself as a glittering, larger-than-need-be playboy. And, boy, did he love his job. He was brazen in his lust for a life that was never really meant to be his. He wanted not just the fast cars and the fast women, but the kudos that came with them. It wasn't enough for him to be seen to be enjoying himself; people had to believe that he meant it, that for him these things were not merely confetti – they were food and drink.

Occasionally ridiculed by the press, he was adored by the faithful. So cool was he when Roxy were in their first flush of success – 'Virginia Plain', 'Pyjamarama', 'Do the Strand' – that he became, almost overnight, a unique arbiter of style, so influential that fans would copy every little detail of his dress, whether he was trussed up like a fifties retro-future crooner, an American GI or a tuxedo-clad lounge lizard. Marco Pirroni, who would become the guitarist in Adam and the Ants, was such a devotee that he once used a magnifying glass to study a photo of

Ferry, just to see what cigarettes he was smoking. 'Even the cigarettes were really good, because they were all white. It was an important statement,' Pirroni says.

Ferry's own style icon was the fashion designer Antony Price, who created many of Ferry's best looks, and is someone who deserves proper recognition. 'Antony Price reinvented the suit so that it was no longer about going to the office,' says the stylist David Thomas. 'He made it rock'n'roll. He started at a time when British fashion didn't have sponsors. It was the era before the superstar designer. They all came after him. Yet he was a visionary. He created that military, dandy, sexy, eclectic men's look. He created rock'n'roll fashion.'

Ferry's fastidiousness played against him. Critics mistook his fondness for archness for phoniness. He was, however, revered by many of those who instigated punk, even though they were reluctant to say so at the time. 'I always do sound tests using Roxy Music, chunks of songs [notably "2HB"],' says the Sex Pistols' John Lydon. 'Bryan Ferry? I mean, he's not the most talented singer, but I love everything he's ever done.'

Ferry had an ability to try a little harder than many of his peers, even if he didn't always convince. The NME*'s revered critic Nick Kent eloquently dubbed him 'the George Lazenby of the Argentinian corned-beef market'.*

Bryan Ferry: Roxy were always about pop art, about accessibility, about the street, and contrary to popular opinion, we were not elitist. Pop art was about celebrating mass culture. We were also quite a lads' band back then, and we appealed to the boys on the street. It's when we reformed that we became a ladies' band. Dressing well is not exactly rocket science. And in my case, it's always been secondary. I have, however, always been a keen student. Antony was the real architect of the Roxy look, and he made these amazing sculpted clothes. Whether he's designing for men or for women, he really understands bodies, understands what looks good, what looks sexy. When I was younger, I was a mod, and I always appreciated the high street – every mod did. Mod was really all about dressing to a certain level, without having to spend a fortune. It was about great design for everyone and being smart.

Antony Price (*fashion designer*): I met Bryan in 1972 at a party. He came up to me and asked if I wanted to get involved with Roxy Music. So, a few days later, he came round to mine with his picture book, and he pulls out the record and I put my headphones on and I hear the first Roxy album. I loved his voice and I could see he was a nice-looking guy and I thought he was going to look good, and that's how it kicked off. Back in the sixties, Stax put a woman on the cover of *Otis Blue*, the Otis Redding album, otherwise it wouldn't have sold to a white audience, but Bryan liked the idea of using a woman to sell a product. For the first Roxy album he wanted this Rita Hayworth look, and [the model] Kari-Ann [Muller] was the closest you could get to Rita Hayworth, as she had this stunning red hair. Bryan also understood that women don't care whether a man is gay or straight. They won't stop fancying them; in fact, it doubles the fun because it means if you can pull him in, then you've really got it. Roxy didn't want to be seen as gay, but they wanted to be seen as exotic. Bryan didn't really care either way, as he knew it was all about how you looked.

Bryan Ferry: The clothes we were wearing at that time would have put off quite a large chunk of people. What I liked about the American bands, the Stax label and Motown, they were into presentation and show business, mohair suits, quite slick. And the cover art, I thought of all the American pop-culture icons, Marilyn Monroe, selling cigarettes or beer with a glamorous image. But it was a bit off-kilter as well; there was something a bit strange about it, futuristic as well as retro.

Antony Price: When the press talk about the early seventies, they always call it glam rock, but we didn't call it that. We just thought it was good taste, dressing smartly and living well. Roxy wanted a glamorous lifestyle and glamorous women. Bryan got it completely, and after a while we used to think almost as one; in fact, after a while his radar was better than mine. He really got the language of fashion and encouraged me to think up ever more glamorous looks. I really liked the military looks we did for the *Country Life* and *Siren* tours. I especially liked the gaucho look, the spaceman look, and the chauffeur look from *For Your Pleasure*. I loved the Caribbean suit we made for the video of 'Let's Stick Together' and the crashed-plane look for *Stranded* – there was just so much glamour. People said we were pretentious, but to us it was just good taste. We both had a sense of perfection, and *Siren* was probably where it all came together best.

Graeme Thomson (*journalist*): There is a case to be made for nominating *Siren* as the first true-born album of the eighties. On Roxy Music's fifth record, you hear stirring pre-echoes of Bowie's *Scary Monsters*, of U2's incipient, pre-stadia rock chimes, of post-punk pop funk, of the glistening synthetic surfaces of the New Romantic movement. If Roxy were the very essence of retro-futurism when they began, embodying the glorious confusion wrought by the possibilities of the space age colliding with the solidly nostalgic sensibilities of the fifties, by 1975 their febrile alchemy had settled somewhat. On *Siren* the sound pushes forward with a relatively solid sense of purpose, rather than shuttling back and forth with mad abandon. The band are cruising into the great beyond with a streamlined purr, well past the halfway point on the road between 'Virginia Plain' and *Avalon*. Some critics asked, 'Where is the Art?' – a grumble that still surfaces periodically – but it's there, all right. You'll find it in the occult guitar, plink-plonk atmospherics and wandering oboe of the first two minutes of 'Sentimental Fool', a song that harks back to the magnificent strangeness of *For Your Pleasure*. It's there too in 'She Sells', a delightful tumble of a track, which begins like the Doobie Brothers fronted by David Niven, then takes a series of lurching handbrake turns into furious urban funk and robotic art rock; and in Andy Mackay's ululating sax solo on 'Nightingale', which otherwise is one of *Siren*'s less arresting songs, despite its prettily folksy intro and Paul Thompson's driving drums. Most obviously, it's there in Graham Hughes' striking cover image. Ferry's soon-to-be girlfriend, Jerry Hall, is presented as a dangerously alluring vision in aquamarine – love very literally on the rocks. 'The cover of the new Roxy Music album is credited to eight people, two more than made the music,' noted *Rolling Stone*, somewhat archly, in their review. There was something reassuring about that. Roxy were changing, but they were doing so with their sense of style intact.

Antony Price: By the time of *Siren*, I had been working with Bryan for three years, and we had done four albums together – *Roxy Music*, *For Your Pleasure*, *Stranded* and *Country Life* – so we were well adapted to working together. Bryan had written this song called 'Siren', and for the cover he decided we should have a mermaid. Bryan always used to call me 'the batsman', because being a Libra I would bat things back at him, building on his ideas. At the time, we were all infected by Linda Goodman's *Sun Signs* book, and you could almost spot people physically and determine their star sign. The cover of *Siren* obviously features Jerry [Hall], who Bryan started seeing soon after. It was shot on the rocks near Holyhead lighthouse, near South Stack on Anglesey, by Graham Hughes. We drew sketches, and then he took the pictures. The idea for the location was Bryan's, after he saw a TV documentary about lava flows and rock formations in Anglesey, in which South Stack was heavily featured. On the shoot, Bryan held an umbrella over Jerry when it started to rain. Jerry at the time was living in Paris with Grace Jones and the fashion illustrator Tony Viramontes, and this location couldn't have been more of a culture shock. On the day of the shoot, it was the hottest day of the year, the sea was completely blue, and as the costume was green, I had to change it to blue by spraying it.

Jerry Hall (*model*): Bryan was at the height of his fame when I arrived in London ahead of the shoot in summer 1975. I loved Roxy Music and thought Bryan had the most beautiful voice, heartbreakingly touching and sexy. One look at his elegant, handsome face and I forgot all about New York. On my first night in London, he took me out to dinner in a black Jaguar with leather seats. When he shifted gears, his hand almost brushed my knees – there was a lot of chemistry between us. The album photo shoot was in Wales, where we stayed in a little seaside hotel. After dinner, I went to bed and curled my hair for the following day's work. I was tucked up in bed in my nightdress when Bryan knocked on my door. I let him in and got back under the covers, embarrassed.

David Bailey (*photographer*): We spent a lot of time with Jerry Hall at this point, as she was Marie [Helvin]'s best friend. But I could never get on with Bryan Ferry, who was then Jerry's boyfriend. I always thought he was a bit silly, a bit stuck up. I get on with most people, but I always found him a bit odd. He'd be perfectly nice at dinner or at home, and then you'd see him at a party and he'd blank you. What's all that about? I don't care one way or another, but you can't say hello to someone one day and ignore them the next. She was much better with Jagger. Mick was more dismissive, but in a sense he was more chivalrous.

Antony Price: Women usually like men who look like girls with a cock, whereas that's not what gay men want. They want scrubbed and shaven and muscle tissue. Jeremy Healy [the DJ] once described my clothes as Action Man meets Barbie doll. I love the crossover. And I think I got it right with Bryan Ferry and Jerry Hall.

David Bowie: In 1975, I spouted some nonsense about the *Young Americans* album being synthetic radio stuff. I don't believe that for one moment now. I was living and breathing soul and R&B at this time. I listened to nothing else. It became America for me.

Marc Almond (*musician*): In my first year at art school, in 1975, I had a bit of a nervous breakdown, and had to be sectioned for five weeks in a special unit. I come from quite an unstable background, and because of my breakdown I knew I wasn't a very emotionally stable person. I was studying performance art at Southport College, and had started to be quite confrontational. My school had been a complete disaster, and I had moved around quite a lot as my parents got divorced, bouncing between Southport and Leeds. I was also off school for seven or eight months with pneumonia and pleurisy because I'd been to a Roxy Music concert. This was 1973. They were debuting their new look, having just released *Stranded*, and they were playing with their new line-up at a festival in Leeds. I bunked off school, just me and my friend, and it was freezing cold. We stayed all night, and I barely had anything warm to wear. So I got pneumonia, was off school and never made up the course work. I ended up playing truant all the time, and I'd go and buy records, anything by Marc Bolan or Roxy. Anything that David Bowie said was good, I was interested in. I thought Bowie was much more of a teacher to me than my teachers because he told me that there was a much more interesting life outside Southport – a life of Jean Genet and William Burroughs and Lindsay Kemp, Iggy Pop, the Velvet Underground and London! So I didn't bother going into school. I went into registration in the morning, went home again, played my records and went back at lunchtime. Then I'd go home again, watch *Lift Off with Ayshea* on the TV. I'd read books, but I didn't get any O-levels, apart from art and English. I wanted to go into the theatre, but I had a terrible stammer, so I thought I was never going to be able to learn to be an actor. So I blagged my way into art school in Southport. They thought I was interesting enough.

Martin Fry (*musician*): It was a great year to be seventeen. I went to see Queen at the Manchester Free Trade Hall because I loved 'Killer Queen' and *Sheer Heart Attack*. They had this new album called *A Night at the Opera*, and that night Freddie Mercury threw a sleeve out and I caught it. So I figured I had a little bit of his magic dust and I took it home. This was the same year I saw the Roxy Music *Siren* tour.

Everybody showed up in their tuxedos, which he'd worn on the previous tour, but Bryan Ferry came out in his GI outfit with Jerry Hall, which was an extraordinary sight – *completely* glamorous. At the time, I saw lots of bands – Dr Feelgood, the Sensational Alex Harvey Band, Steve Hillage, Tangerine Dream and the Jess Roden Band. I was still at school, reading the *NME* and going to the Free Trade Hall every week, just waiting for something to happen. Dr Feelgood were the future for a while. I mean, it's hard to describe Lee Brilleaux, as he was a gear change, and the Feelgoods were suddenly something different. You felt there was going to be a change.

Rusty Egan (*DJ and drummer*): In 1975, I was the runner and tea boy at Dick James Music, at DJM studios, which was in New Oxford Street. I was eighteen and desperate to get into the music business. My parents were musicians, and I was playing drums in the afternoons whenever I could get a chance. I was a real teenage clubber, and there was a club on Friday lunchtimes called the Sundown, which eventually became Busby's, so I would nip down there on a Friday afternoon before finishing work. I looked like a cross between a soul boy and a hippie. I had an Antony Price cap-sleeved T-shirt, but I still had the three-button high-waisted trousers and Chelsea boots, which I absolutely loved. And I had a leather jacket and a David Cassidy-style haircut. I kept bumping into people like Marco Pirroni, who would one day be in Adam and the Ants. Obviously, we all liked David Bowie and Roxy Music.

Siouxsie Sioux (*punk icon*): I was fifteen when I first saw David Bowie. He was singing 'Starman' on *Top of the Pops*, and I was in hospital recovering from a serious illness. I just couldn't believe how striking he was. That ambiguous sexuality was so bold and futuristic that it made the traditional male/female role-play thing seem so outdated. Besides, I'd lost so much weight and had got so skinny that Bowie actually made me look cool! He was tearing down all the old clichés, but he was also having a lot of fun doing it. Bowie was well into clothes and dressing up, and that had a lot of resonance with me, although I was never a Bowie lookalike. A few years later, when he began to withdraw from it all, it really felt like there was something missing. Until then, his albums had been eagerly anticipated. But by the mid-seventies, there was a vacuum. It was no coincidence that so many people involved in punk at the beginning had been inspired by him. Bowie was the catalyst who'd brought a lot of us, the so-called Bromley Contingent, together. And out of that really small group of people a lot happened, including Siouxsie and the Banshees.

As a schoolgirl in Chislehurst, Kent, Susan Janet Ballion – soon to be Siouxsie Sioux – was a determined loner, a reclusive Roxy Music freak with hair 'down to my bum'. Without a peer group, and feeling alienated from her surroundings, she began making day trips to London, visiting Biba, the King's Road, soaking up the urbanity much like another proto-punk, Paul Weller (who used to come up to London and record the traffic). Gradually, she became embroiled in what became known as the Bromley Contingent, the group of friends who would follow the Sex Pistols around, cutting her hair into strange shapes and dyeing it funny colours, shopping at jumble sales, wearing outlandish make-up and generally running riot.

Siouxsie Sioux: It was a form of rebellion, I suppose. I was never happy at school; really miserable, hated it. I was very lonely, but mainly out of choice. As soon as I cut my hair . . . that's when I began to meet different kinds of people. I used to like Roxy Music and Bowie, but I never wanted to emulate them like other people. You have to pay for your independence. When I was at school, my mum bought all my clothes, so I could never get involved in what was fashionable, but then I wouldn't have wanted to. Leaving was the first chance I had to strike out on my own. I got a strange, perverse thrill from looking the way I did – it was like having a massive surge of adrenalin.

Peter York: Now Bryan was wonderful, in and out of Roxy Music. Very clever, agonisingly fastidious, he managed to give the postmodern appearance of standing outside what he did – then a new posture – while at the same time being hyper-involved and passionate. He was ironical *and* sincere. When you heard 'Virginia Plain' for the first time, you knew you were listening to the natural antagonist of Joe Cocker; you were listening to a singer whose whole approach said, 'I'm not *singing*, I'm *being a singer*.' Similarly, *the looks*, all of them said, 'This is just a phase, just a costume for now.' But at the same time, it mattered enormously how you looked. So you got dyed feather shoulders over blue spangles, or you got the white tux with half-tamed forelock, or you got the Antony Price GI combination of 1975 (with matching girl back-up singers – very 'sexy'), and whatever you got, it was done beautifully. And thousands of boys and girls who were sick of the street, sick of the high-street low-life, no-life, did a Bryan and turned up at the concerts wearing the Bryan look (or the gorgeous girl-accessory-to-Bryan look, as in those first wet-dream Roxy album sleeves). People went to the first concerts at the Rainbow, in Finsbury Park, and had their lives changed.

Keren Woodward (*singer*): Sara [Dallin] and I were massive Roxy Music fans, and when I got rid of all my vinyl when I was older, they were the only albums I kept. They were sacred. Every opportunity we'd go and see them. I remember meeting Bryan Ferry outside the Colston Hall in Bristol and nearly fainting. He got out of his car and said hello to us, and I remember going, 'Oh my God,' and just collapsing on the floor. I think the promoter felt sorry for us and gave us tickets for the show, which was amazing. I mean, he was just the coolest person. I knew every lyric of every song. We used to sort of act them all out.

Harvey Goldsmith (*promoter*): I worked on every Roxy Music tour in the seventies, although it soon became very apparent that Bryan wanted to be thought of as a separate entity. He wanted a suite, whereas the rest of the band were content with a double room. He wanted a limo, whereas the rest of the band were happy to be on the tour bus. It was only ever going to end one way.

When Ferry came down to London in 1970, he had been fortuitously introduced to both Antony Price and hairdresser Keith Wainwright on the same evening, at the same party. With an eye on the grand design, Ferry engaged both of them – Price to make his clothes, and Keith (it was always just 'Keith') to cut his hair. Keith owned Smile, Britain's first unisex salon, and it was here that he first cut Ferry's hair. 'He first asked to have it dyed black, which was unheard of at the time,' says Keith. 'It was the late hippie period, when everyone wanted fresh, clean, healthy, natural-looking hair. And in comes Bryan Ferry demanding to be dyed.' Ferry originally sported a 'Budgie' hairstyle, as worn by Adam Faith (another of Smile's clients) in the TV series of the same name, but between them Price and Keith came up with a more suitable long dark quiff. Smile quickly developed a reputation for championing dyed hair, to obvious effect on the gatefold sleeve of Roxy's second LP, For Your Pleasure, *for which saxophonist Andy Mackay was given a green space-age D.A. 'Hair colouring was quite new at the time,' says Keith, 'and when the album came out, we were inundated with people wanting Andy's and Bryan's haircuts. They were the only two in the group who really cared about the way they looked.' For Ferry's first solo record,* These Foolish Things, *Keith made him the ultimate Roxy icon. 'The cover of* These Foolish Things *is just one big combing job. His hair is actually quite long and tucked around the side and back, because he wouldn't have it cut. This haircut was probably more popular and more influential than any other I've done, as so many men – and women – wanted it. But the haircut I used to give people who wanted one was nothing like the one Ferry had himself. It was something quite different.'*

Ollie O'Donnell (*club runner*): Before I worked at Smile, I worked for Ricci Burns. I had seen an interview with him on TV. He was very theatrical, very camp, and I could tell he was also a bit of a rascal. I had already decided I wanted to become a hairdresser, and it had to be a salon in the West End; I had fallen in love with the West End of London from the age of eleven. So I went through the phone book that night and found the phone number for Ricci Burns, in George Street in Marylebone. This would have been August 1975. I wrote a letter for Ricci's attention, and a few days later I got a letter back telling me to come in for an interview. He said, 'I like you, I like your enthusiasm,' and he told me that not only would he give me an apprenticeship, but if I worked hard and was on time every morning, after two weeks he would make me his junior. He was giving me a brilliant opportunity. I was sixteen, and I started work a few days later.

It was a large salon with a lot of staff, and it was very, very busy. They had a very smartly dressed older gentleman in immaculate double-breasted suits who would take the clients' coats. If it was raining, he'd give them umbrellas on the way out. Bianca Jagger was a regular client, and she would come in three to four times a week, just to get her hair washed and blow-dried. Lionel Bart would pop in most days just to hang out, as did Lulu, Adam Faith, Michael Caine, Terence Stamp, Mick Jagger and lots of other people from the sixties.

Ricci had decided that my real name, John, did not suit me any more, and from now on everyone would call me Tara. He said I reminded him of a dear friend of his, Tara Browne, who died in a car crash in the early sixties. Tara Browne was an Anglo-Irish socialite, a playboy and Guinness heir who hung out with all the stars of the early sixties. He was the Tara who 'blew his mind out in a car' in John Lennon's 'A Day in the Life'. Ricci would theatrically flick his hand out in the air and shout, 'Tara!' and I would have to dash across the salon and place his scissors or comb and brush in his hand. It was pure theatre. Ricci was hilarious. Many years later, when my first child was born, I named her Tara.

About sixty people worked in the salon, and they had a large kitchen at the back, run by a guy called Nick. He was the most outrageous-looking person I had ever seen: six feet three inches tall, rake thin and very pale, with a gaunt face and messy, slightly spiky blond hair. He wore white sandals and red jeans with two see-through plastic pockets in the back, and a white tight Serra T-shirt. Both the jeans and the T-shirt came from a shop in the King's Road called SEX, run by Malcolm McLaren.

After a few weeks, Nick invited me to a club called Sombrero in Kensington High Street – down a steep set of stairs, very dimly lit, with lots of alcoves and a DJ booth set up near the ceiling. Lots of gay guys and beautiful girls wearing boiler suits, with short spiky hair, mostly hennaed red or cropped and bleached blonde. Or others with a forties look in smart suits. Some of the guys wore baggy fifties suits; others had winkle-pickers and bowling shirts, with Levi's and either red or white Converse or white plastic sandals. The gay guys all looked the same: Levi's, checked shirts, working boots, and all of them with moustaches. It was all very friendly, and the gay crowd were very accepting of everyone else.

Fiona Dealey (*fashion designer, costumier*): My first nightclub was Intercom, in the Southend shopping precinct. I would have been thirteen or fourteen. I obviously fell madly in love with our hero David Bowie, and also Bryan Ferry and all things Roxy Music. The dream was to look like a Roxy pin-up girl, and we would spend hours studying the make-up and clothes on the Roxy albums, and that's where I discovered Antony Price. Then I started going to Raquel's, again in Southend, and Zero Six, which was at Southend airport. It wasn't in the terminal, it was on the edge of it, on an industrial estate. I used to catch a bus with my friend to get there, and as we were still at school, we'd have to recite our birth dates to make ourselves three years older, because we were having to make ourselves over twenty-one. I started going to the Goldmine, on Canvey Island, which was a very hard place to get to from where I lived – two trains and a bus. I was still only sixteen, so this would have been late 1975. This is when we all started wearing forties clothes, with pencil skirts and lots of fox fur stoles and high heels, and the boys all dressed like they were in the army. Basically, they were copying what Bryan Ferry was wearing at the time, which was the whole GI look. Antony Price told me he and Bryan once went to the Goldmine for the night, and I imagine they were quite shocked at how suburban it all was. They thought it was going to be super-stylish because the Goldmine was in all the papers. We all danced to Glenn Miller and swing music – my friends and I raided second-hand shops for forties clothes . . . One night, Chris Hill was the DJ, and he picked up a Glenn Miller record, cracked it and then put on 'Love Hangover' by Diana Ross, and that's when it all changed. We weren't going to be dancing to swing any more.

Andy Polaris (*singer*): In 1975, I was in a children's home in Stock, between Billericay and Chelmsford, in Essex. I'd been there since I was seven. I didn't really have a family life. My mother was married to a Scotsman, and when they got divorced, as my mum was trying to work I was loaned out, so I went to live with some family, and they were abusive and the school found out about it. So I got put in a children's home and didn't come out until I was sixteen. It was almost like a prison sentence. You didn't have any freedom, and if you wanted to go somewhere, you had to ask permission. That's why I used to sneak out at the weekend to go to Lacy Lady with my brother, who was a bit older than me. I used to get girls from school to say I was staying at their house for the weekend. My brother went to Southend Technical College. I think Tracey Emin was in his class, and he knew people, like Fiona Dealey, who were already into fashion. I also went to the Goldmine, Raquel's and Croc's in Rayleigh, which is where I met Alison Moyet and the kids from Depeche Mode. I remember *Vogue* or *Tatler* did a one-page article on the Goldmine, and that was a big deal at the time. I was a massive Bowie fan before then, though, and I've got dozens of Bowie scrapbooks. That was my escapism: collecting magazines and basically anything that had David Bowie on the cover. We all liked Bowie, T. Rex . . . The home was a real multiracial bag of bad kids, Asian kids and white working-class kids.

Antony Price: The *Siren* tour was an extension of the military look, and I turned Bryan into a GI. The Eurythmics knocked off the whole idea a few years later. The air hostess dresses that the back-up singers wore were so tight and so sculpted they had to be lifted onto the stage, as they couldn't move their legs. The army look was happening at the time, as everything had to look very American. I quite liked it, and I was slightly military-orientated with my design anyway, so that crept into it and Bryan looked good in it. I know a lot of people in the clubs started wearing it, and I actually went down to suss out the Goldmine to see if we could do a shoot there. We didn't; they were doing a forties night and had swing music. Obviously, a lot of people would copy what Bryan wore. At their concerts, I would peak through the curtains, and there would be people in the front row wearing copies of the clothes, so I was aware that the clothes became very important. Bryan was a perfectionist and he would spend months getting the right guitar note or fiddling with some aspect of the music, and then someone would say, 'Oh, I love your trousers.' When the likes of Duran Duran came along later, you realised how important the clothes had been to them when they had been in the audience at the Roxy gigs. The only other person who cared about presentation was Bowie. Freddie Burretti used to dress David, and I used to dress Bryan, and we used to bump into each other at the Sombrero. Bryan and I loved the clothes, but they were very much stage outfits. We preferred the country-gent look as we used to go off to stay in country houses at the weekend. When we did those first shots of Roxy, the record company thought they looked weird enough to go with the sounds. I scraped all the hair back as I was then heavily into men's ears. I swept all Bryan's hair back and put him in my llama jacket, which I made at the Royal College of Art. Bryan loved the models, and they knew he was interested in the fashion business and the make-up and the make-up artists and the whole beauty of presentation. They understood the beauty of presentation, which is make-up, hair and lighting. The thing is, the mainstream media weren't interested in fashion at the time, so it was really just a cult thing. As a designer, I couldn't get arrested, I couldn't get a penny to help me back the business. Nobody wanted to know. It didn't happen in English fashion until Galliano went to Givenchy in the early eighties. It was too early. Vivienne Westwood and Malcolm McLaren were early too.

Malcolm McLaren (*shopkeeper, impresario*): When I left art school at the dawn of the seventies, I ended up on [the] King's Road and went into fashion. It wasn't unnatural or surprising because I came from a family of tailors and dressmakers. But the last thing on earth I was trying to do was make fashion. My aim in life was to make trouble! I saw that King's Road was a wonderful place to make trouble. It was like having a bridge between art school and the street. Art school was a very disenfranchised place, in which we disaffected creatures could separate ourselves from the world and be snobbish about it! It was a safety valve, a hermetic environment where you didn't have to think about the 'real world'. But when we were finally thrown out into this real world, what the hell were we going to do? That was the most astonishing revelation.

Before Malcolm McLaren became notorious as a punk entrepreneur, creating the Sex Pistols – the pachyderm of punk – and forging a career as a cultural disrupter, he was an art student. McLaren actually studied at St Martin's, attending evening classes in fashion and graphic design in 1963, before briefly going to Goldsmiths, Harrow and then the Royal Academy of Art. He left education in 1971, when, with his partner Vivienne Westwood, he started running 430 King's Road, a shop he immediately renamed Let It Rock to reflect their passion for fifties clothing and culture. In 1973, the shop was given a new name,

Too Fast to Live, Too Young to Die, to reflect an emphasis on 'rocker' clothing, and then in 1974, the name was changed again, to SEX, swapping retro clothing for fetish wear. SEX started to attract a small group of disparate customers, including Chrissie Hynde, Adam Ant, Siouxsie Sioux and all four future members of the Sex Pistols. It would soon become one of the crucibles of what would morph into punk.

McLaren's career would be one of haphazard provocation, a career that would pinball around the entertainment industry without apparent rhyme or reason. He became a shopkeeper, entrepreneur, fashion designer, impresario, cultural theorist, showman, pop manager, singer, television presenter, writer and agent provocateur – all of which stemmed from his art-school background and a minor obsession with Situationism. 'I've always embraced failure as a noble pursuit,' he said. 'It allows you to be anti whatever anyone wants you to be, and to break all the rules. It was one of my tutors at St Martin's, when I was an art student, who really brought it home to me. He said that only by being willing to fail can you become fearless. He compared the role of an artist to that of being an alchemist or magician. And he thought the real magic was found in flamboyant, provocative failure rather than benign success. Any survivor of a sixties art school will tell you that the idea of making a product was anathema. That meant commodification.'

McLaren had identified – however accidentally – that the defining characteristic of the mid-seventies was one of neglect. Record companies in particular highlighted the poverty of the present, a poverty of the imagination, and an unwillingness and an inability to do anything about it. Realistically, how could they do anything else? After all, they were responding to the market, and in 1975, the market seemed content with nostalgia, as the charts were full of so-called legacy acts: the Four Seasons, Chubby Checker, Johnny Mathis, Frankie Valli, the Drifters, Roger Whittaker and even, most bizarrely, Laurel and Hardy (with the Avalon Boys featuring Chill Wills) with 'The Trail of the Lonesome Pine'. The album charts, although containing some stellar work that would later be enshrined in the pantheon of 'classic rock' (Led Zeppelin's Physical Graffiti, *Bob Dylan's* Blood on the Tracks *and Joni Mitchell's* The Hissing of Summer Lawns, *for instance), were similarly laden with odourless blasts from the past: Perry Como, Jim Reeves, Tom Jones and Engelbert Humperdinck. McLaren rightly surmised that at this point in the culture, transgression could arrive in many forms, disinterred or not.*

Malcolm McLaren: The origins of punk? One Sunday lunchtime when I was sixteen, I found myself in this little club in Great Newport Street, in Soho, and saw this group called the Rolling Stones. The first thing I noticed was that they were playing looking bored. I'd never seen that before, never seen guys looking like they really didn't care. They were all looking down instead of up and they all looked dirty, not glamorous at all. The music was equally dark, and I suddenly felt that this was actually it, this was the real thing.

McLaren loved Soho and would wander around its streets for hours on end, making friends with traders, vice girls, hustlers, anyone he felt was genuinely part of the 'street'. He called it 'French Soho' and loved the fact it was European, so international. His love affair with the Rolling Stones restored his faith in the power of pop and its ability to be transgressive. He had been brought up on rock'n'roll, loved the initial energy of fifties music, and thought the Beatles had ruined everything. In 1975, he was determined to replicate that excitement.

Vivienne Westwood (*fashion designer*): Malcolm was against everything, for no particular reason. He absolutely hated authority. I cared more about trying to change the world and make it a better place. That's what punk was about – young people figuring out what they wanted from this world. The first thing they have to realise is that they are all victims of propaganda. The only way to do that is through culture. Culture is the antidote to propaganda.

Malcolm McLaren: I'm a product of the sixties, man. The idea of having a career was always a vulgar notion. You never used the word 'career'. If you put that in conversation, you were considered really bad news – it was very uncool. So you just wandered off into the Global Village, you just did whatever came your way. In those days, it was just as hip to be dressing a window on Carnaby Street as to be painting in the attic of the RCA – if not more so. I think that staying at art school was what it was all about. It didn't really matter how many you went to, it was just hanging out, they were all cool in their own way. That was one of the great periods of my life, and I probably learnt everything there. I learnt a lot since through experience, but most of my education was at art school. They taught you how to profit by your eccentricity. They taught you how to get away with murder.

McLaren's only proper job was in 1962, when he was sixteen, when he went off to work as a trainee taster for George Sandeman, the wine merchant. 'The occasional glass of sherry on religious days was the only wine I'd tasted. But my mother, a walking cliché of nouveau riche, thought this sounded respectable enough to boast about at cocktail parties,' he said. He hated the job so much he eventually got himself fired by smoking Gitanes, prompting a letter from Sandeman to his mother: 'Your son is not fit to work in this firm. He's smoking foreign cigarettes, preventing other boys from tasting and smelling our wines. He's a saboteur!' Wasn't he just. When he drank Bordeaux or Burgundy later with his fellow students at St Martin's, he'd find himself saying, 'This one's got a big back on it: the older it is, the bigger the back. A truly heroic, masculine body.' Or that a cheap Beaujolais was 'a young filly, got to watch her – she'll betray you'. His friends would look at him, bemused, as if he were an intriguing, slightly exotic being just off the boat from Burma.

Malcolm McLaren: I left school at sixteen, and my mother got me a job as a trainee wine taster. But one day I followed some girls into St Martin's and saw a voluptuous woman sitting on a stool being sketched. I decided to get myself fired.

Chris Sullivan (*club runner, DJ*): The whole Blitz thing was a continuum from punk, along with those of us who had been soul boys, but the common denominator was a love for David Bowie and Roxy Music, who were probably both at their height in 1975. I used to go to local clubs in Merthyr Tydfil, then we used to go to northern soul clubs, and that's where I met Steve [Strange]. That would've been 1974, early 1975. We went up to Wigan Casino, because there was no alcohol there, so you didn't have to be eighteen. I went to weekenders in Bournemouth, went to the Lacy Lady in Ilford. Then I came up to London in the September of 1975, when I discovered SEX and the King's Road. It was like, 'Wow. This is amazing.' The scene was really working-class. Joe Strummer's father might have been a diplomat, and Malcolm McLaren might have come from a rich family, but most people were working-class.

Ollie O'Donnell: It wasn't a working-class movement at all, as it involved everyone: working-class people, the upper class, people into soul, people into rock, people into fashion.

Boy George (*singer*): I think my first attempt to go anywhere exciting was the Global Village, underneath the arches in Charing Cross. I'd get the train straight from Blackheath and often bunked the fare. I remember a few times not getting in because I was young, so I used to talk to people in the queue, picking up make-up tips about how to look older. There was a local club in the Black Print pub in Bexleyheath which had a soul night that kind of slowly morphed into a sort of weirdo night. But being a local club, there were quite a lot of roughs in there, so if you were a young and feminine boy like me, it was quite scary, especially because I was really popular with girls. I was always with a gaggle of females, and most of them protected me. So

I gravitated towards the West End. There was a DJ at the Global Village called Froggy, and I remember dancing to 'Shaft' by Isaac Hayes, 'Brick House' by the Commodores and 'Fire' by the Ohio Players. Before that, when I was about fourteen, I used to get the Red Rover bus and go up to South Molton Street and the Chelsea Girl, on the corner of Regent Street and Oxford Street. I used to go wandering around the West End looking for exciting people. I had this dream that I was going to become best friends with Bowie and I'd go hang out with him. But I wanted to be part of the bohemian world, which was probably a result of growing up in such a big family where there was very little space. I was always dreaming of buying my mum a big house, so I would do a lot of window shopping to work out what I would buy once I had some money, like what sort of light fittings and furniture I'd get. I would also wander around Blackheath looking at the big houses. So I definitely had a plan to have the life I ended up having, but it was all pretty naive when I was a kid. Clubs were definitely a place where you met exotic people.

Robert Elms: One of the black boys at the Bandwagon started talking about this club called Crackers, in Soho, on the corner of Oxford Street and Wardour Street (and which later, during punk, became the Vortex). I kind of knew where Soho was, but I don't think I'd ever been out at night there. My first trip to Crackers was on a Friday afternoon, because they used to have an afternoon session. I think it started at twelve and went on until three. I bunked off school on a Friday afternoon, and it was a revelation because it was so different to the Bandwagon. At Crackers everyone was either a dresser or a dancer, and everyone was cool. I started going regularly, and towards the end of 1975, a group there started to look very different. I remember seeing a girl with her hair dyed blue, and another one wearing clothes that were a bit ripped and with some safety pins in them. And so this look started to emerge, and after a while you started to hear about places like Acme Attractions and SEX. So it's pre-punk, but we're dancing to funk records. I started going to the Lyceum on a Monday night, and the Global Village, which later became Heaven. And you would see more and more of these little pockets of kids, who I now realise in retrospect were Siouxsie Sioux and her mates, like Billy Idol. I still hadn't really heard the word 'punk' and didn't know anything about bands or any of that sort of stuff.

Ollie O'Donnell: I used to go to the Bird's Nest Club in Muswell Hill, the Royalty in Southgate, and then in 1975, I started going to see pub-rock groups like Kilburn and the High Roads and Dr Feelgood. But the hairdressers had introduced me to a whole new scene: the Sombrero, Crackers, Chaguaramas, and then Maunkberry's and the Embassy in Mayfair. The Embassy was the most glamorous place, with all the young guys in hot pants. It was beautiful. Very chic. Nice cocktails. My biggest influence was Bowie, I suppose, so I wore plastic sandals, pegs, mohair jumpers, stuff bought from Acme Attractions in the King's Road, Portobello Road and Brick Lane market.

Princess Julia (*DJ*): In 1975, I was fifteen, going to Bishop Stopford's School in Enfield, north London, and anticipating leaving school quite quickly. My father was a Hungarian refugee who worked in a metal-box factory, and my mother worked at the BBC as a telephonist in Bush House. My father was quite strict and was already trying to arrange marriages for me – with anyone from the factory! He was trying to marry me off as soon as possible. Obviously, I had other ideas and wasn't having any of it. I didn't want to be judged by my ability to find a mate. Because if you didn't settle down and find a husband, you were considered a failure. I wanted more. My parents rented out the top floor of our house to students, so sometimes I befriended them and would go out to clubs to listen to soul and reggae. I used to skive off school and go to the big Biba in Kensington. I saw an ad in *Miss London* magazine for hairdressing models, so I used to run up to Knightsbridge and have my hair done up into fantastic styles, including the wedge. I was always interested in clothes as they were escapism. Even when I was eight years old, when my mum asked me what I wanted for my birthday, I said, 'Don't get me something, I'll give you a list.' At the time, I wanted to become a make-up artist, but instead I got a job in a hairdresser's called Crimpers. We were all friends with the juniors up at Smile, and one of them was a girl called Kiki, who went out with [Pistols drummer] Paul Cook. So that's how I became aware of the Sex Pistols.

Fiona Dealey: There was a real sense of aspiration. When I was sixteen, I went to see Bryan Ferry play a solo gig at the Royal Albert Hall, and I wanted the whole thing. I loved the way he dressed and was completely in love with him. Then I looked up at the VIP area, and I could see a little group of people who looked amazing, had the best clothes on . . . One girl had a pink parasol perm, and I kept looking up at them and I thought, 'That's the cool gang.' That was what drove me. I've got no idea who they were, although I imagine Antony Price was up there. I was just always driven to be part of the scene, I suppose.

Malcolm McLaren certainly didn't care for Bryan Ferry, thinking him bourgeois and very much part of the old guard. Ferry used to regularly come into 430 King's Road, and McLaren would give him short shrift. 'I think he's leading the kids astray,' he said at the time. 'I mean, Andy Mackay [Roxy Music's saxophonist] comes in all the time and buys clothes for what I think are really "chic", calculating reasons. I think Ferry's stuff is too reserved, too "English". I dislike how he puts it all together. I don't know why half these rock stars come here in the first place.'

Kim Bowen (*stylist*): I used to lie about my age when I went to nightclubs as I was probably about fourteen when my friend and I started going out. We used a very fine eyeliner brush and would draw wrinkles on ourselves. We used to go to the Top Rank in Reading. This was 1975, and we were both at the local secondary modern school. We were very nervous of boys and wouldn't let anyone buy us a drink, although I'm sure people thought we were jailbait. That's about the time I first met David Holah, who went on to form BodyMap. Then I heard about the Lacy Lady, in Ilford. I lived in Farnborough, in Hampshire, so getting to Ilford was really demanding. My friend and I lied to our parents, saying we were staying at someone's granny's. We used to jump on a train to Waterloo station, then dress up like prostitutes in the station because you couldn't leave your house dressed like that. My father, who was a plumber, would have killed me. Punk was just starting, and we were wearing fishnets and leather. The Lacy Lady was an absolutely shitty, ugly-looking pub, but it was miraculous because there would be all these cute guys, who were really good dancers, dressed in clothes from SEX, like giant mohair sweaters and pegged pants and things. We didn't have any money, so we probably had one drink each, but we would just dance all night and then try and get a bus home. One night, I remember we slept in a porn cinema in Soho. Chris Hill was the DJ at the Lacy Lady, and he would sometimes play reggae, so music was becoming more varied.

I'm quite well spoken as my mother was a real stickler for things like that. She was Irish, quite well read and very intelligent, and she was super-conscious of being Irish as people were so racist in the seventies, in that No Blacks, No Irish, No Dogs way. It was important to her to be well spoken and well read because she didn't want to be judged for being an Irish peasant. She was also conscious of all the IRA bombings, as in those days no one wanted to hear an Irish voice. She would be very upset because people would say things like, 'You fucking Irish, go home.'

Andrew Hale (*musician*): The mid-to-late-seventies history of punk and club culture doesn't always reference the influence of the suburbs and suburban soul-boy culture, which was my background. I grew up in Wembley. In 1975, I was thirteen, at school in Hammersmith, and while I was into Bowie, Roxy Music and Steve Harley, I was also listening to Nicky Horne on Capital, and Greg Edwards or Robbie Vincent, immersing myself in soul music. The Bowie I fell in love with was the Bowie of *Young Americans*, and I was also soaking up Stevie Wonder, Roy Ayers, the Ohio Players . . .

I started playing the piano early. When I was about five, a friend of my parents told me I was 'a natural', even though I was just banging my hands up and down. We had a piano in the house, and I started having lessons. A few years later, I remember the movie *The Sting* came out, and I wanted to start playing ragtime. My classical music teacher told me this was a distraction and she didn't want me to do it, and I got pissed off and stopped having lessons. Consequently, my musical education after that was playing along to records in my teens. I was getting influenced by jazz. My best mate's dad had an eight-track in his car which was always playing Stan Getz. I suppose my musical education was about the music I was trying to copy as a piano player, so that's why I got into people like Herbie Hancock and Stevie Wonder. But at the same time, I saw Brian Eno with Roxy and was fascinated by keyboards and electronics being used in a way that looked really cool. Kraftwerk's *Autobahn* also blew my mind, but so did Parliament and Funkadelic. The first time I heard 'One Nation Under a Groove' it had as profound an effect on me as hearing Bowie or Roxy.

Dave Rimmer (*journalist*): The influence wasn't just fashion as such, it was also the tradition of individual eccentrics, going back to Quentin Crisp, the forties dandy, wandering around London with his hair dyed red and his fingernails painted, long before David Bowie or anyone else like that appeared. Then, in 1975, there was a documentary about Crisp on the BBC called *The Naked Civil Servant*, and I think that had a big influence on everybody – the fact that someone was being that flamboyant and challenging everything way back in 1945. People like Boy George and [club promoter] Philip Sallon were as much influenced by him as they were by particular fashion designers.

In 1975, another TV moment was equally important, if not more so. This was the year Kraftwerk appeared on the BBC's science and technology show Tomorrow's World, *their first appearance on British television, and also the year they had their first British hit with 'Autobahn'. In the programme, the presenter, Raymond Baxter, said: 'The sounds are created in their studio in Düsseldorf, then reprogrammed and then recreated on stage with the minimum of fuss.' This appearance would later be heralded as the entire electronic ethic in one TV clip: 'The rejection of rock's fake spontaneity, the fastidious attention to detail, the Europhile slickness, the devotion to rhythm.' Baxter ended the report by stating emphatically that 'next year Kraftwerk hope to eliminate the keyboards altogether and build jackets with electronic lapels which can be played by touch'. Nevertheless, the German technocrats had suddenly electrified synth Britannia. At its best, Kraftwerk's music yielded a sensation of indeterminate depth and expansiveness, while appearing to do just the opposite ('It's good, but is it rock?' asked* Rolling Stone *when they were first exposed to 'Autobahn'). Their passivity was their strength, a refusal to wield guitars, express emotion or, indeed, sweat. Minimal, robotic and exhilarating, they were a teasing glimpse of the future. If Kraftwerk counted as a science-fiction band, the fiction was just as plausible as the science. Visually, they were a conundrum: on the one hand they looked severe and authoritarian, and on the other, as lifeless as the stare of a shop-window mannequin. (*'Kraftwerk' *means 'power station': 'We play our machines into the electrical system and create transformed energy,' said Ralf Hütter. One of the group's nicknames was the Human Machine, another Sound Chemists.)*

Ralf Hütter (*musician*): I think it was more like an awakening in the late sixties of the whole situation. The German term is '*einfach Musik*' – everyday music. It's more like discovering the tape recorder for us; like, the world of sound. Everyday life has a sound, and that's also why our studio is called Kling Klang, because '*kling*' is the verb and '*Klang*' is the noun for 'sound'. So it means 'sounding sound'. That's really what Kraftwerk is about. Sound sources are all around us, and we work with anything from pocket calculators to computers, from human voices, machines and body sounds to synthetic sounds – from anything, if possible. We don't want to limit ourselves to any specific sound, as before with classical music. Then it had be strings, it had to be piano, blah blah blah. We wanted to go beyond, to find a new silence, and from there to progress and continue walking into the world of sound.

Wolfgang Flür (*musician*): My first ambition, musically, was to copy the Beatles. What else could I do? We had no music of our own, and in the sixties, there was no chance to play at any venues other than school halls, garden fairs, gymnasiums or private parties.

Ralf Hütter: We were brought up within the kind of classical Beethoven school of music. We were aware there was a contemporary music scene, and of course a pop and rock scene. But where was our music? Finding our voice, I think that was the use of the tape recorder. Our contact with the tape recorder made us use synthetic voices, artificial personalities, all those robotic ideas.

Wolfgang Flür: The Beatles did something brilliant, but in the end it was not new music. They came from rock and blues, and they liked Elvis Presley and Chuck Berry and everything else. It was not a new invention in music, I must say, even though they were amazing musicians, with their melodies and themes, of course. But Kraftwerk did something more. We developed a completely new music, a new style. The press called it Krautrock, but it's not Krautrock really, it's electro-pop.

Ralf Hütter: After the war, Germany was finished, everything wiped out physically and also mentally. We were nowhere. The only people we could relate to, we had to go back fifty years into the twenties. On the other hand, we were brought up in the British sector, and that was nothing we could relate to. There was no current musical movement other than the fifty-year-old musical thing or semi-academic electronic music, meaning psychologically we had to get ourselves going. And that has only been possible with our generation. You can see the generation before ours, which is ten years older, and they could not do it. The only thing they could do was get fat and drink. There was so much accumulated guilt that it took another generation to be productive, to be willing to say, 'OK, I'm doing a song called "Trans-Europe Express" or something . . .'

Wolfgang Flür: Ralf had a kind of German idea in mind. Something with self-understanding and an immaculate presence, after the ugly wars our parents had inflicted on the world.

Ralf Hütter: We don't have a continuous tradition. But then we realised it was an enormous chance, because there was nothing, there was a void. We could step into that open space.

Wolfgang Flür: I am proud that I said yes to them . . . that I understood the future in this music they showed me. We built so many things together, and we became friends then.

Ralf Hütter: We always thought of ourselves as workers in sound, as studio or musical workers going into the studio to work. Not as musicians or musical artists, but as musical workers. The whole thing was to develop that. At one time we called our Kling Klang studio the Electronic Garden – we bridged the gap between music and technology.

Wolfgang Flür: That was the great release for me, when I saw . . . heard . . . listened to the Minimoog. It was just this fat sound of the ring modulators.

If you take a guitar, it's always the same. But if you tune the volumes and the filters, you can make millions of sounds out of [the Moog].

Ralf Hütter: I think we heard synthesizer sounds in the mid-sixties, around that time. And through our cultural situation, radio from Cologne and electronic music – well, probably mid-to-late sixties, as students. We didn't know exactly which instruments were used, and then I think synthesizers came at around that time. I bought mine . . . I have to think . . . maybe '71, '72, around that time. [Synthesizers were] used for film music, and then we discovered that might be interesting for me. But I also worked with the human voice and speech and language and poetry. It's kind of a concept of making my fingers sing.

Andy McCluskey (*musician*): Interesting year, '75. I was turning sixteen and asking everybody to give me money for my birthday so I could go to the local second-hand shop and buy a bass guitar, which I duly did, except the only one I could afford was the cheapest – and left-handed. To this very day, I play bass with the strings upside down. I was doing my O-levels at Calday Grange Grammar School in the Wirral, and our head boy at the time was Philip May, who became Theresa's husband. Also that summer I went with my big Afro and my long *Doctor Who* scarf and my trench coat to the Anglican cathedral to listen to Tangerine Dream. But on 11 September, I went to the Empire Theatre and I sat in seat Q36 and I saw Kraftwerk for the first time.* Which was one of two Damascene moments for me, the other being 'Autobahn' on the radio that summer. I thought, 'What is that? That is so exciting.' It ticked lots of boxes I didn't even

* Kraftwerk would tour the UK the following year too, and on this visit Ralf Hütter bought himself a beautiful racing-green vintage Bentley and had it shipped back to Germany to be refurbished. Although the legend supports the narrative that the members of Kraftwerk spent most of their leisure time cycling around Europe, they also had a collective weakness for luxury cars.

know I had. It was different, electronic, melodic, continental, and therefore terribly interesting and strange and just intellectually stimulating. This, to me, was what popular music should be, and I was absolutely hooked. That's when I started taking my Sunday-morning paper round money and going to Liverpool to buy albums from the German import bin at Probe Records. I would then take them round to Paul Humphreys' house because I only had a mono record player. He'd built himself a stereo because he was studying electronics. So it was a symbiotic relationship: I had the records, he had the stereo, and we started listening to my German imports every Saturday afternoon, when his mum was at work. I liked Steve Harley – I had a Steve Harley scrapbook – and I liked Bowie and Roxy Music and the Velvet Underground, but it was Kraftwerk who turned my head, and then Neu! They were my gang of six.

Then we decided to try to start making music. All we had was my bass guitar and some things Paul had made by cannibalising his various aunties' old radios. We made weird noises and shoved them through borrowed fuzzboxes and just made this ambient racket for about six months, until we finally got an electric piano and an organ. Because we had no intention of anybody else ever hearing it, it didn't matter what it sounded like. People never believe us when we say we had no aspirations to be professional musicians. It was our Saturday-afternoon hobby, and even our best friends thought the music we were creating was utter rubbish, but bit by bit we started to write these tunes and to construct things that had melody and structure to them.

Paul Humphreys (*musician*): In 1975, I was getting interested in making music. I started out as a roadie for the school band, because my hobby has always been electronics. So I used to build crazy machines. One of the first things I made was a really amazing sounding hi-fi. And I met Andy because we were at the same school in this little town in the Wirral. We've known each other since we were seven, as we went to primary school together. My friends had the school band and they were looking for a bass player, and as I'd seen Andy walking around the town with a bass over his shoulder, I went and knocked on his door and said, 'Do you want to join a band?' He joined, but quite quickly we realised we were the only people we knew who hated the music that was around. We were looking for something alternative. We had both heard Kraftwerk on the radio, heard 'Autobahn', and it was kind of the first day of the rest of my life really. It was like, 'I want to do that.' I bought a piano and joined this school band, but I couldn't play, so I just used two fingers. The rest of the musicians all wanted to be Genesis or the Eagles, but we wanted to do something radical. We used to stay behind after rehearsals and do our own thing, sat in my mum's back room building noise machines. We didn't have any money, as we were two working-class lads. We wanted to be Kraftwerk but we didn't have the money to be Kraftwerk, as synths were so prohibitively expensive, so I used to make these weird machines and we started to make electronic music. Kraftwerk actually played in Liverpool in 1975, and we wanted to go. Andy had turned sixteen, but as I was only fifteen, my mum wouldn't let me go. So he went and I didn't.

I had a lot of aunties in those days, and they always had old radios in the cupboard. I used to say, 'Can I have this?' And I used to go to the local library and get circuit diagrams for drum machines and synths and stuff like that. I just used to bastardise the parts, and scraped some money together for the parts that I didn't have and went electronics shopping. But we didn't dare to go on stage and play our electronic music until '78.

John Foxx (*musician*): I think I could have written and recorded in any period, but of course there's no way to be sure. I started off singing and playing a twelve-string guitar in the Bolton Octagon in 1973, then in a room over a Salford pub, supporting a Manchester band called Stackwaddy. At first the room was empty. Eventually it became full. But there was nothing happening in Manchester then, no scene at all, so I had to leave for London and got the band started [forming

Ultravox in 1974]. The idea was to be London's Velvets. We even had a base in a factory at King's Cross. The synths allowed more possibilities. I was becoming really interested in what could be made in a recording studio that couldn't be rehearsed or developed in any other way. After [hearing] 'Tomorrow Never Knows', I realised the studio was really the most important instrument of the future. That's why we got Eno to work with us. It was either him or Lee Perry.

Gary Numan (*musician*): At the time, I was seventeen, living in west London and working at Heathrow airport as a customs clerk. I was in a covers band called Black Gold, playing at weddings, but I was also writing my own songs at home. I was getting experience, but it was rubbish, and I didn't really enjoy it. We would play 'Proud Mary' and 'Route 66' and all that – just horrible. I was in so many terrible groups, and I suppose it was all about research and development, about pretending to be in a gang. At school I had real troubles. I was at a grammar in Middlesex, and they sent me to a child psychologist in the local area, who then referred me to St Thomas's, in London. It was there they first started to talk about Asperger's. But this is very early days, before the eventual diagnostic criteria for Asperger's were established. For me it was just a day off school. I remember when the Asperger's thing was explained to my mum, she seemed to be offended somehow, as if it was a slight on her as a parent. They had already put me on Nardil and Valium, two drugs designed to keep me calm, because I would get agitated at school and quite troublesome. They put me on those for at least a year. I was eventually expelled.

Daniel Miller (*producer, entrepreneur*): That year I was twenty-four, and spent the winter DJing at a ski resort in Switzerland and the summer working as a minicab driver in London. I'd studied film at Guildford School of Art and was working as an assistant film editor doing commercials, and I'd had enough, so I fled to the mountains. It was a holiday resort, so you'd play Abba, Status Quo, then some German kind of music

– a complete mishmash. I first became interested in synthesizer music at college, where I was in a band. There were three or four bands in my class, and we were definitely the worst. I was in the same class as Paul Kossoff from Free, and he tried to teach me to play guitar. He was a brilliant guitarist: not just a blues guitarist, but a great classical guitarist as well, and we were quite good friends for a while. But he failed to get me to play half-decent guitar. I was also with Nic Potter, who was in Van der Graaf Generator. It was quite a musical class. It was a great time for music, and a lot of people were inspired to make music. And I loved electronic music, especially German electronic music.

Trevor Horn (*musician, producer*): In 1975, I was playing bass in a nightclub in Leicester called Bailey's, seven nights a week, cabaret and dancing. It paid good money. At the time, I was into Yes, 10cc, the Beach Boys – all types of music. I wasn't aware yet of Kraftwerk or electronic music of any kind, and the first time I really became aware of electronic dance music was 'Love to Love You Baby' by Donna Summer, which came out in the summer. That really struck me, and it kind of blew me away. It made me realise that disco could be good.

Malcolm McLaren: Art school had taught me it was far better to be a flamboyant failure than any kind of benign success. I began by digging deep into the ruins of a culture I cared about – the outlaw spirit of rock'n'roll. Armed with certain relics, I began to assemble an emporium where nothing in it would be for sale – a shop that would never open. This was to prove impossible to sustain, and so I persuaded Vivienne to give up teaching children and help me instead. She collaborated in ways I never dreamed possible. The new generation would soon enter my store and want to be part of it. These young, sexy assassins would help spread the word! They became my Sex Pistols: sexy, young, subversive and stylish boys. Anti-music, anti-everything. They would form my critique, help dress a new army of disaffected youth. I gathered my art-school friends to help me plot the downfall of this tired and fake culture.

Ben Kelly (*interior designer*): I was at the Royal College of Art from 1971 to 1975, and while I was there I developed a relationship with Malcolm and Vivienne. The week I arrived in London, I discovered Let It Rock. I had been at college in Lancashire, and when I came down to the RCA I thought everyone would look like David Hockney, but all the product and interior designers looked shit. But I discovered Let It Rock and thought it was amazing. I started wearing crêpe-soled shoes, tight jeans and pink socks. I got to know both of them very well. I remember at the end of 1975, the day he told me he'd got this new band called the Sex Pistols, those two words together freaked me out. He'd found somewhere on Denmark Street for their rehearsal rooms and he asked me if I would do it up for him. So I made it habitable. They had a rehearsal room, with another room above it where they sometimes slept. I lined both rooms out with black MDF, just to make it liveable. Of course, John Lydon came along one day and graffitied all over the walls.

It was at about this time that Vivienne Westwood started to get really evangelistic about the shop's change of direction. Glen Matlock was a part-time assistant at SEX, and he remembers one regular who was part of a crowd that had been coming into the shop since the early days. 'They'd started out as mods but gradually drifted into Alan Ladd suits. One of them looked at the rubber gear and said, "Cor, I don't know about this any more, this is all a bit too weird for me." Vivienne piled into him. "Oi, you, you look like you should be in a fucking potting shed," she said, "not my shop. If you don't like it, get out."'

Malcolm McLaren: People used rock'n'roll as a way to dress up, as it was a way to get out of the house and feel excited about yourself. I was born in a culture of necessity, just after the [Second World] War, but the seventies and everything that came after was about living in a culture of desires.

Midge Ure (*musician*): For most of 1975 I had long hair, until I went to the cinema and saw a rerun of *Dirty Harry*. The minute I came out

I went and had my hair cut like James Dean. I was in the band Slik, as I'd just taken over vocals after the singer had left. They were essentially a boy band, working with Bill Martin and Phil Coulter, who were the songwriters behind the Bay City Rollers. I was living in Glasgow and was quite recognisable as I didn't really look like anyone else at the time. My management team owned the Glasgow Apollo – and this is before Slik had had a record out, when we were just waiting for it to be released – and when bands played there, there were no rental shops, nowhere to hire instruments or equipment in case anything went wrong. So when something broke, they would be sent round to the local guitar shop, 'And Midge is probably there, so go and see him and he'll sort you out with an amplifier or whatever.' So I'm walking out of this music shop, and this guy stops me and says, 'Will you speak to my mate round the corner?' And he was English, which was an unusual thing in Glasgow. I found out later this was Bernie Rhodes, who would go on to manage the Clash. And round the corner, sitting in his beat-up old car, was the most bizarre, effeminate man I'd ever seen in my life, Malcolm McLaren. I didn't know it was McLaren, but he's sitting there in his black mohair jumper and his dog collar, which again is kind of unusual in Glasgow. And they start talking to me, the two of them, and Malcolm says, 'Oh yeah, I used to manage bands,' and he goes on about the New York Dolls and SEX and Vivienne Westwood. And he's telling me all this stuff in his whiny voice, and he says he's putting this band together and, you know, do I want to join? And I thought, 'You don't even know what I do. You haven't asked if I'm a singer or a guitarist or even if I'm a musician.' So I said, 'No, thanks.' And the band was the Pistols. The reason they were in Glasgow is because they had some slightly hot equipment in the back of the car. So I didn't join the Pistols, but I bought an amp. McLaren went back to London and hired John Lydon.

Marco Pirroni: Because I used to go in the shop all the time, Malcolm told me about his new band. They hadn't played anywhere at the time. He said, 'We've got this band and, yeah, come down, boy.' People always say they saw the Pistols and it changed their life and they went home and cut their hair; well, I'd already cut my hair and I already looked right.

St Martin's already had a storied history long before the New Romantics came along, although the college's modern era really began on the evening of 6 November 1975, when the Sex Pistols played their first gig, supporting the pub rock'n'roll band Bazooka Joe on the fifth-floor common room of the art school, in Charing Cross Road. Glen Matlock (the band's bassist) was studying there, and Sebastian Conran, the college's entertainment secretary, who would go on to design clothes for the Clash, helped the Pistols secure the gig (50p on the door!), which would turn out to be one of the most tumultuous debuts of all time. This was the gig where John Lydon famously wore baggy pinstripe trousers with braces, and a ripped Pink Floyd T-shirt with 'I hate' scrawled over it. He looked like a young Albert Steptoe masquerading as a soul boy. Bazooka Joe, on the other hand, looked not unlike many of the bands who would come in the Sex Pistols' wake. They had been formed by Danny Kleinman (who would go on to become a multi-award-winning advertising and movie director, responsible for the stunning title sequences for the James Bond movies, including Spectre*), Stuart Goddard (later to morph into Adam Ant) and John Ellis (who would find subsequent fame as a member of the Vibrators).*

'We knew Glen Matlock, which I suppose is how we came to book them as our support band,' says Kleinman. 'We were doing a lot of gigs at that time, and we were playing all over the place – a lot of art colleges, universities, parties, we had a lot of residences in pubs around London. We played to a lot of half-full rooms – that's how good we were. This one didn't seem to be different to any of our other gigs, but it did have quite a few memorable things about it. We were all art-school boys thrashing away at our guitars, playing rock'n'roll, rockabilly – something edgier than the stadium rock of the time. We were slightly younger than the other bands on the pub-rock circuit [and they bought their clothes in Malcolm McLaren's Let It Rock] and

slightly more aggressive. Maybe Eddie and the Hot Rods were quite in-your-face as well, but it was hard-hitting stuff and there used to be quite a lot of fights at the gigs. Particularly, we played at the Stapleton Hall Tavern in Crouch Hill once a week, sometimes twice a week, and the locals didn't like it because it was quite noisy, we played loudly, there were always fights outside the pub and people were raucous when they went home. The pub manager asked me if I could do anything, so when we finished the gig I asked everyone to be "respectful of the neighbours when you leave, don't make too much noise and go home quietly . . . And here's our encore, 'Someone's Going to Get Their Head Kicked in Tonight'." And the place would erupt with cans and bottles being thrown . . . There were a lot of ageing Teddy boys who didn't like you playing songs unless they were exactly like the original, nor did they like you playing any new material, even if it was within the genre. We had a lot of younger Teds who actually had enough hair to have quiffs, but if you saw a Ted without any hair, you thought, "Hang on, there's a bottle coming here."

'[At St. Martin's] I had no idea who the support act was, but what I did know was that all these gigs we'd been doing around London, all the money we'd earned from playing in pubs, we'd put towards buying our own equipment. We'd bought all these 4 × 12 cabinets, 150-watt amps and a PA system and whatnot, and we were still paying for it on the HP [hire purchase]. So we got to the gig, and the lifts were broken, so we had to carry all this stuff up six flights of stairs, huge cabinets with concrete bottoms. It was a real pain in the arse. We set it up, got it all going, and then the support act turned up and said they hadn't got any equipment and could they borrow our PA, speakers and amplifiers and stuff. And we said, "Sure." I remember not being terribly impressed by the gig. I think they played a couple of cover versions [the Who's "Substitute" and the Small Faces' "Whatcha Gonna Do About It"], and there was some not very competent playing. They played four or five songs and seemed OK, until they started smashing up our equipment. Johnny Rotten started kicking the speaker cabinet, which we hadn't even finished

paying for and had carried up all these flights of stairs and had just lent them out of goodwill. I thought, "You're not Pete Townshend, mate." So I ran in and manhandled him a bit. I'm not a particularly violent person, but it wasn't my finest hour. I think Stuart was quite impressed by their performance, although I think I was too dull to realise this was a game-changing event. Fairly soon after this he left Bazooka Joe and reinvented himself as Adam Ant.'

Stephen Jones: The Sex Pistols played in the student union. I can't remember what date it was, but it was their third-ever gig or something. It was a complete disaster because they turned up really late. They played about two or three songs and, I think, either stormed off stage or the equipment broke down or something. And all the students wanted their money back, and it was actually more of a scene about everybody wanting their money back than the fact that the Pistols played there.

This gig not only kick-started punk, but it set in train a whole sequence of events that would result not just in the formation of the nascent New Romantic scene, but also start a narrative, a long continuum that wouldn't reach a conclusion until Live Aid, ten years later. There were barely thirty people at the Bazooka Joe/Sex Pistols concert, and yet the demographic crossover had already started, with the St Martin's students offering the kind of sophisticated audience the Pistols would cultivate for their first year in business. At their early gigs there was always a smattering of soul boys (just as there was always an enthusiastic hippie contingent), as many bleached jeans and ski jumpers as there were torn T-shirts and plastic trousers. After that, the audiences started to become more institutionalised, not least because they started to ape generic rock'n'roll styles; one of the reasons that traditional rock fans found the original 1976 punks so disturbing is because they looked like demented soul boys rather than US-style rockers à la Lou Reed.

Robert Elms: There was a kid on my council estate called Stephen Marshall – who ended up being a roadie for Spandau – and Stephen was a big guy, a quite tough sort of guy. One day in November 1975, I saw him on my way to the tube, and previously he'd been this very normal straight guy. Suddenly I saw him walking alone, and he's got a safety pin in his ear and he'd shaved his eyebrows and he's really looking extreme, and I asked him what happened. And he said, 'I went to see this group called the Sex Pistols. They're fucking terrible and fucking amazing.' I remember thinking, 'Well, how does that work?' Because I'd gone to see groups that were technically brilliant – you know, went to see War, went to see Brass Construction . . .

At the end of the year, more and more people started going to Chaguaramas, a gay club in Covent Garden's Neal Street. More and more of them were buying their clothes from SEX, and soon they started replacing the club's core clientele.

Robert Elms: Wednesday night at Crackers in 1975 was Bowie night, attracting Siouxsie [Sioux] and [Steve] Severin, pre-punk Nazi chic and plastic trousers, clothing by Acme Attractions and a King's Road shop by the name of SEX. Wednesday night at Crackers was for people with coloured hair and nowhere else to go, and was the start of a scene which was to move on to other gay clubs – Louise's and Chaguaramas.

At the time, Martin Degville was a chef in Walsall. He hated the routine of it all, so he used to dye his uniforms bright colours and spray them all over with whatever was at hand. He would then wear his chef's outfit with ten-inch winkle-pickers, massive shoulders and a huge white quiff. He used to put pillowcases and socks in his T-shirts because he hadn't discovered shoulder pads yet, but he knew he wanted a different silhouette. Big hair, big shoulders, small waist. 'I looked stunning but, of course,' he says, 'I lost my job.'

1976
FIREWORKS

'Even in their wildest dreams, none of the young participants and witnesses of punk shows in 1976 would have thought that these wild, chaotic events would be the subject of history. It felt important – the only thing happening within a moribund, decaying society – but that was not a view that swayed the general public, which regarded it with incomprehension, if not hostility.'

JON SAVAGE

Peter York: Bryan Ferry had a dreadful time when punk came along, because socially he had gone upstairs terribly quick, and those people who used to love him had to pretend that they didn't. All the people who adored him said, 'You traitor.' Certainly, people like Julie Burchill, who had adored him, said he was a class traitor. Bowie was different and he managed these things better, but I think Bryan was wrong-footed by that and rather sort of miserable about it.

Midge Ure: The Slik single 'Forever and Ever' came out at the very end of 1975, so by early 1976, we were on *Top of the Pops*. It had already been a baptism of fire as I had expected to play on the Slik records, although the management thought otherwise. We turned up in South Molton Street in London with a van full of equipment, having driven down from Glasgow, but as soon as we got in the recording studio, they played us the backing track, which they'd already done. The song had been written by the same guys who wrote for the Bay City Rollers, and the musicians turned out to be the same ones who played on their records too. So that was a major stumbling block, because in our minds we were Roxy Music. Of course, the moment you do something like this you are branded as another Bay City Rollers, and that's a very difficult thing to shake.

We were naive enough to think that we'd be able to grow through that, but we couldn't.

The whole thing was bizarre. *Top of the Pops* decided that for their New Year's Day edition, they were going to give four new bands a crack at being on the programme. So we came down, filmed it, and on New Year's Eve I took the train back to Glasgow – because you can't be in England for New Year's Day, you've got to be back home. And by half past two on New Year's Day everything changed because we had appeared on television and everyone knew who we were. It was a weird time, because at that time twenty-odd million people watched it, so it was huge. You couldn't really walk down the street without people recognising you, and all of a sudden you became important for the wrong reasons. Suddenly you were a pin-up, in *Jackie* magazine or *Mates*. All of a sudden you're on girls' bedroom walls, and that's kind of a heady mixture, you know – fame, notoriety, but for all the wrong reasons.

There were moments when girls were jumping on the limo that came to take you to do a radio or TV show, or they threw underwear on stage. But it was very short-lived, and within six months everything changed. The Pistols, the Damned and the Clash came along and upset the apple cart. We'd already started to lag, as while the first single was a No. 1, the follow-up, 'Requiem', struggled to get into the Top 30. I was stuck in Glasgow, four hundred miles from where it was all happening. So we broke our contract. We walked into the studio one day, and the latest song that these guys had written for us was 'The Kid's a Punk', which was a bizarre mixture of the Bay City Rollers meets Johnny Rotten, and it was just wrong from the word go. So we walked, thinking that another company would pick us up, but no one did.

Fiona Dealey: I started going to the Lacy Lady in Ilford, which was a big deal. It remains the best club I've ever been to. It was just so exciting. The place was tatty, upstairs from a pub, but you would get a lot of people from London, so that was when I met the very first punks. It cost one pound to get in, and probably for licensing reasons you were given a raffle ticket or token and got 'free' chips in a basket. This would have been early 1976. They looked really exciting because they were wearing proper punk clothes, but although we were really soul girls, we were wearing similar clothing – rubber trousers, big brightly coloured mohair jumpers. Mum would help me sew a new outfit every week for what I would wear on a Saturday night. I made skin-tight ski pants out of black rubberised industrial shower curtain fabric; harem pants, slashed from the waist to ankle, from curtain lining, worn over fishnet tights; second-hand finds would be cut up, readapted; satin sixties stilettos would be dyed brighter colours with felt pen . . . Anything and everything was possible, new looks conjured up every Saturday night. Never wore the same look twice!

There was a complete crossover on how we were dressing, but we weren't punks. Punks knew that and we knew that, but we just mixed together. And the music was the very best. Chris Hill and Robbie Vincent were DJing. The whole scene there was completely working-class. I was a bit snobby and I started to think that the Goldmine was a bit provincial.

Jan Parker (*musician*): I got into punk while hanging out at the Lacy Lady. It seems that everyone who went there became someone in the media. We were listening to soul and funk at the club but throwing ourselves around and wearing ripped-up clothes. We were deeply interested in anything alternative, but there was no music to go with what we were feeling – until 1976, when the Damned played at the Lacy Lady. We were all completely blown away.

John Lydon (*punk icon*): I read about some disco git in England who theorised that punk actually began in the discotheques. There was, he wrote, a club called the Lacy Lady in Ilford, and he recalled seeing punks there who danced to all the disco records. He remembers it well. Johnny Rotten stole it all from them! Ha! Those punks happened to be me and my mates. Sid, [Jah] Wobble, John Gray, Dave Crowe and

Tony Purcell – a right motley crew. We used to go down the Lacy Lady every weekend because we knew someone who lived nearby.

Andy Polaris: One of the first times I got to escape from the children's home to London was seeing David Bowie at Wembley Arena on his *Station to Station* tour. That was an eye-opener because you saw all his other fans there, the freaks who were all wearing their plastic raincoats and plastic sandals, girls in dustbin liners for the first time, lots of proto-punks and some of the people that used to go to the Lacy Lady. I can remember seeing Billy Idol there. At the time, I kind of self-censored myself as you couldn't really be out and gay, as you felt your friends were not going to be that liberal. So you stayed in the closet.

Fiona Dealey: We started going to the Global Village. I used to have to bunk the fare up, as it was so expensive to get to London. The clothes we wore would often be made the night before, and I'd still be sewing myself into them on the train. The clothes seemed to change quite dramatically at this point. I don't know where we were getting the ideas from. I think we looked at magazines, but it would have been more like *19* and *Over 21* because *Vogue* was a bit dull. It wasn't about us.

I liked the way it changed all the time. So you might go one Saturday night to the Lacy Lady, and you'd see someone in a fluorescent top wearing bright-pink dungarees, for instance. Then we started dressing very fifties, and I'd wear my grandmother's fox fur with circular skirts that I'd made with netting and little slashed home-made tops. The people who lived in London knew how to dress, but we weren't overawed by them at all.

Peter York: By 1976, it's starting to look as though something is changing. I was living in a rather dreadful place on the King's Road. You can't get dreadful places on the King's Road now, but then you could. It was just down at the Crotch [on the King's Road], just before World's

End, literally next door to SEX. I would stop and talk to Malcolm and Vivienne because they were funny talkers – here's this funny art-school couple, and they've got political thoughts and they talk all their stuff. And you could tell they were limbering up for something. Malcolm would talk about the New York Dolls and New York, and I'd actually been to New York and stood in the queue for CBGBs and all that. I'd also read about all these New York bands in the *NME*. I think the *NME* was an absolutely huge influence, and I was reading it obsessively from '75 onwards. I remember going to Andrew Logan's [Butler's] Wharf party, where I met Billy Idol and said to him, 'And what do you do for a living?' And he said, 'I'm a van driver.' And I thought, 'No, you're not,' and, of course, he wasn't. He'd been to Sussex University, he'd cut his hair short, and there were lots of other fabulous people there. Then I met the Pistols through Malcolm and Vivienne. The Andrew Logans of this world knew Malcolm and Vivienne, but then Malcolm felt equivocal about being related to those people because they were too bourgeois and arty for the story they were trying to sell. And certainly they would have been too bourgeois and arty for the Clash, those warriors of W11. At the time, there was that thing about presentation and people wanting to distance themselves from their mentors. You had to be new. I remember going to see *Car Wash* with Malcolm and Vivienne, and sitting in the front row of the cinema, which was funny, because everyone was staring at them. [York says that at the time, the couple were 'plunging themselves into legend'.]

Rusty Egan: I gave up my day job and went professional as a drummer, and started auditioning for the Clash. Every day we went down to the cafe, and they'd talk about politics and no Elvis, Beatles or the Rolling Stones. It was a bit Monty Python, like, 'What have the Romans ever done for us?' I said, 'But I like Bowie.' And they said, 'All right, we like Bowie, but not Pink Floyd and Led Zeppelin.' And I go, 'All right then.' You were allowed to like Lou Reed, but not the Rolling Stones, which I thought was stupid. So I'd be sitting there saying, 'Well, I don't agree,' and they would say, 'Shut up and play drums.' So that's why I was not in the Clash.

Paul Simonon (*musician*): The Clash were the only band with three frontmen. All for one and one for all. It made it tough on Topper [Headon, their eventual drummer] because he wasn't around in the early days, and we were already a unit. It made him feel like an outsider, I don't think he understood what was going on. We weren't a political party; it was all about personal politics. When you've got three blokes in the room and at the end of the day you've done your rehearsal, everybody goes home, but in the Clash nobody did go home; everybody was living it and being it. To the point, well, you know, 'We've got no money, but there's a nice pair of second-hand trousers in Oxfam. We'll get those and paint them.' It was all in-house, and through that environment everybody was double-checking each other. In essence, it was because we were all trying to outdo each other. That's why people say, 'It was like three Eddie Cochrans on stage,' because we were all trying to outdo each other. 'If he jumps this high, I'm going to jump this high.' We were like yo-yos.

Mick Jones (*musician*): We were so of the moment, we never really thought about it, or I didn't anyway.

Paul Simonon: I remember me and Joe [Strummer], as our psychological problems were welling up, saying to each other, 'How come no one talks to us? They always talk to Mick after a show.' After months of agonising, we asked Mick why he thought it was, and he said, 'It's because they are scared of you.' And there's me and Joe having two-way therapy sessions with each other. Nothing much affected us. We had each other; we were an inbuilt system. Mick had his friendship with Tony James [from Generation X], whereas me and Joe had pretty much cut away our lives completely and started from day one with this new ideal: 'We're in the Clash.' I mean, I arrived in the group from nowhere. I had no friends, no baggage, and the same with Joe. The point was that we were doing what we were doing, and other groups were trying do whatever they were doing. It wasn't our concern; our concern was to deal with our stuff. We had an inbuilt integrity within the group and a social conscience. The Pistols were the only people we socialised with at the time. [Class] was something that we had to deal with internally, insofar as Joe went to boarding school, but then again, at the end of the day, does it really matter? By the time I met Joe, he was as broke as I was. OK, he had had a better education than me, but so what? What you're doing with your life now is more important. Whether you're middle-class or not, it's what you do with your life that is important. That's the thing about punk. It changed their [the fans'] lives, and it changed ours too.

Mick Jones: We were very aware of each other. We spent so much time with each other. There was that kind of telepathic thing. We knew things without even saying them; we looked at each other and just knew what the others were thinking. We were a three-pronged attack. We formed in a line, and the line was so strong that we never really thought about it.

Paul Simonon: In the beginning, it was us against them. Most of the audience were not on our side. They wanted to fight you 'cos you were punk, or you looked punk . . . Hence having cages over the front 'cos of the glass and bottles. That's partly why we moved around so much.

Mick Jones: Ducking and diving . . . There's goes a bottle, bang . . .

Paul Simonon: Well, we always did it on our own terms. And that's the magic of the Clash: right or wrong, it was on our own terms. The whole thing about the Clash is that from day one, I was thinking it wasn't going to last. I'm rowing with Mick, and Joe's rowing with Bernie [Rhodes], and so on. We were always so serious about it, the whole idea of being in a group. It was a very fragile thing – to the point that somebody dropped the plate, and that was it.

Robert Elms: I didn't go and see the Sex Pistols immediately, but within two or three months, and I was probably watching the Clash. And then I did see the Pistols, and everything changed. But for many of us, punk lasted about six months. It was very short-lived. I liken it now to a firework display, as it kind of lit up the sky and then just petered out. Suddenly the Pistols are killing themselves or killing other people, and the Clash had gone all American rock, and I remember thinking, 'It's all over now, you know. This is boring, and nothing's going to happen.'

Steve Dagger: I found out about the Sex Pistols from Roger Austin, who ran the Screen on the Green in Islington. Steve Woolley was in my year at school, and when he left, he said he was going to work at the Screen on the Green, and he became assistant manager there and rose to be the manager. So I used to go drinking there, which is where I met Roger. One day, Roger came over in his leather trousers and said, 'My friend Malcolm has got this band – and they're going to be the new Rolling Stones – called the Sex Pistols.' I wasn't keen, but then Steve went to see them and phoned me up and said, 'Actually, they're really good.' So I went to see them at the Screen on the Green, and they were brilliant. Most of the people there were people I'd seen around in various clubs, and they were the more extreme end of the soul fashion crowd. It was a real crossover audience, kids that were looking for something. I thought the bands were fantastic – Sex Pistols, the Clash and the Buzzcocks – and was very excited about it. From then onwards I went to a number of Sex Pistols and other punk shows for about six to eight months.

Gary Kemp (*musician*): Before Spandau Ballet, before the Makers and Gentry and all the other bands I was in, I was in a group of older guys called the Same Band, and we played pubs, doing country rock and Steely Dan covers. Then I went to the Sex Pistols show at the Screen on the Green in August '76 with Steve Norman and Steve Dagger. It was a Saturday night, and we didn't leave until two in the morning. There's no point even describing it now because it has been so fetishised, but I genuinely was there, and it was such an extraordinary thing for a sixteen-year-old to witness these kids who were only a couple of years older than me but seemed like they were other-worldly. It was like an art installation that was so full of energy. They were supported by the Buzzcocks (and Howard Devoto had an arty sense about him), and then the Clash came on in their paint-splattered boiler suits, with their legs splayed. Then you had the oikishness of Steve Jones and Johnny. What's funny is no one was dancing. Philip Sallon was wearing a duster coat, and he got up on stage and danced in this sort of sarcastic way. But I felt that the audience were part of the installation too. I had a rehearsal the next day, and I walked straight in and said, 'I'm out. I don't want to do this any more. I've just seen the greatest thing I've ever seen in my life. I can't play in this band any more.'

Julien Temple (*film director*): I was initially attracted by the ferocity and the originality of the Pistols. Not as musicians, but as a band, an attitude. When the Pistols played Leeds in 1976, all the kids in the audience felt that they had to wear safety pins, tear their clothes and spit at the band. I still remember that amazing image. When Rotten finally came on stage, it was like Agincourt. There were these massed volleys of gob flying through the air that just hung on John like a Medusa. It was like green hair or snakes.

Neil Tennant: A friend of mine, Eric Watson, who later became a successful photographer, took me with him to see the Sex Pistols at the Nashville. This is when I by chance wrote the first piece about the Sex Pistols in the *NME*. I wrote it as a letter, and they published it as a little feature, with this picture by Joe Stevens. There was always an air of violence around the Sex Pistols, and I was scared by that gig. It was so horrible. There was someone being beaten up ten yards from me with a bicycle chain. I didn't go to gigs for five years after that.

Malcolm McLaren: Rotten had terrible shoulders. Round and flabby. Irish shoulders. And his body was the shape of a pear. But in the clothes that we gave him he always looked wonderful. He was a wonderful mannequin for the clothes that Vivienne and I designed for him. He complained about them, of course. I sold a lot of trousers off the back of Johnny Rotten.

Chris Sullivan: Around Easter, punk started to happen, and people got hooked on the shock value because they hated the fact that you had narrow trousers or short hair and winkle-pickers . . . They used to call us 'weirdies'. I saw that more people were starting to listen to the Velvet Underground and the Doors, and Patti Smith's *Horses*. They were all Bowie fans. Then the clothes became a little bit weirder and a bit more sinister, and a schism opened up. I first saw this when I went to see Bowie at the Empire Pool in May 1976. There was one gang that was all pink peg trousers and plastic sandals and Hawaiian shirts. Then the other gang, the Bromley lot, were wearing leather trousers and had dyed hair, with lots of earrings. I thought, 'Something's going on.' Like anybody else, I was into one-upmanship, which is what the whole New Romantic thing was all about. You know, the banter – 'You actually came out like that? And you haven't been beaten up? You didn't take the tube in that, did you?' So anyway, I got right into punk, but it soon became a cliché, created by the tabloids. I didn't even like the Clash at the time as they felt very generic. A lot of people behaved as they thought they ought to behave. Because punk was a fashion. It wasn't anything to do with politics and really angry kids. This was a fashion that emanated from New York, and it was a fashion movement in Malcolm's shop, at St Martin's, with a gay, mixed clientele. The punk cliché got grafted on afterwards. All that spitting was disgusting. I think a lot of people who were involved with it in the beginning were absolutely appalled. Probably one of the finest examples would be Steve Strange, gay, from Blackwood. He loved dressing up. He had all the bondage stuff. He would go absolutely mental if you spat at him, and he'd been a roadie and had worked for some of the bands as well. So he saw it first-hand. So, from where it actually began, which is quite a peacock thing – you know, showing off, red trousers, plastic pockets – to end up with a minging old T-shirt and spitting at each other, with their funny hair, it's quite a journey. In the pre-punk times, you had people wearing Acme Attractions, and if you went to Crackers on a Saturday, you'd see a couple of people looking like Robert Mitchum, you'd see girls in Courrèges and see-through macs. At the time, during the day I'd be wearing a mac and a trilby and a forties suit. Me and my friend went to this pervy shop in Cardiff and bought all this leather stuff. To get into my bedroom, I had to walk through my father's and mum's bedroom. My mother said to me, 'Was I dreaming? Because last night I could have sworn I saw you walking through my bedroom dressed in rubber.'

I had three jobs at the time: I was loading pop lorries, I had a paper round and I had this cancer and polio thing, which was like a pools delivery. I was an avid shoplifter as well, which also helped. We used to get the 7.20 bus from Merthyr Tydfil on a Saturday and would arrive at midday at Victoria station. Then we'd get the Number 11 bus and then walk right down to the end of the King's Road. By the time we got to SEX, we'd have bumped into everybody we knew. And we'd find out where the party was, what was going on. It was almost like the equivalent of Facebook in those days. Everybody you wanted to know was there on a Saturday. So by the end we'd hear about the next Sex Pistols concert or house parties or which clubs to go to. So that's what we did, and we did that a lot.

Dave Rimmer: The key club for those punks who were later to form the nucleus of the New Romantics was Louise's, a small lesbian basement dive on Poland Street in Soho. This was where the Bromley Contingent hung out, and soon they would also introduce it to the Pistols crowd. Siouxsie was one of the first punks to discover it. 'Before it got a label it was a club for misfits,' she remembers. 'Waifs, male gays, female gays, bisexuals, non-sexuals, everything. No one was criticised for their sexual preferences. The only thing that got looked down upon was suburbia.' Soon Soo Catwoman, Berlin, Billy Idol and all the rest of the Bromley Contingent were making it their own. John Lydon remembers taking acid in Louise's and learning that he enjoyed the company of prostitutes. Shortly before the September 1976 Punk Rock Festival at the 100 Club, Malcolm McLaren was in there, worrying that he needed one more band to fill the bill. 'We've got a band,' lied Siouxsie. And thus the Banshees were born. Philip Sallon was a regular and told George O'Dowd to come along. George put on his best black lipstick and sniffed around sheepishly, amazed at how unfashionable it all was. The Welsh contingent, Steve Strange and Chris Sullivan, could also be found in Louise's, where 'Love Hangover' was the signature tune and DJ Caroline would lose it from time to time, screaming, 'Why don't you straights all fuck off? You've got your own clubs to go to!' But they didn't, not really, and they weren't all straight. Safe haven for the crowd that represented the crossover between the dressy end of punk and the nascent new club culture, Louise's was in many ways the first New Romantic club.

Louise's was its own scene, and yet it also encouraged its new denizens to dress up and get involved. In a city which, while having its fair share of important nightclubs, was still unable to cater for those who were deliberately on the fringes, Louise's was somewhere for the sexually fluid, the sartorially inquisitive and the socially mobile (regardless of in which direction) to explore themselves and their peers. One of the strongest leitmotifs at the time was Cabaret, *which managed to fuse so many ideas, both sexually and sartorially, with the likes of Siouxsie Sioux experimenting with fishnets and thigh-high boots, cropped hair, savage* Clockwork Orange *make-up, leather micro-dresses and even the occasional bowler hat. This obsession with the Weimar Republic would eventually result in some of the braver habitués starting to wear swastika armbands, although even for them this felt like a transgression too far. According to Jordan, SEX's infamous shop assistant, one regular at Louise's was Butch Joe, a black woman with a shaved head and no front teeth who wore a beige Burton suit and used to say to anyone in earshot, 'Strap a dick to me, dear!'*

Siouxsie Sioux: By 1975, I was eighteen and had started to become what I wanted to be. I started going to concerts and hanging out with the Pistols, and in September 1976, at the 100 Club punk festival, I played my first gig, along with Sid [Vicious]. We stumbled through a twenty-minute version of 'The Lord's Prayer', and even though we weren't very good, I decided to form a band. I suppose, during the first period of punk activity, I looked quite typical, with a short, sharp shock of hair which was either peroxide or jet black. When the press turned their attention to me, I stepped back, as the worst thing about the whole punk thing was that people were able to call you something on the street. Being caught out spoiled all the fun, as what I really wanted to be was different from everyone else, not the same. So I started dressing in unlikely clothes and tried to create my own face mask and my big headdress. They called me 'a tarantula on stilts'. I knew I wanted something different; it was just a case of trial and error. Someone told me about crimpers, and after using them a few times I realised what you could actually do with them. One day, I just started hacking and came up with the idea for the look – I wanted a haircut which was gravity-defying.

Viv Albertine (*musician*): It [London] was like the Wild West. It felt particularly terrifying for us girls to be dressed the way we were. The police couldn't care less about us; their take was that we had it coming and we looked like aliens, and the skinheads' take was that 'If you're not going to dress like "a woman", we're not going to treat you like a woman.'

The men in suits thought that 'If you want to look like that, we can treat you like shit,' and it was as if all the misogyny that was inside them could come out, because we weren't playing the game of looking like 'a woman', so now they could put all their hate onto us. The whole music business was run by men, whether it was DJs, A&R men, PR people, and the streets, the businesses, the schools, dentists, doctors, everything was run by men, and so we were hated.

Kim Bowen: Louise's was off Oxford Street. My mother and my stepfather dropped us off, and we scuttled off down the road to a pub, went in the toilet and then did the pornographic transformation into whatever filthy outfits we wore. We went into this heaving club, and it was fabulous. It was the first time I saw Philip Sallon, and he was painted gold and immediately befriended us. For so many young people going into London clubs, he was the gatekeeper. There were disco glitter balls, Vivienne Westwood dwarves, men pumping iron in the corners, really loud music, plastic trousers. It was everything I ever dreamed of in a nightclub. There was a smattering of what I suppose were the first punks. We were meant to meet my mother outside so she could drive us home, but we were such horrible children that we hid in the club because we were having such a good time. My poor stepfather had to come in the club to look for us, and then Philip Sallon started to chat him up. He was horrified. I remember when we got in the car to drive home, he wouldn't even tell my mother what he'd seen in there because it was so disgusting, which was very satisfying to us. Then I started going to the Sombrero, Crackers, Bang and the Rainbow Room on top of the Biba store. [Bang opened in 1976 and was London's first proper gay super-club. It was held at the Sundown on Charing Cross Road every Monday, and then, as it grew more popular, on Thursdays too.]

Peter York: I remember being in Louise's. I went with this girl who was a Bowie fanatic, and Malcolm was there, and Sid. Lots of faces you'd see later on.

Graham Ball: I'd started doing security for the Sex Pistols, but didn't really know what I wanted to do. We went to lots of clubs, including Louise's, which was so expensive: four or five pounds for a tiny can of lager. The club was full of attitude. There were real sex workers and groups of gays. Going in as a straight seventeen- or eighteen-year-old, you realised it was a more sophisticated clientele. Certainly more sophisticated than Crackers or the Sombrero. The really sophisticated people were from art school.

In May, the Sex Pistols supported the Doctors of Madness at Middlesbrough Town Hall, in one of their first excursions outside their cosy London media bubble. Richard Strange, the Doctors' lead singer, had blue hair and was well versed in the art of disruption, and yet he saw the dial had moved quite radically. 'I'd obviously heard of them, and I thought, "Yeah, that's all right,"' says Strange. 'They did their soundcheck, and it was all sort of, you know, rough and ready. But when they went on . . . I saw that it was all over for us, that night. I was twenty-four, I guess, and I was finished. I saw the Pistols and I thought, "That's it, that's tomorrow."'

Norman Jay (*DJ*): My clubbing days had started back in 1973, when I was sixteen. I went everywhere, from the blues parties in Brixton, where no white people went, to Crackers, the Global Village, the Lacy Lady in Ilford, the Goldmine in Canvey Island. I was a dancer and a serial clubber and a fanatical black-music fan. However, I think interesting things start to happen when people move from one world to another, so I found it interesting when people who used to go to soul clubs started going to punk clubs, and vice versa. Music scenes in the seventies were segregated because people were so tribal. I was one of those soul boys who used to be on the King's Road on a Saturday morning chasing skinheads and fighting off Teddy boys. They were very anti-punk, so we felt a duty to protect the punks because some of my mates were punks. The skinheads used to come down and bash heads outside the Antiquarius market or outside SEX. I loved the summer of '76 as it was hot. I was unemployed, money was scarce, I couldn't afford to go to football, couldn't afford the clothes I wanted to wear, but it was such an amazing year for black music. Not only was the club scene massive, but I'd started going to gay clubs like the Sombrero, because I realised very early on the gay clubs were playing the best music.

Dave Stewart (*musician*): In adult life I learnt a lot about my childhood, and the longer I strained and looked at my formative years, the more I could remember so many triggers for me to be a musician. You're always looking for things that cause a spark, but you can't believe that everything is an accident. Hearing Rodgers and Hammerstein records on my dad's stereo probably did it for me. Honestly, if I hadn't found a guitar, I would have been a drug addict. Nineteen seventy-six wasn't just the year of punk, it was the year I met Annie [Lennox] and it all changed, as it did for everyone, especially those who would go on to form groups in the early eighties. There was excitement in the air.

Boy George: I guess my cultural development was meeting Philip Sallon in Bang, the gay club at the Sundown on Charing Cross Road. Me and my girlfriend at the time, Laura, went to a soul night at the Lyceum and we were wearing punk clothes, and they said, 'No punks.' So we were hovering around in the street, and this queen just came up to me and said, 'Why don't you go to Bang?' That was really the beginning. That's where I saw Philip Sallon dancing on a podium in a skirt, and I was like, 'Oh my God! I've got to meet that person and become friends with him.' A week later, I went out with him without the girlfriend, and my life began. And it was really that idea that there are other people who think like I do, someone else who had fallen for Bowie! It reminded me of his song 'After All', from *The Man Who Sold the World*. It was sort of a longing for more, really. I loved getting involved with punk. I was a massive Siouxsie Sioux fan – I'd started to see her at lots of clubs – and so I started to wear a lot of make-up. I remember somebody dropping a pint of lager on my head because they didn't like the way I looked, and so there was a bunch of us who kind of knew that punk was becoming something that maybe we couldn't be part of. We wanted something else.

Ollie O'Donnell: In January, Ricci Burns told us he was opening another salon, this time in the King's Road, and in March, I went to work there [by this time Burns was cutting and dyeing the hair of Jordan, the SEX shop assistant]. There was a shop nearby called Acme Attractions, and I would pop in two or three times a week. It was a brilliant clothes shop, but very expensive, as I was on very small apprentice wages. There was a very large market stall in Petticoat Lane which we would go to on a Sunday morning. It sold copies of Acme's stuff, but at a third of the price – pegged trousers, in the same cut, but different colours. We would buy original bowling shirts from second-hand stalls on Brick Lane, which was like a Third World market in 1976 – very run down and very cheap. The top end of Portobello Road was also a great place to find clothes, especially mohair jumpers in perfect condition and big fifties herringbone overcoats and forties suits, which I would get altered. We'd buy plastic sandals in Lillywhites, the big sports store on the corner of Piccadilly. They were sold in the snorkelling and diving department, as they were to be worn underwater. I loved plastic sandals, and they were very comfortable, especially that year, when the weather started to get very hot.

There was a great energy in the air that early summer of 1976. People would go and see *The Rocky Horror Show*, drink in the Chelsea Potter, the Chelsea Drug Store, the Markham. The Roebuck and the Water Rat would also be packed every night. The King's Road was alight. It was electric that summer, fantastic energy. A very creative period in London. My friend Antonio at Ricci's told me he was moving to another salon called Smile, in Knightsbridge, run by a very cool guy called Keith. He said it was a more avant-garde kind of place that would suit him – and also myself – better, with a much more contemporary clientele and more fashionable and more interesting work. So he arranged for me to see Keith, and I started two weeks later. A week after I started at Smile, Antonio was killed coming out of a party by Battersea roundabout. I think it was an Andrew Logan party. He must have been out of it. Apparently, he staggered into the road and a lorry spun round and smashed into him and killed him stone dead. He was only twenty-six, twenty-seven max.

Nell Campbell (*actress*): I worked in Kensington Market, and then got a job as a soda jerk in a cafe in Knightsbridge called Smalls. I had a thirties bob and would sing and dance – the poor customers. One day, Richard O'Brien came in and said he was doing this show called *The Rocky Horror Show* on the King's Road, and before the bill came I was hired. We knew it was going to be a cult hit. The film came out in 1975, and the same thing happened. People forget that all the songs are fantastic, the script is short and tight, and the sex element is major. What other musical has sex where there's cross-gender, bi-, hetero-, trans-, the whole goddamn confusion? It's all there. It liberated people. *Hair* had its fair share of nudity, but it was very dull.

Ollie O'Donnell: At the time, I was going to Crackers on a Tuesday night. You were given a voucher to exchange for a small wicker bowl of sometimes scampi and chips, sometimes sausage and chips. Apparently, that was the only way they could have an alcohol and music licence. This was not uncommon in the mid-seventies. The club itself was a dump. It looked very run down and old-fashioned, but the atmosphere was electric. I had never heard sounds as edgy as this before. Pure funk. I have heard people say it was 80 per cent black kids in there on a Tuesday night, but that's impossible. I am sure I would have remembered that, and also no club in the West End, or even the ones I had gone to in the suburbs – the Bird's Nest in Muswell Hill and the Royalty in Southgate – would let in anywhere near that percentage of black people at any one time. I know that for a fact. From my experience it would not be more than 30 per cent. There was a Friday lunchtime session in the club as well, which was very popular, but I was too busy working in Knightsbridge to get over for that.

People danced wherever they could in the club. It was all carpeted, apart from the small dancefloor. So people did their thing wherever they stood. It was so vibrant in there you could not be in the club and not dance. It was impossible. You had quite a mixed bunch of people, and they would be dressed to dance: very slim, tight jeans; slip-on leather shoes or little suede boots (pixie boots they were called); sleeveless T-shirts; and hand towels to wipe off the sweat from dancing.

There was a small crowd who interested me – maybe only thirty people – who wore very different clothes. They had bleached-blond cropped hair, with crazy red and green streaks through the side. Yet again they'd be wearing black Serra T-shirts from SEX and red jeans from SEX, the ones with the plastic back pockets. These were the pre-punks. There were a couple of Bowie twins from Hatfield in Hertfordshire. They were both tall and razor thin, and looked like a slightly more exaggerated version of David Bowie on the cover of *Young Americans*. Their hair was even more exaggerated: deep red with bleached streaks through the front, but also with pink highlights cascading over their eyes, and slicked back at the sides. Pencil-thin dark plucked eyebrows, very pale complexions, with black mascara. They always wore the shiniest black or red plastic dungarees. Outside the club they would wear these slightly furry leopard-skin bomber jackets, which I thought looked great.

They had a mad, slurry way of talking, and kind of shouted and talked at the same time. They would jump from one subject to another in mid-sentence. They were very unusual people. Every second line was 'Never mind the bollocks.' They would say that three hundred times a night. Everything was 'Never mind the bollocks.' I know for a *fact* that the Sex Pistols got the name for their album from the twins. They both earned a living selling hot dogs. One worked on Charing Cross Road, the other down by Trafalgar Square. They were mad.

If you stopped to talk to them, they would always be arguing with someone. Man or woman, they always had the same line: 'Now listen, sweetheart: never mind the bollocks.'

Princess Julia: At the time, it was all about gay discos and the punk scene, bondage trousers from SEX. Jordan became a role model quite quickly. I know it's hard to believe, but I'm actually quite shy. I was petrified of everything but so into people expressing themselves through what they did creatively or how they looked that punk was like a magnet to me. That's how I made friends and went to gigs, and it was really quite astounding the number of women that were on the punk scene doing amazing things. It was a community for people like me who were disenfranchised. At the time, women were expected to get married and have children and have this sort of life. I just never felt like that was the life I wanted; I didn't want a normal family life. I went to the family planning clinic and asked them to give me a hysterectomy. I said, 'Listen, I think it's time. I think you should take my womb away.' And they looked really sad! I was like, 'I'm not going to have children, and I just want to be sort of androgynous.' I kind of identified as a robot or a puppet of some sort. I'm not sure where I got that idea from. I just felt like quite an androgynous-type person. The initial punk scene was quite androgynous; it was quite fluid, quite gay, effeminate, a lot softer than it became. Boys wearing make-up, girls wearing make-up, lots of drag!

Stephen Jones: Having decided to pursue fashion, I applied to St Martin's, which at the time was known as a sculpture college. But it was right in the centre of London, it was 1976, and it was right at the heart of everything that was happening in the city. I mean, who the hell wants to be in Kingston? You might as well be on the south coast. I had adored Bowie and Bryan Ferry, and London seemed like the only place to enter that world. I had shortish hair. I was wearing suits and was a devotee of the *NME* and *Melody Maker*, and I became aware of punk very early on. There was a place called the Nag's Head in High Wycombe, which was a really super-well-known music venue, and I went there every week, seeing Wayne County and Generation X and all the early punk people, and then eventually I joined a punk band called Pink Parts [with Paul Ferguson, who eventually joined Killing Joke, and Martin Stone from the Pink Fairies]. I arrived at St Martin's in August 1976 wearing black trousers and a black polo neck jumper, with a black beret and chipped black nail varnish. I remember walking into the fashion room, and there were all these girls wearing beige on one side and about five or six punks on the other. So I sat with them. On my first day, I had lunch with a girl called Chrissie Atkinson, whose boyfriend was Shane MacGowan, then in the Nipple Erectors. Kenny Morris from the Banshees was in the room next to me at the Ralph West Halls of Residence. I started to see Siouxsie and lots of the early punks, but we always had a problem with the Sex Pistols because they were manufactured, they were Malcolm's band.

We used to go to a club called Louise's, and then later we started going to Heaven and the Embassy, where I think Rupert Everett worked as a waiter in satin hot pants. Louise's was the place, though, and it's where I met Philip Sallon, Marianne Faithfull, Duggie Fields, Yvonne Gold, Vivienne Westwood, Dinny Hall, Esme Young from [clothes shop] Swanky Modes. That time was all about discovery. I mean, I think it was Kim Bowen who had heard about Nina Simone, and we tried to find some of her records in the Record and Tape Exchange in Notting Hill Gate and spent hours trying to find something. We found one – a 78 or something like that – and that was it. So if you were into something or tried to find out about something, you had to really love it because it was actually quite a difficult thing to do.

Peter Ashworth (*photographer*): I was born in 1953 and had a very strange upbringing. My father was a bit of a violent alcoholic, and it messed my head up quite a lot. He then split just before I was about to do my A-levels, and from this very threatening, restrictive life, suddenly

I was free. So I screwed my A-levels up the first time around because I went a bit AWOL. I'd done chemistry, physics, biology, and I actually really quite enjoyed the sciences, so it made sense for me to pursue a scientific art. Without actually having taken a picture, I decided to become a photographer. So, in 1976, I joined the London College of Printing, at the same time as Stephen Jones was at St Martin's. It was a fantastic time to be in London. I didn't realise when I first came here, because the London I came to was a wreck of a place. I was horrified at the state of London. It looked like it was still in the Second World War, and everyone was in the doldrums. It just felt very grey and negative. It felt like I'd travelled back about five or ten years from Eastbourne, which was a relatively happy-go-lucky place. London was ugly but full of fascinating people. Stephen had actually come to LCP to offer his services as a make-up artist – networking in the first year! It indicated that he knew exactly what he was doing and how he was going to do it.

Ollie O'Donnell: At Smile my name was changed again, as Keith decided to call me Oliver, so everyone in the salon called me Ollie. This name has stuck with me ever since. There would be about fifteen of us that would all go out socialising together. A few of the older ones had seen the Sex Pistols play, and so we all went to one of the two nights of the punk festival at the 100 Club in September. I loved it that night, and the Pistols had a massive impact on me. I loved everything about it: the attitude, the look, the energy, the music. I saw the same twenty to thirty people I used to see in Crackers, and maybe another thirty that I had never seen before. But that was it – fifty people maximum that I thought looked really radical. Everyone else was wearing flared jeans.

A few of my friends from Crackers went, as it was the fashionable thing to do. But they hated it. Straight away there was a division. Most of the soul crowd didn't like the Pistols, and the early punk thing wasn't for them. But then a small percentage of people that went to Crackers and the Global Village on a Saturday stopped going and went to punk gigs and clubs instead, myself included. I had friends that I literally never saw again. They went one way, and we went another. Soul clubs were too mellow for me now.

Martin Fry: At the time, I was just daydreaming about being a singer, and I had no real ambition to be one. Then it changed subliminally when I saw the Sex Pistols play their second show at the Lesser Free Trade Hall in June 1976.

Daniel Miller: I came back from Switzerland around the time when punk was just starting, in the spring of '76, and I was really into it completely. I mean, I wasn't a punk, but I loved the energy and for a moment I loved the music, and then I decided this is a moment for me to do something *with* music.

Simon Napier-Bell (*manager*): In 1976, I started managing two groups: Japan, who I would work with for quite some time; and a punk band called London. I had been living in Spain for two years, but had started to come back to London regularly when I walked into this club – I can't remember which club – and saw this amazing group who played very fast songs, quite tight in a rock manner, and jumped up and down as if they were on pogo sticks. I'd never seen anything like it, so I rushed backstage afterwards and signed them. I gave them £10,000 cash on the spot to sign with me, and then found out the next day that every single group in town jumped up and down like they were on pogo sticks. But luckily I went to MCA Records, and there was a chap there who hadn't been to a gig for about three years, so when he saw them he was as amazed as I was and signed them up. So I got my £10,000 back, and then we went ahead and made an album. They did quite well and had a hit called 'Everyone's a Winner'. They had a very camp, very colourful lead singer called Riff Regan, their drummer was a real loudmouth, a noisy, lower-class person called Jon Moss, and they were all absolutely vile, very working-class. They'd come around to my flat, and they would have trodden in dog shit outside on purpose and they'd put their feet up on the coffee table and things like that. One day, we were offered a TV show at the last minute, so I had to call them all at home. When I called Jon's number, this very cultured woman answered and said, 'Hello?' And I said I obviously had the wrong number. But it was the right number, and Jon was very embarrassed when his mother heard him talking to me in this fake cockney voice. It turned out they were all public schoolboys, and Riff Regan's dad was actually the air vice-marshal, and Riff was actually called Miles Tredinnick. And you can't get posher than that.

Terry Jones (*art director, publisher*): I first started thinking about *i-D* in 1976, although it didn't actually materialise until 1980. The newspapers were full of stuff that was going on down the King's Road, but I'd not seen that many photographers who came to see me with this sort of material at *Vogue*. But then one day this guy came to see me called Steve Johnston, who had just left college in Carlisle. He showed me his portfolio, and it was full of landscapes and sheep walking through villages and stuff like that. I just said, 'Listen, you're not going to make a living out of this. If you want to do something that's really interesting, go and document what's going on in the King's Road.' I said, 'If I had been around at the time, I would have documented the sixties through street photography, and this is exactly what we should be doing now.' I'd started to ask photographers to contribute to this idea, but also I had reached a point where I thought, 'I've been at *Vogue* for four years, it's a repetitive cycle,' and stuff that was happening on the street looked more interesting.

Marc Almond: In 1976, I applied to Leeds Polytechnic to do a foundation course. The guy in charge was Jeff Nuttall, who'd written *Bomb Culture*, and he became my mentor. At the interview, he asked me to perform something, so I did a mime. It was rather embarrassing, but afterwards he said, 'You're in.' I didn't have the qualifications, but he got me. My life so far had been blagging my way into things basically.

So I joined the course, and that was where I eventually met David Ball. I was told to just get on with it for three years and produce a show at the end of every year, and if you don't produce a show, you're out. Jeff said, 'We're not going to tell you what to do, but you've got everything you want at your fingertips. You can make some great films, you can do sculptures, you've got a performance area with lighting and sound. Just make sure you produce something every year.' Jeff liked confrontation, so my performance art became quite confrontational. He was a very confrontational person, and looking back he would kind of molest you and everything like that and be quite full on with you, just to see what your reaction would be and if you could cope with it or not. I suppose this stuff would be totally not on at all now.

The *Anarchy* tour came to Leeds in December. Actually, the first night of the tour. I remember standing by the mixing desk. The Sex Pistols, the Heartbreakers and the Clash. So that was a great time to be at art school, as a lot of students were bringing punk and confrontational stunts into their work – performance, art, paintings. And everyone was excited at what Vivienne Westwood was doing and what was happening in London.

Ben Kelly: In December, Malcolm asked me to design the interior for Seditionaries, which was what SEX was about to turn into. I only did the sign outside the shop as I had to go to New York to do a job. I did lots of work for the Pistols. I did Steve Jones's apartment – his 'shag pad' – in West Hampstead, and I did the Glitterbest office on St Martin's Lane. One day, I was sitting in Malcolm's offices in Dryden Chambers, off Oxford Street, and the phone rang. Everyone had buggered off and I was there by myself. I picked it up, and there was this person called Tony Wilson asking if the Sex Pistols would appear on his TV show, *So It Goes*, in Manchester. I took the message and told Malcolm when he came back from lunch. I was the conduit. And then Tony became obsessed with Malcolm and Vivienne and Situationism.

Robert Elms: In the autumn of 1976, Chaguaramas closed down, reopening in December under a new name, the Roxy. Neal Street, Covent Garden's famous 'birthplace of punk', was thereby born.

Ollie O'Donnell: I went to the opening night of the Roxy. I had been there once before, when it had been a gay–straight crossover club called Chaguaramas. I'm pretty sure Billy Idol and Generation X played the opening night of the Roxy, who I thought were brilliant. We then went there most nights. Sometimes to Louise's, in Poland Street, afterwards. A lot of the fashion punk crowd would hang out in Louise's. Malcolm McLaren would be in there a lot. A lot of the bands were terrible, but a lot were fantastic: Generation X, X-Ray Spex, the Clash, the Buzzcocks, the Jam. I loved it, but I've got to say that the whole thing did not last that long – maybe nine months. It was very intense, extremely exciting, but very short-lived.

Gary Kemp: After seeing the Sex Pistols, we all went back to school in September, our first year in sixth form, and tried to form a band with Steve Norman. We played the Roxy as the Makers, and tried to play a little like the Jam, because power pop had come along. Generation X were my favourites, as I just thought they looked like pop stars.

Karen O'Connor (*clubber*): I had just started working at the Speakeasy, and so had moved up from Dulwich to Chelsea, to a basement flat in Oakley Street. I met Steve Strange a week after moving in; he was urinating in my nearest telephone box, and I shouted at him. He was grubby and homeless, but he was stylish, so I took him home and gave him a bar of soap, and from that moment on we were virtually inseparable. Punk was just starting, and so we used to go to the Roxy a lot, and we immersed ourselves completely in club culture. The early Roxy days were amazing and awful at the same time. There was the ear-bleeding volume of all the bands, the new code of dress and the complete head-rush, counteracted by the skankiness of it all:

the spitting, the sweating, the overall chaos and pogoers gurning and grinding their teeth from the industrial quantities of amphetamine sulphate they all took.

I was severely gobbed on one night when I dared to wear a blue fifties fishtail dress and not the usual black zip trousers and mohair jumper. As I worked at the Speakeasy, I always got in free at all the other clubs, and this was reciprocated when anyone who worked at the Roxy wanted to come to the Speak. Then, it was a real crossover of old seventies and new seventies. You had to be in the music business to get into the Speakeasy, you couldn't just walk in, so when I started there, I served the likes of Tom Petty, Alex Harvey, Rod Stewart or the latest rock group from the US on tour in the UK. All big hair and tight trousers. Lemmy was permanently on the fruit machine. Often Billy Idol and Steve and always too many of their friends would come in when I got them on the guest list. Soon the Speakeasy would book bands like Johnny Thunders and the Heartbreakers and the Only Ones, and it became a bit of a hangout for punk-band members.

As it was, punk imploded before it had really properly started. On 1 December, the Sex Pistols appeared on an early-evening Thames Television magazine programme, Today, *presented by the broadcasting stalwart Bill Grundy. Queen had been scheduled to appear on the show, but when Freddie Mercury developed severe toothache, they cancelled. Eric Hall, the desperate EMI press officer, offered their new signing the Sex Pistols as a last-minute replacement, and so that night the band, accompanied by Siouxsie Sioux and a gaggle of Pistols acolytes, appeared on the show, and immediately sounded the death knell for punk. Goaded by a probably drunk Grundy, the definitely drunk and uncooperative Pistols proceeded to swear their way through the programme, with Steve Jones famously calling Grundy 'a fucking rotter'. The Thames TV phone lines started ringing, the media went ballistic, and the Pistols were suddenly public enemy number one. Quoted in Jon Savage's* England's Dreaming, *the journalist Jon*

Ingham says: 'It became stupid very quickly and no one with any snazz wanted to be associated with something like that.' The early adopters were horrified that something so liberating had been stolen from them by the mainstream media. 'The soul-boy crossover, for instance, was wiped out overnight,' says Savage, 'as the unconvinced returned to their cavernous discos in the hinterlands.'

1977

ENGLAND'S SCREAMING

'Britain's principal export specialities are punk and pageant, the future and the past. The past you know, it's obvious, it's "Queen and Country". You can't write it off as *just* tourism; you can't say it isn't relevant to a discussion of design futures. Because that stuff, the class stuff, the archaic stuff, the great dressing-up box of the past, is massively important in selling things and ideas from Britain.'

PETER YORK

Punk's greatest moments are replayed incessantly. Some people were there, and some weren't, but even those who were didn't see it all, and so we replay those classic moments as though they were part of the Zapruder film of the Kennedy assassination, trying to assign more and more meaning to them, watching them again and again for clues as to the true essence of punk. Was it the time the Sex Pistols played the Screen on the Green, the night the Damned played the Roxy for the first time, the early punk gigs at High Wycombe's Nag's Head, the night Sid Vicious attacked the NME*'s Nick Kent, that extraordinary night at Friars Aylesbury when Talking Heads and the Ramones occupied the same stage, seemingly beamed down from two completely different planets?*

There was a night at the 100 Club when the Jam played that will always stick in my mind. I was standing right in front of the stage, right in front of Paul Weller, as one of the speaker stacks began to teeter. As the bass reverberated through the wooden stage, the stack swung forwards, swung back, swinging away as though it were being pushed back and forth by a wind. I caught the eye of a roadie, who, like me, expected the stack to topple at any minute. He couldn't do anything about it as it was too high, and in the end it just kept swinging back and forth, and even seemed to speed up the longer the gig went on.

This motion seemed to mirror the jutting chins on stage, as all three members of the band kept pushing their chins forward like chickens, metronomically keeping up with 'All Around the World', 'The Modern World', 'Away from the Numbers' and all the others, little horizontal pogos that were copied by all of us in the crowd.

I lost count of the number of times I saw the Jam. The 100 Club, the Marquee, the Nag's Head, the Red Cow. I probably saw them – and their more than occasional support band, the New Hearts – a dozen times, the trio sweating through their suits, jutting their chins and pumping out the likes of 'In the City', 'All Around the World' and 'The Modern World' with the sort of sincerity that these days just looks forced and nostalgic. During punk's pomp, there seemed to be a new development every day, almost as though there was a mandate to splinter. You could look at a copy of the NME*, and a week later every component appeared to have changed: a new cover star, a new subgenre, a new venue, a new way of contextualising what had happened a week ago. It was all about evolution. However, for those who had been involved from the beginning, both on stage and in the audience, there was also the problem of how to deal with the second wave of institutionalised punks, in which the three-chord-leather-jacket-and-sneer template started to very quickly become a cliché. In this environment, it was perhaps no surprise that many of those who had been involved in the very first wave of punk started to look elsewhere for their thrills. In London, Manchester, Sheffield, all over, there were those who felt that while punk had been exciting, there was a world of possibilities out there.*

Still, for the Clash – and for many others – punk was really all about London, and egged on by their manager Bernie Rhodes, they made a point of writing about little else. Jon Savage called their LP The Clash *'virtually a concept album about North Kensington and Ladbroke Grove'. The city became vaguely mythical, a magnet for the future punk royalty, including Paul Weller, who wrote, among others,*

'Sounds from the Street', 'Down in the Tube Station at Midnight', 'In the City', 'A Bomb in Wardour Street' – all of them little snapshots of tough city life. Of course, both Bowie and Ferry had been here before, Bowie with his Swinging London near miss 'The London Boys', and Ferry with Roxy Music's 'Street Life', one of the best songs to celebrate the city as the after-dark glamour capital of the world.

Rusty Egan: I was at the 1 January opening of the Roxy, so I was kind of like everywhere, at every gig on the scene. I started going to the Roxy every night, in the Speakeasy every night, met Glen Matlock, met Leee Black Childers, met Bernie Rhodes, met everybody on the scene. I met the *NME* journalists Tony Parsons and Julie Burchill. I met the guy who would make M's 'Pop Muzik', Robin Scott, who was Malcolm's McLaren's mate. Met everyone.

Don Letts (*film-maker, DJ at the Roxy*): Punk made me realise I didn't want to be just a fan. One of the reasons it's had this lasting impact is that it wasn't just a soundtrack. We were like-minded outcasts who reinvented ourselves as writers, photographers, fashion designers, artists and film-makers. Until that time, I'd never thought about how one thing inspired another. Very little comes out of a total void.

Martin Fry: After the Sex Pistols, I saw everyone – the Clash, Johnny Thunder and the Heartbreakers, Siouxsie and the Banshees, Subway Sect – and suddenly it all made sense. I started a fanzine, as I realised that if you were a journalist, you could get into shows free. It was called *Modern Drugs*. Then I started going to Sheffield University, although there were hardly any punks in Sheffield. It had some incredible young bands like Cabaret Voltaire, the Human League and Clock DVA, bands that were moving on from punk, taking it somewhere else, somewhere more interesting. You'd see them in the local bars, but there weren't that many actual punks in Sheffield in 1977. I ran into Paul Morley, who lived in Stockport and had a fanzine called

Out There, which was mainly about Patti Smith and those people. I interviewed a band called Vice Versa, and they invited me to do a gig with them, so there was no turning back. Two days after the interview, we performed at Middlesbrough Rock Garden and were bottled off. Nevertheless, they offered me the gig, and so we went on tour, opening for Cowboys International. And that's how I started singing. Initially, I wanted to be a journalist, and went up to the *Guardian* in Manchester when I was at school, but I didn't follow it through. It was weird: beforehand it was terrifying, but there's something that makes absolute sense when you're on stage. I remember that feeling of being ignored for the first seventeen, eighteen years of my life, and then suddenly people are checking you out. It's a curious thing, but you kind of feel bulletproof.

Alison Moyet (*singer*): I left school at sixteen, unqualified. I got a hairdressing apprenticeship but was sacked after three weeks for bunking off to see a Tom Robinson gig. Having a grade four in oboe from when I was eleven qualified me for a foundation course in music at Southend Technical College. I passed my theory exam with distinction but was told I'd have to retake the year with a girl that failed. No explanation given, none requested. I just left instead. From here I got a job in a music shop in Romford and got talking to the piano tuner. I applied to the London College of Furniture in Aldgate East to take piano technology – tuning, restoration, building – and was accepted. I knew I could sing because people took note. I didn't start 'singing' to sing (I had been rejected from the school choir). I wrote songs. Words. I was a punk. I was disenfranchised and verbally uninhibited. I couldn't hold down a job, but I wanted to front a band because I was dominant, aggressive. I was not an acceptable presence for a girl in the seventies, and in punk bands I'd seen that otherness. I related to the energy. I came from quite a volatile family. Loud explosions were no strangers at the table. Being a vocalist in a punk band didn't require you to be a singer, and I didn't think of myself as one.

It wasn't about singing, it was about volume. My first band was called the Vandals. It was three girls, a guitarist (who was Vince Clarke's best mate) and whatever drummer we could pull up from our pool. All our mates were in bands – punk, seventies pub rock, speed-lead thrashes, power pop/new wave . . . There was no sense of it being a potential career, not for us anyway. We never got close to a studio. Playing is what we did. It filled the space for us then that gaming does now. We lived in a new town, Billericay. We had no culture. We built our own. I bought into that ethos about punk: that it wasn't about money or fashion or conforming, it was about insisting on being seen, having a presence; rejection of the norms and gender divisions. We had our community. We had lookouts in the town to give us the heads-up when the Teds or the skins or the market boys were seeking us out. And they did. At some point later we made alliances, except for the market boys. They would still give you a kicking for wearing drainpipes and pointy shoes. It was like that then. Shoe-gazing had a different purpose. You lived or died depending on the choices you made knee down.

The most natural home for me then became the sounds of the Estuary. Essex punks had adopted Dr Feelgood, Lew Lewis and Wilko Johnson. This too was a local scene that had a DNA connection with the body of our sound. It was intense and loud and agitating. That's how I took my music: live. You get into Estuary rock and it's natural that you seek out the stuff that informed it. I made mates, I joined bands, I started playing blues, although contrary to the later assumption that it was the jazz classics I was appreciating, it was Billy Boy Arnold that was informing the turns I would use later to embellish the very straight-pointing melodic lines of 'Don't Go' and our club tracks in Yazoo. It was English rhythm and blues in Southend and Canvey Island that was my scene from seventeen to Yazoo. This was what I brought to the microphone. My last band, the Screaming Abdabs, got as far as playing Dingwalls, the Nashville, the Fulham Greyhound and the Hope and Anchor. We often got banned, unfortunately, because the drummer kept drinking our PA contribution. We basically fell apart because the guitarist, a blues fundamentalist, wanted a bloke fronting the band who played harmonica and was not, as I was then, a blues shouter who liked a bit of Janis. I was looking for a new band when Vince called.

Gary Numan: When the punk thing came along in 1977, I wasn't mad about the music, but I saw the opportunities it created. Every record company was trying to sign a punk band, so I thought going into punk music was a way to get going. So I went out and joined a band called the Lasers. I had only recently been thrown out of another band. I'd started a group with my friends and we did three shows, and each one of those was under a different name. That's how argumentative it was. We couldn't decide on anything, but they were doing my songs. I went to a rehearsal for what was going to be our fourth gig and I was slightly late, and when I got there I could hear somebody else singing and began to sense I might not be in the band any more. I walked in and that was it, I'd been thrown out. They didn't have the bottle to tell me; just waited for me to turn up. So then I started to look for another band to join, and found the Lasers. I was slightly burnt from my previous experience, so I had no intention of being the frontman. And then at the very first rehearsal, at my mum and dad's house in Rainsbury, I noticed they didn't have any of their own songs. I said, 'Look, I've got loads. We could have our own songs if you wanted.' So we started doing that. Then I said, 'Everyone's called "the" something. We should try to sound a bit different.' And so they said, 'Well, what do you suggest?' So I listed some of the band names I had, and Tubeway Army was one of them. So by the end of that first rehearsal, where I was intending to stand in the background, I'd changed the name of the band and I was a singer and they were doing all my songs. I began to realise that I was a lot pushier than I thought.

My mum and dad gave me enough money to record a three-track demo at a studio in Cambridge, and we touted that around to all these little pop-up labels. I didn't have the courage to go to any of the big ones. I got as far as Atlantic, but I got so intimidated by the receptionist that I turned around and walked out. Then, by chance, the bass player, Paul Gardiner, went to his local second-hand shop to trade in some of his old albums to get some extra money. It was a Beggars Banquet shop in Earl's Court, and they had just started their own label, and that's how it started. Nine months later, we were No. 1. In the meantime, I discovered electronics. So we went into the studio as a three-piece punk band and came out as an electronic band.

Andy McCluskey: I liked the Pistols because they had great tunes, and I liked the Clash for the sheer energy, but the rest of the punk stuff I thought was crap and the bands were being pantomime punks. You know, 'Oh, you've just jumped on this bandwagon, and if disco was still in, you'd be doing that.' The Clash turned into Led Zeppelin with berets and turn-ups very quickly, didn't they? I always used to laugh when they sang 'I'm So Bored with the USA'. So why are you constantly fucking touring there? But what punk did, it detonated the London-centric music industry for a couple of years. Every regional city had a punk band, except for Liverpool. And every regional city had new-wave/punk clubs. So instead of having to play a youth club or try and get a gig in a pub where the landlord said, 'You're not getting paid unless you play cover versions,' you could actually go to a small rock venue in your town and get up on stage, because there was an open-door policy, and if you made enough noise and got into the *Sounds* or *NME* gig guide and people heard about you, the A&R men from London would have to get the train to come and see you. So punk opened the floodgates of what would come immediately after that. It's no coincidence that all of the bands of our generation come from the provincial, regional cities, not from London.

The Cambridge pub sits on the north-west corner of Cambridge Circus in London's West End – in 1977, just a hundred yards from the Marquee, a hundred yards from the 100 Club and only fifty yards from St

Martin's School of Art. From 1976 to 1980, the Cambridge was one of the most important pubs in Soho, and every band that wanted to leave an impression in the neighbouring venues usually ended up there, pumping money into the jukebox, drinking green and yellow bottles of Pils and throwing shapes in their leather jackets. The downstairs bar often felt like a Parisienne brasserie – long, busy, everyone giddy with expectation – but the upstairs bar was where you went if you knew what was going on. It was always full of demanding people – punks, art students, pop stars and fashion designers – and so you had to be on your guard. Malcolm McLaren had his own stool, the Sex Pistols seemed to be there every Friday night, and Siouxsie and the Banshees took up residency by the jukebox. The Pistols' designer, Jamie Reid, was the coolest man there. He always wore a tight, thigh-length black leather suit jacket, his hair was always fashioned into this greasy truck-driver quiff and he had a bottle of Pils seemingly grafted to his left hand. Pils was the only thing that anyone drank, making it seem as though it was the only thing they sold. Everything happened at the Cambridge: a girl was decapitated by a lorry after she bet her friend she could crawl underneath it before it pulled away from the traffic lights at Cambridge Circus; Peter Doig, a St Martin's figurative painter who would one day auction a painting at Sotheby's for $11.3 million, held court by the bar; and another St Martin's painter called Alan was beaten senseless because he persisted in dressing like Adolf Hitler (floppy fringe, jackboots, leather trench coat and telltale moustache). The first time we saw him we immediately took bets on how long it would take before someone kicked the living daylights out of him. And just two weeks later he stumbled into the Cambridge, covered in the most fearsome-looking bruises. Alan had, to quote a popular Nick Lowe song at the time, been nutted by reality, and soon left the college.

Alan Yentob (*TV executive*): Malcolm McLaren was a great storyteller. He was curious about stuff, thinking aloud all the time, trying to think of the next big idea. He loved all that, so all his stuff was conceptual.

He was a thief as well. He would steal stuff. He had been to Paris in '68, for the revolution, and that really connected with him. He thought, as he moved into the seventies, that they were rather dull and he needed to enliven them. So punk arrived, and he got on the back of that and brought in the Pistols. Music wasn't even his big interest. The thing is, he was quite shy and introverted in a way. He didn't know what to do when the whole Bill Grundy thing happened, when the tabloids went crazy after the Pistols appeared on his show. I think sometimes these things overwhelmed him and he needed to get out. He was a curious combination. Malcolm was actually someone who was always *on*. If he was there, he wasn't himself because he was always on to the next thing. He thought he had liberated young people, though, and he felt he was a revolutionary himself. Like Bowie, he encouraged young people to do it themselves – 'The Pistols did it, you can do it.' Using clothes to transform yourself. But he was also a controller. But every time something went wrong, he sold some records.

Malcolm McLaren: Everything you did, you always wanted to tip the table over.

Alan Yentob: Throughout the sixties, Malcolm flitted around, going from art school to art school, forever searching for something new. When he talked about the sixties, he would always emphasise his quest, always looking for new ideas and trying to get into something. He had a strange sense of self as his mother had abandoned him and he'd been brought up in a very strange way by his grandmother. He was inspired by the Situationists, who were mavericks, anarchists sort of. They encouraged people to reject the status quo, which is what Malcolm did. With the Sex Pistols, he proved that it could work, even though he found it difficult to control them.

Vivienne Westwood: Punk did change youth ideas because it was a celebration. Rebellion, autonomy, swastikas. It was a great stand against authority, but what I'm talking about is, where did all those things come from? They came from culture! What is anti-Establishment? It exists in people's minds, so it must exist. Bondage, rubber and anything to shock – just like the rockers. The Hell's Angels said, 'How can we shock?' One way was to wear a swastika, another was two men French-kissing in public. The motives for being anti-Establishment were already in the culture. A man in rubber stockings is anti-Establishment. Safety pins definitely had an analogy in Third World culture, like putting feathers in your hair . . . or people in Africa who make necklaces out of old car hubcaps. It's the attitude of not looking through the lens of society. I will admit that there's some sort of street culture, but it's never new. For example, when Malcolm and I first started to do clothes, before punk rock, we were looking at our own lifetime's culture and trying to express the rebelliousness, while throwing out all the motives.

Nicola Tyson (*artist*): I grew up in a conventional middle-class nuclear family, in a boring, far-flung suburb of west London. As a lesbian teenager, I found punk compelling. It was such a radical break from the fashion and aesthetics of the mainstream mindset of the time, and most importantly, the oppressive sexual stereotyping. Punk was very liberating for women: you could look aggressive, androgynous, self-created; you could make yourself look purposely unattractive if you wanted to. Radical! I didn't embrace the 'ugly' bit – I'm a sucker for glamour – but enjoyed the androgyny, the opportunity to wear men's clothes in a fucked-up way. Punk really got me through the gender-identity crisis of my teens and allowed me to develop a look on my own terms, rather than what was expected of me. It also introduced me to the London gay subculture of nightclubs and bars where a lot of the early punk scene took place after the gigs.

Peter York: The Jubilee boat trip was completely hilarious because it was full of youthful martyrdom and bad behaviour. Jon Savage was with us and a really charming, very clever person, now dead, called Steven Lavers, who I'd met at a Roxy concert, of course. Jon, Steven and I spent an inordinate amount of time talking about all this stuff – punk – and how important it was. God knows why, but the stations of the cross were nothing on this. And so we went on the boat trip up the river with the Sex Pistols. It was a sort of music-industry promotional trip with subversive overtones. Richard Branson was there, smiling fit to bust. He knew he'd got something good. Anyway, the police eventually came onto the boat and took the offenders away, if they wanted to be taken away. Clearly, you didn't have to be taken away, but obviously Malcolm and Vivienne *wanted* to be taken away. There were lots of people shouting that it's dreadful and all that sort of thing, and then I remember we three went to a pub somewhere in the Covent Garden area, which at that point seemed like the old world, in a slightly cartoonish way. And we thought, 'This is all very, very odd.' And, of course, there it was, it was the Jubilee. Punk was about to be all over. We thought it was completely surreal and atmospheric. I think Jon was convinced that the folk in the pub were out to get him. And it was a good day out anyway, a good time was had by all. It was one of those things where the plates of the decades are crunching, and then it was out. In terms of people being excited by it or horrified or writing tabloid front pages about it, by the end of '77 it was over, and then the music industry developed new wave. There were a lot of conspiracy theories around. People like Jon were convinced that the Police had been invented by the CIA, because they were managed by Miles Copeland, whose father was in the CIA. They were, of course, Pepsi to Coke and were very annoying, like Elvis Costello, who was a very annoying person, but terribly talented when you think about it now.

Alan Yentob: I was on the boat trip. It was kind of mad and noisy, and I got off as soon as I could. I had to be a bit careful as I was working for the BBC.

Neil Tennant: Because I'd had a piece published in the *NME*, I applied when they advertised for some hip young gunslingers, the advert that resulted in Tony Parsons and Julie Burchill getting jobs. I don't even know if I got a reply. I definitely didn't get an interview.

Tony Parsons (*journalist, hip young gunslinger*): The night of the boat trip I shared a gram of amphetamine sulphate – *my* amphetamine sulphate – with John Lydon, and it was the only time I felt really close to him. If you had a few drugs about you, you were very popular. That's why I was never as good a journalist as I could have been, because I was too close to the scene. When I wondered why Tom Wolfe was so much better than me, it was because he always had that distance. I mean, I was never going to shop Johnny Thunders simply for the sake of the truth. He was a heroin addict, but he was also my friend. But that night the police were incredibly violent, without any provocation. McLaren was coming down the gangplank shouting, 'Fascist pigs, Nazi scum!' but he was all mouth and no trousers, as he wasn't going to do anything, and about a dozen coppers got him at the bottom. I don't know how they didn't kill him. I thought they were going to kick him to death. Lydon's gang also beat up some French photographer, which was just as bad. I was called as a witness to Bow Street Magistrates' Court, because some of the band had charges against them, which was quite intimidating. I remember McLaren saying to me in the chambers, 'Don't worry, son, everything's going to be fine, because you look great.' I was peak punk – trilby, SEX T-shirt, Lewis Leathers, zippy trousers and heavy Church's brogues. But I wasn't called in the end.

Ben Kelly: I was working for Malcolm at the time, and Sophie Richmond, who was running his business, said they'd got this thing going on and did I want to come? The river police came along, the boat went to the pier at Charing Cross, and I saw policemen dragging Vivienne by the hair down the gangplank. Then I heard one policeman saying,

'There's McLaren, let's have him.' And so four of them went for him, getting a limb each. I thought they were going to give him a kicking, so I leapt forward to try and help him, and inadvertently knocked a policeman's helmet off. The next thing I knew there was a big arm around my neck. Then I was thrown in the van, to see two girls who worked in the shop, Debbie and one other, lying on the floor. A policeman had his boot on the other one's neck. I spent a night in Bow Street, covered in a blanket with shit on it, listening to Vivienne shouting and swearing at them. It was horrendous. We had to appear at Bow Street six months later, where the policeman lied and said that my girlfriend had jumped on his back and called him a fascist pig. I got a two-year conditional discharge and a fine. A few weeks later, I was outside Seditionaries taking a picture of the shop front, and some kids on bikes from the council flats came screaming up and saying, 'We hate fucking punks,' but of course there was nothing I could do as I was on this conditional discharge.

Graham Ball: I remember Alan Jones, who used to be a shop assistant in SEX, and who was probably the first punk. After the boat trip, he said, 'I'm done.' He got in early and got out early.

Nicola Tyson: There was an air of danger, rather than outright violence. As punks, we were dressed provocatively – aggressively. If you were in a group, doing verbal battle with the jeering public was fun. The danger of violence came from the more organised oppositional groups, like the Teds. I witnessed a few scary bottle fights outside the Roxy in Covent Garden, when Teds would show up for a fight with the punks. Covent Garden and Islington (where there were some other music venues, such as the Hope and Anchor) were run-down areas then, a bit off the beaten track. Their redevelopment and gentrification began a few years later. As a woman, of course, one had to deal with the omnipresent danger of being out and about alone at night in such places, regardless of the pop-cultural moment.

The summer of '77 ('the summer of hate') was not just all about the Jubilee boat trip and the Sex Pistols' 'God Save the Queen'; it also produced the most influential dance record of the period – Donna Summer's 'I Feel Love', produced by Giorgio Moroder and Pete Bellotte. 'If any one song can be pinpointed as where the eighties began, it's "I Feel Love",' says the journalist Simon Reynolds. It was a great beast of a record, as transgressive as it was innovative, a record that invigorated the burgeoning disco scene. Whether you were a dancer, a DJ or a producer, you couldn't fail to be affected by it. The track was also ubiquitous. When the Beatles' Sergeant Pepper's Lonely Hearts Club Band *had been released ten years earlier, if you had walked the length of the King's Road, you would have heard it blaring out of every boutique; and if you'd made the same journey in the summer of '77, the record you would have heard would have been 'I Feel Love'. The traditional narrative of punk dictates that 1977's long hot summer had been co-opted by the Pistols, the Clash, the Stranglers and the Jam, whereas in reality it had been hijacked by Giorgio Moroder.*

Giorgio Moroder (*producer*): I did not compose 'I Feel Love' in the way I usually compose, which is having headphones and hearing a rhythm track, like drums and my voice, and then playing the synthesizer or piano. I didn't really know how to start, so I started with a bassline, which was a C, and then I asked for a G, and then a B, and so I had *dun dun dun dun*. Then I triggered it, so it started to play *dun dun dun dun, dun dun dun dun*. The final piece of the puzzle was simple but critical: we added a delay on that bassline, ever so slightly. It turned the solid *dun dun dun* into a wiggly *diddle diddle diddle*. That changed the whole atmosphere of the whole sound of the song. That was the moment when I thought, 'This is a great song, and possibly something new.' I didn't really think it was something for the future, but I was happy with the sound.

Jon Savage (*journalist*): I can't stress enough how important 'I Feel Love' was, because that was the future, and it blew punk out the water. Punk just sounded really old-fashioned after you heard 'I Feel Love' [which was released in July], it really did. It is one of the best records of the twentieth century, there is no doubt about that. How they made something that still sounds futuristic is incredible. My first real encounter with all this was bumping into Rusty Egan, who took me to the Cage, which was a shop on the King's Road where he was DJing.

Giorgio Moroder: I had already had experience with the original Moog synthesizers, so I contacted this guy who owned one of the large early models. It was all quite natural and normal for me. I simply instructed him about what programmings I needed. I didn't even think to notice that for the audience at large, this was perhaps a very new sound. We did the whole thing in a day.

Jon Savage: 'I Feel Love' defined the period so much more than post-punk.

Giorgio Moroder: Even if you use synthesizers and sequencers and drum machines, you have to set them up, choose exactly what you are going to make them do. It is nonsense to say that we make all our music automatically. Sometimes it was easier to get the sound you were looking for with the new technology, but as often as not it is at least ten times more difficult to get a good synthesizer sound than on an acoustic instrument.

Rusty Egan: While 'I Feel Love' actually came out in 1977, it was still around for most of the following year.

Giorgio Moroder: [In 1982] I produced a song with David Bowie for the film *Cat People*, and he told me he was in Berlin at the point when the song came out. He was working with his partner in crime [Brian

Eno], and they were looking for a new sound. [When they heard 'I Feel Love'] David said, 'Don't look any more, because I think Giorgio found the sound of the future.' I said, 'Wow, this is great.' I didn't realise that Bowie was so impressed by this song, but if he says it, then it must be true. David said they were depressed for a few days, because for weeks and weeks they were trying to find that famous new sound which every artist wants – and especially Brian and David in Berlin – so it was definitely an acknowledgement that it was something new. And here we are forty years later, and we're still talking about it.

David Bowie: One day in Berlin, Eno came running in and said, 'I have heard the sound of the future.' He puts on 'I Feel Love' by Donna Summer. He said, 'This is it, look no further. This single is going to change the sound of club music for the next fifteen years.' Which was more or less right.

Jon Savage: You can still feel the influence of 'I Feel Love' forty years later.

Giorgio Moroder: At the beginning I didn't feel 'I Feel Love' would have the impact, but then months later you'd hear the same bassline on other records. I must say, it is quite difficult now to have an EDM song that doesn't have some kind of 'I Feel Love' bass. Even if you don't hear it, it's usually there, and it's actually quite difficult to not use it at all.

Iain R. Webb (*fashion director, journalist*): I came to London in September 1977, when I went to St Martin's, having just done a foundation course in Salisbury. Being in Salisbury there were probably only about six or eight of us into punk, but I was already coming up to London to see gigs – Elvis Costello at the Hope and Anchor, and Ian Dury, Blondie, Jonathan Richman, Wayne County, Johnny Thunders and the Cortinas at the 100 Club, the Marquee, the Rainbow. Then, of course, there was the big one: seeing Bowie at Earl's Court. At St Martin's I met Greg Davis, who became my best friend, Sade, Corinne Drewery . . . I used to go to Bangs, which was opposite Centre Point, and at the time it was one of the biggest gay clubs in Europe and very eccentric, I suppose. Two floors, a balcony that went all the way around and then a huge dancefloor in the middle at the end. We'd also go to the Sombrero in Kensington and the Embassy in Bond Street, more for dancing than sex. The Copacabana was another gay club over in Earl's Court, and Scandals, which was in Wardour Street, I think. That autumn 'I Feel Love' was everywhere.

Adam Ant (*musician*): We were called the Ants because it's really just a take-off of the Beatles, because I was very ambitious. I thought, 'Fuck it. Insects.' I didn't look like your average seventies rock singer. I wasn't the skinny kind, you know, the wastrel. I was quite thickset and I'd done a lot of physical jobs when I was younger – you know, demolition, I was a groundsman . . . I didn't actually work out, but I was quite strong. I'd seen *Rocky*, and I really liked it. Stallone really inspired me in that film. I kind of felt like Adam, the first man, in some of those Renaissance paintings, like Michelangelo's *David*, so it really started there. Plus, I liked the name. It was, like, the first name. I've always used my body and I very much knew there was a point when I would utilise it, and I did. So that's how Adam Ant came along, and Adam and the Ants just rolls off the tongue. Americans find it very easy to say.

At the time, the Tubes were playing a song about Adam – the first man – who was 'stronger than a tree and freshly moulded from clay', and Adam enjoyed the sound of that too. (Note: Atom Ant was the name of a sixties cartoon character, and Adam Adamant Lives! *was also the title of a sixties TV show about an Edwardian who'd been transported to the future. I always thought they should have been called Adam Ampersand the Ants.)*

Robert Chalmers (*journalist*): Adam Ant, whose real name is Stuart Goddard, grew up on a council estate in St John's Wood. An only child, his father left when he was seven, and he was brought up by his mother, who later remarried. He was educated at Marylebone Grammar and Hornsey College of Art and has retained a London accent, though his intonation and vocabulary have been coloured by his five-year spell on the West Coast: he has acquired an enviably diverse range of alternatives for the word 'man', which includes 'guy', 'bloke', 'geezer' and 'cat'. He got into showbusiness when he formed Adam and the Ants in 1977. Then Derek Jarman noticed him walking through Chelsea with the word 'Fuck' cut into his back with a razorblade and cast him in his film *Jubilee*. In the early days, Adam and the Ants were approached by producer John Walters to appear on the Radio 1 *John Peel Show*, and were briefly regarded as bona fide punks. As a student Adam had become fascinated with the erotic work of painters such as Allen Jones, and his eye was immediately caught by the range of bondage outfits and fireproof caning gear he discovered on sale at the King's Road shop run by Vivienne Westwood and Malcolm McLaren. His body is tattooed with the inscription 'Pure Sex', but he insists that his interest in sadomasochism has never gone beyond an aesthetic appreciation of the imagery, though a certain preoccupation with sexual quirkiness would seem to be indicated by song titles such as 'Whip in My Valise', 'Rubber People', 'Beat My Guest' and 'Human Bondage Den'.

Rob Hallett (*promoter*): Adam was always a little odd, a little bit out there.

Adam Ant: All the Teddy boys used to hang around Sloane Square station, and you'd come out and they'd sit there on Saturday, punk bashing. You'd come out of there wearing bondage trousers and stuff and make-up, and they'd say, 'Well, what are you then?' and they would surround you. I remember coming out of there once and I had leather trousers from Viv's shop, from SEX, and some black suede jodhpur boots with white straps and a 'Cambridge Rapist' T-shirt on and a leather jacket and one eye done up. I had a lot of make-up on. And they just collared me and surrounded me, these big fucking monster Teds, and they started saying, 'So what are you then?' It always started like that. And I said, 'Well, I like Gene Vincent, that is why I wear leather . . .' 'All right then, fuck off!'

I'm not [a fighter], no. I mean, it's not a question of bravado; it's just a question of feeling absolutely disgusted with the human race when you see something like that happen. We played down in Wales once, and the local rugby team turned up and it's all, 'Oh, let's beat the punks up, boyo.' And they were the fucking security on the gig. They got one boy, and they got him against a wall and bent his arm back and smashed it. Backwards. They thought it was hysterically funny. I'm glad those days are over, you know? They're not romantic, they're not glorious. The music was great, the action was great, but there were some fucking absolute atrocities going on.

Vivienne Westwood: Up until the Sex Pistols and punk rock, I'd never thought of myself as a designer. I just thought of myself as helping out Malcolm on his projects, doing research and things like that. But he was crazy in those days . . . He wouldn't let people into the shop who he didn't like the look of. We were supposed to open at eleven, and sometimes Malcolm refused to open till after one. That was his kind of attitude.

Dave Rimmer: Steve Strange has been busily acquiring himself a set of impeccable punk credentials. When still living in Wales, he caught the Sex Pistols' concert at Stowaway Club in Newport on 23 September 1976. Hanging around backstage afterwards, he struck up a friendship with bass player Glen Matlock. Inspired by punk, he arranged concerts for Generation X and the Stranglers at Newport's Roundabout Club, becoming friendly with the former's Billy Idol. Armed with offers of temporary accommodation, he moved up to London and oscillated between the sofas of the Stranglers' Jean-Jacques Burnel and Matlock. Later, he stayed at the Harrow family home of Marco Pirroni, soon one of Adam and the Ants, shared a squat with Billy Idol and Generation X guitarist Derwood, and another with Budgie of the Banshees and Pistols designer Jamie Reid. For a while he also slept at the Sex Pistols' Glitterbest office and worked Saturdays for Vivienne Westwood at Seditionaries. When the Sex Pistols set off on the *Anarchy* tour, he followed them everywhere, getting to know Johnny Thunders and the Heartbreakers. Through Thunders he got to know others in the heroin-dosed scene around the Heartbreakers' flat in Sydney Street, Chelsea, including Blondie and Joan Jett. Rusty Egan has even claimed that for a while Steve Strange had a job cleaning the toilets at the Roxy club. But Strange denied this as one punk credential too far. Desperate to be in a band, Strange ended up working with Chrissie Hynde, later of the Pretenders, on a shock-tactic punk project called the Moors Murderers.

In June 1977, Soo Catwoman, who was already one of the most prominent punks, apparently started telling people that she was thinking of starting a band called the Moors Murderers. 'The Moors Murderers thing was a big joke, to be honest,' she says. 'I was joking about getting a band together called the Moors Murderers and doing sleazy love songs. I had no idea he [Steve Strange] would actually go out and do it . . .' According to the writer Andrew Gallix, Strange claimed to be part of this mythical band in order to secure a photo shoot for the German magazine Bravo.

The Sex Pistols' producer, Dave Goodman, was one of the few who saw the Moors Murderers live. They were supporting the Slits at an NSPCC benefit concert at Ari Up's school in Holland Park, and Goodman assumed that the support band were simply friends of theirs. He remembers Strange being dressed head to toe in black leather, and he recalls seeing Chrissie Hynde. He says they had a certain 'first gig' quality about them, their sound being largely chaotic and the lyrics unintelligible. He was shocked, though, when he found out they were called the Moors Murderers. 'I couldn't believe it,' he says. 'I had lived through that gruesome event, and the darkness it brought to my childhood still felt gloomy. To protect me, my mum would remove any Moors Murderers tabloid sensationalism from the papers, after first reading it herself.' After the show, Steve Strange came up to Goodman at the mixing desk and confirmed the band's name. He'd heard right – it was as he thought. 'We got talking. It turned out that they had this song called "Free Hindley". They had just performed it, but I hadn't noticed. He had my interest – what was his motive? Steve explained. He felt that it was hypocritical of the government to automatically consider other child murderers for parole after a certain length of time, while ignoring Hindley. Being a high-profile case, I believe he felt they were just pandering to public demand. We also discussed change and to what level people can achieve it.'

On 8 January 1978, the Sunday Mirror *published a piece on the band ('Why Must They Be So Cruel?'), based on an interview which had taken place at Goodman's Fulham office. According to the article, the four band members – who included Strange and Hynde – were wearing pillowcases on their heads. In mid-January, the band were featured in* Sounds, *this time wearing bin liners instead of pillowcases. They played a few songs for the journalist ('Free Hindley', 'Caviar and Chips', 'Mary Bell' and 'The Streets of the East End'). The band then played the Roxy on 13 January, before folding a week later.*

Chrissie Hynde (*singer, musician*): Everyone was always mixing it back in those days. I saw him [Steve Strange] in the Vortex club one night, and he came up to me and said, 'I have these songs,' and he started singing these songs to me a cappella there at the bar. And they were all about different criminals. There was one about Myra Hindley called 'Free Hindley'. It went, 'In nineteen hundred and sixty-four, Myra Hindley was nothing more than a woman who fell for a man, so why can't she be free? Free Hindley! Brady was her lover, he told her what to do, a psychopathic killer, nothing new, so why can't she be free? Free Hindley!' And it was absurd. Really. And then he had another song about Al Capone, and a song about the Kray twins. Being a Yank, I wasn't actually aware of the Moors Murderers, and I didn't realise what absolute loathing they evoked in the hearts of all the English. Then he asked me to come down and play guitar, and I was delighted that someone just wanted me to play guitar. We went down to this rehearsal, as he had this record-company guy come down, so I learnt the songs just so I could play. And then he said, 'And now they want to do a piece on us in *Sounds*.' I said I didn't want to be in this thing, so we all wore black bin liners over our heads. But my name was Christine Hindley, so I think people put two and two together. Steve Strange was unknown, but I suppose I had a bit of a name in London by then. The next thing I know, it's in the papers that it's my band. I was mortified, because I had all my friends who were journalists swear that [they wouldn't write about my involvement]. I said that if they ever wrote anything about me at all, I would never speak to any of them ever again. I didn't want to be in the papers until I had finally found my band. And when this thing came out in the papers, people were outraged. They thought it was the tackiest thing in the world.

Steve Strange (*club runner, singer*): By 1977, I'd gotten very bored by punk. It'd become very violent. The skinheads and the National Front had moved in. It was about being creative; we wanted to start something that didn't have anything to do with punk. Nobody should knock escape and fantasy, dressing up like a Hollywood film star, because they're getting away from it, escaping the nine to five.

Trevor Horn: Punk was awful. I mean, I didn't get it at all at first. I understood the liberating aspect of it, but the actual music I detested, although I have to say I thought a couple of the Sex Pistols' tunes were quite clever, especially 'Pretty Vacant': 'Pretty va-cunt!' But it didn't appeal to me much at the time. It wasn't the route for me, as I was more interested in the techno/dance route. I was also more interested in working with keyboards rather than guitars. Keyboards were new, guitars were old. I remember one particular chord I heard on an electronic keyboard, and I thought, 'Fuck me, there's the future. Listen to that, it sounds fantastic.'

Harvey Goldsmith: I can still remember Malcolm McLaren walking into my office with the Sex Pistols and him telling me that they were going to be the biggest thing in the world. I said, 'Not with me they aren't.' I hated punk. To me it was the revolution of the uglies. I couldn't understand why people would pay to be beaten up, as the atmosphere at most punk gigs was one of extreme violence. I didn't understand it at all. I liked the Boomtown Rats, as I liked Bob Geldof's naughty-schoolboy shtick, and I liked both the Jam and the Clash, as they were class acts. But you could keep the rest of them.

Tony Parsons: The audiences during 1977 depended on where you were. I was on the *Anarchy* tour, and it was a student-union audience, so if you were on the road and you left London, like seeing the Clash in Newcastle, as I did, the audience wouldn't be any different to the one you'd see at a Lynyrd Skynyrd, Uriah Heep or Family concert, as it took time to filter through. It was just like the early seventies. Everything moved much slower then. It was also quite dangerous to look like a punk, as people would lurch at you and want to beat you up. They were affronted by you, especially later. At first I was surprised by how stuck in the past everybody was. This was a revolution waiting to happen, and here we were with long-haired, bearded, moustachioed students who didn't realise they were seeing one of the greatest groups of all time. The first person I saw when I went down the stairs of the 100 Club in 1976 was Siouxsie Banshee, and that was quite a shock – stockings and suspenders, swastika armband, the epitome of the punk nightmare. A lot of the kids who got involved in punk were disillusioned rock fans, people who had been schoolkids in the sixties, and almost everybody had some sort of horrible big gig in their past – the Stones at Wembley or Led Zeppelin at Earl's Court. For me, it was Bowie at Earl's Court. It was so disappointing to think you'd missed the party. That was the prevailing feeling. Then, when punk came along, it meant we could have our own party. There was so much great music that you could go out every night of the year. But even at the early gigs, there were still people with flares and long hair. There was no money, there was nowhere to buy the stuff, there was no infrastructure. The only SEX stuff I ever had was given to me; I shopped in Oxfam. I had a pair of Antony Price trousers, but that was about it.

When I left the gin distillery to join the *NME*, I took a massive wage cut. If you went to see the Heartbreakers at the Roxy – and they played there a lot because they played for their heroin money – it felt like the greatest youth club in the world, and it felt like you knew everybody. I saw the Jam once at the Roxy, and the only other people in the audience were the Clash. I even helped them load their gear, because they didn't have roadies in those days, only Paul's dad. You'd see Debbie Harry and the guys from Blondie all the time, and the one time you could be guaranteed to see John Lydon was when the Heartbreakers played. Everybody was doing something – you could be a photographer, or a writer, or a musician, or a designer. The sense of community was probably no different from what it had been in the sixties. But that evaporated the minute you left London.

Don Letts: The smart people moved on. That was when it really got interesting and you could be honest about what records you really had in your record collection.

Princess Julia: By '77, punk had already dissipated. I did go to Louise's a bit, but not very often as I was just a bit too young. I was going to the Sombrero, Bangs, made friends with Steve Strange, Philip Sallon. I started taking a lot of downers and discovered speed.

Steve Dagger: Punk had a kind of built-in obsolescence. It was never meant to last very long. You were kind of looking for a template for your life, and this wasn't it, as it was an art-school installation. It wasn't meant to be the new touch point for another decade or anything of the sort. So that was frustrating, and it became really apparent quite quickly to me and I just got bored with it. I think a lot of the people who were very excited by it earlier on probably felt the same. So the middle of the decade had this spark, and then it went dead. It was a huge disappointment from everybody's point of view. I went wandering around London with various people, still looking for the next big thing but feeling like there might not be one. Punk was one idea, and the big disadvantage of it was it wasn't meant to be good, so how can you make a career out of being involved with something which isn't supposed to be good? And I think it was a big problem for the bands as well, who actually were good. The fact is that the Sex Pistols were a fantastic live band, and some of the records were good as well, but they weren't meant to be. You can see the crisis that those groups had. Some of them, like the Clash, thought, 'Fuck that. We want to be good. We're going to develop our careers.'

Daniel Miller: Punk had this incredible energy, but musically it became very conservative very quickly. It still sounded like sped-up pub rock, and it was very exciting for a moment, not just musically, but also just because it was so disruptive. So I went back to film editing to make some money. I bought a cheap second-hand synth and a second-hand tape recorder and started playing around at home. I had no idea what I would be able to do. I just wanted to try it. And then I started enjoying it.

Gary Kemp: I found myself going back to soul music, so I had this kind of strange double cultural head where I would go to Woodhouse and buy my soul-boy clothes, with my plastic sandals and those fantastic trousers called Smiths and with my mum even knitting me a mohair jumper – that was a soul boy thing as well as a punk thing – but I'd be buying the *NME* and I could see that what I was doing with all these working-class kids in clubs like the Lacy Lady was never written about in the music press. The only black artists mentioned were reggae artists and maybe P-Funk. I saw there was a friction going on culturally between what was more and more a middle-class art form, which was rock music, and what was probably the biggest, most exciting working-class youth culture, soul music.

Nicola Tyson: As the number of fans shot up, punk became more yobbish – Mohicans and all that – and less underground, arty and 'Warholian'. I think we early punks were more interested in the creative aspect – self-invention – than it being a movement as such. It was divided quite early on between those who were into the Clash, say, and those who weren't. I wasn't. The Clash took their 'honest' version of punk mainstream, and it really appealed to your average pub-goer. The early Sex Pistols fans, on the other hand – notably the Bromley Contingent, which included Siouxsie and Steve Severin, Billy Idol and other interesting Warholian/Weimar-type characters – were the idols of the arty punks like me. They were camp and sophisticated, very gay-influenced, and their defiance influenced by the arch flamboyance of Bowie and Roxy Music. Much of the after-hours hanging out, in those very early days, of the then very small scene took place in gay clubs – famously, Club Louise and the Sombrero. These were tiny, old-school, members-only nightclubs, with a dining area to satisfy the then stricter licensing laws and a small dancefloor. It was like going to a private party – thrilling for a teenager from the suburbs! There were some straight nightclubs on the circuit, such as Speakeasy, but the atmosphere in those watering holes tended to be far less relaxed, especially for women, as they were full of anti-punk, boring, predatory, old music-biz types. Not an inspiring milieu.

Steve Dagger: After punk, I went back to the soul clubs. There was an attempt to promote a British jazz-funk scene, the southern soul scene, and create something that was not just people dancing to unattainable music in America. The two most convincing groups were Hi Tension and Light of the World. They were all young Londoners, very British, and the sound was actually different from the American sound, but it didn't work. There were others, like Central Line, but none of them really caught fire in the way that perhaps they should have done, because the scene didn't want them to. The DJs that controlled the scene were obsessed with America. So you could always go to a soul club where you met pretty girls, danced and had fun, but it wasn't going anywhere. It didn't have enough for me to create a career; it wasn't exciting enough. It wasn't about to change popular culture, it was comfort food. Then you had Bowie and Ferry nights, the biggest of which were at Crackers. It was a more extravagant platform for people, who could dress in ways they couldn't elsewhere, so they could let their hair down a little bit more, fashion-wise. In terms of music, you could have Bowie or Bryan Ferry, or anyone that was produced by Bowie or Ferry. It was fine to do this once in a while, but it was ultimately about consuming Bowie and Ferry. I suppose Blitz culture sprouted from all these elements – Bowie nights, the southern soul scene and the remnants of punk.

Martyn Ware (*musician*): Bowie's *Low* was like nothing else, but it still had elements of rock-pop music. Lyrically, it was more like an art installation, for me, like conceptual art. And then, of course, on the second side you had 'Warszawa', and the idea of having an album that just dissolved into pure sonic imagery. It all came back to prog rock, which was something I loved as well, but in a much more futuristic sense. I've always believed that popular music at its best paints vivid images in the mind; that each individual paints their own images different from everybody else's. And Bowie had that capability, leaving enough wiggle room in his work that you can populate it with your own meaning and artistic sensibility.

John Foxx: The point of using synthesizers on the first Ultravox records was to find out what these strange new instruments could do that hadn't been done before. I figured new instruments had always radically altered music in the past – for instance, the electric guitar. Here was the next major shift – the synthesizer. It could make violent extremes of sound, from subsonics to bat calls. At that time, we wanted a total experience. It was a sort of sonic terror, allied to the most extreme guitar feedback possible, plus a battery of megawatt strobe lights. No one walked away unchanged from those mid-period concerts. On the other hand, we were equally into romantic lyrical beauty. The synths could do both. All the bands wanted sonic mayhem, by all and any means. Synths supplied that in a new way.

Midge Ure: Glen Matlock had been kicked out of the Sex Pistols, and he called me as he was looking for a fourth member for his band, the Rich Kids. The writer Caroline Coon had seen Slik perform live, and she told Glen he should meet me. She said, 'There's more to the band than what you see on television.' Had that phone call not happened, I could have ended up driving a bus in Glasgow, as my fifteen minutes had been well and truly used up. So I agreed to go down to London to meet them. I flew down one morning, went into the rehearsal room and was met by these very young, incredibly excitable, chaotic guys. Steve New, the guitar player, was seventeen, and he was so green he walked over to his amplifier and turned it up every time he wanted to play a solo. But Glen was a great bass player, Rusty Egan was a great drummer, and they were incredibly vibrant. At this point, journalists were hailing the Rich Kids as the saviours of rock, and they were getting the covers of the music papers. They weren't even a complete band, so it was crazy. We went out that night to see the Police at the Angel in Islington, and as the support band hadn't turned up, we ended up supporting them. That was my first gig. Then we supported the Boomtown Rats at the Music Machine and went to a warehouse party with Sid and Nancy and the Clash, so in the space of forty-eight hours I'd met everyone I'd been reading about for the last six months. I'm quite a home bird, and I loved Glasgow, but all of a sudden I'm transported into London, where there's racism and violence, and this multicultural city that's a vibrant, wild, mad, noisy scene. I expected a bit of snobbery, especially from the likes of Mick Jones of the Clash, but I didn't get that, and I think it was because they'd all seen me on *Top of the Pops*. Nobody was born a punk, and everybody had been standing there with their tennis rackets in front of mirrors long before they managed to get bondage trousers. They wanted to talk to me because I was the kind of famous one, which was weird. The only one who snubbed me was Billy Idol, who was more of a pop star than I was. I got the sneer when I went to shake his hand; he turned around and walked away. It was weird as I was suddenly the most experienced musician in the band. Not only that, but the Rich Kids' crowd was a bizarre hybrid of Slik fans who'd grown up a little bit and Pistols fans who'd used me as a spitting target.

Dave Rimmer: The Rich Kids were the band formed by Glen Matlock after he left the Sex Pistols and, like the Photons, were supposed to be a power-pop group. Power pop was a dismal music-industry attempt to grab back the initiative and establish a Next Big Thing to follow punk: happy, inoffensive rock groups (there was one called the Pleasers) whose music echoed the mid-sixties golden age of beat. The Rich Kids were the most high-profile but managed only one minor hit: the single 'Rich Kids', released by EMI on red vinyl, which struggled to No. 24 in the January 1978 charts. Midge Ure was now looking for a new project and suggested to Strange that they use some studio time EMI owed him by recording a couple of demos. That was the beginning of Visage.

The biggest insult that could be thrown at you in 1977 was 'poseur'. So many rock consumers had – often overnight, and sometimes in the space of half an hour – reinvented themselves as punks that the way they did it became an important part of the process. Some simply cut their hair, stopped smiling and turned the collars of their shirts up, while others went for the cookie-cutter look, dyeing their hair, buying safety pins and padlocks and covering their jeans with zips from Woolworths. The elegant way to do it was to try and reinvent yourself in a way that didn't necessarily make it look as though you were simply following the herd; however, if you did this, you obviously ran the risk of being called a poseur, simply because you were taking care with what you wore and what you looked like. After all, this was a big moment in many teenagers' lives. Many of the early punks – those who helped create the scene, as well as the first people in the audience – were accused of this when they tried to dress in a way that confounded the emerging orthodoxies of punk. Concerned that the cult was rapidly turning reductive, driven by a media obsessed with stereotypes, they already wanted to move on. Which meant that while traditional punks were accused by ordinary rock fans of being poseurs, so punks were already taking issue with those in their ranks who were already mutating the styles and tropes. Damned if you did, damned if you didn't. One of the cornerstones of X-Ray Spex's live set was their song 'I Am a Poseur', which was included on their debut album, Germfree Adolescents. *Basically a concept album built around a disdain for consumerism and conformity – including punk conformity – it's a genuinely meta artefact. The band's leader had rechristened herself Poly Styrene (born Marianne Joan Elliott-Said, she was the daughter of a Scottish–Irish secretary and a dispossessed Somalian noble), and she was obsessed with the way in which punks had become so clichéd, so quickly. 'In a way, I think posing is a laugh,' she said. 'But just dressing up and having a laugh – and only providing you know the difference between the reality of it and the fantasy of it.' As for herself, she had chosen the name Poly Styrene because it was 'a lightweight, disposable product. It was a send-up of being a pop star – plastic, disposable, that's what pop stars are meant to mean, so therefore I thought I might as well send it up.' (Tubeway Army would soon have their own take on the matter: 'I'm a Poseur'.)*

Terry Jones: I got a call from the *Vogue* reception saying, 'There's a young man to see you called Steve Johnston.' Steve came up, and he had transformed himself, had got orange hair, a ripped jacket, safety pins and a swastika, and he looked like the kids in the *Daily Mirror* and the *Sun* who were causing trouble down the King's Road. And his pictures were brilliant. I called the editor, Bea Miller, down to see them, but she took one look at Steve and walked out of my office. She didn't want anything to do with them. At the same time, we were preparing *Vogue*'s Diamond Jubilee issue, and I wanted to shoot a glass window that was a diamond-cut logo, but I lost the battle to the MD, who demanded we have a red cover. So I resigned. I suppose I was just realising the institutionalised nature of *Vogue*. You know, what was I? Thirty? Thirty-one? I didn't want to miss out on what was happening on the street, so I left.

1978

TRANSITION

'It is emotional. People a long time ago had difficulties finding the sensitivity of electronics. But when you go and see your doctor and he does a heart test, it is electronics that are very sensitive to this. It's the same with an instrument. That's why we should use the tools of today's society to create music – otherwise it is just antique.'

RALF HÜTTER

Peter York: From 1976 on, the British working-class youth ran the pilot programme for the eighties. But out of context, reflected occasionally in freak-show snippets on American TV, the new British styles just came over as a series of separate merchandising hypes: new looks for Seventh Avenue. The one that really caught the American eye was New Romanticism. People I talked to in New York seemed to think it'd come out of nowhere, that it was a bit of fun, like a new movie outdating last year's big thing. They'd bought the idea of a lot of kids done up like old movie stills. They thought these kids represented a reaction against the noisy, violent, nihilistic, underclass punks they'd been hearing about. Well, not only was this untrue, but by the time it came out it was out of date as well. The truth was, it was the same people all along – the first punks *were* the New Romantics.

John Foxx: I felt total affinity with punk, but I was disappointed that it got so conservative, so quickly – it really strangled itself. An old man before it was a youth. Born 1975, died 1977. Never realised its potential. I went out one night for a drink with Mick Jones and Glen Matlock. (I always liked those two – they were truly central to that movement and very sharp. They just radiated.) Mick told me they'd considered asking me to join their new band, pre-Clash. They'd seen

Ultravox at the Marquee and in Islington, but hadn't approached me because Mick felt we were already off the ground as a band. Actually, we were only supporting at the time. The irony was, I'd seen Mick at the Patti Smith Roundhouse gig in 1974 or 1975, and thought he looked right and considered asking him to play guitar. He looked like a young Keith Richards. Then I thought that anyone who looked so good probably couldn't play guitar anyway.

Tony Parsons: By 1978, everything was different. The next wave was scary and dangerous – the skins, the Sham 69 lot, the yobs from council estates who realised you didn't have to go to football to kick someone's head in. I think the New Romantics came along and reclaimed the night – amputated the yob element that smashed up gigs – and gave it back to kids who had heard of Andy Warhol. It was elitist, and that is what made it good.

Malcolm McLaren: Sex had nothing to do with punk. I could never make [Johnny] Rotten look sexy – he *isn't* sexy. But like any movement, in the end it turned into something completely conservative. Punk never succeeded, because it didn't have a cause. The Clash just ended up singing rhetoric at people; all this 'Sten guns in Knightsbridge' rubbish, when they were only worth water pistols in Paddington. I never liked the Clash, never liked them at all.

Tony Parsons: Punk changed when it started to attract non-art-school punks, and when the football crowd came in. It became corrupted very quickly. When the *NME* moved to Carnaby Street, you started seeing punks with Mohawks begging, and to me that was an appalling sight. They should have been forming bands, or writing a fanzine, or doing something for themselves. You had the Finchley boys in the early days, following the Stranglers around, who were football hooligans in everything but name, but as punk grew, the violence grew. John Lydon was always surrounded by his own Praetorian Guard of Finsbury Park thugs, which no one ever writes about, and they were always trying to ingratiate themselves by kicking the shit out of some poor photographer. But when punk grew, attracting people who weren't interested in theories about anarchy, that's when it got rough. When the genuinely working-class lads started turning up, there was trouble. Gigs started to have an edge as the yobs took over. I saw a lot of this because I was sent on the road with Lynyrd Skynyrd as a punishment for taking drugs in the *NME* office. I remember a terrible fight at a Heartbreakers gig in Newcastle.

Jon Savage: I was working for *Sounds*, and towards the end of the year a lot of us on the magazine were getting fed up with punk. In October, we did this editorial, over two issues, called 'New Music', which was basically about synth pop and weird stuff like Wire and Devo. I was really into synth music, and so by early '78, I really wasn't into punk any more. I had the chance to go and see the Sex Pistols at Brunel University in December '77, and I thought, 'Oh, I can't be bothered.' That shows you how much I was into it by that stage. I was already into *Trans-Europe Express* and the Bowie records. I used to get into terrible arguments with people about me writing about this implicitly homosexual synthesizer music instead of the fucking Clash, who by 1978 had turned into this sort of dreary boys' machine. Punk became so macho, with the fucking Stranglers and all that shit, with groups being very aggressive and the Clash just trying too hard to look cool and ending up looking silly. I got threatened very badly twice, and both times the people threatening me had, shall we say, issues with their sexuality which were cloaked in machismo. So punk started to become boring, which is why I liked synthesizer stuff, because it was new. I was into the Normal, Throbbing Gristle, Giorgio Moroder and Donna Summer's 'I Feel Love', 'Magic Fly' by Space, the Bowie synthesizer records *Low* and *'Heroes'*, and Sylvester's 'Mighty Real', which was a huge record for me. I got really fed up when the Sham 69 element came in.

Neil Tennant: I liked anything that had a slightly artificial construct to it. I've never really been that interested by authentic music. I think authenticity is a style. But I loved Bowie when he went electric with *Low* and *'Heroes'*, and I really loved electronic music. Although I wasn't officially gay at this point, I had gay friends who I would occasionally go to nightclubs with, and you would hear what we would think of as gay disco music. That was heavily electronic. I really loved electronic music, like Kraftwerk's *Man-Machine*, and at the same time I loved new-wave music. I liked the pop end of it, the Jam and stuff like that. Then the Human League came along, and OMD's first album was great. Then, of course, at the same time you had Giorgio Moroder, who wasn't, lest we forget, cool at this point. In fact, he was quite naff. There was a designer who worked at Marvel Comics who would put on 'I Feel Love' because he could put it on, go to the toilet and come back, and it was still playing.

One of the defining ideologies of punk was its hatred of anything perceived to be manufactured or phoney. Which obviously included disco, an iteration of dance music that was fast becoming institutionalised in a way that soul, R&B or funk never had been. Disco was the language of the weekend, a lifestyle choice rather than a genuine creative spurt, a musical accompaniment to well-choreographed dance routines. At least this is what the critics thought. 'Eons ago, in the strange time when punks and stoners disagreed about everything except whether disco sucked, rockist sages would complain bitterly about all the ways dance music wasn't alive,' said the celebrated rock critic Robert Christgau. 'It was prefabricated, they charged – mechanical beats and studio thrills stripped of human error, with producers exerting such complete control that the so-called artists were little more than names on a label.'

In the UK, the high-water mark of disco was March 1978, when Saturday Night Fever *finally opened. It had been released just before Christmas in the US, and had turned into a smash, making John*

Travolta a star, confirming the Bee Gees as the biggest stars in the pop firmament, and making the film's writer, Nik Cohn, a very rich man. The whole thing, however, was based on a lie. Cohn had moved to New York as the seventies began, abandoning his journalistic career in London, and started to write a column for New York *magazine called 'Low Outside'. In one of his first pieces, he focused on a nightclub in the New York suburb of Bay Ridge called Odyssey 2001, where disco had firmly taken root. 'Tribal Rites of the New Saturday Night', published in 1976, was such an evocative piece that it was immediately optioned by film producer Robert Stigwood, who, along with Paramount Pictures, turned it into an urban safari of immense proportions. But the remarkable thing was that Cohn had made the whole thing up. Unable to infiltrate Odyssey's tightly knit groups of disco disciples, and believing that 'nasty pieces of work aged nineteen are the same in any country, any generation', he decided to base his characters on the mods he had known in London's Shepherd's Bush ten years previously. Astonishingly, no one noticed.*

Even though Cohn only admitted this fabrication in the 1990s, Saturday Night Fever *had already painted disco as a metaphor for provincial ambition. It would take several years for dance music to be fully appreciated in the same way rock was, years for it to be judged using the same precedents (the Detroit rock radio DJ Steve Dahl would go on to successfully launch his 'Disco Sucks' campaign). To the punks, disco was part of the problem, not part of the solution. When dance music started to be appropriated by first-wave punk bands as they spread their wings and stretched their legs, it was applauded from the balcony – when Talking Heads exchanged their metronomic architecture-student rock for sassy Afro-funk, they were considered to be positively revolutionary – but if dance was your bread and butter, then God help you: there was no room in the church for you. So it was amusing to see how the rock fraternity dealt with a social environment in which dance music wasn't the enemy so much as a means to an end.*

This grudging reappraisal managed to coincide with a purple period for popular dance music, a period best exemplified by Chic. Nile Rodgers and Bernard Edwards' band adopted the Motown ethic of aspiration, appealing to those who wanted their music to elevate them rather than compartmentalise them. They did this not just through lyrical dexterity (the most illustrious example being their anthem 'Good Times'), but also through craftmanship, building dance records with a sophistication that was largely missing from the genre. They rewrote the disco rule book, pumping out dancefloor templates so regularly that they were regarded as running their own hit factory, and were so hyperactive that they produced other people's records as well as their own (most notably Sister Sledge, Diana Ross, and Sheila and B. Devotion). Some said they changed styles so often it was as though they were going out of fashion. But at the time, the fashion was determined by Rodgers and Edwards anyway, who were relentlessly producing upwardly mobile disco anthems that would turn out to be the apotheosis as well as the termination of the Motown dream. Soon rap, hip hop and DJ culture in general would amp up the militancy in black dance music, ironically using the riff from Chic's 'Good Times' as their initial bedrock (it was first sampled to great effect on 'The Adventures of Grandmaster Flash on the Wheels of Steel'). In 1978, however, they were living the dream, a dream that came alive in the nightclubs of central London.

Pop stars were even starting to dress up. Take the B-52's, who took their name from sixties slang for the beehive sported by the band's non-male members, Cindy Wilson and Kate Pierson, and so called because of its resemblance to the vast, phallic B-52 bomber. Their kitsch blend of post-punk dynamics and sixties memorabilia was first heard on their 'Rock Lobster' single in 1978, and all their songs had titles as silly as the girls' hair: 'Quiche Lorraine', '53 Miles West of Venus', 'There's a Moon in the Sky (Called the Moon)', 'Wig', etc. The B-52's were symptomatic of the seventies' reuse and reappraisal of sixties pop and its associated styles. Suddenly Batman, Top Cat, *beach parties, B-movies, the checkerboard twist, paper op art, mini-skirts, pillbox hats, pantsuits, turtleneck sweaters and Nehru jackets, Corvette Stingrays and Barracudas, Mary Quant, flecked mohair, the Monkees and all the other peripherals of sixties US/UK kitsch culture were hip again.*

By 1978, punk had started to flag, and many of those who had been there at the beginning were starting to tire of the relentlessly downward mobility of it all. One day in the autumn of 1978, Rusty Egan was chatting with Steve Strange about how the London club scene had become stagnant. After a brief conflab, they decided to open their own club, alighting on Billy's, a club just off Dean Street in Soho. Popular with local sex workers, it tended to be empty on a Tuesday, so the pair asked the owner if they could start a weekly club night. They printed flyers with the strapline 'Fame, Fame, Jump Aboard the Night Train / Fame, Fame, Fame, What's Your Name?' and very soon they were full. It soon became known as Bowie Night and was popular with a small group of clubbers who had briefly ended their affair with disco to embrace punk, but who had retreated when the scene became overrun by hordes of denim-clad rockers who nine months previously had been nodding their heads in unison to Thin Lizzy and Hawkwind. The club soon started to fill with other disenfranchised night owls intent on reinventing themselves. Fleet Street soon took an interest, calling them the Blitz Kids, and a new movement was born as Soho became overrun by eighteen-year-olds wearing tartan ballgowns, pillbox hats, nuns' habits and deathly white make-up. The Blitz generation took punk and dressed it up, giving it a twelve-inch remix in the process. They anticipated the style-obsessed eighties, when the world became a global catwalk. Narcissism plumbed new depths as haircuts reached new heights. Here, everyone had an alias, an ambition and an aerodynamic haircut to match.

Boy George: Punk had started to feel like a flash in the pan, and so we looked around for other things to entertain us. We knew about Steve Strange, and I once followed him up Wardour Street with Jeremy Healy as he was wearing a pair of Spider-Man boots. We started going to Billy's, which was a fusion of soul, punk and rockabilly. There was still violence, though, and someone tried to beat me up one night when I was wearing a drape and stilettos. I remember going into SEX wearing a drape with Elvis on the back of it, and Vivienne Westwood ticking me off and saying, 'Why are you wearing that?' And I was like, 'Well, it's a pulling look' – because you couldn't pull with spiky hair but you could pull with a quiff. One of the first things that Philip Sallon taught me was, they're just clothes. People are not their clothes, they're just wearing them! It doesn't have to be a uniform. He taught me not to be impressed by people just because of what they wore.

Andy Polaris: The first obviously openly gay club that I went to was probably the Sombrero, at the beginning of '78, and then Billy's started. I didn't really let on to a lot of people about it at the time, and I didn't feel like I started living my life until I came out of the children's home. When I left, I started working in a crappy supermarket, and after that I got a job in a merchant bank in the City. The depressing thing was, they didn't actually look after people that came out of children's homes, and you had to find your own way. But when I started going to places like Billy's, I felt I'd found my home really, because as much as I liked the soul clubs, I couldn't really express myself, and having come from such a restrictive childhood, it was like being in a bit of a straitjacket.

There weren't many black people on the scene, so you did get attention. Most of it was good, but I can remember going to see the Banshees at the Vortex and they did 'Deutschland, Deutschland über Alles', and people took it literally. Sometimes I would be really nervous because there were lots of Teddy boys and skinheads, and people forget how blatantly racist people were back then.

Steve Dagger: Then Billy's happened. I was still searching the West End with Simon Withers, a friend of mine, looking for the next big thing, and he said he'd found this place called Billy's. When I went, what struck me again was that probably two-thirds of the people in the room I knew from various different clubs, parties and art-school events. But you felt that it was the first place where everyone could wear what they wanted. People were there doing what they wanted to and wearing what they wanted to wear. Also, the music sounded completely different. It wasn't just Bowie and Ferry. Rusty Egan was playing Kraftwerk, Telex, and I felt like I was stepping into the future. I thought, 'This is it.' We were both really excited, and Simon said, 'What a great place. This is it. This feeling in this room, this is the future.' I was utterly convinced that this was what the future was going to be. I told Gary and Martin Kemp, 'You've got to come to this club next week.' Gary kind of felt like all the strands were being drawn together. If you break it down into groups, you had people who were out to get laid, who wanted to have a great life, who wanted to enjoy nice things. They were creative. Fashion. Design. Music. Attitude. The club wasn't really important, it was the mix of people inside it.

Gary Kemp: When we started thinking about forming a band, we didn't really have the chops for soul, so we didn't attempt to play it. Plus, soul music was more about liking the uniform and the dancing rather than idolising any particular act. So eventually we thought, 'Why don't we just dress like soul boys and really wind up the *NME*?' Because initially that's what punk had done. We were a weird contradiction. In the early Spandau pictures, we had wedge haircuts and clothes from Woodhouse, but we were playing high-energy pop. I felt that punk had died, while soul music didn't really represent us. So where did we fit in as a band? I wanted to be in a band, and as far as I was concerned, a band had to have a following to be exciting. Steve Dagger loves the history of pop and loved the stories of Kit Lambert and the Who. The Who were never mods, but one day Lambert just said, 'This is what you should wear and this is the audience you can represent.' Then suddenly Billy's appeared, and I went down one night with Dagger and Simon Withers, and I put on my soul-boy finery, thinking that was probably the best clothes to wear. And I was confronted by this

Welshman dressed as a Cossack on the front door, who intimidated me immediately, sexually – probably, you know, like teasing me. I remember the throb of electronic music as I went down the stairs. If you went into a soul club, there was a bpm that was about 120, but this was pulsing much slower than that, much more erotic. This would have been pulsing at about 80 bpm. Maybe it was Kraftwerk, I don't know. I remember going down these stairs, these red, kind of encased stairs. And it was like going down into something very sexual and sinister. And the first two people I saw were Andy Polaris and his mate Kenny, dancing a slow jive that they'd invented together, which was kind of like that sideways thing, holding hands. It was like watching jive in ultra-slow motion. Maybe I'd seen it in the *Cabaret* movie or something, but it was hugely erotic, and those two guys, each one of them could have been the female partner. There was an androgyny about it. There were people from soul clubs, some obviously from art school, some from punk, a lot of guys dressed like Bryan Ferry, and I thought to myself, 'How do all these people know about this?' Midge Ure was there, and Billy Idol, fashion students, literary intellectuals, political people from the LSE, disaffected soul boys, that working-class flash all mixing together. One thing we were utterly sure about was that we were going to make something that was an evolution of what had come before, taking the baton from punk, spitting in its face at the same time and going to the next step. And we could trace it back from the Teddy boys. We were all obsessed with that, that evolution, that drawing of the evolution of man coming out of a gorilla, and here at the bottom was the Teddy boy and right at the top there was the New Romantic.

There was some talk about Baudelaire, but no one was talking about Pete Townshend. So there was pretence in the air, and that was quite beautiful, and people wore their pretence very proudly. I remember seeing this kid with red hair wearing this tight Dan Dare top, and when I asked him where he got it, he said, 'PX.' It was Bob Elms. We hit it off right away. Dagger was absolutely enthralled by it, and said, 'This is it, this is the place for us.' I'd never been to a club with gay people in it before, so it was quite important to be aware of my own sexuality. Suddenly it was contextualised.

I was still living at home, and I got my mum to make me a pair of trousers that were like the ones from PX. I got a piece of paper, drew these panels, found the material I wanted and asked my mum to make them flat-fronted. She put in some belt loops and made them on her sewing machine. So I wore them to Billy's, and then realised they had no flies. I liked the look of them, but they were no good for an emergency.

Ollie O'Donnell: Maybe as a reaction to what had gone on with the early punk explosion, we started going to the Embassy Club on Old Bond Street. This was something else again, with a cross-section of people. Philip Sallon and Marilyn would be there, and quite a few people from the early punk scene, and a very mixed gay–straight crowd – some very fashionable. And then there was Billy's, where I started going every Tuesday night, and where I knew about 80 per cent of the people. Steve Strange I knew from the punk scene, and Rusty Egan I knew from the Rich Kids, with Glen Matlock and Midge Ure. Melissa Caplan was a very good friend of Midge Ure, and she introduced me to Graham Ball and Bob Elms. Chris Sullivan I had met before in Bournemouth. I enjoyed Billy's as it was intimate.

Steve Strange: In 1978, I was briefly in a power-pop band called the Photons. At the same time, me and Rusty had started dabbling in Billy's, because we'd all got disillusioned by the whole punk era and how it had become very regimental and how the nationals basically dictated how to dress.

Rusty Egan: I didn't connect with Steve Strange until we went to Newport with the Rich Kids. And then he started coming to our gigs, sleeping on the floor of our hotel rooms. Midge was never happy about it, but Steve New was always up for it, would get a bottle of vodka or whatever. Then, when we finished the tour, Steve was like, 'Can I stay at your house?' Well, I don't have a house, I've got a room, and then it was the old, 'Can I sleep on your floor?' thing. So he suddenly had somewhere to stay in London. Because of the fashion side of it, we clicked, as I was really into clothes. I was really into looking good and I thought Malcolm McLaren's clothes were great. We went to Acme Attractions, went to Seditionaries – I was mad for looking good. Steve said, 'I've joined a band, we're called the Photons and we're managed by Andy [Czezowski] from the Roxy.' So I went to see them, and I heard him sing 'Tar'. He looked good, and so in my eyes he had passed the audition. I thought, 'You know what? Maybe this guy can really sing, maybe he could do something. Maybe he isn't just a twat from Wales.' He had a mate, Chris Sullivan, who was at St Martin's, and I met all of his connections, all of the people he knew – Andrew Logan, Duggie Fields . . . They were all artists and creative people. And I thought, 'Well, they love him too, and he looks great, and maybe I should think about getting him a job. What could he do?' He didn't tell me he had been in the Moors Murderers, as I think he knew that would have put me off. I didn't know about the drugs, I didn't know about anything that would have put me off. I liked everything about Steve. His 'Can I stay a night?' was never-ending. He might have gone out and not come home, but there he was two days later. So my room became our room.

At that time, the Rich Kids were folding, and I loved clubbing, but I didn't much like the music I heard in the clubs, apart from Giorgio Moroder and Sylvester. And then Paul Cook got attacked in Hammersmith, and it became unsafe to go out. So I decided we should have our own club, a club for all our friends. All I needed was a record collection, which I had, and a sleazy little club, which I could find. People who had been to see the Pistols and the Clash said, 'The scene's over. Where shall we go?' And that's where the idea for Billy's came from. Steve took me to Billy's club in Dean Street, which was run by this guy who looked like a pimp, in a big fedora hat, literally *Starsky and Hutch*: the three-quarter-length leather coat with a fur collar, the gold chains, two henchmen on either side of him. It was one of those 'You definitely don't want to go in there, mate' clubs. There were hookers everywhere – 'You looking for business? Are you looking for trade?' I said to Steve, 'This is kind of sleazy, isn't it? And he said, 'Yeah, it's great, isn't it?' As the club was dark, I decided to make the music very decadent, very *Cabaret*. I found a printer up the street and found a picture of David Bowie with his head in his hands from the *'Heroes'* session, obviously in confusion. And I wrote, 'Fame, Fame, Fame, What's Your Name? A Club for Heroes. Tuesday Nights'. I didn't put an address because we didn't want anyone to know where it was. We wanted to personally invite you. We went to Smile, the hairdresser's. I said to Keith, 'Can you give these to some cool people? You know who they are.' We went to the Paul Howie shop, we went to PX. We went to all of our friends' shops and said, 'Look, we're having a party. It's 50p to get in.'

Now that we were doing it, I thought I'd better go shopping, because I wasn't a DJ, I was a guy with a record collection. I had 'Little Johnny Jewel' and I had the Pistols, Iggy Pop and Kraftwerk, but I didn't have all the extended twelve-inch mixes I needed. I needed more Roxy, more Grace Jones, more Bowie remixes. Then I got told about this bloke called David Claridge, who was a puppeteer, and who had the biggest Bowie collection in London. So I went to Sloane Square to have a cup of tea with him. He had *Stingray*, *Captain Scarlet*, Tangerine Dream and all the movie soundtracks I liked. So I asked him to help me DJ. Then I thought I'd better get Steve on the door to stop all the wrong people coming in. We were in Soho, which was full of drunk people out in the street looking for prostitutes. We don't want that. And the 50p went up to a pound because I thought, 'Well, I've got to pay him, gotta pay security.' A hundred people turned up, so we got a hundred quid, so there was no money in it, but we had enough to go for breakfast.

Princess Julia: I was working at PX, which is where I met everyone – Kim Bowen, Stephen Jones, Boy George. Steve Strange said him and Rusty were going to do a night. Even though Rusty was a pain in the arse, he had an extraordinary, almost encyclopaedic knowledge of music. Honestly, the music he scoured and obsessed about and found out about was really beyond. Billy's was so ahead of its time. Basically, it was like a scene of misfits, with people from the edges of the punk scene, soul boys like Andy Polaris and all these trans girls who worked in Soho. The whole scene was a lot less heterosexual than people say it was now. We were at an age when we wanted to explore different facets of our sexuality. You could be part of that if you wanted to, and you didn't have to make your mind up. There was that sort of undercurrent. It didn't matter. That's probably why so many women came to Billy's, as there weren't so many predatory men around.

Judy Blame (*fashion designer, stylist*): I always loved the Johnny Rotten quote: he said the minute the black leather jacket came in, punk died. The originality had gone a bit. That's when the New Romantics started, because we didn't want to be the same. I mean, no one looked like Princess Julia. She was like the Jordan of the New Romantics. We all used to idolise Julia, but it was more about being . . . different.

Gary Kemp: The first time we went to Billy's, Steve Dagger said we should go and get a synthesizer straight away.

Terry Jones: I had been asked to do a book of erotic photography, but I said what I really wanted to do was a book on punk, because at that time there hadn't been one. But during the process of doing the punk book, I met Al McDowell, and Al was one of the few punk artists I could find who was at St Martin's, and he had done a series of paintings and one of them was called *Dumb Readers Eat Shit*, which was someone shitting in someone's mouth, so his degree show was sealed off from the public. The book was eventually called *Not Another Punk Book*, which was full of Steve Johnston's photographs, and this led to me getting involved with John [Lydon] from Public Image, and I did the newspaper cover for their first single. But it got me thinking that what I should really do is start a street-style magazine, as the Billy's scene was getting really interesting . . .

Nicola Tyson: As punk went mainstream, the younger crowd like myself – the sixteen- and seventeen-year-olds who hadn't joined a band whatsoever – were craving more underground thrills, something new and different. The seventies were a very creatively fertile period, and things moved fast. In the autumn of '78, Steve Strange and Rusty Egan launched Bowie nights every Tuesday at the tiny Billy's club on Meard Street in Soho, and we all showed up to see what would happen. Quite quickly a look started to develop – the other extreme to the monochrome uniformity of punk. Flamboyance and glamour were under investigation. First, a decorative military look was explored, with plenty of diamond paste jewellery . . . if you could afford the gear, much of it leather, from the shop PX, where Steve Strange and Julia Fodor [Princess Julia] worked. Most of us couldn't, so clothes were home-made, and simply anything went. It was important to wear something different every week. Seventeen-year-old George O'Dowd and his coterie excelled at this. Later, once the scene exploded and moved on to bigger venues and, finally, Blitz, a distinct sartorial language had been formulated, embracing many permutations, but at Billy's it was very much just a kind of dressing-up party still, such as Philip Sallon wearing a wedding dress and a police hat. Other soon-to-be celebs of the eighties who went to the Bowie nights at Billy's were Siobhan Fahey [Bananarama], Jeremy Healy [Haysi Fantayzee], Martin Degville [Sigue Sigue Sputnik], Peter Robinson [Marilyn], Andy Polaris [Animal Nightlife], Midge Ure [Ultravox] and members of Spandau Ballet.

As an art student, then on a foundation course at Chelsea, I had a 35mm camera and knew how to use it. I began to document what the others were wearing each week and then sell the colour snaps to them the following week for beer money. People wanted a record of what they were wearing – in colour preferably, because this was a colourful scene, unlike punk, and not just a black-and-white passport-booth photo of their hairdo, grabbed at the tube station on their way there. Good-quality 35mm autofocus snap cameras weren't readily available yet. The press only used black and white in those days or colour slides, so this meant my colour photos couldn't be published until hi-res scanning came along, and consequently they sat in a box for over thirty years! Becoming a passive observer at Billy's suited me, because as the outfits and the look grew more carnivalesque, the less I wanted to participate. I wasn't interested in actually looking like that myself, and hence didn't continue on to Blitz, but years later it came out in my paintings, where I constantly reinvent the body – the female body – in unlikely ways, often factoring in peculiar bits of clothing.

Peter York: Somebody took me to Billy's as an example of the new thing, and I thought, 'Oh yes,' because they were quite clearly people who had come out of punk-land. There was absolute continuity and people trying new things and people wearing chocolate-soldier costumes and so on. And it was a great laugh. I was thinking, 'What are they going to make of that? Where do you go with that? Because as far as I can remember, they're just Bowie people all the time.' I liked it.

Robert Elms: I started at the LSE in September 1977, and by the end of the year it felt as though punk was over, and I was thinking, 'Oh well, that was fun while it lasted, but I've got no cult to belong to any more.' By this stage I'd met Steve Dagger, who was the social secretary of the student union at the LSE. Through Steve I met Gary Kemp, and I'd met Chris Sullivan at Crackers; he used to come up from South Wales most weeks to go to Crackers or the Lacy Lady. It was around the end of 1978 that I heard there was a new clothes shop called PX in Covent Garden, a wasteland yet to be colonised for upscale retail. I was wearing winkle-pickers at the time, and old Seditionaries stuff, and I remember walking into PX, and Steve Strange – who was employed by the shop's chief designer, Helen Robinson, as a shop assistant – commented on my trousers or my shoes or something. He said he was starting this club with Rusty Egan on a Tuesday night, at a club in Soho called Billy's. So I went to the first night with Graham Smith, and what was weird was I saw loads of those kids who I hadn't seen since the very early days of punk. In this room there were probably only fifty people, but I sort of knew by eye at least half of them. And that night, I think, set the tone for the next few years. You suddenly knew something was happening, and that it was going to be exciting.

At the start, Rusty didn't have many records to play, so he played Kraftwerk, Bowie and Roxy, going back to where we all started. Within weeks, Steve Dagger comes down and brings Gary [Kemp] with him, and then, you know, everyone starts to talk. A lot of the people there were slightly too young for punk, but it was an absolute continuum of punk. That's one of the big points about the Blitz scene: it wasn't a reaction to punk, it was a reaction to everything that came after it. I liked the dressing-up side of punk but hated all that lying in the gutter being sick on yourself. The first punk clubs were always about elitism, as was Crackers. You had to be a really good dresser or a really good dancer to fit in there. They had that sort of very competitive edge. So I think Billy's came partly from that. I also think it was a sort of working-class, urban aristocracy, if that makes any sense. It was kids who were faces; it was that mod thing again. 'Oh, I know the best jokes, I've got the important records, I know I'm the one.' It was either people like us from LSE or art students from St Martin's or disaffected people from the punk and soul scenes. Gary Kemp was training to work as a printer in Fleet Street, there were hairdressers . . . all these people who were part of an urban elite. People who aspired to work in the West End, who thought they were the best, in that mod way. They didn't just think they were the best, they sort of knew they were. They knew they were the best dressed, the coolest.

Graham Ball: I was at the LSE with Robert Elms and Steve Dagger, and when we went out, we started bumping into all these people from

St Martin's, like Fiona Dealey and Chris Sullivan. The scene started coalescing around Billy's, when that opened. That was the first time that soul boys really started mixing with art students, and the fashion started changing too. People like Chris would change their outfit every day, and you'd go round to his flat and he'd spend more time getting ready than actually going out. You'd start to see people looking like extras from *Casablanca* or trying desperately to copy Marlon Brando. For me, Wednesday was a half-day at the LSE, so it meant you could have a big Tuesday night and skip Wednesday completely. We'd go for a steam in Porchester baths and bump into people like Terence Stamp or the occasional cab driver. There were no other clubs at the time, so most weekends were spent looking for parties that didn't exist. I remember going to Andrew Logan's warehouse party, down in Butler's Wharf, and that gave me the idea of doing nightclubs on a bigger scale. We all wanted peer recognition, although not everyone knew what they wanted to do. The idea of making money from nightclubs became very interesting, a career option. The unifying edict was that none of us wanted anything to do with the straight world. Back then, if you didn't go out, you didn't exist. So, as you went out, you had to make very quick decisions about who you wanted to spend time with. You'd get up at lunchtime, and your day would be vinyl, tea and cigarettes, until you went out and had another go. There was a trip to New York that year, when we discovered a different level of nightclub, which were already being done an industrial scale, with proper promotion and props and doormen and name DJs – very bright people who took clubbing seriously. The scale of those places was incredible. For us, it was a lightbulb moment.

Fiona Dealey: In 1977, I had gone up to Coventry to start a fine art course, but I hated it. It was a cultural wasteland. There was a big problem there, because I was quite friendly with the black students and there was a lot of racism. This was the first time I'd come out of my comfort zone of Essex and London. I'd already made my mind up that

I didn't want to stay in Essex and I didn't want to get married. I wanted to be part of a group. So I'd seen all that, and then I'm up in Coventry and I felt like I'd landed on another planet.

So I left there, and then started at St Martin's, on the fashion course, in September 1978. Sometimes when you're growing up you find yourself with the wrong group of people, so getting into St Martin's and being part of a scene in Charing Cross Road – how bloody exciting was that? It was just all incredible, and I felt like I'd met my 'band'.

I'd met Chris Sullivan at a house party in Basildon a few years earlier – I remember he was wearing a black fifties jacket with red slubbing – and as we were both staying at the Ralph West Halls of Residence, we reconnected. In the first week there, I got into the lift with a Welshman, and it happened to be Chris. He was talking about how many seconds it took to move between one floor and the next, and I said, 'I've met this jacket before.'

This is when we started going to Billy's. And suddenly there were all these people I knew from the clubs. I remember driving a van full of people to go to Billy's, and there were people who I knew from the Lacy Lady, the Goldmine . . . And we were all dressing up. We weren't following celebrities or anything like that. But the atmosphere at Billy's was always very competitive, and you wanted to look your best, every week. You didn't want to look like anyone else, so it wasn't about fitting in. Sometimes you get peer-group pressure where you've got to be wearing the same jeans, the same leather jacket, but at Billy's it was all about looking different, and you couldn't really wear the same thing too often.

The address of the Ralph West Halls of Residence was 45 Worfield Street, although they were actually on the west side of Albert Bridge Road, facing Battersea Park. They serviced all the art schools in central London: Camberwell, Central, Chelsea, the London College of Printing and St Martin's. If you were from the provinces, and you were in your first year studying at one of those colleges, and you could afford it or were lucky enough to have a grant, this is where you stayed (this is where Joe Strummer lived in the early seventies, when he was at Central School of Art, as did Glen Matlock a few years later). A nine-storey Inner London Education Authority tower block overlooking a council estate, to me this felt like the centre of the known world. Just a five-minute walk from the King's Road, Ralph West was like New York's Chelsea Hotel, reimagined as a youth hostel.

Walking along the corridors of Ralph West was like being inside an enormous musical advent calendar, as out of every bedroom there poured everything from Genesis to the Ohio Players, from Neu! to the Sex Pistols. It was as though you were turning a radio dial as you walked along the floors, as rhythms smashed into each other with complete disregard. There was some convergence, though little consensus. As for myself, David Bowie's Low *seemed to take precedence, and while my cheap little turntable hosted everyone from Joni Mitchell and Steely Dan to U-Roy and Glen Campbell, for a while the second side of* Low *– the largely instrumental one – appeared to be equipped with the right kind of dystopian top notes, music that seemed to mirror so much of what was going on at the time, from nascent industrial noise and spiky new-wave disco to DIY futurism and scratchy punk.*

I moved there in August 1977, fresh from High Wycombe, and spent a year immersing myself in punk London. In August 1978, a new tranche of students moved in, including Chris Sullivan, all the way from Merthyr Tydfil (and whose life always seemed packed with incident), and Fiona Dealey, all dolled-up from Southend. I got to know them both, with Fiona and I becoming fast friends. We spent hours in each other's rooms, moaning about St Martin's (she was in the first year of the fashion course, I was in the first year of graphics), gossiping about the sex lives of people on our floor and working out which parties we were going to gatecrash at the weekend. Young love was everywhere, and there was one couple – Marjorie and Karl (although obviously not their real names) – who were having so much sex, usually up against the doors of their respective rooms, that Marjorie used to say she had forgotten what to do with her legs. I was still going to gigs, dashing out most evenings to the Marquee, the 100 Club, Hammersmith Odeon, the Hope and Anchor, the Moonlight Club and the Nashville to watch an increasingly disparate bunch of post-punk groups (Siouxsie and the Banshees, Wire, Joy Division, Gang of Four, Slits, Pere Ubu, Cabaret Voltaire, etc). Fiona, meanwhile, would be dressing up to go out to nightclubs, which soon included Billy's. On those nights when I wasn't going out, I'd sit in my room playing Iggy Pop and Buzzcocks records, while Fiona would sit on the end of my bed, looking like a Bond Street Valkyrie, complaining that she had nothing to wear. I'd often ask her, in strong vernacular terms, what she thought she looked like, jokingly wondering aloud how she had the audacity to go out looking so extreme. In truth, I thought she was one of the most exotic creatures I'd ever seen, and I became intoxicated by both her and the world she moved in. I found the whole thing fascinating. Soon I started going to these clubs too, and found them as exhilarating as the early punk clubs. Not that I was dressed for the part. I can still remember what I wore the first time I went to the Blitz: black studded leather jacket, black T-shirt, black skinny-legged jeans and black patent winkle-pickers. In hindsight, I could pretend that I was channelling one of the early-sixties Warhol gang or a Tom of Finland leather boy, but in truth I was simply wearing what I always wore. I would soon learn that this wasn't really good enough.

Kim Bowen: Billy's started the same autumn I went to St Martin's and is where I met Stephen Linard and Lee Sheldrick. We lived in the vilest of places in East Ham. It was so awful, our first college landing spot. So Lee, Stephen and I started going to Billy's, but they were always picking up boys and going off to get laid, and I was still hanging after Lee. I thought he was going through a stage, but he wasn't. So I'd catch a night bus home, as they were off having sex, and dressing like I did, this was quite scary, as you'd attract a lot of attention and people would be abusive and rude, you know? I went and found a squat in Warren Street.

Chris Sullivan: I had been on the foundation course at Camberwell School of Art, and then applied to St Martin's. I wrote down five courses at five different art schools, and then my friend Graham Smith pulled one out. 'Oh, fashion at St Martin's. You'll never get in there, there are five thousand applicants per place!' I said, 'I will. You watch!' Of course, I did. I regretted it almost immediately, as I'm not exactly fashion-designer material. You have to be quite exact to make clothes; I'm rather approximate. A few weeks later, I bumped into Steve [Strange] one night on Oxford Circus, and he had the long leather coat on and a little hat to one side, and he said, 'Come along to this new night I'm doing at Billy's.' And that was it, the first night. The reason we started all these one-nighters is because none of the West End clubs would let us in. We got refused service in a few pubs in those days, so we all wanted somewhere to go, a safe haven where there wouldn't be any fights and the DJ would play whatever he wanted.

Iain R. Webb: I think I went to Billy's on the first night, because I met Stephen Jones and Princess Julia at PX, down in Covent Garden, that week. It was much more industrial because back then Covent Garden wasn't Covent Garden. PX sold military clothes, leather trousers, pegs, big army overcoats and macs. At that time, Stephen had big fright–horror hair, a big leather coat and a leather queen's cap, and Julia was in her tight leather jacket, with a pencil skirt and a huge beehive. The original ethos of punk for me was always DIY, where everybody did their own thing, but by the time I reached London it had just become a uniform. So a lot of people who were the original nucleus of punk, especially from the art-school world, had moved on and were dressing in their own way. So when Steve Strange opened Billy's, it was all about dressing up. You might buy some medals or brooches from PX, with something from my old auntie's jewellery boxes, bits of diamante jewellery, or I'd go to

John Lewis and buy a metre or two of patterned ribbon and wear it as sashes. We were influenced by *Cabaret*, *Myra Breckinridge*, *The Boyfriend*, *The Night Porter* and watching old films on Saturday afternoons with the curtains drawn, when everyone else was outside playing sport. Billy's was a place where all that could manifest itself and we could dress as characters from films or books or from the imagined lives that we all wanted. That whole thing about reinvention is very important, plus the fact that it all grew out of punk, which a lot of people don't think it did. You have to remember that London was very grey at the time, grey and bland and conservative and locked down, and there weren't the outlets for people that there are now. The New Romantic idea, with its flounces and the big bows and the crimped hair and the whatever, in this fancy-dress kind of way, was a reaction to our surroundings as much as anything. Self-expression through adversity. To me that was key during that Billy's period. Someone would be in full religious garb, someone else dressed as Little Bo-Peep, someone else dressed as a Left Bank existentialist. You could have somebody in a leather jacket and torn jeans. You could have a biker in full leathers, and some kids just in Harrington jackets. And it was all OK. In a sense, we were rejecting fashion and just doing it ourselves. It was about not only rejecting the Establishment, it was about rejecting what we were being sold as fashion. We were being ourselves and dressing as other people, although this contradictory nature, I think, is part of it anyway. The contradiction of finding yourself and dressing up as a character isn't a contradiction because through that experimentation is how you find yourself anyway, and how you express yourself, and the fact is that none of us are purely one thing.

Peter York: Billy's was really the start of the new portable clubland. In 1978, after the first London punk scene fell apart, the various constituent parts went back to first base, who were . . . David Bowie, Bryan Ferry, soul music and posing for the haircut kids. The style punks went down the popular gay clubs, which was no big deal. They let in straights, they let in girls. Billy's was this little nothing gay club in

Meard Street, a Dickensian cross-street in Soho with girls in the windows and 'French Model, First Floor' in the bell pushes, and Maltese boys in Travolta suits down at street level – old tyme Soho. Billy's was another little box club, until Steve Strange and Rusty Egan changed it all. Steve and Rusty took over Billy's on Tuesdays, when Rusty was DJ and Steve was on the door, and they played futurist music, as it came to be called.

While one of the biggest changes in London nightlife in the late seventies was the shift from the likes of the Marquee and the 100 Club to nightclubs such as the Embassy in Old Bond Street (which opened in April 1978) and Legends in Old Burlington Street – as we started going out to dance rather than going out to watch bands – so there was also a shift from pubs to cocktail bars, as the proto-Blitz Kids started wanting more glamorous places to drink.

And the obvious place to go was Mayfair. Yes, you could have gone to Peppermint Park or Rumours in Covent Garden, and yes, you may have wanted to scoot all the way down to the King's Road occasionally, but the most esoteric place to drink your Tequila Sunrise, your Singapore Sling or your Pina Colada (drinks which might sound incredibly naff today, but which were considered to be exactly the opposite back then) was the Beachcomber Bar in the Mayfair Hotel.

The Beachcomber had originally opened in July 1960, created by the semi-legendary Danziger brothers, Harry and Edward, American film producers who had moved to London and bought the hotel. The Beachcomber was the first London iteration of the American Polynesian restaurant phenomenon, opening three years before the London outpost of Trader Vic's. At the time, the capital had never seen anything like it, with plastic palm trees, rainstorms over a pond of caimans, parrots in and out of cages, and oceanic art all around.

I first went there in 1978, and at the time it was one of the most ironically glamorous places I'd ever been. As you sat sipping enormous pink drinks in extravagant glasses, life-size animatronic crocodiles crawled around the pink plastic foliage beside you. It was a world away from the warm lager you'd find in the pubs in Soho.

I seem to remember my clothes becoming rather outlandish too. In the space of a few months, I went from wearing a leather jacket to suit jackets and pointy shoes. I wasn't alone in this, as people all over the country started to dress up and be more ambitious about the way they looked. Whether they had come out of the soul scene or the punk clubs (or both), they wanted more.

Nick Rhodes (*musician*): My parents would often watch *Top of the Pops* with me, as they were quite turned on by knowing what was going on in the charts, and I remember they actually liked Bowie. They liked him so much they took me to see him when he played the Empire Pool in Wembley, in London, in 1976, on the *Station to Station* tour, not once but twice. I'd become such a fan, and he had become such a focus of what I thought I wanted to do with my life at the time. They were very indulgent of Bowie because this was the person who inspired me, and the rest of Duran Duran, and most of the rest of the British music industry that exists now, to do what we all chose to do. I told my parents when I was ten that I wanted to be a rock star when I grew up, which they laughed off and said, 'Yes, well, that's very nice, darling, but let's not talk about it now.' But when I was still saying it at fourteen, it was a little more worrisome for them. At fifteen, I could already play guitar, and a year later I formed a band. At the time, I wore huge, wide trousers, bum-freezer jackets with wide lapels covered in Anabas badges, and shirts with unforgivably large collars. I accessorised and adapted everything. I remember during punk I would pin my tie back with paper clips to make it look thinner. You just adapted whatever you had. I remember in assembly at school the headmaster announcing that 'Just because Nicholas Rhodes is doing this to his clothes doesn't mean all of you have to do it.'

Simon Le Bon (*singer*): I think we were a symbol of music and fun and parties. And the weekend, driving in an open-topped sports car with music blaring and a pretty girl driving, hair blowing in the wind, and who knows what's going to happen? That's what Duran Duran meant to me.

Nick Rhodes: When I was asked to DJ at the Rum Runner in Birmingham, I basically just played all my David Bowie records. This was in 1978, and we were just about to form Duran Duran, and all of us loved Bowie. Most of the other members of the band were working at the club in some capacity – cooking, cleaning or washing up – but I actually got to play Bowie's records. Duran Duran had a single vision of what we wanted to do: we wanted to mix glam rock and punk rock with a little bit of disco, although the prime motivation for forming in the first place was David Bowie. It always was. An entire generation of groups who formed in the late seventies or early eighties only happened because of David. He is basically responsible for British music in the first half of the eighties. There was a decadence about him that was appealing; something dark, something German, but something very exciting.

Simon Le Bon: We were just never really into that grey, small-time, independent thing. Our heart was in the early seventies.

Nick Rhodes: In 1978, Birmingham was finally creeping out from under the shadow cast by the IRA pub bombings of 1974, despite continued unemployment, power cuts and the three-day week. Allegedly, this was the UK's second city, but you couldn't help but wonder at the gaping disparity with the capital. If this was the second city, what might life be like in the thirteenth? I was a teenager at the time, trying to remain optimistic about the future, despite the Sex Pistols' curse that there was not to be one. When the punk bubble burst, its residue splattered far and wide. The Pistols imploded. Some bands clung on, only to wither slowly. The Cure and the Banshees made the natural migration to goth; the Clash became a spectacular rock band. But a new guard was already rising. Birmingham's clubs had been a casualty. Barbarella's and Rebecca's were quickly displaced by the Rum Runner and the Holy City Zoo. DJs scoured the musical no-man's-land for clues to what would be the new soundtrack.

When we formed Duran Duran, it was really a melting pot of new wave mixed with electronic dance music, disco and glam rock. It was all the things we knew as teenagers, and we somehow wanted to make a hybrid to create our own sound and our own look, to launch ourselves, and we knew we didn't want to do anything that wasn't stylish. With the background we'd come from, we wanted something that was going to have a strong visual impact. We always chose our own clothes and put things together ourselves. I remember the first time we encountered a stylist was in the late eighties. We hadn't had a clue that people like this existed. [Before that] it was all very naive. We didn't really have to think about it. We'd just go and find things that we liked, and somehow we grew together. It's like being in a gang, being in a band. Nothing was manufactured, as many things are now. We got together from school. It was definitely in our mandate [to find our own look], but we weren't looking for something unnatural. We were actually just searching for things that we thought were cool, and often we'd find women's clothes, because actually men's clothes weren't particularly flamboyant at that time, so we'd literally go to small women's boutiques and buy jackets off the shelf or a shirt that buttoned the wrong way for us, but it didn't really matter. And you'd mix that up with leather trousers that you'd managed to find in Birmingham or from a biker shop or something, and then you'd find a shop like Kahn & Bell, which was a dream, because everything they made, we wanted to wear. Probably John [Taylor] and I subconsciously guided where we went stylistically as a band, but everybody in the band, without exception, had their own vision and style. For example, Roger [Taylor] and I always laugh now when we arrive at a photo shoot and there are rails of clothes there. I can literally go through them, as he could, and pick out something – 'Oh, that'd be for John. Oh yep, there's a Roger one there. Yeah, that's mine. OK, Simon will like that' – and literally separate them all, and when everybody arrives it's very rare that there's a squabble over a jacket or a pair of shoes or something, because we are pretty much defined by the things that we like.

Post-punk was in full bloom in the US, and during the summer of 1978 there was a veritable new-wave heatwave. Devo. Suicide. Talking Heads. The B-52's. Blondie. All of them were key disseminators of electronic pop, moving their own dials, building on a series of musical developments that in some respects were way ahead of what was happening in the UK, and all of them sounding decidedly exotic to British ears: Devo making arch, angular rock that bordered on dance; Suicide experimenting with futuristic noir; Talking Heads deftly moving their preppy pop to the dancefloor; the B-52's exploding with full meta retro; and Blondie fusing power pop and disco. Their disruption was attractive, and probably more so because it was all so disparate. A lot of it sounded vaguely electronic (Vaguely Electronic actually being quite a good name for a group in 1978), and bound only lightly to the past, much of it floated in time, although if you took any time to analyse it, you could see that all they were really doing was starting to acknowledge the 'beat' – i.e. dance, black music, R&B, funk, etc. – and in that sense the music could be easily slotted into a continuum. Nothing was coalescing, though, and there was nothing to frame what was going on other than a definite move towards the margins: dancing this mess around. The only thing that really soldered them together was their complete lack of anything approaching agitprop. Here, pleasure was the law.

Devo were perhaps the most subversive, which actually made them seem a little old-fashioned. 'When I was in high school, I dressed like a punk rocker and people would scream "Devo!" at me – because Devo infiltrated the mainstream,' Kurt Cobain would say in 1993, when the post-punk period was being re-evaluated yet again. 'Out of all the bands who came from the underground and actually made it in the mainstream, Devo is the most challenging of all. They're just awesome. I love them.'

Though Deborah Harry, with her metaphorical and literal appropriation of platinum-blonde hair, spray-on micro-skirts and melodic, monosyllabic pop, became the most acceptable – and ultimately the most successful – of all the punk pin-ups, she never tried to hide the fact that her iconographic hair was dyed; she was a punk, after all, and on the cover of the first Blondie LP you can clearly see her brown roots. Blondie were deliberately ironic. Even their name was a giveaway – a band called Blondie fronted by a girl who obviously wasn't. From the beginnings of the group, Harry was always toying with the ambiguity of pop iconography and the implications of sexual role-playing. Like the boys and girls in Billy's, she was dressing up.

Deborah Harry (*singer*): The whole thing was kind of obsessed and mad, and . . . purposeful . . . [Pop art], that's what Blondie came out of. We all had that influence. Chris [Stein] and I came from an art background, and it's part of the way we think. There was also our association with [Andy] Warhol, and Chris was very friendly with William Burroughs. Chris went to art school and would either have become a photographer or a painter – and then the music evolved. At first, there was considerable indifference to us, and then a considerable amount of resistance – resistance and fear – to me as a female singer. To me, the idea of presenting a strong female singer had finally found its time – it was inevitable. I felt a lot of female singers were always being victimised or used, and that a lot of their lyrics reflected that. And I remember thinking how much I liked the blues of Janis Joplin or Billie Holiday, but how I really did not want to portray that sort of woman – the sort who was always going to get her ass kicked by love or whatever. And I actually think that me doing that was part of the reason why Blondie were treated so badly by people in the industry and in management. Because it was all men, and it was like they were saying, 'We're gonna fuck her up,' because I didn't portray a particular type of woman singer. Or maybe we were just stupid. I know that Chris was extremely idealistic and not very interested in business, and that although we were partners, I would follow his lead. But actually, I think that perhaps I was the better business person. We were experimenting a lot; usually, bands have just one style, but we were trying out lots of different styles of music. So it took us longer. That's the only thing I can put it down to. When you look at the Ramones, they did their style of song and perfected it. We were doing lots of things, so they took longer to perfect. Does that sound logical? People thought I was just a bit of fluff. Well, maybe I was, but there was more there than that.

Kraftwerk were not only counter-intuitive as far as their music was concerned, but with The Man-Machine *they also fundamentally redefined what a rock group should look like: four men, all dressed alike in red shirts and black ties, their hair short and lacquered, their faces white (and frozen), pouting in red lipstick, confounding all consumer expectations (some said they dressed like aristocratic European businessmen). Everything about their expressions, their posture and their uniforms screamed artifice and studied cool, so it was perhaps not so surprising that their identity became a template for boys at Billy's, who could identify with a look that mixed conformity with effeminacy and took the punk ethic and put it into a suit. The image was beyond reproach, not least because the music Kraftwerk made was peerless. In its own way it was more inventive than punk, and certainly more influential. (In New York, they were already having the kind of effect that would soon reshape black dance music.) It is almost impossible to overemphasise how important it was. It wasn't so much that it was vaulting in its ambition, but rather that Kraftwerk decided to breathe a different kind of air, and to dress in a completely different way while they did so. In that sense, it was kaleidoscopic in its execution, both musically and visually. Many critics and consumers accused them of irony, although this could not have been further from the truth. As David Stubbs says in* Mars by 1980: The Story of Electronic Music,

'Only retrospectively can we see how, in 1978, Kraftwerk stood four-square at a threshold that would determine the course of both black and white cultural identity, pop and art, soul and artifice, the impending structures of pop, as well as broaden considerations about work and leisure in an increasingly automated age whose volatile anxieties were in stark contrast to the studied, bland serenity affected by Ralf Hütter's vocals.' And it was The Man-Machine *that did it.*

David Cavanagh (*journalist*): Nobody ever believes me, but I was watching a talent show on ITV one night in the late seventies when four blokes came on dressed as mannequins and danced robotically to Kraftwerk's 'Showroom Dummies'. I think they were from Yorkshire, and no, they didn't win. But what an act! They live on in my memory as a totem of The Bizarre Ways That Britain First Heard Kraftwerk. My own first encounter was in 1975, when 'Autobahn' entered the charts the same week as 'Wombling White Tie and Tails' and West Ham's FA Cup song. Truly a Top 40 to die for. These days we're all thoroughly accustomed to Kraftwerk. They're the grand dukes and sovereign rulers of electronic music. They inspire awe for the glittering pop palaces they built with their tisky-tisk drums and singing, swinging synths ('Europe Endless', 'Spacelab', 'Neon Lights', 'Computer World'). An alphabet of the people they've influenced would run to 2,500 names before it even got to Cabaret Voltaire. And yet, for all our clinical theories about innovative electro-pop and minimalist man-machinery, what's striking about Kraftwerk's catalogue is that it still comes down to a very basic, non-scientific response: the immediate alertness, pleasure and fascination that Kraftwerk's icily beautiful textures trigger in our hearts and brains. Ralf Hütter and his since-departed colleague Florian Schneider were famous for pioneering tomorrow's technology today, but they also wrote romantic music that will dance in the air forever. And that's a clinical theory.

As an adolescent in 1978–79, Kraftwerk were seldom far from my radio. The local station used to play 'Kometenmelodie 2' (from *Autobahn*) and 'Airwaves' (*Radio-Activity*) on its Sunday-evening programme for hi-fi buffs, along with audiophiliac Moog voyages by Tomita, Jarre and Vangelis. You switched off your bedroom light, angled your face to the night sky and imagined your small transistor radio to be emitting the pulsating symphonies of faraway planets. Today the second side of *Autobahn* (1974) still takes me back to those spooky Sunday broadcasts, and I get a Proustian thrill from the rock'n'roll chords on 'Kometenmelodie 2' that sound like Hot Butter playing Status Quo's 'Caroline'. However, the main attraction of *Autobahn*, of course, is its twenty-two-minute title track, a virtuoso sound-simulation of a motorway journey – from the car door slamming and the engine starting, to the hypnotic white-noise patterns of 130 km/h driving. While Kraftwerk can sound metallically stern when they choose to, 'Autobahn' is freckled with warmth: sunny vocal harmonies ('*... mit Glitzerstrahl*'), a carefree flute solo (Schneider) and clever modulations (denoting gear-changes) to break the tension.

As the likes of Bowie and Eno listened attentively, a dark triptych followed. *Radio-Activity* (1975) begins like a heartbeat in the void, accelerating into the pulse that will form the spine of the title-song, an eerie tribute to the intangibles (music, disintegrating atoms) that linger in the atmosphere. The LP has a musty scent of Old Europe, which proved a hit with the synth groups of 1980–81 (e.g. Ultravox and Visage), and it retains a blood-chilling, Wagnerian quality even now, thanks to Kraftwerk's use of the Vako Orchestron, a choir-like relative of the Mellotron.

Trans-Europe Express (1977) and *The Man-Machine* (1978) are most people's idea of Kraftwerk. They move with mother-of-pearl grace, each with a wry pop satire in the centre ('Showroom Dummies', 'The Model') that allows the grandeur either side to breathe. The sparse lyrics lend themselves to considerable interpretation. Who are the real automatons – the humans or the robots? – is one of the central questions of Kraftwerk. It might be argued that, in an age when we stare into screens for years of our lives, sending emails to people sitting at desks six feet away, a line like '*Ya tvoi sluga, ya tvoi rabotnik* (I'm your slave, I'm your worker)' is not so much cute as close to the bone. At least the dummies had time to go dancing.

Michael Bracewell (*writer*): On 30 June 1978, a seven-inch single was released. It came in a cheap paper sleeve the colour of tinned salmon. On the front was a line illustration of two young hipsters dancing – the kind of figures you might expect to see on an artist's impression of a swinging 1967 nightspot. The Letraset aesthetic of the typography – 'Electronically yours . . . THE HUMAN LEAGUE' – pronounced the record, 'A FAST PRODUCT', to be low-budget and therefore of interest in the lost, edgy months following the collapse of punk. The single was called 'Being Boiled', the B-side 'Circus of Death'. Fast Product was a small label run by a man in Glasgow called Robert Last. His other releases had included a clear plastic bag with a piece of orange peel in it. The Human League came from Sheffield. Back in the late seventies, due to the specialist nature of its steel industry, Sheffield had escaped the full assault of unemployment which had hit so many northern cities; but despite this, the city had a post-industrial air, as though it lingered in a curious kind of time warp between the past and the future. Science-fiction strangeness and melancholy was grafted onto the ruins of civic grandeur. It was the perfect 'alienated synthesist' backdrop and from 'Being Boiled' onwards, the League made a soundscape for this collision of time zones. The young Phil Oakey, bright at school but bored with 'having no money and being pushed about', had been working as a hospital porter – legend has it (fuelling the Human League's reputation for fetishising the synthetic) in a plastic-surgery ward. A fan of David Bowie and Roxy Music, he recalls being thin enough to buy women's clothes in Sheffield, which he customised into radical one-off garments.

Phil Oakey and Martyn Ware become fast friends while in the fourth form at King Edward School in Sheffield. They often rode around the Derbyshire countryside on motorbikes, and shared formative sexual and chemical experiences. Although Oakey was quiet, he didn't seek approbation from his peers and appeared almost other-worldly. He turned Ware on to Frank Zappa and Carla Bley, and they both became unusually obsessed with anything electronic and experimental. Ware thought Oakey could be conceptually right for what he had in mind for the group he was starting, the Human League, although he says he never had any idea if Oakey could sing or not; but he knew he looked great, with his floppy haircut and interesting clothes. He also wasn't sure if he could write melodies to the backing tracks he was making. Ware gave Oakey the instrumental demo of a tune called 'Being Boiled' and told him to go away for a couple of days to see what he could come up with. What he came back with were perfectly obscure lyrics and a singing voice that was almost deadpan (he sounded like an odd cross between David Bowie, Neil Diamond, Peter Hammill and Leonard Cohen). Between them they started experimenting with what they called 'the banality of disco', mixing their electronic music with deliberately arch sci-fi narratives. Towards the end of the year, they started to get interest from the Fast Product label, and so set about recording their first single. Ware's most vivid memory is rushing down to his local stationer's to buy some Letraset in order to do the cover.

Martyn Ware: Eno was a massive influence. He did an interview in 1975 in which he said that rock'n'roll was dead, and that all you needed to be in a band was a tape recorder, a microphone and a synthesizer. We took that to heart. Punk? We were a little bit sniffy. We thought we'd already gone through this with the New York Dolls. We just thought punk was a bit old-fashioned. Sounded like pub rock.

All of the Human League's equipment was bought on hire purchase, and so when they started touring, they built a protective structure out of steel and Perspex. 'The journalists at the time were going, "What a powerful indication of the alienation of contemporary youth," but it was just to stop the skinheads from gobbing on them.' Martyn Ware was bamboozled by the positive reaction to 'Being Boiled', as he thought it was actually quite a difficult record, a 'novelty'. When John Lydon reviewed the single for Melody Maker, *he just said, 'Trendy hippies.'*

At first, Ware was upset, but then thought that if Lydon's taking notice of them, they must be doing something right. It eventually sold 5,000 copies, which was a lot for an independent single, and then they signed with Virgin, who promised them more independence than their other suitor, EMI. The band had a manifesto of sorts, which included a clause that stated they would never write a lyric that included the word 'love'. So as they had ruled out writing about love, sex or human relationships, they were creating more and more songs based on science fiction and theology, inspired by Kraftwerk, A Clockwork Orange *and all dystopian points in between.*

On 13 October, in her speech at the Conservative Party conference, Margaret Thatcher invoked her own kind of inner-city dystopia: 'When a rule of law breaks down, fear takes over. There is no security in the streets, families feel unsafe even in their own homes, children are at risk, criminals prosper, the men of violence flourish, the nightmare world of A Clockwork Orange *becomes a reality. Here in Britain in the last few years that world has become visibly nearer.'*

Martyn Ware: We [the Human League] played the original Marquee Club towards the end of 1978. It was the hottest gig I think I've ever played in my life. It was ridiculous. It was rammed, and it must have been a thousand degrees in there. [A while ago] I heard from somebody who went to that show, and they said that while they were waiting outside to go in, they saw David Bowie and Iggy Pop, both with their full entourages, getting turned away by the door staff. It could have been a disaster. That could have been that. But then a couple of weeks later, we were in London again to play the Fulham Greyhound, and about twenty minutes before we were due to go on stage, David Bowie suddenly appears in our dressing room, totally unannounced. We were just four lads from Sheffield, and there was Bowie and his entourage, something like eight people, turning up out of the blue in this tiny dressing room with no door on it, a room about twice the size of your average toilet cubicle. Can you imagine?

We knew it went down well and we were pleased with it, but you just don't know. And then there was Bowie in the *NME* the following week, saying he had seen the future of pop music. You'll never get a quote like that again, will you? I'll settle for that. It's a shame Iggy didn't turn up again, but we ended up touring round Europe with him the following summer, probably because of Bowie's recommendation, I should think.

Phil Oakey (*musician*): We laughed at the other bands learning three chords – we used one finger.

Daniel Miller: I loved the whole DIY thing, so I thought, 'Fuck it, I'll put out a single.' And that was it. Having worked with a lot of film processing, it was quite familiar to me; it wasn't that complicated or expensive to do. A friend had given me J. G. Ballard's *Crash* to read, and it all came from there. So I made the Normal single 'T.V.O.D.' and 'Warm Leatherette'. I was shocked by the positive response I got, as before that there hadn't really been any electronic music, only the Throbbing Gristle album, *The Second Annual Report*. I had no idea what people would think. I got some test pressings from the pressing plant in east London, and as I didn't really know what to do, I went to a couple of record shops to see if they wanted to buy some. I went to Small Wonder, who took five copies, and then went to Rough Trade. They listened to it in the shop, which was scary for me because all these very cool people were there, but they loved it and said they wanted to distribute it. I didn't really know what distribution was, and they said, 'How many are you going to press?' I said, 'Well, I was going to press 500, because that's the minimum you can press.' And they said, 'We think you should do 2,000.'

I went back to see some friends I'd been working with in Switzerland, and I got this phone call telling me that Jane Suck, who was reviewing the singles for *Sounds*, had called it the Single of the Century. I thought, 'What the fuck is going on?' It got really good reviews in the four main papers, and on John Peel, and my life changed completely. I didn't think of myself as a recording artist particularly; I just wanted to make this one single. So I did the Silicon Teens project, which was a virtual electronic group, and then I was introduced to Fad Gadget and Robert Rental, and I liked the music so much I thought I'd start the label proper, and that's when Mute really came into being. The name came from mute film, which is film that hasn't got any sound on it, and the logo came from Letraset.

I basically formed Mute to release the Normal single, and it grew from there, and from then on I had a label I could use for whatever I got involved with. The whole thing was accidental. I had enjoyed punk, but I liked the energy and the enthusiasm and the DIY nature of it rather than the actual music. I found a lot of punk music to be quite repetitive, and having always enjoyed the likes of Kraftwerk, Neu! and Can, I thought modern electronic music was the way to go. When Roland and Korg started producing cheap synthesizers, I really thought that electronic music could be more punk than punk. You didn't even have to learn any chords; you could just hit the keyboard on the synth and something interesting would happen.

Thomas Leer was also responsible for kick-starting the DIY indie-techno boom. His single 'Private Plane'/'International' (Oblique Records) was released in September 1978, over six weeks before 'T.V.O.D.'/'Warm Leatherette' by the Normal. 'International' is my favourite post-punk single, but more importantly, it encouraged a whole generation to explore electronics in a completely new way. This was cut-and-paste music in a cut-and-paste sleeve, a lo-fi masterpiece recorded in Leer's bedsit without even an entry-level synth. Not only did he have to sing in a hushed voice so as not to wake his girlfriend (Leer was 'the original one-man bedroom band', according to the Independent*'s Andy Gill), but also the music was created by heavily processed instruments, tapes and extremely primitive electronic gizmos. Released on his own label, it was the* NME*'s Single of the Week* *and caused a stir throughout the industry – 'compelling pop with a dark heart, swooping between the pretty and the pretty disturbing', according to one review. It influenced the Human League, ZTT, The The, Throbbing Gristle, Thomas Dolby and everything that came in its wake.*

Born Thomas Wishart in Port Glasgow, in October 1953, Leer played in several local experimental pop groups in the early-to-mid-seventies, moving to London during punk and forming the punk band Pressure. Influenced by Kraftwerk and Can, he recorded 'Private Plane', and would later release the album The Bridge, *in collaboration with Robert Rental.*

Andy McCluskey: After doing a foundation course on the Wirral, I was going to go to Leeds art school, but then I took a gap year, and that's when the band started. It was the summer of '78. Three things happened: the Human League released 'Being Boiled', and we were like, 'What?'; 'Warm Leatherette' came out by the Normal; and our mates gave up being a punk band and turned themselves into Dalek I Love You. They played Eric's club with a drum machine and a tape recorder, and they dressed the set like an art-rock happening. Paul and I were there, and we just went, 'Man, we can do this. We're getting left behind.' So because I'd taken a gap year and Paul had just accidentally failed to tell his mother he'd been offered a BT scholarship to be a telephone engineer in London, we started OMD. I briefly sang with Dalek I Love You because they needed a singer, but after about four gigs, I said, 'I want to sing my own songs.' We went and knocked on the door at Eric's and asked if we could come and play on one of their Thursday nights as a two-piece doing electronic music. And they went, 'Yeah. What are you called?' So we invented the name Orchestral Manoeuvres in the Dark, for one night only: 12 October 1978. Then we got asked to play at Factory in Manchester, and Tony Wilson, after being encouraged by his wife, said he wanted to make a record of one of our demo tapes. He said, 'But they're just these hairy Scousers whining about electricity,' but she made him sign us. He said, 'Would you like to do a single, as you are the future of pop music?' Tony was always very good at rewriting history.

So we recorded 'Electricity', it was played on John Peel, and it sold out all 5,000 copies in one week. Tony said, 'Factory is too small, and you should be on *Top of the Pops*.' And he sold us to Dindisc, which was owned by Virgin, for £5,000. Peter Saville [Factory's graphic designer] said we were the only band on Factory that ever actually adhered to the original founding ethos, as all Factory wanted to do was to develop young artists and move them on to big labels. Dindisc was started by Carol Wilson, who worked for Richard Branson. He said [to her], 'What can I give you as a thank-you for signing Sting to my publishing company?' She got Dindisc. 'Electricity' wasn't a hit immediately, but it was re-released several times.

We were consciously in love with Kraftwerk. Because we thought so many things were clichés, we wanted to avoid them. So let's have a synth melody instead of a chorus. Cymbals, cliché. Using the word 'love', not going to happen. All these things were banned in our musical vocabulary. Kraftwerk taught us that you can do beautiful melodic music with intellectual lyrics, and I think we welded a three-minute pop mentality onto the top. Paul and I didn't sit in the back room of his mum's house going, 'Right, what we're going to do is, we're going to add the melancholic emotion of Neu! to the rigid structure of Kraftwerk,' but that's what we did. At the time, I was very difficult, a little precious, pretentious – some people would say I haven't changed – but this was our art. It seems preposterous to describe it as such now, but this was what I was doing instead of going to do sculpture at art college. Orchestral Manoeuvres in the Dark were a two-piece conceptual art project in the guise of a musical band, and I think that nobody was more surprised than us when we started to have hits. We were budgeting for failure from day one, which is why we spent all our advance on a studio – we didn't think we'd make more than one record.

Paul Humphreys: Punk was fantastic because it opened up a lot of clubs around the UK. There weren't enough punk bands to fill the punk clubs every night, so they used to do alternative nights where you didn't get paid, but you could get up and play as long as it was something different. On a Thursday night at Eric's in Liverpool, you could get up and do different things. We loved punk, but we discovered our alternative music before punk happened: electronic music. You can look at some of our songs, like 'Electricity' for instance – it's almost like punk on synth really. One of the great things about punk was that pre-punk, to be in a band you had to be a great player or a great musician; like if you were a keyboard player, you'd have to play like Keith Emerson. Whereas when punk happened, it was all about expressing yourself, about the statement you were making. It didn't matter if you could play or not. Andy and I were terrible players, but it didn't matter whether you were musically proficient; it was what you were saying.

We were in Eric's one night, and we heard 'Warm Leatherette' by the Normal, and we looked at each other and were like, 'Wow, other people in England are making electronic music, and we need to just get up on stage and do it.' And so we got up on stage, just us and a tape machine. There were thirty people in the audience, but there was a guy there from Manchester who saw us and said, 'Why don't you come and play at the Factory club in Manchester?' We had only meant to do one gig, but we thought, 'Why not?' So when we did, we gave Tony Wilson a copy of our demo of 'Electricity'. All of a sudden we were on Factory Records.

At the time, we looked like a couple of hippies. I had really long hair, and Andy had a big Afro, and we weren't interested in image. We had this kind of anti-image that we developed to look like bank clerks, because we didn't want to sell ourselves on personality, it was all about the music. And we didn't even care about the videos. So our anti-image actually became an image. That was the thing about the eighties, they're sort of remembered for the big hair and the big shoulder pads and the

New Romantics with all the fluffy sleeves and stuff. We didn't want to be part of that. We just wanted to be as different as we could be.

Before the eighties, before the UK had its own style magazines, our reading matter in this area was principally American, and our perceived sense of style largely came from magazines such as Interview, New York *or* Punk. *We might have taken a lead from something in* Sounds, *the* Melody Maker *or the* NME *(which was then selling in excess of 250,000 copies each week and was probably the most influential music paper of the time), or maybe* Tatler *or* Vogue, *but there was no magazine for the generation of young people who had been inspired by punk. Sure, there was a fanzine industry, a thriving independent sector that was responsible for some of the most passionate music journalism of the time, but there was nothing that had a wider brief. The music papers had a huge demographic, and they were very much in their pomp in 1978, although there was also another, smaller and more particular set of magazines at the time that appealed to a more select group. Today, they are long gone, gone to the great reading room in the sky, available only in libraries, vintage-magazine shops and in those dark corners of the Internet where few dare to venture. They are the style magazines that time forgot.*

And what wonderful things they were: New Style, *David Bailey and David Litchfield's* Ritz, *the ridiculously large (four foot by three)* Midnight, *and* Viz *– not the scatological comic, but a London-based monthly that featured what all these magazines featured: art (usually home-grown stuff by Allen Jones, Duggie Fields or Peter Blake), fashion (Antony Price, Claude Montana and a newcomer called Jean Paul Gaultier), furniture (Tommy Roberts), sub-erotic photography, nightclub vox pops, arch celebrity profiles, restaurant reviews, gossip (back when gossip was a novelty, not a publishing genre), lots of articles* about The Rocky Horror Show *and dozens of ads for long-forgotten King's Road boutiques. In these post-punk gazettes the motif was always leopard skin, the cultural touchstone Biba (which* *had closed down a few years before, in 1975), the club always the Embassy, the Bond Street haunt that was Mayfair's answer to Studio 54. In broad brushstrokes, these magazines were a cross between* Tatler *and the* NME*, a mixture of uptown and downtown, of street life and park life, of toffs and commoners colliding in a giddy world of fashion, music, cocktails and lifestyle, before lifestyle became what we know it as today.*

One of the most impressive titles was Boulevard*, a monthly large-format, London-based style magazine that was launched at the end of 1978 by someone called Baron S. Bentinck. Containing the usual* Ritz/Viz/New Style *mix,* Boulevard *also had about it a certain hi–lo punk pizzazz, a certain sense of what was right for the times, a certain energy that was missing from the others. The 'baron' managed to cajole a number of soon-to-be-important people to work for him too, including photographers Helmut Newton, Michael Roberts, Terence Donovan, Neil Kirk, Johnny Rozsa and paparazzo Richard Young; fashionable illustrators Jean-Paul Goude and Connie Jude; and writers Nik Cohn (*Boulevard *published his seminal travel story '24 Hours on 42nd Street'), Craig Brown and Nicholas Coleridge. Now the chairman of the V&A, Coleridge, who wrote book reviews for* Boulevard*, remembers the operation with understandable fondness: 'There was a very cool atmosphere in the office' – which, naturally, was situated on Sloane Street, albeit above a pub. 'There were all these friends of Duggie Fields and Andrew Logan lolling about on black vinyl desks, making phone calls to their friends.'*

Kerry Sewel was a St Martin's student at the time, and she produced illustrations for Boulevard*. 'It was the only magazine to work for,' she says. 'There was* Ritz*, of course, but* Boulevard *was the only magazine that was big and glossy, the only one produced on shiny paper. It might not have been the greatest magazine in the world, but it felt like it at the time. It captured something, whatever that might be.'*

These magazines didn't last long, as there was yet to be the kind of critical mass to support them. They were too early. All were owned by entrepreneurs who were acutely aware of how easily new magazines (like new restaurants) haemorrhage cash, and the stark reality of 'vanity publishing' was compounded by the fact that many of these magazines were such odd sizes that, unable to fit them onto their shelves, newsagents simply put them on the floor. Which is no place for a glossy magazine. 'One got the impression that not a lot of work was being done, which seemed like quite good fun,' says Coleridge. 'And there didn't appear to be any clear policy. I got the impression, perhaps unfairly, that things were out of control.'

One day, I turned up with my portfolio of St Martin's illustrations, dressed in my black leather jacket, skinny black designer trousers, winkle-pickers and my Kensington Market T-shirt, and sat on a black leather sofa until the 'baron' came out to tell me that the magazine was closing down. Boulevard *managed just half a dozen issues, and though* Ritz *carried on well into the eighties, the other magazines were gone by the time the New Romantics arrived, when mass elitism, lifestyle careers and the commercialisation of youth culture became the defining elements of the early-to-mid-eighties. The underground went overground, and with the launch of* i-D, The Face *and* Blitz *in 1980, suddenly far more people had the opportunity and – apparently – the desire to be a trendy. Suddenly everyone was mediagenic. The big difference between the style magazines of the late seventies and those of the early eighties was the fact that* Viz, Boulevard, Ritz *and* New Style *were all exclusive – they were preaching to the converted and didn't appear remotely interested in adding to their flock. They were aimed at the 'Them' crowd, that hip, smart London set who all looked as though they were living inside a Roxy Music album cover. Art students, fashion designers, hairdressers and magazine journalists, they were the London equivalent of the Warhol New Yorkers – the women trying to look like Jerry Hall (even though most of them resembled Cruella de Vil), the men trying to pass themselves off as Bryan Ferry or Antony Price. If you picked up any of these glad mags, they'd be full of photographs of Andrew Logan, Justin de Villeneuve, Bill Gibb,*

Derek Jarman, Tchaik Chassay, Zandra Rhodes, Peter York or Keith 'from Smile'. The congregation had a restricted membership, which is why these magazines – great though they were – ultimately failed. Unlike Nova, *the phenomenally influential sixties women's magazine, which eventually closed in 1975 and whose formula many of these publications tried to emulate,* Viz, Boulevard *and the like were unable, or unwilling, to tap into the public's tastes. All sizzle, then, and no sausage. All polish and no finish.*

Boulevard*'s closing-down party was a riotous affair, with enough champagne to sink the* Titanic. *One wag, a staff writer who was a little peeved that he had just been downsized, felt he owed the owners a parting gift. And so, as he left the office that night, walking away from the boulevard of broken dreams, he called the speaking clock in Los Angeles (something you were still able to do in those days) and left the receiver off the hook. It's not known when it was replaced, but one wonders if the bill was ever paid.*

In a way, Ritz *was the real harbinger of change, the magazine that made it possible for the launch of* i-D, The Face *and* Blitz, *and which really kick-started celebrity and style culture in the eighties. In the early seventies, the legendary photographer David Bailey was briefly the photographic consultant on a magazine called* The Image, *which was edited by David Litchfield. It focused on graphic design and photography, and featured the work of Andy Warhol, Richard Hamilton, Allen Jones, Peter Blake, William Burroughs and Don McCullin. The magazine was how Bailey met Litchfield, and although he thought Litchfield didn't do a lot on the title, he could tell that Litchfield was pretty good at what little he did do. Which was just as well, as Bailey wanted to start his own magazine. He was sick of working for other people and wanted to do something for himself, wanted to do a magazine that he was totally proud of. And* Ritz *was the magazine he came up with, a stylish fashion and photography magazine that 'evoked the style of Fred Astaire'.*

Bailey wanted it to be like a newspaper, but the more he developed it, the more he thought that what he really wanted to do was a cross between Interview *and* Rolling Stone, *but very much for the British market. He'd been there at the birth of both magazines, and he thought a mix of the two would be perfect for London. He wanted* Ritz *to be artier than* Interview, *and wanted it to be more positive and less cynical. He wanted all the interviews to be strictly Q&A, 'without the journalist getting in the way', said Bailey. 'I certainly didn't envisage the magazine as being full of paparazzi pictures of chinless wonders running around ripping each other's bras off.'*

David Bailey: Partly, *Ritz* was meant to be a competitor to British *Vogue*, as I'd briefly stopped working for them. I'd fallen out with [the editor] Bea Miller and wanted more freedom to do my own things. At this point, I'd been working for them for over fifteen years and I felt I'd had enough. I wanted a raunchier magazine, one with more sex appeal. I felt I was being taken for granted at *Vogue*. I was too available, always doing reshoots when other photographers had screwed things up, always flying off to Africa or the Caribbean to do some shoot I didn't really want to do – and at that time I wanted to do some more experimental work. I've always said that I don't know what I'm looking for until I see it, and partly I wanted *Ritz* to be an outlet for that side of my photography, the photography that didn't have to fit into a particular commission. I wanted everything in the magazine to be marvellous, as I was fed up with the English attitude of always knocking anybody and everybody. I liked the American can-do attitude, not the build-them-up, knock-them-down attitude of the English. And having met David Litchfield, I thought he'd be the perfect guy to be the art director. Stupidly, I gave him half the shares, and regretted it almost immediately.

Bailey & Litchfield's Ritz – that was the registered name – launched in December 1976, as a monthly. We featured everyone from the likes of Bianca Jagger, Manolo Blahnik, Amanda Lear, Frank Zappa, Oliver Reed, Kraftwerk, Lartigue and Tatum O'Neal to Ossie Clark, Jasper Conran, Patti D'Arbanville, Sylvia Kristel, Antony Price, Paul McCartney, Jack Nicholson and Marisa Berenson. We featured celebrities, fashion designers, models . . . people generally on the scene. We also started shooting all the New Romantics and the new club kids, like Steve Strange and Boy George. *Ritz* had everyone from Tennessee Williams telling us he was just a sad old queen to Bob Marley being asked what hair products he used. We once had Man Ray, Lucrezia Borgia and Gary Glitter in the same issue. We used writers like Peter York and Craig Brown, and stylists like Caroline Baker, who had worked on *Nova*. The offices were deep in Covent Garden, right next to *The Lady*, right around the corner from Joe Allen's, up a couple of flights of rickety stairs, and it was always full of hangers-on and kids who wanted to get involved to get a step up the publishing ladder. We only had two little rooms, yet they were always full of people hanging around – little worker bees who wanted to get involved in the magazine.

I wanted to use a lot of photographers who weren't getting their work shown elsewhere. I also got Helmut Newton and Lartigue to work for us, and I started to interview people too, everyone from Mick Jagger to Nic Roeg – anyone I wanted, really.

At *Ritz* we did quite a lot of stuff with Gore Vidal, who I knew from just being around. I first met him in Sardinia, where I was shooting a commercial, and we were both staying at the Aga Khan's hotel. He used to call me his 'little bunny', although I never knew why. I was always a bit in awe of Gore – he was a big chap, and he had such a vicious tongue. I liked him as he was funny; at least, he never gave anyone else the chance to be funny because he wanted the stage to himself. He probably thought I was just a bit of good-looking rough trade. Nothing sexual, but we were friends. We'd occasionally have dinner, and I'd shoot him for *Ritz*. You didn't want to make a fool of yourself in front of Gore; you couldn't be flip, you always had to be in control of what you were saying, or else he'd go for you, and when he went for you, that was it. He was a cunt, but he was a cunt with the biggest brain of anyone I ever met.

When we launched a trial issue, the newsagent's WHSmith took some to see if they could sell them in sufficient numbers to stock it all the time, and we found out which shops they were in and we went and bought them all, every issue we could lay our hands on. So Smiths thought *Ritz* was a runaway success! We had our meetings either in Langan's – lunches and dinners that I always seemed to pay for – or else at my house in Gloucester Avenue, in Primrose Hill. We couldn't really afford to hire studios when we started, so I shot a lot in a big room at my house that I'd turned into a studio specifically for the work I did for *Ritz*. Langan's was our greasy spoon. All the Hollywood lot sat in the window seats – Jack Nicholson, Tony Curtis, John Travolta, Mick Jagger . . .

Clive James worked a lot for us in the early days. He wasn't really my cup of tea as I found him a bit creepy, and he was always sniffing around the girls. A few years later, after I'd married Catherine he even tried to kiss her. He said, 'Don't worry, I won't tell Bailey.' And she said, 'Yes, but I probably will.' He was just obsessed with sex and women.

People used to think I was doing the magazine with Patrick Lichfield, which annoyed me no end, although I think David liked it enormously. He was a good designer, and very good with type, but he wanted to be more than that – he wanted to be Diana Vreeland. He was also quite jealous of me and was no good at dealing with people who weren't beholden to him. He'd always say things like, 'Why are you going to dinner with Jack without me?' 'Can I come to the Mick Jagger dinner you're doing?' 'No! Fuck off!' He always used to get upset. He wanted to be in the thick of it, but why would I invite him to dinner?

We had four gossip columnists at one stage, which I could never understand – Nicky Haslam, Frances Lynn, Stephen Lavers and Amanda Lear. I really didn't like the negative side of the magazine. Why go to the bother of asking someone to be in the magazine and photographing and interviewing them and putting them on the cover, and then tear them to shreds? It just makes no sense to me. If you're nice to them, they'll come back. And actually, it's harder to be nice, as it's so easy to be nasty. Why put Jack or Elton on the cover if you're going to be bitchy about them inside? You either want them or you don't.

Nicky Haslam (*writer, interior designer*): With *Ritz*, I was amazed to find how many people who liked to be thought of as highbrow, or to give the impression of being a 'recluse', were eager to be questioned and quoted in such a flippant manner.

David Bailey: *Ritz* invented the British paparazzi, which I knew about from Rome. I wanted the magazine to be full of photographs of people at parties. I always used to ask them to get as many paparazzi pictures in as possible, as then everyone would buy a copy for their uncle! Richard Young got his break taking pictures for *Ritz*. He was a sweet guy then, and he's a sweet guy now. Dave Benett, the other London paparazzo, he's a nice guy too. Richard and Dave's photography is a lot more important than people might think it is, as it's a genuine social document of what people wore, where they went and how they behaved when they got there. I suppose you could say that we were responsible for the obsessive paparazzi magazines that came after us – *Hello!*, *OK* and *Heat*, and all the others – but the *Ritz* world was somewhat more refined, and the people in our world weren't the sort of bottom-feeders you see in paparazzi photos today.

1979
THE BLITZ

'I always feel more comfortable in chaotic surroundings. I don't know why that is. I think order is dull. There is something about this kind of desire for order, particularly in Anglo-Saxon cultures, that drive [*sic*] out this ability for the streets to become a really exotic, amorphous, chaotic, organic place where ideas can, basically, develop.'

MALCOLM MCLAREN

Rusty Egan: After a bit of success at Billy's, the management doubled the price of the drinks. I said, 'You can't do that, they're students, they haven't got any money.' So Steve said he'd heard about this club called the Blitz in Covent Garden. We go and have a look, and meet this lovely Irish guy called Brendan, who said the club was like a morgue on Tuesday because there was nothing in Covent Garden, not even street lights. We liked it because it was a bit of an industrial Alphabet City, dark and weird. With the neon blue light it was like a forties film noir. And don't forget, the only other thing to do at night at the time was go to the Notting Hill all-night cinema and watch beautiful old films in black and white. So I said, 'It's brilliant.' They said we couldn't have it for a few weeks, so I went to Berlin to buy some records. That's where the music was, as far as I was concerned. I also wanted to meet Kraftwerk. I had this girlfriend at the time who was a student from New York, and she had her daddy's plastic. So we went to Düsseldorf, and it was freezing. It was Oktoberfest, and we went walking up and down the streets, asking for Kraftwerk. I was wearing a German leather coat, a black shirt and a red tie. We got directed to this club, and I said to the barman, 'I heard Kraftwerk come here.' And the guy said, 'Yeah, they're here now, over there, Ralf and Florian.' And they were drinking beer in the pool room. I knew who they were, obviously, from the album covers. I said, 'I've come all the way from London searching for you, because you are the sound of the future.' And they were more than welcoming. They were surprised, like, 'Is this a TV show or something? This is a joke.' And I was going, 'No, no, I have a club in London and I'm a drummer, and when I play Kraftwerk records, I can mix them into each other because they're in perfect time, because they're done with machines.' So anyway, I buy a lot of records and go back and open the Blitz.

Robert Elms: I think Billy's lasted for about three months, and then Steve and Rusty launched the Blitz, again on a Tuesday. The place was actually quite tacky and run-down. It was an old Covent Garden wine bar with gas masks on the wall, but it was what they could get. And although everyone who went thought they were very elite, they didn't have a penny. I think it was 50p to get in, and if you didn't have it, Steve would let you in. People had the money to buy one drink, if that. So they weren't getting drunk. I mean, there might have been a bit of speed or something, as it was student days. No one in that room was over the age of twenty-two or twenty-three, and apart from Midge Ure, no one was well known in any way, but obviously they all thought they were.

There was a point when the 'Them' crowd dipped their toes in the water and came down to have a look – the likes of Andrew Logan, Duggie Fields and Peter York – and God bless them, they were really encouraging. They started inviting us to their parties, so I'm suddenly going to posh people's parties. Peter was great to me, and he sort of took me under his wing. He really encouraged me to write. I remember going to a party at Andrew Logan's, when he had the place by the river in Butler's Wharf. I'm a kid from a council estate, and that was the most extraordinary, extravagant thing I'd ever been to in my life. They had canapés! They struck me as being a real throwback to the old seventies King's Road, and suddenly I saw that we were practising the same tradition, realising that we were not the first people who had done this sort of thing. Looking back, what we did have was an extraordinary degree of front. More front than Selfridge's!

But the movers and shakers – Steve Strange, Boy George, Marilyn, Fiona Dealey and Melissa Caplan – they were all teenagers. They were eighteen, nineteen, and students who were skint, living in squats. I mean, it was much less 'glamorous' than people think it was; it was do-it-yourself. Most of the clothes were home-made or cobbled together, while the biggest clothes' supplier was probably Laurence Corner, selling old wartime army surplus. I think the Blitz was probably the most important nightclub in Britain since the 2i's in Old Compton Street. In many ways it was very similar: in the sixties, if you'd have gone to the 2i's, you'd have seen Adam Faith, Cliff Richard, Tommy Steele, Screaming Lord Sutch, all these kids who were going to become the first wave of British rock'n'roll.

Karen O'Connor: I remember the Blitz being formed. I moved into a flat in Notting Hill Gate. It was so run-down it was christened 'the Regency skip'. Billy Idol was going to move in but decided to try his luck as a solo artist in the States. So Steve and Rusty Egan said they would take the other room instead. Unfortunately, there was only a single bed in there, so Steve basically shared with me, as their room consisted of a bed, clothes and records. Rusty started talking about opening 'a club of our own', with him DJing and Steve on the door. The Blitz was approached, and they offered the Tuesday night – notoriously the quietest night of the week – and in a few weeks it became *the* place to go. Consequently, the flat had a constant stream of visitors. I went on holiday for a fortnight, and came back to find Steve had given all my clothes away. It didn't help either watching most of the people on the dancefloor at the Blitz the next Tuesday having a good time in all my clothes.

Stephen Jones: Kim Bowen took me to the Blitz one night, and I knew everyone there, like Stephen Linard and Fiona Dealey, Steve Strange,

Rusty Egan, Ollie O'Donnell, all the boys who would form Spandau Ballet. You knew them from all the disparate clubs we'd been going to. I think even Brian Eno went at one point.

Peter York: Towards the end of the seventies, I was spending a lot of time in Great Queen Street, for entirely bourgeois reasons. There was a big new ad agency that I knew very well at the top of the street called Wight Collins Rutherford Scott, just at the corner of Drury Lane. We knew them terribly well and did lots of stuff with them. But then there was the other bourgeois watering hole, Zanzibar. I was in Zanzibar practically every night. I loved Zanzibar, and I think it should be a listed building. That wonderful curving bar was really very clever, and I had a lovely time there. And then, just down the road . . . I don't know what drew me down there, but it wasn't far to go. During the day, it was a sort of nothing wine bar with a sort of retro theme, like British Railways or something. And then on Tuesday nights it became wonderland. Run by Steve Strange. The Blitz. I remember thinking in those early days that he knew exactly what he wanted, that he knew his way around older, experienced people. He knew how to handle them, so cleverly that one was terribly impressed, and he seemed to be very much in charge of his life. Of course, I had a grown-up life to lead, but I loved going to the Blitz. I think the people there were talented, or about to become talented. I'd say they were fifty–fifty art school and Canvey Island. I don't remember any fights, and the people were all well behaved. It was all about identity politics – every possible sort of identity, dramatising identity. You dramatise, and then you normalise. So you can be wonderful, you can be your own star, you can do anything. There was dressing up, and you thought immediately, 'I know what this is, the dressing up.' It's because you watch old movies in black and white on the telly, because those kids had grown up watching thirties and forties films, pirates, eighteenth-century France and all that sort of stuff, they'd grown up watching that as art-school people. So I thought it did prefigure the modern world in certain ways.

Jason Cowley: When I was an adolescent, idling my way through empty days in the suburban drablands of the Essex/east London border, Steve Strange was a figure of considerable wonder. To enter the Blitz, you had to negotiate your way past Strange on the door; he once correctly turned away the ridiculous Mick Jagger for arriving dressed in a baseball cap and trainers. You also had to look different, extravagantly different, which meant dressing up, wearing make-up and experimenting with gender roles (and that was just the boys). Those bands that were inspired by the Blitz crowd were later packaged and promoted as New Romantics or futurists, but there was nothing calculating about the early pioneers of the scene: they were sincerely, uninhibitedly weird. This was a time of rapid change in British youth culture. A libertarian punk attitude was being fused with a Thatcherite, consensus-breaking entrepreneurism to create an entirely new social phenomenon: the style-driven nightclub. Before Strange and his collaborators came along, the nightclub as currently understood did not really exist; there were only discos and pubs. Blitz called itself 'the Club for Heroes', after the great Bowie track, and there was indeed something heroic about the posturing and ambition of the young people who gathered there, most of whom were from tough working-class families and had long since dropped out of school, abandoning all hope of a conventional career. The anarchic energy of the punk scene had liberated them into rebellion: where once perhaps only football, boxing or crime offered a way out from the low-horizoned impoverishment of their inheritance – the pit, the factory, the building site – the future was becoming an index of thrilling possibilities. They seized the day.

Ollie O'Donnell: The Blitz was the next club that everyone went to, and it was packed from the off. I liked Steve and Rusty, but the music was not club music. Yellow Magic Orchestra and Kraftwerk I liked, but not in a nightclub. It wasn't soulful enough for me and it didn't have the energy of early punk, so it left me cold. But I did meet some very interesting new people there, genuinely flamboyant, eccentric characters with a lot of personality. However, there were also starting to be these boring poseurs, the sheep in wolves' clothing. They would be all dressed up head to toe in the latest clothes from PX, and it would become apparent to me very quickly that they had no energy.

David Johnson (*journalist*): Every Tuesday for a year, Strange declared a 'private party' in the shabby Blitz wine bar. Outrage secured entry. Inside, precocious nineteen-year-olds presented an eye-stopping collage, posing away in wondrous ensembles, emphatic make-up and in-flight haircuts that made you feel normality was a sin. Hammer Horror met Rank starlet. Here was Lady Ample Eyefull, there Sir Gesting Sharpfellow, lads in breeches and frilly shirts, white stockings and ballet pumps, girls as Left Bank whores or stiletto-heeled vamps dressed for cocktails in a Berlin cabaret, wicked witches, kohl-eyed ghouls, futuristic man-machines.

Shrouding any pleasure in ritual magnifies its intensity, and the Blitz was all ritual. Everyone supped and danced on the same spot every week according to some invisible floorplan: downstairs near the bar stood the boys in the band (no make-up), their media and management by the stairs, credible punk legends such as Siouxsie Sioux along the bar, suburban wannabes beside the dancefloor. Deep within the club, around Rusty Egan's DJ booth, were the dedicated dancing feet, the white-faced shock troops, the fashionista elite – either there or near the cloakroom, ruled first by Julia Fodor and later by George O'Dowd. Downstairs, the women's loo was hijacked, naturally, by boys who would be girls. Upstairs on the railway banquettes might be respected alumni from an earlier London: film-maker Derek Jarman, artists Brian Clarke and Kevin Whitney, designers Antony Price and Zandra Rhodes.

When Steve Strange eyeballed you at the door of his club, your look alone did not guarantee admission. He did not want passive consumers but 'people who created unique identities'. By taking Bowie at his word to be 'heroes just for one day', you were expected to become one of the new names to drop.

It took a good year before the media caught up. In a ring-fenced page of cool that I edited in London's *Evening Standard*, I had dubbed these preening egos the Now Crowd since they lived so much for the moment. Two of the Blitz's tyro journos – Perry Haines and Robert Elms – had proclaimed them Herald Angels and Dandy Dilettantes. The national press came up with New Dandies, Romantic Rebels and the Blitz Kids, which is what stuck. Finally, in September 1980 this prompted the New Romantics headline (ouch!) in the music weekly *Sounds*. Everybody winced and denied membership.

Eve Ferret (*cabaret performer*): People were already going to Blitz before Steve Strange discovered it. I started performing there in November '76. I was desperate to be a singer, but in those days everything was so proscriptive. You'd see ads in the *Melody Maker* for 'singer wanted to front a band, size ten'. I also saw an ad in *The Stage* for Blitz, saying they wanted singers in the style of George Formby and Vera Lynn. I thought, 'Well, I'm not like Vera Lynn, but I'm a bit like George Formby.' So I started a few weeks later. Chris Corbin, who would launch Le Caprice and the Ivy with Jeremy King, was the chef, and Liam Carson, who went on to run the Groucho, was a barman. There was a great atmosphere at the club as it encouraged women to come by themselves, which wasn't always the case in those days. I had always wanted to be a singer, but a singer like you saw in the Frank Sinatra movies, so the Blitz was perfect because it had that old feel, and although it was a canteen, at night-time it would transform itself, and there was lots of Glenn Miller music, like there was at the time at the Goldmine in Canvey Island. So people were already going there before Steve and Rusty. It was Helen Robinson from PX who told Steve to go and look at it. Paula Yates used to come, Gilbert and George . . .

Blitz was operational throughout the punk time, although I wasn't fazed by that at all. I'd seen all that black-lipstick look at Biba and *The Rocky Horror Show*. At the time, we were hanging out at Country Cousins on the King's Road, which is where Freddie Mercury and

Marc Bolan had all their parties. But when Blitz got going in '79, it really felt like a tribe – Chris Sullivan, Fiona Dealey, Stephen Jones, Billy Idol, Michael Hurd dressed as a *Thunderbirds* puppet. We all dressed up. I went once with a saucepan on my head as a member of the Home Guard. I even went as Demis Roussos one week. We had a common thing, which was partying and a laugh and good times. Don't wait for Christmas, parties should be every day.

Steve was smart, though. When he started hosting nights there, it was empty inside, with a huge queue outside. I said, 'Why don't you let them in, as there's no one here?' He said, 'But they don't know that.'

They were such beautiful people. I remember standing in the DJ booth with Rusty one night, looking out at the crowd and just imagining what their lives would hold for them. I cried as I looked around at all these fabulous people with a kind heart. Never mind how they looked, it was their heart. It was such a weird juxtaposition of all this glamour inside and the desolation of Covent Garden outside. It was like a huge empty warehouse, it was dark, there was nothing there, and you could feel the tension on the streets. Especially if you looked like I looked. It was certainly tough if you were overtly gay. I was with Biddie [Eve's cabaret partner] one night, and I leant over to put my arm around him, and I thought, 'Oh my God, he's wet.' Somebody had just come up to speak to him, but as they went away they slashed him across the face with a small blade because he was gay. We went off to the hospital, and all I was saying was, 'You have got to make the scar look good,' because he's so beautiful.

Steve Strange was a lot smarter than some gave him credit for, as he understood that clubs were driven by people, not just music, and that while many of those he didn't let into his clubs thought he was just being spiteful, it was all about curation. Not that the lucky ones were exactly overflowing with empathy. To those left outside on the pavement, the lucky ones could appear snotty, the sort of people who might cut you dead if you saw them again in daylight. In truth, the denizens of the Blitz were adopting the modus operandi of Andy Warhol's Factory, never responding to anything or anyone around them. The lesson learnt was never to get excited about anything and just stare instead. The mantra was simple: look at it, and let the looking at it become the thing that you're doing. This was called the silent shrug, and it was employed by many of the lucky ones inside. Being one of the chosen few encouraged a certain unnecessary conceitedness.

Stephen Jones: The Blitz ruled people's lives. Exactly that. A nightclub inspired absolute devotion, of the kind previously reserved for a pop idol. I'd find people at the Blitz who were possible only in my imagination. But they were real.

Chris Sullivan: Young people were no longer prepared to be sold clothes they didn't like or go to clubs playing records they didn't want to hear, being run by grunters three times their age, and having to pay for the privilege. When the Blitz opened, for a start it was cheap, but it was also extraordinary to have someone aged nineteen vetting the door.

The world of luxury has become so pervasive that it's often difficult to imagine what life was like before it, when we lived in a world without social media, and where we blithely lived our lives without the constant, relentless bombardment of fashion imagery. Back in the seventies, London may have been a sophisticated European capital, but it certainly wasn't considered to be a cultural or sartorial hub. Savile Row was where the Establishment had its suits made, and Bond Street may have been a jet-set enclave, but for anyone seeking anything out of the ordinary, and who was unimpressed with the institutionalised glamour of Oxford Street, Carnaby Street and the King's Road, the only solution was the Oxfam shops and the likes of Euston's Laurence Corner, where you could buy army surplus clothing.

These days the word 'vintage' covers a multitude of sins, and in fact has become so abused, and is such a cliché, that it's difficult to believe that it still has any cachet. Back in the late seventies, though, second-hand clothing was what you wore if you wanted to either approximate or initiate, and it was the shonky charity shops you went to if you wanted to look like a character from a forties movie, say, or needed to create something new in order to impress your peers in the Blitz. The look of the period, with its plethora of styles, had no particular meaning, and yet it coalesced into something significantly identifiable. In the same way that futurists, or at least those experimenting with electronic music, had to flex their DIY muscle by building their own instruments, so the wannabe pop stars and art-school show-offs who were making their name in London needed to scour the high-street Oxfam and Help the Aged stores in the hope of finding a solution to their sartorial conundrums.

This exercise was called 'looking for dead men's clothes': finding an old double-breasted suit that had been retired not because the owner didn't want it any more, but because they had moved on to a higher plain. There seemed to be a deep discrepancy in the clothes to be found in these places, as there were never any contemporary clothes and almost nothing from the recent past; in fact, in many charity shops you'd find such a huge array of suits from the forties that it looked as though they had perhaps simply been dumped there by a wardrobe assistant. Of course, many of these suits had been owned by men who hadn't come back from the war, and whose wives and girlfriends – and boyfriends, perhaps – had had to eventually divest themselves of their wardrobes. The Second World War was when charity shops became widespread, with the Red Cross opening their first shop in Old Bond Street (coincidentally) in 1941, and over the next four years opening hundreds more. They would also soon become full of demob suits, which were given to servicemen who were demobilised from the forces. The fact that in 1979 hundreds of these suits would have been destined to be worn in the Blitz only added more poignancy to their appropriation.

Stephen Jones: The Blitz was absolutely electric. It was the dawn of the New Romantic scene, and I felt like I was at the vanguard of something. I was in my early twenties. I graduated from St Martin's in June 1979 and opened my first shop, in Endell Street – around the corner from the Blitz – a little later. You couldn't just turn up, no matter how good you looked. It was a select crowd, very judgemental – you would never get away with a look you hadn't quite sorted out. There were pop stars in our midst: Boy George, Marilyn, Duran Duran. When someone as famous as David Bowie came down, of course we were very aware of him, but we weren't really interested in other people's fame. We wanted to do new and interesting things, for us. So no one wanted to wear a label someone else had designed because it meant you couldn't come up with your own. The Blitz gave me my first clients. The hats were home-made; I'd loan or sell them at a discount. Quite often we'd do a trade: I'd make a hat for someone, and they'd take photos for me. None of us had money, but we had a certain amount of talent. The club was also the reason I went on to open my first shop, in the basement of PX, where Steve Strange and DJ Princess Julia worked. I had no business plan, but I had a wonderful collection of hats. I still work from Covent Garden. It's right in the middle of everything. A hat is a central London purchase, and I've always thought, 'If you're going to be in London, you may as well be *in* London.' For me, the Blitz years were a time of great uncertainty, a weird time of flux. It was scary, but fortunately I met this group of people and entered the melee of London clubland. We considered it our duty to support one another, like a family. We'd put on a beautiful costume, and it would often hide insecurities and uncertainties. We were like any other group of like-minded people, but what made us unusual were the times we were in. We'd come out of the nanny society of the seventies and were told that self-expression was OK. You could do your own thing. A few years later, Aids happened, and it absolutely decimated us. A quarter of the people I knew died.

Boy George: Steve Strange, you see, him and I we loved each other, but we were also sworn enemies. I was living in Birmingham when Steve started the Blitz, so I was going to the Rum Runner a lot instead. We weren't speaking when he opened the Blitz, and I was banned, which was like having a nail shoved into your brain. I remember discussing it with people, saying, 'What if I look amazing? He's never going to turn me away, you know what I mean?' So it'd be like, 'OK, what can I do that is so beyond as a look that he would just be embarrassed to turn me away?' We were always at war with each other around that time. Then, eventually, he gave me a job there, so I think he realised I was quite popular. I started going to film premieres uninvited, because if I looked brilliant, they would never turn me away. There were some great people around at the time – Stephen Jones, Kim Bowen, Fiona Dealey, people that had gone to art college who kind of felt like they were more legitimate than people like me and Jeremy Healy. Steve used to wear designer clothes, and we always felt like we were at odds with those people, and it wasn't until Jeremy started sleeping with Kim Bowen that there was this mad sort of coming together of us ragamuffins from south-east London and the ritzy St Martin's people.

Steve Strange: There was always bit of rivalry between George and me, because we were all very competitive. We all clambered for pole position to be the most outlandish, girlish and outrageous. I gave him the cloakroom job in the Blitz because I knew times were hard for him and he needed all the money he earned from taking the coats. Eventually, we had to sack him because he was caught stealing, yet I still employed him a year later, when I did the club Hell, because I believed in him. He was just one of the Blitz regulars who went on and did really well – there are so, so many. There's been a lot said about my strict door policy at the Blitz, but all I wanted was to create a haven for all these individuals where they could be free to be themselves without the threat of trouble from those who didn't get it. It was heavy back then, and if you walked down the street dressed like we did, you would almost certainly be attacked.

Iain R. Webb: One week I would go to the Blitz wearing bondage trousers, a tuxedo jacket, nothing underneath and biker boots. The next week I would be in skinny ripped jeans, an Afghan cardigan, nothing underneath. I didn't wear that much; it was easy access. You didn't want to look exactly the same as anyone else, but then the religious thing happened, and you had Judith Franklin, Stephen Linard, Michelle Clapton, Fiona Dealey and George all doing their own version of it. The main people at first were those from the gay clubs and students from St Martin's. Steve was the Pied Piper, and we just followed him across town. We all came from mostly odd places all around the country, where we would have been the village idiot or the freak. Suddenly we came to London and found each other. I can remember standing at the top of the stairs at the Blitz, that little bit of a balcony, and looking down on everything.

Robert Elms: If you went to the Blitz and wrote everyone's name down . . . well, it's extraordinary. I would say from the early contingent of the Blitz in the first few weeks, at least 60 per cent would go on to be either famous or world recognised for what they do. They were also climbing on each other's shoulders. It was simultaneously incredibly bitchy and kind of individualistic and also a support group, because often those people couldn't walk down the street on their own without getting beaten up. London back in the late seventies was homophobic, and you could get chased down the street for wearing the wrong trousers, let alone looking like we looked. It was a tough place. So this was a self-preservation group as much as anything. The Blitz was one place where you could go looking like that and feel safe, and so therefore we sort of stuck together. That environment produced Boy George, it produced George Michael, John Galliano, Cerith Wyn Evans. Britain was so broken, and it was a time of extraordinary opportunity. If you decided you wanted to start a nightclub, well, you just took that place over for the night. It was a product of decrepitude. I really think the whole urban renewal that London has gone through started right there, because that was where the next generation of designers were, the entrepreneurs, the journalists, the architects, the photographers, the artists. These were people who understood what it meant to be urban – who loved being in London, who wanted to live in a squat in Warren Street, who wanted to take over central London. Soho and Covent Garden became the playgrounds. There was also a strong gay element, which is something not everyone talks about. I was only used to it because of the type of clubs I had been going to previously, where there were always a lot of gay people; punk had been kind of like that too. Punk is portrayed as a democratic movement, but it was actually one of the most elitist movements of them all. If you did not have the right Vivienne Westwood clothes on, you were not a member of the Bromley Contingent, for instance. Punk in its earlier days, which is what I think the Blitz was kind of harking back to, was incredibly elitist. The message was, you can do it, but what you were doing had to be interesting. It was incredibly liberating for all sorts of reasons. The fact that suddenly everyone around you is saying, 'I'm going to be a fashion designer,' 'I'm going to be a film-maker,' 'I'm going to be a musician.' People were pouring out of art schools and wanting to be noticed.

Anita Corbin (*photographer*): I was studying photography at the Polytechnic of Central London [now the University of Westminster]. It was a Tuesday night, and I had just blagged my way past the door, carrying my Olympus camera plus a 35mm lens, a huge Braun flashgun, a heavy battery and a bag of film. I was wearing a US Air Force jumpsuit from Flip, an American recycled-clothing shop, and I had bleached blonde hair. It was the second time I'd ever been to the Blitz, and I had gone there specifically to hunt out New Romantics for my *Visible Girls* project. I knew that the Blitz had a reputation for being full of 'peacocks' – people who like to show off and really dress up. There was a lot of make-up and hair experimentation going on. I was interested in photographing the 'informal' uniforms that young women were adopting. As a young woman myself, I was also seeking my identity. I was interested in women's choice, and this was reflected in the eighties itself and its active women's liberation movement and subcultural experimentation. I wanted to create a series of images that showed how young women had a choice in how they expressed themselves, from shaving their heads to becoming a WOW [woman-orientated woman] to being an ultra-feminine New Romantic. And executing this in a way that was exciting, colourful and engaging – as a piece of art and not a dry social document.

Oliver Peyton (*club runner, entrepreneur*): I was studying textiles in Leicester, and so I used to go to the Rum Runner in Birmingham each week, where every room had a different kind of music – soul, Bowie, etc. Even now I can remember the faces of people who were there – Simon Le Bon, Nick Rhodes, John Taylor . . . Anyway, we started going down south, to London and the Blitz, but we could only get in if someone from the Rum Runner had arranged it, otherwise we'd be standing outside waiting not to be let in. I can still remember what I wore when I first went: a white double-breasted jacket with a Nehru collar that I got from Leicester market. The Blitz was great fun, but it was a bit formal, and I started to enjoy London clubland when it loosened up a bit. The Blitz may have been where it all started in terms of what happened later in the eighties, but the clubs that came afterwards were always more exciting. I ran lots of clubs in London in the eighties, but I think my favourite of all of them was maybe Cha Cha's at Heaven, and then [Leigh Bowery's] Taboo. I liked the wild clubs.

Paul Smith (*fashion designer*): Whereas some young designers were borrowing a lot of money or getting backed by large companies, we were never like that. So the transition from the seventies to the eighties – we almost didn't notice it. But by that time, the difference was I didn't just have a shop in my home town of Nottingham, I had a shop in Floral Street in Covent Garden, which I opened in the winter of 1979. By the time I got into the eighties, that shop had started to be a little bit settled in, a little bit well known with a certain group of people: young architects, graphic designers, musicians – quite a creative group. The shop was designed in a very minimal way – it was probably one of the first minimalist shops in all of London, because it was before Issey Miyake, Yohji and Comme des Garçons came to Europe – and it attracted a lot of attention because it was in Covent Garden. You have to remember that Covent Garden was empty. There were no other shops at all. There were two pubs, two fruit-and-vegetable stalls, a ballet school, and virtually nothing else. Everything else had closed in the seventies, when the fruit-and-veg market moved away. So it was this sort of little oasis in the middle of an area that had been so full of hustle and bustle. I chose the location because it was the only place I could afford, and also because I liked the character of Covent Garden. It was an outback at the time, but it felt good, it felt new, it felt very young. Most people thought I was mad coming here and said, 'You know, you'll never do any business,' and 'It'll never happen,' and 'You'll need a passport to go to Covent Garden, it's *so* far out.'

Fiona Dealey: At the Blitz we were always allowed to go to the head of the queue because I knew Steve Strange. We would occasionally make clothes for him, so he was nice. I suppose it's just like being part of 'the cool crowd', isn't it? You'd see all the other people in the queue and you'd naturally want to go to the front. We were so wrapped up in ourselves, you'd walk past someone and you'd think, 'There's no way they're gonna get in.' It was our own version of Studio 54. And the other thing is, Steve Strange would let good-looking boys in. We did have an extraordinary sense of entitlement, and if you want to know the truth of it, I think anyone who is involved in that still has that sense of entitlement deep within them. We were rebelling, but we were entitled at the same time. No one could tell us anything. It's quite funny looking at the old photographs of us at the time, as some of them are quite extraordinary. But it was all just about the arrival, the going in, the dancing. It was a great time to be young, and it was such a small scene. I know who was actually in the Blitz, and a lot of people who say they were there weren't there at all. It's like the people who say they saw the Sex Pistols at the Screen on the Green: they can't all have been there, as it wasn't big enough. There were probably only about a hundred people, or a hundred and fifty tops, who actually went to the Blitz. But there seems to be an awful lot of people who were never there who say they were there. At the Blitz there was just this interesting fusion of people, as you had St Martin's fashion students, some sculpture students, like Holly Warburton, and then the Middlesex fashion students, like David Holah and Melissa Caplan, and randomly the LSE boys who started pitching up, like Bob Elms, Graham Ball, Graham Smith . . . And then Spandau Ballet pitched up, but we were there before Spandau Ballet were. We were all a bit miffed the night they played at the Blitz, because we weren't going there to see bands, we were going there because we thought we were just as important. Steve Dagger was really clever doing something like that, because then it was like we were following Spandau Ballet, which we weren't.

Peter Ashworth: I found myself at the end of the course at the London College of Printing really not knowing what the hell to do, so I started assisting. One of the studios I worked in was in Covent Garden, just around the corner from the Blitz, right near PX. So I met Steve Strange and started taking his picture, and then I started shooting Rusty. I knew Steve very well, but he could be difficult. When you're a doorman, you develop a certain attitude, and he was a hard doorman. I don't think I would have ever gotten into the place if I hadn't been a photographer working next door or Stephen Jones hadn't walked me in.

So many of the Blitz Kids were art students, those who were more interested in exploring professional creativity than they were in pursuing academia, and the art-school experimentations of the late seventies would turn out to be as important to the cultural development of the time as they had been to the sixties. At the time, art schools functioned as a state-subsidised bohemia, where, in the words of critic Simon Reynolds, 'Working-class youth too unruly for a life of labour mingle with slumming middle-class kids too wayward for a career in middle management. After graduation, many turned to pop music as a way to sustain the "experimental lifestyle" they'd enjoyed at college.'

The generation of young men and women who went to British art schools in the seventies didn't come from a line of iconoclasts or stubborn outsiders. Mostly they came from upper-working-class or lower-middle-class families who had no idea how their offspring were going to turn out. Like most of their generation, they probably just wanted them to occupy one of the rungs above them on the social ladder. The offspring themselves seemed mainly committed to exploring a legitimate extension of their adolescence. For many seventeen- and eighteen-year-olds who went to art school between 1970 and 1980, this was a goal in itself. Like many of those lost souls who ended up at art schools at the end of the fifties or at the dawn of the sixties and then went on to form second-generation, post-Beatles pop groups – everyone from Pete Townshend and Keith Richards to Syd Barrett and Roger Ruskin Spear from the Bonzo Dog Doo-Dah Band – they wanted a taste of bohemianism, a taste of adventure.

In Art into Pop *(1987), Simon Frith and Howard Horne analysed the significance of art schools in the development of the pop music of the sixties and seventies, a book that was itself analysed by Mark Banks and Kate Oakley in a study they produced for Leeds University called 'The Dance Goes on Forever? Art Schools, Class and UK Higher Education':*

> *Art schools provided a particular context for people who had few qualifications or class credentials, and little cultural capital, but whose social 'awkwardness' – as Frith and Horne [described it] – seemed to have some sort of creative*

potential. Art school was where erstwhile 'council estate yobs and truants' such as Keith Richards could find an outlet for their latent talents, and where a 'bright, disruptive, lower class grammar school boy with no O-levels' like John Lennon could find a temporary location that was 'better than working'. Art schools therefore welcomed the 'talented but academically unqualified', who were encouraged to be self-expressive, and 'find their way', but also embody the virtues of the idea of art as a practice – as an open-ended, indeterminate and materially-specific process of inquiry.

The time between 1975 and 1985 is such a rich period in post-war culture, and so many of the people involved were nudged on their way by the art-school experience. Many of the protagonists in Sweet Dreams *went to art school, and it was there that they learnt to grow and met like-minded souls. Many of the synth groups of the time grew out of higher education, having first been inspired by the likes of Kraftwerk and Neu! – Soft Cell and Orchestral Manoeuvres in the Dark included. (So potent was the art-school fix, it even produced an insecurity in those who hadn't been to one. 'Some bands went to art school,' said Bono a few years later. 'We went to Brian Eno.')*

Art schools have changed dramatically in the last forty years, and they are no longer the chaotic incubators they once were. Nowadays prospective art students often have to prove their academic credentials to compete for a place at some of the most prestigious colleges, which somehow defeats their purpose. And saliently, tuition fees have made higher education in Britain more expensive than anywhere else in Europe, with art schools being no exception. Colleges make more money from attracting international students, while the high fees mean that the all-important social and economic mix is disappearing. It is well known that students from poorer backgrounds are a lot less inclined to take out loans for non-vocational subjects. These days there are approximately 175,000 new art students every year in the UK (out of 2.3 million students in total), whereas back in the seventies that figure was closer to 5,000 (out of a total of 75,000 students in total).

It meant a lot more to be an art student in the seventies than it does now.

It is no coincidence that this period of cultural experimentation was part of a wider bohemianism, a petit haute bohème *driven by a generational sense of dissatisfaction, curiosity and ambition. London, which in the late seventies was still considered to be the crucible of professional adventure, was somewhere young impoverished people could afford to live and play, a city that was still finding its feet barely thirty years after the war. If the sixties were thought to be the decade of transformation and transgression, the social shock waves administered at the end of the seventies would prove to be no less seismic.*

Keren Woodward: I left home in 1979, at the age of eighteen, and moved to London from Bristol. Before that, Sara [Dallin] and I used to come up to London and pretend to our parents that we were staying at each other's houses. We'd get on the train and put on a pair of high heels. We were do-it-yourself punks. I used to wear my uncle's policeman's shirt and my dad's skinny tie, and safety pins. I loved punk. I remember going out one day looking like Farrah Fawcett Majors and coming back with a black crop, and my mum refused to speak to me. I was walking down the street, and if she saw a friend, she would push me in a doorway. She hated it.

So when we moved to London, we stayed at the YWCA in Great Russell Street, in Covent Garden. You couldn't choose your room, but we engineered it so we ended up sharing. I think we were quite noisy, and I'm not sure anyone else wanted to share with us. And then we just started going clubbing. The first club I remember going to was Studio 21, on Oxford Street, where we met Paul Cook from the Pistols. You weren't allowed men at the hostel, but one day he turned up to see us, and there was this announcement: 'Paul Cook to see Keren Woodward and Sara Dallin.' We just went, 'Oh God, he's come to see us!' So we started going to a lot of gigs with him. I got a job working in the pensions department at the BBC, as I was good at maths, but every night we treated the West

End like our playground. We eventually got asked to leave the hostel, and so we stole all the furniture and pushed it down the road to Denmark Street, where Paul had offered us the flat above the Sex Pistols' rehearsal room, which was very rough and ready. We were eighteen, living in London with the coolest people in the world. The walls had Johnny Rotten's drawings all over it, all this graffiti . . . All the furniture was from *The Great Rock'n'Roll Swindle*, and we used the 'Who Shot Bambi?' headboard as a coffee table. There was no hot water, an outside toilet, but we loved it. Paul Cook was asked about us recently, and he said, 'I don't know where they came from, but suddenly they were everywhere.'

There was a girl we met at the YWCA who called herself Ziggy and went out in full Bowie stuff every night. One night she took us to the Blitz. I remember Boy George standing outside. A few years later, just after we started to become successful as Bananarama, he'd see us out and say, 'One day I'm going to be more famous than you.' And he hadn't even started a career at that stage.

It was Paul's suggestion that we start singing. Along with Steve Jones, he was in a new band, the Professionals, and we would just mess around singing backing vocals, pick up instruments, and when they didn't lock up the rehearsal rooms, we'd come in from clubs and smash the drums around and stuff. We used to mess around doing cover versions – including 'Venus', actually – and Paul suggested we make a demo.

Terry Smith (*photographer*): I got assigned by *Time* magazine. They had done a famous cover in the sixties on Swinging London, and this was meant to be a seventies version. When I was given the assignment, I went to meet Steve Strange in his flat in Baron's Court. I wanted to put him at ease, as there had been rather a lot of unkind coverage in the tabloids that was incredibly sarcastic. I wanted to put his mind at rest that this was a serious look at what we thought was a cultural trend. Up until then he'd only been featured in the tabloids and a bit in the music press. I thought he was bit like the Joel Grey character in *Cabaret,* although he always seemed to have a thing for straight men.

I think a lot of the press thought it [Blitz] was a place where people went in fancy dress, but it was nothing of the kind; people didn't go as Charlie Chaplin or Joan of Arc, they went as themselves and wore extraordinarily creative clothing – colourful, exotic and flamboyant. A lot of the crowd were St Martin's students, so I knew that kind of crowd, and I liked the general vibe straight away from the moment I walked in.

It was a bit scuzzy, it had a terribly dirty floor, and I don't even think there was a carpet. It was a cement floor, I think, or maybe old floorboards. Whatever, it was pretty grubby. The furniture looked like it was kind of utility-era table and chairs, which may have been deliberate because, after all, it was the Blitz club and there were posters from the Second World War on the wall and a picture of Churchill. It obviously wasn't a very cool bar, but that was just what they inherited. They didn't try to dress the place up in their own image. That wasn't the interesting part of it; the interesting part was the crowd they got there.

I found everyone to be very friendly, there was no violence whatsoever, and I didn't see so much as an argument. There were a lot of gays, both male and female, and there was a lot of necking and flirting, male on male and female on female, but I never saw any nastiness, I never saw anybody drunk. I never saw any drug-taking. I heard there was a little bit of hanky-panky in the toilets, but I never went to investigate.

I didn't point a camera at anybody who didn't want their picture taken, and most people were more than happy to be shot, although sometimes they would pose a little too much. As soon as they did start hitting poses, I stopped taking pictures. I tried my best to catch them as they were.

You had to have a very specific look. One guy turned up with a kind of mask you might expect a robber to have worn, and he was turned away straight away. Steve's way of doing it would be to put his hand across the door and say, 'I'm very sorry, but this is a private party.' I saw him turn away a little party of Japanese girls one night who looked immaculately dressed, in really smart clothes with angular lines and smart haircuts. I felt really sorry for them, but it wasn't the look. You had to invent your own.

Fiona Dealey: What motivated myself and other people was a sense that having found somewhere we considered 'home', we wanted to move on and succeed. We were all incredibly ambitious, but we just didn't talk about it. I was motivated because I wanted to be someone more glamorous. I think a lot of people were running away from things, like the gay ones, because in London they could be openly gay. I didn't have bricks thrown at me when I walked up Charing Cross Road, but I did when I was in Southend high street.

Chris Sullivan: When that space age look was going down, I went to the Blitz dressed as Clark Kent – I even had a Kent cigarette packet in my top pocket and a notebook in my hat. The next week people were turning up in suits and hats. I couldn't believe it – I only did it for a joke.

Steve Strange: I ran a very tight ship in terms of my door policy. I wanted creative-minded pioneers there who looked like a walking piece of art, not some drunken, beery lads. The best move I made was turning Mick Jagger away at the door. He was wearing trainers.

Fiona Dealey: When we went to cocktail bars, you'd make sure your outfit matched the place, you know, smoke a Sombrero cigarette. We'd go to the Beachcomber bar, Joe Allen's, Rumours. We used to go to Peppermint Park for lunch, and we were students! I remember after my first year at St Martin's I got a call from my bank manager, who called me into the local bank that my parents banked at, and he got my cheque book out and asked what Rumours was. And I told him it was a fabric shop. Billy's? Fabric shop. The Embassy? Fabric shop . . . In those days you wrote a cheque for everything. I did have a Barclaycard, and he asked to see it. When I gave it to him, he took out this big comedy pair of shears and cut it up in front of me. 'You can't live like this,' he said. I remember I went back to my car, and I'd locked myself out, so I had to ask a mechanic to break into the door, and the bank manager came out just as I was giving the mechanic a fiver. I remember with my first grant cheque I went out and bought three pairs of Manolo Blahnik shoes. That's what we did.

Kim Bowen: I was at St Martin's by this point and going to the Blitz every week. I liked it, but I preferred the getting-ready part and I used to get quite annoyed with all that music. I much preferred soul music and didn't much care for Rusty Egan going on for five hours with electronic beeping. It really irritated me. And then I met Chris Sullivan and everyone else. I think there was a whole contingent of people that definitely loved old soul and jazz, so I think that was quite a backbone, aesthetically. Because I'd been going to clubs for some time, the Blitz wasn't as amazing to me as it was to other people. I actually loved the Embassy, as they used to play quite good music. It's funny to think that people started taking pictures of us, because none of us could really afford to take pictures and have them developed, as we didn't have money to spend on things like that. But I felt ugly, anyway. I look back at some of those pictures today and they're beautiful, but I felt really ugly. Which is so stupid. Of course, like all people you look back and think, 'No, you weren't.' It's an affliction that lots of young women have, I think. I appeared to be an extrovert, but actually I was incredibly shy. One of the things that dressing up gives you is wonderful armour. I could come across as quite frosty, but I wasn't.

Andy McCluskey: Soon electronic music seemed to be everywhere. We eventually found other people were doing the same thing, and in addition to the Human League and Daniel Miller you had Cabaret Voltaire, Ultravox and Gary Numan, obviously. Then, of course, as soon as Numan was successful, suddenly all the labels were like, 'Get me a synth band!' And so we got signed, the Human League moved from Fast to Virgin, and then there was the second wave – Depeche Mode, Soft Cell and then eventually the Pet Shop Boys. Vince Clark openly says they [Depeche] heard 'Electricity' and decided they wanted to play synths. I think we all had a respect for each other, but we were also kind of going, 'Hmm, they're riding a horse. How did they get that horse? Get off that horse, it's our horse.' I think there was a wave of bands that came out of the UK who had been to art college, and everybody was united in a desire to try to do something different, because punk had detonated the formula. But then somebody else had to pick up the pieces, because punk was kind of nihilistic.

Paul Humphreys: In some ways it was a bit annoying when we found out about the likes of Gary Numan and the Human League, because we thought we'd found our alternative music, and all of a sudden we realised that all around the north of England people were listening to the same things we were – Kraftwerk and Neu! and Bowie and Roxy. Everyone had discovered synth. Synth was this new way to make music, this huge palette of sounds that had never been heard before. Our biggest influence was Kraftwerk, because they were classically trained musicians and so included harmonic structures in what they did. They were brilliant, but they did it in the simplest way. Simplicity, but with great melodies. We took that blueprint and decided to make it even more concise. Kraftwerk were the leaders in using keyboard lines as the chorus rather than the sung chorus, so we took that too. If you look at a lot of our early singles, they never had a chorus. 'Enola Gay', 'Electricity', 'Souvenir', 'Joan of Arc' and 'Messages' all had keyboard melodies, and we took that directly from Kraftwerk. Andy and I both had a knack for writing hooky tunes. When Tony Wilson heard our first few songs, he said, 'This is the future of pop music.' And we said, 'Fuck off, this is experimental music.' We thought 'pop' was a dirty word; it was like an insult.

We were all out to slay the rock'n'roll dragon, and we saw electronic music as the future of pop music, as we hated rock'n'roll clichés. We were so naive. We also couldn't believe we had got a seven-album deal, and kept expecting to be found out. So we thought, 'Let's spend all the money we've got from the advance on building a recording studio in Liverpool, so that when they drop us, we'll have a business.' Because at that time recording studios were a good business to have. So we just budgeted for failure, and it was a real surprise that we managed to keep going. We still viewed OMD as an art project, but we kept getting bigger.

Phil Oakey: Back then our biggest problem was we used synths to make bass drums, and they would do two good hits, then two dodgy ones, then two good ones . . . But we couldn't do anything about it; we didn't have a sampler, we just had to stick with it the way it was. So the basic palette was the one we single-mindedly just stuck at. It got into my head with Wendy Carlos, Giorgio Moroder, Donna Summer and even Keith Emerson. It was around that period that it occurred to me: analogue synths may change a little bit while you're playing them, but you don't have to play them too much. You can have a little think about it while you're doing it. And then we just added drum machines later on. We made two albums [*Travelogue*, *Reproduction*] without drum machines. Then we got a Boss DR-55, a drum machine with four skins on it. It had four crap sounds, but that's exactly how we still work now.

I like science fiction. I still think J. G. Ballard is the greatest British writer of the last century. We did a tribute song to J. G. Ballard very early on. Because Roxy Music had done '2HB' for Humphrey Bogart, we did '4JG'. Was science fiction an influence on the Human League? I'm afraid it was. I try to pretend that it isn't and try to look like a sophisticated urbanite. I hide all my toys and science-fictiony stuff in the attic now, so if anyone comes round, they think I'm a BBC2 type. But when Amazon recommends anything, it's amazing how science-fictiony it is.

Martyn Ware: In the early seventies, with my best pal [Phil Oakey] I discovered all sorts of things – early computer music, Xenakis, free jazz, like Carla Bley. We sought it out. Before the soundtrack album of *A Clockwork Orange*, I'd already bought *Switched-On Bach*. When I first heard that, it was like a light went on in my head. I'd always loved classical music, especially Bach. I was really into Kubrick: we'd seen *2001: A Space Odyssey*, of course, so when news came out that the next film he was working on was *A Clockwork Orange*, we rushed out and bought the book. When we read the section where the bands are mentioned, we were always wondering, 'What do the Heaven Seventeen look like? What do they sound like? Are they a gospel band?' Another name we were toying with in those days was Monolith, taken from *2001*. When I saw the film of *A Clockwork Orange*, it all clicked. Electronic music, futuristic imagery: it was a perfect storm for us. It's still my favourite film. It really spoke to us. Looking back, a lot of it is misogynistic and wrong, but that sense of teens against the world, its transgressive nature, the dysfunctional gang culture, it was very exciting, but it had intellectual depth and was designed to make you think. The music was a massive influence on us. I was astonished when Wendy Carlos released the rest of the material she composed for the score. The track 'Country Lane' is fantastic, and why that wasn't used in the film, I don't know. Because the film was withdrawn in the seventies, it wasn't showing in any UK cinema; I actually went to Amsterdam to see it. I reviewed it in the Sheffield fanzine *Gun Rubber*, under the name Art Zero. I also went to see *Deep Throat*, but that's another story. Later, I remember trying to track down a VHS copy of it. You couldn't buy a legit copy, so you had to get dodgy bootlegs. In the end, Martin Fry got me a copy. It was something like fourth generation, really crackly and fuzzy, but that gave it even more of an illicit feel.

Phil Oakey: Our first tour was with Siouxsie and the Banshees, and they were from Bromley. They were very, very supportive. There was the Banshees, Spizzoil and us. That was when we were getting our ideas together. We had nothing at that stage. Even if we went as far as somewhere like Bristol, we'd have to go back to Sheffield that night, so the Banshees would pay for us to have a hotel room. It was really incredible. And immediately after that tour we went to Europe with Iggy Pop. It was the *Soldier* tour. It was an eye-opener. It was while all the drugs were still going on. You'd come to breakfast in the morning, and there'd be a couple of people missing. And the others would be like, 'Yeah, they got taken to hospital.'

It seemed to make sense that science fiction might be the perfect antidote to the urban deprivation of 1979. It also seemed to be perfectly apt that the public sector strikes that straddled the new year had taken on a Shakespearean hue, contributing to the Winter of Discontent. The term was first used to describe the events of the winter by Robin Chater, a writer at Incomes Data Report, *but then it was misguidedly used by Prime Minister James Callaghan himself, and subsequently picked up by the tabloids. Fuelled by the attrition between the unions and the Labour government – the unions demanding larger pay rises, and the government demanding they be kept below 5 per cent – there were widespread strikes by public sector bodies. The industrial action included an unofficial strike by gravediggers working in Liverpool and Tameside, and, saliently, strikes by refuse collectors. It was the rubbish that did for the government, as the mountain of frozen black bin bags in central London not only created terrific visuals for the television news crews, it also gifted the Right with a bombproof political metaphor. Our great city was being allowed to morph into a rubbish tip, an act of negligence that had seemingly been sanctioned by the government. While the strikes were largely over by February, the government's inability to contain them cast Callaghan in a bad light and helped add momentum to Margaret Thatcher's bid to oust him in the May general election.*

Not only did Thatcher win with ease – the Conservatives won 339 seats compared to Labour's 269, while the 5.2 per cent swing to the

Tories was the largest since 1945 – but the result would prove to be a political watershed, marking a break in post-war British history. If the era from 1945 to 1979 had been characterised by a 'consensus' style of politics, in which the main parties mostly agreed on certain fundamental political issues and concepts, such as the mixed economy, the nature of the provision of public services, the need for an incomes policy and the role of the trade unions, this was now to change. In fact, Thatcher's first term would redefine the very nature of what one meant by 'change'. What she set about delivering wasn't so much an adjustment as a revolution. In essence, Thatcher hated consensus politics, distrusted pragmatism, and didn't see why she had to pretend otherwise. 'Our economic weakness has been partly caused by failure to accept that the interests of all classes within the nation are ultimately the same,' ran the draft of the 1979 Conservative manifesto. As she was editing it, the Conservative leader scored a line through the offending sentence and wrote in the margin: 'No it hasn't – it isn't.' In that context, and perhaps anticipating what was to come, maybe science-fiction fantasy seemed an entirely rational response.

Trevor Horn: It was science fiction in a way, as in my own way I was being experimental, making things up as I went along. By the time I made 'Video Killed the Radio Star' with Buggles, I had already started making records, working for two or three different publishers; they would sign somebody, and I would make the demos. That was the only way to get into a studio. I had heard Kraftwerk by this time, and the Normal, and so pretty early on I made myself a very basic drum machine on a sixteen-track tape and a drummer to play separately over the top, just making a very straightforward dance beat. Of course, the drummer hated it and said, 'It sounds like a fucking machine.' And I said, 'That's kind of what I'm trying to get it to sound like.' It was perfectly in time. So I started trying to make records without a drummer. I had been reading a lot of science fiction, and 'Video Killed the Radio Star' was actually inspired by a J. G. Ballard short story.

It was good song, but Buggles was a bad name for a group. We'd have been much better off calling ourselves something like Orchestral Manoeuvres in the Dark or the Human League. We threw everything at that record, tried every trick in the book. We did crazy stuff on it, like for a snare drum we hit a telephone with a wooden spoon and put it through a fuzzbox. The interesting thing about it is, it's all played. There's not a single thing programmed on it, even though I was starting to experiment. Anything that sounded like a sequencer was just because that was the way Geoffrey [fellow Buggle Geoffrey Downes] played it. But it was a hit, and having a hit gave me lots of options, not that I knew what they were immediately. So we kind of took a sideways step and went off to join Yes, which was a completely different world for us, but not something that we felt we could turn down. It was like one of those things in your life where somebody offers you something, and you think, 'Well, I can say no, but if I say no, I'll regret it, and if I say yes, I'm sure I'll still regret it, but if I say no, I might regret it more later on.' The thing was, I wasn't really up to it. I did pretty well with the record, but live I couldn't take doing all those shows across America. After doing three nights at Madison Square Garden you become fearless, but what I wanted to do was be back in the studio. There was so much electronic music happening, and I wanted to be part of it.

Midge Ure: By the end of 1978, I had purchased a synthesizer, hoping to introduce it to the Rich Kids, but it proved to be the thing that broke the band up. Glen and Steve absolutely hated the idea of a synthesizer. At this point the Blitz had started, and Rusty was running it with Steve Strange. We'd go there and listen to a lot of this music coming out of Europe, a lot of Neu! and Can and Kraftwerk and all of that stuff. And I was fascinated with the sound of this instrument, what you could do with it within the context of a rock band, using it as another colour. Rusty and I were listening to other things; we were hanging out and dressing differently. Glen wanted what he called 'good old rock'n'roll', and I wanted rock'n'roll with a modern edge, and that's when Rusty and I finally wanted the band to split. We were wandering the streets of London, skint, Rusty buying me dinner because I had no money and he was making some DJing. Rusty came up with a million ideas a day, and one was, 'Wouldn't it be great to have a band with all our favourite musicians in it?' And I went, 'OK, stop. Let's do that.' And that was Visage.

Rusty Egan: Midge wasn't sure about Steve initially, but I said, 'Look, John Lydon can't sing, but he is an amazing frontman, and so is Steve. This guy is going to be someone.' The truth is, I started Visage because I'd run out of records to play at the Blitz. We'd been playing the same records every week, and I had this album by the Yellow Magic Orchestra, and I was like, 'Listen, this is the future.' I'm basically telling everyone, 'Punk is over, and this is the future. This is the sound.' And everyone's going, 'Yeah, sure.' Then I hear 'Life in a Day' by Simple Minds, and I was like, 'No, somebody's doing it! They're ahead of us.' And then I got the Human League and I was crying. I was going, 'Ah, this is the sound!'

Midge Ure: All the musicians we wanted to work with in Visage were working in other bands. Dave Formula, Barry Adamson and John McGeoch were in Magazine, and Billy Currie was in Ultravox. So Rusty approached them, and they were all up for the idea of doing this simply as a studio project, as a collective. It was never meant to be a band as such, but we needed someone to sing, and Rusty said, 'My mate Steve is in a band, and he'd love to do something.' So it worked on many levels. Steve was the only person in the Visage set-up who wasn't signed, who didn't have a band. Everyone else was contractually tied up with their own set-ups. So we started throwing these ideas together when we could, and beg, borrow or steal studio time. The Rich Kids had been allocated some demo studio time as part of the contract, and I took my two or three days and went in with a synthesizer and did a cover version of the Zager and Evans song 'In the Year 2525'. I didn't want to sing it, so we got Steve in to do it. For me, the big thing was being in the studio, controlling the studio, being a producer, creating something I wanted to create as opposed to something other people wanted me to do. I didn't feel I had control in the Rich Kids, as it was Glen's band. But this was something that I could control – I conceived it, I drew the graphics, I designed the Visage logo, I did all of that. It was like my baby. Because we weren't a live band, Steve didn't have to have massive stage charisma, he didn't have to be Bono or Bowie. It wasn't about that. He was the blank canvas, him and his connections and, I suppose, the buzz that was coming out of the end of Billy's and the beginning of the Blitz. That whole thing was invaluable. That was his contribution. He didn't write the lyrics and he wasn't a really great singer. I had to sing the songs first and then pump my voice into his ear, and what came out of his mouth was a close enough representation. His value was the face, the connections, the make-up artists, the clothes, the style, the look – all of that stuff was just as important. So there was no question of me doing this as a vehicle for myself.

Visage served a great purpose, and I learnt an awful lot in the studio. There's something really weird about making something specifically to play in small clubs. It was never designed to become commercially successful, but it did despite itself, thanks to 'Fade to Grey', but then again, you've got to remember it wasn't just the music that was important. All of a sudden we had moved from looking at fashion, style, current fads or whatever in magazines and started watching it on videos. We started having this vehicle that didn't really exist before then, and it became more and more important. The Godley and Creme video that accompanied 'Fade to Grey' was just as important as the song because it presented the look, it presented something other-worldly, and it sent that look all across Europe, right round the world, saying, 'This is what's happening in this little club in London right now.' That was pivotal to our success.

Steve Strange: Midge Ure invited me to record some songs with him as he had some free studio time. I got into it so much when we did that cover of 'In the Year 2525', I was literally acting as if the world was coming to an end. I was holding on to the vocal booth, bellowing it out. All the tracks we were recording, we would play at Billy's, and later at the Blitz, and that's when the record companies started coming to the club. We were getting a lot of kids from St Martin's; not just bands and musicians, but all these designers like Stephen Jones, John Galliano, Stephen Linard and Melissa Caplan, who would go on to do the costumes for the 'Fade to Grey' video and went on to do costumes for Toyah.

The scene was largely white – there were as few black faces among the Blitz contingent as there had been in London during punk – while many of the strongest voices were female. Sexuality ceased to matter much, and the abiding atmosphere was always one of tolerance. The toxicity of punk 2.0 was a world away from the carefree New Romantic dance-floors of central London in the late seventies, and while the movement had a rather inchoate manifesto, it made up for this by exuding a sense of social energy through experimentation, transgression and inclusion. The New Romantics were fluid.

Fiona Dealey: The gay scene was huge. Dencil [Williams] was fabulous, as he was one of the most extravagant creatures I'd seen in my life. On the first day at St Martin's, I got the tube back with him to Ralph West, and he used to wear ballet pumps and he'd walk on the balls of his feet and he had these really tight trousers on and full make-up – I mean, he looked amazing and spoke in that really fabulous American drawl. He was from Hawaii or somewhere like that. He was black and he was really, really beautiful, exotic. I mean, he had the body of a gymnast. And beyond camp, absolutely beyond. So we're sitting on the tube, and he was like, 'Why are all these people looking at us?' I knew gay men in Southend who used to go up to London, to the Coleherne in

Earl's Court or Louise's in Wardour Street, and they wore transparent plastic trousers, they were buying clothes from SEX and they were beautiful-looking men. I associated gay men with real glamour. They were more sophisticated than straight men of their age. As I'd always known gay men, being at St Martin's just meant there were more of them. But they were prettier and better dressed. Billy's and the Blitz were always everything – no gay or straight, we just all mucked in. There were never any fights, not at the beginning. As there were a lot of gay men around, all that fighting that you'd get in previous clubs just disappeared, and I never remember any gay men getting beaten up by any straight men at any of these clubs ever. It was all really harmonious. I only went to a couple of punk gigs, and I just couldn't bear the violence. But even at the Lacy Lady there would be violence, but it was mainly with the doormen, with the people who were coming in.

One of the first gay disco records was 'I Was Born This Way' by Valentino, which had been released in 1975, although it would be another three years before the genre would find its first real anthem, Sylvester's 'You Make Me Feel (Mighty Real)', which he sang in an exuberant falsetto. Gay disco would soon take on a more exalted mantle, as it started to appear genuinely transgressive. The Sylvester record was released at the end of 1978 and became the sound of 1979 – all *of 1979. While gay disco produced huge crossover hits, it was nevertheless an underground scene, promising decadence, freedom and connection. In the UK, and in London in particular, it also felt incredibly sophisticated, as the scene offered a direct relationship with America, and with the far more mature, other-worldly gay environments in New York and San Francisco. Andrew Holleran wrote about the unifying passion of these clubs in his 1978 novel* Dancer from the Dance, *which became known as a kind of gay* Great Gatsby*: 'It was extraordinary, the emotions in those rooms . . . everyone was reduced to an ecstatic gloom . . . we lived on certain chords in a song, and the proximity of another individual dancing beside* *you, taking communion from the same hand, soaked with sweat, stroked by the same tambourines.'*

Dencil Williams (*model, artist*): In 1977, I was still in Nassau, in the Bahamas. I'd just got my first modelling job, in Lima, a swimwear shoot. I'd just turned sixteen. I had been accepted by both Parsons in New York and St Martin's, and opted to move to London to do the foundation course. After a year I joined the fashion course, which is when I met everyone. I felt like I'd arrived. The city was a lot smaller then, and having come halfway round the world, I suddenly found myself mixing with all these extraordinary people – Mario Testino, Fiona Dealey, Stephen Jones, George O'Dowd. They thought I was strange, but they were just as strange to me. I was free from my parents, even though my mother controlled me with her money, as Mummy always paid for everything. My father was just an accountant, and my mother was a stay-at-home mum. His great-grandparents would have been slaves, so they didn't have this silver-spoon life that I did; my father did everything to make my life and my brothers' and sisters' lives perfect. He made our lives his. We were so pampered. As much as people in the Bahamas were exotic, it was such a peripheral place, and I was brought up with religion forced down my throat. Everything was about God, it was all this black culture. What was interesting to me at the time was that you either lived in a hole in the ground or in a palace. You were rich or poor; there was no in-between.

My mother would send me all this money, and I would go straight down the King's Road, and Manolo Blahnik would see me coming! I was terrible with money. I got a job at the Embassy Club washing dishes, but I think she paid them to employ me. The dishwashing only lasted a few weeks, until the owners asked me to go upstairs to entertain people. I remember putting on a wig and a mini-skirt and singing 'Bad Girls' by Donna Summer. London was so sexually liberating. Oh my God, wasn't it? All those public toilets. You could walk anywhere and have sex with anyone at any time. That was incredible. I remember the first fuck club I went to. It was just in Leicester Square – I think it used to be a cinema. It looked like a normal club from the outside, but then you would go down to the bottom and sex would be everywhere. Sometimes the police would raid the place and the red light would come on, and you would see the person that you were having sex with and it was like, 'Oh, it's you!'

Quite often in these clubs I would be the only black person. Sometimes I would do fashion shows, and I would be the only black person. That was odd. Also, I couldn't understand why all the black people walking around London made themselves small. I suppose that's one of things that made me, you know, 'Say it loud, I am black and proud.' I couldn't ever understand that. I was going out with this boy once, and he started talking about Paki bashing. That's when I found out he was in the National Front. I asked him why he was going out with me, as I was black! He said, 'Because you are different.' I mean, how was I different? But London was racist then, and it's racist now. I can remember being stopped by the police going into Harvey Nichols. I said, 'Why are you stopping me?' It was because I was black. He was like, 'You don't look like a normal Knightsbridge shopper.' What the fuck should a normal Knightsbridge shopper look like? It's because I am black.

At the time, I was pretty, though, and my pretty little smile could open any door, and it did.

Rusty Egan: How would I describe the Blitz club to people who weren't there? It was magic, like punk in 1976. In those days, people didn't have any money, but they could customise their clothes. They could put pictures of Karl Marx on an old suit that they'd bought. You could make your own magazine, you could be a band or a manager. We carried that on, so all the kids at St Martin's could go to Blitz and for one night they could be a hero. That was our song: '"Heroes"' by David Bowie.

Michele Clapton (*costume designer*): The first time I went to the Blitz I just felt an enormous sense of relief and excitement! Finally, a place where people celebrated how you looked rather than laughed at or baited you . . . So yes, it was a community. While at college, I worked part-time at the ICA in the evenings as an usherette. Once the audience were watching the film, I would prepare myself for a night at the Blitz, and my friends would come, ready to leave for the club directly after the film. When the audience came out, they were confronted with this spectacle . . . it never went down better than after a John Waters film! We just loved running round as a group; it made us feel brave. We were so used to being picked on individually. I lived in Brixton at the time, and it was probably the most accepting place to live – there and Soho. The Rastas seemed to accept me, and the drag queens identified with us. I guess we were all minorities. Stephen Linard was brilliant, as a designer and as a person, incredibly funny and dry, and modelling in his final show at St Martin's was fabulous: Myra, Fiona, my lovely friend Lee Sheldrick and George, I think. It was such a great moment . . . it felt like we were all on our way. Other memories? Just dancing and gossiping in the club . . . fighting over the same boy with another boy – it was pretty gender-fluid . . . Making films with Cerith Wyn Evans and falling asleep repeatedly while he filmed me! And he didn't mind! Being Miss Frozen Assets at the alternative Miss World.

Spandau Ballet was born in north London in 1979. Their clothing was paramount to their appeal, but then so were their good looks – so much so that the bidding war to sign them was fevered (Chrysalis won). 'We were not just another band,' said their singer, Tony Hadley, and in this instance, he was right.

Robert Elms: I seem to remember thinking, 'I could be a journalist,' one night at the Blitz. I remember Steve Dagger talking about people Vopping, which meant, 'I'm doing a Variety of Projects.' He came up with this silly acronym for when someone would ask, 'What are you doing?' They'd say, 'I'm doing a variety of projects.' You know, 'I'm starting a magazine,' 'I'm opening an agency,' and half the time they weren't. I was just saying that on a Tuesday night while wearing silly clothes, but it made you think, 'Maybe I can do this! I better start a magazine. I better get Graham Smith to take the photos. Gary's got a band, so maybe we should ask them to play.' And it was like that. I wouldn't say it was entrepreneurial, because no one was making any money, and it was before anyone realised you could make money out of it, but what you could make was a name for yourself, you could make a reputation. You could become a face.

In the summer of 1978, myself and Chris Sullivan, Graham Smith, Graham Ball and Ollie O'Donnell had been to Berlin for a long holiday, and I saw the words 'Spandau Ballet' written on a wall. Before that, they were called the Gentry, but although it was a terrible name, it at least showed their aspirations. There was that sort of Teutonic thing going on, and they said, 'Yes, that's a great name, we'll call ourselves that.' So by that stage I'd already been sort of recognised within the group as someone, like Bob does words, Graham Smith does pictures and Melissa Caplan does tabards. Graham started taking all the pictures at the Blitz. Melissa was designing clothes, and so I thought, 'Well, I'd better do something, and all I can do is write, so I'll start doing that.' As Gary had his band, I wrote an article about their first gig and walked into the *NME* and said, 'Right, I've written an article about Spandau Ballet.' Steve Dagger asked me to write it, so I sat in his parents' council flat in Holborn and wrote something in longhand on a bit of paper, and he walked me to the *NME* offices in Carnaby Street, because we didn't have the fare. We said, 'You should print this. Your paper is shit; you don't know this is going on. There's this whole scene.' And they did. They asked if I had any pictures, so I called Graham. And that's where it started for me. So I was already flash enough to think, 'They'll print what I write.'

Steve Dagger: By now I wanted to be a manager. I had read about sixties management and was obsessed with the likes of Andrew Loog

Oldham, Kit Lambert and Brian Epstein. That was the job I wanted. And when I stumbled into Billy's, I thought there needed to be a band, a great group that could actually mean something to popular culture. I knew Gary [Kemp], as he had played guitar with a lot of older guys in an Islington group called the Same Band. I would have bet my house on this scene becoming culturally important, and in the context of that I wanted a band to go with it. I was absolutely convinced that in a year's time, the whole of London and the UK would be moving in that direction musically. There were so many creative people at the Blitz – graphic designers, clothes designers, DJs, journalists. Spandau formed quickly. They changed their name from Gentry and started putting their look together. We did an initial showcase for our friends at a rehearsal room in Holloway. Steve Strange and a number of people came, but Chris Sullivan was also there, and both of them offered me shows straight away. Chris asked us to play the second Mayhem warehouse party gig, and Steve asked us to play the Blitz. We did both. I started to get the national press interested, but by then there was a buzz about the band – this feeling that the Blitz was the hottest club in London and there was a group in it, with all these people that were incredibly talented. I went to the *Daily Mirror*, I went to the old *Evening News* and I went to the *Standard*. The *Daily Mirror* gave me two pages, the *Standard* gave me half a page and the bloke at the *Evening News* didn't really like it. Record companies started to become interested, and I knew it was going to work. I had absolutely no doubt at all. At the Blitz show, Chris Blackwell was there. He came up to me when I was on the mixing desk. In the end we didn't do a deal with him, but it was that kind of momentum. Every day you got up and there was a phone call from somebody. On a broader level, the media were picking up on the way people looked, what people were saying in the press and the general attitude pervading in the club. There was a succession of journalists that came to the Blitz, and there was an etiquette amongst all of us that quickly developed. If somebody got in touch, we would always say, 'Yes, there's this journalist, this designer, this DJ, this film-maker.' We were all trying to help each other. We turned people towards *i-D*, which was just about to start, towards our friends at St Martin's, towards Jon Baker, who had just opened Axiom. Jon absolutely got the whole thing immediately, which is why Axiom became the place everyone bought their clothes. You could go for the Fritz Lang *Metropolis* look, you could look like Clark Gable, you could look like Boadicea.

Peter York: I remember the manager of Spandau Ballet being frightfully serious about all of this stuff. There was someone who didn't crack a smile.

Gary Kemp: We had no interest in the rest of the music scene, as we grew out of club culture. We started at Billy's, then the Blitz and all these places where you didn't rub up against the rock world. We were very particular in those days. It was a gang mentality, and one that kept us very close.

Rusty Egan: Steve [Strange] loved Spandau Ballet because he fancied them, especially Martin Kemp, and he wanted them to play in the Blitz. He was going to go along to a rehearsal, and I said I'd come too, as I wasn't going to have them play in the club unless I'd seen them. Then Gary Kemp came up to the DJ booth in the Blitz, saying, 'So, you're going to come to the rehearsal?' I said, 'Yeah, I'm going to come see you guys. I hope you've got a synth.' And he goes, 'Yeah, of course we've got a synth.' I know they went out and bought it; they didn't have a synth. So I went to Holloway Road with Steve, and they played 'To Cut a Long Story Short' and 'The Freeze' and 'Instinction', and they were good, five young, really good-looking boys.

Gary Kemp: We didn't talk to the music press, as we had no interest in trying to persuade them that what we were doing was good. They didn't believe we were working class and tried to paint us as middle-class

Tories. The music papers at the time were full of middle-class white boys who didn't like the fact we were from council estates. They wanted to believe we were right-wing, but we were anything but. We all came from the Essex Road in Islington, and we had no sympathies with anything remotely Thatcherite. We were also commercial, which in those days was a political act in itself. We just wanted to get on and improve our lot. We wanted to be successful, we wanted to be famous, and we didn't see why we should be embarrassed about it.

Spandau Ballet tended to espouse success, wallowing in extravagant and escapist pop promos and behaving like minor members of the royal family. The music press didn't just dislike them because of their music, they also hated the way in which Gary Kemp would continually point out the inconsistencies in many rock stars' back stories, especially those of white, middle-class heroes such as Bob Dylan and Bruce Springsteen. Spandau were the sort of working class the largely white middle-class music journalist couldn't cope with.

'The collected rabble-rousers, cynics and savage wits at the NME *lost little time in deflating any ego I might have been nurturing since getting in front of the cameras,' says Danny Baker, himself a former* NME *hack. 'They found particular joy in my apparent endorsement of Spandau Ballet – a group who, though generally unknown, were already veterans of the review-room toasting fork. When I presented a similar show about some other newcomers called Iron Maiden, they all but debagged me and made me walk up Carnaby Street wearing a bell and a placard around my neck.'*

Simon Napier-Bell: Spandau's speciality was intellectual bullshit. Marc Bolan and Bowie had both done it better, and at least they'd always laughed at themselves, but that was something Spandau were incapable of. Their debut album was released in a pure white sleeve with a perfect Aryan torso. The sleeve notes spoke about the 'soaring joy of immaculate rhythms' and the 'sublime glow of music for heroes'. The press accused the group of 'toying with Nazi chic'. Their column inches grew. It was just what Spandau wanted.

Gary Kemp: Class was certainly an issue, as you had the working-class kids who were aspiring to something culturally better than what they were probably being offered or that people thought they deserved. Intellectually, it was about aspirations outside of our class and certainly outside of what I would have grown up with – spending all your money on clothes and making yourself look grander than a kid in a council house should be looking. I think for the middle-class kids it was about being outrageous, doing something different from anything their parents wanted from them maybe. At the time, there was a lot of talk about politics, a lot of talk about the old Left being wrong, the old Trotsky Left not understanding the aspirations of working-class people. None of us [Hadley aside] were Tories, and we all ended up hating Thatcher, but we also hated the idea of the sort of London School of Economics Trotsky mentality. There was this anger amongst working-class kids like me and Elms that punk had been a piss-take on what the working-class kids were looking like, this sort of ripped jeans, leather jacket, flat-cap mentality. And we didn't think that the inky press got us. I think we were challenging those old ideas of what the working class deserved and who they were. And I think what came out was the idea that punk really had been a middle-class art-student invention, and we felt we were being condescended to, patronised.

David Johnson: Spandau Ballet sounded defiantly un-rocklike by playing the new synthesized electro-pop and singing about being 'beautiful and clean and so very, very young'. Gary Kemp claimed pointedly: 'We are making the most contemporary statement in fashion and music.' In those early days Spandau bassist Martin Kemp, who learnt to play because his big brother asked him, used to say: 'I'm not really a musician. I belong in a club dressed as sharp as a razor. That's the thrill – just being there at 3 a.m., excited by where you are and the people sharing the night with you.' When Spandau Ballet emerged, their strategy was to enlist their entourage of creative night owls not only to stage-manage the fastest launch yet of a new band but also to redefine youth culture in the working-class terms prescribed by the late George Melly, author of the essential paperback *Revolt into Style* (1970). He claimed the first duty of pop is to 'trap the present' and express the aspirations of society 'as it is', not as others would wish. Spandau placed fresh emphasis on clothes and presentation, on self-respect conveyed both by the voice of Tony Hadley, and by dislocated lyrics underpinned with streetwise conviction. Spandau Ballet defined the new direction of pop by opening a debate about the credibility of 'pure pop' as a celebration of the sexiness of youth, then claiming to have relegated 'rock' to the album charts for good.

Peter York: Spandau were driven along by a strange new mix of fantasy, style yearning, preciousness and entrepreneurial zeal. Now *that* was something else, the way Spandau simply couldn't be bothered with the conventional approaches into music-land: find some backers, see if you can get the A&R men to turn up, do it the normal way. Instead they worked out a completely different strategy, involving contracts, networking, an awful lot of self-reliance, and an instinct for DIY publicity. They had no ideological baggage whatsoever. Entrepreneurial zeal. As John Ranelagh notes in *Thatcher's People*, 'Entrepreneurs, notably in the fashion and pop culture worlds, only began multiplying in the seventies. The pop and fashion worlds provided nearly all of Britain's success stories in that decade.' However grim things got between 1979 and 1981 (and those were the years when the number of people out of work doubled to well over two million), it was clear that this group was going to do what it wanted anyway. Partly, it was because this was the last time anyone could surf into any kind of college on a student grant – so make the most of it – and conversely, because they were realistic enough to understand that soon they were going to have to do some fairly serious hustling, not least because they were a load of obsessives, fanatics, dream believers.

But quick to spot an opportunity. When Charles Fox, the Covent Garden theatrical costumier, held its closing-down sale, the Blitz crowd descended in one fluid movement and bought up everything glamorous, old-filmy that they could find. Steve Strange and Stephen Linard bought a pair of matching ankle-length wolf-fur coats for five pounds each. When the big world started to invite the Blitz Kids to flavour up their own parties, the Blitz Kids said, 'Thank you very much,' did their stuff – i.e. acted up for the host – then disappeared into the night. At Paul Raymond's party, they stayed for about half an hour, before returning with carrier bags full of chicken and salmon. *They worked at it.*

David Johnson: Before Blitz culture, there were no 'style gurus' to propose what to wear. You dressed either as a Top Rank disco kid, a new-waver in black drains and narrow tie, or one of those mutants like Mohican punk or skinhead. That's why dressing up at the Blitz became an act of affirmation. The Blitz Kids were the first children of the television age, wise in the ways of the popular media, and they set out to subvert the realms the young know best – music and fashion. Gary Kemp said, 'A cultural identity is a great outlet for people's frustrations. Kids have always spent what little they have on records and haircuts. They've never spent it on books by Karl Marx.' Spandau were the vital extra ingredient that pushed the Blitz into its critical phase. Their mission: to return pop to what Kemp called a 'visual extravaganza', in the spirit of Ziggy Stardust. Steve Dagger determined to outwit the moribund A&R men ('There wasn't one that I rated') and change the way bands were signed. Kemp, who despised the racism of the anti-soul music press, determined to outflank these self-regarding gatekeepers. The entourage of otherwise unemployed Blitz Kids suddenly found careers in the tax-free world of what Whitehall started calling 'the economically active' by dressing, photographing, staging and promoting the band. What united this collision, in Robert Elms's words, of white face with white sock? Dagger was clear: 'We were all in it together to cause a revolution.'

Before winning access to Spandau, Dagger subjected all interviewers to discreet vetting. Applicants wearing denim or Doc Martens never reached the shortlist. Such was the rigour that Spandau's coalition of twenty-year-old talents brought to executing the whirlwind wind-up that it became a template for every New Romantic 'rumour band': (1) They staged secret 'tease dates', never 'gigs', at clubs and venues calculated to annoy the rockists, such as the Blitz, an art-house cinema, or a warship on the Thames. The audience got in only by looking good – which applied to critics too. (2) They refused to send demo tapes or invite record companies to shows, so few insiders actually knew how the band sounded. (3) Seemingly a band with no past, Spandau crafted an artful creation myth around the Blitz's postmodern themes: Bowie's 'just for one day' notion of disposable identities, and of bricolage in which the band's baffling name was supposedly plucked arbitrarily by Elms from some graffiti in Berlin. The Blitz's motormouths and myth-makers were a gift to the media.

Concerts were put together with loving care. The most OTT secret date they played was the first of two at the arty Scala cinema. Following two surrealist Buñuel films, Elms stepped up to declaim some toe-curling blank verse, then Spandau were revealed casting stark expressionist shadows on the screen, fully romanticised with blousy shirts and wing collars and an insouciant cigarette in the raised hand of their tall, striking singer.

The fallout from the flurry of press included a TV documentary built around this group of obsessive dressers for *20th Century Box* on London Weekend Television. The Scala spectacle was restaged, and after its transmission in mid-July the music bizzy-bodies set Dagger's phone jangling. Spandau Ballet had played only eight live dates before signing an unrivalled contract. In the end only two record companies 'got' what Spandau were about, CBS and Chrysalis, and the second won by agreeing to greater creative freedom. The band secured an unprecedented package: 14 per cent against the norm of 8 per cent;

their own record label, Reformation, to manage publishing rights and merchandising; a promotional video and a twelve-inch club mix with each single, which were firsts for a British band. And they agreed in the spirit of democracy to a six-way split of the proceeds, Dagger being de facto a member of the band.

Two weeks after release, their first single, 'To Cut a Long Story Short', entered the charts and reached No. 5. It was danceable, melodic and the vocalist could sing. As cult sounds went, this was unique. They called their new genre 'White European Dance Music'.

Neil Tennant: The whole renaissance of British pop starts with Gary Numan and 'Are "Friends" Electric?'. He took the David Bowie thing and reduced it to a black shirt and a pair of black jeans.

It would be easy to say that the British charts of the first three or four years of the eighties were full of young men and women either pretending to be David Bowie or using one of his many characters as a blueprint for their own tawdry space-faces, but few copied so obviously as Gary Numan. When pushed for a comment, Bowie witheringly said that Numan had successfully filleted 'The Man Who Sold the World' (alienation, a hint of space), and left it at that. He also had Numan thrown off the set of the Kenny Everett Television Show *Christmas special. Numan had already filmed his segment and was hanging around to see Bowie film his. 'Before then I thought he was a god,' he said. 'I used to get into fights at school protecting his name. Then, all of a sudden this bloke I'd adored for years was throwing me out of a building because he hated me so much. It really upset me at the time, especially when I thought of how many thumps I'd taken for him. I can only imagine he was going through an insecure patch. At the time, I was outselling him about four to one.'*

Before going solo, Numan (who was basically what Bill Wyman would have been like had he become famous in 1979 rather than 1963) was in Tubeway Army (a band with an unusually magnificent name), who had a surprise UK No. 1 with a wonderful creation, 'Are "Friends" Electric?' (a song about a robot prostitute), and who for a few weeks struck many as exemplars of magnificent desolation. On the cover of his 1979 album The Pleasure Principle, *Numan stands behind a shiny counter wearing a badly cut double-breasted suit, a convention-ready tie of indeterminate hue and eyeliner. And the way in which he tries to impart his enigmatic qualities to his fan base, the way in which he attempts to semaphore his postmodern otherness, his colour-by-numbers existential angst? That's right, by staring at a small illuminated plastic pyramid. (The* NME*'s Danny Baker said Numan was 'just a ham with a synthesizer . . . making intelligent music for people who aren't intelligent'.)*

Gary Numan: When we went into the studio to record Tubeway Army's first album, we were a punk band. It was meant to be our live set, ten songs, even though we'd only played three or four times. But when I got to the studio, there was a synthesizer in the corner, and I tried that and loved it and converted all of the songs over the next two or three days to pseudo-electronic songs. So I went back to Beggars Banquet with an electronic album, which they didn't want, didn't expect, so we had a really big argument. Making electronic music didn't feel brave to me, either because I was too stupid to realise what I was risking or I was too confident. I mean, I was absolutely convinced, having tried that synthesizer, even though I couldn't play keyboards. I'd never seen a real synthesizer before, I'd only heard of things like Kraftwerk, but when I heard that first little Minimoog in the studio, it just sounded like the future to me, it was a completely different type of music. I realised then that my interest in music wasn't really musical; I'd never had enough interest to want to learn how to be a really good player. I liked noise, sound, and the synthesizer had that. You could press one key, and by manipulating the dials you make this most enormous sound, do things and change and evolve without doing anything musical at all. It was all about atmosphere and mood, and it was just a completely different experience for me, and yet hugely powerful at the same time. And haunting and atmospheric. It was a real revelation to actually sit down and clumsily play one for the first time. I was ignorant of the fact that there were plenty of other people out there trying to do the same thing, people like Orchestral Manoeuvres in the Dark and the Human League. So I understood the record company's resistance to it, but I really was adamant. It almost resulted in a fist fight. I was going to punch the men that owned the record company. I'm not a fighting sort of person at all, but I was absolutely convinced that that was my future, and they were trying to stop me, and I really did believe that if that album didn't come out, then three months later somebody else would be doing it.

It was only subsequently that I found out that I wasn't at the front end at all. I mean, Ultravox had done three albums before I'd even done my first. I was very much at the end of it. OMD's Andy McCluskey used to say I was a johnny-come-lately to the electronic scene, and yet luckily I was the first one to have the big No. 1. But that was luck, to be honest. When we were recording 'Are "Friends" Electric?', I hit a wrong note because I'm not a very good player, and I thought, 'That sounds better, I'll keep that.' So I kept the mistake. It was actually two different songs that I stuck together, two bits of songs I couldn't finish, stuck together with a bad note, and I got to No. 1 with that. And so I realised quite early on that luck plays a huge part in this.

Top of the Pops had a section called 'Bubbling Under' – a song just outside the charts – and that week it was either me or Simple Minds. I think I was at No. 180 and they were 160 or something, and it was down to somebody in the office at *Top of the Pops* to choose between us. And he chose Tubeway Army because he thought it was a more interesting name. The other thing was that 'Are "Friends" Electric?' was released as a limited-edition picture disc, at a time when picture discs were very rare. They decided to put out 20,000 picture discs of a band that was completely unknown, doing a sort of music that no one had really heard before. That was a bit weird and wonderful, on a single that was five minutes, fifteen seconds long, so way too long to get on the radio. And a band that had only sold 3,000 copies up until that point. I got on *Top of the Pops*, which made me famous, thanks to the unbelievable generosity of two people I've never met. So you don't come out of that thinking that you're God's gift to music; you come out of that thinking you're the luckiest guy in the world.

Jon Savage: I got Gary Numan immediately, and he was very important, as both 'Are "Friends" Electric?' and 'Cars' are terrific. I remember I really stood out against all my contemporaries. 'Friends' was the song of the summer. I looked at the credits and thought, 'Oh, he produced this and he wrote it – he really knows what he's fucking doing.' I went off to interview him for *Melody Maker*, and it was a big step because everybody else was dissing him frantically, and I gave him a very long piece and they put him on the cover.

Gary Numan: Fame was a mixture of being absolutely brilliant on the one hand and terrifying on the other. These sudden rises to fame – literally overnight in my case – are very difficult. I'm not a natural showman. I've had to learn how to do it over many, many years of overcoming nervousness and lack of confidence and so on. I became successful without really having a great deal of confidence in what I actually did. I felt lucky to be there. I felt it had happened too soon. There was no progressive rise. People that become successful over a series of albums, that's the way to do it. As each new level comes along, as each album does a little bit better than the one before, you get used to the public's reaction to you. They know you better, but they know you better in a slower kind of way. It's almost like going to school: you come out at the end of it qualified and knowing what you're talking about. I just wasn't prepared. When it comes quickly, like it did for me, everything is sort of overwhelming and difficult, and you don't feel as if you know what you're doing and you don't know how to deal with crowds. The biggest crowd I ever had up until then had been about thirty people at a pub, and that got stopped because a fight broke out. And then the next thing you know you are doing three or four thousand people at these great big theatres. I also went from no money to a ton of money, and I went mad. And I was young – I had only just turned twenty-one when it happened and was still living at home, with my dad still making all the decisions for me – and I've got Asperger's, which just adds to the problem. So I found it really difficult, to be honest, but I was sharp enough to realise that this was a life-changing moment. So it was a mixture of being great on the one hand and pretty horrible on the other.

The black-and-white music weeklies (the 'inkies'), which were all extremely influential at the time, were downright hostile towards Numan and what they would soon start calling 'synth pop'. How dare these poseurs dress up and stand behind a synthesizer? In their minds, this sort of thing had been done before by Kraftwerk. Electro-pop acts were largely treated with suspicion, as they were thought to be reductive and inconsequential. Punk had created a whole new set of hierarchies, which were determined by almost slavish notions of authenticity. And swapping a guitar for a synthesizer was deemed unacceptable, as was wearing outlandish clothes or make-up.

During punk, the synthesizer had been viewed almost with mistrust, largely because it was so closely associated with prog rock. Perhaps as a result of this, when post-punk bands started to use them more frequently, they tried to make them synonymous with urban deprivation, an instrument to be used when trying to expose the underbelly of society or espousing the allure of concrete jungles. Of course, elsewhere synths were also starting to be associated with gloss, sophistication and fashion. For many die-hard rock critics, this would always be tantamount to decoration. However, punk's DIY ethos was actually carried on by the likes of Soft Cell, OMD and the Human League, who bashed out singles on hastily assembled banks of rickety synthesizers, creating a rash of pioneering independent record labels in the process – Mute, Factory, Some Bizarre, etc.

Elsewhere, the post-punk world was full of ideologies and samizdat manifestos, thoughts and ideas that were mostly theoretical. Angst was hip, introversion a prerequisite, while an emphasis on pop and melody was only allowed as a contextualised return to the jingle-jangle purity of sixties pop. Post-punk was a world that was fit to bust, entertaining everyone from Devo to Cabaret Voltaire, from the Pop Group to the Gang of Four, and yet this boom time – a 'space of possibility' – was almost deliberately fragmented, as bands went out of their way to differentiate themselves. The New Romantic scene that started to develop out of clubland contained its own particular narrative, one involving a sweeter, more commodified type of pop transgression.

*Many post-punk artists immersed themselves in the narrative of political oppression, the difficulties of human existence and the iniquities of societal development. Some railed against consumerism, sexism, racism and, as Simon Reynolds says, 'the way in which "the political is personal" – how current events and the actions of governments invade everyday life and haunt each individual's private dreams and nightmares." This period was rich in invention, as bands such as PiL, Scritti Politti, Magazine, Joy Division, the Fall, Throbbing Gristle and the Specials dedicated themselves to fulfilling punk's unfinished musical revolution. And while critics have always been keen to include the likes of ABC, Heaven 17 and the Human League under this benign umbrella, the '*Smash Hits *groups', with their sheer pop efficiency, fared less well, criticised for their adherence to a traditional framework in a climate where pop was developing kaleidoscopic ambitions.*

George Chesterton (*journalist*): It's a tough job to assess Gary Numan's place in British pop. He has been seen as everything from little more than a Bowie-aping joke to a vital influence on music as varied as the early hip hop of Afrika Bambaataa and the restless experimentalism of Damon Albarn. One thing hard to dispute is that he has made some music that will live long and prosper. His earliest work with Tubeway Army, with whom he found chart success in early 1979 with the No. 1 single 'Are "Friends" Electric?' and the band's second album, *Replicas*, was followed a few months later by his first solo album, *The Pleasure Principle*. On that was one of the mightiest, grandest, most enigmatic songs ever to reach No. 1 in the UK: 'Cars'. Listening to *The Pleasure Principle* now it is hard not to feel sorry for Gary. Every song is dripping in paranoia and neuroses. Each lyric is a tale of claustrophobia and/or agoraphobia. He seems afraid of pretty much everything. His stage persona – caked in make-up – reflected this too. He would hide his face like a gawky teenage android who has been scolded by his parents. But that only tells half the story of 'Cars', one of the greatest singles in the history of pop. Firstly, 'Cars' has an electro riff that would not be out of place on Jimmy Page's Les Paul. This is backed up by the powerful drumming of the late Cedric Sharpley. Secondly, the force of the multi-layered Moog synthesizer parts is almost overwhelming. Using effects usually associated with heavy guitars – reverb, flanging and phasers – Numan drenched the gliding synth lines so they flow over you like wave after wave of ice water. These build throughout the song until the fantastical 1'30" fadeout, during which the Polymoogs – used as elements of a string section – are folded on top of each other in hypnotic harmonies that reinforce the song's sense of eerie dystopia. The synth-pop brigade looked to J. G. Ballard for images of the near future, and many now seem merely quaint, like old episodes of *Tomorrow's World*. But 'Cars' contains a bit of futurology that was rather sophisticated. Numan positions the car not as a mode of mechanical transport, but as a fetishised, abstract interface with the rest of the world. This is – in a pop form – what the French philosopher Jean Baudrillard had been writing about a few years earlier. To be fair to Numan, this notion of the car in relation to individuals and society has only deepened in the decades since. *The Pleasure Principle* has many other great tracks on it, especially 'Metal' and 'M.E.' (the basis of Basement Jaxx's 'Where's Your Head At'), but 'Cars' is literally something else.

Gary Numan: I went solo immediately. Tubeway Army had always been my thing anyway: I wrote everything, did the sleeves, I was the singer. I wanted a clean break from punk and to go off on my own. Beggars Banquet didn't want me to, obviously, and wanted to keep Tubeway Army. But I didn't want to compromise and had realised that being in a band involved compromise and having to listen to other people's ideas and see them ruin yours. At the time, the press were quite harsh, as I think they thought that electronic music was going to be a flash in the pan and then we'd go back to guitar rock. Almost certainly, they didn't think I was very good, so I wouldn't last very long. There was a strong resistance to it because it had come out of the punk thing, which was a very anti-hero, anti-pop-star thing. And I was saying the very opposite, so I think that annoyed them quite a bit. As I said, I had Asperger's. I was young, so I was being brutally honest, but shooting myself in the foot while doing so. So I don't think I helped my situation at all. I've got no kind of axe to grind about that. Certainly got no chip on my shoulder about what was said about me then. I think some of it was harsh and unfair, but some of it was true actually.

David Bowie: What Numan did he did excellently, but in repetition, the same information coming over again and again. Once you've heard one piece . . . It's that false idea of hi-tech society and all that, which is . . . doesn't exist. I don't think we're anywhere near that sort of society. It's an enormous myth that's been perpetuated – unfortunately, I guess – by readings of what I've done in that rock area at least, and in the consumer area television has an awful lot to answer for, with its fabrication of the computer-world myth.

Gary Numan: The bulk of the songs on the Tubeway Army album were based on science-fiction stories I'd been writing. I'd been trying to write a book, a collection of short stories that together described a particular world: a London of the future. So I looked like one of the characters in the book, a Mach man, which is half machine, half man. That was my look. When I was about sixteen, I went to London to buy my first proper guitar, and I was with a friend of mine called Gary Robson, and we saw a ghost. We got off the train, and there was a man in front of us and a group of young people in front of him, and as we got to the top of this escalator in Piccadilly Circus station this man went to the left, and we just followed him around without really taking much notice, and as we got around the corner there was a wall, and he wasn't there. We both saw him, and it freaked us out and we ran, and I've never forgotten that. And what the man was wearing was a long grey coat with a grey suit underneath it and a fedora, and he was smoking a cigarette. And so when I got famous I started to use that as an image. So, on *Pleasure Principle*, which was the first Gary Numan album, I started to dress like the man, the ghost that I'd seen.

David Bowie: He stole my entire act.

Bowie was always good at holding grudges, and he displayed his displeasure in fairly orthodox ways: by occasionally being blithely bitchy with interviewers and carefully pushing people out of his life or, worse still, embarrassing them at close quarters. Once, as a guest on Chris Evans's radio show in the 1990s, the DJ asked the star which of his records he'd like to hear. Bowie chose 'Cars' by Gary Numan. 'That's a good one, isn't it, eh?' he said, cattily. At the 2002 Meltdown festival, which he curated and where he performed his 1977 album Low *in its entirety, he was asked to make his usual selection of people to meet after the show. Like all entertainers of his magnitude, Bowie would normally be given a list of friends, journalists and boldface names who were at his shows, and he would then decide who would be asked backstage and in what order they would be received. At the Meltdown concert he was told that both Nick Rhodes and Simon Le Bon were in the audience, but only Rhodes was invited to meet him after the show. Another example of Bowie's ability to diminish those who had met with his disapproval involved an extremely senior BBC arts producer, who, having worked with Bowie early in his career, was always at pains to keep pally with him. When the producer flew all the way from London to New York to gatecrash a meeting about a BBC film instigated by a rival, he was left to stand for a full fifteen minutes before finally being acknowledged by Bowie and offered a chair.*

Gary Numan: I remember Brian Eno was a bit shit about me, as was Mick Jagger. And David Bowie said something like, 'With three albums in the charts, I thought there would be more going on.' I still had three albums in the charts, though, didn't I?

David Bowie: Electronics are rewarding in terms of playing around with atmosphere and trying to reach different parts of the mind, funny corners of the mind, but it's very hard to use those instruments without a kind of preconditioning already being there: that if you use a synthesizer, it means this particular thing, that I'm part of this angular society. Experimentation can be rewarding for finding awkward stances musically, but it just isn't satisfying after a while. And it's not satisfying because it's not very useful, except – as Brian Eno would say – for setting up a new kind of vocabulary.

Gary Numan: After a while I started to lose the plot a little. I didn't meet many people, to be really truthful, because of the Asperger's thing, as I always found talking and having conversations with people face to face quite difficult. So I wasn't really much of a one for going out and mixing and hanging out, you know? I just didn't. I was very much a stay-at-home. I was work obsessed as well, always trying to come up with new things. So I was a loner, I guess, partly for being shy and awkward, and partly because I was happy with my own company.

For a brief period, Numan was much in demand, and one day towards the end of the year he appeared on the Saturday-morning children's TV show Swap Shop, *where he was quizzed by viewers during a live phone-in session. The one question that the callers wanted answered was a simple one: why did he never smile? Fidgeting nervously, Numan (again not smiling) gave a very good impression of someone who would have been happy never to appear on breakfast television ever again.*

Midge Ure: Towards the end of 1979, I was asked to join Ultravox. Billy Currie was already doing Visage with me, so I saw the demise of Ultravox at first hand, with John Foxx leaving and being dropped by the record label and all of that stuff. The guitarist stayed in America, and it was just a nucleus of a great band. I would have loved to have joined them, but I was kind of shy. I didn't see that I was the guy to be in the band. Rusty did it for me. He said, 'Here's the guy – guitar, he can play a bit of keyboards, he can sing, he can write songs.' So that was something I kind of hoped for. There was no plan; I kind of fell into it. When I joined Ultravox, I wanted to be part of a rock band. I wanted it to be something experimental. I wanted it to be art rock. I wanted to be more Roxy Music than Kenny, so this was a great thing for me. I was allowed to kind of experiment and play and be led along by these three other guys who had much more experience in that world than I had.

Keanan Duffty (*designer, educator*): I lived in Doncaster, which had a small youth-culture scene, but we used to hang out a lot in Sheffield, Leeds and Manchester, sometimes even Birmingham. Doncaster had this really great music venue called the Outlook, and so all of the first wave of punk bands played there. I was thirteen in 1977, so I was a little bit too young to go to the Outlook, but the following year I started to go to gigs in and around the area, whether it was Leicester, De Montfort Hall, or City Hall in Sheffield, or whatever. My friends were at least four or five years older than me, so they were dragging me along to local punk shows. A few of them were already going to London and to Billy's, and getting the 125 train down and sleeping at King's Cross and coming back the next day and telling me all these great stories. When the New Romantic clubs started up here in 1979, we'd go to the Rum Runner in Birmingham, Pip's in Manchester, the Warehouse in Leeds or Primo's in Leeds, which is where Marc Almond used to DJ. Soft Cell played the Futurama festival in Leeds in 1979, along with the Banshees, Joy Division and A Certain Ratio. This was the first time I'd seen two people with a synthesizer since Suicide, but they were this whole other thing. It wasn't punk and it wasn't post-punk, and we didn't know what it was. It was a bit like fashion at the time, which went from black and white to colour. It was the same with the music. It became political, but with a small 'p'. You could say that it started with the glam thing, but it was only really the bands that could get away with wearing those looks. I mean, it was very hard to walk down the street dressed as Ziggy Stardust, but it was much more possible when the beginnings of punk happened, and I think that spirit re-emerged with the beginning of the New Romantics.

Martin Fry: Slowly Vice Versa turned into ABC. I just thought it was important to compete with James Brown and all those incredible R&B records, Motown, Stax, etc. We were playing Futurama and all those festivals with the likes of Depeche Mode, and we could have continued as a three-piece, but it just felt right to make it more organic and physical, more danceable. Of course, if I had known then what I know now, I wouldn't have attempted it, because it's completely naive to try and compete with the likes of Earth, Wind and Fire. We chased Alex Sadkin to produce the early ABC records because of all the work he'd done with Grace Jones, but those albums had Sly and Robbie on them, and we were never going to compete with them. We were also obsessed with David Bowie's 'Stay' and trying to work that art-and-funk hybrid. Later, we'd find out that there were other bands doing the same thing, people like Haircut 100 and Stimulin. So we became quite militant and determined to do whatever it was we were doing, well. We wanted to get as far away from rock'n'roll as possible, away from leather trousers, and redefine it all. Even in Vice Versa we had a manifesto. We had a postcard with a manifesto on it about what we liked, what we hated. You either hated stuff or loved it. It was really dogmatic, cheeky. But that's how you define yourself when you're that age. There wasn't a designer or a stylist or a record-company voice saying, 'Do it this way.' It was home-made. When I think about it, I think the eighties were truly revolutionary – politically, sexually. Not ABC so much, but the whole idea of the eighties. Having said that, I'm very proud of the records we would go on to make.

Nick Rhodes: I grew up with glam rock, so mascara was no big deal to me.

Martin Degville says that when he used to go to the Rum Runner, Duran Duran would come running up to him, asking for his autograph. 'They were like these spotty little kids who didn't have any idea . . . until they met the Berrows guys [the band's future managers].'

Midge Ure: I think this period had the same ethos as punk, just different tools. It was all about DIY, it was all about making it up. The kids who went to the Blitz hadn't got anything. It was the start of Thatcher's Britain – strikes, there was nothing going on. The club itself was in a really seedy part of town, and when they went there, they raided their granny's wardrobe or did whatever they did without having two pennies to rub together. It was entirely DIY. Make your own music, borrow a synthesizer, record it, do whatever – and that was the ultimate punk ethos.

Andrew Ridgeley (*singer, musician*): I was thirteen in '76, so punk kind of passed me by, as it did George [Michael], and it only really entered my life when the Sex Pistols did their TV interview with Bill Grundy. But it wasn't really on our radar in Bushey Meads. We were far more interested in disco and *Saturday Night Fever*. That was our perspective. Sylvester, 'Mighty Real' – stuff like that. We'd been to see Queen at Wembley in '77, and George and I had been to see Genesis at Earl's Court. We both loved Queen. How could you not? We liked Elton John, Roxy Music, the Eagles too. Lots of glam, lots of soul. But punk wasn't melodic or musical enough for me. I much preferred new-wave artists like Elvis Costello, XTC and the Jam. New wave went in parallel with disco, which we loved – Michael Jackson, etc. What punk did was liberate how people thought about creativity in the musical sense. It did for us. Punk gave birth to all these styles and varieties: ska, white reggae, Steel Pulse, the Police, UB40, the Selecter. We went to local clubs in Watford, Bogart's [in Harrow], places like that. I did A-levels, but all I wanted to do was perform and write songs, and we'd already formed a band, the Executive. I'd wanted to be in a band since I was about fifteen, and that's what the punk message was. Anyone could do it. The Executive played white reggae, ska, influenced by the Beat, the Police. We looked a little bit mod, a little bit ska, although George and I actually looked like penniless teenagers and got most of our clothes from the Sue Ryder shop in Watford.

There was no sense that we were rebelling, and there was no sense in the music either. Our parents probably thought we were going against the grain somewhat, but there was no artistic motivation to rebel. We had nothing to rebel against. Even though it was a tumultuous period in history, we had nothing to rebel against. Growing up in the suburbs, perhaps there wasn't the same kind of friction you had in the cities. We weren't the Specials. You could argue that the Sex Pistols were a rather confected rebellion, but Paul Weller, for example, was famously anti-Establishment. But for us it wasn't a pastime or a hobby; we had genuine ambition. A desire to make music, first and foremost, writing songs and performing them. The Executive did a couple of demos, and we thought we were close, but nothing came of it.

If anything was a harbinger of change, it was the Futurama festival that was held on the second weekend of September at the Queen's

Hall in Leeds. Billed as 'The World's First Science-Fiction Music Festival', the event showcased Joy Division, Orchestral Manoeuvres in the Dark, Simple Minds, Soft Cell, Echo and the Bunnymen, and Public Image Ltd, among many others, all of whom could be said to be making soundtracks for the future. The festival also featured film screenings, laser shows and a small futuristic army of people dressed up as robots. (One punter said that the sci-fi component didn't amount to much more than 'a genuinely futuristic 50p for a can of Coke'.) Science-fiction tropes were everywhere at the time, perhaps best exemplified stylistically by the retro-future ideas employed by the B-52's, who accessorised their bleep-bleep lava-lamp pop with Populuxe art direction and costumes beamed straight up from the sixties. The fictionalised future became a place where new groups would happily place themselves, especially those wielding synths rather than guitars, a fertile breeding ground for acts who were keen to explore their post-punk possibilities without being quite sure how to do so. Technology screamed progress, a modernist sensibility in a postmodern environment where cultural advancement could be measured in electronic drumbeats and wailing synthetic sirens. Bowie's sci-fi progeny were suddenly everywhere.

John Foxx: It was 1979, and I was living in a flat in Tollington Park, north London. I'd just left Ultravox, deciding to go solo at the end of the US tour for *Systems of Romance*, the band's third album. If I remember rightly, the last gigs were at the Whisky-A-Go-Go in LA. By this point, I was a bit of a cinder. *Systems* had been a joy to record, not least because we had Conny Plank as co-pilot. It was great to be working in Germany with the man who'd recorded Neu!, Cluster, La Düsseldorf, Can and Kraftwerk, all our heroes, and finally getting the big, sprawling sound we'd always wanted. But then came the touring. I love writing and recording – it's all to do with ambushing instinct with invention. Sure, it takes its toll, but it's touring that does the real damage. You get to feel like a ghost by week three and the Invisible

Man by week four. After that, I'm in for repairs. It was unfortunate, because all this coincided neatly with the very moment the band was at its peak – a proper organic unit, all plugged in and fizzing. We were meshed up with synths and drum machines and running at high voltage. But although it was frustrating to leave after reaching that point, I had to let it go and figure something else out, just in order to survive. So I left the band with the name and caught a plane back to London. I was certainly a bit nuts at the time, but I had a stack of new songs in my notebook. Something else was happening in the world, you see, and it had been nagging me for a while. It was important. For the first time ever, you could buy very cheap and totally portable synths. There was a new drum machine too, which had these great, awkward rhythms. It was a non-dancing genius Japanese programmer's drummer-replacement strategy – the Roland CR-78.

I had one at home, along with a few other bits: an ARP Odyssey, a Space Echo and an Elka string machine, plus an MXR flanger and phase pedal. With this magic kit, I realised I could make an album all by myself. This was an entirely new development. Bands were a pain, and the future looked mobile and agile. One or two guys with a synth, a drum machine, a tape machine and some imagination, and you were away. There was also a whole new language to be devised, as you had to rethink every element of a track and replace them all with synth functions. The old sonic hierarchies suddenly bit the dust. The dynamics were different, with very few chords and often no bass. Everything was skeletal now, everything mercilessly naked. The subjects of the songs had changed too: there were no love songs and no jolly stuff. Sure, there was a kind of humour, but it was far from light. It was urban, angular and dark, an architecture of longing and mystery, and it was all implicit in the natural sound of the machinery.

I began to notice a number of other musicians were on the same mission, although we were mostly unknown to each other. In 1978, Daniel Miller and Thomas Leer put out their home-made singles 'Warm Leatherette' and 'Private Plane', both pure DNA. Then there was Cabaret Voltaire, who had been ferocious pioneers for some time. Also in 1978 came the Human League's first record – well on the bleep in Sheffield – while Chris & Cosey were busy conspiring inside Throbbing Gristle.

An entirely new stream of music was emerging, and it was going to change everything. A genetic splice at first, then a complete technological mutation. It was around this time Gary Numan managed to distil the entire emerging scene into a couple of perfect singles that blew the door wide open for everyone else. It was brilliant and completely unforeseen. We were all on the launchpad now. The music suited the times perfectly. London was a half-derelict mash of roads and grey concrete, pretty grim, and so were all the northern ex-industrial cities. We'd been out there on our own, making the soundtrack of the era, but everything was starting to move into some weird kind of synchronicity. I could feel this was our time. It was urgent. It made my bike wobble with excitement.

I'd already decided that I had to design a whole new project and a whole new me. After punk's brief burnout, the job was to transmute that anger into a cool, blank fury – more efficient, more effective. Instead of a quick little ball of flame, this was a slow burn that could last for years. Technologically enabled primitivism. It needed to be psychopathically disciplined, ruthlessly minimal, and as cold as London concrete. All you needed was three instruments, a couple of effects boxes and an eight-track tape machine. In my wee head, I was the Marcel Duchamp of electro-pop. Fully charged. No mercy.

I booked Pathway, a demo cupboard in Islington, and a swift cycle ride from my place in Tollington Park, initially just to see how it might go. It had an eight-track machine and a home-built desk, but the sound was dead accurate, and you could dub on the desk. There was no switch delay. It cost a fraction of the big studios, the sound was more accurate, and you could experiment, take lots of chances.

So this was the start of the making of my first solo album. The music was firmly based on the noise and feel of London, plus a few other cities. Beautifully awful places. Plazas, cenotaphs, motorways.

Abandoned cars and abandoned industries, all lit by dusty, crackling neon. Perfect.

Metamatic was also a state of mind. A sort of exhausted romanticism. A man, a woman, a city. Alone and adrift in the metropolis, quietly attempting to maintain dignity and ever hopeful of romance. As for the tracks themselves, the idea for 'Underpass' came from a scary walk through an underground passageway after my car had broken down in Brussels one night. We got a great sound on the CR-78 by gating it hard, then Gareth [Jones] dubbed it up with plate echo to make the odd snare crash. The feel of the track was intended as a kind of electronic dub. We'd been listening in on what else was happening at Pathway, including a group of West Indian guys who were turning stolen Channel One tapes into dub twelve-inch singles, which were a very new thing at the time. These guys would dive into Pathway for a couple of hours to knock out a couple of mixes, and we were fascinated by what they were doing. A lot of the album was influenced by the fact I'd been reading sci-fi since seeing the film *Robot Monster* at the Royal in Chorley when I was a kid. I'd also picked up on T. S. Eliot and William Burroughs, mixing them up with Marvel Comics. Plus, of course, J. G. Ballard. A weird form of personal culture initially accumulated through uninformed and random grazing on market bookstalls. I especially liked the way Ballard got the link between the near future and now. I sometimes think he's still around, re-employed as a ghostwriter for the TV news. Splice all that with growing up in a northern industrial town, an art-school imagination, bad food, shabby old London, a sense of deep inadequacy, a fear of the immediate future and a sonic overexcitement. The result was 'Blackpool Neon Tango'. Or *Metamatic*, as it became. I suddenly realised this was it – science fiction was over. We were living there now.

As usual, the record company changed the schedule, holding over the release of the album until after Christmas, which meant *Metamatic* came out in January 1980. It happened to be the first synth record of the decade.

On Foxx's 'Underpass', the backing singers sounded as though they were shouting 'Underpants!', which managed to undermine Foxx's portrait of dystopian urban alienation somewhat. Elsewhere, the emergence of 'industrial' music was also making the post-punk scene rather complex. Some may have thought that the period was becoming more proscriptive, inching away from a top–down band/consumer experience to one revolving solely around the dancefloor, but this wasn't the case at all. In January 1979, I went to see Throbbing Gristle play the Centro Iberico, a disused school just off the Harrow Road in north-west London, and the audience was full of St Martin's students and people who were regulars at Billy's. This was a genuine event, one of the most enticing moments of the week (during a period when there were dozens and dozens each month), and the so-called cognoscenti didn't want to miss it. They were not disappointed: the sound was so loud it was almost barbaric, dry ice swelled throughout the crowd in such a sinister manner that there was a sense that it was deliberately threatening, and ABBA's 'Dancing Queen' disrupted proceedings halfway through the band's performance, jolting everyone back into their own reality. This was a time of Anything Goes, and so anything went . . .

Marc Almond: I'd go down to London with my friend. We thought we were very provincial, and went down trying to get some of that vibe. I ended up starting clubs in Leeds at the Warehouse, being influenced by what I saw in London. I stayed with actors I knew, and I was taken a lot to Soho. I was going to the early days of the Blitz club and things like that. I was friends with Molly Parkin, and I stayed with her most of the time, at her house in Cheyne Walk, which was owned by Keith Richards. She took me to all the discos, and we both wore black turbans and black coats – a kind of Taliban glam. I met her when she came up to Leeds with her artist husband Patrick Hughes to judge the degree show. Her daughter Sophie had started at the art college. Molly kind of adopted me.

This was around the time I met David Ball. Dave started in my last year at the art college. I was doing performance-art pieces and experimental theatre, coming from that punk ethic that used to shock people. Lots of nudity. Dave started making soundtracks, and he roped various people in, including me.

Ball was entranced by Almond's theatricality. 'His main piece was called "Mirror Fucking",' says Ball. 'He'd be naked in front of a full-length mirror, smearing himself with cat food and shagging himself. It provoked quite a reaction.' Their experimental minor-key pop followed soon after.

Marc Almond: David came along with this thing called a synthesizer, which at that time we only really knew from the likes of Keith Emerson and Rick Wakeman, who had huge banks of them. Eno had used one in Roxy Music, and I remember them on *The Old Grey Whistle Test* playing a ten-minute version of 'Ladytron', one of the greatest things I've ever seen on television. Then, of course, came the microchip, which made it possible to have small electronic instruments, including synthesizers. The first time I'd seen a synthesizer close up was when David Ball brought one to college. He was writing these little songs on it, and these were the very first Soft Cell songs. They were about TV advertising, subliminal messaging, suburban nightmares and things like that. I kind of blagged my way into Soft Cell really. I said I'd like him to do some music for my shows, 'And if you do some music for my performance shows, I wouldn't mind doing the vocals on some of your tunes.' And that's how it started, the genesis of Soft Cell – the future.

Antony Price: One day towards the end of the year, as the decade drew to a close, I was with the illustrator Tony Viramontes. He was messing about with some ideas, and he drew a picture of Grace Jones and Arnold Schwarzenegger, with all this muscle and texture and perfection and all these beautiful, sturdy lines, and I looked at it and said, 'That's what the eighties is going to look like.' And it did.

1980

THE CHARMS, SUCH AS THEY WERE

'*The Face* reflects the aspirations of a generation who no longer see a chic lifestyle as the sole birthright of the idle rich.'

SUNDAY EXPRESS

Rob Hallett: So, it's 1980, and suddenly colour appears.

Adam Ant: I was very much from this kind of underground thing, and then one performance on *Top of the Pops* – bang! I mean, a quarter of a million records . . . When you get into entertainment and you become a public figure, let's not forget you are *inviting* the public to acknowledge you, so you can hardly turn around later and say, 'Oh no, I want to be alone.' You know, if you want to do that, be like Greta Garbo – chuck it in and fuck off.

Harvey Goldsmith: The new bands were all about glamour. After the swirling, dark music of the early seventies, when you had all the bombastic music from the likes of the Pink Floyd, Genesis, Emerson, Lake & Palmer and Yes, and after all the aggression of the punk era, these new acts wanted to bring glamour to an industry that didn't need all the histrionics of the seventies. They were also far more professional largely, and if they were taking drugs, they were taking recreational drugs. They weren't on life support.

The Pretenders' 'Brass in Pocket' was the first No. 1 of the new decade, a song about money and ambition. Though it was a love song, the lyrics contained the kind of quiet determination found in material by Joni Mitchell, say, or Millie Jackson. By 1980, apparently, even affairs of the heart had become transactional. Peter York's Style Wars *was also published in 1980, and was just as prescient. More than any other British writer, York was responsible for inventing what became known as 'style journalism'. Writing in* Harpers & Queen, *York's new school of journalism was a 'mock-heroic' exercise in understanding society by reading its surface. Pigeonholing then became something of a 'thing', as yuppies (Young Urban Professionals) were heralded as the unacceptable face of professional success; few synthesised concepts of class and status have acquired so much amoral resonance so quickly. They were followed in quick succession by guppies (gay urban professionals), dinkies (double income, no kids), dockneys (east Docklands London yuppies), poupies (Porsche-owning urban professionals) and buppies (black urban professionals). As for the New Romantics, they were now firmly established in Fleet Street circles, as figures of both extraordinary glamour and, of course, fun. London itself suddenly became a hot topic too, as the media started to acknowledge it as a shape-shifting city, celebrating its old brick and stone while applauding its new steel and glass, witnessing a cultural capital that was experiencing yet another rebirth, a slip from the dank and dismal seventies to the seemingly limitless possibilities of a decade rapidly adorning itself with shoulder pads and warpaint and the occasional pantomime pop star. The world of commerce was initially unsure as to how to react, eventually boiling down 'the look' to frilly shirts, satin knickerbockers and make-up.*

One of the ways to see the shift from the garish riotousness of punk to the flamboyance of the New Romantics is through the prism of Adam Ant, a performer who went from being a kind of camp renegade to a popular entertainer in the time it took to visit a theatrical costumier. There was a fundamental difference between those who became successful during the first flush of punk and those who started being noticed during the New Romantic era, three years later: the punks didn't know how to embrace popularity without negating their cool quotient, while the New Romantics would turn out to be more like the pop groups of the early sixties, more than happy to encourage success in pretty much any form. Their credibility seemed entwined with their commercial appeal, or at least the two things weren't mutually exclusive. The Clash were one of the few early punk bands to achieve true supergroup status, and part of their appeal – indeed, part of their DNA – was their struggle with the existential notion of being popular on a global scale. Adam Ant wanted to be successful, but when that aim appeared initially to have eluded him, he sought help in the form of the man who had masterminded the Sex Pistols, Malcolm McLaren.

The original Ants weren't what you would call accomplished – in 1977, few people were, and you would have been suspicious if they had been – but they knew what to do on stage: namely, create a din that spoke of every transgressive act one could imagine. Before 'Adam' successfully reinvented himself as a dandy highwayman and short-term pin-up, he actually made some interesting records, most memorably 'Young Parisians' and 'Dirk Wears White Sox'. None of them were the type of thing you were ever going to hear at a wedding, however, which is one of the reasons he decided to enlist the help of McLaren in order to turn himself into a star.

In 1979, having agreed to become a managerial consultant to Adam for the princely sum of £1,000, McLaren had given him a mix tape that was meant to suggest where the singer might go next creatively. It included 'Wipe Out' by the Surfaris, 'Mystery Train' by Elvis Presley, 'Rave On' by Buddy Holly, 'You've Got to Pick a Pocket or Two' by Ron Moody (from Lionel Bart's Oliver!*) and, saliently, 'Burundi Black' by Burundi Black, 'Hello! Hello! I'm Back Again' by Gary Glitter and 'Cast Iron Arm' by Peanuts Wilson, three songs driven by drums. Even so, McLaren wasn't impressed with what Adam then produced, and proceeded to steal his band, forming a new one around them, Bow Wow Wow (as he had rechristened them), whose new lead singer McLaren found in a dry cleaner's in Kilburn – Annabella Lwin, a fourteen-year-old half-Burmese girl whose real name was Myant-Myant Aye Dunn. McLaren named Bow Bow Wow in honour of Nipper, the dog who was known as the mascot of HMV (His Master's Voice), the music retail division of EMI.*

Adam Ant: I think everybody has to go through a very honest situation of imitation to discover themselves fashion-wise, music-wise. What I tried to say is that those ideas weren't mine. They were never mine. Any ideas I had at the time were someone else's. The only originality I had was the way I put it together. And that's the beauty of fashion – by the time a fashion is established, it's dead, so you're always behind yourself.

David Hepworth (*editor, journalist*): A big factor in the new pop of the eighties was video, which is why Adam Ant was so popular. He was the first big act for *Smash Hits*, and he was absolutely huge, all thanks to video. Around this time Felix Dennis used to do unlicensed poster magazines, and he did one of Adam and the Ants. Because Adam had copyrighted his look, with the beauty spot, Felix just flipped the image back to front with a projector.

Adam Ant: I originally liked the name because it suited my physique. My real name's Stuart Goddard. When you're naming a group, the more ambiguous the title, the better. Names are very critical, they are very, very important. The sort of energy I was drawing upon at that stage had nothing to do with insects. It was later that I used the insect imagery in the lyrics, because it was right in front of me, but I started using slogans, if you like, 'sales points' or 'ear points', because I was influenced by the [Phil] Spector sound and felt that the most difficult thing to achieve was a sound people would recognise. You hear an ABBA record on the radio and you know it's ABBA, it can't be anybody else, and I think that's the hardest single thing to achieve in music.

Chris Salewicz (*journalist*): For at least the last two years of the seventies, Adam and the Ants had led the league as the group name most favoured by mutant punks for spraying on the backs of their Lewis Leather jackets – the absurdly titled *Dirk Wears White Sox* album had been a considerable seller ever since it was first put out on the independent Do-It label on 1 January 1980. Even so, there had long been a suspicion that Adam and his chaps were really rather silly – or, perhaps, a little sinister. Certainly, it had not been good for Adam's reputation to have been featured in Derek Jarman's precious *Jubilee*. That apart, however, his punk credibility was pretty unblemished: formed at the Roxy, managed by Jordan, apparently stitched up by Malcolm McLaren . . . Adam, of course, is yet another rock'n'roll product of the English art-school system. He quit Hornsey in 1976, two-thirds of the way through his graphics course: 'I didn't see the point in spending the bulk of the third year writing a thesis – it had no relation to what you were going to be earning your living doing. I'd done all the graphics for the Ants, though: I was lucky to be able to incorporate the skills I'd acquired into my *work*.' His worship of *style* found its Godhead early on in another example of British art-school rock'n'roll output: 'Bryan Ferry was like a mentor to me, even though I never met him. He had so much attention to detail, and he never lowered his standards. I think that is something admirable in any artist, whatever they're doing.' The Antmusic For Sexpeople motto under which he traded seemed more like a Freudian glimpse of Scorpio Adam's psyche than a true definition of the heavily percussive music of this version of Adam and the Ants, a noise that was really closer to camp than smouldering sexuality, more Gary Glitter than Jim Morrison.

Malcolm McLaren: I found my way back to London and into the arms of Adam and the Ants. Vivienne was at that time nestling thoughts of recreating clothes from eighteenth-century pattern books, clothes that had a kind of ethnicity and a kind of piracy about them, so this idea of fusing all the imagery together with the Burundi drumming was creating something particular. There was a sense that in order to reinvent the cultural spirit of punk, you needed to create something not black, but colourful. At the time, it was more to do with gold; a little bit more theatrical, the opposite of all the black and chrome that was so strong with punk rock. I happened to notice some pictures of Geronimo, and apparently when the Apaches used to go to war, they would paint this white line across their face, and that looked very powerful, and I liked the marriage of that with the black look of Adam. I thought, 'This boy is really going to be a big hit.' I could sense it then. When he put that on, he was made, really. My job ended right there.

Adam Ant: Malcolm McLaren had come in with these ideas, you know, heroics, and he was more into the Indian stuff. During the ten-day period that I worked with him before he basically got the band to kick me out, I paid him £1,000. And anything I got out of that particular time I felt equipped to use, and I did. McLaren said to me when he met me, 'You have got two things going for you: you look good and you've got muscles.' But I couldn't work with him because I didn't want to make a porno film with the Slits [whom McLaren was managing at the time] in Mexico, which was one of his ideas. Because Malcolm is a voyeur. He was [going] on about the homosexual Apaches. Lyrically, if you listen to Bow Wow Wow, most of the lyrics are Malcolm, and they're not very good. Because Malcolm can't sing or write. He's an agent provocateur. He's a good tailor. He knows a lot about rock'n'roll. I wouldn't take that away from him, but he cannot sing and he cannot write. And he could never deal with that. And he [got] a kick out of getting young, usually working-class people to go do the work for him, then taking the credit. I mean, he ends up on television with Melvyn Bragg. I think he wanted the Adam and the Ants audience because we could sell out the Lyceum and places like that, the Electric Ballroom, without a record company, without a record out really. But basically we had this amazing audience. It was very hardcore, the real thing. And McLaren always wanted that for the Pistols. Left alone, the Pistols had it. But with him, they got into the whole . . . Malcolm to me is Laurence Harvey in *Expresso Bongo*. And he can't get away from it. He's a spiv, with a very strong opinion of himself, which is fine. But if you've got a good idea, you'd best keep it to yourself.

Having stolen Adam's band, McLaren needed some kind of ideology to wrap around them. He had already decided to focus on the cassette tape's ability to bring about the downfall of the record industry, principally by espousing home taping; and he had also decided to co-opt the Burundi-drumming idea that he had already suggested (and sold) to Adam Ant. But this wasn't enough. For a while he wanted Bow Wow Wow to be a 'gay band', in his own words, at least according to the band's guitarist, Leigh Gorman. 'Homosexual Apaches is what he wanted us to be. He took us to Heaven when it first opened because he wanted us to be gay for a while – he thought gay bands would be in vogue – and he'd say, "Come on, boys, I want you to try it, you'd be great as a gay band."' Bizarrely equating homosexuality with sexual perversity, McLaren encouraged his charges to explore the carnal delights of Soho, but only managed to amplify their innate heterosexuality, according to Gorman, and they spent an inordinate amount of time with prostitutes (as did McLaren himself). It seems sex obsessed McLaren at the time, which is why he enjoyed the furore over Annabella.

When McLaren had first envisioned the Sex Pistols, he had imagined a group who were young, childish, anarchic and what he called 'sexy assassins'. At the time, he was obsessed with the Situationist slogan 'autonomy for kids', while many of his designs for SEX and Seditionaries (which was what McLaren and Westwood rechristened their shop in December 1976) involved sexual themes. With Bow Wow Wow, though, he took sexual transgression too far. He laid out his stall by recreating Édouard Manet's famous painting Le Déjeuner sur l'herbe, *starring Annabella Lwin as the naked central figure (traditionally described as a prostitute), but his big idea for the band was to use them as an excuse to publish* Chicken *(originally titled* Playkids*), which, removed from McLaren's contextualisation, was ostensibly a piece of paedophile propaganda. For the arch manipulator, this was the last taboo: the sexualisation of children. 'I find sexuality in children a really potent way of them laying claim against this society,' he said. 'Sex, ultimately, as you know, is one of the most powerful selling forces* *in the world. It's something everybody cares about, and it has a lot of magic and a lot of taboos.'*

Bow Wow Wow's first single, 'C-30 C-60 C-90 Go!' was released on cassette – the numbers referring to the standard running times of cassette tapes – in a bid to encourage and promote home taping, 'pirating the goods of the big corporation'. Ironically, the band's record company was EMI, who had famously signed, and then unceremoniously dropped, the Sex Pistols. The subtext of all the promotional material, as well as many of the lyrics of Bow Wow Wow's songs, referenced the empowering of children, although inevitably McLaren simply looked as though he was exploiting them, and in particular the girl he was supposedly managing. Fred Vermorel, an old friend of his, thought his strategy was to create a child-porn scandal, pointing out the hypocrisies of the industry by highlighting the record business's habit of exploiting children – and not just sexually.

Alan Yentob: It must have been late 1979, early 1980, when I first met Malcolm properly, probably at some party in the West End. We started having coffee together occasionally, as after the Sex Pistols he was starting to come up with new projects, one of which was Bow Wow Wow. I was doing the BBC arts programme *Arena* at the time, and we must have decided to make a film about him. Either that or he approached me. This was just after he'd gone and worked with Adam Ant, who clearly was his practice run, using the Burundi drumming. Basically, what happened is, he decided he was going to use all that somewhere else, so he stole Adam's band and found this girl, Annabella Lwin, in a dry cleaner's. Or at least that was the story. So we started making the film, but then her parents complained to the BBC about it, and clearly there was a sexual dimension to this. So we stopped the filming, as I thought, 'We can't go ahead with this,' because the implications were that if we carried on . . . Well, Malcolm was a mischief-maker, that's what he did. That was his vocation: a disruptor and an artist. The notion that it was provocative didn't worry him at all.

This was the whole *Chicken* thing. 'Chicken' was a colloquial term for underage boys and girls, and Malcolm wanted to produce a pleasure mag for adults, featuring kids as objects. It was there to incense people. The proposition was to make a magazine based on the same ideas as he was conceiving for Bow Wow Wow. In other words, provocative, sexual, teenage and subversive. And if you think of those images of her, she had no clothes on. And she was thirteen [*sic*] at the time. He dressed this girl, or undressed her, kept her looking the way he wanted her to.

Malcolm had a complex upbringing. His mother . . . there was even talk of prostitution. He didn't get on with his mother, was brought up by his grandmother, was always interested in clothes. 'Sex' was a word which came out of his mouth continually, all the time. Why were the Sex Pistols called the Sex Pistols? He had undermined the conventional music business once, and he wanted to do it again, wanting to address what he thought was unspoken about sexuality and music. Just look at the song titles – 'Hello, Hello Daddy', 'Sexy Eiffel Tower', 'Giant-Sized Baby Thing', 'Radio G-String'. We thought, 'Oh my goodness, something's going on here.' I could see it was going to be an issue, so we stopped. It was very unusual for us to abandon a film, because the thing about documentaries is, you could make them all work if you spent time in the cutting room. Somebody said he had trapped me in it in some way, but I don't think that's true, but being the BBC, with a young girl in these circumstances and the parents not liking it, I had to stop.

Adam Ant: Malcolm McLaren just said to me, 'What do you want, Adam?' I said, 'I'd like to be a household name and have everyone know and like Adam and the Ants.' He said, 'You're making it very difficult for yourself.' And he was right! He sorted me out. He went through my first album word-by-word, note-by-note, and just said what was what. I think he realised early on there was no way I was going to sing about cassettes or sing his lyrics, which is what all the Bow Wow Wow words are. I did try, but I couldn't work under those conditions.

McLaren once attempted an autobiography with the journalist Barry Cain, and though it remains unpublished, those who have read it have been shocked by some of its sexual content. One salient passage sees McLaren wandering into his bathroom at home, aged six, to see his mother and a male companion defecating on each other in the family bathtub. If this was the atmosphere at home, then it's no surprise he would develop a complicated relationship with sex.

Adam Ant: From my point of view, my success was due to the songs. Which Malcolm had nothing to do with. The imagery, he had very little to do with. He may have sparked off a few ideas, but he delivered it in a completely different way, around Vivienne's collection. I did it much more, if you like, crudely. I went to Berman's and Nathan's and got David Hemmings's jacket from *The Charge of the Light Brigade* and studied the Apache and declared war on the music business. That's what I did. But I had been fucking about with make-up for two years, which was at the base of it. The kabuki face had been over two years. I just put the line across and it was there. [After being on television], the next week we sold a quarter of a million records. I mean, I'd waited three fucking years to get on TV.

Marco Pirroni: I'd already played with Siouxsie and the Banshees in their debut gig at the Roxy, and I'd been in the Models and various other bands, but in 1980 Adam asked me to join the Ants. I'd gone to audition for the Banshees, as they wanted me to play with them full-time, but I didn't really want to do it. And the next day, I had a note through the door from Adam Ant. I thought, 'What the fuck does he want?' He was doing this white-sock thing but couldn't shake off the punk audience, and it was holding him back. We met in this cafe in Covent Garden, and he said his favourite band was Roxy Music. I said, 'Yes, mine too.' So that was it, and we started from there. Adam and the Ants obviously had millions of other influences as well, but the core of it was always Roxy Music. We didn't do Roxy quite as literally as Duran Duran or Spandau, and we didn't look like Roxy, but it was all about taking those disparate elements and putting them together. That was the idea. We took Ennio Morricone, the Glitter Band and the ideas that Malcolm had sold to Adam – including Burundi Black, glam-rock guitars and tribal chanting. We were told we were anti-synth, but we just didn't know how to use them, and other people were doing it better.

As for Adam's white stripe across his face, it was basically his version of the *Aladdin Sane* lightning bolt. We knew we needed something that kids could copy, so it needed to be really simple. We desperately wanted people to come to gigs dressed as us, and they did.

Alan Yentob: I think even Malcolm knew he'd gone too far with *Chicken*, not that he was embarrassed in any way. He just moved on.

Annabella Lwin (*singer*): My mother was used as a publicity vehicle for the album, and unfortunately it caused a huge rift between me and her while I was still in my teens. It was quite a difficult period both for my mother and myself. I guess somewhere along the line I have to thank my source in the universe for protecting me from the sex, drugs and all the rest of it.

Adam Ant: At the time, it was devastating [when Malcolm stole my band], because obviously we were buddies. Dave [Barbarossa] and Matthew [Ashman], myself, and Leigh Gorman was the new kid who had just joined. One thing's a band splitting up, but with that there's a friendship and the camaraderie, and that came into question. I think Malcolm saw a situation where he could conveniently get a really good band to back up the idea he had. A lot of water has gone under the bridge since then, but it was devastating on a personal level. On a professional level, it turned out to be pretty good for both parties. I couldn't have seen it happening without that. We were very close doing our thing, and then someone else came in and started casting doubts amongst us. That created a kind of mutiny, if you like. But they did Bow Wow Wow gladly, which I thought was a really good project and sounded great, and I did *Kings of the Wild Frontier*, which was my view of things. We'd all sat around listening to hours and hours of philosophy by Malcolm about taking rock'n'roll back to its basics, and him playing us all kinds of records, from Django Reinhardt to Charlie Parker, through to various ideas Malcolm had in his head. He'd talk to you for about an hour on something, and if you were lucky, you would understand a minute of it. Making those kinds of ideas turn into reality just involves a lot of work. I just sat there and listened, and it sparked off certain directions for me. But what he was talking about in those meetings was pretty much what you hear when you hear the Bow Wow Wow sound. Mine was more . . . There are timpani drums in *Kings*. There are thirty layers of vocals on it, which I did, so I didn't fit into that idea that Malcolm wanted us to fit into. I had to put my hand up and say, 'This really isn't working for me. I'm not quite getting the vibe off this.' When he got the band to say they wanted to leave, I certainly had the name and I had these threads of ideas, but nothing that fitted in with what they were doing, so I came out of it and went and started again. There was still a competitiveness. I thought, 'I'm not going to waste all this time sitting listening to this lot and not use it, because I paid for it.' I think I got my money's worth.

Marco Pirroni: I remember going into meetings with CBS when we first signed, having to explain the concept of Adam and the Ants because all the record-company guys were Clash fans. I had to explain that we wanted to be pop stars: 'You know what pop stars do, don't you? They go on stage in make-up and stuff and they sing songs, and their songs sell lots, and then they make lots of money and then they buy cars and houses and things. That is what we're doing.' I mean, it's very traditional. I don't think Spandau or Duran or Bananarama gave a fuck about credibility. We didn't. We were into showbiz, not politics.

Peter Ashworth: I ended up doing the Adam Ant album *Kings of the Wild Frontier*. Adam was just about to get his first-ever gig on *Top of the Pops*. He hadn't seen himself on film before, and video had basically been invented while I was at LCP. For the film he booked an office not far from Brixton Town Hall, and he and the band were basically faking it. The guys with guitars had guitars, but the guy who played drums just had drumsticks, with Adam standing in front, with a video crew in front of them. I was there to shoot stills. Of course, I couldn't see anything because the video crew was standing in front of me. But there was a bloody great monitor to my left, and I realised the pictures on the monitor were actually quite interesting. So I started shooting off the monitor when I couldn't get a look-in. The record company thought this looked really interesting, so a week later we booked the video suite at CBS in Soho Square and did it properly. I spent the entire day shooting off the video. I was going to get the next sleeve, the one where he moved from being whatever he was to being a pirate. He was going to do it on a ship, and we met for a quick chat about it. He told me, 'We're going to be on this old ship.' And I said, 'How about if . . .' And he said, 'Get out!' Because I had dared to suggest something. He didn't even let me finish. He basically didn't want to hear anyone's opinion.

Marco Pirroni: Before the tour, I wasn't famous at all, but we just exploded. We started in fairly small venues, and by the end we're doing three nights at the Dominion. We started off playing Manchester Students' Union and ended up playing the Manchester Apollo. It just got bigger and bigger, and in six weeks our lives had changed completely. We hadn't had any money yet, but we were seeing things like pictures of Adam and the Ants on Weetabix packets.

Boy George: Everybody was starting groups, and I was just looking around me. I had seen Steve Strange jumping on stage with Chelsea at the Vortex, and I was just watching everybody starting bands and I knew people who'd picked up the bass and learnt to play it in a couple of months. I knew Matthew Ashman from Bow Wow Wow and Adam and the Ants, and he was a really good friend of mine, and one day he heard me singing. He said I had a good voice and said he wished he could have me in Bow Wow Wow. Malcolm McLaren later tried to take the credit for choosing me to sing with the band, but I think he just asked me to sing to upset Annabella, because I looked like a girl. He only used me to piss her off, because she wasn't doing what she was told. So I did these two gigs with Bow Wow Wow, one at Manchester University and one at the Rainbow. Vivienne desperately wanted me to wear Seditionaries clothes, but I was trying to get them without having to wear them [on stage], so I could take them home. I remember being aware that I didn't want to be just another person dressed head to toe in Westwood. I was pushed on stage and immediately thought to myself, 'Oh God, I love this.' So it was a bit accidental, a little bit circumstantial. I definitely knew I wanted to be known. I don't think I would have used the word 'famous' then, but I certainly wanted people to know who I was. I remember from the age of fourteen riding the train from Blackheath and seeing all those lights on in people's houses and just thinking, 'Oh, it's really sad – all these people will never know who I am, and I won't know who they are.' So I was in Bow Wow Wow for five minutes, before Malcolm fired me because he thought I was trying to take over. After that I was like, 'I've got to prove him wrong.' He obviously didn't see me as anyone worth bothering with. I always loved Malcolm. I was always so impressed with him. I used to go around telling people he managed me, when he didn't.

Adam Ant: I think punk had become very much a caricature of itself, and it got very grey and very political. The kids were wearing the same kind of drab outfits. I've never been a political artist. I keep that out of my work. I've never been interested in that. I think it had become quite excessively violent, the gigs were getting more violent because of that, and it was just not enjoyable. Post-punk brought out some interesting music, but I felt that I just needed a way to suddenly make it a bit more colourful. Up until that point, I'd only used black and white in the graphics, in the handbills and record covers and stuff like that. So I suddenly just wanted to do the opposite of that, something heroic and celebratory, really. That's where *Kings of the Wild Frontier* came in: I wanted to be like a king, not just some guy hanging on the corner moaning about everything and spitting and wearing safety pins, which I've never been interested in!

Antony Price: In 1980, you had Vivienne on one side of the King's Road with punk, and you had me on the other with Plaza, which was all glam. So we've got these two things going on, and the new groups are starting to cross the road all the time, from one to the other.

Nick Rhodes: The moment we saw Adam Ant dressed as Prince Charming, we knew the New Romantic look was all over. When EMI gave Duran Duran our first clothes budget, we went straight to designer Antony Price and blew it on suits. In those days they cost £300, which was a lot, but I think we got the 'cute young band' discount.

Steve Dagger: In early 1980, I heard there was another group in Birmingham: Duran Duran. As I perceived it, they had a disadvantage as they weren't in London. My whole thing was we had to be quick because there were starting to be a lot of others. There were similar sorts of clubs in every big city – you had Pips in Manchester, the Rum Runner in Birmingham, Maestro's in Glasgow, Valentino's in Edinburgh, and there were various clubs in Sheffield. The idea of playing keyboard-orientated electronica came from those clubs. And so it was very quick. Some of these bands already existed – Depeche Mode. We [Spandau Ballet] had the first hit record, but we were followed very quickly by Duran Duran and also by Visage, Soft Cell, but I wasn't in the least bit surprised.

Duran Duran's name was inspired by the villain played by Milo O'Shea in Roger Vadim's 1967 sci-fi spoof Barbarella, *starring Jane Fonda. The band's bassist, John Taylor, remembers sitting at home one night watching the film on the BBC. 'I'd always liked the film, thinking it was so sexy, but this time was struck more by the words "Durand Durand", which kept getting repeated. A man's name, in fact, was what it was. Well, I had a little combo of extrovert nature happening at the time, centred at our Birmingham City Art School. There was myself, Nick Rhodes, Stephen Duffy, and a forgotten clarinettist, Simon Colley. The sounds we were making were quite out of the way and required an out-of-the-way moniker. After some small deliberation, the shoe fit.' In their first interviews, Duran Duran liked to repeat that they were influenced by the Sex Pistols and Chic (although Nick Rhodes would also refer to his band as 'a cross between Kraftwerk and the Monkees'), while always referencing Bowie and Roxy Music as the reasons they all fell in love with pop in the first place. In this they weren't alone, although they were the first New Romantic band to actually ask Antony Price to design their clothes for them. In reality, they owed an even bigger debt to Roxy. In May, Roxy Music released their seventh album,* Flesh and Blood, *which contained one of their finest latter-day singles, 'Same Old Scene', a production that sounded more modern than most of the records that surrounded it in the charts. If many of the New Romantic bands claimed to have been influenced by the style and panache of Roxy, in a more prosaic way Duran were actually influenced far more by this record, as sonically it became something of a template for them, with its shiny amalgamation of clattering disco drums, glistening keyboards and mannered vocals. The critic Paul Stump rightly says that the song 'was imprinted upon every new popster's eardrum almost immediately, most notably Duran Duran, who first built a debut single ("Planet Earth") and then a career upon this one brief moment of Roxy Music studio harmonisation'.*

Betty Page (*journalist*): After I'd done the big New Romantics interview in *Sounds*, I became a magnet for every ruffle-shirted chancer in the country. The letters, demo tapes and grainy snapshots poured in. I'd never seen such a parade of badly applied blusher and sucked-in cheeks. So, when I received a phone call from the manager of a Birmingham-based band called Duran Duran, I had, understandably, developed a healthy cynicism. But Paul Berrow was a smooth operator. 'Come to the Rum Runner,' he said of the club he co-owned with his brother Michael. 'We've got a scene going on up here to put the Blitz to shame, and a band to go with it.' He had singled me out to be the first journalist to write about his band – and they actually wanted to be called New Romantics (fancy that!). I knew from talking to Steve Strange that there was plenty of fine posing going on in Birmingham and I wanted to investigate it further. On that basis, I agreed to take up Berrow's offer. The Rum Runner was impressive – smart, spacious and futuristic – unlike most of the clubs in London at that time, which were cubicle-sized and decorated with flock wallpaper that hadn't been replaced since the sixties. The Berrow brothers were charming and knew exactly what they were doing, which was packaging a pop band in the fashion of the moment. But they weren't Svengalis – just a pair of clued-up businessmen who'd found themselves a bunch of smart boys – average age nineteen – who all had the potential to become teen idols. In the beginning, there were three Taylors – John (bass), Andy (guitar) and Roger (drums) – joined by Nick Rhodes (keyboards) and Simon Le Bon (vocals). Nick was the most obvious New Romantic – a bouffant blond David Sylvian lookalike who sported frilly shirts and shiny suits – but the style sat rather uncomfortably on the rest of them. The alarmingly pretty, floppy-fringed bassist John drew the line at satin shirts and a shoulder sash. Le Bon, a former drama student at Birmingham University who was a little on the podgy side, took up the look enthusiastically but rather theatrically, in velvet and a selection of miniature jingle bells. Andy, whose natural style prefigured Jon Bon Jovi, clearly had to be bribed into wearing a tunic and pixie boots.

And the shy but smouldering drummer Roger just looked profoundly embarrassed by it all and stuck to his trusty leather trousers. I worked out pretty quickly that they were not on the same sartorial planet as Spandau Ballet. Their claim to be a New Romantic band fell down when they took the support slot on a Hazel O'Connor tour – a smart marketing move, but not high on the credibility scale. Duran, however, saw it as a way to reach a wider audience. Not for them the Spandau-style secret gigs to an invited elite.

Rob Hallett: I'd done the 'Punky Reggae' nights at the Vortex and had worked with the Sex Pistols, X-Ray Spex, the Damned, the Killjoys [Kevin Rowland's first band], Johnny Thunders, lots of punk bands. When Joe Strummer asked me to book Tapper Zukie, I started promoting a lot of Jamaican bands and got a reputation as the reggae guy. Which is probably why I got a call from UB40, who wanted me to look after them. I said, 'You're white boys from Birmingham, I'm into the real reggae from Kingston, why should I be interested in you?' But they had made a great record, and I started booking them. Then they told me about this group that were rehearsing in the same place as them that I probably wouldn't like but should check out anyway. It was Duran Duran. I knew we ought to start marketing them to fourteen-year-olds as well as twenty-year-olds, because you could immediately see their appeal.

Alan Edwards (*publicist*): I was managing Hazel O'Connor, who had just had a huge hit with *Breaking Glass*, which was a British post-punk movie. She was about to go on tour, and a few weeks beforehand I got a cassette in the post. It was a tatty envelope and there weren't enough stamps on it, but nevertheless I played it, because in those days that's how people sent you new music – by cassette. It was sent from the Berrow brothers, these guys from Birmingham who ran the Rum Runner and who were quite aggressive in business. So I stuck the tape on and I quite liked it, and I booked them for the tour, to support

Hazel. It was when we played the Birmingham Odeon that I realised we might potentially have a problem, as they were going down much better than a support act should. And as we moved closer to London, every night they were getting more and more applause, and Hazel was getting less and less, so I was unwittingly responsible for the slowing of her career and the acceleration of Duran's. A few weeks later, they were the biggest thing to come out of Britain since punk.

Nick Rhodes: I'll tell you what, that tour we did supporting Hazel O'Connor did us so much good. It meant we played everywhere from Manchester Apollo to the Marquee, tested them out, learnt how to win an audience. Like Chris Spedding said to me, 'If you rehearse nine days a week, you become very good at rehearsing; if you play nine dates a week, you become very good at playing live.'

Rob Hallett: Harvey Goldsmith was very quick to try and steal Duran Duran off me.

Dave Ambrose was the A&R man who signed Duran Duran and who immediately saw their potential, thinking that Simon Le Bon looked like a born-again Elvis Presley, albeit an overweight one. 'Margaret Thatcher and Milton Friedman came along and offered a new vision of right-wing thinking: "Every man for himself and let's make lots of money." Duran Duran and Spandau Ballet, I think, up to a point, suggested a celebration of "Let's go out and get it, let's go and enjoy it, and who cares?"'

At this time, Depeche Mode were still performing as Composition of Sound and building up a strong local following at Croc's, a former Tesco store in Rayleigh, Essex. Croc's is where many of the New Romantic bands played their first gigs. John Fatman, who was one of the original DJs at the club, remembers how 'Spandau Ballet came one night, stood in a huddle for an hour, and left in a huff as no one acknowledged or hero-worshipped them. If you wanted to pose, you went to the Blitz, Hell, Heaven or the Mud Club. For a great night out, the same people came to Croc's.'

Depeche Mode were the boys from Basildon – Vince Clarke, Andy Fletcher, Martin Gore and Dave Gahan – who formed what would become 'the most popular electronic band the world has ever known', and who would go on to have such poppy electronica hits such as 'New Life', 'Just Can't Get Enough' and 'Get the Balance Right'. They had geometric haircuts, clothes that could have come from Gerry Anderson's costume department, and always looked terribly serious about what they did whenever they were on television. In a way, they were a synth-pop bromide.

Daniel Miller: Betty Page from *Sounds* was a big supporter of Depeche Mode in the early days, as before she started writing about them they hadn't had any press, apart from something in the *Basildon Echo*, for which the headline was 'Posh Clobber Could Clinch It for Mode', which meant that if they had a half-decent dress sense, they might make it, which has been a running joke for forty years.

I saw Depeche play at the Bridge House in Canning Town. I liked the early Human League singles, Cabaret Voltaire and OMD, but I wasn't hanging out with these people. I got to know Throbbing Gristle a bit, but for me people like Ultravox were already kind of old school in a way. A terrible thing to say. So I didn't really have any pop aspirations at all, but when I saw Depeche I couldn't quite believe what I heard or what I saw. I was excited that there was a new generation of kids who were using synthesizers in the way they had once used guitars. This was genuinely new, and I was excited at the prospect of what might happen with that new context. When I saw Depeche, they were very young – sixteen, seventeen, eighteen – playing very simple, cheap synthesizers perched on beer crates. They were like home-made New Romantics, playing these brilliantly arranged, incredible songs with a drum machine. They had a very shy, gothy lead singer who didn't move throughout the gig. He looked about twelve at the time, and I just couldn't quite believe the combination of their age, the music, the way they put the songs together. Afterwards I went and had a chat with them, and after a while asked if they wanted to put out a single. I made the same arrangement I'd made before with artists, a strict fifty–fifty profit share. I said, 'No long-term contracts, let's do a single and see how it goes,' even though I knew they had more potential pop crossover than anyone else I'd worked with. And so it started.

Then the major record companies started sniffing around, offering these big deals, and the band turned them all down. They wanted to stay independent, even though they were being offered all this money. I mean, they were all working-class kids. Martin and Fletcher had low-level jobs in the City, Dave was at college and Vince was unemployed, but even though they were offered these stupidly good deals, for whatever reason they decided to stick with Mute.

Kate Mossman (*journalist*): When Dave Gahan – the future singer of Depeche Mode – was ten years old, he came home from school to find a man sitting at the kitchen table who, his mother told him, was his father. The person he thought was his father had died a year earlier. The man at the table took him and his sister out for the day – 'bought us a gift; I think he bought me a sweater' – and didn't come back. The man, a bus driver called Len Callcott, of Malaysian ancestry, had left the family when Gahan was six months old. 'I am told I sort of *knew* about this?' he says. He later found out that Len used to call a neighbour, Mrs Clarke, one of the few people in the neighbourhood who had a phone, and ask after him. The messages were not relayed by his mother. 'I could have done with that information. But everyone has these stories, don't they? My mum was raised by an aunt she thought was *her* mum. It was a generational thing. And Martin Gore has a similar story.' Gore discovered, as an adult, that his father was a black American GI. Gore, chief songwriter, and Andrew Fletcher, the synth player, attended the James Hornsby School in Basildon. Alison Moyet was a classmate; she was, Fletcher once said, the best fighter in the school. They had a band with their friend Vince Clarke. Fletcher and Clarke were Christians; they didn't know Dave Gahan, who was a pupil at the Barstable School three miles away – periodically, spending his weekends at an attendance centre in Romford as payback for joyriding and theft. He eventually gained a certificate from Southend Technical College that qualified him for window dressing. Gahan was spotted by Clarke while performing David Bowie's '"Heroes"' at a jam session, and joined the band 'because I had absolutely fuck all else going on'. As a child, he had done Mick Jagger impersonations on *Top of the Pops* nights for the benefit of his aunts.

Stephen Dalton (*biographer*): Vince Clarke was the songwriter and driving force behind Composition of Sound, but a reluctant frontman. One day, after hearing Dave Gahan belting out Bowie's '"Heroes"' in a school rehearsal room, he offered Dave the post of singer in his group. 'About a week later I got this phone call from Vince,' Gahan recalls. 'He said, "Was that you singing?" And I said, "Yes" – it was actually a bunch of people singing, but I said it was me. They were already gigging as well, and I had this bunch of friends who liked to dress up and go to gigs. So we almost had a ready-made audience of about thirty people who were the cool people of Southend. Friday-night people. The oddballs.' Gahan was the band's missing jigsaw piece. Although a mere mouthpiece for songwriters Clarke and Gore, his laddish charisma sent a jolt of punky rock'n'roll through their electro-pop machine. Always a sharp dresser, he rechristened the quartet Depeche Mode after a French fashion magazine – translated literally, the name means 'fast fashion', although it simply sounded cool at the time.

Martin Gore (*musician*): To us, the synthesizer was the punk instrument. It was an instant, do-it-yourself tool. Because it was still new, its potential seemed limitless.

Stephen Dalton: The founding members of Depeche Mode all grew up in working-class, religiously inclined families. Gore and Gahan were both raised by then stepfathers, only meeting their biological fathers later in life. They were weaned on glam rock and soul, David Bowie and Gary Glitter, Sparks and Kraftwerk. But when punk hit Basildon, it changed everything. Thanks to newly cheap synthesizers, working-class teenagers with limited musical ability could suddenly make arty, avant-garde pop.

In August, the Observer *said that 'a small synthesizer now costs less than a good electric guitar, and it doesn't take years of practice to get something good out of it. The synthesizer sets the musical imagination free very quickly. Not surprisingly, the new generation of musicians is taking to it in a big way.' A revolution was in play. For instance, as synths became smaller and cheaper, at the time an EDP Wasp synthesizer could be bought for as little as £200.*

Martin Gore: I really hated Basildon. I wanted to get out as quickly as I could. I think being in a band was an escape. There was very little to do. It's one of those places where you go drinking because that's your only option. I hear it's a pretty horrible place these days. When I was about seventeen or eighteen, me and my friend were walking back from a party in Laindon, which is close to Basildon, and we heard this running behind us. We didn't think anything of it, but suddenly we were surrounded by six guys saying, 'Which one of you called my mate a fucking wanker?' One of those, you know? So then they started punching and kicking us . . . They weren't fun times. Dave used to get beaten up all the time for dressing out of the norm.

Dave Gahan (*singer, musician*): I just wanted attention. I put my mum through a rough time – in and out of juvenile court. It was petty crap – joyriding, criminal damage, theft. My mum did the best she could if the law showed up. I remember one time when this police car pulled up outside. She said, 'Is it for you?' And I said, 'Yes.' I distinctly remember her saying, 'David's been in all night.' But I'd written my name on a wall in paint! [Gahan ended up in weekend custody at a sub-Borstal attendance centre in Romford.] It was a real pain in the arse. You had to work – I remember doing boxing, stuff like that. You had to have your hair cut. It was every weekend, so you were deprived of your weekend, and it seemed like for ever. I was told very clearly that my next thing was detention centre. To be honest, music saved me. Seeing the Clash just made me think, 'I can do that.' I've always been a bit of an exhibitionist, and when I was really young the aunts would come round and I would entertain my mum by doing my best Mick Jagger or Gary Glitter impression across the room, make everybody laugh. I wasn't really good at anything else, but I saw that that really got a reaction. I rehearsed a couple of times with a few bands. There was one that my friend Tony Burgess played drums in. He didn't actually have a drum kit; he played biscuit tins. Never played a gig; just rehearsing after school. They were called the Vermin. They were very famous in that one area of Basildon. In our own minds we were going to be the next Sex Pistols.

Andy Fletcher (*musician*): We came out of a time where prog-rock musicians were completely the opposite – public schoolboys. Punk came along when we were sixteen, and it all changed – working-class kids, coming out of art colleges all over the country, wanting to make music. Vince [Clarke] and I were born-again Christians from the age of eleven to about eighteen. Dave wasn't, and Martin just used to come along because he liked the singing. That was where we learnt how to play instruments and sing – we learnt our trade, I suppose. We used to go to Greenbelt every year from the age of eleven, which is a massive Christian rock festival. In fact, I once saw U2 there, in 1980. To be honest, it was more the social aspect of the church and the music. It was quite a big social scene, and in Basildon there wasn't much else to do. You had to either steal cars or go to church.

Jon Savage: From April 1979, I was working for Granada in Manchester, so I was busy with Joy Division and Tony Wilson and Factory and all that stuff, so my only real contact with the birth of the New Romantic period was reading about it in *The Face*, Robert Elms and Spandau Ballet. I never went to Billy's, never went to the Blitz. I think after punk I was burnt out on going to nightclubs. I had just had enough, as it had all been very intense. So I wasn't aware of those nightclubs at all. I was aware of strange-looking people, but then we like strange-looking people, so that wasn't an issue for me. Of course, you had Duran Duran and the Rum Runner in Birmingham, but Manchester was a lot grittier and more downbeat – perhaps too downbeat. There were similarities, of course, and Joy Division certainly were interested in disco and synthesizer music, but it was a very different world. In fact, I remember thinking that this was really a London thing. Then I saw Spandau Ballet play at Heaven, and I thought they were not very good. I ended up laughing at them, actually. I have to say I feel a bit mean now, because of course I was wrong, as I went to see them a year later, when they were doing 'Chant No.1', at Le Beat Route with Beggar & Co., and they were great. But I still had the punk hangover, and I was still like, 'Manchester's better than London.'

Gary Kemp: At the beginning, we were accused of being fascist because we were elitist, as we didn't let certain journalists into our gigs, and because we played in places that weren't regular clubs, where ordinary people could go. It was only our followers who could go. So we were seen as being elitist and, therefore, reactionary. I think that was part of what we were trying to sell. That's what pop music tries to sell to you; it's what youth culture tries to sell to you. It tries to sell something unique: a club that's very difficult to get into. Once everyone is in, like punk, you don't want to be there any more, you want to go somewhere else. When we look back at our idols, like Bowie and Ferry, it was their aloofness that attracted us. If you look at all the bands that were successful in the eighties and came out of that movement, most of them came from ordinary backgrounds. All the other kids cleverly went into better jobs, like fashion or journalism.

Adam Ant: Richard James Burgess was producing Spandau Ballet, and he coined the phrase 'New Romantic', and I think it applied to them. And they are good guys and I like them, but basically, to me, it sounds terribly twee [and] Byronic . . . You know, council-flat boy buying arty French films on a Friday and buying a Super 8 camera and getting deep. Which is fine. We all do that. But it was such a load of crap, and because we'd really made it at that point, there was more to it than frilly shirts and things like that.

Fiona Dealey: I look at all the photographs taken when we were at the Blitz, and it looks like we had really bad teeth, because we never smiled. I think we all looked ferocious, in different ways. I was always told I was really intimidating, and I never thought I was intimidating at all. I always thought I was quite friendly. We were photographed for *L'Uomo Vogue*, which was quite good, but it wasn't quite cutting it, you know what I mean? It was nice to have an article written about me, but really? There were loads of those funny sorts of magazines, but again you'd be in a club, and somebody would say, 'I'm starting up a magazine,' and you'd think, '[small groan] OK.' There was *Viz*, *Boulevard*, *Ritz*, magazines like that. Then *The Face* started, and *i-D*.

In 1980, in the space of three months, three magazines would launch that would help to start to define the decade. Nick Logan, Terry Jones and Carey Labovitch started a small publishing revolution by launching, respectively,* The Face, i-D *and* Blitz. *Logan, a former editor of*

*Actually, there was a fourth magazine that launched this year: *ZG*, a folded, tabloid-size, cross-cultural title, intended by its founder and editor Rosetta Brooks to focus on 'self-consciously borderline activities'. The first few issues included features on Antony Price, fascist symbolism in popular culture, Cerith Wyn Evans, the photographs of Helmut Newton, John Maybury, the transgressions of social taboos and the adoption of Nazi imagery, Gilbert and George, *The Great Rock'n'Roll Swindle*, Dick Hebdige on Sid Vicious, and, of course, the Blitz Kids. In its own words, *ZG* 'paused, repeated, and above all reframed the culture of power'. As a vehicle for avant-garde thought, it went unchallenged.

the phenomenally successful NME *and the creator of* Smash Hits, *and Jones, a former art director of British* Vogue, *both independently realised that style culture, or what was then simply known as 'street style', was being ignored by much of the mainstream press. Labovitch, an Oxbridge graduate, was thinking similar things, although* Blitz *was initially more of a magazine dedicated to culture. These magazines were launched not only to catalogue this new explosion of style, but also to cater for it.* i-D, Blitz *and* The Face, *which were aimed at both men and women, reflected not only our increasing appetite for street style and fashion, but also for ancillary subjects, such as movies, music, television, art and zeitgeisty things in general – everything that was deemed to have some sort of influence on the emerging culture. They soon became style bibles, cutting-edge manuals of all that was deemed to be cool. Fashion, nightclubs, art, pop – if it clicked, it went in.*

Nineteen-eighty was Year Zero in terms of independent British magazine publishing, in much the same way that 1976 was Year Zero in the music industry. It was the date when lifestyle suddenly became an end in itself rather than a by-product of success, and when magazine publishing houses started to realise that men and women might be able to buy the same magazines. The Face, i-D *and* Blitz *were magazines that came from wildly different places, but which together forged a new micro-sector of the magazine publishing industry.*

'Style magazines' was what they would soon become known as, magazines that defined a decade that would soon develop an ability to care unduly about how it looked. In a pejorative sense, this obsession with the surface of things, this analysis of presentation, was perceived to be a shallow pursuit best suited to being bundled up in the pages of magazines devoted – or so the uninitiated thought – to an intoxicating mix of fashion, music, film, sport and lifestyle. But these magazines not only covered a much wider section of the cultural waterfront than most people realised, they became the culture itself.

Of the three magazines, The Face *was initially the most orthodox, being a glossy monthly that incorporated some associated content, such as fashion and film. In the space of a few months, it became the benchmark of all that was important in the rapidly emerging world of British and – in a heartbeat – global 'style culture'.*

I can still remember buying the first issue from the corner shop opposite my first-floor flat (above a greengrocer's) in Stamford Hill, north-east London. It was a Sunday, back when Sundays really were Sundays, when little was open but pubs at lunchtime. Having been a long-term consumer of the NME, *and having spent a year at Chelsea School of Art, and being halfway through a graphics course at St Martin's, I was a slam-dunk target reader.*

I loved The Face *immediately.*

The man who started it, Nick Logan, was already a peripheral hero in my eyes, as he had reinvented the NME *in the early seventies, making my adolescence, and the adolescence of 250,000 other like-minded music fans, a rich and vibrant time. The* NME *was how we discovered everything, from esoteric pop music to galvanising politics and cynical OTT cultural criticism; it was our own national newspaper, a place where passion and cynicism were encouraged in equal measure.*

After I left St Martin's in 1981, I would join i-D, *first as a writer/gofer/professional ligger, but then as an editor, immersing myself in a world that I rather grandly thought I was partially responsible for. We had a friendly rivalry with both* The Face *and* Blitz, *although collectively we thought we were better than anyone else.*

i-D *started, naturally enough, with a wink, which is often the way with relationships, particularly ones that last. A wink, a smile and the promise of a great new tomorrow. The original idea was a simple one, something Terry Jones hatched while still art director of British* Vogue. *Terry was at* Vogue *from 1972 to 1977, only leaving when it became evident that his colleagues didn't share his enthusiasm for the fresh and exciting new direction in street style that exploded in tandem with punk. So he left the magazine, eventually starting* i-D *in the summer of 1980. Initially looking like little more than a punk fanzine*, i-D *was essentially an exercise in social documentation, a catalogue of photographs of 'real' people wearing 'real' clothes, what Terry liked to call 'straight-ups'. People on the street. In bars. In nightclubs. At home. And all of them on parade. And although in the decades since* i-D *has developed into an internationally renowned style magazine, full of fancy photographers and the very fanciest models, this 'straight-up' element has never been lost. Above all else,* i-D *has always been about people.*

When it launched, i-D *didn't look like any other magazine on the shelves, and in many respects it still doesn't. Turned on its side, the* i-D *logo resembles a wink and a smile, and every cover since the first issue has featured a winking, smiling face, a theme that has given the magazine an iconic identity as strong as the one developed by* Playboy *in the fifties (which always included a bunny silhouette somewhere on the cover). I can still remember where I was when I saw the first issue, in September 1980. I saw it on a friend's desk in the first-floor, second-year graphics department at St Martin's. Having long been an avid reader of domestic style magazines (the aforementioned* New Style, Viz, Midnight, Boulevard, Ritz, *etc.), as well as their American counterparts (*Interview, Punk, *etc.) – all of which focused on tightly knit groups of micro-celebrities – it was refreshing to find something which plugged right into British subculture, a heat-seeking style-sheet which found room for every fledgling youth cult in the country, from punks, soul boys and New Romantics to psychobillies, rockers and penny-ante trustafarians. Along with* The Face, *which had launched a few months previously,* i-D *was suddenly the voice of a generation – a generation with no name. I also liked it because it was full of people I knew, and in some respects it was an in-house magazine for the flotsam and jetsam of London nightlife.*

Terry Jones felt that the best way to reflect the creativity he admired in street style was through 'immediacy', through visual imagery rather than just straight text, and so the magazine used typewriter fonts, ticker-tape headlines and wild, often perverse graphics. And although this was a style born of necessity as much as any ideology, it gave the magazine an identity that it has preserved ever since.

*The magazine was always A4 in size (slightly thinner than most glossies), although in the early days it was landscape as opposed to portrait and opened – somewhat annoyingly – longways. The first issue was just forty pages, stuck together with three rickety staples, and cost 50p. A bargain. 'Fashion magazine No. 1,' it said on the cover, and that was all you really needed to know. Inside were several dozen 'straight-ups' of various upwardly and downwardly mobile exhibitionists: some fairly dodgy-looking Blitz Kids, a rockabilly or two, a goth and some Teddy boys from Brighton. A girl called Pennie, interviewed about what she was wearing, had this to say about her jumper: 'I got it from some shop in Oxford Street. I can't remember the name. I get so mesmerised when I shop along Oxford Street I never notice the names.' (For the first few issues, Terry only allowed photographers to shoot two frames per person, so the 35mm contact sheets became works of art in themselves, a sort of sartorial police file.) There were also a few fashion ads from Fiorucci, Robot and Swanky Modes. It even had a manifesto of sorts: '*i-D *is a Fashion/Style Magazine. Style isn't what but how you wear clothes. Fashion is the way you walk, talk, dance and prance. Through* i-D *ideas travel fast and free of the mainstream – so join us on the run!'*

To print the magazine, Jones turned to Better Badges, a London-based company largely responsible for producing most of the fanzines in the capital. He told them he wanted to produce the world's first fashion fanzine, and they agreed to print 2,000 copies, on the condition that Jones himself bought the entire print run. The launch was rather troubled as newsagents complained about the staples: people were apparently piercing their fingers and getting blood over the other magazines on the stands. This proved to be such a problem that there were only two newsagents who agreed to stock the second and third issues. Then Virgin stepped in, guaranteeing nationwide distribution, enabling the magazine to increase its print run exponentially. 'It just grew from there,' said Terry.

Jones was keen to reflect the fact that street style was a democratic, amorphous process. And i-D *wasn't ever, if truth be told, anything like a barometer of style. Even though the magazine originally branded itself 'The Worldwide Manual of Style', it was never – has rarely been – prescriptive. Sensibly, Terry always believed that it's important to like the bad stuff too.*

Terry Jones: I wanted to get the concept over that we don't lay down the rules about what you wear, the idea of 'in–out' fashion.

Jones was never particularly keen on drive-by journalism, not interested in ring-fencing people in arbitrary social groups. For the quintessential style magazine, this was ironic, seeing that the 'style' magazines and newspaper lifestyle sections that came in its wake seemed devoted to the reductive. i-D *has been many things – irritating, infuriating, wilfully obscure, over-extravagant and often impossible to read – but it has rarely been without substance.*

In a world that soon became awash with style magazines aimed at every different type of demographic, it was easy to forget that in 1980 magazines like i-D *just didn't exist.* i-D *was the first street-fashion magazine, a pick'n'mix grab bag of punk fashion and DIY style, a pop-cultural sponge soaking up everything around it with inelegant haste. During a decade when the safety net of society was gradually folded away,* i-D *catalogued a culture of self-sufficiency, even if that culture was at times only sartorial. Sure, the eighties was the decade when 'designer' became not just a prefix but also an adjective, but it was also the decade of unreconstructed, and often rabid, individualism.*

The eighties had a lot to live up to. If the sixties had been a decade of confrontational happiness, and the post-punk seventies full of agents of social change, the eighties were crowded with a generation seemingly devoted to self-empowerment and self-improvement. It was a decade that couldn't wait to get ahead of itself. Reinvention became almost a prerequisite for success, as soap stars became pop stars, pop stars became politicians and politicians became indistinguishable from their Spitting Image *puppets. Everyone was a party catalyst, everybody a star. When Andy Warhol said that in the future everyone would be famous for fifteen minutes, he wasn't simply talking about New York in 1973; he was unwittingly describing London in the early eighties. A vortex of entrepreneurial hedonism, London hadn't swung so much since 1966.*

Enjoying the freedom of a magazine that was bound by no constraints, Terry could often be perverse in his art direction and design. Contrary. Bloody-minded. If a picture suggested that it should be used full frame, full bleed, then Terry's inclination would be to crop it in half and print it upside down, with a 30 per cent cyan tint running through it. The best picture from a session would be used small, while the worst one would be printed across a spread. When asked why he did it, he'd cut back with, 'Why do it like everyone else?'

Usually he was right. Not always, but often.

Video grabs and TV stills were used to provide a sense of speed and the unexpected. Body copy and headlines were unflinchingly distorted, while computer type became one of the magazine's defining characteristics, a decade before it arrived in such publications as Wired *and* Dazed & Confused. *Jones liked to describe his graphic discipline as 'instant design', a saturated 'mash' of photography and graphics, of colour and type. But although the result often looked as though it were arrived at randomly, this belied the rigour of the execution.*

Terry Jones: I don't like the concept of perfection, because it implies finality. I like the end product to look easy, and that takes a lot of effort. Instant design is [actually] a lie. It is never instant.

If you left anything lying around the office for long enough, it would probably end up in the magazine. Passports, address books, taxi receipts . . . Terry would find a use for them all. I once made the mistake of showing him some old family snapshots, only to come back from holiday and find they were in the magazine. Heigh-ho. If you couldn't get an original copy of a particular photograph, then why not just photocopy the book you found it in? It was unlikely anyone was ever going to notice. It was a very democratic place to work too, where a receptionist could be fired one day and hired the next as a features writer. One particular receptionist ended up being the television critic of the Observer. *Which is just as well, as she was a lousy receptionist.*

Because i-D *was a vehicle for art direction as much as journalism, the magazine found itself being haphazard, irrational and wildly pretentious. The readers understood this and somehow went along with it. Some of them, anyway. In the fifth-anniversary issue – which also contained Nick Knight's unforgettable studies of a hundred of the most 'influential' personalities ever to appear in* i-D *(a bizarre-enough group, including boldface names like Patsy Kensit, Morrissey and John Peel, as well as some of the least tightly wrapped people you could ever meet and a couple who shouldn't have been included at all) – various readers were asked how they'd sum up the magazine. 'You discover all the secret talents and mad scientists,' wrote Michael Odimitrakis from Kostas, while J. Dominic from Deptford compared the magazine to Marks & Spencer's Continental Biscuit Assortment (a rare accolade indeed). My favourite comment was sent anonymously and is nothing if not succinct: 'You are a stupid lot of wanking ignorant trendies.' Charmed, I'm sure.*

For a journalist, Terry's often total disregard for the printed word was, on occasions, supremely painful. I remember the first time I was victim to his vagaries. As a cub reporter on the magazine in 1983, I had just returned from an assignment – no doubt interviewing some equally artless fashion designer, club runner or nascent pop star – to find Terry laying out the next issue. As I glanced at the layout of one of my articles, I saw him cutting the bottom three inches off the galley, so my piece ended inelegantly, slap-bang in the middle of a sentence. Sensing my apprehension, he turned to me and smiled: 'Well, it won't fit.'

It was to be the first of many such arguments, most of which Terry won. I was there from the end of 1983 to the end of 1987, four years in which we tried – relentlessly, religiously and, I must say, with a modicum of success – to reinvent our own particular wheel. Using guerrilla graphics, cutting-edge fashion photography and tongue-in-cheek text ('Why did God make homosexuals?' asked one gay fashion editor in a particularly flippant editorial. 'To take fat girls to discos'), Terry Jones's i-D *quickly gained a reputation as the complete Situationist tip sheet and street-fashion bible. Terry not only gave me a career, he gave careers to hundreds of other teenage and twenty-something wannabes: from photographers Nick Knight and Juergen Teller to journalists Caryn Franklin and Alix Sharkey; from photographer Corinne Day and art director Robin Derrick to stylists Simon Foxton and Ray Petri; from jeweller Judy Blame and writer Kathryn Flett to photographers Marc Lebon, Richard Burbridge and Donald Christie. To name only a few.*

The real stars of the magazine weren't the contributors, they were the subjects, whether it be Leigh Bowery cavorting about in the depths of Taboo, a Japanese cycle boy in an Eisenhower jacket or some UK garage DJ whose name no one could ever remember. Or Sade, Madonna, Björk or Kate Moss, all winking as though their careers depended on it (often they did). Any fashion designer, photographer, stylist, hairdresser, film-maker, actor, model, style journalist, make-up artist, club runner, DJ or pop star in the eighties who contributed anything to what is laughingly called the zeitgeist was, at some point or another, profiled or photographed in i-D. *'How much do I spend on clothes?' Frankie Goes to Hollywood's Paul Rutherford told* i-D *readers in 1984. 'Is Jean Paul Gaultier a rich man?' The* i-D *story is the story of pop culture in the eighties, a roll call of the great, the good and the unseemly, a litany of bad behaviour and unhealthy diets. While* The Face *could claim to be no less influential, no magazine has produced such a rogue's gallery of achievement as* i-D.

As he showed by giving Madonna her first magazine cover, Terry was always good at exploiting pop, but then, during the first three or four years of the eighties, most publications were. Pop music was vital in disseminating this new visual culture of fashion and arrogance, and the emergence of the new pop groups, such as Duran Duran, Frankie Goes to Hollywood, the Eurythmics, Spandau Ballet and Culture Club – who, in a move away from the punk ethos (more like a volte-face, actually), began spending their vast royalty cheques in the designer boutiques along Bond Street and the King's Road – gave rise to a new-found tabloid interest in anything to do with pop.

Terry Jones: By the end of 1979, I was convinced I wanted to do a street-style magazine, not just to catalogue punks, but everyone. I grew up in Bristol, and the estate where I lived was predominantly full of greasers and rockers. The minute they were old enough to ride a motorbike, they'd be getting a 125 or a 250. I had long hair in the mid-sixties, and the only place you could drink was a beat bar called the Three Tonnes. But I also had a lot of friends who were mods, but I hated the way that everyone was pigeonholed. I didn't like the idea that everyone was given a label or a uniform. To me they all felt like school uniforms. So, by the time of punk, I just felt there was a rationale for a magazine that took the breadth of the street and started mixing it up. You know, if you look on the street, you don't see everyone walking around all dressed the same. The idea is it's all mixed up. So that's how the idea for *i-D* came about. In the early days, I think the person who was much more understanding of the London scene was Perry Haines, as he was a man about town, while still being a student at St Martin's. He was completely involved in the scene and was something of a catalyst. Like a lot of people, once Perry started coming to my house in West Hampstead, where we were putting the magazine together, he didn't go back to college. It was very important to me that while we were cataloguing what was going on in London – and obviously with the Blitz scene you had Fiona Dealey, Boy George and Stephen Linard – it was imperative that we took stock of what was going on in Cardiff, Leeds, Manchester, etc. I made sure it wasn't London-centric and wanted to expand it into a global language, so it felt like it was a language without borders. That fashion could become the language without borders. And I wanted the magazine to be like that. So it was not wanting to do something which was over-intellectual, and more about breaking down barriers. I could see that something was going on with independent publishing, but I felt *The Face* and *Blitz* looked more like conventional magazines, whereas *i-D* was deliberately anarchic. I'd always say the magazine had three levels. You'd have the immediate rush, which was a kind of graphic impact; then you'd have the other sort of like fast gratification; and then, you know, sitting on the toilet reading it three months later, you'd still find something that you had missed out on. So you weren't being given the whole story. We weren't forcing our opinions on people, but more like provoking. I was also careful not to have criticism, as I didn't see the point of publishing something and then being sarcastic about it. There came a point when we wouldn't put skinheads in any more because they came up with so many racial slurs. There were a few of them in the early issues, and very quickly we started saying, 'OK, well, we didn't actually want to give them a voice.'

i-D grew and grew, and we started becoming competitive about writers and photographers. I was like a football manager. I might have inherited a little bit of that attitude from *Vogue*, in that you had your stable, you had your key players, and you try to be protective about those key players. But we had no financial incentive for people. So it was purely the passion and the integrity of what we produced that would actually attract people. We were taking liberties with a lot of the material coming in, and so the photographers had to be totally on board. They had to believe in what we were producing. It was before the celebrity of the photographer took over from that of the subject, as the subject was still more important. We didn't rely on advertising, as opposed to *The Face*, which already had a serious advertising manager. I don't know about *Blitz*, but our funding was like a hobby, and that went on for a bunch of years, till I thought, 'I can't keep paying the bills.' Then Tony Elliott [from *Time Out*] came on board, bailed us out, set us up with a proper office. Tony was the saviour. We needed one because everything was so hand to mouth.

i-D happened at a very important time, because there was so much going on. Everyone down at the Blitz was going to Angels, the costumiers, and all the post-punk activity was so exciting. Some people look back upon the fifties as being very interesting in Soho, others focus on the Swinging Sixties and punk, but when you look back on the eighties, it was a decade of ideas. Before the money came in, when money was actually tight, before the corporations came in, before youth TV.

Stephen Jones: *i-D* for me, and for us, was so important because that was the magazine of our generation. Just simply that. It was our voice. When it first came out, we were all a bunch of freaks from the countryside who had ended up in London. We always thought how lucky it was for people who were growing up as the freaks in their local town that they could actually buy something like *i-D* magazine and realise that they weren't the only ones, there were other people out there like them, so they should get to London quick and make their fame and fortune.

I knew Nick Logan long before I went to work for him, having spent four exhausting years at Terry Jones's i-D. *When I joined* The Face, *both it and* Arena *(the men's magazine that Nick would launch in 1986, and which caused another tsunami of publishing activity, including* GQ*) operated from a converted laundry in Ossington Buildings, just off Marylebone High Street. For a while this was the citadel of London cool, a place where everyone from Robert Elms, Nick Kent and Tony Parsons to Ray Petri, Jean-Baptiste Mondino and Boy George would congregate, all of them metaphorically tugging their forelocks whenever Nick himself appeared. Logan was, like Jones, one of the least demonstrative people you could ever meet, and yet he had a very tight and exact idea of what was right and what was wrong.*

The Face*'s* raison d'être *was simple: what was the right thing to do? We would all sit in the downstairs 'War Room' and discuss exactly that, on a daily basis. In the year leading up the hundredth issue in 1988, we spent many nights in here, excitedly compiling a list of the* *most important events of the decade, from the emergence of go-go to the proliferation of the Filofax.*

And having shouted at each other for an hour or four, we would then trudge down to the Soho Brasserie in Old Compton Street to drink expensive imported beer and carry on arguing late into the night. What The Face *invented was a new way of looking at the notion of cool. And though this wasn't initially proscriptive, after a while the contents of the magazine almost became self-selecting: you could look at a layout and know immediately whether or not it was 'right'. In a sense, this collective idea of what was the correct thing to do was not only a reflection of the decade, it was a product of it too. Hey,* The Face *even had a trendy estate agent to find its new premises within the recently gentrified parts of London – David Rosen at Pilcher Hershman, which employed the magazine's superstar designer, Neville Brody, to design its logo.*

The Face *was incredibly hard work, and it was a hell of a lot of fun. I think some people imagined the staff walking around in Regency fancy dress, perhaps with monocles or aggressively tinted sunglasses, leafing through fashion magazines and laughing at photographs of the great unwashed. Nothing could have been further from the truth. The people who worked on* The Face *were not only small in number, but rapidly developed all the skills you needed to put a magazine or newspaper together. Logan could do everything – he had almost single-handedly put out the* NME *week after week during a strike at the paper in the mid-seventies – and everyone who worked for him was expected to learn on the job. The entire staff were also resolutely left-wing, as anyone who expressed an admiration for the Tories was put into the toxic box quite quickly. Eventually, politics would play an enormous role in the magazine, and yet the editorials were socially liberal rather than particularly strident. The Left would often criticise* The Face *for exemplifying elitism, yet this was a massive oversimplification of what it, and its staff, stood for.* The Face, i-D *and* Blitz *all espoused liberal sensibilities; they just did it with a certain panache.*

Logan was exacting. When I went to work for him, I remember sitting in our repro house up in Kilburn late one night during the final week of production, watching him spend over an hour carefully editing the intro to a tightly worded column on the back page. Having worked his way through yet another packet of cigarettes, he passed the page over, sat back and said, with as much satisfaction and enthusiasm as I ever heard him muster, 'There. Now fifty more people might read it . . .'

This may have been the decade of the power lunch and the cocktail hour for some, but in the world of Wagadon (Nick's small publishing company), all hands were needed on deck at all hours of the day. We arrived, we worked, and then we left. Many times we went out, gallivanting around town, but often we simply went home to finish an article we couldn't afford to commission anyone else to write. With The Face, *as with* i-D, *there was a certain amount of growing up in public, and our enthusiasm was often enough to get us from gun to tape. I think we all felt enormous privilege in being able to – largely – write about anything that took our fancy, whether it was an esoteric new nightclub, a beer bar in Barcelona, a hitherto obscure sixties movie or the contorted prose of a forgotten nineteenth-century hipster. What these magazines offered was a sense of freedom, for their readers as well as their contributors.*

It was a tough office in some respects, at least inasmuch that any hint of pretension was seized upon as a weakness. Express the wrong opinion about a film, a song or someone's appearance on Newsnight *(which Nick was obsessed with), or turn up to work in an unnecessarily jaunty hat, and you would be laughed at for weeks. Sometimes longer.*

The Old Laundry was fun, though, and there were times when, huddled around the lightbox – no doubt peering at some awful fashion photographs a hapless photographer had sent in – with Neville Brody, Robin Derrick (who would go on to art-direct Vogue*), Christian Logan (Nick's son), Kathryn Flett (the features editor) and Rod Sopp (the extraordinarily un-PC ad director), I thought I might never stop laughing.*

I remember the day we got our first fax machine. A member of staff had successfully sent The Face*'s first-ever fax, only to see the original piece of A4 paper still languishing in the tray.*

'It's still here,' she said, incredulous.

'It's not matter transfer,' said Rod, on his way to force someone at TAG Heuer to give us another page of advertising. At times like this, Logan would smile indulgently and then disappear up into his office to fiddle with the flatplan, creating magic out of industry.

Nick Logan (*journalist, publisher*): When I left the *NME* in 1978, I really didn't know what I was going to do. I just had to get out for my own health, but I knew I didn't want to work for a corporation ever again. I thought I might be able to form some kind of relationship with a smaller publishing company, one in which I might be on a more even footing financially. I was poorly paid for all the stress that came with the job of editing what, for IPC, was a huge money-maker. *Smash Hits* happened almost by accident. For EMAP I'd come up with three or four ideas for music magazines [including a British version of *Rolling Stone*], but I didn't want a potential publishing partner to think I was simply offering them a rival to the *NME*. So, to widen the range of ideas, I threw in a teen song-lyric mag based around improving on a pretty poor existing title. I was surprised and thrown by EMAP's reaction: the teen magazine was the one they leapt at. I edited it for a year or so – with other staff by now, of course – but it was never something I wanted to do on a long-term basis. What I discovered from *Smash Hits* was the joy of working with a small team after all the hassle at the *NME*. And also working for the first time with colour photography and quality paper stock. When I started *The Face*, the photographers I used were people I had discovered through *Smash Hits* – like Sheila Rock, who did brilliant colour photography, and she pretty much did the first-ever fashion and style pictures for us. And others like Chalkie Davies and Jill Furmanovsky, who shot for the *NME* and gave me outtakes in black and white and shot for me in colour. What I wanted with

The Face was to have the production qualities of, say, *Tatler* or *Vogue*. It was kind of 'Why should the devil have all the best tunes? Let's have that quality with this subject matter, historically only ever seen before in grainy newsprint.' So I learnt a lot from *Smash Hits*. Another important lesson from *Smash Hits*: it validated my theory that most of the bands the *NME* covered – acts that had commercial potential and integrity, everything from the Clash to the Jam to Blondie – also held appeal for a younger audience.

I thought there was a gap in the market for a publication I would want to read myself. That's been my philosophy for everything I've done – everything that's been successful, that is. And that gap was for a glossy magazine that acknowledged the fashion end of music, which was always important to my mind, and that was kind of what I wanted for myself almost from the time that I was fourteen, when, having left school prematurely, my mother moved out of London to live in Lincoln, where I was marooned for a whole summer, at the time when youth culture and the Beatles and the Stones and American soul was happening – Tamla Motown and Chess – and there I was, stuck in this backwater (apologies to Lincoln). I was reading Alan Sillitoe and David Storey, hanging around the small modern-art section of Lincoln Art Gallery, desperately trying to make a connection with a culture that was developing elsewhere. I was desperate for knowledge but had to scratch around for scraps. Mainstream music papers were only interested in chart acts who were predominantly pop/white. As a proto-mod, I was into black music – soul, R&B, blues – but looking to white pop acts for fashion. One of the weeklies, *Record Mirror*, started a tiny, two-hundred-word series called 'Great Soul Heroes' – Solomon Burke this week, Otis Redding the next . . . Then, maybe in something like *Beat Instrumental*, there'd be an offstage posed pic of the Stones, where you could study their haircuts, Cuban heels, leather coats . . . That relationship of music and fashion always fascinated me. That pic would only have been in *Beat Instrumental* because it was a free PR shot. Most of the music press used live shots because the editors thought they caught the excitement best. The posed photo (outside of the cheesy PR shot), believe it or not, was a rarity; the unposed, informal offstage shot so familiar now . . . it barely existed. One of the first things I did at the *NME* was to drastically reduce the live photos. They did little for me – so many of them were clichés. I didn't want to see Roger Daltrey's tonsils; his jacket was more interesting to me. Paul Weller walking through a crowd of mods on the way to a gig . . . that was far more interesting to me. I started *The Face* with £3,500, or around that, of savings from my *Smash Hits* payments and royalties from my part in the *NME Encyclopedia of Rock*.

Robin Derrick (*art director*): Nick Logan was the editor of the *NME* for some time during the punk movement. The *NME* was a black-and-white newspaper. Photographers decided to shoot colour pictures, although there was nowhere to put colour pictures of pop stars. The first issues of *The Face* included a large amount of content that was colour pictures of bands. You could have a colour picture of the Specials. It was just a picture with a caption; no need for an article because no one else was publishing it. There was *Top of the Pops*, but that was it. I moved to Milan a few years later to launch *Elle* magazine. I was welcomed with positive cries of 'You worked for *The Face*!' We knew we worked for a cool magazine, but I had no idea of the effects. We had no idea of the repercussions. How people reacted was part of the work. The viewer completes the picture.

Simon Tesler (*publisher*): *Blitz* was born in September 1980, the brainchild of Carey Labovitch, then a twenty-year-old student. At the time, the youth press was dominated wholly by the fading star of the music tabloids. After an unstable period during the mid-seventies, the music papers had found their niche with the emergence of punk in 1976, a form of music and youth culture perfectly suited to rough-and-ready tabloid newsprint. But by 1980, punk had been superseded by something altogether more ambitious, a culture that had grown directly out of punk but that was more concerned with extravagance, visual style, creativity. The same people who had spent their time going to punk gigs were now growing up and trying to make some sort of interesting, preferably independent, living – writing, perhaps, or making clothes or acting; anything, in fact, rather than going to work as a bank clerk or a secretary. There was the beginning of an explosion of 'alternative' arts – theatre companies, street entertainment, film-makers, independent clothes shops, stand-up comedians, performance artists and so on. Interest in photography boomed, recapturing some of the excitement and creativity that had grown stale as the photographic *enfants terribles* of the sixties became the seasoned old hands of the seventies. Yet the music press, still stuck in the rut of music, seemed to be doing little to reflect the change.

The emphasis of this new feeling was on appearance: the look or visual feel of things; image, style and design as a way of transmitting ideas; photography as a way of reflecting mood and style far more succinctly and effectively than written copy. New Romanticism, the vaguely defined culture of a fashionable circle centred around a succession of Soho and Covent Garden clubs, formed only a small part of the whole, but it served in some ways as the hardcore of the new feeling, a sort of reference point, particularly as fashion became a central part of this new creative energy.

Part of the idea behind *Blitz* was that it would reflect what this new and disparate group of people were trying to do, and in covering them would give space to the creative abilities of those capable young writers and photographers unable to get work in the established magazines because they lacked, not ability, but cuttings in their portfolios. And instead of covering simply music it would reflect the whole range of subjects affecting this market – design, film, politics, theatre, art, video, fashion and much more. The magazine also offered exhibition space in the form of a regular 'portfolio' feature, which each month presented work by a new and promising photographer. And as the style and the fashion of the times became more eclectic – snatching ideas at random from the dress and moods of the last sixty years – so too the style of photography that reflected it in the pages of *Blitz* became more eclectic.

Carey Labovitch (*publisher*): In the autumn of 1979, I was nineteen, at St Hilda's, Oxford, studying French and Italian, completely away from London. I'd always been interested in magazines, and as a ten-year-old I did a magazine called *Optic*, which was full of my own cartoons, and I got loads of school friends to write articles and do crosswords, and I produced it on the school Roneo machine. I can still smell the ink on it, to be honest. I used to sell it in the school playground, and I attached a boiled sweet to make sure people bought it. I just loved writing and I loved drawing and I loved taking photographs, and it was just my creative juices. I then edited the official school magazine, and when I went on to Oxford, I thought I would like to write for one of the Oxford magazines. There was *Isis*, but they were full up of 'would-be' writers, they didn't need anything. I got a couple of cartoons in it, but that was it.

I used to buy magazines avidly, but I was disappointed that all my own interests weren't being covered. I'd look at *NME*, but obviously that was all about music, and there were lots of girls' magazines, which I wasn't interested in. I'd been to a mixed school and was interested in anything that girls and boys were interested in. I didn't feel I wanted to be segregated into just a girls' magazine. Magazines like *Vogue* were a bit too grown up for me then, as I couldn't afford half the things in them. So I thought I'd start my own magazine. I went to my college and asked them to help. I have this sort of mentality that if you don't ask, you don't get. I managed to get a grant of £250 from the college, which was based on my presentation and a mock-up dummy. They asked me what the name was, and I couldn't think of anything. I knew I wanted something short, something with a 'z' in it, because 'z' sounded quite snappy. So I came up with *Blitz*. I had no idea about the Blitz club in London because I wasn't part of that. The first issue was also funded by advertising, because I went to all the local shops and showed them my dummy, and I said, 'Will you support this? Will you take a quarter-page or half-page ad?' I found a printer and used a college payphone to make all my calls. I found a local place in Didcot where the husband and wife did typesetting on galleys and then posted it back to me. I had to cut it out and get some cow gum and stick it onto these page grids I had made. Friends of mine helped me get it into local newsagents, so I think we did about 2,000 copies for the first issue.

I was really pushy and wrote to lots of important people, telling them I had launched this magazine, hoping I could get some free publicity. I even wrote to Rupert Murdoch. I have still got letters in a folder back at home. I wrote to anybody I could think of – actors and journalists and editors – and I got these letters back saying, 'Great first issue,' 'Thanks so much,' 'Keep up the good work,' and it gave me the push to carry on.

Iain R. Webb: That's what people forget, how few people were there at the beginning, and through *Blitz* and *i-D* and *The Face* we sent those messages out to the rest of the world. I remember getting a phone call from a magazine and saying, 'What do you mean by styling?' – because at that point that didn't exist as a career option.

Carey Labovitch: After I graduated, I moved to London and took a small office in Soho. I loved journalism, but with *Blitz* I never ended up doing much because I was so busy being the publisher, art director, editor . . . everything. I had no idea there were any other magazines doing similar things, but then *i-D* was more about fashion and *The Face* was more about music. *Blitz* was probably more journalistic, a bit more serious. So I didn't ever feel they competed, but what did excite me was that there was a trend, and I thought that was great because that could help push sales for all of us. It was difficult to get work at the time, and *Blitz* became a place where young photographers and writers could get noticed. People's hobbies were becoming their professions. The first few issues we didn't pay anybody, and Simon [Tesler] and I didn't pay ourselves for many years, to be honest, as the staff came first. We just existed on bank loans. The banks would always address Simon in meetings, so I made him grow a beard because he was very youthful-looking in those days. It was really tough. Not only tough because I was young; I was a girl, and people thought because I was a girl, I was automatically a secretary. I think that's why I fought so hard, because I felt I had to prove to people I could do what they could do. I was a lot more naive than Nick Logan or Terry Jones because I had never worked in the industry before. I've never met Nick Logan, but he had it in for me right from the start, and I didn't know why. I didn't know that *The Face* existed when I started *Blitz*. I would have loved to have met him. We had a lot of journalists and photographers in common, but if they ever worked for *Blitz*, they weren't allowed to work for *The Face*. I just never understood it. We stayed fiercely independent. IPC tried to buy us once, and we were offered a million or something for the company, but we didn't want to come and work for a corporate organisation, so we passed.

Jon Savage: *The Face*, *i-D* and *Blitz* became more than magazines; they became, as *i-D* sort of ironically noted, 'style bibles', models for emulation rather than communication, as the celebrants of the clubland myth became the new aristocracy.

Robert Elms: Punk had brought in people like me: soul boys. And you'd put on a leather jacket. But then, after punk, the music was awful. I hated all that northern gloom, all that post-punk stuff, like the Gang of Four, which just wasn't fun. So I think that divide was there. And I think clothes were the dividing line, as the *NME* hated anything that dressed well. Always had done. They thought clothes were beneath them. 'We don't write about trousers,' is what they said, whereas Nick [Logan, at *The Face*] always wanted to write something about trousers. And I've always said, it's the primacy of style. When you're a kid in particular, your main weapon is what you wear. It was all we had.

We had the records that we bought and clothes that we wore. And I think the other thing is that although lots of bands came out of it, the Blitz wasn't really about bands. When you go to see a band, they're the entertainment, but when you go to a nightclub, you're the entertainment – how sexy you look, how well you dance. The Blitz was the ultimate statement. Everyone in there was the entertainment for all the others, and that's why it was so competitive. After the Blitz, Chris Sullivan started a club, then Ollie O'Donnell, and suddenly Soho starts to change. Then you had *i-D*, *The Face*, *Blitz*, people start talking about design, and London started to change.

Peter York: When did I meet Bob Elms? I met him through Nick Logan. Nick said, 'Here is Bob Elms, and he's terribly clever.' And then Bob went into absolute hyperdrive and told me all this stuff, and I just nodded. I thought, 'This is wonderful.' He wrote all this hyperdrive stuff about the real working-class culture. So he totally thought he'd made his mark on me. He was, in fact, a publicist – the informal publicist for his friend Steve Dagger and their group. And his friend was hilarious. He used to say things with such conviction. They'd been at the LSE together. People like Bob started on the same patch, I suppose, writing about all this stuff, becoming style journalists, but I didn't think, 'Oh, come on, sonny.' Most of it was being done by people I sort of knew and liked, so I didn't think, 'You're knocking me off, you little bastards.' And, of course, it made the market for me better. It's like the rule of retail attraction: you know, you have an anchor store, then you get more stores, and then you get more trade for the anchor store. So it was fine by me.

Peter Ashworth: Al McDowell was a young student at Central who got thrown out for creating a degree show to do with shit and stuff, and he started this design company called Rocking Russian, and they started getting me work. He started employing Neville Brody, who went on to work for *The Face*. Then, all of a sudden I got asked to do the Visage album, which is the kind of thing that happened back then, just out of the blue. I then got grabbed by Polydor, seemingly because I was the hot young photographer who was in touch with everything, when in actual fact I just happened to be in the right place at the right time. So I started doing all sorts of things for them. Once you're seen as hot by one record company, you're seen as hot by all of them. Everything I touched became gold. I did six platinum albums in my first six months. Suddenly I was the most in-demand person: Visage, Stephen Jones, Ultravox, David Sylvian, the Clash, Adam Ant and, when it launched, lots of work for *The Face*.

Obviously, not everyone liked style culture. British sociologist Dick Hebdige accused The Face *of elitism, describing it as 'the embodiment of entrepreneurial Thatcherite drive' and accusing it of being 'hyper-conformist . . . [it has] flattened everything to the glossy world of the image, and presented its style as content'.*

This was a criticism that was aimed at the whole Blitz movement in general, an aesthetic that was demonised for rejecting the austerity and anti-fashion stance of punk. The perceived narrative suggests that many of those who came in the wake of the Blitz Kids were symptomatic of the vacuous money culture that would define Britain in the eighties. Their emphasis on style and conspicuous consumption gave them an affluent, materialist swagger. In other words, they were seen as punks on the make, representing what some would call an upstart social mobility, 'an outré example of the Thatcherite self-made man or woman', as Hebdige put it.

The metaphors were obvious to see. 'Their love of the high life reached a peak with the movement's most successful band,' wrote Ludovic Hunter-Tilney of the Financial Times. *'I'll take my chance because luck is on my side,' Duran Duran sang aboard a yacht bedecked with fashion models in the Caribbean, in the video for their 1982 hit 'Rio'. A generation of City slickers, soon to explode into pinstriped life in the Big Bang of financial deregulation, took notes.*

Some of those who emerged from the Blitz cast themselves as pop rebels, with an emphasis on inclusiveness and bohemianism. It was a strong counter-argument. 'Many were inspired by the punk upheaval that swept London a few years previously,' said Hunter-Tilney. 'They led extravagant alternative lifestyles, fuelled by decadent potions and powders. Any adherence to the Thatcherite virtue of thrift was well hidden. Despite the Blitz's exclusiveness, inside was a zone of tolerance. Lesbian, gay, bisexual and transgender culture played a crucial role. Boy George's appearance on Top of the Pops *in 1982 singing Culture Club's "Do You Really Want to Hurt Me?" in make-up and lipstick, dreadlocked hair festooned with ribbons, was one of the most sensational in the BBC television programme's history. Tabloid headlines the next day summed up Fleet Street's bemusement: "Is it a girl or is it a boy?"'*

Were they early adopters of Thatcherism or social dissidents? As Hunter-Tilney said, 'The answer is both and neither.' There were too many personalities involved, too many different pop-cultural strands being dragged through the streets. 'Like London itself, the city in which they were brought to life, the New Romantics can't be boiled down to a single meaning.'

They embraced a cultural gentrification that at first glance would have been anathema to the ideological guttersnipes of the punk generation. However, a quick second look will tell you that the initial instigators of punk – Sex Pistols manager Malcolm McLaren and Clash Svengali Bernie Rhodes – were old-school wheeler-dealers. For them, shock value meant money, and in this they were no different from any of the iconic music managers who had gone before them, tussling with their clients in the ever-heroic battle between art and commerce. As punk came complete with its own self-destruct button, having an inbuilt obsolescence, success in any regard was going to be a disappointment, or at least at odds with what rebellion had traditionally looked like.

So perhaps the aspirations of those who came after were slightly less compromised. Many of them certainly seemed to have more control over their aspirations, even if they were just as inept at putting them into practice. Success, for some, was quicksilver in their hands. What came afterwards was in many ways magnificent, however, and whether or not one considers the cultural growth of the eighties to be politically complicit or co-dependent, it's impossible to deny the extraordinary effect this period had on the wider culture.

Initially, the New Romantics were thought to be a considered reaction to the anti-glamour of punk, but in one sense they had a kind of nostalgia for the future. Coincidentally, this was the way David Bowie described the atmosphere he was trying to achieve in the video for his 1980 Pierrot-style reincarnation in 'Ashes to Ashes', which featured four ecclesiastically attired Blitz Kids solemnly walking along the pebble beach in Hastings. This backward–forward thing was all the rage. Back in the Blitz, they danced to futuristic sounds in Elizabethan garb, while others cooed along to Siren*-era Roxy as they paraded up and down, dressed like* Thunderbirds *puppets.*

If the decade of 'style culture' started in 1975, in parochial southern nightclubs and northern art schools, it also grew in parallel with the ska movement, electronica and goth, sub-cults which flowed in and out of each other like silk ribbons. The post-punk New Romantics have often been disparaged, but actually they were a crucial part of a pop-culture continuum, as well as being responsible for some of the most compelling music of the post-war period. Many of the bands associated with the genre thought they were the new bastions of the underground, although a few became tied up with imperialism, escapism and dressing up. The television adaptation of Brideshead Revisited *was screened in 1981, and while obviously a fairly ruthless examination of aristocratic values, on a surface level it was also an endorsement of fantasy, one that plugged right into the wedding that summer of Charles and Diana. Fiddling while Brixton and Bristol burned. This framing was developed by the likes of the* NME*, which considered New Romanticism to be the enemy of progress, indicative only of a new centre-right sensibility. The editors of* Smash Hits*,* i-D *and* The Face *begged to differ.*

Not only did this period act as the shop window for one of the most creative entrepreneurial periods since the sixties, not only did it have a huge influence on the growth of print and broadcast media both here and abroad, and not only did it visually define the decade, it was the catalyst for the second British invasion, when the US charts, not to mention MTV, would be colonised by British pop – Duran Duran, Spandau Ballet, Culture Club, the Eurythmics, Depeche Mode, the Human League and Wham! all vying for teenage hearts (and dollars), from Pennsylvania to Santa Barbara. Before the turn of the decade, pop had appeared on the features pages of newspapers, but by 1983 it regularly appeared on the front page, making it one of our most powerful cultural exports.

Fundamentally, the New Romantics were the result of a groundswell of entrepreneurialism, a DIY ethos that, in the space of about eighteen months, produced an entire generation of creatives. As the critic David Stubbs says, 'The New Romantics were partly a counter-cultural celebration of free play in a post-industrial world, in which you defined yourself not by the job you had but what you decided, stylistically, to become.'

There was an ancillary army too, of journalists, film-makers, fashion designers, illustrators, publishers, promoters. This entrepreneurial spirit was one that continued as the seventies turned into the eighties, and as times became tougher, so people had to be more attuned to their surroundings. As society's safety net was swiftly reeled in and folded up, a pioneering spirit became the order of the day. Punk had also encouraged many to take more care with how they dressed, as they began to understand that the way you looked determined not just how you were perceived, but also how you might be employed. Blitz Kids mainly wore hand-me-downs and second-hand clothes, and while many of them were fashion students who could create their own little mini-masterpieces, they were all part of a generation which had become accustomed to 'making do', scouring charity shops and altering high-street designs in order to create their own looks. Some of the denizens of the Blitz could afford to spend their money in Bond Street, South Molton Street and Beauchamp Place, but not many. Nor did they necessarily aspire to do so, as the Blitz Kids had far more of an entrepreneurial DIY spirit than people thought. In many respects they were alchemists, turning trinkets into jewellery, making a demob suit look like evening dress and often conjuring something out of nothing much at all. 'I'll take a piece of rubbish and make it the chicest thing you've ever seen,' said the stylist and designer Judy Blame, a man who was at the core of both the early-punk and New Romantic scenes. Christened Christopher Barnes, he was still called Chris when I met him in his Brixton squat in 1981. Like many Blitz Kids at the time, he lived from hand to mouth, from club to club, and from outfit to outfit. To meet him you wouldn't have thought that he would go on to become one of the most influential stylists of his time, but then people didn't really think like that in 1981. Not all of them, anyway. Some of the people in groups had a far more ambitious streak in them – a streak that Spandau Ballet's Gary Kemp, for instance, is justly proud of – but for the majority, their lives were spent looking for some kind of definition and acknowledgement. Success, if it arrived, would come later.

'I've always said nightclubs really were like my school, because you used to go out and you'd see lots of people you knew,' said Blame, 'and we had our own looks going on and everything, having a really good time.'

David Hepworth: In 1979, I was being kept by my wife, a teacher, when Fred Dellar at the *NME* told me that Nick Logan was starting a new magazine. So I rang Nick, and he pretty much asked if I could start the next day. He'd put the first issues of *Smash Hits* together on his kitchen table, but by the time I joined, in 1979, they'd just gone fortnightly and even had an office. When Nick left to start *The Face*, Ian Cranna became editor, and then I followed him. We were in Carnaby Street, and it was an incredibly small team. That was actually one of my first glimpses of what became the New Romantics, as there used to be a clothing shop called the Foundry, just off Carnaby Street. And Boy George used to sit in all his finery in the window. I don't know if he worked there or what. I used to see Marilyn as well. They really were odd creatures from a different galaxy. If you saw anybody like that in those days, they'd made it up themselves; they hadn't gone and bought it from anywhere.

Stephen Jones: One minute we were unknowns and the next we're bumping into David Bowie at the Blitz.

David Bowie was spending more time in London, and one of the things which had started to fascinate him was the capital's nightlife. Having immersed himself in the Berlin club scene, he was intrigued to see how London compared. 'I was upstairs at the Embassy Club when I spotted Bowie,' says Marilyn, one of the stalwarts of the Blitz. 'Naturally, I went over and sat on his lap. Imagine my surprise when he turned around, grabbed me and started sucking my neck. He was a bit forward, I thought, so I pushed him off. But it wasn't long before he'd managed to plant a big red love-bite all over me. He was around a lot at the time . . .'

Chris Sullivan: You'd occasionally see David Bowie at the Sombrero in High Street Kensington at the end of the seventies, but I didn't meet him until he came down with Bianca Jagger to Hell one night, which was a one-nighter I was running in Soho in 1980, at the same time as the Blitz. He had this soul-boy haircut, peg trousers and a brown tweed overcoat. It was empty, maybe only about six people there. My friend Christos [Tolera, the painter] went up to him and said, 'Hello, mate, how are you doing?' He thought he was an old soul boy he knew from Essex who used to go to the Lacy Lady. Christos is asking him how he is, and David Bowie doesn't really know what's going on, eyes looking around the room. I think he may have been chemically enhanced at the time. Christos that is, not David Bowie. I think Bowie went off that night with Helmut Newton. After he left, Christos came up to me and told me all about this guy he used to know at the Lacy Lady – which was an old soul club in Essex – and he was mortified when I told him he'd been talking to David Bowie for half an hour. I think Bowie was too polite to say anything. He said, 'I thought there was something funny about him, because of his eyes. It must have been the drugs.' I said, 'The drugs he took or the drugs you took?'

Steve Strange: I was working on the door of the Blitz, and as usual we were up to full capacity, when I saw a black stretch limo go round the corner three times. At the time, we had already been given two warnings from the council over fire regulations and the number of people we had in the club. In fact, the week before I had to turn Mick Jagger away from the door because we were up to capacity. He was with Sabrina Guinness, and Jagger said to me, 'Don't you know who I am?' I said, 'Of course I do. Please don't make this any harder than it is.' Luckily, I knew Sabrina, and she calmed him down. So this time the limo pulls up and this really stroppy woman called Coco informed me, 'I've got somebody very important in the back of that black limousine.' Because she was so stroppy I gave her quite an arrogant answer. But when she said it was David Bowie, I went into meltdown. I thought, 'Oh my God, what do I do now? If the kids queuing to get in the club even know he's in that limo outside, he'll be mobbed.' So I went into overdrive, thinking how the hell are we going to get him into the building without causing too much of a fracas. I called security, and we opened up the back level of the club, which was the fire exit, and got him upstairs and put him into what we thought was a quiet area, away from prying eyes. However, word spread from the queue, and we had to get security downstairs to stop people coming upstairs. Everybody wanted to be near him. At one point Coco came up to me and said, 'David wants you on his table.' I wasn't being arrogant, but I said, 'Excuse me, I have my job to do. I take my job very seriously. This is not a goldfish bowl. The kids that are in this club are here because they feel at home. My shift doesn't finish until 1.30 a.m.' When I finally went up to him, he said to me, 'I've been watching you and love what you've been doing and the sound that you're creating musically, and I'd like you to be in my next video.' He asked me to style and choose the extras for the video, which was 'Ashes to Ashes'. So four of us were told to meet outside the Hilton Hotel in London at 6.30 in the morning, and we were all thinking we're going somewhere fabulous, and then we're told we're going to Southend! They'd closed off the whole beach, but it was freezing. Bowie was known as a very clever thief; that's why he turned to the Blitz, because he wanted to be part of London's most happening scene.

Midge Ure: I was there the night God turned up, because all those kids were massive Bowie fans. When Bowie turned up at the club, suddenly all these cool, haughty people melted. Just went into absolute hysterics and wet themselves. But it's great when you get someone like Bowie going there to choose Steve and three others to be in the 'Ashes to Ashes' video. That's influential. As flippant and as silly as it might seem, that was making its own little statement.

Marco Pirroni: Steve said, 'Bowie's here,' and he walked up the stairs, and there were people standing on chairs and tables. And maybe I'm just imagining this, but I saw him through the crowd in the middle of a long table. It was the Last Supper, with him with a white suit on. He was like Jesus. Because he was, that's exactly what he was: he was Jesus.

Tracey Emin (*artist*): I was there the night Bowie came down, and I was one of those chosen to sit on the table with him upstairs. That was the first time I met him. I was one of Steve Strange's pets. He always let me in, because I think he thought it was funny to have these two fifteen-year-olds there, in our fringed cowboy tops and ski pants. And false eyelashes. We are the robots! We loved it when he would point at us – me and Maria, my best friend from school in Margate – and say, 'You and you,' and then we would jump the queue . . . and sometimes we didn't have to pay. I used to go to Billy's, but the Blitz I used to go to most weeks. After going to all the soul clubs I started to look for places that played my kind of music, which was more obscure, places that were more sexually ambiguous. My hair was in a quiff at the time, and I dressed like a boy but looked very much like a girl. I wore very short skirts. I used to hang out with Kim Bowen a lot at the Warren Street squat, along with Billy Idol's sister. I used to model for Melissa Caplan and [designer] Willie Brown too. I got to know George, and later he even asked me to join Culture Club and play bass guitar. I could play bass a little as I'd learnt a bit, but I didn't actually want to be in a band at the time. George said not to worry as they were going to have violins, nuns, harps and all sorts in the band. I loved the Blitz, and I think people liked me because I was so young, and homeless, and because I danced a lot, every week, like a robot!

Edward Bell (*artist*): A visit to the Blitz club was not something I relished, in the light of only recently having been denied entry by the host, Steve Strange. Flanked by bouncers, this fastidious arbiter of a particular genre of fashionable dress would, on club night, stand at the door and, scanning the crush, identify with a languid finger the 'chosen ones' for that night. Things were different when David [Bowie] persuaded me to tag along. We sailed in. The place was packed, and all the high priests and priestesses were in attendance (Boy George, Marilyn, Gary Numan et al.). As we entered, the crowd gave off an air of being on the verge of a collective nervous breakdown, but parted like the Red Sea to allow passage for their god. David occupied himself by having fun in picking out those he deemed suitable to appear in his 'Ashes to Ashes' video. As he circulated, so the closely packed crowd followed. Thus, if I stood as far as possible away from him, I was able to breathe, even find space at the bar to have a quiet drink and a fag. The only discordant note that evening came while we sat in the gallery, surveying the massed congregation below. One of the elect approached David offering to procure any, or every, drug under the sun, should he so wish. David didn't even bother to look at him. 'Fuck off,' he said without emphasis.

Eve Ferret: Sophie Parkin was there the night Bowie came. She says he sat next to her and said, 'So, tell me what's happening, what's going on?' And she was so upset by that because she was a huge Bowie fan. She didn't want him to ask her what was going on – he ought to have known himself.

David Mallet (*video director*): I first met David when I was producing and directing *The Kenny Everett Show*, and we had him on the show performing a rehash of 'Space Oddity'. This must have been January 1980. He liked what I did for him and asked if I would make some videos. He was completely un-strange, absolutely charming, highly intelligent . . . I think I would actually say that the biggest plus point was that he just wanted to collaborate. It started off as, I guess you could say, mutual suspicion. Rock'n'rollers aren't mad on television people, and television people are normally slightly in awe of, or expect the worst from, someone with his reputation. But everything I found was completely the opposite to what I would have expected. I probably learnt from him a lot of stagecraft and showmanship tricks, particularly stagecraft, because he'd obviously learnt from people like Lindsay Kemp. If he said, 'Blah blah blah,' and I said, 'Oh bollocks, that won't work,' he'd say, 'Oh, all right then,' and we'd come up with something else. We talked about old television a lot, ridiculous things, obscure British nostalgia. We had a little obsession with an English harp player called Shirley Abicair, who was always on TV in the fifties. God knows what she was; just a ridiculous name that we both remembered from our childhood. Stupid things like that. In those days, video was regarded as the top form, as opposed to a bit of wallpaper, which it is now, so you did your very best to make a film that was to a lesser or greater extent illustrative of the song. On

'Ashes to Ashes', David said he wanted to be a clown on a beach with a bonfire, and wanted to include all the New Romantics, all these characters from the Blitz club. I said, 'Great, but I can improve on that,' because I'd recently found a process which made the sky turn black, and it made the whole thing look like some hallucinogenic dream. 'Great,' says David, 'we'll do that.' The norm for a video in those days was a day, but 'Ashes to Ashes' broke the record, at three. There was a beach, there was a studio, there was a building site . . . you know, on and on. It was epic. [The filming was interrupted at one point by an old man walking his dog, looking for driftwood. Mallet asked him if he wouldn't mind moving, and pointed out Bowie sitting outside the catering van. 'Do you know who this is?' he asked. Sharp as a tack, the old man responded with, 'Of course I do. It's some cunt in a clown suit.' Sometime later, Bowie remembered, 'That was a huge moment for me. It put me back in my place and made me realise, "Yes, I'm just a cunt in a clown suit."']

Diane Wagg (*studio director*): In the eighties, I was director of record producer Tony Visconti's companies, acted as his PA and managed his recording studio, Good Earth, in Soho, for five years. It was an era when there was plenty of money, and we were very young and full of confidence. You could do anything you wanted if you had drive, energy and passion. Good Earth clients included the Boomtown Rats, Thin Lizzy, George Michael, U2, Duran Duran, the Stranglers, Hazel O'Connor and many more. It was party time (our Good Earth parties were legendary) and there was a 'scene' that everyone belonged to, and we hung out together at the Blitz club and the like. In 1980, Visconti was co-producing *Scary Monsters* with Bowie. Bowie was a long-time friend of Visconti's, as well as them having worked together on earlier albums, of course. The stories Visconti would tell were mesmerising and we would all spend hours listening, and David joined in with anecdotes when he was with us. Many stories are out there; others are not and never will be.

So they started recording in New York and then moved to London. We were used to major artists coming through our doors and knew how to take care of everyone, but of course David was going to be extra-special. I'd not met him yet, but Coco Schwab, David's PA and fierce protector, was in touch in preparation for the sessions. We got the Colombian coffee in, the Silk Cut cigarettes, ordered his favourite drinks and food, made the studio immaculate, did extra maintenance, got in supplies, extra equipment, flowers everywhere . . . anything we could do in preparation for our soon-to-arrive guest. I double-checked the insurance for the studio to make sure that if David should cut his finger and not be able to play an instrument, we had more than our usual high cover (in retrospect, I think Coco got me to do that – it would have been on her 'tick list'). The day arrived, and an air of expectancy, excitement and a little nervousness vibrated around the studio. We so wanted to make it a smooth and warm family feel for David and to be a credit and support to Tony. So you know the rest – the album came out, the iconic video with the kids from the Blitz was made and the miracle that is Bowie carried on.

David Bowie: I got the same woman who used to do all the costumes for the Lindsay Kemp mime company, Natasha Korniloff, to make this outfit for me. It was based on the Italian Pierrot. It was pretty well authentic. With a cigarette. The make-up was designed by Richard Sharah, which I smeared at the end of the video. That was a well-known drag-act-finale gesture, which I appropriated. I really liked the idea of screwing up his make-up after all the meticulous work that had gone into it. It was a nice destructive gesture. Quite anarchistic.

Jon Savage: [Bowie] made heavy use of Steve Strange in the 'Ashes to Ashes' video – the most absurd, yet *the* most magnificent, exponent of the Suburban Pose which never dies.

Iain R. Webb: In 1980, when Bowie planned to make a video to accompany 'Ashes to Ashes', he visited the Blitz to handpick his co-stars, among them Steve Strange, wearing designer Judith Frankland's black wedding dress. Frankland walked alongside Strange, behind Bowie, who was dressed as a clown by his long-time collaborator Korniloff. The Blitz's New Romantic crowd had started life at a Bowie night at Billy's nightclub in Soho. It was Bowie's original flamboyance that caught the imagination of the hardcore style snobs that formed the New Romantic scene, and what secured Bowie's credentials as a style icon was his elitist standpoint.

It is somewhat ironic that the success of 'Ashes to Ashes' (Bowie's second No. 1 single in the UK – the first had been 'Space Oddity', to which 'Ashes to Ashes' was the maudlin sequel) coincided with a raft of, if not exactly matchy-matchy songs, then at least a seam of modern electronic pop that took a lot of its tropes from Bowie – everything from excessive styling and arch outsider status to cute androgyny. Ironic because 'Ashes to Ashes' is symbolically the end of Bowie's purple patch, the end of his imperial period. It signalled the end of the queer chameleon, the leopard-skin messiah and the glam apocalyptist, the last anti-rock hurrah before the arrival of the custard-coiffured yuppie, the man who wanted to stay in and get things done. And as Bowie abdicated – or at least stepped down from his perch – the crowds below were full of acolytes who started making records that sounded as though they were made in order for Bowie to like them. It wasn't just Gary Numan who aped Bowie's otherness, but also everyone from the Eurythmics and Spandau Ballet to Visage and Depeche Mode (who were starting to define themselves as a sort of children's television Kraftwerk). A lot of pop is indivisible from the times around it, whereas a lot of early-eighties futurist pop was indivisible from the idea of David Bowie.

David Bowie: *Scary Monsters* was a very obvious way of ending the decade, a way of trying to bring everything full circle, of tying up some loose ends and bringing some harsh realities to my ideas of characterisation. I brought back Major Tom, as I wanted to bring some depth to him, some character. I'd been toying with the idea of bringing Ziggy back, and had actually spoken to Mick Ronson about getting involved again, but when it didn't work out, I thought about reimagining 'Space Oddity'. *Scary Monsters* also turned out to be a big record for me, something commercially viable, which wasn't expected. I was enjoying the video medium, and I could sense that soon everything was going to be about the promo, about the image, about the way you looked as you mimed. It was very odd going down to the Blitz club and seeing all these kids who had grown up with me, who were dressing like me, trying to make records like me! Which is why I wanted some of them in the video for 'Ashes to Ashes'. We also had Gary Numan at one point! Ha! Bless him.

Gary Numan: I had been treated so badly by people, and let down by some people I admired, that when anyone became successful and had any kind of electronic element, I would always write to them and say, 'Congratulations, and welcome to the rat race.' Because my thinking at the time was there was too much animosity between bands. Bands are always having a go at each other. It was always very negative. I think the media played on these band rivalries quite a bit. I didn't like that. I always thought we should be tight, the musicians should all be together and try to find a common bond to deal with all the negativity around us. The music business seemed so hostile. You'd read a review of something, and it was wicked, really cruel and nasty; and you heard people doing interviews, and they'd be slagging off other bands for not being original and whatever. When you were doing interviews, people were genuinely pretty nice, and then they'd write the nastiest things about you. At first, I had no idea that I was going to get fucking crucified, because people seemed quite complimentary, and they are chatting about your stuff and it's jokey and so on. I was just stupidly honest, giving them all this ammunition. So after a while it started to make me really nervous. Every question you were trying to figure out what they were really getting at, and it made you doubt everything you said. And so it was a bad experience, actually. For instance, I was slightly jealous of the fact that Ultravox seemed to be very popular with the press, and Visage. Anyway, I started well, but then my success began to fall away.

Midge Ure: Nobody in their right minds would sit down and think, 'Right, let's write "Vienna".' There isn't a less commercially successful song you could imagine, this long, slow, meandering thing. It was a fluke. It's a fine piece of music, but it's too long, it's the wrong format, it doesn't fit, it speeds up, slows down, it's got a violin solo . . . Everything kind of goes against it. So for anyone thinking I came in and I changed everything about the band, all I changed was the dynamic. Just like you do with any set-up, anything that involves a team. When you change one member of the team and bring someone else in, the entire team changes just because of the nature of the beast. And that's what happened. I suppose we got slightly rockier, maybe more melodic. I had no great plan to walk in and say, 'I can make Ultravox commercially successful.' It was people hearing that song that made it successful.

Rusty Egan: Steve [Strange] had been in a group called the Photons, and they all wore the Bowie suits, like off the back of *Pin-Ups*, except Steve. Vince Ely, the Psychedelic Furs' drummer, was in it. He left, the guitarist went back to Wales, the bass player married a Swedish girl . . . I saw Steve on stage with them, though, and he looked amazing. It was in this little Covent Garden theatre. Some girl had made a special outfit for him. He could sing too. I didn't think he could at first, but there he was. I thought, 'Right, he can sing, he can write songs, he's worked in a nightclub, he looks amazing, he's wearing all the latest fashions.' He was a great person to focus a band around. Midge Ure and I had some ideas for some electronic-sounding songs. I told him I didn't want to play gigs any more. He couldn't understand that, and said, 'You can't give up being a musician.' But I wanted to be in the studio, not touring and being in a rock band. I hadn't been into that for the whole of the previous year. I'd been going to discos and clubs, so we ended up getting Steve and forming Visage. Steve knew exactly what he wanted to do by then; he wasn't put up to it by Midge and I. The basic boot came from me, but he found the direction. He just thought, 'Great, I'll get all those bastards who used to treat me badly.'

Midge Ure: Visage were a studio band, and we were never meant to play live. We were just making music to play in Rusty's clubs.

Steve Strange: We did actually do quite a few bits of jamming [on the first Visage album]. In the sense of how I used to write, some of the songs I had to put lyrics to, so although I had been in a band prior to Visage, it was quite new to me, being in a studio and writing lyrics and actually writing the first Visage album in that way. To be quite honest, when we actually wrote the first Visage album, if it wasn't for the likes of Godley and Creme [who directed the videos for 'Fade to Grey' and 'Mind of a Toy'] and Martin Rushent [their original producer] from Radar, it wouldn't have happened.

I knew we had something with the album. In the studio, Midge taught me that Bowie technique of creating lyrics by cutting up newspapers, and to shuffle those cards like Eno – Oblique Strategies, that sort of thing. When the album came out, I was like, 'Why haven't I got a credit on "Fade to Grey"?' [But] it was my idea to put the French girl in, and it was supposed to be a five-way split. Our first pay cheque from that was £350,000, every one of us. And that was because of me getting out of bed and going to five countries in a day, and all they did was moan about me going to too many fucking parties. I was pissed off. I was the only one not signed to a record contract. I didn't know how these things worked; I was pretty naive. But I was the one going to five fucking countries in one day, while everyone else got to lay in bed. Nobody did anything to help me promote the album. The thing is, I would never have dreamed of telling Midge how he should play or anything like that, and once my vocals were recorded, done and dusted, it made much more sense to me to be out at a party. I mean, why should I be locked in a studio, when I can be photographed out and about? Midge would be like, 'Oh, you've done your vocals now. I suppose you're fucking off to a party.' I went, 'Yeah, I am actually, to get us more press, to sell us more records!'

Keanan Duffty: Everyone was forming bands. I was the guitarist in a Doncaster band called Wonder Stories, which started in the winter of 1980. We were a dandy band of merry men in pixie boots, out to rob the riches of the music industry. One of the band had been to the Blitz and had passed the test of style enforced by the club's promoter and doorman Steve Strange, while simultaneously facing down the catty remarks of coat-check boy George O'Dowd. Now we were all on a mission to avoid the drab conformity of our northern English town and live like it was Studio 54: thrift-store chic and cut-price Kraftwerk. The audience at the New Outlook club in Doncaster contained a strange bunch of style misfits, all fleeing from the mundane: a male nun, a Cossack, a Che Guevara lookalike, a bloke in a wedding dress and the Chip Shop King of South Yorkshire, looking like he had escaped from *Game of Thrones*. I had to live down the howls of laughter and disapproving barbs from the neighbours as I waited at the bus stop, looking like Little Lord Fauntleroy in crushed velvet, eyeliner and Cuban-heeled winkle-pickers. I didn't care. In my mind I was walking down a catwalk, not the high street, and every day was a voyage in a parallel universe. I looked like a discount Andy Warhol. *The Man Who Fell to Earth* had landed in *Coronation Street*. I have fond memories of that era, as in retrospect it seems joyfully naive. Anything seemed possible. We have come to an impasse in contemporary culture, and the sheer vacuous nature of contemporary celebrity culture makes the New Romantics seem like intellectual giants. It's a simple analogy: the late seventies were black and white; the early eighties seemed to transform the world into vibrant colour. The sixties had been swinging, but only for a few hundred lucky people. By the seventies, it was pretty bleak. Punk offered an alternative, but its nihilism hit a brick wall, while the Blitz Kids embraced a more positive, upwardly mobile politics.

Iain R. Webb: 'Dressing up' has definitely been used pejoratively, but I believe dressing up can often be viewed as a provocative political statement. It was, after all, the drag queens who changed the world at Stonewall. In the mid-eighties, I remember getting grief from the rockabilly regulars at the Bell gay pub when me and my best friend, the androgynous model Martine Houghton, took to dressing flamboyantly like the bastard children of Oscar Wilde.

The Blitz lasted until October 1980, by which time other clubs had started to crop up, not just in London, but all over the UK. Chris Sullivan, Robert Elms and Graham Smith (who was developing into the scene's in-house photographer) had already had some success with a number of warehouse parties at Toyah Willcox's Mayhem Studios in Battersea, and so in January 1980 they partnered with an old friend of Sullivan's from Merthyr Tydfil, Stephen Mahoney, and opened a Monday-night club at St Moritz, a cellar in Wardour Street. Here, the music reflected the retro leanings of the Blitz crowd, being somewhat old-fashioned and camp. St Moritz lasted until March 1980, and two months later Sullivan joined forces with Strange and Egan in a new venture, Hell, in Henrietta Street, again in Covent Garden. This closed the same week as the Blitz, a month before Sullivan, Elms and Smith started another one-nighter at Le Kilt, where the tropes were tartan and funk (two things which were previously thought to be mutually exclusive).

Chris Sullivan: I had started doing the warehouse parties at Toyah's Mayhem Studios, and then we opened one-nighters at Kilt, St Moritz, Hell . . . The reason we did St Moritz was because the whole Blitz gig had got a bit silly. There were people coming in with writing down their faces and silly make-up and daft clothes. The reason we had door policies was because your normal person couldn't cope with people like Philip Sallon walking around in a wedding dress and a policeman's helmet, or George as a geisha with a green face. One night, Jock McDonald slipped in. He was in a band called the 4" Be 2"s with John Lydon's brother, Jimmy. And he used to bully Steve and go around PX and take clothes without paying for them, and he had his little gang of Arsenal tearaways. They came down the Blitz one night and they were bullying Stephen Linard and Princess Julia. So I took Jimmy outside and I basically beat the three of them up, and it was all over very quick. So they start making death threats to Steve. Next thing you know, about twenty-five of them come down mob-handed and storm the door and come running through the club. I got hit on the head with a chair, I had a glass on the side of my face. Then there's a roar from the back, and all of the Animal Nightlife mob get stuck in, all these heterosexual tough geezers, the Ealing contingent who fought the punk–Ted wars. They came from the back and completely battered the living shit out of them. I've never seen such a hiding given to a group of people. It was incredible. They were just completely annihilated. Of course, it did rather spoil the night.

Nick Rhodes: Chris Sullivan's Hell was very cool and perfect. Everything seemed in its place, with everyone in their little rooms . . . full of immaculately dressed people talking away, while Marlene Dietrich played in the background. It was nothing like the mad-crazy party scene in Birmingham.

Iain R. Webb: Antony Price had a shop in the King's Road called Plaza that we all aspired to. I've got a photograph of me standing outside, with a massive screen in the window. The screen meant that you couldn't see inside, so you didn't really know what was going on. In a way, that stopped a lot of people going in. To him, it meant: 'If you're not ballsy enough to come through the door, you're not ballsy enough to wear my clothes.' That was incredibly modern. Even when you went in, the clothes were stapled onto a board, with a drawing and a number, and you'd have to ask the assistant, and they would go away and bring them back to you, and then you go into the little booth and try them on. Everything was art-directed.

The Them crowd, the Chelsea set, were very important because it was them who actually allowed us to do what we did, because they'd been there before. People like Andrew Logan, Duggie Fields, Luciana Martinez, Zandra Rhodes, Antony Price, Keith from Smile. They were important because they had a big gay strand, which is something that's often forgotten about punk and the early Blitz days. It was fuelled by gay people and gay culture, but as most pop historians are straight, it's always seen through the eyes of straight men. But the Blitz culture was all gay. I don't think the writers do it deliberately, but I think there's an element of gay infrastructure in punk, as well as the New Romantics. When I'm talking about self-expression at the Blitz club, you can relate that right back to things like the Cockettes in San Francisco.

Peter York: New Romantics was a marvellously cynical name, wonderfully memorable and inappropriate for a group of little stylists, kids who'd grown out of the twentieth century.

The entire history of post-Second World War pop culture is rife with cultural appropriation, from Elvis Presley onwards, and yet it wasn't until the noughties that 'intersectionality' – the idea that discrimination takes on different forms depending on the race, class or gender of the person discriminated against – took hold. If you were a white girl with cornrows, you were no longer considered naff but offensive, immediately the victim of Internet outrage.

The sensitivities surrounding the Blitz Kids' dressing-up would no doubt cause a media flurry today, and yet even at the time there were boundaries that were being pushed. One prominent second-wave Blitz Kid took to wearing Hasidic clothing, including heavy black overcoats and a wide-brimmed black velvet hat. He drew the line at wearing a shtreimel, *the tall, cylindrical, Russian sable hat that Hasidic men wear on the Sabbath, but probably only because they were more difficult to get hold of. He saw no reason not to wear this ensemble as he didn't think he was being in any way offensive, although after six months or so, having been accosted by various Orthodox Jews who accused him of insensitivity, it was returned to the dressing-up box. I can't remember anyone taking George O'Dowd to task for his wildly extravagant ecclesiastical garb, but I would imagine that was only because he looked so intimidating.*

'My granddad, a lovely man and always very smart in a suit, I met him once outside Waterloo station and he refused to sit in the same carriage as me,' says Spandau Ballet's singer, Tony Hadley. 'I was wearing ballet slippers, white socks, wraparound Iranian Cossack-type trousers, tight at the ankles and baggy, with a flap like Aladdin up the front, a silk shirt with Greek imprints, make-up and a headband. And this was only going to see my mum and dad in Pontins.'

Midge Ure: In Slik, there were just girls in the audience. In Ultravox, the boys started to come too, in mackintoshes and moustaches. There were always lots of men at Ultravox concerts.

Blondie were so successful in Britain that the country almost took ownership of them. They were always on television, always in the music press and touring up and down the country. The privilege of access was not treated lightly by the band, and while many US groups tended to be rather patronising towards the UK, Blondie embraced the country and its people. Deborah Harry and her partner, Chris Stein, were driven by ambition: what was the point of being a professional musician unless you were going to be successful? The question was completely rhetorical. They had a reverence for Mike Chapman – the Parallel Lines *producer who had previously helped define the glam era (almost single-handedly) – and they adored the British bands who came in the wake of the first punk explosion. But they really had a lot of respect for Giorgio Moroder. The legendary producer had originally asked Fleetwood Mac's Stevie Nicks to supply the lyrics and sing the theme song to the 1980 movie* American Gigolo, *but when she turned him down because of contractual issues, he approached Harry. Moroder presented Harry with a rough instrumental track called 'Man Machine', and she supplied the lyrics. Thus, 'Call Me'.*

Deborah Harry: Giorgio was great. He's a funny personality. In a way, he's a scientist. A bit like Leonardo da Vinci, he's this multilayered artist, a scientist, a curious person. He's kind of a mathematician, and we were all sort of in awe of him. He had done all those tracks with Donna Summer by then, including 'I Feel Love', which I completely adored. The music completely fitted with what we were trying to do, that mixture of hot and cold. The Blondie character I created was always meant to be androgynous. Obviously, I don't think that I am physically androgynous, but I wanted 'Blondie' to have more supposedly male traits. I've always been frustrated by the idea that I grew up in an era when women were not expected to have a career or to have strong opinions. I felt akin to a more kind of liberal mentality and I always felt angry about being told, 'Oh, you can't do that because you're a girl.' The idea of not having that authority was something that probably pushed me into being a punk. It might not have looked like it at the time, but I was all about androgyny.

In John Lennon's last radio interview, on 8 December, he said, 'Wasn't the seventies a drag, you know? Here we are. Well, let's try to make the eighties good, you know? 'Cos it's still up to us to make what we can of it.'

1981

VIDEO KILLED THE RADIO STAR

'I can't stand rock'n'roll. I like Giorgio Moroder because I like pop. Moroder met a mad professor in Germany who had built a machine that could make all kinds of sounds, and Giorgio said, "With this, I have hits!" He made "I Feel Love" soon after that. I like commercial music, and we certainly wanted the Human League to be commercial. The idea was that people could go into a record shop and say, "I want the record by that bloke with the hair on one side." It had to be as easy as buying a bar of chocolate.'

PHIL OAKEY

Midge Ure: After 'Vienna', with the 16mm, Cinemascope, grainy, black-and-white film noir, everyone wanted a video – Duran, Spandau, McCartney . . . everyone.

The future kept arriving. This was the year in which MTV started to supplant radio as the main conduit for pop, while also helping to sell bands who put more of an emphasis on the way they looked, and who, had they not done this, would otherwise have been 'shelf death'. The channel was launched on 1 August, with the words, 'Ladies and gentlemen, rock'n'roll,' played over footage of the countdown to the launch of the first space shuttle, Columbia *(which had taken place earlier in the year). The first music video shown on the channel was 'Video Killed the Radio Star' by Buggles, a song that had been written three years previously.*

Soon it became imperative for pop stars to be videogenic, to have a 'style', a story they could tell through their clothes, their hair and the location of their videos. The channel quickly developed a style of its own – brash, colourful, fast, cool – a unique visual language that was immediately appropriated by the creatives responsible for the advertising that MTV wrapped around the pop promos. Whether they were selling sports shoes, hair mousse, breath freshener, jeans or even cars, they cast the consumer as a smooth suburbanite with street smarts, the kind of generic US pop consumer who probably felt that Daryl Hall and John Oates might have been as transgressive as they were prepared to be themselves.

In the space of six months, MTV also seriously disrupted the US payola system, which had ruled the industry for decades. The American record business had been built on payola, and if you wanted your single to enter the charts at No. 5, say, all you had to do was pay for it. You simply paid your $50,000 to the relevant parties, and the job would be done. Frequently, British acts with absolutely no media presence in the US would find themselves in the American Top 10, having been included in some management deal with the radio stations, often when they hadn't pressed, let alone shipped any vinyl. As the US charts used airplay as part of their sales' calculation, if the right stations were 'flattered', so their lists would be full of thousands of imaginary plays. When MTV became a thing, payola became far less powerful as an industry tool, as the process became far less opaque.

The look of MTV was deliberately retail-focused, as every flat surface, every moving image or ragged animation looked like the kind of thing you might see in a clothes shop or shopping mall. The graphics were bright, colourful and energetic. Every image suggested movement or a party or celebration of some kind. This was brash visual merchandising aimed at the young pop consumer, a look that coincided with the launch, in Italy, of the Memphis Group, a design and architecture agency set up by Ettore Sottsass in 1980, and which premiered at the prestigious furniture fair the Salone del Mobile a year later. Memphis was the base camp of postmodernist eighties design, a brash and fragmented look that borrowed heavily from graphic interpretations of pop art and art deco, bundled together with unapologetic and often meaningless elements of kitsch. Critics lampooned the Memphis style for being 'a shotgun wedding between Bauhaus and Fisher-Price', which was a good approximation of the visual tropes utilised by MTV. This, however, became the visual vocabulary of the first half of the decade – bright colour, geometric patterns, seemingly random, child-like shapes, lurid illustration and a heavy use of irony. It was faux chic. Plastic. An aesthetic based on poppy abstraction.

This entry-level postmodernism also shaped many of the videos MTV were so keen to show, fantastical dreamscapes that appeared to acknowledge their superficiality, while striving for a stylistic authenticity. The British pop video of the early eighties was postmodernism come to life – a dayglo world of juxtaposition, irony and ambiguity. Or, more prosaically, wild hair, 'fun' clothing, typographic gymnastics and knowing smiles. And if not a smile, then a smirk or a designer frown. Design trends of this period included po-mo deco, neon noir, popsical cyberpunk, tropical pastel (which was very popular with restaurants) and geometric rainbow. Jazzy palettes one and all.

MTV became part of a slogan the minute it launched, as the company had spent months working with the Madison Avenue legend George Lois trying to come up with one. The winner, 'I Want My MTV', was used in idents featuring David Bowie, Mick Jagger, Madonna and Pat Benatar, and, most famously, was later sung by Sting on Dire Straits' 'Money for Nothing'.

Predictably, not everyone liked it. Greil Marcus, the cultural critic, was savage in his denunciation. 'MTV is the pornography of semiotics,' he said. 'Available around the clock, a closed system where nothing outside its frame of reference is ever allowed to intrude, it most closely resembles the lowest porn commodity, the loop: a circular repetition of signs whose meanings have been frozen long in advance.'

Peter York: Video style bundled up all the key factors in one go: pop music, clothes designers, young film directors (usually trained in TV commercials), set designers, graphic designers. Any time you see the following motifs in a film, TV, music, packaging or graphics, remember where they come from: spiky hair, white faces (Jackson Pollock's paint splash?), very red lips, girlish boys, boyish girls, cross-dressing, period clothes, rocking horses (think of Robert Palmer's 'Addicted to Love', where those girls' lips vibrate like a volcano designed and shot by a British photographer). All these clichés of popular modern design – the video style – started in late-seventies British design in music and fashion and graphics. When I think of the English promo video, I think of Adam Ant's 'Stand and Deliver', at the height of the New Romantic style. It featured Adam as a 'dandy highwayman' in eighteenth-century kit, tricorn hat, brilliant make-up and Walkman, swinging though post-modern English period settings to music stolen from African Burundi drummers at the suggestion of Malcolm McLaren.

Neil Tennant: MTV meant Adam Ant could have a visual manifesto that brought together all the bits and bobs he'd learnt in art school and put it on children's television at 10.30 on a Saturday morning.

Gary Kemp: The only reason MTV became so successful in America, and then globally, was because there were these pretty beautiful, visual-orientated bands coming out of the UK. That was all they showed, British bands – us and Duran, Culture Club. In a way, this was more interesting than the first British invasion, as we were going up against established American artists who didn't really understand the medium. It was only when Bruce Springsteen did 'Dancing in the Dark' that rock bands realised they all needed videos.

Peter York: Video made it a saleable style. I think it's the fact that you had all that stuff, you combine it with video – and slick, high-cost videos were very much an eighties thing – and you made it saleable. Absolutely everyone talked at the time about what the whole shtick was – what the video looked like, who was doing the styling, all that stuff. It was a total package. People who understood the look of things got their shout . . .

Deborah Harry: Our success in the UK was a huge boost for us, and the general atmosphere in the country at the time was amazing. The way in which the media and broadcasting works here created this wonderful ambience, and it was a new experience for us because our country was so regional at the time. We didn't have a unified presentation of what the music scene was. There was the East Coast, the south, the west and the central states. So everything was always sort of divided. That all changed with MTV. When MTV happened, the US was a lot easier to reach.

One video that MTV never showed is considered by some to be the greatest New Romantic video of all, first broadcast on BBC2 in February 1982. Featuring an assortment of Blitz Kid archetypes – a cartoon Nazi here, a Cavalier there, a bloke in a beret at the back – the song's deliberately meaningless lyrics were the very height of parody: 'By the river of blood, the children cry, their egos ruined by an alibi.' The band were called Lufthansa Terminal, the song was titled 'Nice Video, Shame About the Song', and it appeared in the sketch show Not the Nine O'Clock News.

Midge Ure: When the *Vienna* album came out, there was a marked difference in the dynamic within Ultravox. The band became a real band, which was really quite interesting. There wasn't a leader, there wasn't a dominant character; there were four individuals pulling together and making a sound that only those four individuals could make. So once we came out with 'Sleepwalk', people got it. Because it wasn't the same as the previous Ultravox; something had changed, and they could hear that something, whatever it was, and they kind of accepted it. And, of course, once 'Vienna' came out as a single, we crossed over to an entirely different audience, and they didn't know the previous Ultravox, the one with John Foxx. Ultravox to them was the band that they'd heard on the radio that day.

There was an obvious through-line from the likes of Ultravox, Visage, the Human League, Depeche Mode et al. right back to the origins of pop art in the fifties. Whether you look at the slightly parodic work of the British pop artists or the more immersive imagery produced by the Americans, they were both dealing with everyday subjects, like comic books, advertising, Hollywood, product design and pop music – all of which were mass-produced, designed for mass-market appeal, and which often involved mechanistic, generic sex appeal. What these groups appeared to be suggesting was that it was easier to digest transgressive attraction if it was presented in a robotic, mediated way: i.e. if it's not real, it can't harm you.

Phil Oakey: Image is a really great thing, I think. I was almost coldly clinical about making sure I got on top of an image. I'd done that before I had a chance to be in a group. Because I loved David Bowie so much, because I loved Marc Bolan and Rod Stewart so much, and they all had haircuts, I had started looking for one. Maybe also because I was shy. I wasn't very good at speaking to people at parties and I needed something to make them come to me.

The Human League were a peculiar compound of the familiar and the exotic. Their name was deliberately arch – it came from a board game called Star Force ('Alpha Centauri – Interstellar Conflict in the 25th Century') – although they felt very familiar. While Duran Duran and Culture Club delivered slick, straightforward pop, Phil Oakey seemed unable to produce material that wasn't in some way meta.

While being one of the first post-punk synth groups, the Human League had found it difficult to get any quantifiable commercial traction. Both their 1979 album Reproduction *and 1980's* Travelogue *sold modestly, and they were so marginalised they were even lampooned on the Undertones' Top 10 single 'My Perfect Cousin'. Steadfastly determined to stay true to their art-house ethos, they managed to screw up their big opportunity of 1980, when their management secured the support slot on the Talking Heads' UK tour. Bizarrely, they decided to suggest a fully automated show, which meant they could stand in the audience and watch 'themselves' on stage. 'We'd got these new synchronisation units that operated the slide show in sync with the music,' says Ian Marsh. 'We guaranteed that while we wouldn't be on stage, we'd be at every gig, talking to the audience, shaking hands and signing autographs.' Martyn Ware was equally enthusiastic. 'We'd gone a long way down the line: all the programming was done, it was going to be this big multimedia show, almost Exploding Plastic Inevitable. But Talking Heads changed their minds; it was too much for them. Maybe they thought they were going to be upstaged.'*

At the tail end of 1980, Ware and Ian Craig Marsh acrimoniously left the Human League and launched an independent mini-corporation called the British Electric Foundation, a loose-knit group with a slightly arch/meta agenda who set out to act as freelance producers, encouraging the likes of Gary Glitter, Sandie Shaw, Bernie Nolan and Tina Turner to record unlikely cover versions. At the same time, Ware and Marsh also formed Heaven 17 with Glenn Gregory (who had been their original choice when looking for a singer for the Human League), a group that was responsible for half a dozen classic early eighties anthems: '(We Don't Need This) Fascist Groove Thang', 'Play to Win', 'Let Me Go', 'Temptation', 'Come Live with Me', 'Crushed by the Wheels of Industry' and 'This Is Mine'.

In Stanley Kubrick's film version of A Clockwork Orange, *the movie's anti-hero Alex DeLarge sweeps through the aisles of his favourite record shop (it was actually shot at the Chelsea Drugstore on London's King's Road, which is now a McDonald's). He strolls by an illuminated chart of fictional groups: Johnny Zhivago, the Humpers, the Sparks, the Legend, the Blow Goes, Bread Brothers, Cyclops, the Comic Strips, Goggly Gogol and, of course, the Heaven Seventeen.*

Michael Bracewell: The Human League's 'alienated synthesist' period lasted two albums, *Reproduction* and *Travelogue*, before Marsh and

Ware left the group in December 1980 to found Heaven 17 and BEF. It was at this point that Phil Oakey recruited Ian Burden to play bass and Jo Callis – formerly of the Rezillos – to play guitar. Then, most famously, in the Crazy Daisy nightclub in Sheffield he found two teenage girls – still at school studying for A-levels – who looked like Sheffield's answer to the models Bryan Ferry had recruited to sing on the Roxy Music *Siren* tour. Joanne Catherall and Susanne Sulley were the magic ingredient which turned the Human League's cult recognition into the stuff of multimillion-selling albums. By feminising the masculine, dare we say 'geekish', appeal of the early League (boys in long raincoats reading Penguin Classics and the *NME*), Catherall and Sulley managed to empower the group's ability to make pure pop. Suddenly, the bookish boy fans of the Human League would discover that girls liked the group as well. It was the final triumph of combining ingredients which shouldn't work. With their hip-swinging, hand-clapping dance style, always looking like they were having a laugh, the girls humanised the Human League and, in so doing, paved the way for *Dare!* to sell five million copies. Notably, the sleeve was based on the cover of an issue of German *Vogue* – the final summation of all those boys and girls who had lived out their dreams of Roxy Music glamour and fashion-magazine style through provincial nightclubs and Saturday-afternoon shopping trips in the rain. *Dare!* became a fixture in one generation's record collection, just as Carole King's *Tapestry* or David Bowie's *Ziggy Stardust* had become standard-issue records for earlier generations. Along with its smash-hit singles 'The Sound of the Crowd', 'Love Action (I Believe in Love)', the Christmas 1981 No. 1 'Don't You Want Me' and its clutch of glossy videos, *Dare!* became a kind of multimedia package: a definitive statement of its times, ushering in a new pop sensibility after punk and post-punk, which would quickly lead to the whole jazz revival. And problems for the Human League. Interviewed in the early eighties, Oakey cited his favourite singles as teen stompers by Dollar and Abba.

Phil Oakey had the perfect postmodernist haircut for the perfect postmodernist pop group of 1981, and in fact his haircut almost became the band's logo. Always Sheffield's finest exponents of ironic pop, this regrouped band of post-pop/postmodern futurists embraced three-minute synth pop and fashion-house imagery. Throughout these changes, one thing remained constant – Oakey's ridiculous 'piste', a haircut that was short on one side and long on the other. By 1981, many fledgling bands had started using all kinds of weird haircuts as a means of getting themselves noticed by the press. No longer was a haircut representative of a particular group of people, and if, in a nightclub, you bumped into someone with a gigantic sixteen-inch, charcoal-black conk, it by no means meant that they had anything to do with the music industry. As their meanings became more confused, more diffused, as their codes became scrambled, so haircuts became more idiosyncratic, losing some symbolic importance along the way. (Pejoratively, the press started to call young groups 'haircut bands'.)

Michael Bracewell: The Human League are on a kind of mezzanine between immortality and pop kitsch. On the one hand, they are regarded by pop historians as seminal; on the other, they seem trapped behind the glass of eighties revivalism, a decade which Oakey himself can no longer remember, in his words, as anything more than 'a psychological fog'. Oakey's role within the Human League has become one of the signature performances in British pop. His 'geometric' haircut – trimmed neat to the left, nearly shoulder-length to the right – became almost as famous as his group. Seen now, Human League videos from the early eighties present what seem like miniature New Romantic dramas, with swathes of moody mist, lots of enigmatic technology and, of course, the quietly erotic presence of Joanne Catherall and Susanne Sulley. It is Oakey's triumph and burden that he is remembered for one song, 'Don't You Want Me', the video for which played off the business of making a pop promo against the supposed private affairs within the group. And yet beneath the surface of early-eighties culture there is a secondary cultural history which tells a different story, or at least sheds light on the other. This was the cult of what Oakey described as 'the alienated synthesists', in which young people living in a bright new Britain still found themselves walking through poorly lit concrete subways, feeling displaced and emotionally chilled. Oakey cited Gary Numan's 'Cars' and 'Underpass' by John Foxx as other exponents of this condition. It was the music of the wet, deserted precinct or the bus station at midnight. Back then, the cult of alienation was all to do with looking like the glamorous protagonist in your own film noir.

The way in which Phil Oakey reinvented the Human League as a vehicle for po-mo kitchen-sink dramas has become something out of legend. In June 2019, in the New Statesman, *the Irish novelist Kevin Barry was asked what his specialist subject on* Mastermind *would be. 'You'd be a long time trying to catch me out on arcana concerning early-eighties electro-synth bands from the north of England,' he deadpanned. ('Outside which Sheffield disco did Phil Oakey of the Human League first meet Susanne Sulley* and Joanne Catherall?')*

Joanne Catherall (*singer*): It was just a regular Wednesday. We had certain clubs that we went to on certain nights, and Wednesday was the Crazy Daisy. It was always a bit of a mad place, and Philip didn't actually talk to me that night; he talked to Susan because I was dancing. I remember, of course, going home on the late-night bus and being really excited and saying, 'Ooh, it was lovely of him to want to ask that, but our parents are never going to go for it.' They were quite strict, and you had nothing like *X Factor* in those days. Like now, I don't know if anyone would think it was out of the norm for someone to ask something like that, because people actually seek that sort of stuff. But in 1980, it was a case of, 'Someone in a *band* wants you to go on tour with them! And are we going to let you go?' Certainly, at the beginning of the recording

* Sulley now goes by the name of Susan Ann.

of *Dare!*, Susan and I were still in school, so we just used to hop on the train down to Reading to do bits, then we had to get a train back. We couldn't have days and days off. [The commercial success] wasn't due to just Susan and myself, though; Jo came on board at that time, Ian Burden came on board, and obviously one of the most important people was Martin Rushent. You can have great songs, but if you don't have a good producer – we didn't have anyone within the band who could produce – it can't get finished off to the level of loveliness that Martin did it. We had the songs there, but he finished them off and made them commercial. Because we weren't too way out there, other girls could relate to us. We were down to earth, we were northern, so people could read articles where we'd said things and think, 'Oh, I know what she's going on about there.' People could dress like we did, and I think it was quite important that we weren't just seen as . . . what tended to happen at the time was that girls were singing, but they were very much in the background. Groups at that time were male-dominated; you had female singers, but they tended to be solo singers within a group. Obviously, you had your exceptions, like Abba and Blondie, but it wasn't completely the norm, and I think we helped that change. We were right up front doing backing vocals and dancing, but as a proper part of the band. I think a lot of people, when *Dare!* was a hit, thought it would be a one-hit wonder because synthesizers were not looked upon as proper instruments. If you didn't have a band that had someone playing a guitar and a drum kit in it, you weren't a proper band. We had no qualms about the fact that we wanted to do pop music, but we wanted to do it our way. We didn't have anyone who could play guitar until Jo came along, and he could, and then we didn't let him play his guitar! But then, as he will say, he came out with something like 'Mirror Man' through doing it in a more difficult way than he would have if he'd just been doing it on his guitar. It made it different, and I think it made it better.

Susan Ann Sulley (*singer*): I remember going to Los Angeles to record the TV show *Solid Gold*, and we wouldn't allow them to have their dancers on with us. That wasn't our thing at all; it was way too . . . I don't know, showbiz. And I can remember leaving the set with the guy from the record company shouting at us, going, 'You'll never, ever work in this country again!' Two weeks later, 'Don't You Want Me' was No. 1. We actually didn't want it released as a single. None of us did! On the vinyl, it's the last song on the side, and if you listen to it, you'll hear that there's quite a long gap between 'Don't You Want Me' and the song before it. And we did that on purpose. We felt that 'Don't You Want Me' was not very representative of the rest of the album. But we also knew that the record company thought it was fantastic, and even though we didn't want it as a single, they said, 'Sorry, we're overruling you.' And I'm quite glad they did. And yes, Philip did spot us in a club on the eve of a Human League tour. He never really asked us to join the group. He just asked us to go on that tour with them. They were contracted to do a tour, or else they were going to lose an awful lot of money. And Martyn Ware, who had been in the previous version of the Human League, had a very high voice and used to do all the backing vocals. So Philip actually was looking for just one girl, but then he saw Joanne and I together, realised we were friends and thought we could look after each other. I mean, we were just kids at the time. But we got on really well, and when Philip started writing *Dare!*, he asked us if we wanted to pop over to the studio and do a few vocals. And it happened, just like that.

Phil Oakey: For some reason people think 'Don't You Want Me' is a love song, and it's not. It's a power song. Mostly, there wasn't a lot of love in our records. They tended to get a little bit mawkish if they got towards that. Our songs were about disputes. Love in the band? It happens. [Oakey had a relationship with Catherall.] Romance in the workplace. I think we're lucky to have gone beyond it, and we still get on really well.

Ironically, 'Don't You Want Me' immediately humanised the group, giving them more than a patina of warmth and empathy. Here was a record you could hear in Woolworth's as well as in a nightclub, something you might hear on both John Peel and daytime Radio 1, a walk-you-through-my-story song that moved a banal domestic to-and-fro up onto the big screen. This was the perfect New Romantic macro/micro-riposte to the genre's previous tropes of isolation and elitism. You could sing along with it too. The objective, after all, was ultimately success.

David Stubbs (*writer*): Heaven 17 were preoccupied with immaculacy and detail, all three members pitching in on all aspects of the material, music and lyrics. Meanwhile, in what seemed like a side project, the British Electric Foundation was making an impact. This, in fact, was the label, the package, that Virgin had signed, with Heaven 17 as its first project. BEF were in keeping with a tendency at the time to break away from the convention of the band as mere industry pawns, to take on the contours of 'business' themselves, an evolution of punk's DIY aesthetic. PiL, with the 'Limited' in their name implying corporateness, were playing a similar game. They too had a penchant for suits and ties.

Martyn Ware: When the split happened, it was engineered by the record company, who wanted two bands for the price of one. And, to their credit, it worked. I was presented with a fait accompli; they'd signed Jo Callis, for example. Also, they had Martin Rushent on board. None of this could have happened had the League not split. Meanwhile, Heaven 17 were basically the three of us and a few session musicians, with complete control written into the contract. There was massive rivalry [with both bands working in the same Sheffield studio, recording *Dare!* and *Penthouse and Pavement* at different times of the day]. There was an arms race: who could sell more, be the more snappily dressed.

Glenn Gregory (*musician*): It really wasn't pleasant between Martyn and Phil, because they'd been at school together. Martyn felt really angry. So there was a fire lit under all our arses, to prove ourselves. As for me, I'm very happy that I was never the singer of the Human League because it would have been a completely different kettle of fish. I love the League, especially those first two albums, *Reproduction* and *Travelogue*. I took photographs of quite a lot of their early gigs for *Sounds*. I saw quite a lot of them. They stayed at my flat in Ladbroke Grove.

Heaven 17's first album came out in September. Penthouse and Pavement *featured the band ironically dressed as captains of industry, shaking hands, making deals on the telephone and looking for all the world as though they were building the country's brave new dream. The record obviously required a certain amount of promotion, and the band all needed to look the part. When they were approached about their first photo shoot for the* NME, *Glenn Gregory panicked. As he didn't want to look like a 'rocker', and knowing he had another session scheduled for the album cover, he turned to his grandfather for help, asking if he could borrow one of his old suits. Having found one he liked (and that fitted), his grandfather said he could keep it, including the old £10 notes he found in the pockets, as well as a random packet of condoms. Gregory declined the additional items but wore the suit on the covers of both the* NME *and* Penthouse and Pavement.

Stephen Dalton: Throughout 1980 and early 1981, Depeche Mode became local legends in Essex clubland. Vince Clarke honed a catchy, hook-laden, upbeat pop formula that sat somewhat incongruously with the band's emerging leather-and-chains uniform. Martin Gore, especially, was developing a taste for skirts and make-up, which would lead to endless speculation about his sexuality.

Martin Gore: I honestly don't know what was going through my head when I was doing that. There was some kind of sexuality to it that I liked and enjoyed, but I look back now and see a lot of the pictures and I'm embarrassed. But it never crossed my mind that I might be gay.

I always knew I was heterosexual. Over the years I've met so many people that have naturally assumed I'm gay. I don't have a problem with that. The fact that I'm not is neither here nor there.

Stephen Dalton: Mute Records boss Daniel Miller, who eventually signed Depeche Mode, argues that fetishism and bondage was key to the Essex post-punk underground. Derived from Lou Reed and Suicide, it was the region's hardcore answer to goth and New Romantic. The Mode were never New Romantics. Miller calls them 'futurists – a very subtle difference'. They appealed to his vision for Mute as a modernist, Eurocentric, pro-electronic label. Mute were far from the obvious choice, but Vince Clarke persuaded his fellow Mode members that Miller's left-field pop instincts would serve them well in the long term. Martin Gore recalls being offered 'ridiculous amounts of money' to sign with various major labels, but they chose Miller largely because they admired Mute artists like Fad Gadget, the Normal and Silicon Teens. 'We were very lucky that we did,' says Gore. 'One of the people after us was Mark Dean, who went on to sign Wham! – that whole fiasco. I'm sure if we'd have signed to any one of those major labels, we wouldn't be around today. We'd have been dropped by our second or third album.' The foursome agreed a handshake deal with Mute at the start of 1981, accepting a fifty–fifty profit-share, which later became the gold standard for artist-led labels. They would not sign a formal contract for twenty years. Although their unorthodox Mute deal would eventually prove hugely lucrative to both band and label, the Mode spent their early career watching the pennies. Even while gigging and recording their debut album *Speak & Spell* in 1981, Fletch and Gore stuck with their banking and insurance jobs in east London. When their second single, 'New Life', shot to No. 11 in June, they travelled to their debut *Top of the Pops* appearance by tube.

Andy Fletcher: I didn't have a choice. There was no advance at all. I think Vince got a small publishing advance, and we got a hundred quid, so we didn't have any money. All we ever wanted was our beer money and to give our mums ten quid a week, and that was it. It was a bit peculiar – I think for the first two years we went to *Top of the Pops* on the tube with our synths and things. I'd go into work the next day and get a standing ovation.

Just as success loomed, the Depeche Mode masterplan faltered. Vince Clarke announced his decision to quit the band even before Speak & Spell *became a Top 10 album in October 1981.*

Daniel Miller: The first Depeche single came out in February, and the album came out in October. They did a little tour for it. I was driving them and doing the sound, and I noticed that Vince just wasn't communicating with the rest of the band. He was fine on stage, but I didn't know them well enough, I didn't really know what was going on, and it was around that time he announced he wanted to leave. We asked him to keep it quiet until we'd signed with Seymour Stein from Sire, who were about to sign them for America. It was very odd. Everybody outside the band wrote them off at that point. If you think about it, the guy who writes all the songs has left the band, but Martin had been a songwriter before, and they all stepped up. They were pissed off with him, obviously, so they thought, 'Well, we'll show him we can do it without him.' And they did. It was a bit of a conflict for me because Vince was still on Mute with Yazoo, and for a while they were more successful than Depeche, although that was a very short-lived project. When you're in the middle of it all, you just get on with it somehow. It was a crazy time anyway, because I was learning so fast. I was lucky to find some people, to have professionals around me to help me. I think that's one of the reasons Vince saw the potential when he left Depeche Mode: he was like a technology hoover; he realised that with the technology at his fingers he could do everything, without being in a band. The synth duo was the thing. Vince was just like, 'Whoa!' I don't think he liked the band dynamic, just because it's too much discussion and too many egos – 'All I need is a good singer and I can do the rest myself.' And so the synth-pop duo was born – the Eurythmics, Soft Cell, Pet Shop Boys, Yazoo . . .

For his sins, Vince Clarke had never expected Depeche Mode to be so successful, and he 'didn't feel happy. Or contented. Or fulfilled. And that's why I left. All the things that come with success had suddenly become more important than the music. There was never enough time to do anything.'

Martin Gore: Maybe it was personal, maybe there were frictions – minor frictions compared to what we've put up with for the last twenty years. One thing that might have been a turning point was when he came along to rehearsal with two new songs, and he was teaching us how they went, and when he went to the toilet we just looked at each other and said, 'We can't sing these, they're terrible!' [One of the new songs, dismissed by the group as derivative rubbish, was 'Only You', later a huge hit for Yazoo, the pop duo Clarke formed with Alison Moyet after leaving Depeche Mode.]

Andy Fletcher: You had to be careful with Alison because she'd just beat you up. She was in our class at school and she was the best fighter in the year. Once, when we were in this small Mute office, she thought we were laughing at her, and she said, 'Fletch, if you laugh at me once again, I'll kick you in the bollocks.' Never laugh at Alison Moyet. She will kill you on the spot.

Stephen Dalton: Gore says the Mode were 'in shellshock' after Clarke left, but it was also a 'godsend' for his songwriting ambitions. The band advertised in *Melody Maker* for a replacement keyboard player. West Londoner Alan Wilder was recruited on a weekly wage of £50 in late 1981, initially for live shows only. He would not become a full band member for eighteen months. At first, Wilder's more middle-class roots created distrust in the band.

Daniel Miller: They were very 'Bas'. All their friends were from Basildon, and Alan came from a slightly different – slightly posher, in their eyes – background. He was musically very adept and, at the beginning, slightly snobbish about the fact that everything they played was one-finger monophonic stuff.

Stephen Dalton: Alan Wilder came on board just as Depeche Mode's honeymoon with the pop press began to curdle. As their dirty electro sound hardened, chart music softened. The gleefully synthetic new pop generation was being supplanted by Thatcherite fluff and windy, worthy stadium rock. The synth-pop trend withered, but the Mode stuck unfashionably to their guns. Although their commercial profile would build steadily throughout the eighties, UK critics consistently dismissed the band as comically pervy lightweights. They were a Casiotone Cure, a Toytown New Order, but without the credibility or mystique of either. Reviewers were savage.

Martin Gore: If I'd been writing reviews at the time, I'd have given us a bad review. At least the first couple of albums, and probably a bit longer. But we also really suffered because of our image. We had a really awful image. Once people hate something and get a bee in their bonnet about it, you have to really work to gain their trust back.

Alison Moyet: It was while I was completing my first year at the London College of Furniture that Yazoo came about. I had known Vince since I was eleven, as we both went to a community, council-funded, Saturday-morning music school that was held at Laindon High Road School, Vince's newly enrolled comprehensive, the rival school to me and the other Depeche boys – Nicholas Comprehensive. I was in the same classes at school as Andy Fletcher and Martin Gore from Depeche Mode. I was

Tick tock: in 1975, punk was already simmering away in London, but it took Malcolm McLaren and Vivienne Westwood to give it form, and to give it a purpose. Here is McLaren outside their first proper shop, Let It Rock, in 1972, before it morphed into Too Fast To Live, Too Young To Die, SEX, Seditionaries, and then World's End. (Alamy)

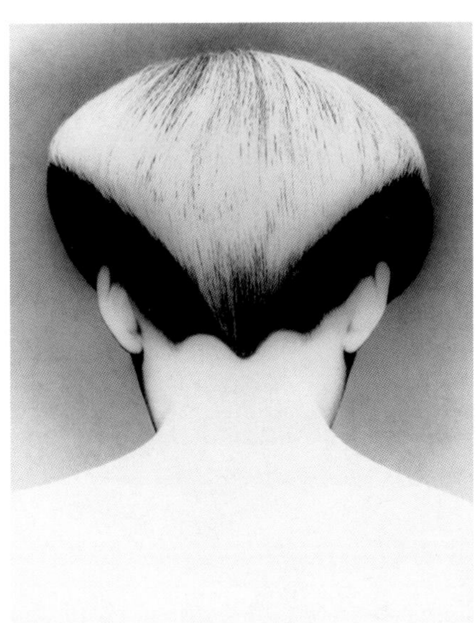

Haircult: the wedge was the most significant hairstyle of pre-punk Britain, worn by both soul boys and girls alike. It looked so alien, and yet so suburban. (Trevor Sorbie)

In the mood: the swing revival in 1975 meant that clubs like the Goldmine on Canvey Island were full of dancers in GI uniforms, swingers who had also been swayed by Bryan Ferry's adoption of the look. (Brian Longman)

The motherlode: David Bowie and Bryan Ferry were the common denominator for everyone involved in the early punk and then New Romantic scenes. They were such arbiters of taste that throughout the seventies they were beyond reproach. Future Adam and the Ants member Marco Pirroni even studied what cigarettes Ferry smoked. (Author)

I'm in with the in crowd: it took a lot of people to create and maintain Bryan Ferry, here with (left to right) stylist Antony Price, designer Nicholas de Ville, photographer Karl Stoecker, and writer and publicist Simon Puxley. (Terry ONeill/Iconic Images)

Steve Strange at the Blitz, where the Cult With No Name were eventually given their moniker, 'Blitz Kids'. Strange was the doorman as gatekeeper, the maître d' as social conductor, a working-class Welsh Gatsby. (Terry Smith)

Fiona Dealey soon became one of the queens of the Blitz, one of the original core gang, and someone who had done her time in the nightclub trenches of Ilford and Canvey Island. Stephen Jones was an ex-punk from High Wycombe who would go on to become the most famous milliner in the world. (Terry Smith)

Rusty Egan was Strange's partner in crime, a musician-turned-DJ who espoused the scene like no other participant. He enjoyed his reputation as a motormouth, but in truth would become renowned for being one of the architects of 'Synth Britannia'. (Terry Smith)

Boy George would soon become the public face of the New Romantics, first as the scariest member of the Blitz Kids, and then as a global pop sensation who became as popular as the Queen Mother, and who famously said he preferred a cup of tea to sex. Seen here with George's friend, Claire. (Terry Smith)

The Ralph West Halls of Residence in Albert Bridge Road, opposite Battersea Park, serviced all the art schools in London, and was where you stayed if you were a student who didn't come from the city. During 1977–79 it became a hotbed of iniquity. Left to right (and opposite): Chris Sullivan, Fiona Dealey, Lee Sheldrick, Stephen Linard, Kim Bowen and Graham Smith. (Graham Smith)

Dencil Williams (pictured with Marilyn, who started life as Peter Robinson) was one of the most glamorous Blitz Kids, with a voice, a dress sense and a sensibility that was equally at home in the hallowed portals of Studio 54 as it was in Soho or Covent Garden. (Graham Smith)

Reluctant émigrés: Christos Tolera, Dylan Jones, Chris Sullivan, Daryl Humphries, John McKitterick and Jimmy O'Donnell channelling Stephen Linard in the summer of 1981. (Author)

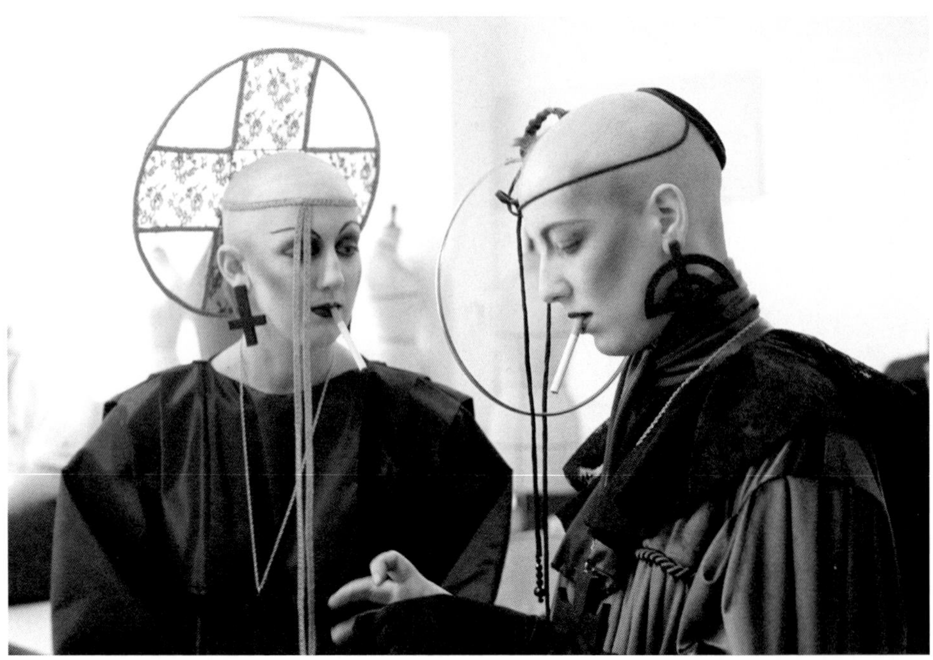

Stars on Sunday: appropriating religious garb was one of the great taboos, one which was exploited by the denizens of the Blitz, including Myra Falconer and Michele Clapton. Michele would go on to be the much-lauded costume designer of *Game of Thrones*. (Graham Smith)

Soon there were one-nighters every night, as the Blitz scene grew like a family tree. This was the flowering of the latest iteration of Swinging London, growing right before your eyes. (Graham Smith)

In the space of three months in 1980, the style press was born, with the publication of *The Face*, *i-D* and *Blitz*, three magazines that would, one way or another, define the decade to come. They appeared to leapfrog existing magazines such as *Ritz* and *Frizz*, while music magazines such as *Zig-Zag* had no choice but to try and catch up. They would soon be joined by the teenage sensation *Smash Hits*, and then by dozens of one-shots devoted to particular bands. Mentioned in despatches: *ZG* and *New Sounds New Styles*. (Author)

Terry Jones was the ex-art director of *Vogue*, who wanted to produce a fashion fanzine like *Sniffin' Glue*. So he invented *i-D*. Pictured with staffers Caryn Franklin, Marion Moisy and Dylan Jones. (Author)

Publisher Simon Tesler and editor Carey Labovitch putting together an early edition of *Blitz*, laying out a feature on Gerald Scarfe (using a tube of Cow Gum). When she launched the magazine, Labovitch had no idea there was a 'Blitz' scene in London. (Carey Labovitch/Guardian)

Ex-mod Nick Logan had been the inspirational editor of the *NME*, one of the most influential publications of the seventies and the paper that launched the careers of Nick Kent, Tony Parsons and Paul Morley. When he left, Logan launched *Smash Hits* before inventing *The Face*, a magazine that would become synonymous with the eighties, and what the eighties wanted to be. (Getty)

Under Steve Dagger's tutelage, Spandau Ballet ran rings around the music industry and even greater rings around the music press, who didn't know how to respond to them. Here they are, taking matters into their own hands in St-Tropez in 1980, along with their in-house spokesman Robert Elms (one of the most important chroniclers of the period), and the unofficial Blitz photographer Graham Smith. (Graham Smith)

David Bowie said that with 'Ashes to Ashes' he was 'wrapping up the seventies', with an epitaph that reunited him with Major Tom from 'Space Oddity'. The accompanying video was a brazen attempt to co-opt the burgeoning New Romantic scene, which was ironic given the entire movement was largely based on him in the first place. (Author)

She was called Sade Adu, the band were called Sade, and they went on to become Britain's most resolute export of the time. Sade not only became a global phenomenon – selling millions and millions of records all over the world – but Sade herself was a very peculiar kind of celebrity: she had absolutely no interest in being famous. (Author)

This was the sound of the late seventies and early eighties, pop singles which meant more than they had done since the sixties, pop records that defined a generation, that elevated the art, and juggled post-modernism without losing any commercial acumen. Some artists wanted to be artists, others just wanted to be popular, but all of them wanted to leave their mark on the new decade. (Author)

The eighties exploded in a riot of pastel, post-modernist hues. The Memphis Group was an Italian design company founded by Ettore Sottsass which specialised in colourful, ephemeral designs and abstract decoration as well as asymmetrical shapes, much of which alluded to already existing forms but which also managed to look insincere and shrill. Very eighties. (Wikimedia)

MTV reinvented pop by placing an emphasis on what it looked like. Where did you get your clothes? Who did your make-up? Why did you decide to define yourself in this way? Answers on a postcode, please . . . (Author)

The eighties had a design sensibility that placed a huge emphasis on decoration. The question was often asked of graphic designers, interior designers and creative directors everywhere: if Duran Duran were a shop logo, crisp packet, pair of earrings, media strategy – what would they look like? (Wikimedia)

In the era of New Pop, when the British media started genuflecting in front of everyone from Alison Moyet and Simon Le Bon to Boy George, the narrative arc was simple: the more famous you became, the more equity you accumulated. This was an era in which pop stars were more willing to play media games than they had been since the sixties. (Alamy)

THE Sun

ONLY 5 DAYS TO GO
£80,000 Sun BINGO

Wednesday, August 15, 1984 16p TODAY'S TV: PAGE 12

BOY GEORGE HIT ME SAYS GIRL, 16

Pop fans in 'fattie' fury

By NIGEL FREEDMAN

A TEENAGE girl pop fan last night accused superstar singer Boy George of punching her on the nose—for calling him a "fat poof."

Sixteen-year-old Alison English claimed that Boy George went berserk in the street when he heard the insult.

Several of her friends backed up Alison's allegation that she was punched square in the face—leaving her semi-conscious with blood pouring from her nose.

EXCLUSIVE

GUTTER

Shocked onlookers say Boy George then had to be dragged away by his chauffeur, still screaming.

Trouble flared when the chart-topping idol, lead singer of smash-hit group Culture Club, arrived at the EMI headquarters in London.

Alison and eight other girls were waiting outside . . . hoping to catch a glimpse of their pop pin-up Duran Duran singer Simon Le Bon.

The girls say Boy George spotted one of his record promotion posters torn up in the gutter and accused them of being responsible.

Sixteen-year-old Michelle Bains, of Raynes Park, South London, said: "He was furious with rage and said we were stupid for following Duran Duran. He said the

Continued on Page Two

Flat out . . . Alison in a photo taken by pop fan Jan Cracknell

IT'S A GIRL'S BEST FRIEND

So keep your new £10million card in a safe place—it could win you a Concorde trip too—Page 7

CATCH THE BINGO BURGLAR AND WIN £500 Page 2

Today's numbers—Page 21

Miner dies in 'scab' storm SEE PAGE 2

The media bites back: you may have been popular, you may have been *really* popular, but in a decade when pop stars moved from the gossip pages to the front page, the trade-off was simple. In the early eighties, pop stars replaced politicians as taking points. (Author)

In 1985, David Bowie was one of the many stars to play Live Aid, the culmination of a ten-year history that in many respects had all been about Bowie in the first place. And here he was, King of the Hill, celestial without being imperious. (Getty)

The second British Invasion. The Beatles? Who the hell were the Beatles? And who cared when the US charts were full of Culture Club, Duran Duran, Spandau Ballet, the Thompson Twins, the Human League, Wham!, Soft Cell, Bananarama and the Eurythmics? Honestly, it was like punk had never happened. What on Earth would Malcolm McLaren say? (Author)

friendlier with them, and later Dave Gahan at Southend Tech, than I ever was with Vince. He and I were townies who would recognise each other, but we weren't mates. We hadn't hung out.

Depeche materialised with the futurists. I went to see them with our mates at Sweeney's, a club at the top of the escalators by the big clock, which was our meeting place. They were pretty and glossy. I'd not seen any of them look like that before. I was impressed by their industry, but I didn't find their chintz compelling. Later, Depeche did it for me very much, but *Speak & Spell* I found too pleasant. I was very much about Canvey Island by then. Music was live. That's how I mostly engaged with it. I didn't listen to the radio, other than any tannoy feed in a factory job, and I never followed the charts.

My mates were my mates. It was an interesting mix. One ended up joining the Cure, another became a well-known international milliner, some died young. Most worked as barely waged care workers. I didn't seek out people on the high-life scene or try to install myself with the up-and-coming stars. I never liked being around that much pleasure. It smelt of snark and privilege, but that could have absolutely been my prejudice. I just didn't trust it. I didn't trust that I wouldn't be rejected as the oddity that I felt myself to be.

When Vince called me, it was to ask if I would sing on a demo for him. He'd know better what I sounded like. He'd seen me. I hadn't. The song was 'Only You', which had a nursery-rhyme quality. There was no talk of starting a band. I was excited to be recorded, as it was something to do. I was impressed at how he had got a ball rolling. Had an open goal but saved his own shot nonetheless. He'd got something away and dismissed it. That's always going to be interesting. As I didn't listen to chart music, I didn't think in terms of a vanguard. I didn't know what was flying. I didn't have a goal or any ambition, other than gigging on the London pub scene. I wasn't even aware that Dr Feelgood had troubled the charts. They were a local royal headliner who helped lots of us out and gave us support slots at the Shrimpers club.

So I did the demo. Vince said Mute would record it and release it. We went in the studio, and the B-side Vince had quickly written, 'Don't Go', was too good for a B-side, so we wrote 'Situation' together quickly and used that instead. In America, they flipped the single, and 'Situation' was a massive club hit. Vince's publisher then said we should make an album, so that's what we did. We put on the table various ideas we had, and we recorded them. Three days per track in studio down time – night or early morning – to both program and record and to mix. It was tremendously exciting. It was marching powder for both of us. Until we started fucking each other off.

Dave Gahan: Oh, they [the press] hated us! They *hated* us. We were a joke. But we were also misunderstood.

John Lydon: Because we were so adamant and took such a definite stance, it obviously had to happen that the backlash would be dreary, wimpy, homosexual disco music – nail varnish on the keyboards. The good side is that Marc Almond has continually made me laugh – he is hysterical! His tongue-in-cheek attitude is great.

Marc Almond: My confidence probably came from when I was at school. I was at a grammar school in Leeds, and when I was thirteen we had to do a project about leaving home. I had problems at school with dyslexia and I couldn't write very well, so I bluffed it again. As I couldn't write my piece, my teacher asked what I was going to do. I said, 'I'm going to sing a Beatles song,' and I stood up in class and sang 'She's Leaving Home'. I didn't get bullied so much after that, because everyone was so flabbergasted. It was a moment where everyone had a respect for me afterwards. And so I thought, 'Well, I can do something where I can kind of get people's attention.' I'd been in a couple of bands when I was sixteen, in Southport, singing. I bluffed my way into that as well, because the guy I worked with at a fruit-drinks factory in the summer holidays looked like Marc Bolan and Roger Daltrey and wore velvet jackets, and I kind of hooked onto him because he was the most interesting person. He was a singer in a local band, playing 'Suffragette City' by David Bowie and hits of the day. I asked to come along and watch them rehearse, and started singing backing vocals. He stormed out one day, saying the band were terrible, and I stepped in. We did two or three gigs at local pubs, and I got a taste for it.

But singing in a proper band seemed like a million miles away. When I was at art college, first of all, you have these dreams. I was never a good painter, I never was a sculptor. I was trying to find what I wanted to do, whether it was film or theatre, and then along came Dave Ball with a bunch of songs. I thought, 'Well, here is an opportunity for me to take this kind of feeling I've got from performing and actually make it into something.' There was a northern electronic-music scene happening at that time in Sheffield and Leeds, and I thought, 'If I'm really lucky, maybe we'll get to support Cabaret Voltaire or the Human League.' So I just seized the opportunity.

We did our first concert in the college common room, which was quite safe ground, and because we'd seen the Human League use projections and slides, and as they had a technician as part of the group, we had to have one too. So we roped in one of the other art students, as we thought we'd have films on one side and slides on the other. We started to do little concerts in Leeds and Bradford, and then Dave's mum paid for a little recording, a terrible, scratchy recording which we thought was fantastic. It actually got a mention in *Sounds* in their futurist chart. Next we did 'Memorabilia'. I said, 'We should do a song based around a James Brown record, that's just repeated over, over and over again with a synthesizer, and I'll make up some raps and put some words over the top about consumerism or something.' Then it became this record, and Daniel Miller produced it. And then Rusty Egan started playing thirty-minute mixes of it at clubs around London.

Those early days were quite exciting, but we still felt like art students from Leeds. We started playing in London and got a bit of a reputation, although we were still poor northerners who couldn't afford decent outfits. We played Croc's in Rayleigh, supporting Depeche Mode, and they had great New Romantic outfits and equipment, while we had a battered old Reebok tape recorder. Spandau were there, and they threw coins at us. But they were exciting times that were very exciting for us. I think it was when the success happened that it all seemed to go quite sour quite quickly. We always thought we would be a kind of arty cult, sort of an experimental band. I don't think pop stardom ever really entered our minds at that time.

Dave Ball (*musician*): We were a weird couple. Marc, this gay bloke in make-up; and me, a big guy who looked like a minder.

Jon Savage: I absolutely adored Soft Cell and wrote a big piece about them for *The Face* around the time of 'Bedsitter', which, of course, was a completely synth-based tune – they were part of that wave of posing groups. And I liked Adam Ant as well – 'Ridicule is nothing to be scared of' is such a fantastic line and seems to apply to most of the New Romantics. I thought 'Dog Eat Dog', 'Antmusic' and 'Prince Charming' were great pop music. I think Robert Elms did such a good job of propagandising the whole scene, but when you're young, these things get more polarised, as I do remember at the time being quite anti. As I said, I still had a hangover from punk, which took a long time to go; I only really shook it off with *England's Dreaming*. Anyone who worked for the *NME* or *Sounds* or *Melody Maker* took against this new type of music, but all that was about was the post-punk hangover, and it should be treated with the contempt that it deserves.

There was this huge groundswell of gay pop, and it was fantastic. I mean, Soft Cell were an outrage. I remember seeing Marc Almond do 'Tainted Love' on *Top of the Pops*, and it was just completely outrageous. And he knew what he was doing as well. Yes, it was the time of the gender benders, with Annie Lennox and Grace Jones and Marilyn and Boy George. I did like George, as I found him fascinating and, again, it was just a lot of fun. It was a sort of golden age for gay or non-standard-sexuality pop music, just before Aids really kicked in. If you're being holistic, you regard the rise of gay pop and the androgyny of the time as a whole, and if it's a bit blurred around the edges, it's a lot more accessible to everybody. As soon as you come up with a programme, then you've got something that people can reject. And so when I asked Marc Almond in September 1981 whether or not he was gay, he quite rightly fudged the issue, and I didn't mind him fudging the issue. It was very cheeky. I got told off by a very good friend of mine afterwards. He sat me down and said, 'Jon, would you like somebody asking you that?' And I said, 'Well, not particularly.' And he said, 'Well, why did you do it? You shouldn't do that sort of thing.' But Marc was fluttering about too much and getting on my tits probably and being very provocative, and I wanted to see how far it went.

The New Romantic period is a continuum, because a lot of the people who got involved in punk in the first place were stylish and a lot of them were soul boys, so it had this tremendous crossover. Plastic sandals, angora sweaters, the Clash playing the Lacy Lady. It was also really diverse: you had the narrow New Romantic scene, with Robert Elms, Spandau Ballet and George and Billy's and Blitz, but in fact it's a lot wider, because you have Soft Cell, you have early New Order doing 'Everything's Gone Green', you've got the Human League in Sheffield, and of course you've got Duran Duran in Birmingham. I don't think the period was specifically Thatcherite, not least because that was not a thing quite yet, as it came in with the Falklands War in 1982 and her second premiership. I suppose it was quite honest, in a way, using punk's techniques not to change the world but to change *their* world. Plus, in a cultural sense, all the gay, gender-bender stuff was implicitly against Tory morality and bellicosity.

Marc Almond: Dave [Ball] was a huge fan of northern soul. Coming from Southport, there were always lots of northern soul clubs, like the Twisted Wheel and the Wigan Casino. I never knew what the records were but I loved the music, and Dave had a big northern soul collection.

Electronic music had become quite straight-faced, what with everyone busy being robotic and sucking their cheeks in and being very kind of Berlin about the whole thing. And so we thought, 'Let's do something a little bit different.' Dave said, 'What about doing a northern soul record?' – because we loved that mix of electronics and emotional vocals that Giorgio Moroder had done with Donna Summer, and we loved the idea of doing cold electronic music with passionate vocals. We thought about doing three or four songs, including 'The Night' by Frankie Valli, before we tried 'Tainted Love'. There were two versions: one by Ruth Swann and another by Gloria Jones, who I, of course, had heard of as I was a T. Rex fan [she was Marc Bolan's girlfriend]. 'Tainted Love' is a fantastic title as it seemed to sum up the time and everything we were about at that moment, and that's why we thought it would be a culty record that we would play live as a special encore. We never thought it was going to be such a massive hit. We thought that no one would really know what it was, and everyone might think it was our song. And amazingly, in some parts of the world, they still do. They all probably still think I'm heterosexual as well.

Peter York: I loved the music. There would be things you'd like quite a lot, but you want it as a video, you want the pictures to go with it. So there were a number of parallel strands emerging, and they didn't necessarily come out of the same culture or the same town. Adam Ant was pretty much parallel in terms of the timeline, but he wasn't really out of the Blitz. And then Duran came from Birmingham, and people were very cruel to them about it. And then there were extraordinary people like Marc Almond. Because Marc Almond was a sort of tortured torch-singer type, naturally Jon Savage thought he was wonderful. Then there was Billy MacKenzie, who had the most extraordinary voice.

Marc Almond: There was something innocent about sexuality in the eighties. Back in the seventies, even lorry drivers liked the Sweet, and you had this kind of flamboyance – male peacocks, dandies, blending masculine and feminine. But it was all play-acting. Even [Boy] George said he preferred a cup of tea to anything else, and he didn't really have a sexuality. So I think I came across as quite a threatening figure, quite aggressive.

Marc Almond's success in the early eighties with Soft Cell owed more to the band's quirky electro-pop image rather than his innate good looks and well-groomed hair. But he was a pin-up just the same, whose image was festooned across bedroom walls all over the country. There was always a tendency to describe Almond as having a 'ghostly pallor', a 'gothic screen wash' . . . Mixing the icy precision of Kraftwerk with the warm emotion of northern soul, Soft Cell made electronic punk, happy sad music that mixed glamour with squalor. They could almost have been called Flotsam & Jetsam. Their first big hit, 'Tainted Love', was No. 1 in seventeen countries, while their single 'Bedsitter' was the first UK Top 5 single to feature the soon-to-be-ubiquitous sound of the Roland TR-808.

Neil Tennant: The early singles by Soft Cell sum up a time in London when clubbing was creative and music was dominated by art students – a great period, in other words.

Marc Almond: It was terrifying suddenly being famous, because I've never really coped very well with big groups of people. I still find it very hard to cope in a lot of social situations. It was exciting, thrilling and terrifying all at the same time. Fame is obviously very seductive, but – and this is an old cliché – fame is a mask you can't take off. And when you finally put it on, you're there. Everybody suddenly knew who I was. I'd been on *Top of the Pops*, we had a stylist choosing clothes for us . . . it was weird. The first time we were on, I remember I'd seen this photograph of this socialite called Nancy Cunard, and she had all these bracelets going up her arm, and I thought, 'What a great look.' And I'd seen this spoofy, jokey film called *The Artist* [starring

Tony Hancock], where they have these existentialists with these black polo necks and black eye make-up. I love Juliette Gréco and I love that whole French Left Bank thing, and I mixed it up with punk and a Scott Walker haircut. This mishmash became my look. I remember the record company saying, 'You can't go on like that.' But I said, 'This is how I'm doing it. I can't think of anything else.' Suddenly people were dressing like me and looking like me and wanting to be me, and at first I found it very, very frightening. I just wanted to run away. Then I kind of remembered that devil-on-your-shoulder thing, saying, 'You can use this. You can do this and do something with it.' I realised it was a great opportunity to make mischief. I remember watching David Bowie put his arm around Mick Ronson on *Top of the Pops*, when no one was quite sure about Bowie's sexuality, even though Mick Ronson was a bloke from Hull who was probably roped in to wearing all these silver outfits. But it had this huge effect on people in their bedsits, and so I kind of respected that and felt a huge, enormous pressure to do that, just as David Bowie had showed me there was another world out there. But I didn't know if I could really cope with the enormous pressure to be that person. I didn't want to be a role model, and I certainly felt I wasn't really equipped emotionally to deal with it.

Peter Ashworth: I always used a lot of props in my pictures, and during this period it seemed to be appropriate. I'd grown up watching Desmond Morris, and I was fascinated with body language and gestures and what they mean and inferences. So props helped frame a picture. For Soft Cell's 'Bedsitter', even though there were only two people in the band, I wanted a narrative. Bedsits were pretty basic, and it was all about kitchen-sink drama, knives and forks, pots and pans. It was a very simple shoot: it was a piece of blue Colorama [paper], and I stuck a lot of knives and forks and pots and pans to it. Every time I took a shot, one of the props would fall off, and Marc started exploding. So there was a real tension in the air, and you can see the tension in the pictures. It actually looks like there's rods up their arses and they're about to get a cattle prod, a taser shot or something. There's something really weird going on. Also, Dave used to go off into a dream. He sort of used to not be there sometimes, and I think in one of the sleeves I shot for them he's actually asleep.

Neil Tennant: At the time, I was still writing songs, and in 1981 I bought a synthesizer, a Korg MS-10. I assumed it had a speaker in it. [It didn't], so I went to the Chelsea electronic store, and they made a lead so I could put it into my stereo system, and that's where I met Chris [Lowe]. Which I suppose is the very start of Pet Shop Boys.

Norman Jay: In the early eighties, suddenly this generation of kids are not playing instruments, they are playing computers. You have got a group of people calling themselves a band, when you are not a band, you are a group, a collective of people. A band to me is a collection of people who come and play with instruments. A group is just a collection of people, which is what bands became in the eighties – groups. It wasn't their fault, because technology had moved on to a stage where you didn't need to be a keyboardist or a drummer; if you could work a computer, you could recreate the same sounds. After all, the drum was the first instrument, and it doesn't matter how you make that noise; it's still a beat.

Dismissed by the inkies – Sounds, Melody Maker *and the* NME *– as little but pastel-suited fops with no standing in the pop firmament, Duran Duran were catnip for the glossies, for* Smash Hits, Number One *and* Record Mirror. *They were never particularly fashionable – even when they were meant to be fashionable themselves, ironically – yet they made classic pop that defied (and annoyed) the critics. Even if you hated what they stood for, it was difficult to say objectively that they didn't write extremely good songs: 'Is There Something I Should Know?', 'Rio', 'Save a Prayer', etc.*

'I treated Duran Duran as if it was an airline traversing the globe,' says Malcolm Garrett, who designed many of their sleeves. 'They had

a distinct international flavour. The band had picked up the "doing everything and controlling everything" vibe from punk and then applied that through a big label.'

For many who wrote for the weeklies, the whole New Romantic scene was Pollyanna-ish, full of gurning makeweights who had no interest in either current affairs or the cultural equity of pop. In 1981, Paul Morley wrote a ferocious piece for the NME *in which he called Duran Duran 'glammed-over techno-rock twits', portraying them as facile poseurs with no grasp of, or interest in, reality. The interview took place in Birmingham, as a riot erupted in the city. Later that night, onstage at the Birmingham Odeon, Simon Le Bon addressed the crowd: 'I want you to remember what's happening out there has nothing to do with what's happening in here.' As Morley pointed out in his piece, 'He could easily have said, let them eat smoked salmon.'*

Simon Le Bon: [What do I think of the Paul Morley piece?] The 'let them eat cake [*sic*]' one? Yeah, it's funny, I was thinking about that recently. I think my head *was* in a funny place. I can see where he was coming from. The thing was, we were so intent on our career and making something happen. We were so focused, and we were kind of blind to everything that was going on around us. And now I can really see that. And I think he was right. We were in this theatre, talking, and we could hear the riots going on outside. And we thought, 'If they could harness that energy into doing something useful, there wouldn't *be* a fucking problem.' Which sounds like a very callous statement, but that was very much our attitude: don't wait for somebody else to change your life, don't sit there complaining, 'Why isn't my life better?' Do it *yourself*. And that was very much part of the core of eighties thinking, and possibly Thatcherism as well. And in some ways, it's very good, but it had a real downside as well. And I can see what Morley meant.

Rob Hallett: At the time, it was trendy to be negative about anything, and I'll never forget when the *NME* put Duran on the cover, when they were one of the biggest groups in the country. It was a picture of Nick eating an ice cream and three pages taking the piss. It was like, 'What the fuck?' I think writers like Paul Morley have got a lot to answer for.

Simon Napier-Bell: I'd known about Duran for some time. They were dedicated Japan fans and had been hanging around the office begging me to persuade David Sylvian to produce them. If he had done, Duran Duran probably wouldn't have happened, but because he refused, they hit on something much more commercial. The end result was a tribute to marketing – a triumph of packaging over substance. There were five of them, all with copycat versions of David's haircut and strangely shaped trousers.

Simon Le Bon: We had a sexual tension and threat. Boy George said we were 'like milk', which I just thought was stupid. 'Girls on Film' was actually *political* in a way. It was a feminist statement, for sure. It's about the exploitation of women. And you had all these little girls singing along with it in their bedrooms . . .

John Taylor (*musician*): We thought we were an *art* band. We thought we'd slot in somewhere between [early] Simple Minds and [early] Human League. But it never really went according to plan. We fell into a different bag, and the pop thing kind of happened. We got jumped on. *Smash Hits* was in the ascendancy, and the serious music papers hated that, so they positioned themselves against us and we never really got it back. We could have taken a million different routes, but we chose that one. The one thing you can't control is how you connect with an audience, when millions of people fall in love with you. We had no idea. That was the unknown quantity.

Mark Ellen (*editor*): *Smash Hits*' sales shot up to 250,000 a fortnight in 1981. Four years later, it was 600,000. The acts that mostly drove that were Duran and Spandau, Soft Cell, the Human League, Wham!

and Culture Club. The arrival of video had changed everything. Until then, bands had to make it through relentless touring; now, they could be seen by more people worldwide via a promotional clip than they could possibly reach in a lifetime on the road, so how they looked was the key. It had never mattered more. Music-paper sales were reliable indicators of any golden age and press-invented, twin-act dogfights often a key part of the equation. The press started the Cliff vs Elvis ding-dong in the fifties, a huge sales boost for records and papers. Then it was Beatles vs Stones. Then Hendrix vs Clapton and Bowie vs Bolan ('T. Rextasy'!). Then the Clash vs the Pistols and, later, Oasis vs Blur. We stoked the fires of Duran vs Spandau, a big tribal war eventually picked up by the news press – the *Mirror* talked excitedly of 'Durandemonium!'. A much-trumpeted special edition of the BBC's *Pop Quiz* pitted Spandau against Duran, as if it was a Middle East peace accord. The two singles-chart superpowers gamely pretended to dislike each other. New Romantics still get a bit of a kicking – unfairly, I think. Tedious purists got their pants in a twist about whether some of them actually played on their records, but why did it matter? The whole era began the liberating drift towards machine-made music, the greatest revolution of the eighties, the age when sound was freed from all its traditional shackles and the studio became the instrument. I didn't imagine it would be so enduring. Some of those New Romantic acts still fill arenas; some are on eighties package tours. Virtually every early-eighties pop act that had a hit is still touring – even Marilyn, for God's sake. There isn't the same level of affection for nineties artists. Shows you how massive the eighties record market was and how many people are still attached to it.

Smash Hits *assumed that the young, intelligent pop stars of the time had learnt the lessons of punk and decided to link them to the glamour of pop stardom and international nightlife. A stylish, thoughtful, hedonistic pop era flourished, and in a way* Smash Hits *was its house magazine. The* NME, Melody Maker *and* Sounds*? Why, they were* *just 'rockist'. Published every fortnight, in the early eighties* Smash Hits *was the biggest pop magazine in the world.*

David Hepworth: So I became the editor of *Smash Hits* in 1981, and the magazine was going from strength to strength, as each time you put on more copies, you managed to retain quite a significant number of them. We were probably selling around 240,000 copies every two weeks, and if you had a spike and put on another 30,000, you might keep around twenty [thousand]. Big numbers. *Smash Hits* would eventually go on to sell a million copies every two weeks, but I was there when it really started to grow. We covered a lot of the same people as the *NME* – the Jam, Blondie, whatever – but when the New Romantics came along, we started covering them, and the *NME* went off to do Bauhaus and teenage-suicide covers. We were fuelled by a really buoyant singles market, and we were recruiting a lot of teenagers who were coming to the market. And also *Smash Hits* was better than the other titles, like *Disco 45* and *Jackie*. We featured Spandau Ballet, Depeche Mode, Duran Duran and Toyah – she got on the cover of *Smash Hits* quite a number of times. She was pretty popular but not madly popular, and the reason she got the cover was she always had fantastic pictures. You would call up her PR, and they would do special pictures for you, so you always used them. It wasn't simply about popularity, otherwise Shakin' Stevens would have been on the cover every week; it was about the way the bands looked. Every new single would bring with it a new look, and that was great for a colour magazine like *Smash Hits*.

Mark Ellen: I remember looking down into the *NME* from the *Smash Hits* office in 1981, literally the other side of Carnaby Street, and being so relieved I'd switched sides. Thrilling though it was, *NME* seemed full of twitchy and insecure, highly competitive blokes agonising over whether their musical taste said the right thing about them. The least relaxed place imaginable. It was the rise of political punk benefit gigs and their slightly dour opportunities for 'radical fun' and 'dancing with attitude', and the covers featured joyless, spine-stiffening fare, like Cabaret Voltaire, the Scars, Deutsch Amerikanische Freundschaft and Jello Biafra. It was all a bit tense and black and white and soul-plumbing, and the sales were on the slide. But obviously *Smash Hits* was about pop singles and colour and videos and fun, and we were mostly ex-*Sounds*, *Melody Maker* and *NME* writers in our late twenties, so way too old for Duran, Spandau, Wham! and Visage. And that was a relief. It wasn't about you or their effect on you; it was about them. You didn't have to take it seriously. We just thought about how the acts might appeal to the teenagers who bought the singles by remembering how we felt when we were that age and liked the Beatles or T. Rex or whoever. It was a hoot, and the sales were sky-rocketing. Pictures of New Romantic acts didn't suit the smudged newsprint of the weeklies and only really worked in the high-gloss colour stock of *The Face* and *Smash Hits*, so we both played a big part in the whole movement. The more outlandish the act, the more we'd want to run shots of them. We welcomed them with open arms and fondly sent them all up in the office. David Hepworth always called Steve Strange 'the Welsh dresser'. I'd been at the *NME* during punk rock, or the end of punk rock, and at the time I didn't think any of those punk-rock stars really were going to last the distance. I think I was largely right. Punk rock was just a huge press thing and it wasn't quite the extraordinary cultural event in the real world that people claim it was. Whereas the eighties was the reverse of that in many ways. Everyone was saying, 'This is synthetic. This is fake. This is manufactured. This is a load of idiots who probably can't even play their instruments, dressed up in preposterous clothes.' And, actually, that decade produced some incredibly durable music. Neil Tennant and I were about twenty-six or twenty-seven when we were at *Smash Hits*, so clearly we were too old for some of the records. They weren't aimed at us. Certain things like Adam and the Ants were clearly aimed at twelve-year-olds or whatever, and you could still admire what was involved . . . but some of the records were terrific. We really liked the ABC record, we really liked the Frankie Goes to Hollywood record. The Human League. There were just so many good songs. I'd worked at the *NME*, and I thought it was really vicious and really cruel, actually. It just wasn't in my nature to be like that. I'm not that kind of person. I found working at the *NME* quite hard, actually, because I just didn't have the required cynicism. I was slightly sarcastic but I wasn't cynical. I think everyone else at the *NME* really enjoyed laying into yesterday's news. Obviously, we were keen to promote tomorrow's news – but having promoted them, for me there was a little too much pleasure in pulling the rug out from under their feet. It was a harsh environment, really. So with *Smash Hits* the idea was that you can't take pop music (and, to an extent, rock music) 100 per cent seriously all the time, because half the fun of pop music is that it can be colourful, it can be over the top, it can be shallow. And it's populated with very exotic and charismatic and often rather peculiar characters. It's good to encourage them to be like that, because that's what you want them to be. Also, pop is full of preposterous pretension a lot of the time. It's very easy to laugh at pretension, but often pretension is just people trying to do something different, willing to go out on a limb. They might make themselves look ludicrous, but they might succeed, you know? I always used to think Queen were pretentious. A lot of people really liked what they did, and good luck to them, ha ha . . . So part of the *Smash Hits* thing was that we were trying to suggest the landscape was filled with these kind of cartoon characters, really. And all of the musicians really liked it. Well, Morrissey didn't really like it. He didn't particularly like the way we wrote about him and felt he was above *Smash Hits*.

Nick Logan: It took about eighteen months for *The Face* to develop a personality. I was really trying to do a picture magazine with an international flavour. I was reasonably happy with the first two issues, and then the New Romantic thing happened. I had launched on a wave of 2-Tone, but the weeklies weren't covering the New Romantic thing; plus, of course, it was very colourful, which was perfect for us.

I think we were the first place where the term 'New Romantics' was mentioned. I couldn't really afford proper writers, so I tried to make writers out of non-writers, like Gary Crowley and Vaughn Toulouse, but I spent too much time rewriting copy. So in the end I had to get proper writers in, like Jon Savage, even though we didn't pay very much. There was a point when Jon Baker from Axiom [a New Romantic clothes shop] wanted me to move into an office in Newburgh Street with him and Melissa Caplan and some others, but I didn't want to do that as I wanted to remain independent. Essentially, I was just looking for pockets of interest, although when we started writing about what people wore, we weren't sure what to call it, as nobody really did that back then. So we called it Style, as it wasn't really fashion, and anyway fashion magazines were a long way away from what we were trying to do. I remember a friend called John Carver brought me in a picture of a dentist's chair that was converted into an armchair, which looked fantastic, but I didn't know how to run it in the magazine. So we got a lot of disparate photos and ran them all together on a spread. I was just feeling my way, I suppose. I was really concerned what the messaging was, and so I analysed every page, every advertisement, as I wanted to make sure that we were sending the right messages to the reader. 'This magazine is about music, fashion, art; this magazine is straight; this magazine is a bit gay.' Every nuance was analysed. I tried to be the reader and see it from their perspective. However, at no point did I think we were making history.

Mark Ellen: I thought acts like the B-52's were the way forward, but Joy Division were the *NME*'s sacred cows. Say anything bad about them and you half expected an on-the-spot fine or to be hung out of the window by your ankles. I reviewed them once and just couldn't get it. And I got a very cool reception in the office when the issue came out. I was way off message. I was off brand, in fact. Various acts were office favourites and still sound terrific – the Human League, ABC, Soft Cell, some of the Culture Club singles, Wham!, Thomas

Dolby. There were some that were precisely right for their audience, and you could see the appeal – Ultravox, Spandau, Duran, Adam and the Ants. Some seemed embarrassing from the start – Belouis Some, Classix Nouveaux, Sigue Sigue Sputnik, Kajagoogoo. And some were just too complicated to decode for the age group buying the singles. *New Sounds New Styles* magazine was based in the *Smash Hits* office, a New Romantic monthly edited by Kasper de Graaf and designed by Malcolm Garrett, and their house band seemed to be Blue Rondo à la Turk, a goateed Latin/salsa gang who took to breezing into reception in their Zorro hats and zoot suit finery and making a colossal racket. Their name came from a Dave Brubeck track, they had a single called 'Klactoveesedstein' and they dropped forties fashion and jazz names in interviews. The mass market hadn't the faintest idea what they were on about.

Chris Sullivan: With Blue Rondo, I very much wanted to do something different. I was fed up of people wandering around with make-up and big shoulder pads and frills, fed up of electro music. I wanted to do something with men with big moustaches, in suits, without a synthesizer in sight. I wanted to do something that represented the heterosexual side of the scene. It was also about turning the clock back.

The annals of London's rock history are filled with impassioned stories about the best surprise gigs of all time, whether it's the Sex Pistols playing on the Thames in the summer of 1977, Dr Feelgood stepping up unannounced at the 100 Club, the Libertines playing the Albion Rooms or Paul McCartney busking in Covent Garden. In 1981, Blue Rondo à la Turk, the salsa brainchild of Chris Sullivan, played a gig in a warehouse in Clerkenwell on the eve of the royal wedding. This was the first time the band had performed as a ten-piece, and they put on such a sensational display that they were immediately signed by Virgin Records for £500,000. Those who were there say it was one of the best gigs the country had seen since Pere Ubu and the Red Crayola played the Chislehurst Caves two years previously, although this might have been due to the fact that a substantial percentage of the crowd had taken large quantities of MDMA that had been imported from America that week. Earlier in the year, Steve Dagger had orchestrated another PR stunt by shipping a dozen Blitz Kids over to New York in order to try and launch Spandau Ballet in the US.

Robert Elms: In May 1981, Steve Dagger took Spandau to New York. Actually, the trip was done to launch Spandau in New York, but Steve Dagger being Steve Dagger decided the best way to do it was not to sell Spandau, but to sell the whole scene. He'd studied Andrew Loog Oldham and knew how to make a splash. That trip to New York, it does show the extraordinary arrogance of us all. We didn't have a pot to piss in and yet we arrived, swanning around New York, getting into the *New York Times*, all of this sort of stuff on a wing and a prayer. People squatting on people's sofas and yet dressing up to the nines and appearing on national television.

Steve Dagger: In America, they have a more developed entertainment industry than us, and what I learnt very quickly is how much could be achieved, because the music industry is much more connected to film and TV. We were initially told that the radio stations wouldn't play our records, and then we started to be played on the black stations. Then, of course, British electronic music started to influence not just black radio, but American rap acts. This coincided with the whole 'disco sucks' movement and the rise of MTV. Before music television started, there was something called Rock America, which distributed a monthly selection of European music videos to hundreds of clubs and bars all over the country. There were all these state-of-the-art clubs that had been built for disco but no longer had anything to play in them, and they all had these great sound systems and huge video screens. Everything was far more sophisticated than Le Beat Route or any of the London clubs. Suddenly, the Americans were getting interested in eighties dance music – 'new eighties music', they called it – and it was initially all European. Mainstream fashion in America started to change too, which was a big deal. Then the music started to appear in teen films. When John Hughes used us in *Sixteen Candles*, we could not have been happier.

Robert Elms: When I started to see Spandau and Blue Rondo in the papers, Stephen Linard and Fiona Dealey in *i-D* and *The Face*, it somehow felt correct, felt like this was our due. I think we had what I describe as the arrogance of ignorance. We had no idea you couldn't do what we did. Britain at the end of the seventies was broken, grey, grim; it's got strikes. Well, you can have two responses to that: you can either get really grumpy or you can put on your best clothes and dance, and that's what we did. There is no doubt that we were fiddling while Rome burned. On the one hand, we were all terribly left-wing, and yet on the other, we were all baby Thatchers. There was an entrepreneurial edge, an individualistic edge, but I would say that in the early days, at least it wasn't about making money. The first warehouse party that Chris Sullivan and I did at Mayhem Studios, we didn't even charge people to come in. We had no conception that you could make money out of doing this. It was only later on that it started to be about people making money. For me, it was about being perceived in that small world. I didn't realise that you could reach out to a bigger world until quite a lot later, but I absolutely thought, when it started happening and all my friends started to get famous and be on *Top of The Pops* or designing this and doing that, that it was fair and just. Media became important once we started to go beyond our own group. At first, you're doing everything to impress [Animal Nightlife's] Andy Polaris, because he's a great dancer on the dancefloor and always dresses well, and you want him to be impressed by you. Then you're doing it to impress Nick Logan, and then you suddenly realise actually you're now on *Newsnight.* It sort of went like that. I never, ever remember thinking, 'This is weird, as all my friends are famous.'

Andy McCluskey: We were trying to change the world with our music, and we thought Spandau Ballet and Duran Duran were just a bunch of glamourpusses. I struggled with the fact that we were selling our art and it was perceived as pop music. And so we were determined to evolve, which is why every album after the first one was different. The idea that we thought we were going to change the world just by modifying popular music styles now seems ridiculous, but when you're steeped in the power of popular culture as a teenager, it's incredibly important to you. You know, the clothes you wear, the haircut, the music – that's how you're going to change the world.

Andy Polaris: I didn't have any aspirations to be a singer at the time, although one of my biggest influences was probably Poly Styrene from X-Ray Spex, as it was great to see a mixed-race girl on the stage. So that really kind of changed things because I kept thinking, 'If she can do it, maybe I can do it.' But at that time I didn't really see myself in a band playing rock music. In the early eighties, people used to go down to Bournemouth for the weekend, and I think I'd been really drunk and I was singing in a cab, and someone heard me singing and said, 'Oh, your voice isn't too bad. Do you want to be in a band?' So I ended up going to a rehearsal, and it all started from there. [Boy] George was starting, Sade . . . In a way, I think Animal Nightlife kind of satisfied the attention that I needed after spending all that time in a children's home and not really having any fun. I was making up for all the things I missed out on before. You're getting all the attention, you're up there on the stage, you're being creative. I had confidence, but there was also a lot of support from people, and thinking about it, it was almost like a collective.

Fiona Dealey: Every night we went out. I've got no idea how we could afford it, as no one had any money. Of course, we got in for free and people would buy us drinks, and we were probably drunk before we got there – we used to buy a bottle of gin and drink it before we went out. For me, the best London club was Le Beat Route, which opened in the spring of 1981. I loved that place. I did the door, and I got £100 a night, which was a lot of money in 1981. I wasn't allowed to use the cash machine on the counter as the management didn't trust me, so they paid for a cashier, and I had to sit there looking glorious and say, 'Yes/no, free/one pound,' depending on who I was letting in. The important thing was who got in for free and who didn't, and I had the power to decide. You'd let your mates in and any man you fancied, but then there would be other people pitching up, and you really wouldn't know who they were. I remember George Michael and Andrew Ridgeley turned up and said they were from Wham!, and I laughed and said I'd never heard of them and made them pay. Grace Jones, Bob Geldof . . . I mean, all those people, they all turned up. You just took it all for granted. Le Beat Route went on for two and a half years, and it was the longest-running club, until the Wag opened. Every night there were people queuing all down Greek Street, and you wouldn't be able to let them in – you'd be full – because of fire regulations. If they didn't get in, they would hate you. I can go out today and I'm on a film set, and some gnarled old man will come up to me and go, 'You didn't let me into Le Beat Route.' And I think to myself, 'I was right.' They hold a grudge, those people.

Ollie O'Donnell: Le Beat Route was my favourite club. The most important part of the club was the door, I think even more important than the music. Women like a club with slightly more women than men, and men prefer a club with more women than men, as it gives off a softer, more attractive vibe, so you'd work on 40/60 per cent. You also needed an edge, a group of people standing around the entrance making it look as though the club was really full. Passers-by would stop to look and join the crowd. The harder I made it for people to get into Le Beat Route, the more desperate they were to get in. More than twenty times I must have said to a very good-looking girl, 'You can come in, but the guy you're with can't,' and the girl would walk straight in and leave her date for the night outside in the street. Shocking. Grace Jones turned up one night with a massive entourage of about twenty people, and I told her they weren't all coming in. She had a big Jamaican bodyguard with her who proceeded to try and intimidate me, skinning up his teeth. I told her the bodyguard was definitely not coming in, and she stormed off angrily. Twenty minutes later, she came back, just her and four girls, as sweet as could be. No bodyguard, no entourage. She stayed in the club all night and then came back the following week with the same four girls.

Toyah Willcox (*singer*): I always think of the eighties as the alien tearing itself out of the body of punk. In 1979, you had this whole underground movement wanting to be slightly more refined, as a backlash against the torn clothes, the gin and the vomit. Suddenly, vanity started to come in and boys started to wear make-up well, as opposed to badly. From 1979 to 1981, you had Steve Strange being extreme, me being extreme, Nina Hagen being extreme, and Boy George was exactly the same as he was in 1984. There was incredible freedom. At the same time, there were only three or four females in the chart at any one time. So it was really freakishly strange for me, Kate Bush, Hazel O'Connor, Kim Wilde to be in the charts. It was almost gimmicky. And Clare [Grogan] too. I remember she always slept in female fans' homes to save money. She once woke up in the morning and found herself in bed with the fan and the fan's mother. I said to her, 'Clare, how can you be such a cheapskate?' She must've been earning *some* money back then!

I did have seagulls painted on my face and I had limited appeal because of the extreme images, but I was still in love with the punk ethos, and to see what then happened was like being out in a strait-jacket. Every time I appeared in a newspaper, it was about 'my new image'. If Madonna went out with her hair up, it was her 'new image' or a 'comeback'. But that's one thing the eighties changed: women were finally allowed to come forward.

It was a highly political decade, and we were one of the few bands that would go to Northern Ireland. Our security was always really good, but around 1982 we got to The Europa in Belfast – the most bombed hotel in the world – went up to the third floor, and there's three hundred fans in the fucking corridor waiting for me. The security was so bad half my audience could get in there. A month after, a bomb went off in the reception area. Wouldn't happen now.

The Neo Naturists were started by Christine Binnie, Jennifer Binnie and Wilma Johnson in London in 1981, a small group of feminist body painters (sometimes including Grayson Perry) who grew out of, and often were in conflict with, the New Romantic scene. They were quixotically bohemian, forged at St Martin's, and fully espoused the grand ideals of lurid cultural expression rather than conforming to what, to all intents and purposes, had become a clique. As living, naked paintings they joyously performed ad hoc rituals, gatecrashing trendy clubs – '. . . red and shiny and smiling, and a bit too fat' – and pretending to be feral, when everyone around them was pretending to be matinee idols and screen queens. Beneath their coats they perfected a number of looks that were painted directly onto their bodies, including trompe l'oeil *lingerie or blue jeans, as well as wild, grinning faces that transformed breasts into eyes and belly buttons into nostrils. Their bodies were almost cubist.*

For Christine, a visit to Berlin in 1979 was the initial spark of inspiration, as she saw lots of tanned German punks sunbathing nude around the lake, whereas in Britain the punks were very pale, wore black and stayed indoors. Then, when Wilma Johnson asked to paint her body at a life drawing class, the Neo Naturists were born. 'Part of the thing of doing the Neo Naturists was using women as women, rather than there being a sort of object,' says Johnson. 'Historically in art, the woman is the model and the muse, and not the person who's actually making the work about women's naked bodies. So we were turning that around.'

They were part of a large cultural network that included the dancer Michael Clark, film-maker John Maybury, performance artist Leigh Bowery, avant-garde musician Genesis P. Orridge, superstar painter Peter Doig, conceptual artist Cerith Wyn Evans and painter and model Dencil Williams. Everywhere they went, they were naked, firm believers in the radical and subversive potential of body painting to unnerve, annoy and inspire. Critics rushed to define them, although, in essence, in the Neo Naturists' performances 'the body was both spectacle and metaphor for the social body'. They contributed to a celebration of the self, at a time when the very idea of the self was becoming increasingly reliant on being mediated. The image presented was an unerotic one, a deliberate move away from restraint and exaggeration, both literally and metaphorically. They were born to flaunt ('Just wear a big coat,' Christine Binnie once advised would-be flashers. 'It's easy!').

Wilma Johnson (*painter*): When I started the foundation course at St Martin's in 1978, I thought everybody was going to be completely wild and crazy, and when I got there I thought, 'Oh shit, I am the crazy one.' I loved the Clash – I'd been on an early date with Joe Strummer – but punk had become so proscriptive. You couldn't do this, you couldn't do that. It was very trivial, I think. Then, when the New Romantics thing happened, in a way it was completely the opposite, as no one was telling you what to do. You could wear a turban, wear a headdress . . . whatever you wanted. For me, I was a girl from a private school trying to be a punk, getting yelled at by skinheads, but I was told I didn't have the right to be involved because I was middle-class. The New Romantics were more creative and free, but there came a point when I started rebelling against them, which is what the Neo Naturists were.

One day, Christine Binnie came to my studio as a life model, and we started talking about body paint and we did some photographs. It started off as an art thing, as in part we were trying to find a more outrageous outfit than Boy George's for her to wear down the Blitz.

It was a bit like have a laugh, have a dare, drink something inside, and then, 'Do you guys dare us to go out naked?' I remember the first time we did it, we went down to the Venue in Victoria. We were like, 'What if we go down to the club with half our bodies painted yellow and nothing else on?' Everyone else was like, 'You would never dare.' We were like, 'Just watch us.' That was the beginning of it. We felt the New Romantic thing had become quite precious, and everyone was wearing their nice white ruffles. We were even banned from Spandau Ballet gigs! After that, we started doing performances, and we became the Neo Naturists. There was me, Christine Binnie and Jennifer Binnie, then Grayson Perry was in it for ages. I look at it now and think half of what we were doing was what is now called 'body-positive' – love your body; you don't have to look like a model to take your clothes off. That was a strong motivation. Looking back on it, it seems really weird when you look at the reviews and what people were saying. 'Oh my God, you're so hideous. I can't believe you would take your clothes off. You're so fat . . .' I thought we looked fabulous. We did have a laugh, as it was hilarious. We would just come up with some crazy idea and sit round in hysterics: i.e. what if we sing 'Chirpy Chirpy Cheep Cheep' dressed as Maoists? A lot of the stuff we were doing was taking the piss out of women's roles. There was one performance where we were dancing to Rod Stewart and sweeping up the floor and pretending to be housewives. They tried to chuck me out of St Martin's for being a Neo Naturist. They were like, 'Oooh, naked women!' So I got a friend to carry Christine in a blank canvas, tie her to a stretcher and add an abstract painting onto her, and the external assessor loved it. He gave me a first, which caused a lot of upset. We even got a really hard time from the feminist establishment at that time, as we were the wrong shape to be feminists. You couldn't be a feminist if you wore a C cup or an F cup.

Christine Binnie (*artist*): We were into being provocative and causing confusion. There was never any titillation in our being naked. It was more, 'Here we are, nude, with our big bosoms and tummies. Take it or leave it.'

Jennifer Binnie (*artist*): We weren't careerist in any way, though neither was anyone else back then. And we didn't really fit. We confused the art world, as well as our audiences. There was always this question as to what we were exactly – cabaret or performance art?

Louisa Buck (*art critic*): After stripping off for an impromptu Neo Naturist performance with the androgynous pop star Marilyn at Henley Regatta in the early eighties, Christine Binnie and Wilma Johnson were approached by the *Sun* to pose for Page 3. 'When we got there, we refused to put our knickers on and Wilma refused to take her glasses off, so they got very grumpy and sent us home,' remembers Christine, adding that 'they wanted us to pose with an enormous spooky teddy bear'. 'Everyone was quite outraged that we accepted the invitation to go to the studio, but we thought it would be brilliant if the *Sun* inadvertently published a photo of feminist performance artists on Page 3,' recalls Wilma. 'I think of it as one of our most subversive performances! Perhaps they'll ask us back for Page 3 online!'

Wilma Johnson: We were quite naive, actually. People would come up to me and say, 'You have a great body.' And I would be like, 'Fuck off. How dare you say that just because I'm naked?'

Louisa Buck: Their image of female nudity was unerotic. Instead, they distanced themselves from the sexualised ideal of the nude feminine and sought 'family values'.

Grayson Perry (*artist*): I particularly remember the pain of trying to wash off body paint that was welded to my body hair. It had been mixed with Scott's porridge oats.

Dave Rimmer: Nobody would ever call themselves a New Romantic. Not just that, but nobody even knew what to call it. Were they Blitz Kids? Were they Bowie kids? Were they futurists? As soon as anyone was called a New Romantic in the press, they'd instantly do an interview to deny that they were New Romantic. As soon as frilly shirts were identified as being a part of the New Romantic kit, bands immediately stopped wearing them.

Club for Heroes was probably the last club to be labelled 'New Romantic', as the scene was quickly morphing into something else. Nestling next to an upmarket estate agent's in Baker Street, it was one of the chicest venues Steve Strange and Rusty Egan had ever hired. Everything was changing, though. Music was becoming looser, funkier (something even Kraftwerk acknowledged), fashion was becoming less strident (influenced enormously by Vivienne Westwood's appropriation of historical global styles), and people were becoming slightly less uptight. There was certainly a more relaxed attitude towards drugs, something the Who's Pete Townshend realised when he visited Club for Heroes.

Pete Townshend (*musician, guitar hero*): I loved [Club for Heroes]. The only thing was, I nearly died there one night. The first night I went, I was with a couple of friends, and I ended up going blue – my heart practically stopped. I thought at the time that I'd probably gotten so drunk I didn't know what I was taking, and that I took some terrible drug. But I think I actually drank so much brandy I gave myself alcohol poisoning. I just went black. And that was my hero's entrance to a Club for Heroes: a seven-foot bouncer carried me out like a sack of potatoes. But I did get to know Steve Strange quite well as a result of that, because I went back later to apologise. And he turned out to be an absolute sweetheart. Very, very ego-less, in a real sense. Superficially, totally preoccupied with image and everything, but underneath, not like that at all.

David Cavanagh: Having clanged a whole lotta metal on *Trans-Europe Express*, Kraftwerk turned their attention to commerce, with outrageous elegance. *Computer World* is as sensual and soulful as Roberta Flack and Donny Hathaway, yet it keeps up a chattering commentary on its comings and goings ('Business! Numbers! Money! People!') like an arrivals and departures board in a busy airport. *Computer World* was criticised for its repetitiveness and short running time (thirty-four minutes), but it's now rightly regarded as a masterclass in how to construct an exquisite electronic song-suite from the most unsexy ingredients.

Vivienne Westwood: The Pirate collection was a continuation of the cult thing we had started with the drapes. We wanted to get out of the underground-tunnel feeling of England, that dark feeling where people like the Clash were taking a pride in being working-class. That wasn't a celebration; it was a polarisation of something old hat. After Seditionaries, I didn't know what to do, and Malcolm just looked at what was happening on the streets, and he saw people wearing fancy dress and old clothes, just like they did in Paris in 1972. He said, 'Do something romantic. Look at history.' And I realised that I'd only looked at my lifetime's culture and all the rebelliousness. Pirates were very English, very empiric . . . I was very into anthropology then. After that it was the savage look and then the hobo look . . . taking the idea that the tramp could look like the king.

The Specials' 'Ghost Town' was not only one of the most important records of the early eighties, it was also one of the most evocative. While punk was largely a cultural insurrection, repeatedly using thematic working-class imagery – the Brutalist modern tower block being the most obvious manifestation of this, a symbol of post-war progress that very quickly became a totem of social deprivation – 'Ghost Town' was a direct response to the deprivation that the Specials' leader, Jerry Dammers, saw around him. The band had already had huge success as the standard-bearers of the 2-Tone organisation and had had hits with

'Gangsters', 'A Message to You, Rudy' and 'Rat Race', among others. Inspired by punk, they had their own grudges to articulate, and they were doing it through the medium of ska.

This was realism.

Jerry Dammers (musician): Britain was falling apart. The car industry was closing down in Coventry. We were touring, so we saw a lot of it. Liverpool and Glasgow were particularly bad. The overall sense I wanted to convey [in 'Ghost Town'] was impending doom. There were weird diminished chords. Certain members of the band resented the song and wanted the simple chords they were used to playing on the first album. It's hard to explain how powerful it sounded. We had almost been written off, and then 'Ghost Town' came out of the blue.

The Specials were advocates of late-seventies postmodern ska, the inventors of 2-Tone and quite simply one of the coolest, most important British bands of all time. In the space of just two years, from 1979 to 1981, the original Specials managed to embody the new decade's violent energies, morals and conflicts – though always with an ironic and often sardonic detachment that kept the band cool as the eighties grew increasingly hot. Their records defined a generation who weren't sure they wanted to be defined in the first place. Sure, the band were earnest, but they were studiedly sarcastic too, which endeared them to everyone at the time who mattered. Not only that, but they came from Coventry, Britain's very own answer to Detroit, the epitome of the post-war urban wasteland, the quintessential concrete jungle, and felt they had a right to bleat about anything they wanted to, especially the onslaught of Thatcherism.

The 2-Tone movement attempted to do more for racial integration than any previous youth movement. Musically, 2-Tone had its roots firmly in black culture, although the fact that ska had previously attracted a fierce skinhead following in the UK meant that gigs featuring the Specials, Madness, the Selecter, Bad Manners and other 2-Tone groups turned into opportunities for mass skinhead violence. The more the groups espoused racial harmony, the more the skinheads took umbrage. As racial tensions heightened and then escalated into riots, the ska revival was seen as a complex kind of salve.

From a distance, it looked as though 2-Tone was the polar opposite of everything that was happening in the frilly-shirted nightclubs of central London.

Nineteen eighty-one was a desperate year in the UK. Youth unemployment was rife as the country felt the bite of Margaret Thatcher's cuts. This was an apocalyptic portrait of inner-city oppression set to a loping beat, offset by an unsettling and vaguely Middle Eastern motif: 'Government leaving the youth on the shelf . . . No job to be found in this country . . .' The single sounded like the fairground ride from hell, complete with strident brass, madhouse wailing and dub-style breaks. The video was just as bleak, featuring a road trip through some of the least salubrious streets of central London.

The week after the song was released, there were riots and civil disobedience all over the country.

Pauline Black (*singer*): It wasn't a surprise when it went to No. 1 – most things 2-Tone became hits. 'Ghost Town' epitomised the 2-Tone idea that black and white can operate in the same unit and speak to the youth. And its sense of melancholy spoke clearly: there were the 'sus' laws [the informal term for the 'stop and search' law that enabled the police to stop, search and potentially arrest suspects], inner cities not functioning, racism dividing the working class. There was fighting at Selecter gigs; there were lots of National Front people around. There was frustration about 2-Tone falling apart. We were seventies bands in a time of two-man synth bands. The record companies were happy to leave 2-Tone's problems behind.

Simon Price (*journalist*): Seventeen months separate the Specials' two No. 1 singles, and a million musical miles. Their first, a live recording of

'Too Much Too Young', was essentially the Sex Pistols' 'Bodies' gone ska, but the intervening year saw the Specials ditch that punky-reggae template. Jerry Dammers experimented with lounge-noir on their second album, causing intra-band friction. 'Ghost Town' initiated a strand of spooked British pop that has lived on in Tricky and Portishead' trip-hop and the dubstep of Burial and James Blake.

Realism? This was urban decay writ large, accompanied by a kick drum and a muted horn.

In some respects, 1981 was defined by the riots as much as by the music they inspired. Yes, there was a royal wedding, in sharp juxtaposition to inner-city decay, a wedding that would produce a genuine royal superstar; yet the riots – the worst for a century – would resonate throughout the country for years. Motivated by racial tension, a perception of inner-city deprivation, and heat, the defining factor was the ongoing war of attrition between the black community and the police. The four main riots occurred in Brixton in London, Handsworth in Birmingham, Chapeltown in Leeds and Toxteth in Liverpool, although there were disturbances in at least twenty other towns and cities, including Derby, Bristol and, almost unbelievably, High Wycombe.

The worst were in Brixton, between 10 and 12 April. Dubbed 'Bloody Saturday' by Time *magazine, the main riot took place on the eleventh, and resulted in a mass confrontation between the mob and the Metropolitan Police. There were forty-five injuries to members of the public, and nearly three hundred to the police; over 5,000 rioters were involved, many of whom had simply come out to fight as they had nothing better to do, and nowhere better to do it.*

The riots were more than a collection of urban disturbances; they were a media flashpoint that drew international attention to the huge rift in ideologies between the Left and the Right in the country, as well as the gap between perception and reality in terms of how the government was coping with the economy. There was also a growing sense that the Tories had no understanding of, and no pastoral interest in, the have-nots under their care, those who hadn't benefited from financial deregulation, privatisation or Thatcher's changes to the welfare state. While she would always say that she was empowering those who had previously been beholden to the state, Thatcher was criticised most often for having no idea of what to do with communities when the safety net had been withdrawn.

Living in London, you certainly got the feeling that you were somehow living under siege. In south London, conflict gave an edge to every transaction in a corner shop, every late-night walk home from the Underground. Walk into a Brixton pub and you felt eyes upon you. Television coverage of the riots painted them clearly as battles between residents and the police force, although what they really did was create even more racial tension between blacks and whites on the street, between neighbours of different ethnic backgrounds, between people who knew each other and those who didn't. I had a friend who was chased down Gresham Road, near Brixton police station, by some of his black neighbours just because he happened to be white at the wrong time of day. He sought refuge in a (black) neighbour's house, who promptly called out to the gang chasing him, who ran in and kicked the living daylights out of him. Police aggression made everyone paranoid, and made people who had previously lived quite happily side by side turn against each other for no other reason than it seemed like the safest thing to do.

The morning after the first 1981 riot was almost as bad as the riot itself, as the mess and the devastation made you feel as though you were living in a place that was never going to improve, that was only ever going to get worse. And so you started treating the place with the same disdain. What was the point of throwing an empty cigarette packet in a bin, if the bin was going to be thrown through the off-licence window later in the day? Back in 1981, walking around Brixton's Electric Avenue and Atlantic Road after the first night's disturbances was nothing if not surreal. You couldn't quite believe that things would ever return to normal, what with the broken glass, the boarded-up windows, the dozens of overturned cars, the smoke billowing from the shops in the market. The carpet shop always seemed to suffer, not that any of the stock was ever taken. What had the rioters got against carpet shops? The looters concentrated on the electrical shops, on the ghetto blasters, television sets and radios. Coldharbour Lane always looked like a fairly unforgiving place at the best of times, but for weeks after the riots it felt as though it had been transported directly from some post-apocalyptic wasteland, a tunnel of terror. Walking down the Lane at night you felt a little like Orpheus walking out of the underworld, too anxious to turn around and see what might be behind you. Everywhere there was tension. One afternoon that autumn, a few months after the riots, I had walked from a squat in Peckham up to the Oval, and was just about to enter the Underground when I was approached by a gang of about a dozen skinheads. They were all over the place at the time, although they tended to leave Brixton and its immediate environs alone, so whenever you saw them in the area, you suspected there might be trouble. I assumed that my dyed hair, red bandana and Chinese slippers had probably caused my shorn-haired friends to think I was a lily-livered liberal with a penchant for Afro-Caribbean culture, so as soon as I saw one of them reach into his pocket for his knife, I turned on my heels and ran. All the way to Brixton. And, unlike Orpheus, without looking back – I had recently been stabbed by a gang of casuals as I left the Hemingford Arms in Islington, and didn't fancy repeating the experience.

When Mrs Thatcher first arrived in Downing Street in 1979, there were many who thought she would become as much of a prisoner of the Whitehall machine as her predecessor, Edward Heath, yet she quickly used her abrasiveness to slap down the mandarins. 'She gives the civil servants hell,' said one observer, soon after she became prime minister. 'She writes these brusque, caustic notes accusing them of woolly thinking, and they are absolutely terrified of her.' The Cabinet were terrified too, as her treatment of her colleagues was appalling.

There would be no woolly thinking in Mrs Thatcher's government. Elected against a background of rotting refuse and unburied bodies following the Winter of Discontent, she took her mandate for governing as a mandate for change.

No woolly thinking.

Thatcher dismissed the idea that racism, heavy-handed police tactics and unemployment were behind the Brixton disturbances – even though police brutality and the continual harassment of young black men had been one of the prime motivators behind the riots – saying, 'Nothing, but nothing, justifies what happened . . . What aggravated the riots into a virtual Saturnalia was the impression gained by the rioters that they could enjoy a fiesta of crime, looting and rioting in the guise of social protest. They felt they had been absolved in advance.' She was criticised for this outburst, but she wasn't entirely wrong. She was wrong, however, when she claimed that money couldn't buy either trust or racial harmony. What many forget about the peace process in Northern Ireland was that it was as much to do with prosperity as political and sectarian will.

Spandau Ballet's 'Chant No.1 (We Don't Need This Pressure On)' was, in its own way, as important to the summer of 1981 as 'Ghost Town' – a canny mix of contemporary funk and bottom-heavy agitprop. It is one of the most important records of the early eighties, and this is not an opinion solely justified by hindsight. By the spring of 1981, the all-powerful music press already had it in for Spandau. In their eyes, they were simply a bunch of muscle-bound poseurs, led by an overripe costermonger who sounded as though he was going through his vocal exercises while giving a dinner call. But then that was the music press, who at this moment in time were all too keen to kick anyone they suspected of having any fun. And one thing that Spandau engendered was fun. They were hated by the Left, especially

when they found out that Tony Hadley voted Tory (regardless of the fact that the band's leader, Gary Kemp, was a card-carrying Labour supporter). 'But the link between Spandau Ballet and Thatcherism is about more than the personal politics of Tony Hadley,' said the Guardian, *pompously. 'It's about the emptiness of Spandau, the aspiration to do nothing more than look good in a nightclub, the happy embrace of style over substance. Billy Bragg has even attributed his decision to become a performer to them: "One day [I] saw Spandau Ballet on* Top of the Pops *wearing kilts and singing 'Chant No. 1' and something in me snapped. I was waiting for a band to come along to play the kind of music I wanted to hear, and none was forthcoming, so it was that moment I finally realised it was gonna have to be me."'*

'"Chant No. 1" was all about urban paranoia,' says Kemp. 'I wanted to make a Soho film noir song, something that was evocative of an urban experience. Dark shadows, dark corners. A fear of living on the edge in an urban environment as a young man. The early eighties were rough for most people, and I wanted to reflect that in the song. It's a very dark track, and one that mirrored the economic plight of the time.'

The promotional video for the song was filmed at Le Beat Route. The night the video was filmed, the Blitz crowd came out in force – many of whom would go on to form bands of their own: remarkably, in the club that night were various members of Wham!, Sade, Culture Club, Haysi Fantayzee, Blue Rondo à la Turk, Blancmange, Pigbag, Ultravox and Swing Out Sister, to name only a few. George Michael actually spent so many Friday nights in Le Beat Route that he would eventually compose a song about the place: the decidedly upbeat 'Club Tropicana'.

Pop culture in the UK at the time appeared to be obsessed with mixing the past with the future, perhaps because the present seemed to be so depressing. Elsewhere, pop simply became giddy with its own possibilities. Take the metallic reggae of Grace Jones. Jones acted as a kind of po-mo cypher, packaged to within an inch of her life by the

French photographer and graphic designer Jean-Paul Goude, while her music was an animatronic fusion of exotic funk and brittle electronica. She was one of the strongest personalities to emerge from the period, a larger-than-life approximation of what a modern pop star could look and sound like, Goude's illusory style being perfect for Jones's assault on a pop audience still wary of emancipated soul divas. They met at Studio 54 in the late seventies, when Jones was still trying to make it as a performer. 'I always loved the mixture of threat and beauty. I just thought it was time for Grace to stretch out,' says Goude.

As it was, the reinvented Grace Jones (she had been a model and partially successful disco singer) was one of the most transgressive figures of the eighties. At the time, she made many of the small British electronic bands seem quite parochial.

'I've heard it said that Grace Jones is a human being,' wrote Matthew Sweet. 'I've yet to see the evidence. Human beings don't have vanishing points. The planes and angles of the jacket [on the cover of her album Nightclubbing*] seem less a product of couture than of her own internal architecture – as if we weren't looking at fabric, but at lustrous slate cladding on the embassy of some rising nation.'*

For many, she was an acquired taste – there are those who say that her voice has always had the animation of the Speaking Clock – but she quickly became the ultimate disco queen, a mirrorball icon who was completely sure of herself. I interviewed her at the time, at the height of her fame, and it's an experience I've never forgotten. She was in London to have a cast of her body made for Madame Tussauds, which obviously made it easy for me to accuse her of being self-obsessed.

'You think I'm narcissistic?' she growled at me. 'Well, thank you very much. For a while I was terribly vain, but not any more. When I was modelling, I spent half my life staring at thousands of perfect reflections. It got to a stage where I was losing all sense of reality – so after I quit modelling, I took all the mirrors out of my house.'

Feeling emboldened by too many cups of coffee, I asked her if this hadn't caused havoc with the way she looked.

'That's why I started dressing like a bum. I'd be walking around the house in rags, and then I'd go out without stopping to look at myself.'

For journalists of my generation, an interview with Grace Jones was always a poisoned chalice, because while you would certainly come away with great copy, there was always the danger that she might belt you round the face or shout at you for being less than she expected. Only four days before my interview, she had allegedly punched a French journalist for probing too deeply. When I arrived at her hotel suite that morning, she acted as if she had already drunk half a bottle of champagne . . .

'I've had more misrepresentations than I can handle, and people have told the wickedest lies about me,' she said. 'A lot of them have taken their frustrations out on me, and I don't like that because it can wound. Not necessarily me, but those around me. Journalists can be so bad.'

She was extremely beautiful, outrageously thin, with an Azzedine Alaïa waist and amazingly chiselled legs, although her voice was disconcertingly masculine, with an odd cockney lilt – 'Alroit?' She smoked incessantly too, ate her club sandwich with both hands and stirred her champagne with one of last night's dirty chopsticks.

I told her she had become renowned for being intimidating. Did she need constant recognition?

'No, not constantly. I like a bit of honesty every now and again.'

But not too much.

'But not too much.'

1982

WAKE ME UP BEFORE YOU WHISKEY-A-GO-GO

'Fame is a funny beast, because no one really understands it. It's a little bit like love, a little bit like God. I remember in 1982, when I was doing the classic, "I'll never change, I'll always be me," and this friend of mine said, "Everyone will treat you differently." So you go through this period of losing the plot, and sometimes that suits people. Some people really get into it and they like it. And other people go, "Oh no!" I guess I was one of the second lot. I just went, "Not for me."'

BOY GEORGE

Michael Bracewell: The pop climate of British music experienced a touch of global warming when ABC's *Lexicon of Love* revived the zoot suit and kicked out the synthesizers.

In some respects, Martin Fry's ABC pre-empted the entire ethos of new pop, creating a thoroughly convincing pop property with a light sense of irony – earnest backing vocals, gold lamé suits and snarky lyrics. Their first album, The Lexicon of Love *(1982), said it all: on 'The Look of Love', when Fry encourages us to help each other, you just know his tongue is firmly in his cheek. 'It was like disco, but in a Bob Dylan way,' said the record's producer, Trevor Horn, although it was actually much better than he made it sound. With 'The Look of Love', 'Poison Arrow', 'Tears Are Not Enough' and 'All of My Heart', ABC managed to create totally modern-sounding records that celebrated the delusory idea of pop itself. If the Buzzcocks' Pete Shelley had written songs for Motown, they may have sounded like this. In a way, ABC were doing what Roxy Music had done ten years previously, which was create a shiny pop environment, slightly at odds with the times. In ABC's world, men wore suits and women were grateful – before breaking their men's hearts. The defining quality of their music was its intelligence, driven by a desire to elevate the pop genre rather than simply turn it into a commodity. Former Buggles member Horn had only recently produced a series of clever singles for the slightly naff pop duo Dollar, yet the collaboration with ABC worked wonderfully well. Fry introduced Horn to New York records by Defunkt and James Chance and the Contortions, while Horn introduced Fry to the wonders of the recording studio. 'He gave us the keys to the candy store,' said Fry. 'Trevor would say to us, "If you want pizza, I'll get you pizza; if you want a string section, I'll get you a string section."' Demos were made using a Minimoog, a sequencer and a drum machine, with the band recording over the top. 'It was like tracing,' said Horn. 'Which meant that we got it really spot on and snappy and in your face.' Fry, meanwhile, was the lonely mountaineer of the heart.*

Martin Fry: The look of ABC came from jumble sales. It came from going to shit bars full of old guys in Sheffield and Manchester and thinking, 'God, there's a world out there somewhere.' So a lot of it was pursuing a fantasy, a Vegas fantasy about what show business could be like. It wasn't on your doorstep, so you had to find it. When people think of *The Lexicon of Love*, they'll see the red velvet curtains. I really liked Jerry Lewis in *The Nutty Professor*, when he transforms, and I wanted that kind of feel. The reinvention. All those bands and all those musicians, they were seeking attention. It was escapist, and there was a lot to escape from.

Trevor Horn: After playing with Yes, I was at a point where I didn't know what to do next, and my late wife said to me, 'You should forget being an artist because it's not your thing at the moment, but if you went into production, you could be the best producer in the world.' So that's what I did. I worked with Dollar and made 'Give Me Back My Heart', 'Mirror Mirror' and 'Hand Held in Black and White'. That's what led me to ABC, as Martin Fry was a big fan of 'Black and White'. To me, ABC sounded like sophisticated dance music, but a lot of my friends heard their early demos and just thought it was disco. I said, 'Listen to the lyrics!' ABC basically wanted me to make a record they could play in the club they went to! They wanted it to compete with the American records they heard in their club in Sheffield. But they were great people to work with because they were all bright guys. It really makes a difference when you work with bright people. They were intelligent and funny. Martin said that if I worked with them, I would become the most fashionable producer in the world, as they were the most fashionable band. When we started making 'Poison Arrow', we got it to a certain point, and they were still sounding like an English indie band. I asked them if they were happy with it or whether they wanted to make something better. They said, 'Better,' so that's what we did, completely stripping everything out and starting from scratch. We made *The Lexicon of Love* sound American. By the time it was finished, we'd already had hits with 'Tears Are Not Enough' and 'Poison Arrow', and the record company was waiting for the album. Even when it was finished, I went back and remixed four of the songs because I didn't think they were quite right. We were trying to get it to sound as slick and as tight as we could. We spent so long on it that after a while I couldn't tell if it was any good or not. I was asking the guys in the white coats at the pressing plant if it was any good, because I just didn't know any more.

Martin Fry: The instant success was terrifying. We knew we'd stumbled across something – a vision of the pop future. One minute John Peel was phoning to tell us he was playing our single, the next we were off to Studio 54 to meet Andy Warhol.

Julien Temple: ABC owed everything to video.

Martin Fry: I'm enormously proud of *The Lexicon of Love*, as it's a great record conceived by a great many people. It was a wonderful collaboration. Every molecule was conceived. It's very focused, so each bar something seems to happen lyrically, melodically or sonically. I was really into the barbed love song. I loved Joy Division's 'Love Will Tear Us Apart', as I thought that was like a revolutionary Sinatra song. When Ian Curtis hanged himself, it was a tragedy, not just personally, as I thought they were going to go on making records like that for ever. I suppose we were doing the same thing simultaneously. 'The Look of Love', 'Poison Arrow', 'All of My Heart' – they are love songs, but there's a lot of hate in them. I suppose we were trying to give the love song some dignity. I loved Sinatra and all those wonderful songwriters, like Sammy Cahn and Jimmy Van Heusen, and it just felt right not to be singing about electric pylons. There was a lot of material about the future at the time, but ours was a more emotional future. That's what *The Lexicon of Love* is about. It did seem shiny and brand new at the time, but it could almost have been a country-and-western album. When we did 'All of My Heart', we demoed it, and it was like a country-and-western song, in the sense that it's a bit of a tear-jerker, but obviously we wanted to make it sound more grandiose, widescreen and cinematic. That was the name of the game.

Trevor Horn: In 1982, I also produced a Spandau Ballet record, 'Instinction'. I did it while I was still making *The Lexicon of Love*, and of course ABC were very cross with me. They said, 'How can you work with Spandau Ballet when you're working with us?!' I'd heard the Spandau album – *Diamond* – and hadn't liked it very much, but they asked me to choose a song and remix it for a single. I always had a real soft spot for Spandau Ballet because Gary's a great writer, and some of their songs were very good. So I just picked one and did it in a day, put some extra keyboards on it, redid Tony's vocal, and away we went. I think somehow the guy that had worked with them before had given Tony a bit of a complex, and Tony's a hell of a good singer. I know you either like his voice or you don't, but you can't take it away from him – the guy can sing. I happen to like his voice because he's got one of the great English voices. And so the remix was a hit.

Martin Fry: It didn't feel like any great community. I met the Duran Duran guys, and they were really personable, really nice guys, but artistically on a different canvas. That's why we wanted to work with Trever Horn. What he did was very different to what you would hear on John Peel, very different to what everyone else was doing. So it was never like a pop community. But we were very competitive. It was like the Premier League, where there are only four places to play Champions League football. And it's only one act that can get to No. 1. That's how I saw it. There was also competition between north and south, although in the end everybody ended up in London anyway. If you are really honest, as soon as you have success, it's not so regional, is it? You're all in the lounge at Heathrow having a drink.

ABC seemed to be appreciated by both *Smash Hits*, because we were popular, and by the *NME*, because of what we were trying to do. We played the A to Z club in Bayswater some Sunday night, and a lot of journalists from the *NME* were there, prior to us getting a recording contract. I think one of the reviews, maybe by Ian Penman, said our songs were like the lexicon of love, and that's where the title of the album came from. The beautiful thing about selective memories is that you remember the good stuff, but there was a lot of stuff around at the time that we didn't like. To be honest, Duran Duran and Spandau were better at the *Smash Hits* stuff. It was hard to do that stuff with a smile on your face.

Mark Ellen: All the acts played the game, as they had to, really. The weekly press detested artifice and gimmick and wanted things raw and 'real', so they thought the New Romantics were laughably shallow and pretentious. Which made them even keener to get into *Smash Hits*. At the *NME* you'd always be sent a band's new record and asked if you'd interview and photograph them. At *Smash Hits* you tended to get sent colour transparencies of a band's 'new image' first, then the new video, then the new single. In a way, the music was just the soundtrack to the look. At *Smash Hits* the idea was to create a language of our own and make the readers feel part of a club or secret society, a sort of Facebook of its time. Our take on the New Romantics was applause for their courage and for bringing a ray of sunshine to the page, plus a gentle lampoon for being preposterous. A photo caption for Blue Rondo à la Turk would say, 'Look at the STATE of the Turks!' One for Soft Cell would say, 'Poptastic trilby £276 (a snip!). Hair by Keith at Scowl. Dog collar with metal spikes, model's own'. Anything majorly over the top – like Nick Rhodes, in a powder-pink suit and top hat, with a live flamingo – was captioned, 'It's like punk never 'appened!' [Assistant editor] Neil Tennant always said any hit act whose new single flopped was 'down the dumper'. If the next one sold, they were 'up the dumper' or 'back, *back*, BACK!'

Marc Almond: There wasn't a collegiate atmosphere as there were intense rivalries between all the groups, and so I felt alone at that time. Duran hated Spandau, Spandau hated us, and we hated them. I remember staying at the Columbia Hotel, on the Bayswater Road in London, where everyone stayed when they came down to do television, and everyone would be sitting at their breakfast tables ignoring each other. Everyone tried to be their pop star selves, and there was this intense rivalry. I think that kind of competitiveness was encouraged. You'd go on radio shows and you'd be encouraged to be very bitchy about someone's record. *Smash Hits* loved all that, people slagging off each other's records. At that time, Neil Tennant worked for *Smash Hits*, and he came to do some of my very first interviews. I think he came up and lived for a while in a bedsit in Leeds. He was very much championing Soft Cell, but we didn't really like that world. They had a Christmas issue, and they wanted Dave and I to pose with party hats and party poppers on the cover, and we just felt utterly demoralised by the thing and just looked at each other and thought,

'What are we doing this for? And I said, 'Is this what it's come to?' Mariella Frostrup was my PR at the time, and she was always trying to invent girlfriends for me and send me on dates with Siouxsie or Mary Wilson or someone like that. She once said to me, 'Have you heard of Bebe Buell?' And I said, 'She's a famous American groupie, isn't she?' Mariella said she could come over and pretend to be my girlfriend. That's how it was. They said, 'Your record will not get played on Radio 1 [if people think you're gay].' That was the climate. You really wanted to kind of blur it, because you'd get people saying, 'You are, aren't you?' Eventually, you just scream out to the world because you've had enough. I remember the first time I ever said, 'All right, if you insist blah blah blah,' and I wished I hadn't done that. I liked the kind of blurring that Morrissey had. I know it's a terrible thing to say, but I remember the first time I heard Neil Tennant describe the Pet Shop Boys as a gay band, and I wished he hadn't. I took that blurriness from the seventies, in a way, and even though you knew that Bowie and Bolan had wives, you never *really* knew, and that was really exciting. I never wanted to be pigeonholed, but I always thought that when I died, the headline would be: 'Gay eighties singer dies'. I always felt blurry about my own sexuality as well. I've not just been purely gay and I've had all sorts of different liaisons in my life. I went to see Morrissey at the Albert Hall a couple of years ago, and he came on and had this thick make-up on. I was amazed at how camp he kind of was, and he was backed by this blokey band. It was like Larry Grayson fronting Skrewdriver. But I love that old Hollywood blurriness.

Boy George: The first gig Culture Club ever did was in Croc's in Rayleigh, which was the Essex New Romantic club where Depeche Mode started. Then we played Heaven when 'White Boy' came out, and I went on stage saying, 'You cunts didn't buy our records . . .' and really swearing. And so that carried on for a while, until I started getting letters from people's mothers, saying, 'I brought my daughter to your show, and you were effing and blinding.' And my manager said, 'You really can't talk to the audience like that.' That was the beginning of me learning how to conduct myself on stage, because I was quite desensitised. I'd walk down the street and people would make comments, and I'd tell them to fuck off. I suppose I was quite intimidating, and that was because I was probably quite intimidated. 'Do You Really Want to Hurt Me?' got played on Gary Crowley and by David Hamilton on Radio 2, and then we got on *Top of the Pops* by accident. We were in the low forties, and so we weren't eligible for *Top of the Pops*, but then there were two stories about why we got it: one was that Elton John wanted to play his video, and they wanted him to play live; and the other was that Shakin' Stevens wasn't well. So whether it was Elton or Shakin', we got their slot. So the night before, I got a phone call from my manager, saying, 'Do you want to do *Top of the Pops*?' And we were just like, 'Aaaaaagggghhh.' We knew that was going to be the beginning of everything. I stayed up all night doing my hair and working out what I was going to wear, and literally from that performance on my life was never the same.

Neil Tennant: My world opened up when I joined *Smash Hits* as a writer. I always remember when Dave Hepworth gave me the job, I went into the office, and Mark Ellen said, 'Welcome to the world of free records.' I would learn a lot by going through the discarded records in what was known as the 'dumper box'. I just couldn't let these free records go. I was going to have to listen to them to see if they were worth keeping. So I'd often just sit in the office after hours going through records, and that's when I discovered this producer Bobby Orlando. Chris and I wanted the Pet Shop Boys to sound like him, so he was always the person we wanted to produce us. Before I went to *Smash Hits*, I was already writing with Chris, and we'd already made a demo. When I was at *Smash Hits*, I heard a lot more music and I got more and more interested in electronic pop, the kind you heard in the gay clubs. What we wanted to do was take that electronic sound and put with it lyrics you wouldn't expect to hear on a record like that.

We would have singer/songwriter lyrics that were more reflective, that could be political or satirical. Like, 'I've got the brains, you've got the looks, let's make lots of money.'

David Hepworth: The group that took us by surprise in terms of popularity were Duran Duran. We always felt they had no mystique because they came from Birmingham and always looked a bit desperate. But they were hugely popular, and the key person was John Taylor. He was incredibly good-looking, and the girls absolutely adored him. In the early days of *Smash Hits*, we were pretty much fifty–fifty in terms of a gender split, but during the Duran Duran days there were definitely more girls involved. We slightly exaggerated the war between Spandau and Duran, but it was easy. One was London, one was Birmingham. One was more popular, one thought it was a bit of a cut above. They were both perfectly balanced – chips on both shoulders. *Smash Hits* was this fabulous puppet theatre, and it was our job to fill the stage with as many characters as possible. Personally, I didn't particularly like the music, but a lot of people in the office did. But I think generally what turned us on was being successful. The golden age of anything is the period of inevitability, the period when things work in such a way as to make you think they'll work this way for ever. That's probably what we thought. What you learn over a period of time is, you're not a genius when it's going well and you're not useless when it goes the other way. But that's what turned us on, wanting to sell more copies. When I became editor, we did our first readers' poll, and so we printed something in the magazine on the best male, best female, best record, best video, most fanciable, etc. We read and counted every single last one of the votes ourselves in the office. We didn't send them out to a finishing house, didn't think anything like that was beneath us. We used to come in on a Saturday to count them, and there were 55,000 responses. We were a very small team – me, Mark Ellen, Bev Hillier, Tom Hibbert, Neil Tennant – and also we all really liked each other. We all got on, and that makes such a difference. Still, to this day, Bev

Hillier, Mark Ellen, Neil Tennant, whoever . . . all these people will ring you up and they will say, 'Man.' We'd call each other 'man' as it seemed like the most ludicrous thing to call each other. We developed a vernacular, as we wanted everything to be funny. We thought pop stars were rather absurd and developed a way of dealing with this supposedly glamorous world in an extremely mundane style. Adam Ant was called 'Alan Ant', Paul McCartney 'Fab Macca Wacky Thumbs Aloft'. What made it work was that we were dealing with a subject which was ostensibly cool, and therefore we dealt with it in the least cool way possible. It was Molesworth, it was Famous Five. *Smash Hits* was always the one going, 'Cool, look at this, it's weird,' you know what I mean? *Smash Hits* was never comfortable on the other side of the red rope. We called Simon Le Bon 'Lardo' because he was a bit chubby, we called Tony Hadley 'Foghorn'. It was the language of a school magazine. Neil Tennant would ask someone if their mother played golf, as this revealed if someone was posh or not. We would fall out with people too, as it became a kind of struggle of 'We're more important than you' on both sides. Paul Weller – or 'Paul Welder', as we called him – said, 'It's like punk never happened,' but he kept talking to us. There used to be a lot of struggles about photographs. I can remember having a problem with the Human League over some cover pictures, and they just turned up in the office, as they thought it was some sort of conspiracy. Jimmy Pursey from Sham 69 once came to the office and pinned me to the door and said, 'Don't ever write about me ever again,' and we took great delight in honouring that request. We used to joke that some people were impossible to get hold of, while others would be in reception. One year, we decided to tell the story of the Human League as a comic strip, and when we started looking into it, we found that it is actually very hard to do. We eventually found this guy called Harry, and we had to book him six months ahead because he spent most of his time sitting in a bungalow at the Beverly Hills Hotel, storyboarding for Spielberg films. We got him to draw Phil Oakey at home, with a hank of hair, and his father also has got a hank of hair, and the budgie in the cage behind also has a hank of hair. And that was *Smash Hits*. We took you down a peg or two and we made you part of the great British soap opera. That's why it never took off in America. There was pressure on us to make the magazine weekly, but we stood our ground and said that the quality would suffer if we went weekly. Also, don't forget that there's a very long, honourable tradition in this country of fortnightly publications – just look at *Private Eye*. It's the perfect bridge between a weekly and a monthly.

In the eighties, Duran Duran had fifteen Smash Hits *covers, more than any other act. Wham! would go on to have ten, the Pet Shop Boys would have seven, while Culture Club and Frankie Goes to Hollywood managed five each. ABC, Depeche Mode and the Human League? Four. Spandau Ballet, the Eurythmics and Orchestral Manoeuvres in the Dark? Three. Adam Ant and Gary Numan managed only two each.*

Neil Tennant: We were strictly apolitical at *Smash Hits*, although it was apolitical with a left-wing slant.

Duran Duran's songs sounded like glossy-magazine spreads come to life, but if anything was a harbinger of how the eighties would soon start to be seen, it was their video for 'Rio', which was shot in Antigua in May 1982 and released six months later, the fourth single from the Rio *album. Directed by Russell Mulcahy, who had directed 'Video Killed the Radio Star', it captured the band dressed in colourful Antony Price suits, aboard a yacht speeding across English Harbour bay, literally living the dream. With salt spray in their nostrils and the wind in their hair, Duran Duran were as sure of themselves as any British pop stars had ever been. There was no irony involved here, just a beautifully filmed travelogue that immediately moved the band away from any post-punk New Romantic milieu. Presented as a gang of wannabe playboys, they were defined by their playfulness and ambition. When the video was first shown on British TV, the response among those who expressed an opinion (and who weren't appalled by its self-indulgence) was exactly what the band had hoped for: no one could believe how expensive it looked. Here was a music video that didn't pander to anyone's idea of pop-cultural 'meta'. This was a celebration that was completely free of inverted commas. Nick Rhodes was seasick during the filming and, unapologetic to the last, said, 'I hate boats unless they're tied up and I'm having cocktails on them.'*

Eve Ferret: I kind of giggled at them being on a yacht. Not in a horrible way, but I just thought it was so funny, these young boys with floppy blond hair pretending to be on someone's boat, pulling faces.

Gary Kemp: The videos bands like us and Duran made were all purposely set in other countries – in Hong Kong or Sri Lanka or New Orleans. Because what that was saying was, 'We are global. We're not interested in the petty politics of one country. Not only are we global, we're not even available because we're always abroad.' These videos were little postcards, saying, 'While you are getting on with all that, we're out here because we're an international band.' I remember talking to Paul Weller, who was very cross with me at one point for not writing songs about miners. Steve Dagger, on the other hand, in the late seventies was on the picket lines when all that was going on. My dad was a Labour voter, and so was I, and a lot of middle-class people in the music press just didn't get what our parents had gone through.

David Bailey: Duran Duran all looked the same to me, apart from the one who thought he was Andy Warhol, Nick Rhodes.

Paul Morley (*journalist, provocateur*): All through the eighties, I hated Duran Duran, when for some they were the kings of pop. I hated them because they acted as though they were minor members of the royal family, but those that loved them did so because they made grand, escapist music, reflected in escapist videos celebrating their own playboy riches. When I interviewed them in 1981, they were already lording it over the charts and playing ornate pop rooted in the otherness of Bowie and the cool of Roxy Music, but somehow also in the scarves of the Bay City Rollers and the barnets of Slik. I was so angry at their self-importance that I could never bring myself to call them by the name they lifted from Roger Vadim's *Barbarella* – they seemed more soap than space opera. I used different names for them, my favourite being Diana Diana. Even then, they resembled the freshly minted Princess of Wales; you could see where her look as a fan came from, certainly her hair, eyeliner and posing genius. You could see Diana as a female member of Duran Duran, as Cilla was the female Beatle.

Antony Price: Duran Duran started their career believing that clothes were 50 per cent of their success, because they were in the audience at Roxy Music gigs. That was the big difference between bands in the seventies and bands in the eighties. Now I had spent a lot of time in the Caribbean, and so I understood the importance of colour in relation to the sea and the lighting of Mustique and the Bahamas. So when they came along saying they wanted to do a video in the Caribbean, I knew all about it, and I knew what I was going to do. Nick Rhodes had been to a lot of Roxy gigs and he understood the importance of the clothes, and he wanted Duran to have the same vibe. So we did all these wonderful electric suits. I loved Nick. I ended up doing his wedding.

Nick Rhodes: Britain's best-kept secret is Antony Price. I've worked with him for years, and his clothing is beyond any couture I've ever seen. It belongs in the Victoria & Albert Museum.

Paul Morley: I hated them from the point of view of a rock critic taking pop seriously, even when it was just for fun. They fancied themselves as not so much the made-up boy band they clearly were – the pretty one, the chubby one, the moody one, possibly the talented one, etc. – but as Peel-listening pop conceptualists mixing the Sex Pistols with Chic (wanton English energy and brazen processed disco, an interesting formula I may have stolen when working with Frankie Goes to Hollywood, my personal chart retort to Dreary Dreary). Duran Duran, though, sounded forced, lacking the subversive swagger of the Pistols and the transcendent swing of Chic and leaving behind an embellished melodic sludge. They were perhaps more Sweet crossed with Abba. To understand them you need to understand the times. Duran Duran arrived only a few years after punk transformed the idea of what rock could be, in a Britain dragging itself out of the bruising, disorientating seventies. Things were intellectually and spiritually tightening up inside the iron grip of Thatcherism, and at the same time loosening up economically and socially. Music magazines turned glossy, gossipy and colourful, requiring new sorts of fairy-tale cover stars, a backlash against the highfalutin weekly inkies containing thousands of intense words about Cabaret Voltaire. All new pop then made by those interested in being the latest thing had to be influenced by punk, if just the look, the clothes and the expression. One consequence was an experimental sonic elaboration of punk's ideological spirit and aesthetic vision, but a rejection of the safety-pinned visual cliché; this became known as post-punk. Another consequence was more theatrical, with dandy tabloid-labelled New Romantics looking back longingly over the spiky heads of the harsher, angrier punk to the showy costumes and window-dressing camp of glam, when pop stars looked like pop stars. Some groups could float, sometimes self-consciously, sometimes serenely, between those two camps – Human League, Japan, Depeche Mode, ABC – and others occupied a more purist, thoughtful zone, advocating mental glamour – Gang of Four, New Order, Associates, Magazine, the Smiths. The hardcore New Romantics were definitely all about the clothes, cosmetics, travel and showing off; as a response to grievous, turbulent times, Steve Strange, Spandau Ballet, Wham! and Duran Duran preferred the dolled-up posing in pampered cliques inside VIP sections of exclusive nightclubs. They weren't privileged, but pretended they were, which could be annoying if you didn't get the joke, and especially annoying and complacent when it isn't a joke. New Romance wasn't all about the fancy dress, shaky pretension and cocktails. There were those displaying convincing signs of resistance to the mediocre, to the restrictive and ordinary – the presence on *Top of the Pops* of daring Boy George blurring the sexes and positively confusing the mainstream mind, Soft Cell's northern sauce, and something deviant dripping from Adam Ant's painted brow was a sign of intact subversive punk spirit filtered through a kinky dream of Bowie.

'The merry-go-round stands rusting and lifeless. An elaborate floral display that used to stand proudly at the front of the mansion has wilted, leaving just bare earth. The tepees are collapsing in on themselves and a tent covering the bumper cars is falling to bits . . .' As a snapshot metaphor for the tragic demise of Michael Jackson, Eric Munn's 2008 piece in Rolling Stone *about the ruins of his Neverland playground is hard to beat. The aerial photographs of the ranch show a deserted and lifeless playground, with scorched earth and untended gardens, an abandoned circus, tumbledown and sad. In this blasted, dusty landscape, the only movement came courtesy of a tennis court – its net wilting under the harsh Californian sun. The elephants, giraffes, lions and monkeys were all gone, the horses were at a nearby children's riding school, and Jackson's own pet monkey, Bubbles, was in a sanctuary. But then you squint, flex and start moving your toes from left to right as 'Rock with You' starts folding out of the speakers, followed by 'Billie Jean', 'Off the Wall', 'Wanna Be Startin' Somethin'' and one of the greatest dance records ever made, 'Don't Stop 'Til You Get Enough', and the vision becomes blurry.*

The scandals that started to erode Jackson's legacy are still in play, making it difficult to look back at his career with the same appreciation we once did. He will be forever tainted, and yet his achievements in the early eighties still stand. Not only was he one of the few US artists at the time to use video as a proper marketing vehicle (even though he initially found it difficult to get them played on MTV – black music and anything hip hop-related was largely excluded from corporate patronage), he surpassed them in terms of both sophistication and ambition. Thriller *may have been Jackson's sixth solo album, but when it was released on 30 November, it immediately set itself apart from anything that had come before it. In just over a year,* Thriller *became the world's best-selling album (it is the second-best-selling album in the US, behind the Eagles'* Their Greatest Hits (1971–1975)*), winning a record-breaking eight Grammy Awards and producing seven singles: 'The Girl Is Mine', 'Billie Jean', 'Beat It', 'Wanna Be Startin' Somethin'', 'Human Nature', 'P.Y.T. (Pretty Young Thing)' and 'Thriller' itself. In an odd way, Jackson and his producer, Quincy Jones, somehow validated the British acts, personifying the pop sophistication many of them were striving for.*

Simon Napier-Bell: The colours of pop androgyny were a perfect match for the new television technology, so MTV jumped on the British bandwagon. Very soon, for a male entertainer to be wearing colourful make-up seemed totally unsurprising. And once people got used to men wearing make-up in videos, it was only a small step to get used to them wearing it elsewhere, which made Michael Jackson seem much less odd than he might have been otherwise. Yet Jackson himself was missing from the videos that filled MTV's screen each day, and when CBS executives asked why, they were told, 'His music's not rock.' Well, nor was Boy George's, nor the Eurythmics', nor even Duran Duran's. MTV argued that rock nowadays could mean pop, providing it wasn't trite or trashy. In which case why wasn't Michael Jackson being played? Was it because he was black? Absolutely not, said MTV. CBS boss Walter Yetnikoff decided it was. He became enraged because MTV refused to play Jackson's videos. 'I said to MTV, "I'm pulling everything we have off the air, all our product. I'm not going to give you any more videos. And

I'm going to go public and fucking tell them about the fact you don't want to play music by a black guy."' MTV relented and played 'Billie Jean' in heavy rotation. Afterwards, the *Thriller* album went on to sell an additional ten million copies.

David Hepworth: It's not stuff I listen to much. I think a lot of it just sounds as if it's got no bottom to it. I used to really like *Dare!*, but now it just sounds a bit shrill. Those records sounded quite amateurish, but that was part of their charm. It was supposed to be music that sounded good on *Top of the Pops* and on a small radio speaker. I mean, is *The Lexicon of Love* as good as we thought it was? I listened to Culture Club recently and I thought it was amazing that it was so big at the time, because it's so insipid. But, you know, the visuals were such an important part of it. Actually, Eurythmics records, they were pretty good, as were Michael Jackson's, obviously.

Gary Crowley (*DJ*): I was fifteen in 1976, and started a fanzine called *The Modern World*, where I interviewed the Clash, the Jam and the Pistols. I was mainly going to gigs and didn't start going to clubs until Bernie Rhodes started Club Left at the Whiskey-A-Go-Go in 1979. Vic Godard played there as a sort of reinvented crude crooner, and it's where Bananarama first got up on stage, singing 'High Hopes'. I left school in '78 and eventually got a job as the receptionist at the *NME*, where I took over from Danny Baker. Around the same time, I got to know Steve Dagger and Gary Kemp, who was in a power-pop band called the Makers. Radio 1 asked me to come and compère a couple of *In Concert* programmes featuring younger, edgier bands. Then one of the producers jumped ship to Capital and offered me a job as a DJ. At that time, Danny Baker was doing a few bits on TV, but as far as radio was concerned, there was nobody with a strong regional accent. I wanted the show to be different right from the beginning, so I thought we should make it a club, and we called it *The Tuesday Club*, which meant we could do it live as well and get bands in to play or do a

PA. This was when dance music was really coming to the fore, and so, as well as playing the likes of the Bluebells, Everything But the Girl and the Style Council, I'd also play Animal Nightlife and things like 'White Lines'. I remember bowling down Old Compton Street, and Joe Strummer was coming towards me. I was all smiles, and he was like, 'You've sold out, man. I can't believe you're working for Capital Radio.' I said it wasn't me who signed to CBS! By this time, the *John Peel Show* was almost unlistenable, and there was so much great music coming out of the clubs. I wanted my show to reflect what I was listening to, that mix of guitar bands and synth pop, and all this exciting stuff that was beginning to filter over from America. I played Culture Club's first single, Bananarama's first records, Haysi Fantayzee, Wham!, Blancmange. With 'Do You Really Want to Hurt Me?', I remember telling the producers that not only did nobody sound like Boy George, no one looked like him either. And, along with David Hamilton on Radio 2, we made it a hit.

Kate Garner (*singer, photographer*): I met Jeremy Healy when I was photographing some Stephen Jones hats for the *Sunday Times*. He was masquerading as a hairdresser, but he didn't even know how to put a clip into the model's hair. I told him I was writing music, and he said he'd do it with me. He took me to a council flat, where Boy George knelt down in front of me and sung me a Marvin Gaye song, and then on to the Warren Street squat, where John Maybury was filming boys dressed as angels, in a room filled with swathes of billowing cheesecloth. All of a sudden I was very happy. I had no aspirations to be a performer, but I just kept getting asked to do it, culminating in me being chased through the north London streets by Malcolm McLaren, who wanted to audition me for Bow Wow Wow. But, after that, Jeremy and I went and made some demos, which eventually led to Haysi Fantayzee being signed. The instant fame was difficult to cope with because the musical foundation of our house was actually quite shaky. If I look at old photographs of me at the time, my eyes look quite mad.

The bigger we got, the scarier it became, because I didn't feel able to fulfil the expectations being placed upon us.

Gary Crowley: I used to ask bands to do jingles for me. Elton John did a slightly homoerotic one. It went: 'If you fancy Gary Crowley, if you drive a Morris Cowley, if you are a rower, if you are a cox, wouldn't you like to get your hands on Gary Crowley's *Magic Box*?'

Keren Woodward: Our name came from 'Pyjamarama', the Roxy Music song. Someone from the record company wanted to call us the Pineapple Chunks, so we rushed to find a name. Paul Cook produced our first demo, 'Aie e Mwana' [a cover of the Black Blood song, sung in Swahili], and Terry Hall from Fun Boy Three heard it on *John Peel*. They'd just split from the Specials and took us under their wing. Everything happened so quickly. I was brought up playing the piano, and Sara and I sang in all the school musicals and used to write songs in the summer holidays and record them on cassette, but I don't think we ever seriously thought about it as a career. We used to sing Frank Sinatra covers at Club Left, but we weren't professional. We used to force our way onto any stage that would have us. We recorded with the Fun Boy Three, went on *Top of the Pops*, and then it went nuts. We had a hit with 'Really Saying Something' and never looked back. We just threw ourselves into it and learnt as we went along. I think we really had the punk mentality, like anyone could get up and do it.

Gary Crowley: I was a big early supporter of Wham! There used to be a big Sunday football game in Regent's Park with Spandau Ballet and Blue Rondo, and Andrew and George came down a few times. I remember reading Tom Wolfe's piece about the noonday underground, and so I started a Saturday lunchtime disco at Busby's for all the Topshop girls in the West End. I asked Andrew and George to do a PA, but they outnumbered the audience, so we just hung out and chatted. When I started DJing live, I'd bring in a whistle or a cow bell with me. I'd play a record, then jump down onto the dancefloor if people weren't dancing, trying to get people onto the floor. We used to do a club night at Bogart's in Harrow, and George and Andrew would come along, and they'd be dancing with secretaries, girls who worked in the Wimpy or post-office workers. This was the time when kids were screaming at bands again, and they certainly screamed at Wham! It had started with Adam Ant, but by 1982 it was Wham!'s turn. People wanted to be pop stars again. Even Bowie. They wanted to be successful. It was a golden period of pop. People were galvanised by the excitement of it all, and many of them had come out of the clubs, like Spandau, Wham!, Blue Rondo, Bananarama, Culture Club. Lots of them had been in punk bands that hadn't made it.

Keren Woodward: Initially, it wasn't important to us that we were taken seriously, because we were just having fun. One minute we're on the *NME* and it's very cool, and the next we're on the cover of *Smash Hits* holding balloons. We got tarred with that *Smash Hits* image, where they would just make a pretty set around you because you were three girls, so we had a massive reaction against that and started writing more serious songs. So we kind of taught ourselves to write songs, and we learnt everything in the public eye. I'd never been on a flight before Bananarama; in fact, I think it happened the same week I signed off the dole. We used to steal knives and forks, toilet paper . . . everything. We were so broke, even though we were on *Top of the Pops*.

We had no stylist, no make-up artist, and just did everything ourselves. We obviously had the bird's-nest hair too, which I suppose was a leftover from punk. But everyone had their own style at the time. Antony Price made a few things for us later, but usually we just did our own stuff.

The big problem was, the music business was like a boys' club, and we were continually being exploited. Everyone in the record company was male, apart from the secretaries. It was a constant battle, which is why we were so combative and confrontational in interviews. I think journalists used to be quite scared of us, because we were tough and wouldn't take any crap. We used to have a lot of fun, but just because you're having fun doesn't mean you're an idiot. And we were treated like that a lot, so we all ganged together. We had the power of three, so we moved as one person and had each other's backs. It was us against the world. We were inseparable. If one went to the toilet, we'd all go. We moved as a group. I don't think we could have contemplated doing what we did as solo artists. I wouldn't say I have any regrets about that period, though. I mean, I've been in some sticky situations, really silly stuff, like getting in cars with people, saying, 'Take us to a club,' and ending up down an alleyway running for our lives. We were probably a bit naive. But again, you've got to be super-careful when you're a girl. There were so many bitchy comments: 'You can't dance, you can't sing, you look a mess . . .' I used to get upset because some of the worst things said about us were written by women. They were the bitchiest of all, which I've never really understood. I'm very proud of the fact that we became successful on our own terms, wearing dungarees and Doc Martens and not flaunting our sexuality. I think we were positive role models in an industry that is so sexualised. The industry was worse in the States. I remember some bloke from a company putting his hand down my trousers, and I just screamed and pushed him off. And he said, 'Don't you want to be No. 1?' And I said, 'No, not that much.' The States was a giddy time, though. I remember Andy Warhol being asked what the coolest thing in New York was at the time, and he said Bananarama. And then going to LA, and Mike Tyson serenading us with 'Cruel Summer', word perfect. I mean, both our dads worked in factories.

As British pop continued to fracture as the eighties progressed, two themes seemed to coalesce. The first produced dozens of willowy-looking groups seemingly intent on making records that aped classic sixties pop singles, complete with jingle-jangle guitars, muted horns and winsome vocals: the Pale Fountains, Aztec Camera, the Bluebells, the Suede Crocodiles, Fantastic Something, April Showers, etc. The second affected bands who seemed desperate to semaphore their innate funkiness by covering songs by William DeVaughn, Sly and the Family Stone and James Brown. Bass guitars would be mixed to the fore, as would scratchy guitars and bubbling keyboards. These acts would appear in both Smash Hits *and the* NME, *slipped in among the synth-pop duos and the New Romantic bands. Haircut 100 were the most obvious example. The new pop was not just a collage of every kind of pop that had been before it, but also any number of new splinters, calculated postmodern slices of everything from scratchy post-punk to the popular avant-garde, from black electronica to gender-bender pop.*

And the biggest new act of the year was Wham!

Two suburban boys with West End aspirations, Wham! were second-generation immigrants, Andrew Ridgeley coming from Italian/Egyptian stock, while George Michael (real name Georgios Panayiotou) was Greek. Hailing from Bushey in Hertfordshire, in the heart of the disco belt, they were high street through and through: their white T-shirts and socks came from Marks & Spencer, their blue jeans from Woodhouse. For years they danced themselves stupid at the New Penny in Watford High Street, moving on to the Camden Palace as soon as it opened in the spring of 1982 and immersing themselves in London's holier-than-thou nightlife. To west London sybarites, they looked oddly naive in their quasi-naff clothes and floppy fringes, yet anyone with eyes in their head and loafers on their feet could tell they had a very spangly future ahead of them. Wham! seemed to fulfil the tabloid shibboleth of 'picking a winner'.

George Michael (*singer, musician*): Andrew and I became fully fledged suburban soul boys at fifteen [in 1978]. We wore dungarees and bright colours and got sent home from school. All this shitty minor rebellion. I loved all that 1977–8 disco stuff, but then it started getting into jazz-funk, and I thought, 'Fucking hell, all those seventeen-year-old kids haven't got a clue about jazz music. They just think it's the trendy thing to do.' We just got out of it, stopped going to those clubs. We got into 2-Tone because that was the next thing that happened that was young and energetic. Then, when that faded, we were flailing around for about a year in terms of what we liked and what we wanted to write. Then there was a resurgence of soul-pop, stuff like 'Burn Rubber on Me' by the Gap Band, and we decided that was what we wanted to do. 'Wham Rap!' was meant to be a piss-take of rap records, it was meant to be a parody – 'I am the most beautiful.' Rap was quite funny at first, but it got really boring. 'Punk disco' they called us. The ridiculous things they called us!

Andrew Ridgeley: After the Executive folded, George continued writing songs, as did I, but I don't think we had thought about doing another band. It was all home recording. The '81 demo for Wham! had 'Wham Rap!', a verse and chorus of 'Careless Whisper' and about half of 'Club Tropicana'. We had had a complete musical rethink. The New Romantics had come in, which had changed things a bit, so our music and image changed too. There was so much happening, with lots of things crossing over. Haircut 100, ABC, more dance acts, rap, soul boys . . . George's and my tastes were very broad, and we weren't confined to any particular genre. It all informed what we wanted to do. We didn't feel like we needed to fit in, and we didn't feel defined by any one thing. We had quite an individual spirit. My mum had me when she was only eighteen, and she was quite liberal. My father was rather more conservative, but there was a sense of freedom at home. Like I say, we weren't rebelling.

We already had the name Wham! It came from 'Wham Rap!', which had come about when we were rapping along to a song in a club. We didn't know what to call ourselves, and it just sounded suitable. The exclamation mark came later, from Roy Lichtenstein.

Success came quickly, and it was odd. We released 'Wham Rap!' in May of '82 and it did nothing, and it was anticlimactic. So that was a knock to our confidence. Then we did 'Young Guns', which was a marked improvement and a considerably better song, and we were doing a lot of PAs. Then a researcher from *Saturday Superstore*, the TV programme, saw us at one of these PAs, and she recommended us to the production team. And after that, someone cancelled from *Top of the Pops*, and as we were just outside the Top 40, we got our chance on the show. Then we were off and running. It was an incredibly fast ascent, although we still couldn't afford to leave home. It was a weird juxtaposition, being very successful but having no money. We still had the same social lives as we didn't have any money for a very long time.

There was a lot of criticism from the music press at the time, who felt slightly nutmegged that we weren't the new standard-bearers for disgruntled youths. I mean, even John Peel played 'Wham Rap!', although I don't think he ever played anything else by Wham! The music press felt duped. We told them all along; they just weren't listening. It didn't fit other people's narrative.

Simon Napier-Bell: Wham! discovered themselves. They just arrived on my doorstep. I saw them performing 'Young Guns (Go for It)' on *Top of the Pops* in 1982, and they had this amazing dance routine. You could tell they'd done it themselves. *Top of the Pops* used to always direct everyone, so to see a group come across that well, I knew they'd done it themselves. They had worked out how *Top of the Pops* worked and went home and rehearsed it to make it look amazing. So it went through my mind at that moment that they might be an interesting band to get involved with.

George Michael: At the beginning with Wham! there was a real sense of humour. You go from being two kids who have got this chance they weren't expecting to being . . . professionals. My absolute all-time low career-wise was the video for 'Bad Boys', because by the time we got round to making it, I had forgotten it was meant to be a joke. That video is the worst thing in our entire career. We look such a pair of wankers in it. How can anybody look at those two people on screen doing what they were doing, with all those camp dancers prancing around in the background, and think it's good? We lost a lot of ground with that video.

Simon Napier-Bell: Jazz Summers came to see me and asked if I wanted to manage Wham! with him. I didn't really want to do more management and told him that I wanted to go and live in Asia and write books. And he persuaded me to have another go, so I went to meet George and Andrew. Instantly, I knew they weren't the identical-twin couple I'd seen on television, as they had very different personalities, with Andrew being very much what you saw, and George being more careful, distrustful and cautious. Andrew picked up a copy of my first book, put his feet up on the coffee table, started reading it and said, 'This is the guy for us, as in the sixties he was either drunk or having sex!' But George started asking questions: 'Who are you managing?' 'What do you do?' 'Why will you be good for us?' Andrew was an easy pull, if you like, but George was intelligent and wanted you to understand that. The only artists you're ever really going to be successful with are the ones who want to know how the business works. If they're leaving it all to you, then they're going to be impossible, and the sooner you can teach them how the business works, the sooner you're going to have somebody you can work with. And so George was immediately attractive to me to work with.

He had to work at his persona, though, as this was obviously why he was with Andrew, because Andrew was front of house. When they first did their first tour, when Andrew walked out on stage, everybody screamed, but when George walked out, they didn't. Andrew had blond hair, George had black, and by the end of the tour George had blond hair too, and they started screaming. George was learning all the time about stage presence, learning it from Andrew, because Andrew had this extraordinary, carefree confidence. George had to learn to project an image of that confidence, while never actually having it.

Andrew and George had met at Bushey Meads School and had remained best friends ever since. At school George had found himself something of an outsider – a podgy boy with glasses and curly hair. In his first term, he found himself sitting next to Andrew, the boy everybody wanted to know – good-looking, brainy, athletic and funny. To George's amazement, Andrew befriended him and became his best mate. Probably, it arose from something they had in common. Despite the differences in their looks, they both had immigrant fathers. George's was from Cyprus, Andrew's from Egypt. George rose to the challenge of being Andrew's best friend. He bought hair straighteners, took the curls out of his hair, put in contact lenses, threw away his glasses and lost weight. Soon Andrew and George looked almost like twins. People often ask me what Andrew contributed to Wham! They thought of him as a non-singer, non-musician and non-writer. But in a group, the thing of greatest importance is the image. Backing singers and musicians can be paid by the hour, professional songwriters can be brought in to provide the songs, producers can be hired. Only the image has to be real, and Andrew provided it.

Andrew Ridgeley: 'Young Guns' was the springboard, and from then on it went big. We were pretty rough around the edges, but we became polished quite quickly, although George hated 'Bad Boys' as he thought it presented us in a bad light. He wrote it after 'Wham Rap!', and you could see the continuity, in image and theme, but it wasn't us. Artistically, he didn't like where it was taking us. He thought it was too camp. It was a dead end. Luckily, we had 'Club Trop', which for us was a complete rebrand. We used to go to Le Beat Route all the time. We weren't part of the inner sanctum, but it was a great club. It was a slightly oblique look at that scene, a slight pastiche. But we loved it, and the club meant a lot. As did Ibiza, where we made the video.

Simon Napier-Bell: Childhood trauma seems to be the major cause of someone becoming an artist. There's some kind of pain inside from when they were a child. That's where the creation comes from, looking back at that pain. If I see an artist and there isn't any trauma, I know if I search, I'll find it; it just hasn't been talked about. Childhood trauma pushes that creativity out of people. I never discussed anything with George that touched on his personal life, nor discussed the source of his frequent depression. I just dealt with it as best I could, as I've done with any other artist I've ever managed. I try to help them find an infrastructure on which they can build success. As a manager, I'm hired to exploit their talent. I'm not a psychiatrist hired to treat the source of it.

George Michael: I had all the things not going for me that thirteen-year-old kids don't have going for them. Apart from the spots. But I was well overweight, taller than everyone else. I had really frizzy, curly hair, very thick glasses . . . Nobody looked at me, absolutely no girl ever looked at me. Then suddenly, when I was about fifteen, I cut my hair and got contact lenses. The optician was saying I was too young, but I wanted them so badly. It's not vanity to not want to have specs, is it? There was no doubt about it, I wanted Andrew's style. When we were younger, people used to ask me if he was gay; it was only when we grew up that people started asking him if I was gay. When the soul boy thing came in, he wore cherry-coloured satin trousers and had those three little plaits in his hair, almost Red Indian-style. And I said, 'I'm not walking down the street with you like that! This is Bushey!'

Le Beat Route was perhaps the greatest club of the entire period, bang in the middle of Greek Street and just behind St Martin's, so it attracted not just the ever-growing Blitz crowd, but a new influx of art students, as well as younger soul boys who were now pouring into Soho at the weekend. It was here, in Le Beat Route, that the eighties truly began to cohere, in terms of music, style and attitude. Steve Strange and Rusty Egan also bounced back with something of an upmarket vengeance in June 1981, moving out of Soho and Covent Garden to the Barracuda Club in Baker Street with Club for Heroes, in some ways having come full circle. It would close in November 1981, the last hurrah for the puppet masters of the one-nighter club. In April 1982, they would open the Camden Palace on Camden High Street, a gargantuan Titanic *of a nightclub on the site of the old Music Machine. The one-nighter had become an all-weeker, and the underground club culture that had started in the smallest of Soho echo chambers was now a lynchpin of global pop culture. When Madonna made her first appearance on a London stage, it was at the Camden Palace.*

Jason Cowley: In 1982, Steve Strange opened a new club, the Camden Palace, described by Boy George as a 'tacky deco-style posers' parlour', which I used to attend while still at school. Thursday night was best, when Strange would be on the door and Rusty Egan spinning the records. You would have to dress at your most outrageous simply to get in, and then, when the club closed, spend dead hours hanging around the streets because you had missed the last train back to the suburbs.

Fiona Dealey: There were three big club openings in 1982. There was the Wag, which was Chris Sullivan and Ollie O'Donnell's club in Wardour Street, and then you had the Camden Palace, which was the old Music Machine, but it had been taken over by Steve Strange and Rusty Egan. There was also the Dirtbox, which was opened in the spring by these guys called Rob and Phil above a chemist's in Earl's Court. Both the Wag and the Camden Palace felt as though they were the logical next step to mainstream culture, especially as so many Blitz people were now becoming famous. The Dirtbox was definitely not mainstream, though!

In the spring, in London clubland at least, you started to see less of an emphasis on dressing up, as people began dressing down with a vengeance. The generic look was simple to describe, simple to achieve: torn, worn jeans; Vivienne Westwood tops; little leather caps; big studded leather belts; white socks; Chinese slippers, plimsoles, espadrilles or biker boots. At clubs like the Dirtbox (an itinerant, moveable feast which bounced around the city, from an Earl's Court walk-up to warehouses and squats), everyone looked like this, boys and girls alike. Even though this was a faux blue-collar look, it was obviously androgynous, mixing the sexual codes up again (one way to spot the girls: short, dyed, peroxide hair). In one sense, it was driven by music, as Chic's 'Good Times' gave way to records like 'Money's Too Tight to Mention' by the Valentine Brothers and 'The Message' by Grandmaster Flash, twelve-inch epics that openly referenced recession and urban deprivation. The look was a bit rockabilly, a bit clone, and very street. This seemed to be a genuine reflection of the economy, mirroring the political insurrection that was happening elsewhere in the music industry, a cultural environment that had been kick-started by the Specials' 'Ghost Town' the summer before. 'Hard Times', The Face *called it, and while it was seemingly inconsequential, a largely white consequence of the influence of hip hop, it would prove to be extraordinarily prescient. Club culture was spreading, broadening out, and the hard-times look not only reflected the fact that a lot of people couldn't afford to dress up and go out, it also had a genuine ironic quality. This was a nod towards* nostalgie de la boue, *the nineteenth-century French term meaning 'nostalgia for the mud', which had already been appropriated by Malcolm McLaren and Vivienne Westwood.* 'Nostalgie de la boue *tends to be a favourite motif whenever a great many new faces and a lot of new money enter Society,' wrote Tom Wolfe, a decade beforehand. 'New arrivals have always had two ways of certifying their superiority over the hated "middle class." They can take on the trappings of aristocracy, such as grand architecture, servants, parterre boxes, and high protocol; and they can indulge in the gauche thrill of taking on certain styles of the lower orders. The two are by no means mutually exclusive; in fact, they are always used in combination.' Which, considering that aspirations were going in both directions, like escalators in a tube station, was a pretty fair summation of London clubland in 1982.*

Vivienne Westwood: The enemy of individual expression is the high street. My generation was politicised by the hippies, while punk was trying to achieve the look of an urban guerrilla. For me, next came pirates. The only subversion is in ideas, and ideas come from the past. It's about culture, as you can't throw away the past.

Marco Pirroni: Soon we were competing with ourselves, because once you got into it, you had to get bigger and bigger. You had to keep going. But obviously, after a while it became unhealthy – you know, the crushing defeats when singles only got to No. 2. We began to think it was starting to tail off after 'Prince Charming', when we were on another tour with a ridiculously expensive stage set. We should have gone to America at that point, but we couldn't afford to take our fucking stage with us. I didn't know how much we were spending as we never took any notice of how much money we were making on the road. After 'Prince Charming', the band relations were very bad, and I was caught in the middle because Adam decided he didn't want to talk to the band. It was all very much, 'Tell him to pass the fucking salt,' and it was all bollocks, you know, but Adam had decided in his head that the band was against him and all that, and there was no reasoning with him. So it's like, 'Oh well, I'm not doing this any more.' We jettisoned the Ants at the beginning of '82.

If any example were needed of just how esoteric London nightlife had become by 1982, you only had to consider the Gold Coast Club, a one-nighter opened by Christian Cotterill and Joe Hagan in the basement of Gossips at 69 Dean Street, the former home of Billy's, three and a half years earlier. Essentially, this was a night dedicated to all kinds of African music, which to an audience reared on Quincy Jones and Roy Ayers should not have been in the least bit esoteric, but actually appeared transgressive to a clientele who were now dancing to the likes of Wham! and Spandau Ballet. Here, Ghanaian DJ Hagan would play Manu Dibango, Fela Kuti and Gaspar Lawal, mixed in with the Philadelphia International All Stars and even the occasional track from Young Americans.

The most important club launch of the year was undoubtedly the Wag, the Wardour Street club Chris Sullivan and Ollie O'Donnell opened in the spring. They started by packing out the Whiskey-A-Go-Go every Saturday night with their own crowd, until the club's new leaseholders asked them to run it with them full-time. So they rebranded it, lowered the drinks and door prices, pulled in specialist DJs, and the place took off, becoming a Soho institution almost immediately. They had only been open a few weeks before they hosted the first ever hip hop club event in the UK, the Roxy Road Show, featuring twenty-five artists who flew in from New York, including Afrika Bambaataa, Grand Wizard Theodore (widely credited with inventing scratching), Jazzy Jay and Fab 5 Freddy, skipping-rope stars the Double Dutch Girls and legendary breakdancers the Rock Steady Crew. They soon developed a name for themselves by booking the likes of De La Soul, the Jungle Brothers, Queen Latifah, Eric B and Rakim, Kool Moe Dee, Grandmaster Flash and Doug E. Fresh. It's no overstatement to say they were complicit in breaking hip hop in the UK. The Wag became a drop-in too, and a strict door policy meant that boldface names largely felt safe, mixing with Sullivan's carefully curated crowd – a crowd containing many famous names of the future. Thus, on any given night you could be guaranteed to bump into – literally – anyone from John Galliano and Jonathan Ross to Tracey Emin or David Bowie, or perhaps a combination of Leigh Bowery, Grayson Perry, Boy George, Joe Strummer, Neneh Cherry, Mick Jagger, Keith Richards, Prince, George Clinton, Stevie Wonder, Robert De Niro, Brad Pitt, Karl Lagerfeld and Jean Paul Gaultier. Unsurprisingly, Sullivan had time and a word for all of them. 'One night, George Michael had a fight with our DJ, Fat Tony,' he says, 'and Grace Jones had to be physically restrained after laying out an irritating bloke with a single punch.' Sometimes it felt like the VIP room of a benign approximation of the Mos Eisley cantina in Star Wars.

Alix Sharkey (*journalist*): When the Wag Club opened, it became a focus for clubland innovation, a catalyst for racial integration and a temple to unremitting hedonism. But more than this, this tiny nightclub also symbolised how profoundly our culture had changed over the previous two decades. Soho during the mid-seventies was a very different country. Anyone frequenting the area was, by definition, of a dubious character. The area was known for brothels, strip-clubs, gambling and drinking dens, and nasty-looking blokes with big fists hanging around in shop doorways. There were no gay pubs, no fast-food restaurants, no twenty-four-hour espresso bars, no trendy members' clubs or all-night supermarkets. Neon signs were confined to Piccadilly Circus. Restaurants were few, snotty and expensive. Pubs were approached with caution if you weren't a local. As per the rest of the country, everything was shut by eleven.

Except nightclubs. Which is why, aged seventeen and yearning for life beyond closing time, I set out from Essex for the West End. My mates reckoned the return ticket was a waste of money. 'You'll get cut,' they warned, as I boarded the train to Fenchurch Street.

In 1974, the Wag was still called the Whiskey-A-Go-Go. A huge black man who looked like an extra from *Shaft* stood outside in a black leather jacket and a black fedora with a white silk band, hissing the words 'coke, mary-jane' at passers-by. Very few, I think, got his drift. Inside, up a steep flight of stairs, one wall was entirely covered in mirror tiles. The ceiling had been plastered crudely and painted silver-grey to resemble a lunar surface, while the supporting pillars were rough approximations of stalactites. On the dancefloor, a skinny bloke with a patchwork leather trench coat and flared jeans strutted his syncopated footwork, while gazing at the reflection of his own hennaed perm. A few girls in clogs and minidresses shuffled around him. Soft drinks only, no licence, they said at the bar. A weasly-looking geezer at the next table put me straight. 'Ask for a can from under the counter,' he grinned. This advice earned me a light ale. Illegal drinking in a black dance club where people wore patchwork leather coats. Could it get any better?

It did. After I had sidled onto the dancefloor and spent an hour copying the bloke with the perm, there was a ruckus at the top of the stairs, followed by shouting and a mad scramble as everyone in the club seemed to dash into the men's toilets. By the time the police had actually gained admission, there were discarded joints all over the floor, and the sound of cisterns being flushed could be heard above the music. Two uniformed coppers half-heartedly frisked a couple of punters, while a detective in a mac disappeared into a back room (presumably to get his 'drink'). They left as quickly as they had arrived. Fantastic. My first night in Soho, and I had witnessed a police raid.

Best of all, the Whiskey lasted till 1 a.m. – desperately late, in those sad, forgotten grey days before punk, New Romantic and acid house. It seemed impossibly exotic, this former Soho R&B club which had been popular with mods and had since fallen on tough times, and was now the home of an underground scene where young urban blacks and whites mixed together, rubbing elbows with drug dealers and pimps, dancing to records that were never played on radio, a new kind of brassy, sweaty dance music by people such as James Brown, Fatback Band, Ohio Players and Kool & the Gang.

And when you got talking to [the] doormen, they'd tell you how the Who and Jimi Hendrix would drink here, sometimes even jump on stage and jam, if they were in the mood and there was a decent act playing. But in truth, the Whiskey had never been as glamorous or as popular as the Flamingo, the jazz and R&B club which occupied the ground-floor premises beneath it. And towards the late seventies, it seemed a mere shadow of itself, haunted by memories of better times.

Chris Sullivan: We started the Wag Club initially on a Saturday, but then we got asked to take it over all week, and it became a career. I have to say, I wish I could turn the clock back to savour those times a bit more, because I was too busy having fun. Someone said to me the other day that the whole scene was quite Tory, but it was actually the opposite, as the first thing we did was lower the cost of getting in and lower the cost of the drinks. We actually made the whole experience more egalitarian. It was more of a community thing. We had a door policy, but it wasn't elitist; it was meant to protect those inside. If you go on a tube and it's packed and they can't get any more in, then you can't get on, can you? And the door policy worked: in eighteen years we only had half a dozen fights. We had brilliant door staff. We had Big Louise and one girl called Marie, the trans sex change who used to dress like Margaret Thatcher. The bouncers all knew but they never gave her any ribbing. They just took it in their stride: 'Isn't he the one who used to come down before and used to be a geezer, innit?'

Chris Sullivan's fastidious door policy wasn't always as stringent as he makes out. One night, I was there, propping up the bar, and these two loud Americans pushed by me, each wearing black leather jackets, and each with two tin cups looped through the epaulettes on their shoulders. Needless to say, they looked ridiculous; they could only have looked sillier if they had turned up with traffic cones on their heads. Years later, I read Scar Tissue, *the autobiography of the Red Hot Chili Peppers' vocalist, Anthony Kiedis. In one passage he recounts going to the Wag Club while on a trip to London with another member of the band. What were they wearing? Tin cups attached to the epaulettes of their black leather jackets.*

Ollie O'Donnell: Me and Chris sat down to come up with a name for the new club, and Chris suggested the Wag Club. It never occurred to us that people thought we called it that because of the name Whiskey-A-Go-Go. It was pure coincidence. Then, because the Saturday night had been such a success, we were offered the club for the whole week. We thought, 'Why not?' We had a lot of people who wanted to go out, all very sociable, a lot of people at St Martin's. You'd go to drink upstairs at the Cambridge, go to Jimmy the Greek, Bar Italia. Soho felt empowered. And then when the Wag took off, it was a whole new thing altogether. The other thing about the Wag was the colour bar, as we didn't have one. At the time, people would still be frightened of having too many black people getting in their clubs. And the music at the Wag was all black, all soul, all funk.

Winston was the chief security guy, a lovely man who had a great history. He had been great friends with Marvin Gaye and toured all over Europe as his minder. He had also worked with the Stones during the early seventies, and he used to tell me stories about Mick Jagger's mad tolerance for drink and drugs and how he would be awake for two days at a time. Winston was the nicest man you could meet, but he could only be pushed so far. He was notorious for his knockout punch, and both left and right hand were just as effective.

Norman Jay: For years I played records in and around west London, in Shepherd's Bush, Acton, Ealing. More often than not, we weren't paid, so I suppose the first time I played records for money was in 1979. Thanks to Freddie Laker, I managed to save enough money to go to New York that summer. I think it was £99. I went to meet some of my family, who were living there, and to check out the clubs. I spent four months there. I used to stand outside Studio 54, which was the first time I had seen a club with a rope outside, and this was completely alien to me. I also went to a lot of clubs in the boroughs, in Crown Heights. When I first went there, this was the black ghetto, and it was the first time I'd ever gone to a place where there's no Asian people, no white people, no Jews, no Italians, and I was quite uncomfortable with that. Then I went to the Labor Day Carnival, which had all these floats playing different music. I had an epiphanal [*sic*] moment, thinking we should have a carnival like this at home. But I knew that the Notting Hill Carnival wouldn't initially be the right place to mix everything up, especially not with the gay, fag disco I liked. But I thought it could work in a club. I loved the fact that all these heavy black clubs were playing white music – Gary Numan, 'Another One Bites the Dust', stuff like that. In London, you weren't allowed to stray from the music narrative, as all the clubs were controlled by white gatekeepers. They ran everything. We never got a sniff. For whatever reason, whether it was race, whether it was the fear we might threaten them, you couldn't stray from the music narrative. So I reached out to a whole new audience, started being more experimental at Carnival, and that's been the basis of my career. I didn't want to play just to the traditional crowd, I wanted to be able to invite my gay friends along. I have never been intimidated to take musical risks when I really believe in it. So I started with the sound systems and then ended up on Kiss FM when it launched in the UK. The thing is, the black music press ignored me, and I had to wait to be picked up by *i-D, The Face* and the *NME*. London really had the best crowds: the aspirational, the creative, the subculture junkies, the marginal. I like the freaks who come out at night; I didn't want to swim in the mainstream. I liked to be the straight guy in the gay club. I liked to be the only black guy in a white club. I wasn't intimidated by any of that. I would just go there and accept things for what they were and embrace it and love it for what it was.

Hector Heathcote (*DJ*): Before moving to London in 1979, I had been a northern soul DJ in Derby – although we didn't call it that, we called it 'rare soul' – but London was a different scene altogether as there were so many clubs to play. I knew Chris Sullivan as I'd played the Blue Rondo royal wedding warehouse party in '81, and that's one of the reasons he asked me to play at the Wag. Basically, it was my dream job, because the crowds were very demanding, which made me more competitive. This was such an extraordinary period for creativity, and there were so many talented people who used to congregate at the Wag, although I would like to think it contributed in some small way to getting rid of the racist door policies that were prevalent in the West End at the time, the 'Sorry, we are full up tonight' kind of attitude. The Wag was a conscious statement against that. The only people we turned away were the ones who said, 'Don't you know who I am?' Classic. There's a guy here who doesn't know who he is!

Chris Sullivan: At the time, all the West End clubs were playing terrible pop music, so I wanted somewhere with a great mix of music, whether it be jazz or funk or disco or reggae – a different vibe every night. We were also playing a lot of electro, which is where electronic funk was moving.

By 1982, the synth had become so pervasive that it became the subject of a dispute initiated by the central London branch of the Musicians' Union. When Barry Manilow toured the UK in January, he used synths to simulate the orchestral sounds of a big band, after which the union passed a motion to ban the use of synths, drum machines and any electronic devices 'capable of recreating the sounds of conventional musical instruments'. They were particularly concerned about the possible effect on West End theatrical productions, imagining orchestra pits full of 'technicians' instead of musicians. Roy Eldridge, who was then the A&R director of Chrysalis, said, 'The proposal is totally unrealistic. It would mean ruling out half the records in the charts.' The MU eventually saw sense, and even though the decision was discussed by the executive committee later in the year, it was then quietly forgotten. It was later pointed out that the original call for a ban was logged on 23 May, the birthday of Robert Moog.

Alix Sharkey: Sullivan's idea of a club that changed atmosphere, music and clientele every night was a fresh and radical departure, and soon there were queues down Wardour Street, a hip young crowd of art students, musicians, designers and shop assistants. On the dancefloor, regulars included Boy George, John Galliano, Jean Paul Gaultier, Neneh Cherry, Michael Clark and Leigh Bowery, as well as any number of 'fabulous nobodies'.

Sullivan was convinced that dance music would start to be the lingua franca of pop, and every night in his club you would hear the latest US imports. The three records that cartographically defined the start of the new decade were all American: 'The Adventures of Grandmaster Flash on the Wheels of Steel' by Grandmaster Flash (Sugarhill, 1981), 'The

Message' by Grandmaster Flash and the Furious Five (Sugarhill, 1982) and 'Last Night a DJ Saved My Life' by Indeep (Sound of New York, 1982). The first personified the scratching, sampling and stop–start techniques that would affect every record in some way for the next twenty-five years; the second was a forerunner of gangsta rap and the whole culture of complaint; and the third was a coronation of the DJ as the axe hero of the eighties. The best club music of the decade's early years tended to be gay disco: Coffee's 'Casanova', Lime's 'You Love', 'I Can't Take My Eyes off You' by the Boys Town Gang, and any hi-energy record you cared to mention. How could it not be? Dance music during this time was all about transgression and euphoria.

Kraftwerk would obviously have a hand in the creation of hip hop, via Afrika Bambaataa and the Soulsonic Force's 1982 'Planet Rock'. The record built on the work of the Yellow Magic Orchestra and George Clinton, as well as that of Kraftwerk, combined with the soon-to-be-distinctive beats produced by the Roland TR-808. Along with Kool Herc and Grandmaster Flash, Afrika Bambaataa Aasim – named after a nineteenth-century Zulu chief, obviously – was one of the most influential New York DJs in the mid-seventies. Brought up in the Bronx, he eventually became a gang leader, but he started a community-spirited social network which gave him access to the crowds he would soon seduce with his entrepreneurial skills. He was also one of the first to swap his record decks for the recording studio, helping to create electro by mixing Kraftwerk-inspired beats with breakbeats, rap and funk. 'Planet Rock' came out in April 1982, and was one of the most influential records of the year. I met him once, when he came to London to play the Camden Palace, and he was a great bear of a man, looking like George Clinton might have done if he'd swallowed a large fridge. Softly spoken, direct and quite mad-looking in his octagonal sunglasses, big old hoodie and 'tennises' the size of small boats, all Bambaataa really needed to assume the disposition, if not the mantle, of an African potentate was a throne. He had a sub-Mohican haircut and the word 'FUNK' razored into the fade.

Afrika Bambaataa (*hip hop artist*): Hip hop has been hijacked by a Luciferian conspiracy. People have used hip hop in a lot of ways that cause a lot of mind problems. They use the word wrongfully. They use it to mean a part instead of a whole. My definition of hip hop is taking elements from many other spheres of music to make hip hop. Whether it be breakbeat, whether it be the groove and grunt of James Brown or the pickle-pop sounds of Kraftwerk or Yellow Magic Orchestra, hip hop is also part of what they call hip house now, or trip hop, or even parts of drum'n'bass.

Not everyone liked the Wag Club, as many felt it was simply yet another excuse to be elitist at a time that called for a more egalitarian, democratic spirit. One critic was the NME *writer Charles Shaar Murray. 'I always associated the Wag Club with that very Thatcherite London club culture and despised it. I remember going there with a friend once, and after about an hour, we turned to each other and said, "We're standing here drinking over-priced beer, surrounded by fools, listening to records we've got at home." I'm always sorry to see a venue close down, but the Wag Club was so associated with everything I hated about the eighties, so I have to say in this case I'd make an exception.'*

Others liked it because of what it wasn't. 'I was a punk, so I hated the whole New Romantic scene, and the Wag became a bit of a home for me,' says Jah Wobble, who had been one of the original members of Public Image Limited. 'I used to do a residency there. It was a very busy club with a charged-up sort of atmosphere. The door policy was pretty good because there were still lots of pretty girls down there. The eighties were a horrible time, but of that period it was the only club that still seemed to have a slightly bohemian edge.'

Alix Sharkey: The regular Friday-night slot, Black Market, spawned the rare-groove scene and did so much to fuel the growth of hip hop and rap in the UK. It also disproved the 'elitism' tag. 'All the other

West End clubs at that time turned young black kids away,' said Sullivan. 'The Wag was the only place that wanted them.'

Robert Elms: It was never some super-slick place. I even DJ'd there a couple of times. I was one of the world's worst DJs.

Andrew Hale: By 1982, I had moved from London to Brighton to go to Sussex University. I'd missed out on the Blitz scene because I was a couple of years younger than everyone else, so my first clubs were Le Beat Route and, of course, the Wag. I remember coming up from Brighton for the opening night. By that time, I'd already met Bob Elms, who was going out with Sade. Lee Barrett was managing the band Pride at that time, which had Sade as a backing singer. I had been to see them play in Barnet, which was where I met Sade, Stuart [Matthewman] and Paul [Spencer Denman] for the first time. They had started doing a set with Sade as lead singer, almost as a side project, and after a while Lee and my mate Alex told me they were looking for a keyboard player. It was crazy, because I was still in my second year of college. We were all so incredibly young. We didn't know anything. And it was a big decision for me because I left university to join a band. It sounds silly to say that now, but at the time I didn't know where it might lead.

All the new pop stars in London appeared to know each other. The early eighties were the years when you'd bump into George Michael in the Wag Club dancing to one of his own records, or stand behind David Bowie in the queue for the gents' at the Mud Club, or see one of Spandau Ballet chatting up Bananarama. There was one particular party in Harrods, bizarrely enough, when the department store decided it wanted a bit of designer jus *itself. The group of luminaries included Labour leader Neil Kinnock – slumming it for a bit of tabloid and style-magazine exposure – Duran Duran's Simon Le Bon, PR guru Lynne Franks, Boy George, fashion designers Jean*

Paul Gaultier and Katharine Hamnett, the American artist Julian Schnabel and one of London's most notorious transsexual prostitutes. Oh lordy, it was as if social boundaries had yet to be invented, as though social mobility was the birthright of anyone in a loud jacket with shoulder pads and wearing a pair of bulbous patent leather shoes.

Pop stars were everywhere, propping up the bars and piling into toilet cubicles. Walk into Club for Heroes, Heaven or the Wag Club, and you'd see someone from Heaven 17 or Duran Duran, or Madonna, Shane MacGowan, Depeche Mode, August Darnell (from Kid Creole and the Coconuts), the Pet Shop Boys, Boy George, Spear of Destiny's Kirk Brandon, Pete Townshend, George Michael and Andrew Ridgeley. If you went to Rio, Monte Carlo, New York, LA, Tokyo or Toronto, the chances were you'd bump into them there too, propping up the bar and nodding as you walked in, as though they were still drinking cocktails in Soho.

Keren Woodward: I loved making the music and doing the shows, but I was always very uncomfortable with all the attention. I never really enjoyed going to premieres and stuff like that, and I've always preferred clubbing with my friends. When Bananarama started travelling, wherever we'd been, if we got back in time, we would race to the Wag on certain nights when Fat Tony was on the decks.

Kathryn Flett (*writer*): I remember once drunkenly wandering over to George Michael at the Wag Club and saying in a rather sentimentally drunk way, 'Thank you for writing "Everything She Wants",' and he looked utterly horrified at this weaving woman. I think it was the last time I was there. Aside from the Camden Palace, there wasn't a designated place of cool. There weren't members' clubs then, but the Wag was a sort of unofficial members' club, with a horribly strict door policy, so when you went there you made a bit of an effort.

Chris Sullivan: When we launched the Wag, David Bowie started popping in a lot, often with Julien Temple. He seemed to like Soho, loved seeing what was going on, soaking up the atmosphere. He used to say that he loved the Wag, as it reminded him of what it was like in the sixties, when he was a mod. He loved the music, the interior. He said, 'There's so much style in this room.' Imagine: you're in your mid-to-late thirties, out of the loop, and you come back to London and there's this little scene going on, a scene where a lot of people thought he was a god. I was there the night he came down to the Blitz, and it was embarrassing. Even though I'd met him before, I stayed away from him that night as people were fawning all over him. He was a god to all of those people. But you wouldn't have known he was at the Wag as he didn't really want to show off. You wouldn't have noticed him at all. He was very casual and just a really nice bloke. He'd talk about art, music, Miles Davis, sit down and have a pint of bitter. Loved bitter. He wasn't just interesting, he was interested, and always wanted to know what you had been up to, what was going on. If someone is interested in you, then you sort of forget who they are, don't you? But the eyes never let you forget that you were talking to David Bowie. He knew people in Soho too. We went to dinner at L'Escargot one night, and *everyone* knew him. He asked me to get involved in a couple of projects, which obviously I did; I mean, you're not going to say no to David Bowie, are you? Even if he is asking you over a drink in the bar at the Wag. For one video, I helped him get Sade and Slim Gaillard, Eve Ferret and lots of Soho faces. I'd bring people straight from the Wag, and they'd be out of their minds on the set; people would be selling lines of coke for a fiver, going to the bar at lunchtime, having sex on pinball machines. I'd spend a lot of time on set and would often babysit Duncan [Jones, Bowie's son]. He'd never heard a Welsh accent before, and I think he loved being there. He later told me it was those daily trips to the set that made him want to become a film director. His dad would take him around, show him what was going on, introduce him to the cameramen. A proper dad. No wonder Duncan turned out to be so level-headed. Bowie was doing some filming at the Wag one day, and because he was using my office as a dressing room, he insisted on making me cups of tea. I said, 'You don't have to do that,' but he insisted. He'd never pass you in the street, always said hello. I'd bump into him in St Martin's, Vogue House, anywhere, and he'd always say hello. He had a great ability to make people feel special. He was the most amazing man because you'd be chatting to him, and then he'd be called up for a take, and suddenly he'd turn into David Bowie. He'd just turn it on. Amazing. Boom. 'Now I'll be David Bowie.' He'd come back and say, 'How was that?'

Eve Ferret: I met Bowie when I was in the 'Jazzin' for Blue Jean' film. I was one of the few people who wasn't a huge fan, maybe because when I looked at him, I thought, 'How can you go to bed with such a person? He's so thin.' He said, 'Ferret, why did you choose that name?' I said, 'It's my name. My mum and dad are Ferrets,' and he really liked that. Then, for some reason – and I hadn't realised his Anthony Newley connection – we started singing a song that my nan used to sing called 'Call Around Any Old Time', and he knew all the words and sang it in a very cockney way. He knew it off by heart.

In terms of ambition, these London clubs were nothing when compared with the Haçienda, which in 1982 was transformed by Tony Wilson, New Order, Peter Saville and the interior designer Ben Kelly from a cavernous warehouse in the centre of Manchester into one of the most extraordinary nightclubs ever conceived. The name came from Wilson's obsession with Situationism, an interest initially fuelled by his relationship with Malcolm McLaren: 'The Haçienda Must Be Built' was a slogan for the radical alliance Situationist International, from Formulary for a New Urbanism *by Ivan Chtcheglov. Grand in scale, grand in ambition, when it opened in May 1982, the Haçienda looked like an enormous installation, an exhibition or a gallery waiting for its public. When you walked in, what impressed you wasn't just the fact that it was beautiful, or that it was clever, or that it contained visual jokes; it was the fact that the building so obviously respected the people who were meant to use it: us, the punters. I visited the Haçienda three times in its first couple of weeks, and it felt more modern and more forward-thinking than anything I had seen in London up to that point.*

Ben Kelly: I had designed the Howie shop on Long Acre for Paul Howie and Lynne Franks, and it was through them I first met Peter Saville. In the Zanzibar, I think. Out of that came a collaboration to do an album cover for Orchestral Manoeuvres in the Dark. His idea was to make a cover with the least amount of cardboard possible, so I told him it should be perforated, and said he should go and look at the door of the Howie shop. Then I started working on a freelance basis for Factory, working for like-minded people and wackos. The ripples that came out of Factory were extraordinary. The big thing was having independence, and the independent record labels at the time symbolised that attitude – 'Fuck it, we're just going to do it.' I suppose to a degree it was giving two fingers to the Establishment. To me, my design had an attitude, and I ploughed a certain furrow that had nothing to do with the corporate world. Creatively, you always wanted to bring about some kind of change, to make sure that people's peripheral vision was catered for.

Working with people like Tony Wilson gave you confidence, although the weird thing about him was that he had two jobs: his day job and his 'other' job. He'd walk around Manchester, and people would shout, 'You fucking twat!' and he loved it. He played on that. He was a very bright man and had one foot in the anarchy world and one foot in the television world. He had an education but he smoked dope. At the time, he was one of the few people who understood about employing designers, and he gave you free rein. As he used to say, profit was not their remit.

As for the Haçienda, New Order had been to New York, to Paradise Garage, and they came back and said, 'We fucking want one.' So we built them one. Rob Gretton, their manager, meanwhile, just wanted somewhere he could 'ogle the birds'.

On a very simple level, one of the most important things about the Haçienda was scale. It was a big space. Before that, clubs in the UK had either been shitty, dirty basements or they were designed by Peter Stringfellow, with flock wallpaper and chandeliers. And because Factory had already set a precedent with their design work and their sensibility, Peter Saville had been given free rein. It was almost expected. They wanted Peter to design it, but he went there and said, 'I can't design this, but I know a man who can.' So I met Tony Wilson and Rob Gretton, and they gave me a tour of this huge space in a pretty poor state, and at the end they said, 'Do you want the job?' They thought all I was going to do was give it a lick of paint and tart it up, but I could see that you needed to start from the beginning. I said, 'Of course I want the fucking job.' It was the biggest thing I'd ever undertaken, and I think the key to it was that not only had I never designed a nightclub before, but they'd never commissioned a nightclub before. We were all naive and inexperienced, so there were no preconceptions. We knew it had to have a bar, toilets, a stage, and I was adamant that the stage couldn't be at the end, or else it would just turn into a venue. We had arguments about the stage, the sound system, the eyeline from the balcony, the lighting system . . . we had arguments about everything. So, in the end, the Haçienda became a hybrid: is it a bird, is it a plane, is it a club, is it a disco . . . what is it? Because it was none of those things but all of those things; that was one of its secrets. We had a hairdresser's, an inflatable swimming pool, fashion shows, exhibitions, theatrical productions . . . we had everything.

Some people said it looked better in the daytime, as there was a fair amount of colour in there, which in the evening you didn't see so much. I was interested in geometry, and I wanted a journey and a narrative when you walked in. I wanted you to have to walk through these weird monolithic slabs – which was my reference to *2001: A Space Odyssey* – before coming into this cathedral-like space. Then you were steered around the dancefloor by roadside bollards and cat's eyes. The only identification outside was a small hand-carved granite plaque saying 'Fac 51 Haçienda' in silver leaf. People started travelling there from all over the world, and when they arrived, they weren't sure if they'd found it. So there was a mystery, making people think. I thought calling it the Haçienda was the worst thing in the world, until I found out it came from the Situationist manifesto, leaving the twentieth century. And Tony was obsessed with the Cambridge spies because he went there to study, calling the cocktail bar the Gay Traitor, after Anthony Blunt. Then we had the Kim Philby Bar. There were games being played everywhere. I wanted it to look industrial, which is why we had ribbed rubber on the floor, which you would only ever see in an industrial space. I painted stripes on the columns because the columns supporting the building had been moved to the middle of the dancefloor, and I thought they were hazards. So I used the language of the factory, the workplace, to colour-code things. To me, it felt like building a big piece of sculpture that happened to be a nightclub.

Of course, when it opened, they knew nothing about management, so they were basically throwing money down a hole in the ground.

Bernard Sumner (*musician*): If the Haçienda hadn't existed, we wouldn't have been under so much pressure. There's good things about it and bad things about it. I'm not complaining. I live in a nice house, I've got a nice car and I'm not bitter about it. It was ego that wouldn't let go of it. It was gambling on a horse that couldn't win. To save face, you kept putting money into it. The Haçienda changed the country. It was Rob Gretton's baby. And the reason he went into it was not to change the country, but to change Manchester, because his thinking was, 'This is where we live, let's make it a better place,' but it ended up changing the country.

Ben Kelly: One of the other important things was the fact that the Haçienda was in Manchester and not London. Tony Wilson had an obsession with Manchester, and it's acknowledged by Manchester

City Council that it was the Haçienda that kicked off the city's regeneration. There was a bit of 'Poncey gits down there. We can do it better.' There was Mancunian pride and industry and independence. I think we felt more allegiance to New York. London did their version with the Ministry of Sound, and then you had Cream in Liverpool, but there was nothing to touch the Haçienda. It was a very special part of a crazy decade.

Steve Strange: For me, there was no one moment that summed up the eighties. The whole decade was extraordinary. I was courted by the world's biggest fashion designers – Thierry Mugler, Karl Lagerfeld, Montana. They flew me in, gave me prime position in the front row of all their fashion shows and treated me like royalty. Eventually, I realised they were milking all our looks and watering them down for the Paris catwalks – and the more outrageous we were, the more they liked it.

Midge Ure: Visage was fine until we'd finished the second album, *The Anvil*. I was doing two projects at once by this time, because by the time the second album came around, I was running Ultravox, and it got really silly after a while. What happens with success is that it breeds hangers-on, and Steve was surrounded by hangers-on, surrounded by people living in his ear – 'Oh, you don't need these guys. We can produce this record. We can make a movie with you and we can do this . . .' That's heady stuff and very difficult to control. So I was in my management office when Steve was in New York to launch the second album, and I heard this one-sided conversation about a camel being stuck in a tunnel in New York, and I'm saying, 'What camel?' This was one of Steve's ideas, which he hadn't run past anyone. He was going to arrive in this nightclub in Manhattan on the back of a camel, in front of all the media, and they'd all think, 'Wow, this is amazing,' and bow down and kiss his feet, and then we were going to crack America. And I said, 'If he gets on that camel, I walk. I can't do this any more. This is a Punch and Judy show. It's just nonsense.' So he got on the camel, and I left.

And the reality was it rained, Steve's make-up ran and the camel shat all over the floor outside the club.

Rusty Egan: Visage ended because of management. Bottom line, Midge's managers took over the contract, and then it was all about Midge. We stayed friends throughout everything, but it was difficult.

Ollie O'Donnell: I spent a lot of time with Steve [Strange] after Visage started, and there was an unbelievable amount of money being thrown around. We were in Paris for a Helmut Newton shoot, and there was this mad expenditure of money. Steve was actually very eccentric, and he could be quite straight and provincial. We were staying at the George V, just around the corner from the Champs-Élysées, but he had no interest, as long as there were bottles of champagne coming into the suite and everything was fabulous and glamorous. The fact that we were in Paris, it didn't even register. We got drunker and drunker and kind of ignored Helmut Newton. He was like Benny Hill, this big chubby German guy just talking about how big the models' tits were. Steve was so famous then. In Paris, people stood up and applauded when he walked into a room. He wasn't equipped to deal with it, though; he was just a kid from South Wales.

Steve Strange: *The Anvil* got mixed reviews, as they tried to say that by using Helmut Newton and his stark black-and-white photography, I was actually trying to promote the Hitler Youth. His photography style was very monochrome – he had certain criteria to his photography. I only chose Helmut Newton because he was the most hip and happening photographer at the time. What really blew it with Midge was when we were in New York. We were going to be at this event, and there was going to be Andy Warhol, the Talking Heads, the B52's, Blondie, and I thought, 'Right, I've got to make an impact at this super-cool party.' So I decided I wanted to come in on an elephant. I said to the record company, 'I want an elephant!' 'What?!' they said. 'I've got to blow all these people away! I want an elephant!' 'Where the hell are we going to get an elephant?' they asked. 'Well, there must be zoos in New York,' I said. Later, I get a call: 'We can't get an elephant, but we've got a camel.' Anyway, it did the trick – it was on every TV station and newspaper. But Midge blew his top. He said, 'I'm getting on Concorde if you come in on a bloody elephant!' I said, 'Oh, get on fucking Concorde then. They can't get an elephant anyway, I'm on a camel,' and I put the phone down.

Rusty Egan: This was the year we opened the Camden Palace, but right from the start I didn't feel good about it. After a while, the company who owned it were going to take it public, but they said that Steve was too volatile and took too many drugs, so 'We want to do a deal with you, Rusty.' And they took me to the Churchill Hotel and said, 'Forget your partner, forget Steve. You're the guy that books the bands, you're the DJ, you promote it all . . .' And I said, 'You mean, put Steve on wages?' They said, 'Rusty, if we go on the stock market, overnight you'll be worth millions.' And I go, 'So you're saying dump my partner?' And they were going, 'Well, you keep rewording it like that, but you're missing the point. Steve gets drunk every night at parties with all his friends, and you're in the office in the daytime booking the bands and the DJ's playing all the music. We don't need Steve getting drunk every night.' I said, 'Well, you did when you were empty, and I'm not going to dump Steve.' So they had him arrested in the club and dumped us all. So overnight I lost millions.

Steve Strange: With the success of the Visage record sales, it was all done. Well, a lot of it was done purely on cocaine. Which was supplied by people connected to the record company, who basically see you as a commodity. The more countries you're in in one day, doing this, that and the other and all the press conferences, obviously means the more records you're going to sell.

Stephen Jones: It was the Camden Palace that signalled the end of the Blitz scene. The night of the opening – I think it was around May 1982 – the following morning I was going to New York, so that was the end of one thing and the beginning of the next. I met somebody, and we were really making out in the stairway, and I thought, 'I need to go and finish packing now,' and that was a very conscious decision. The eighties had arrived, and it was all about work.

Nick Logan: For me, the thing began to finish when the Camden Palace opened, as it just seemed anathema to what had gone before.

Ultravox were another band who were disregarded by the traditional music press, not least because of their fondness for eyeliner, duster coats and wantonly enigmatic pop videos. The band had passed through a Bowie 'beam' (in the words of the NME*'s Paul Morley), but then every band at the time had done exactly the same thing. They came along at a point when meaning was everything in pop, and to only pretend to have meaning, or to disregard it completely, was deemed unacceptable. It didn't help either that a lot of the records were often rather mediocre, many of them simply capitalising on ambience. 'Ultravox always attempted to blend their influences into something as provocative as early Roxy, as challenging as early Floyd,' said Morley. 'They never had the art or the heart and, despite themselves, never looked the part. They tried to be so much more than just a pop group. Ure was never quite there, Ultravox was never quite there, together they make inessential but stylish synergic pop.' He described them as 'something sweet to play after you've sweated through Cabaret Voltaire and want to flick through some magazines. For everyone else, the thing is not to take them seriously, and then for the first time you might see a point in Ultravox's existence. This is pop, with style, within reason, without too much pretension.'*

Midge Ure: I think the period does hold up. I think you can date anything, especially electronics. You can hear a drum sound and say,

'Oh, that's a CR-78,' or, 'That's a LinnDrum,' or whatever, and it does become very dated. It grows old and becomes a product of its time. But there's something quite magical about what we did, because it wasn't all just electronics. It was a combination. What they saw on television were these kind of stoic, po-faced, thin young men looking very dark and moody behind a bank of synthesizers, and that's what they heard. Even though the sound may be dated, we didn't just press a button on a machine that everyone else could press. We created those sounds. There was a whole different ball game. We made those sounds from scratch. There were lots of bands doing similar things – Japan, Depeche Mode, New Order – but I think what we did was special.

David Sylvian's Japan moved through our lives without leaving much of a trace: a ghost ship, the Flying Dutchman *of modern British pop. Too late for glam rock, reviled by many during punk, nevertheless there were quite a few New Romantics who were fans of the band. Unfortunately, Japan didn't appear to reciprocate. 'I don't like to be associated with them,' said Sylvian. 'Their attitudes are so very different. For them, fancy dress is a costume, but ours is a way of life. We look and dress this way every day.' So yah boo sucks.*

Simon Napier-Bell: Nineteen eighty-two was a big year for Japan. I met them in 1976, and signed them up at once, as I thought, 'Nothing can be more fantastic and amazing than their look.' But then I'd never seen the New York Dolls, and I didn't know they looked exactly like them. It took me six years to make them successful, but I knew they had something. Like all great artists, David Sylvian didn't need much steering, and didn't want much steering. It was like trying to control a car. If you told David something was a good idea, he'd immediately do the opposite. So in the end I started suggesting bad ideas, and he'd do the opposite, which is exactly what I wanted. David's voice was originally a cross between Marc Bolan and Rod Stewart, and if you go back and listen to their first album, it's actually very good. There's a great version of the Barbra Streisand song 'Don't Rain on My Parade'. Then they turned up one day, David Sylvian and Mick Karn, and they'd both changed their hair. David previously had long blond hair down below his waist, and Mick had matching long red hair. And they turned up one day with the hair that Duran Duran took, a sort of dual-tone strawberry blond. My secretary at the time looked at the pictures of them and said, 'You should say he's the most beautiful man in the world' – meaning David. So I immediately made her their press officer. She called all the newspapers in Australia and said that David Sylvian had been voted the most beautiful man in the world, and one of them fell for it and printed the picture, saying David Sylvian was the most beautiful man in the world. Then she took the cutting and went to all the English papers, and suddenly David was in every newspaper as the most beautiful man in the world. And that was really the beginning of getting some sort of grip on publicity for Japan. They kind of benefited from the whole New Romantic thing, even though they had nothing to do with it. More importantly, we broke them in Japan, as I thought it would be funny to have an English group called Japan actually have some success there. I spent three months learning Japanese in order to do so.

I went off to Japan and took the album, went to see the record companies and showed them all the pictures I had taken of the group, and they said, 'We'll use them.' Until they heard the album, which they said was absolutely useless. So we thought of another way of selling them. We settled down and made a plan whereby we would form a fan club, and at the end of six months we'd made them the number-one foreign act in Japan. They had a fan club of 50,000 members and were the most popular group in Japan, but no one had ever heard a note of their music. On the first morning of release, the album sold 50,000 copies, and by the evening, of course, there were 50,000 tiny disappointed Japanese girls. But they'd spent their pocket money on the album, so they obviously played it until they liked it. Shortly after that, we went and played the biggest gig Japan had ever played, to 14,000 screaming Japanese teenagers, and previously their biggest gig had been playing to forty-two people in the Red Lion in Hammersmith. The money they earned in two weeks in Japan was enough to keep them for a whole year – not extravagantly, but they could live. I invested £300,000 to £400,000 in breaking Japan, which in those days was an incredible amount of money. So we made another album, they changed their hairstyle, and David Sylvian got a new voice If you listen to the second album, it's a completely different voice, as he forgot Rod Stewart and Marc Bolan and sort of Bryan Ferry-ed himself. Eventually, they became the most influential group, as Duran Duran stole their hairstyles, and Gary Numan stole David's voice.

Danny Eccleston (*journalist*): Nineteen eighty-two was a baffling year for Japan to call it quits. The dandified Catford four-piece had just released *Tin Drum*, their first album to breach the UK Top 30, and their most lucrative tour beckoned. More crucially for a band derided in the music press as Dolls/Bowie/Roxy wannabes, they had grown into their own, markedly minimalist sound. Credibility *and* popularity seemed in their grasp. Perhaps the damage had already been done. David Sylvian (né Batt) looked like he'd been designed to be a pop star, but found the attention jarred with a personality that could be described, most politely, as standoffish. He was now deeply involved with bassist Mick Karn's ex-girlfriend Yuka Fujii – a classic source of friction. Meanwhile, the success of *Tin Drum* and its spooked single, 'Ghosts', prompted reissues of LPs and singles from Japan's 1978–9 apprenticeship on Hansa Records (home to Boney M.) – glam rock and disco juvenilia from which the sensitive Sylvian recoiled. In spite of the group's growing progressive pop dimensions, their fan base leaned to teenybop. It was as if Japan embarrassed him.

Simon Napier-Bell: For twenty years, Hammersmith Odeon had been London's principal medium-sized music venue. When Japan were doing their final UK gig there, I'd arranged for David Bowie to see the show and come backstage afterwards, something Japan wanted very much. But when Bowie turned up in the back of a stretch limo and lowered the window, he was confronted by a snarling security guard.

'Who d'you think *you* are?'

'I'm David Bowie,' said David Bowie.

'Well, I'm President Reagan,' the guard sneered scornfully. 'So you can piss off.'

And he did. Which left Japan quite upset.

Soon there would be a swathe of second-generation synth duos, including Blancmange, the Pet Shop Boys and Tears for Fears, who featured songwriter Roland Orzabal and singer Curt Smith. Their first hit was their third single, 'Mad World', released in November. 'I wrote it when I was nineteen, on the dole in Bath,' says Orzabal. 'We're known as a synthesizer group, but back then I just had an acoustic guitar. I was listening to Radio 1 on this tinny radio, and Duran Duran's "Girls on Film" came on. I thought, "I'm going to have a crack at something like that." I did, and ended up with "Mad World".' They recorded it using a borrowed synth, changed their haircuts – Orzabal going asymmetrical, and Smith getting plaits – and started wearing black eyeliner à la Gary Numan.

If the average cultural experience encourages the suspension of disbelief, then what are we to make of synth-duo relationships? There was always something oddly fetishistic about the synth duo, triggered, perhaps not unreasonably, by a suspicion that said duo's relationship might not be completely platonic. Boy/girl, boy/boy, it didn't matter, as any tension – real, implied or imagined – simply suggested a love gone wrong/hidden/lying in wait. In the early eighties, synth duos were as ubiquitous as rah-rah skirts: the Eurythmics, Pet Shop Boys, Blancmange, Yazoo, Tears for Fears, the Associates, Buggles, Soft Cell, Erasure and Orchestral Manoeuvres in the Dark – and all of them British to the core. Neil Tennant called them 'fire-and-ice duos', with one emoting while the other one glowered. In his book Love Is a Mix Tape, *Rob Sheffield recalls how he was once fuelled by synth-pop fantasies, and how, every time he had a crush on a woman, he would imagine the two of them as a synth-pop duo: 'The girl is up front, swishing her skirt, tossing her hair, a saucy little firecracker. I'm the boy in the back, hidden behind my Roland JP8000 keyboard. She has all the courage and star power I lack . . . She moves the crowd while I lurk in the shadows, lavishing all my computer-blue love on her, punching the buttons that shower her in disco bliss and bathe her in the spotlight. I make her a star.' He came up with names for these mythical dalliances too: Multiplex; Metroform, Angel Dust, Unpleasant Pleasures, Schiaffiano, Criminally Vulva, Indulgence, Appliancenter, etc. It was all about the boy and the girl, says Sheffield, together in electric dreams.*

'We each had different bands at college,' says Neil Arthur, who was one half of Blancmange. 'I was in a band called the Viewfinders, and Steven was in M.I.R.U. The only similarity between the two bands was that we both used to try and cover the stage with tons of machines just to look good. We had washing machines, lawn mowers, the lot. Just to fill the stage.'

Paul Humphreys: *Architecture & Morality* had sold about five million, but then two things happened. Journalists criticised us for not being overtly political; when they talked to us, we were quite political and had strong views, but it never appeared in our music. The other thing was some idiot at the record label said to us, 'All you have to do is do *Architecture & Morality* number two, and you'll be the next Genesis.' So we thought, 'Right, we're not going to do that, so let's do something different.' So we did an album about the Cold War, without our usual sugar coating, and people went, 'What the fuck?', and we lost 90 per cent of our audience. Looking back, it was a very brave record, and it's still one of my favourites, but it bombed. It was a bit of a shit-fight at the time because new bands were coming out all the time, the quality of the songwriting was really fantastic and everyone was trying to be different yet compete in the same kind of world. We would constantly hear records on the radio and think, 'I wish we'd done that.'

It was a time when fashion and music were very linear and one thing replaced the next, and the music they listened to, the clothes they wore, the haircut they had defined them as a person.

Alison Moyet: I didn't like being famous, as people stared at you. Staring, in my experience, led to a fracas. Fame turned me into a freak who couldn't fight back. I felt disarmed. I couldn't hang with my mates because it drew too much attention, and I didn't want to be in those places famous people populate. I stopped going out for a very long time. I met a couple of people who were nice, but I didn't follow it up. I was socially inept and awkward, so I kept to myself.

At *Top of the Pops*, more often the fresh up-and-comers were full of it, the old guard much more chilled and grounded. I remember Paul and Linda McCartney always went out of their way. I got a feeling most of the other bands connected in some way. Who knows? I didn't. I don't remember faces. I don't know a single musician who would call me, or I them, who is not in my band . . . even then. Journalists at the time were a little divisive, and actually it was often me who came out better in the early days. Detractors dismissed Vince as somewhat twee and were kinder about me. Obviously, that was revised, as it always is. Sometimes we were the thousandth Second Coming, and for some an ungainly glitch in the mainframe. On the whole, I'd say we were lucky. We made an impression. The mainstream press didn't know what to make of me. There weren't loads of feminists writing for the red tops, and they were befuddled by my lack of comeliness or seeming desperation to fix it. One massive red top called my mother and told her they were doing a piece outing me as a transsexual. Desperate for me, she offered to show them my passport. That was the worst. I could easily take the sneer, as that was nothing new. It's when they land on the people you love, who feel they need to defend you, that it leaves its mark.

Gary Numan: *I, Assassin* was the second-worst album I ever had. So it went pretty bad, pretty quick. I recovered from that one a little bit, but there was this general decline for the next ten years. And each album did worse than the one before. The tours were getting harder to sell, and I went from selling out great big places to not selling out quite small places. So it was increasingly demoralising and desperate as the years went by.

Alison Moyet: It was reported at the time that I left to be a solo singer. That's what all women want, eh? Limelight? The girl? Never truly a fit in a band. Either ego or decor – that's us. I never wanted to go solo. I always was, and always wanted to be, in a band, and Yazoo was less like a band than any I had been in. Vince left Depeche because he wanted to be autonomous. He didn't intend to start another band yet. He had a point to prove. Vindication. We were not a fit. I was a scrapper, and he was uncomfortable around combustion. We didn't have the time to understand one another or the love to give us the reason to want to. He'd had a hit with Depeche. He had a hit with me. He had no reason to think he needed anyone to have a hit, until later he found that he did. You need a fallow period to know the wood from the trees. It found him quickly in a better place, but I was nowhere I wanted to be. All our contacts were his. Not his fault. I knew no one well enough and didn't push to. I was always a confident stage presence. I was fearless until I became famous. Fame is a thousand lying lights. It can make you look good, and it can make you see nothing. It also makes you a bit of a cunt for a while.

Heaven 17 were too reluctant to be proper pop stars, yet they nonetheless confidently churned out consistently high-grade, if brittle, funk. In 1982, they produced an album under their British Electric Foundation banner that consisted of cover versions featuring Tina Turner, Paula Yates, Billy MacKenzie, Hank Marvin, Paul Jones, Bernie Nolan and Gary Glitter. Music of Quality & Distinction *helped resuscitate Turner's career, and Martyn Ware, Ian Craig Marsh and Glenn Gregory were hired to produce her next single, a cover of Al Green's 'Let's Stay Together'. When she went into Abbey*

Road Studios to record her first song with BEF, a cover of the Temptations' 'Ball of Confusion', Turner walked into the studio expecting to see musicians, but there wasn't a human or an instrument in sight. When she asked where the band was, it was explained that the new Wall of Sound was being built by something that looked like an enormous X-ray machine. All she had to do was sing along to a giant computer and smile while she did so.

David Stubbs: Dedicated to 'Music of Quality & Distinction', the British Electric Foundation's early releases were radical in the extreme. The thirteen-minute verse-less, chorus-less 'Optimum Chant' from *Music for Stowaways* could have been released by Cabaret Voltaire at the time. But their most notable achievement, commercially at least, was to relaunch the career of Tina Turner.

Glenn Gregory: We were asked to write a track for her, but we were working on *The Luxury Gap*, the follow-up to *Penthouse and Pavement*, so we said we didn't really have enough time, but we could do another cover. That's when we did 'Let's Stay Together' [eventually released on her 1984 smash *Private Dancer*]. I kind of wish we'd written her an original song now . . . She was in the doldrums at that point. She was playing tiny little places in Vegas. We went to LA to meet her, and I remember knocking on the door and Tina Turner answering, and it was like, 'Fucking hell, it's Tina Turner.' She cooked us dinner. She was genuinely such a lovely person and completely happy to work in a different way from the way she'd worked before.

The Human League, who were having more than their fair share of problems trying to best Dare! *– wanting to repeat it, trying not to repeat it – released a couple of one-off singles while they struggled with a sequel. One of these was '(Keep Feeling) Fascination', something of a generic synth-pop record, albeit with an accompanying video that showed the band actually playing together. Phil Oakey said* *the aim of the promo was to help them in America, where they were believed to be a purely manufactured proposition, like the Monkees.*

George Chesterton: The Human League's '(Keep Feeling) Fascination' walks in the room with a plodding bassline but then starts leaping all over the place with what appears to be a discordant, jarring synth riff. But listen again – rearranged with a horn section, it would sound like the opening bars of a Stax or Motown showstopper. Even the lyrics, consciously or otherwise, allude to this incongruity: that synth pop from the English regions and forgotten industrial towns (the bane of every music-loving parent who'd grown up in the sixties) had a meaningful relationship with its forbears. 'Just looking for a new direction in an old familiar way,' they sing. Susan Ann Sulley and Joanne Catherall's vocals were wondrous precisely because it was what the girls in your school sounded like when they sang along to it. Every time I saw Sulley's blonde flick on the head of a supermarket checkout girl or through a hairdresser's window, I thought of her and of what her group meant. Their fantasy of the high life was exactly the same as yours. Oakey was all drama, quietly spoken but a tall baritone fit for England's urban operas. When he sang, 'And so the conversation turned until the sun went down,' he was echoing the symposiums from a million teenage bedrooms: that time and place where young people make their first profound connections, where they learn together, where innocence slowly turns to experience. Just like any great pop music, '(Keep Feeling) Fascination' seemed new at the time to the people who mattered, namely, the people who didn't know any better. They are who pop is for. The something, in this case, is joy. The whole message of the song is just that: fascination, passion, love, moving on. It's only when we stop moving on that we start to see this kind of music as throwaway, silly or unsophisticated. And what a tragedy that is.

One of the salient reasons Paul Weller disbanded the Jam in 1982 was because of their success, and the fact that the crowds at the band's concerts often turned ugly and had started to resemble those at football matches. The cultural aggression felt at early punk concerts had swiftly morphed into a gang mentality that made the crowd at a Jam gig not that much different from the crowd at one by Sham 69. The political sentiments broadcast from the stage may have been poles apart, but the crowds were nearly as unruly. So, sensing a change in the zeitgeist, and enjoying the sort of cross-fertilisation between New Romantic pop and jazz-funk that he'd heard on records such as Spandau Ballet's 'Chant No. 1', Weller decided to ditch the Jam, buy a pair of white socks and reinvent himself as a sort of tongue-in-cheek new-wave soul boy. His next vehicle, the Style Council – a great band with a terrible name – was often mannered and gauche, yet they sounded like the eighties, all spic and span and shiny. Keen exponents of faux jazz (they were the Nescafé Society), they enjoyed getting up the noses of those fans and critics who would have preferred Weller to have kept on making Jam records in perpetuity. They emerged as the pop promo started to grow in reputation and influence, and Weller used the medium completely to his own advantage: in their ironic Summer Holiday*-style videos, he had the appearance of a fey sixties boulevardier, a creature of cheekbones and colour, frequently in motion and tantalisingly throwaway. The Style Council may have been born out of pastiche, but their identity was actually incredibly well defined.*

Unlike many of his generation, who hadn't got a clue how to further their careers after punk began to wane, Weller had talent, tenacity and a thirst for change. And the Style Council turned out to be extraordinarily successful, and for many are remembered with more fondness than the Jam.

Not that he was a patsy. Along with his partner in crime, Mick Talbot, Weller went out of his way to distance himself from the game of self-promotion. One way in which the Style Council combated their image as a 'quirky Eengleesh pop band' was to send the whole thing up. Irony was always big in their world, and what was often seen as gross pretentiousness was actually a giant wind-up. It was in this way that Weller defused a lot of the contradictions thrown up by him being on the one hand a recognisable icon in Smash Hits, *and an opinionated political animal on the other. For the maudlin Pied Piper, donning a silly hat let him off the hook, although for many of the Style Council's fans the irony was lost. They just liked their records.*

While the band often looked as though they got dressed simply in order to appear on children's television – all tennis whites, blazers and primary colours – ironically Weller's lyrics became angrier. He was initially as distrustful of Labour MPs as he was of their Tory opponents. Having fleetingly expressed some admiration for the Conservatives when the Jam first started attracting attention in 1977, in a volte-face Weller quickly embraced the Labour Party, almost to the point of obsession, turning himself into a class warrior in the process. The rise of Thatcher only exacerbated this. His lyrics would often sound idealistic and naive, although this was forgivable considering how sweet his melodies were. A self-proclaimed 'moody bastard' (whenever I hear the Style Council song 'My Ever Changing Moods', I think, 'Ah yes, all the way from taciturn to grumpy'), Weller was the champion of everyone he knew with a 'bingo accent'.

He was eighteen in 1976, and almost fully formed when he became famous. There were three principal punk figureheads: John Lydon, an unreconstructed sociopath; Joe Strummer, a slumming busker; and Weller, who managed to articulate the desperate aspirations of the suburbanite while cataloguing the striplit nature of late-seventies Britain. However far he thought he'd come from the punk ethic, and from the punk noise, Weller was still a surly punk at heart and rarely dropped his caustic mien. He may have had a strong sense of balladry, but throughout the eighties he retained a true punk sensibility. No, he didn't get a Mohican like Joe Strummer, during the Clash's death throes, and no, he didn't drink and swear a lot like John Lydon, but he remained true to his intransigent nature. For a while, he appeared to assume prejudices the way some people collect shoes. And vice versa, actually. There is nuance, though. Like Van Morrison a generation before him, Weller has always had a reputation for grumpiness and for being anguished; and, like Van, it's not strictly true. What Weller is, is particular.

The eighties is a decade that Weller would prefer to forget, however, even though it was good for him. 'I think a lot of our problems now stem from the eighties and Thatcherism,' he says, perhaps predictably. 'We lost so much during the eighties – community spirit, trade unions. Even big hair!'

Siouxsie Sioux was one of the few from the punk days who managed to surf the change in the zeitgeist. In the process of developing the Banshees' sound, she slowly developed a completely new genre, one that would soon start to be defined as 'goth'. Along with the Cure, Bauhaus, the Cramps, the Birthday Party, Killing Joke and the Sisters of Mercy, she inadvertently created a phantasmagorical and nihilistic sound, and a fashion sense that consisted of clothing and hairstyles that suggested a gothic-romantic allure. Her deathly pallor, electro-shock hair and feline eyes became as famous as her wailing voice. Siouxsie and the Banshees were Edvard Munch's Scream *made flesh, and they became harbingers of a post-punk movement which would outlast many of the others, becoming an indie alternative to heavy metal almost, with introspective and romantic lyrics replacing songs about the devil and young girls. Goth was macabre, but it didn't play with satanic imagery, while stylistically it was almost unisex. By the early eighties, when the Banshees were one of the biggest groups in the country, Siouxsie's image was ubiquitous. Siouxsie herself became the ultimate goth reference point, and while kohl-eyelinered Siouxsie clones were a feature of many British high streets – gothic nymphs – her most talismanic element was her hair. As one journalist said, 'As she transformed the role of a female frontwoman into something powerful, mysterious and dominant, teenage fans were painting their bedroom walls black, and acquiring the singer's deeply-held interest in the supernatural.' She claims that the Banshees would have happened regardless of the punk explosion, and that while many of the primary punks had been influenced by the likes of the Stooges, the MC5, the New York Dolls and the Flamin' Groovies, Siouxsie herself liked Bowie, Roxy Music and Kraftwerk. Lyrically, she focused on disturbed childhoods, urban paranoia and personality disorders, although the band's rather opulent sound was modish enough – this was basically sensual psychedelica – to appeal to those who were more interested in Spandau Ballet or Depeche Mode. Around this time, she told me that she hadn't seen her real hair since she was sixteen. 'I catch glimpses of it every now and then,' she said, 'and I've seen the odd grey hair, but I really don't know what colour my real hair is now. I've kept it dyed since before punk. I hope I helped change the way in which women present themselves. In the early part of the twentieth century, in the twenties, women looked very strong. This was a very bolshie period for them, with their austere bobs and straight up and down lines. Women then looked powerful. I always tried to be the antithesis of the curvy, tanned, blonde bombshell. I can't do much about the curves, but everything else . . .'*

Nineteen eighty-two felt a long way away from the mid-seventies, since when there had been as many changes in the culture as there had been in politics, a period which had seen hard-headed punks slowly morph into professional entertainers, becoming commodities in the process. Paul Weller was significant in that he actually became more strident than he had been at the height of punk. Like many on the Left, he was appalled when, in April, Britain suddenly went to war. What soon became known as the Falklands War was a ten-week conflict in the South Atlantic between Argentina and the UK over control of the Falkland Islands and its associated dependencies. It started on the second of the month, when Argentina invaded and occupied the Falklands (and, the following day, South Georgia and the South Sandwich Islands) in an attempt to establish sovereignty. Three days later, the British government dispatched a naval task force to engage the Argentinian navy and air force, before making an amphibious assault on the islands. The war lasted seventy-four days and ended with the

Argentinian surrender on 14 June, returning the islands to British control. In total, 649 Argentinian military personnel, 255 British military personnel and three Falkland Islanders died during the hostilities. The British press was understandably conflicted, with some papers deploying an incendiary rhetoric that was perhaps best exemplified by a front cover of Rupert Murdoch's Sun *in May, celebrating the sinking of the ancient Argentinian battleship the* General Belgrano *by a British submarine. The* Sun *gleefully reported the first deaths of the war (368 conscripts, many in their teens) with the headline 'GOTCHA'. At the time the headline was written, the paper's editor, Kelvin MacKenzie, thought that as many as 1,200 Argentinians might have died. According to the* Guardian, *those present say he considered replacing it with the weaker 'DID 1200 ARGIES DIE?' but was overruled by Rupert Murdoch himself, with the words, 'It seems like a bloody good headline to me.'*

One of the greatest songs of the period was Elvis Costello's 'Shipbuilding', which he and the producer Clive Langer wrote for Robert Wyatt. It was a blistering condemnation of the Falklands conflict and a brutal – if elegantly composed – sideswipe at government policy. During 1982, former ship workers could talk about little else other than the possibility that the shipyards might reopen, solely because Britain was at war with Argentina over the Falklands. And so Costello turned this into a devastating piece of social realism. As the Financial Times *would comment, this was pretty much the last time a popular song about war made a mark on the public consciousness in Britain. 'One reason, perhaps, why Costello's lyrics are so measured is that the Left in Britain was unsure how to react to the war,' it said. 'The initial impulse was to see it as an imperial adventure; on the other hand, there was a risk of being seen as objectively pro the Argentinian junta. Hence, perhaps, the decision to focus on the human cost of the conflict rather than explicitly taking sides.' As for Costello, he simply said, 'I wasn't being alarmist or trying to be morbid in any way.'*

Gary Kemp: I was very much in two minds about the Falklands. Initially, I thought you couldn't just let another country walk in and change the culture of an entire island that didn't want to be taken over, but once the blood started to spill, it suddenly seemed unnecessary, while it was increasingly obvious that Thatcher had done it for political reasons. However, I think any prime minister would do the same thing today, regardless of the complications.

1983

THE CRADLE OF CHORUSES

'We were an avant-garde outfit when we began, but we were also very ambitious. But when the media came into contact with us, particularly journalists who had a grounding in what came after punk, which was very austere, political, industrial and had no colour to it, I think they felt what we were doing was a betrayal. But we wanted colour, flamboyance, romanticism, aspiration and optimism after all that pessimism. Punk to me was fucking bright colours. It went grey after punk. But we wanted to bring the spiky hair, the dye, the make-up and the fun.'

SIMON LE BON

Alan Edwards: Duran Duran supported David Bowie on the Australian leg of the *Serious Moonlight* tour, and they were the quintessential party animals. We played the cricket ground in Sydney and 120,000 people turned up, as David was probably the biggest star in the world at the time, and Duran were on a vertical trajectory. David had chosen them for the tour because not only did he like their music, he also found them very approachable, which they were. They were great fun and always looked fabulous, and they were very naughty boys. The promoter threw a party every night in whatever hotel we were in – and this was during the period when the record industry was flush with cash – and literally no expense was spared. There would be dozens of glamorous girls every night – and I mean *dozens* – limos, champagne, cocktail parties in each other's rooms and more girls. I've never seen so many girls. When you're on the road with a rock band – and I've toured with bands for nearly fifty years – you get used to a certain amount of excess. But Duran were something else. David's band included Carlos Alomar and Tony Thompson, and they both had a great relationship with Duran and could party just as hard. It was an extraordinary period, and it was the very height of rock'n'roll excess, with wall-to-wall models and all the shenanigans that you might imagine. The Duran guys were uncomplicated, friendly, English, down to earth, and there was great chemistry between them and David. I became Duran Duran's PR for a while, and I still had quite a punk approach to the industry, so my attention to detail was perhaps not what it should have been, and my press releases were possibly not constructed with the amount of finesse they ought to have been. So I did this release for Duran, and it came back annotated in red pen by Simon Le Bon, who gave me marks out of ten for spelling, grammar and construction. It was actually incredibly impressive, if brutal, and the cumulative score was two out of ten, signed off with the words 'You're fired.' I was incredibly upset and quite angry about it at the time, but of course I now think it's very funny.

Rob Hallett: Rock'n'roll excess? Andy Taylor's wedding at the Chateau Marmont, with girls *everywhere*.

Reading interviews with some of the more contemplative bands of the period, you could be forgiven for thinking that they spent so much of their time honing the theoretical aspects of their manifestos that they had forsworn all pleasures of the flesh. Obviously, this wasn't the case, whether you were a brash new pop sensation or a navel-gazing post-punk radical. In 1983, I approached New Order about contributing a new song to a 'Scratch' video I was helping i-D's *Terry Jones produce for the Japanese market. We had hired half a dozen directors and fashion photographers (including John Maybury, Jeffrey Hinton and Marc Lebon) to shoot short street-style videos, which were then going to be edited by Terry and synced with various commissioned tracks. I'd had various conversations with New Order's manager, Rob Gretton, and then had two meetings with the band – one at their PR's offices in Ladbroke Grove, and the other in a private lounge at Heathrow airport. At this second meeting, after a few drinks Peter Hook and Bernard Sumner regaled me with a story involving an enthusiastic female fan that wouldn't have been out of place in the ribald Led Zeppelin biography* Hammer of the Gods. *Girls wanted to sleep with synth-pop bands in the same way they wanted to sleep with any rock band. One story doing the rounds that summer involved the singer of a prominent synth-pop group enjoying a groupie in a trailer backstage at a large European festival, as said groupie blithely looked out of the window. After several minutes of being entertained from behind, she saw the singer walk in front of the trailer on his way to Catering. His place had been taken by the keyboard player.*

Rob Hallett: Duran had the best time. We all did. They were chased by girls all over the world. The girls slept outside hotels, broke into hotels. I mean, it was a phenomenon. They were very exciting times, and the band certainly enjoyed it. They actually called themselves 'the band to dance to as the bomb dropped'. Hence the designer suits, the gorgeous girls.

There was a high-energy attitude towards sex. There was a certain sexual liberation back then that we seem to have lost. They were getting all the girls the *NME* writers didn't get. I remember being in the back of a cab with John and Roger [Taylor] one night in Tokyo, with hundreds of girls chasing us in the street, and we all spontaneously burst into a chorus of 'I Love Rock'n'Roll'.

Nick Rhodes: We were probably the biggest band in the world at the time, and when you can have everything, you tend to take everything. For a while, anyway.

In June, Duran Duran were in Cannes, at the same time as Elton John, who was shooting a video for 'I'm Still Standing', which was planned to be the first single from his forthcoming album Too Low for Zero. *In between shoots, Elton bumped into Simon Le Bon in the Negresco Hotel, where the singer encouraged Elton to try his first vodka martini. According to those who were there, Elton proceeded to drink another seven martinis before having a couple of lines of coke and then tearing all his clothes off and smashing up a friend's hotel room. So much for going out drinking with Duran Duran.*

Jon Savage: By 1983, most of the groups had pretty much cut loose from any subcultural beginnings, and they had become mainstream pop music. I didn't like 'Gold'-period Spandau very much, as they really got on my tits, and Duran I never quite understood, as they seemed a bit lumpy to me. I thought the Wham! singles were really good on *Top of the Pops*, and Boy George was completely fascinating. In a way, George, to me, is the key figure in the whole thing. He had the biggest hits and he is the link with punk and he is the link with the subculture and he was the global superstar. There's something really fascinating about George. He was a soul boy, and then he went through punk and he went through the squatting scene and he did all that. The Eurythmics made a couple of terrific pop records, and then they went all authentic and started making really shit records. As soon as those groups stopped making synth pop, they all turned to shit. It was really embarrassing when Tears for Fears, who had made a couple of pretty good synth records, started going all authentic. I remember talking to Neil Tennant about this; if you strayed from synth pop, then you were a traitor, basically.

The whole period is fantastically important. When I was younger, I wanted everything to be serious and heavy, and now I'm older I'm really appreciative of fun and good times, and there's a lot of fun and good times in those records. The whole New Romantic period is deep with meaning and has great resonance, but it was also a lot of fun. Obviously, the whole gender/gay element is incredibly important, so that gets a thumbs-up. That whole period is important, from the Normal's 'TVOD' and the Silicon Teens through Depeche Mode and Yazoo, the Human League's 'Sound of the Crowd', 'The Chase' by Giorgio Moroder, 'Just an Illusion' by Imagination, 'Love Resurrection' by Alison Moyet, the Divine records, Telex, Japan, 'Torch' by Soft Cell, 'Rock the Box' by Sylvester, and then, of course, you have early rap, like Grandmaster Flash. In a historical sense, the period provided a great positive look forward after the demise of punk, and it was bright and it was colourful and it was pop, and I mourn the loss of those records. The records were of the moment but also commented on the times. I mean, just look at 'Bedsitter', which is about the emptiness of club life, and which is a very emotional record.

David Hepworth: *Smash Hits* became a way for all these groups to grow from the margins to the charts.

Jon Savage: *The Face* and *Smash Hits* were quite close and there were all these links between us, and we went to the same parties. I remember being very irritated by Robert Elms, but time heals all wounds.

The success of Spandau Ballet generated a kind of A&R feeding frenzy, as record company scouts started scouring London nightclubs in search of 'rumour bands'. Everyone was looking for the Next Big Thing, and if you were approximately good-looking and had appeared in the pages of i-D *or* The Face *at least once, and you claimed to be in a band, then you were automatically a record company target. This was originally how Chris Sullivan's Blue Rondo à la Turk attracted so much attention, making their success something of a foregone conclusion. However, while they were certainly an intoxicating live attraction, the Latin movement – such as it was – was successfully hijacked by singalong popsters Modern Romance. They had little of the credibility, but all of the hits. Blue Rondo's failure caused the record companies to instigate a collective sense check, which initially made them suspicious of Boy George's Culture Club. After all, while George was ostensibly the public face of the New Romantics, who knew if he had any of the right ingredients to be a pop star? After Culture Club's first two singles performed poorly, Virgin, who had signed them, thought the band were a busted flush, but then things suddenly changed.*

When 'Do You Really Want to Hurt Me?' hit No. 1 in the British charts in September 1982, the pandemonium that greeted their success had distinct echoes of Beatlemania, and by the time they replicated this success in the US a few months later, Culture Club were genuine global celebrities. Well, sort of: it was George O'Dowd who became the focus, George who appeared on most of the magazine covers, and George who became the group's spokesperson. By the time they played London's Dominion Theatre at the end of March the following year, Culture Club couldn't move without escorts and security. The scenes outside the Dominion on 31 March were nothing if not extraordinary: the ambulances were on hand, ready to deal with the inevitable high spirits, and a cordon of police were hanging back in case the 2,000 identikit teenage girls – who had all come to the theatre dressed as George – suddenly decided to move en masse. I saw a similar scene in Tokyo a few months later. I was there working for a fashion designer called Takeo Kikuchi, who fronted a company called Men's Bigi, and who appeared to specialise in minesweeping London nightclubs looking for interesting flotsam and jetsam to use in his fashion shows and ad campaigns. Hence, I was in Japan with a dozen other nightclub habitués, and none of us could quite believe our luck. Every night we were taken to a succession of bars and clubs, one of which was on the fifteenth floor of a tower block in Shinjuku. As we stepped out of the lift, right into the club, we walked into a sea of young girls who all looked like Boy George, and this being Japan, the attention to detail was granular: each of them looked perfect, almost as though they had been styled by the same team. It was an impressive, if slightly bewildering, sight, all these girls dressed in an approximation of their supposedly asexual idol, presumably to impress their friends and pick up boys. George's appeal was one of the cornerstones of the media's interest in Culture Club – his ability to project an image of benign asexuality, while at the same time looking like the most transgressive pop star of all time.

Elsewhere, the new pop's appeal was rather easier to grasp, and when I soon started travelling the world as a music journalist, I worked out quite quickly that the cultural equity of any writer for one of the glossy weeklies – Smash Hits, Number One *or* Record Mirror *– was based solely on how well they knew the members of Duran Duran, Wham! or Spandau Ballet. At least among fans. I remember being at a Hall and Oates concert in Cedar Rapids, Iowa, and the mere fact that I worked for a glossy magazine in London – England! – coupled with the fact that I had not only just met but interviewed Duran Duran, meant that I was – fleetingly – almost as important as the Queen (at least to the twenty-something girls in the Five Seasons Center that night). This was the golden period of British pop, when domestic stars could really do no wrong, as MTV transported them from the relative insignificance of London's club scene to TV screens in bars, clubs and frat houses all over the US. For the big groups, this was the imperial phase, when British pop stars had a global media influence that far outweighed their domestic relevance. The likes of John Taylor, Martin Kemp and Andrew Ridgeley (the three pin-ups of the period) may have been famous in the UK, but in the rest of the world they were treated as genuinely international sex symbols.*

For a while, it seemed as though everyone involved in clubland was dabbling in alchemy and being signed by a record label. Against all odds, Monroe-lookalike Marilyn secured a contract, as did Philip Sallon, who, having been born in 1951 and so was at least a decade older than everyone else, was almost like the guardian angel of the whole scene. A loyal friend of George ('Even though he used to call me Boy Gorge and sing "Do You Really Want to Eat Me?" at the top of his voice'), he perhaps deserved it more than most. His record wasn't a hit, an unsurprising situation when you consider how uninterested he was in the whole process. I interviewed Sallon in EMI's Manchester Square headquarters when the record came out in 1985 (Sallon was dressed head to toe in an outfit that appeared to have been fashioned entirely from old newspapers), and he seemed to have absolutely no idea why he was there or what was expected of him.

Boy George: When Culture Club started to become big, I didn't really see myself as a pin-up. I didn't ever think little girls would scream at me, and that was the most shocking thing. If people had seen me before I was famous, there is no way they would have thought I was straight. I was kissing Jon Moss [Culture Club's drummer] in public, and there were photos in magazines of my tongue in his ear and him flirting with me. It was only when things got more successful that Jon would start to pull away from me. No one ever said to me, 'You can't be gay,' but you just got the sense that you weren't going to be appreciated by everyone around you. You just had to learn to conduct yourself in a more commercial way. When we landed in America and there were all these screaming girls, it just felt like validation, but it was kind of at odds with so much of what I was as a person. In terms of gay culture, we all learnt how dark and murky the seventies were, which we never really thought about at the time because it was all about not frightening the horses. Even in my own family. I came out when I was a teenager, and it was, 'We know what you are, but don't keep going on about it, don't shove it in our faces.' But, of course, I did do that, I did sit in my parents' living room back-combing my hair into gravity-defying shapes, putting on more and more make-up. And my mum would be like, 'Jerry, look what he's wearing.' And my dad would just look over his newspaper and be like, 'Well, if he wants to get beaten up . . .' I forced them to accept who I was. The thing about being gay is that when you're six or seven, you don't really know there's anything different about you. It's other kids who point it out, because you're not interested in the same things they are and maybe you've got too many girlfriends, and in my case you collect broken jewellery and you like songs from musicals and you're not aware there's anything wrong with you. When Bowie came along, it was like a light at the end of the tunnel – like, 'Oh my God, this guy is just telling the newspaper that he's bisexual.' I remember reading that 'I met my wife because we were dating the same man,' and all those things . . .

Mikey Craig (*musician*): It was amazing, because *Top of the Pops* encompassed everything about Great Britain at that time. Every genre of music was played there, from the ridiculous to the brilliant, and the great thing was that everybody watched it. You would even set your video recorder to tape the show if you weren't around. If you managed to get yourself onto *Top of the Pops*, then you were guaranteed to have a hit record because everyone was watching you.

Norman Jay: I loved it when Mikey Craig joined Culture Club. I was properly pleased for him – you know, 'My mate's playing in a band with Boy George.' A kid from Hammersmith – wicked.

Neil Tennant: The arrival of Boy George was the moment when androgyny came into mass-market pop music, and that changed everything, because before that it was just straight boys dressing up.

Simon Napier-Bell: From the moment Culture Club had their first hit, George was constantly pushing for more column inches. Jon Moss, the group's drummer, was less appreciative of the media's attention. He and George were having an affair, but George was effectively cheating on him by having a simultaneous affair with the media.

Neil Tennant: One of the good things about punk was the way in which it suddenly edits the pop song back to two and a half, three minutes, it brings back the songwriting discipline that develops into power pop. Then you add in elements of the avant-garde and politics and style, and then finally electronics. And so you have a renaissance of British pop that lasts until 1985. I loved all the synth-pop acts of the early eighties, but then I loved Motown and lots of sixties pop, especially the Beatles. I loved Soft Cell when they came along and had that amazing run of five or six brilliant singles. The New Romantic scene takes the lessons of punk, with well-crafted pop songs, but now they're looking for glamour. Then, of course, as with Bryan Ferry – who was the first to do this – it becomes the thing it imitates. Pop music in the early eighties was actually very alternative. It's made in bedsits, it's trying to do something original all the time. After that, the formula comes in. Bryan Ferry starts off as art rock and then begins wearing a white tuxedo, epitomising the poignancy of wealth. He was obsessed with the aristocracy. Ten years later, he's got children at Eton. He's become the thing he dreamed of. It was the same with fashion in the eighties: it starts off with Kensington Market DIY cool, and then by the end of the decade it's all being made in Paris. It's the same with electronica: it started off in bedrooms, and now EDM has taken over the world. My favourite pop is what I always call 'aspirational' pop, i.e. it doesn't just celebrate what's there, it celebrates what *could* be there. All of the groups from the early eighties had cultural aspirations. You'd see Boy George walking down Carnaby Street, or Steve Strange walking around in full Moroccan gear, and there was something special about this idea that people were going to create new versions of themselves, and maybe even do it quite a few times – taking this, of course, from David Bowie. The other thing is that you had people who'd come from an alternative or punk background who decided they wanted to be Abba. Around this time, it became very fashionable to want to be Abba and to have a manager who wore a suit and carried a briefcase, like Steve Dagger. People started realising they could push their success even harder by taking control, or at least by looking like they were taking control, of the agenda.

Martin Fry: It had all started to get very competitive, with Culture Club, Duran, Spandau Ballet . . . all the big bands. When it was time to record *Beauty Stab*, the follow-up to *The Lexicon of Love*, we wanted to work with Trevor Horn again, but he was working with Yes. He took me to meet Malcolm McLaren, but then we decided we wanted to change our sound completely. Now is that arrogance or naivety or both? We saw David Bowie reinvent himself, and film directors did it all the time, so why not us? Bowie did it in increments, in a funny kind of way, and he wasn't always successful. It's all there in the song 'That Was Then but This Is Now', which was the first single from *Beauty Stab*. But the reception to the album really shocked me, and not in a good way. It was a disaster.

Trevor Horn: After *The Lexicon of Love*, I had the opportunity to work with ABC again, but the thought of working with Malcolm McLaren was just so enticing. Malcolm played me something in our first meeting, and it totally blew me away. He had some scratching sampler, which I had never heard before. Scratching! Imagine. When he said the DJs pull the needle across the record, I was like, 'Get the fuck out of here. Really?' And then I heard it, and loved it. Then he played me some township music, and he wanted to mix them together. So I was intrigued. I didn't know what part Malcolm was going to play, and it turned into an odyssey, going around the world to record it all, but there's some great stuff on the record. We recorded in South Africa, had Cuban drummers . . . the lot. Then we came back to England to make 'Buffalo Gals'. Malcolm had a fixation about buffalo girls, and we recorded it in Tennessee, using utility pickers in a little studio. And it was just fucking awful. We couldn't make this song work, as it sounded like a cowboy song. Just terrible. But thank God for Malcolm – he got the World Famous Supreme Team to come and scratch on it. So these two African American tough guys arrived from New York and took one look at me, as if to say, 'Who the fuck are you?' Then it turned out they hadn't brought any gear with them, so we had to get somebody in New York to buy these decks. Then we spent ages – four hours – trying to get their favourite beat. When it came to rapping the song, they said they couldn't do it. I said I could, and went into the studio to show them. After I was finished rapping, I went back into the control booth, but I couldn't see them, so I thought they'd gone back to their hotel. But the reason I couldn't see them was because they were rolling around on the floor laughing. After that, *Duck Rock* really started working. They would be scratching, I would come up with some music, and Malcolm would come up with some talking. The problem was, Malcolm had no sense of rhythm, so we would get something going, and he would dive in and kill it. That's the first time I ever heard the phrase 'vibe killer': the Supreme Team would say, 'Malcolm, you're a vibe killer, man.' When it was finished, I took it to the record company, and they were stunned, as they didn't know what to make of it. Legend has it that one of the mail boys said, 'What's that? It's fucking great.' Then, of course, we had a big hit with it. I mean, not a No. 1, but mad for a record as weird as that.

John Lydon: I learnt nothing from Malcolm. He learnt from me, if anything. I wrote the songs, I gave it all the direction, I was the brains. Not him. Malcolm wouldn't know one end of a console from another. To him, it's a big lump of metal with flashing lights . . . and he's got a cheque by putting his name to all those records that were made by Trevor Horn and all the rest.

Alan Yentob: After the Sex Pistols and Bow Wow Wow, Malcolm started being a performer. He started entering the narrative himself, and he saw the parts he could play. He was always looking for himself, looking for his future. So he had encounters with people he thought might be interesting and might provoke some response, which would take him to the next step. I felt in some ways he was searching for something he wasn't really finding, because although people think his career went somewhere, actually it sort of ground to a halt. He had a reputation, people were prepared to take him on, but it never made a big impact culturally. Once it was a provocation to mix high and low culture. But not any more. He needed an audience. He needed someone to listen to him who would be the trigger for him to be able to open himself up. But his influence faded.

Boy George: I look at fame in a really different way now, and I think I've probably made my peace with it, but at the time I had all this incredible financial freedom, but I didn't have any *real* freedom. I think everybody who is famous wants to have fame that comes with an off button, and it takes years for you to really have a relationship with what you've created and what you crave. At the beginning with Culture Club, it was exciting and annoying at the same time. It was everything. I've always been quite a personable person, and when I was in a hotel I would go down and talk to the kids, and they would just scream in my face. That's when I realised it wasn't necessarily about me. I think in the beginning, when you're the hot new thing, a lot of people just latch on to you because it's what everybody else is doing. As artists we go out of our way to get people to worship us, and then we're uncomfortable with all the attention because we can't control it.

Mikey Craig: There were disagreements [about 'Karma Chameleon']. George came into the studio with the song. He had the melody and asked the band to work on it. We put more music to it, and the song was written in four minutes flat.

Andy Bell (*singer*): I liked Culture Club, but I really liked Depeche Mode. I moved to London, to Ealing, from Peterborough – I grew up on a council estate in Dogsthorpe – in 1983, with the intention of joining a band. I was in the sixth form at school, but I didn't really want to go to university, so I left before my A-levels. I wasn't really concentrating. OMD were probably the most popular band in the sixth form at the time, and I loved all the synth-pop bands. After I moved, I worked in a bar, in a sandwich shop, and then worked at Debenhams for a while, but the whole intention was to join a band. I formed a local band with a bass player, but after two gigs answered an ad in the *Melody Maker*, and it was Vince Clarke, post-Depeche Mode, post-Yazoo. Weirdly, I had thought about writing him a letter anyway, as I loved what he did, so the coincidence was amazing. I had started experimenting sexually when I moved to London. I had a girlfriend at the time, and she was really sweet as she used to encourage me to go out and experiment. So I started going to gay clubs – the Embassy, Pyramid at Heaven. I used to go to the Bell in King's Cross, which was a real hub, and loads of singers went there – Morrissey would be there and Jimmy Somerville and Marc Almond. You could feel the power, and when I first started going out, seeing Divine, Grace Jones, Frankie Goes to Hollywood . . . it was intoxicating. Being a young gay man, you could just feel this energy on the dancefloor. There was a camaraderie. Going out and seeing Boy George and Marilyn and all this cross-dressing, you felt the world was your oyster. You almost became fearless.

Stephen Dalton: After their transitional post-Clarke album, *A Broken Frame*, Depeche Mode recorded a trio of albums which marked Martin Gore's coming-of-age as a songwriter, heralding a new lyrical darkness and hard-edged sound. Its 1983 sequel, *Construction Time Again*, was mixed at Berlin's Hansa Ton studios, the 'hall by the Wall' famous for Bowie's *'Heroes'* and, later, landmark albums by Nick Cave and U2. Hansa became their regular studio for the next three years. The studio was recommended by Gareth Jones, the band's long-term engineer. A strong pound also made it significantly cheaper to relocate the band to Germany rather than pay London rates. Besides, Berlin was a twenty-four-hour party city and the Basildon boys were starting to live a pop-star party lifestyle. Martin Gore's growing interest in S&M found an outlet in Berlin's famously bohemian club scene, and it was there he would compose sado-erotic anthems such as 'Master and Servant'. The band's reputation as small-town synth-pop lightweights still dogged them during the Berlin years. While Gore flirted with gentle S&M symbolism, Frankie Goes to Hollywood would soon start to take a much more upfront and marketable leather-clone look to the top of the charts. When Depeche Mode began tinkering with industrial rhythms, they were overshadowed by hardcore metal-bashing hipsters such as Test Department or Einstürzende Neubauten. Unlucky timing and critical disdain conspired to belittle their progressive pop agenda.

Nick Rhodes: MTV obviously brought another dimension to music, and there were artists of our generation who embraced it because it was exciting and new. It was state-of-the-art at that time. There were older artists who were a little more hesitant to get involved. I think they felt it had perhaps turned the seriousness of some of their songwriting and musicianship into showbiz, which wasn't as appealing to them. But eventually you've got a lot of those artists making videos – and some of them made some really good videos too. We were part of that wave, along with a lot of other British artists, particularly, who made interesting videos at that time, like the Cure and Billy Idol. And obviously, in America you had mega-artists like Michael Jackson and Madonna and Prince who also moved into that medium. I'm not sure how much it really changed things. But it was exciting for a time. When somebody told me about MTV for the first time and said, 'It's a twenty-four-hour music channel, and they just play music non-stop,' that was unbelievable. 'Wow! How has this not happened before and how *great* that we've got a channel that we can turn on any time to see music.' It was a revelation.

Boy George: MTV became our friend very quickly, as it did the job globally for you.

Jim Kerr (*musician*): The eighties were a great time for dreamers. Whether it was Billy MacKenzie, New Order . . . everything seemed possible and everything seemed up for grabs. Of course, video changed everything. Your video could travel to places you could never even imagine. But MTV did create a monster. Everyone was trying to be more outrageous than the others and to look the part. You had stocky guys like me in eyeliner, trying their best.

By 1983, MTV was on a roll and had started to become famous for its crazy contests and incredible prizes. There was almost a frat-house sensibility about the new network, as it continually tried to top itself in terms of its outlandish, boyish stunts. One MTV contest winner described how he won a wild weekend with Van Halen when he was just nineteen (and so legally not allowed to drink). He and his friend were flown to Detroit and greeted with Jack Daniel's, cocaine, weed and their very own groupie, Tammy. 'This was the Wild West of the cable era and [MTV executives] were doing anything they could to connect with viewers,' says one of the network's former directors. Other prizes included an entire town in Texas, shooting a Madonna pop promo and winning Jon Bon Jovi's childhood home. Nuts.

Gary Farrow (*publicist*): Television was so huge at that time that it would give you an instant sales lift. When I was looking after Heaven 17, they did *Crackerjack*, *Basil Brush* . . . anything that was on television.

Spandau Ballet's drummer John Keeble would say that they spent most of their time in the early eighties on television, 'miming to small children'.

Nick Rhodes: I think we've always been pretty pragmatic about the industry. MTV certainly was fantastic timing for Duran Duran, and when it started it was all you could ever wish for: twenty-four-hour music on television, with videos, interviews and bands popping in . . . It was really something. But once they decided that game shows were gonna be more successful and they only wanted a playlist of five songs a week . . . The quote I'll always remember – I saw it on the front of a newspaper – was 'Toys 'R' Us Wants to Get Out of the Toy Business', and I thought that was so applicable to MTV. 'MTV Wants to Get Out of the Music Business' would've been the appropriate headline.

Andy Taylor (*musician*): When it came to establishing a foothold in the States, there's no doubt that our videos gave us an edge over other British bands. We had a strategy for doing well in America, and we believed we could make it there, but it involved a lot of commitment and hard work, and we knew we had to make more effort than any other band. It involved touring in as many American cities as possible, and we were careful to always try and keep the American media on our side. Video was at the heart of our success. We couldn't have done our first American tour were it not for the MTV following that we established. During '81 and '82, we broke into markets in the rest of the world, but initially it was very hard to get radio airplay in America. But we were conscious that lots of nightclubs there had TV screens in them, and as our videos took off in the clubs, it created a talking point.

Midge Ure: It was a heady period, but you've got to remember that while you might try and say all the bands were part of the New Romantic scene, they were all wildly different. Culture Club were radically different from Duran, who were different from Spandau. Spandau were soul boys, Duran were a bit of whatever and Culture Club were playing soft reggae. They all had a look, they all had a style. What they all had in common was the ability to experiment in an environment that allowed them to be creative. The big thing was the video revolution. We were making videos before there was a vehicle on which to show them in America, so when MTV started, the only content they had was from the UK. So they blasted the hell out of Duran, Spandau and Ultravox, until they started making their own. For the first six months, year or whatever of MTV existing, it was all British acts, and that was an incredibly powerful thing. All of a sudden you were getting to homes in the Midwest, these guys with make-up on and bouffant hairdos. There they are in Arkansas on someone's television, and that just never happened before. It encouraged some artists to do it more and more, and the ones with the bigger budgets made bigger and more extravagant videos, until Michael Jackson came along and did 'Thriller', and nobody could compete with that. But there was a desire to be bigger and better. And there was also a kind of Beatles/Rolling Stones-type rivalry between Duran and Spandau, who were constantly trying to outdo each other. Funnily enough, often with the same video director. However, I don't think any of the artists thought, 'Let's make the video, and then write a song to suit the film.' It all stemmed from the music. So if the music wasn't good, it didn't really matter how much you spent on the video because it wasn't going to get shown. So it was like a catch-22, but it did become a bit of a race to see who could have the most outrageous or the funniest or the quirkiest video. There was a video I directed with Ultravox, 'Love's Great Adventure', where I actually stopped the backing track in the middle of the film, breaking the fourth wall. I was hacking through the jungle, huffing and puffing, when I said, 'Hold on a second . . . OK, let's go,' and the track started again. You were constantly trying to think of little things that would make your video a bit different, but the video wouldn't have existed if the music hadn't existed in the first place. So it was never a case of 'Let's write any old crap to make this fantastic video.'

Boy George: It was such a whirlwind, and it all happened so quickly that it was difficult for us to really grasp what was happening. We became famous, but we didn't have control over it.

Simon Le Bon: All that mattered was the image, as that's what people got, and people got this amazing, incredibly glamorous feeling from the whole thing, and that's what they wanted at the time. We've been the kind of band who have always divided opinion, and it's always been an extreme kind of reaction. We're not a band about whom people say, 'Oh, I like them.' They say, 'I *love* them,' or 'I *hate* them.' So we've grown up with quite a lot of criticism, some of it constructive, some of it not. And one of the things you do is you start to not take any notice of it. I would say, 'Yes, it's nice that we got nice reviews,' but I don't really read reviews. It's no huge deal to me, because what I feel when I walk out on stage, what we feel from the audience, means so much more than what people write about us. We can tell whether we're playing a good show or not because the crowd tells us right there and then. Sometimes you have to not give a fuck about what people think about you. You just get on with it.

*By 1983, Duran Duran had grown accustomed to their jobs, treating the success, the acclaim, the non-stop travel, the adoration and the constant press intrusion as the ever-rolling constituent parts of their day-to-day existence. They were pop stars, and they appeared to be very good pop stars. Having spent much of the previous twelve months living abroad as tax exiles, in August they flew back from Miami to the UK, where they were due to play two charity concerts: one at London's Dominion Theatre, before the Prince and Princess of Wales, for the Prince's Trust; the other at Aston Villa's football ground in Birmingham (their home turf), in aid of MENCAP. As it was the silly season for the press, what with parliament being in recess, the Duran visit was a godsend for the tabloids, who constructed various meaningless headlines relating to their visit: 'LOVE AND DURAN MANIA' (*Daily Star*); 'DURANDEMONIUM – IT'S JUST LIKE THE SCREAMING SIXTIES AS FANS MOB FAB FIVE' (*Daily Express*); 'DURANTASTIC – BEATLE-STYLE MANIA AS PRINCESS DIANA'S FAVOURITE POP GROUP FLY IN' (*Daily Mirror*).*

Following the Prince's Trust concert, the band were introduced to Charles and Diana, and their reactions afterwards were pitch perfect. 'I think we've got a lot in common – we've both got a lot of fans,' said Simon Le Bon. 'To begin with, we met them before the show, a very formal presentation, and answered a few questions, which was nice because it was like breaking you in very gently. They must know how nervous people like us would be. Then afterwards there was a reception upstairs. It was much less formal and much easier to talk. They were a very pleasant couple indeed.' Nick Rhodes was equally respectful: 'They were very nice. Very human, actually. Prince Charles liked our "gear" – "I rather like your gear – what do you call it?" They chatted about Montserrat. They seemed to know quite a lot about us – they'd obviously been briefed well. Everybody was impressed with them. She was chatting about the other gig we were doing and how tired we were and when were we coming back again. She looked great. Really pretty.'

Here was a pristine eighties media moment, with pop, royalty and popular journalism all working in complete harmony. The arrangement had echoes of Beatlemania, and its co-dependency suited all parties involved. As for the band, it was all in a day's work, another day espousing the good life, and a message of pure pop escapism. Neil Tennant, who was still working for Smash Hits, *interviewed Simon Le Bon after the show, and ennui deluxe had yet to set in. Quizzed about whether or not he ever got fed up with his cosmopolitan existence (that week the band were due to fly from London to Montserrat and then Sydney), Le Bon said, 'We've got to do it. If you choose this kind of living, that's what you've got to do. It's like saying you want to be an accountant, but you don't like doing maths. You can't do that. You have to find ways of enjoying it, or it becomes very tedious. And you build up this nomadic sense of pride of being able to move from one place to another very quickly. We're like a commando team: we move in and out very quickly.'*

After a while, Duran became something of a soap opera. 'We called it Duranysty,*' says Nick Rhodes. The press were so obsessed with the band that everything they did, no matter how inconsequential, was used as collateral in the papers – whether to build them up or knock them down. Anticipating the inventory of fake news that bubbled up during the 2016 US presidential campaign, when truth became a media variable, the British tabloids of the eighties never let a robust denial get in the way of a good story. Rhodes was bewildered by the attention: 'Which restaurants is John going to? Will Simon have a new girlfriend this week?' Because Duran Duran sold newspapers, the newspapers were full of Duran Duran. Always attuned to the suspicious British sensibility, journalists were ever mindful of anything approaching hubris. 'The English love to see Americans succeed, they love Hollywood and they flock to movie openings,' says Rhodes. 'But if another English person gets too successful, they can't bear it.'*

The press coverage got to such a level and the expectation was so constant that you would begin to worry if there wasn't a Duran story in the papers. What had happened? Had one of them had an accident? Had Simon been run over? The intensity was such that the PRs would start announcing (literal) non-events: 'DURAN TAKE WEEK OFF'; 'DURAN TAKE BRIEF SUMMER BREAK'; 'DURAN'S SIMON HAS LUNCH WITH PARENTS'. As we all acknowledged, this really was Beatlemania all over again.

Consequently, Duran – and all their new pop rivals – were constantly at the mercy of the markets, and at this point in their trajectory it really didn't matter if their singles were any good; it mattered how successful they were. And success was so expected that if a new record 'only' went in at No. 4 or 'only' reached No. 2, then the papers started whispering about dusting off the gallows: 'I mean, really, how long have Duran Duran got left?' As John Taylor says, 'Everything had to be No. 1.'

The band would start to feel like part of the process rather than the reason everyone was there in the first place. On tour, they became even more institutionalised. The photographer Denis O'Regan was with them a lot during this period. 'I remember driving down the road past these girls, and Simon saying, "Let's see what happens." He opened the window, and they went, "Oh my God!" And one of them just keeled over.'

These fans were incredibly resourceful, and often the band would be in the middle of a hastily arranged meeting in a hotel lobby or backstage at an arena, and a girl would just appear from under the table or walk out of a closet or a broom cupboard. Usually, the girls wouldn't bother being so devious. After the band played Madison Square Garden as part of their first arena tour, and as they were taking their encores, one girl held up a home-made poster. The message was a simple one: 'Fuck me John.'

As fame started to supplant musical appeal, so the British charts began to fill with phenomena rather than pop stars, and the likes of Duran, Culture Club and Wham! were treated as forces of nature, the kind of organic phenomena it was impossible to control. You couldn't catch it, you couldn't stop it and you couldn't divert it; all you could do was chart it, which the tabloid press did with great alacrity. At this level – the above-the-clouds altitude of Simon Le Bon, Boy George and George Michael – the fame was all-consuming and almost completely self-referential. There was no relationship with any culture other than their own, and the interesting thing about their success . . . was their success. Boy George may have presented a new kind of 'probably gay' entertainer to the public, but fundamentally the new pop's appeal in 1983 centred around popularity rather than anything else. This wasn't medicine, wasn't a panacea; it was spectacle, plain and simple – good old-fashioned institutionalised hysteria.

What did success look like? Nick Rhodes, as ever, condenses the answer perfectly: 'Every dinner one would go a little further down the wine list.' (Rhodes was in good company. 'Somebody said to me, "But the Beatles were anti-materialistic,"' says Paul McCartney. 'That's a huge myth. John and I literally used to sit down and say, "Now, let's write a swimming pool."')

Malcolm McLaren: That early-eighties period was just a big pantomime, a playpen, a bunch of kids just dressing up for the sake of it. Boy George and Duran Duran and the Spandau Ballet – it was all theatre, man. Plus, everyone was suddenly making disco records.

Lee Gale (*journalist*): Bernard Sumner was born at Crumpsall Hospital in north Manchester on 4 January 1956. His mother had cerebral palsy; he never knew his father. During his childhood, Sumner lived in his grandparents' house in Lower Broughton, Salford, along with his mother and stepfather. His grandad, John Sumner, was an engineer. 'He showed me how to do a few electrical things,' Sumner says. 'This may have started my love of technology.' After the death of Joy Division singer Ian Curtis in 1981, Sumner, piratical bassist Peter Hook, dry-humoured drummer Stephen Morris and recent addition Gillian Gilbert (Morris's wife, who played keyboards and synth) vowed to keep the band going under a new name, looking to America to develop their sound. After a trip to New York later that year, New Order started mixing traditional rock instrumentation with the synths and beats of New York and Germany. Joy Division had become New Order. A contest was held to determine the band's most able singer, and Sumner drew the short straw. 'I like singing now,' he says, 'but I didn't at the start. I didn't think about singing, didn't know how to do it, so I hit the ground stumbling. I had four lessons, which helped. The teacher showed me that my breathing was wrong. I stopped going when he used Tony Hadley of Spandau Ballet as an example of a good singer, that I should study his voice. It's experience. If someone throws you in a pool and you can't swim, you're going to struggle.'

Bernard Sumner: I don't remember much about that 1981 visit to New York. I was tripping at the time. But we felt New York was a second home, a bit of an escape from Joy Division. We were going to all the clubs and having a fantastic time. It was a mixture of English new wave with American dance, like Sugarhill Gang, and early rap, like Kurtis Blow. It was a good mix, and I thought, 'Wouldn't it be great to hear one of our own tracks?' In fact, we did – they played 'She's Lost Control', the twelve-inch version, which is dancey anyway. And it wasn't just New York; we were hearing stuff in London. There were clubs playing four-to-the-floor dance music, but done with instruments. I thought, 'I know what they are trying to do, they're trying to play precise drum loops and bass loops, but you could do that with a sequencer and synthesizers.' Music was on the cusp of change. We managed to grasp that early on and then take it out live, when no one else was doing it because the gear was so unreliable. We saw an opportunity. When we toured America that year, we were using technology that wasn't designed to be used in a live performance. A lot of the time we were fighting the equipment. Usually, one of the roadies would come and say, 'The synthesizer's not working. Can you come on stage and see what you can do?' Our roadie Terry [Mason] wasn't technically minded, and he used to have colour-coded cables because he didn't understand what the synth was doing. But we had blue lighting, so . . . 'Bernard! I'm trying to plug it in, but the stupid lighting gear means that the green looks like blue and yellow looks like red.' Just before we plugged the ARP synth in, I'd have to get on stage in front of the audience with my screwdriver and toolkit.

I remember in Toronto, backstage, I said, 'Right, what is it tonight?' 'Nothing's working at all. Everything's broken. Even the echo unit. Nothing's working.' Then we had a gig where the gear didn't turn up. We were playing with Simple Minds. We were going on before them, and Terry came back and said, 'The gear's just not here. Something's happened at customs, and it's not here.' 'We go on stage in an hour.' 'Yes, it's not here, we've got no gear.'

So I dealt with that one by drinking a complete bottle of neat Pernod, which wasn't a good idea. So we said to Simple Minds, 'Can we go on after you, because we've got no gear? We believe it's on its way from customs.' And they were, 'Oh no, we can't do that.' So the whole show got put back later and later. We were supposed to be on at 9 p.m., and we went on at 11.30 p.m. Terry went, 'The truck's just pulling up now!' And they were going mad, Simple Minds. Rob [Gretton, New Order's original manager, who died in 1999] came in and said, 'Look, I've worked it out. What we should do is go on and play all the acoustic tracks that don't use electronic equipment. As the gear turns up, we'll put it on stage. You go on, start playing the drums first, and then we'll bring Bernard's amp on, and he can play guitar, and then Hooky's bass.' So that's how we did it.

We even took a boffin out on a tour to Australia, a guy called Martin Usher. He did a lot of telecommunications. He worked on the first Sony camcorder. He was brain-drained to work on artificial intelligence in

California. He was a top guy. It's funny how I got to meet him. During the making of [Joy Division's] *Unknown Pleasures* – and I'm rather ashamed of it – I used to drink brown ale. There was a logic behind it. I would drink drinks that nobody would touch in dressing rooms. I wouldn't dream of drinking that now. I then moved on to Pernod with blackcurrant, and then Pernod with orange. So I started on *Unknown Pleasures* and spilt a bottle of brown ale into my amp. Martin Hannett [Joy Division's producer] got Martin Usher out to fix it. He was an interesting guy. When we were doing the early electronics, we couldn't afford to buy some of the equipment. To buy a sequencer would cost the same as buying a semi-detached house, so I used to build electronics kits, and Martin would advise me.

Stephen Morris (*musician*): If there is one piece of equipment that has a special place in my heart, it's the drum machine that we did 'Blue Monday' on: the Oberheim DMX drum machine. Bernard said, 'What the bloody hell did you get that for?' It's hard to explain, but it's just so much fun. You can't do much with it. It's difficult to explain how a machine has a human feel. You can fall on it, kick it, and it'll still sound like Prince. You can do anything on it. It's like a toy. I do enjoy it. It was a pain at the time, though.

Bernard Sumner: New Order brought about a change in our relationship with pop, and 'Blue Monday' defined this. It's a convergence of rock and dance. 'Blue Monday' was made by post-industrial progressive-rock musicians from an alternative label bravely bringing together what everyone really wanted: thinking beats. It was more than an audio experiment. 'Blue Monday' changed our fashion and the way we look. It was coming anyway, but 'Blue Monday' brought the moment together.

I did most of the work on it, but obviously other people contributed, and Hooky did his bass. It was on the cusp, working with new equipment. It was done with the little sequencer I'd made, and we got a Moog and a new drum machine we'd bought, a DMX. We didn't play encores, and we were getting into a lot of trouble over it. Rather naively, we thought we'd write a song that could be played by machines, and all we'd have to do was press the button. They'd get what they wanted, and we'd get what we wanted. It was an exploration into pure electronic music, so we took the machines to the limit to see what we could do with them. What we could do with them was very basic at the time, so it was making the most out of what little gear we had. I would whack the sequencer to make it work, and Stephen would whack the drum machine, as I remember. He spent all day programming a backing track, and then he caught a power cable to the DMX drum machine with his bloody foot, ripped the power cable out and lost all the drum programming. So we had to start again on the drums. We managed to get most of it, but we lost the original drum for 'Blue Monday'. It was different. It's funny that it's become one of our most famous songs.

It's not really a song, the way I see it. It's more of a machine that sounds good on club systems. I was doing some work with 52nd Street, a Manchester group on Factory Records, kind of funk music, and I was doing some keyboard effects with them. I was going to a lot of clubs with them, clubs I wouldn't normally go to, and listening to the sound systems, the sub-bass frequencies. It never occurred to me to listen to that frequency when I was in Joy Division. We never used *bass* bass really, because Hooky's bass was all middle. We never used bottom end. So we went to a club that had a fantastic sound system, with all this sub-bass, and we used that knowledge on 'Blue Monday'. There was a lot of trickery going on in 'Blue Monday' that you don't realise. It's not just the bass; there are quite a lot of subsonics.

Matthew Horton (*journalist*): Let's be honest – 'Blue Monday' wasn't made in a vacuum. It might've influenced decades of dance and rock music, but it scavenged the archives for plenty of 'inspiration' itself. That drilling bass drum sound, for a start, was an attempt to emulate Giorgio Moroder's pulsations on Donna Summer's 'Our Love'. The rhythm track as well – that's a ringer for Italian post-disco dons Klein

+ MBO's 'Dirty Talk', a record that caught New Order's collective ear when they heard Hewan Clarke playing it at the Haçienda, and the monks' chorus is a straight swipe from Kraftwerk's 'Uranium'. But the genius is in taking elements learnt by osmosis and turning them into something new. Bernard Sumner cites Sylvester's immense disco classic 'You Make Me Feel (Mighty Real)' as a touchstone too, another slice of joy going into the machine and coming out blank.

In the pop world, the 12" single was all about zero imagination. The average extended mix consisted of the 7" with an extra minute of drum fills stuffed in the middle or the intro played twice over or – if the boat was really being pushed out – a spoken-word interlude. 'Blue Monday' realised the possibilities of the form: you could bankrupt yourself with a die-cut sleeve! But you could also write a song fit for purpose, a sprawling monster that could only be accommodated on a massive slab of vinyl. New Order took a practical clubber's format and turned it into an artistic statement.

It wasn't meant to be this pivotal. It was supposed to be an entirely automated excuse to hit the bar early. One of the four would press the button and the track would take care of itself, allowing the band to leave the audience to it. That was before they realised how complicated it was to try and get all these sequencers and drum machines to actually talk to one another. There were dry runs in 'Everything's Gone Green' and '586', but nothing would have the same stark attack. They'd vanquished their own ghost, shaken off any lasting memories of Joy Division and obliterated all preconceptions of what a rock band could do. Even the gloomiest overcoat-sporting rockist could cut a rug to 'Blue Monday' without risking indie points – and that might be its greatest achievement.

The 1983 general election was held on Thursday 9 June, giving Margaret Thatcher's Conservative Party the most decisive victory since that of the Labour Party in 1945. After three years of instability following the 1979 election – during which time the government lowered direct taxes while increasing taxes on spending, sold off public housing and instigated severe austerity measures as rising inflation and unemployment caused Thatcher's popularity to temporarily wane – her first term had started to look shaky and perhaps unsustainable. But victory in the Falklands War had given her personal popularity a boost, while the economy had also started to recover. Thatcher had morphed into the Iron Lady (so called by a Soviet army newspaper), a peacetime victor and trade union slayer. Her landslide gave her a real mandate, one she immediately set out to implement, while the passage of her increasingly radical agenda was now secure. More trade union reform was promised, as was a programme of privatisation that was to include British Telecom, British Airways, British Steel and Rolls-Royce.

Thatcher would also become a keen ally of US President Ronald Reagan, describing him as 'the supreme architect of the West's Cold War victory' (and a firm believer in American exceptionalism). Her relationships with European heads of state were rather more circumspect, not least because she didn't believe in the European Union as a political endeavour. In her book Statecraft, *she would write: 'That such an unnecessary and irrational project as building a European superstate was ever embarked upon will seem in future years to be perhaps the greatest folly of the modern era.'*

Her second term would underscore the divisive nature of her policies, framing her for ever as the most schismatic British leader of modern times. In the words of the former political editor of the Guardian, *Michael White, 'It was Thatcher's misfortune that her insights were not tempered with much sympathetic imagination for people unlike herself – "Is he one of us?" in the famous phrase – or by humour or emollient wit, by homely style or evident personal weakness. Even among the party faithful it made her more admired than loved. Among those she worsted in political battles it all made it much easier to hate her. Few prime ministers in Britain have been burned in effigy.'*

As it was, the Labour Party didn't really stand a chance in the 1983 election, as their vote had already been split by the breakaway Social

Democratic Party. The SDP had been founded in 1981 by four senior Labour moderates, nicknamed the Gang of Four: David Owen, Roy Jenkins, Bill Rodgers and Shirley Williams. Essentially a centrist party, they advocated a mixed economy, European integration, decentralisation and electoral reform. The SDP believed the Labour Party had become too left-wing, what with its commitment to nuclear disarmament and withdrawal from the European Economic Community. They formed an electoral pact with the Liberal Party, but while they took over 25 per cent of the vote, they won only a fraction of Labour-held seats. The damage was done, however. The Labour leader Michael Foot accepted responsibility for his party's defeat, adding that 'the fight to win the next election starts immediately'. Foot would stand down as party leader later in the year, to be replaced by Neil Kinnock.

Nick Logan: We were making it up as we went along on *The Face*. I don't think we started nailing it until around '83. Sales started well and then began to fall away, which is the normal pattern. You launch and then lose, say, 30 per cent, then another 10 per cent. Finally, sales stabilise and climb to a level ahead of where you started. But mine went down, stayed down, and I was desperately worried. 'What do I do? What does it take?' And I couldn't find the answer. But two things definitely moved us forward. One, when Robert Elms came by after the *NME* showed him the door. He wanted to write about the burgeoning club culture and his friends Spandau Ballet. I could easily relate to clubbing culture, if not immediately to the participants. Better still, the *NME* is ignoring it, it's highly photogenic, and I have a young, enthusiastic writer. Then there was Neville Brody. I came across him when *Smash Hits* was looking for an art director. He was fantastic, very talented, but too 'punk' for *Smash Hits*. I thought I'd keep in touch with him and, jumping ahead some eighteen months, we end up sharing office/studio space, him doing his freelance design for books and record companies, me editing *The Face*, by then with a staff of three. Watching us work, Neville wanted to contribute to the magazine, did a few pages and then covers, and that was a huge jump forward. Previously, I'd been doing most of it myself.

Neville Brody (*art director*): *The Face* was a living laboratory where I could experiment and have it published. Our golden rule was to question everything. If a page element existed just as taste or style, it could be abandoned. Page numbers could be letters or shapes increasing in size. We could start the headline on the page before. The office was in this cavernous basement, with Nick Logan's desk in the corner. Half the carpet was wet from flooding. It was far from glamorous. We had an intern turn up in a purple velvet Jean Paul Gaultier suit – he stayed less than a week because he was so disappointed.

David Bailey: With all these new magazines like *i-D* and *The Face*, everything had changed. I eventually got fed up with all the deals I felt we were making at *Ritz*, and I thought the magazine had become too compromised. There were too many freebies, too many holidays and cases of Bordeaux arriving at the office. On the other hand, it was becoming too obsessed with celebrity. I suppose we were anticipating, maybe even helping create, the awful celebrity culture of today, but at least when we were doing it, we tended to celebrate people who had actually achieved something. After a while I'd had enough and wanted out, and so I gave my half of the magazine to David Litchfield for one pound. In hindsight, I was crazy to do it, but by then I'd really had enough and just wanted to walk away. I was so annoyed with the way *Ritz* had turned out that a few years after I walked away, I threw my entire collection into a skip outside my studio in Brownlow Mews. I regret it now, but I just wanted to rid myself of them. Stupid.

After *Ritz*, there came many similar magazines, but they came with another point of view. I always felt *Ritz* was an incredibly sophisticated magazine for its time. The covers were iconic – great covers of Jack Nicholson, Mick Jagger, the great Jordan punk cover, Blondie, Charlotte Rampling . . . dozens of seriously good covers. But we were also starting to feature people like Michael Jackson, which I wasn't sure about. We were also the first magazine to catalogue the Blitz crowd. The magazine was fun while it lasted. I was on the cover of our sixth-anniversary issue in 1982, but that was one of the last times I was involved with the magazine. The last issue was in 1983, No. 78, but by then I was long gone.

Chris Sullivan: What marked the era was that many of us, having seen our friends create successful bands when they could just about play an instrument, seeing other friends promote these bands armed only with an address book and having seen young designers making a name for themselves by creating clothes in their mum's kitchen, we were unafraid to go out on a rather shaky limb and try and do the unexpected. We were not hindered by fear of failure or the need to make fortunes, as we existed in a bubble where everyone was having a go at 'something'. And some succeeded more than others, but none were criticised for trying, only applauded. After all, we were being featured in *i-D* and *The Face*. It was a time of liberation, when all of us felt that nothing was beyond us, that we could be anything we wanted to be, and when many started getting big record deals – Spandau, George Michael, George O'Dowd, Haysi Fantayzee, Sade – and some hit the top of the charts worldwide. That empowered us even further. We knew that we had something special – our youth – and that that was a marketable commodity. And we all helped each other. Young people who promoted nightclubs got their friends to DJ, design flyers, make backdrops, put on fashion shows, read poetry, perform, and allowed many of our pals in for free, while young bands, such as Spandau, got their friends to manage them, cut their hair, design their clothes and album covers, promote their gigs, photograph them, direct their promos. It was a time when if we needed something done, we found a friend to do it.

Robert Elms: Blue Rondo were playing on Barry Island, and we were all in this van, driving to Wales. Somewhere on the M4, around

Reading, Lee Barrett, who was managing this band from Barnet called Pride, asked Sade – my girlfriend at the time – if she could sing. And she said, 'Yes.' Sade, who was wanting to be a clothes designer at this stage, says, 'Yeah. Of course I can.' We stopped at the next service station, and I said, 'What do you mean, you can sing?!' And her exact words were, 'Well, it can't be that hard, can it?' There was just this assumption by that stage that you could do anything. It's like everyone could sing. Bloody hell, if Chris Sullivan claimed he could sing, literally anybody could. Then suddenly people in New York were talking about *The Face* as if it were a bible. *i-D* too. That period felt like you were in this engine and anything was possible.

Betty Page: In May 1983, when I was assistant editor of *Record Mirror*, my good friend the late Gill Smith asked if I would interview a new band she was trying to generate some press for. Odd name: Seona Dancing. Not easy to pronounce – never a great career move. I quite liked their debut single, 'More to Lose'. It wasn't particularly distinctive and was hampered, as I recall, by a glaring Bowie influence, but I agreed to speak to the band as a favour to her. That's the way things worked with record company press officers in those days: 'You mention my tiddlers, and I might catch your magazine a bigger fish some time.' When I met the duo, I found them both engaging. Bill Macrae was tall, shy and quietly spoken, and his partner was small, dark and beyond chatty. His name? Ricky Gervais.

Ricky Gervais (*comedian, actor, director*): I went to university to study biology, and after two weeks I thought, 'Hold on, I didn't come to university to study, I came to join a rock band. I was thin, with great hair and a jawbone . . . I tried to be a cross between David Bowie, Roxy Music, Tears for Fears and Japan. I wore make-up.

Betty Page: The pair had met the year before while studying philosophy [Gervais had switched from biology] at University College

London. Bill heard that Ricky could sing and asked him to put words to his music. After a cabaret-style residency at a cafe in Brussels, they made a demo and got a deal with Decca. This was pre-Pet Shop Boys, but there were several notable duos around – Soft Cell, Yazoo and Blancmange being three of them. When I interviewed them, Ricky was certainly entertaining, but I saw little evidence of the comedy genius to come, when he would again pair up with a tall bloke. 'We're a duo, we're young, we write songs, we've got a disco beat, piano, synth, and you could draw comparisons with anyone,' Gervais told me. 'You could say we're like Blancmange, because I'm short and he's tall, but it's not really relevant. We're definitely more passionate than the average duo.' Passionate *and* sensitive, it seems. Said Gervais, 'I just think generally it's more sensitive . . . But that's pretentious! The technical side comes easily, so we concentrate more on songwriting. That sounds pretentious too!'

Ricky Gervais: We got signed on a demo tape, released two records, and they failed. I was dropped. That was the end of it . . . I was a pop star for a year. I saw David Bowie perform '"Heroes"' on TV when I was about sixteen. I thought, 'Oh wow, this is amazing. I want to do that.' [So] I learnt to play guitar. I ripped off David Bowie badly.

Betty Page: When I asked the inevitable, if lazy, pop writer's fall-back question, 'What are your influences?' he said, 'Well, I really like our music, actually. I quite enjoy listening to it. I've never bought a record in my life, so I haven't got any others.' Aha – the first sign of irony twinned with arrogance . . . 'I went through a phase when I was fourteen, fifteen, when things had to mean something and be deep, and my favourites were always Cat Stevens and Simon and Garfunkel, deeper music that wasn't very commercial.'

(Cat Stevens and Simon and Garfunkel in 'not very commercial' shock . . .)

Ricky Gervais: After the success of *The Office*, David Bowie and I became pen pals and started exchanging funny emails about art and everything. When he came over to England, he invited me to dinner 'with some very old friends'. So me and my girlfriend went along to this place in Richmond, and there was us and these people – David Bowie, Richard E. Grant, Pete Townshend – all having dinner. The night before, I'd been on Paul Merton's *Room 101*, and they'd showed a clip of Seona Dancing, the New Romantic band I was in forty years ago, which is me basically doing a Bowie impression. So at dinner the next night, David Bowie comes up to me and says, 'Seems I owe you an apology. I saw you on TV last night and I think I've been ripping you off for the last thirty years.' I went, 'Yeah, all right, calm down, it wasn't just me, it was everyone else in 1983 ripping you off.'

It was just really sweet, do you know what I mean? I remember asking him a few things about his work [in my emails]. I think I told him once that he was my favourite, but then never again. Then I plucked up the courage to ask him to be in *Extras*. I said, 'I thought the joke would be that I bump into you, and you're just really awful to me.' I thought, 'Wouldn't it be funny if he was an arsehole?' He liked the idea, and so I sent him the lyrics for 'Little Fat Man'. I then called him up and said, 'Can you do something retro, like a "Life on Mars?"-type thing.' And he said, 'Oh sure, I'll just knock out a quick fucking "Life on Mars?" for you.' I just started laughing – like, who am I to be telling Bowie what to do?

When Gervais and his writing partner Stephen Merchant were in pre-production for Extras, *their follow-up to* The Office, *they were both amazed at how self-deprecating the celebrities they asked to be on the show could be, and how prepared they were to laugh at themselves. Of all the people they asked to cameo – Patrick Stewart, Johnny Depp, Chris Martin, Kate Winslet, etc. – the one who had the most effect on them was David Bowie. In fact, they acted rather like the Blitz Kids had done twenty-five years earlier. Stephen Merchant:*

'Ricky had somehow got David Bowie's number, and he called him and was on speaker phone, and he answered and said, "Hello, Rick, I'm just eating a banana." And we're like, "Whoah! David Bowie eats bananas! I eat bananas!" Just the idea that he's at home with his supermodel wife – "Iman, have we got any bananas?"'

Ricky Gervais: I loved Japan, and my first attempt at New Romantic make-up was copied from David Sylvian. I did all this white make-up on my face, but then I forgot about doing my neck, so I ended up looking like a mime. Never mind. We did two singles and then we were dropped, probably because Tears for Fears had become successful. They had fifty groups like us, and I'm not surprised they dropped us, and actually now I'm rather glad they did.

The successful groups were moving from a place where the emphasis was on the particular to somewhere where the focus was on the universal. In Spandau Ballet's case, the band that recorded 'Chant No. 1' were a very different proposition from the one that delivered 'True'. Around this time, Spandau's club-centric image changed too, and they swapped their harsh New Romantic threads for smart, expensive, tailored pastel suits, at exactly the same time as David Bowie – who, on his Serious Moonlight *tour in 1983, with his custard-coloured hair, could easily have been the sixth member of Spandau. Their biggest hits are part of the pop radio continuum.*

Gary Kemp: 'True' was written about Clare Grogan. She was the inspiration, and she also gave me a copy of Nabokov's *Lolita*, and I used a couple of lines out of it for the song – 'seaside arms'. We were an underground band for eighteen months, but then we were on *Top of the Pops* six times, so it's very difficult to be alternative when you're on TV all the time. So *True* was a conscious effort to try and write a pop album, to try and write some blue-eyed soul that would get us into the charts. I stopped worrying about the rhythm or the sound of the synthesizer and started worrying about the melodies. We were becoming bigger and bigger, and when you start to play bigger halls, you need different types of material, which is why we changed our sound so much. We were a really great live band – we had a terrific sound, a terrific live show, and Tony's voice was better than anyone else's at the time. And I stand by all of that.

Jon Moss (*musician*): One of the most magical things was meeting George, because he showed me so much. I was into the whole punk phase, but I missed out completely on the Blitz scene because I couldn't be bothered and I didn't understand it. So from two separate poles came these two people – and George was this wild thief, this crazy nutcase, this fucking lunatic. And for some strange reason we got on instantly. It was like a love affair. We found ourselves getting caught up with each other, never touching but running parallel. When Culture Club started, the energy was formidable . . . it was the first time in my life I felt as though nothing could stop me. Real power!

Mikey Craig: It's hard to talk about because it was Jon and George's relationship. But I think when there are two members in a band who have a relationship, it becomes this kind of dominating force. It worked in a good way, in that I think a lot of creativity came out of it, but at the same time, it was quite destructive. That's kind of why we fizzled out.

This was the year when the tabloids went Pop!, when the lives and loves of Boy George, Simon Le Bon, Annie Lennox and the Kemp brothers became front-page news. The pop stars believed their own publicity too, and many – particularly Duran Duran – began living the life of dilettantes and new-moneyed aristocrats, poncing about on boats and dating catwalk models. They had taken reinvention to its natural conclusion. Five years before their huge success, they had looked as though they were made of money, even though their pockets were empty; now, the good life was theirs for the taking. And they took it, each with both hands. Greed was good, after all, and credit so easy to come by, while dreams and wishes seemed so readily obtainable. In a way, success became democratised, and worlds that had once been available only to certain sets of people became accessible to, if not everyone, then at least anyone with enough luck and tenacity.

'Our legacy has been underplayed over the years,' says Culture Club's Roy Hay. 'Without us, you don't get Madonna, Lady Gaga or Marilyn Manson. We opened up those barriers and we didn't need to say anything. We just stood there, and it was obvious the message was, "Here we are, check this out." If you grew up with a Culture Club poster on the wall in eighties America, I doubt you're voting for Trump now.'

The pop world wasn't just fashionable, it was sexy too, and the arrival of androgynous celebrities such as Boy George and Annie Lennox put a whole new spin on Swinging London. Pop stars began hanging out with fashion designers and frequenting the many nightclubs that were springing up all over the capital. PR agencies were beginning to exploit this new-found confluence of art and commerce, and the high street began taking notice of all the new money.

As pop became big business, the tabloids began encouraging readers to phone in with stories about celebrities. Had they seen one misbehaving? Had they grown up with one? Consequently, the features teams of the nationals became less averse to the telephonic ramblings of overexcited readers. One night at the Daily Mirror, *one of the phones on the news desk rings. The night editor picks it up, only to find a very excited chap on the other end.*

'Hello, is that the Daily Mirror? *It is? Oh good. I just wanted to let you know that I've invented a time machine,' said the man.*

'Aha, a time machine. I see . . .' said the night editor, with a heavy heart.

'Yes, it's a rather good time machine as it goes forward in time, backwards in time, and sideways in time. It really is the most amazing thing you've ever seen.'

'Well, that certainly does sound interesting. What would you like us to do about it? How about you bring it in to show us here at the paper?'

This chap can't believe his luck, and stammers for a while before answering, in typically breathless fashion, 'Yes, absolutely. When would you like me to bring it in?'

Just a split second before he quietly replaces the receiver, the night editor says, 'Yesterday.'

David Johnson: Insolence and narcissism lit a torch that led a generation through what might have been a dark age, for by 1983 one-third of Britain's jobless were under twenty-five. The blitzkrieg took a giant leap for everyone on the right side of forty, especially in TV and publishing, which had lost touch with the young, just as the politicians had. Crucial magazines lit the way, television launched edgy 'yoof' programmes that broke taboos so every clubber who wasn't 'putting a band together' was 'submitting a treatment to Channel 4', which had decided close to its 1982 launch to target a fifteen–thirties audience. Marketing and retail too had to have 'one of those kids with blue hair'.

Jon Cummins (*TV researcher/chairman of Channel 4*): In 1982, I was at university in Durham, and I was obsessed with television and kept sending ideas to companies, trying to get a job. In the end, I was lucky enough to be seconded as holiday relief to the production team of *The Tube*, which was launching at the end of the year, so I felt desperately inadequate at the prospect of being around the lethally hip researchers and the fearless reputations of the presenters, Jools Holland and Paula Yates. *The Tube* would reinvent youth television and became one of the most influential TV shows of the decade. It went out live at 5.30 on a Friday night for ninety minutes and was the start of the weekend. Jools turned out to be eccentric and charming and always cracking jokes, dressed in a three-piece suit and riffing on lots of different subjects, from ancient history to jazz, blues . . . whatever. Paula was pregnant but insisted on wearing a tutu, and was outrageous and lovely. I'd go down to Paula's dressing room, and she'd get changed while I was there, which nearly gave me a heart attack. But I fell in love with them at first sight, and they were so kind to me. Like everyone else on the show, they cared about the quality of the material, about the quality of the live bands and about the authenticity of everything we did. The team were unbelievable – Malcolm Gerrie, Andrea Wonfor, Paul Corley . . . It was such an intoxicating time – not only the revolution that was happening on television on Channel 4, but what was happening in clubland, in fashion, in music. For instance, Frankie Goes to Hollywood were discovered by *The Tube*, not by a record company. We were the first people to do Prince. *The Tube* cared passionately about the music, and it was all about reverence for the artist. I soon got involved in content, and we'd do things like getting Jools and Peter York to do a history of the Jaguar motor car, told through popular culture. It was a big bet, but it worked. Channel 4 was trying to do dramatic things for young people, and we even had a commissioner for youth. The charter articulated that we had to innovate in form and content, serve audiences and minorities, those not served well elsewhere, and bring different voices to the screen. Channel 4 invented youth programming, because there wasn't a single TV company on planet Earth that had a department of youth. Anything edgy was late at night, and we wanted to be mainstream. So if you were a young person, it was the first time ever in your history you saw yourself reflected on TV, you saw your passions reflected on TV and you saw your heroes reflected on TV. It was a new thing for people both to feel part of that and to go and start their own band or do their own thing or start their own club or whatever it was, because we were rejoicing in this era of difference in innovation and this pioneering spirit. It was very much a celebration, as opposed to an analysis, of these things. When I was at Channel 4 myself, Jeremy Isaacs would come round to my and most executives' offices at least once a week and basically say, 'Where the fuck is the new stuff? What are you doing that is new? What are you doing that's never been on television before?'

The high-water mark of the new pop was November 1983, when Boy George appeared on the cover of Rolling Stone, *with the cover line 'SPECIAL ISSUE: England Swings. Great Britain invades America's music and style. Again.' The issue was designed to celebrate the fact that the US charts were once again full of British acts – everyone from Culture Club, the Eurythmics, U2, Big Country, the Alarm and Aztec Camera to Duran Duran, Kajagoogoo, the Police, Madness, the Human League, A Flock of Seagulls and Soft Cell. There were more British artists in the US charts than there had been at the height of Beatlemania, nearly twenty years earlier. 'A revolution in sound and style – lying somewhere between artful ingenuity and pure pop fun – has taken root in this country over the past year and a half,' sang the editorial. 'Much like the first explosion of pop culture upon mass consciousness, which commenced with the Beatles' arrival in America in February 1964, the primary impetus for all this has been emanating from the far side of the Atlantic. We are in the throes of a second British invasion.'*

On 16 July, there had been eighteen British singles in the American Top 40, which topped the previous record of fourteen, set on 18 June 1965. 'This term new music – an umbrella for everything from punk to synth pop, New Romantic or Oi – does not so much describe a single style as it draws a line in time, distinguishing what came before from what has come after. New Music betokens a kind of pop modernism with a British bias, without getting too specific. It can be said to have originated in the UK around 1977 with the noisy infidel insurrections of the Clash, the Sex Pistols and the Jam, and it continues in a broken line and through all manner of phases and stages – to the present day, with such artists as Culture Club, Duran Duran and Big Country . . . [And] when it came to MTV, the British won out, hands down. Next to the prosaic, foursquare appearance of the American bands, such performers as Duran Duran seemed like caviar.' (The week Rolling Stone *was published, twenty of the entries in the US Top 50 album chart were British.)*

The Brits weren't just feted in public, they were loved by celebrities too. Andy Warhol struck up a very public friendship with Nick Rhodes, a man who was said to have based much of his persona on Warhol. In an interview in The Face, *Warhol said, 'I love him. I worship him. I masturbate to Duran Duran's videos.' Rhodes's appreciation is more measured: 'I loved Andy. I often think about him. Now, he's become so much larger than life, even more so than he was then. And it's amazing how prophetic his personal vision was. He pretty much invented the twenty-first century, with his imagery and his obsession with fame. He would have loved these reality-TV things.'*

On Duran's first trip to New York, Rhodes was asked what he'd most like to do, and having said, 'Meet Andy Warhol,' the next day the band's record company, Capitol, made it happen. When Warhol was taken to their show, he went backstage to meet them. 'I told them how great they were. They all wore lots of make-up, but they had their girlfriends with them from England, so I guess they're all straight, but it was hard to believe. We went to Studio 54 in their white limo, and [co-owner] Steve Rubell was really nice to them. He took them to the booth and gave them drinks.'

Dave Stewart: In 1982, Annie and I went to Australia with the Tourists, but the band broke up and we ended up in a hotel in Wagga Wagga. I had a little black and yellow Wasp synthesizer and was making didgeridoo sounds. When Annie started singing along, we thought, 'Maybe we could make weird and experimental electronic music?' On the flight home, we split up as a couple but kept on with the music, carting the gear in a second-hand horsebox. At one gig, we played to four people, drove home through the night in the snow and had to stop the car. It was 6 a.m., and Annie was crying. I realised we needed some proper equipment, so we went to see the bank manager. Sat in his office, we were this odd couple. I was taking speed. Annie wasn't. Amazingly, he lent us £5,000. I couldn't get any of the new equipment to work. By this point, Annie was totally depressed. She was curled up on the floor in the foetal position, when I managed to produce this beat and riff. She suddenly went, 'What the hell is that?' and leapt up and started playing the other synthesizer. Between the two duelling synths we had the beginnings of 'Sweet Dreams (Are Made of This)'. It's the most misheard lyric in British pop. People think I'm singing, 'Sweet dreams are made of cheese.' It was a juggernaut rhythm, but it wasn't a song. Quickly, Annie did this startling rant which began, 'Sweet dreams are made of this . . .' It was mind-blowing, but depressing, so I suggested the 'Hold your head up, moving on' bit to make it more uplifting. We thought we'd done something miraculous, so we were disillusioned by other people's initial reactions to it. The record company said there wasn't a chorus, so they didn't see it as a single. But when a radio DJ in Cleveland kept playing it from the album, his studio phones lit up. The label relented, and it was a global hit and No. 1 in the US. People went bonkers for the video, which was constantly on MTV. I wanted to make a commentary on the music business but also something a bit performance art – weird and dreamlike. So we mocked up a record company boardroom in a studio in Wardour Street and put a cow in it, to signify reality. There we were: Annie and I laid flat on a table, and this cow, which was peeing everywhere.

Annie Lennox (*singer, musician*): We'd come out of the end of the Tourists battered and bruised. We were massively in debt, and I'd come across some real monsters in the music business. I'd lived in so many bedsits and was desperately unhappy. We'd survived, kinda, but it was tough. I felt like we were in a dream world, that whatever we were chasing was never going to happen. All this poured into 'Sweet Dreams'. From that first line, it's not a happy song. It's dark. 'Sweet dreams are made of this' is basically me saying, 'Look at the state of us. How can it get worse?' I was feeling very vulnerable. The song was an expression of how I felt: hopeless and nihilistic. 'I travelled the world and the seven seas, everybody's looking for something' was about how we're all in this perpetual state of seeking. It's about surviving the world. It's not a normal song so much as a weird mantra that goes round and round, but somehow it became our theme song. We wanted our visual statements to be strong and powerful, because we knew they'd be there for ever. I wore a suit in the video, with my cropped hair. I was trying to be the opposite of the cliché of the female singer. I wanted to be as strong as a man, equal to Dave and perceived that way. Wearing wigs and taking them off again was about the affectations that women create to become acceptable or beautiful to men, about removing masks and how none of it is real. People didn't always get that or understand the irony of it. Because of lines like 'Some of them want to use you . . . some of them want to be abused,' people think it's about sex or S&M, and it's not about that at all.

Peter Ashworth: I was going out with Annie at the time, and I think she got a bit freaked that it was going to break the band up because Dave was still madly in love with her. I think Dave was always in love with Annie, actually, so it was a surreptitious relationship. The famous *Touch* album cover actually started out as a cover for *The Face*. It's the one that people think 'Sweet Dreams' is on, the androgynous one. She did her own make-up, she bought a bag of clothes – I mean, literally just played about. She had the idea for the mask already. She wanted to play on the strong-arm pose. I don't know if the mask came in because I'd started to do my fetish work. I did do a couple of shots with Annie in PVC, which were never used and I've never released, because I tend to promise everyone I photograph, 'Let's try something out, and if you don't like it, no one's going to see it.' And I actually always kept to those promises. This was one of my best days ever, because it was so productive. There was no faffing about, there weren't other personalities involved. We were just there to do a job.

The cover of Touch *was one of the most iconic, and certainly one of the most memorable, album covers of the decade: a photograph of Annie Lennox with cropped orange hair, blindfolded, with her fists raised in a strongman pose, possibly ready for combat. It's often thought of as the cover of* Sweet Dreams, *and has actually become the defining image of the Eurythmics, the picture people conjure up when reminded who they were. It plays with contradiction, with vulnerability and power, with masculinity and femininity. And for an image produced in the middle of the designer decade, its graphics were strangely ad hoc. The sleeve's designer, Laurena Stevens, added a deft graphic touch to the cover by using a mixture of typefaces, in what was largely a happy accident. 'I'd run out of most of my Letraset,' says Stevens, 'so I just created the titles for each of the tracks on the album using whatever I had, mixing upper case and lower case with different fonts.'*

Simon Napier-Bell: In 1983, the Eurythmics topped both the British and American charts with 'Sweet Dreams (Are Made of This)'. They were a duo, and the mainstay of their image was Annie's masculine hairdo. But when MTV executives saw what Annie looked like, they got themselves into a tizz. They refused to play the group's video until a birth certificate had been sent from England proving that Annie wasn't an unusually dressed male.

Fiona Dealey: You'd go to the Wag Club and you'd see all these famous people, as it became the club where all the bands went – Culture Club, Wham!, Sade, Eurythmics, Blue Rondo, Bananarama . . . I used to go to the Wag quite a lot then, but never when they had bands on. I'd rather bump into George Michael at the bar than watch JoBoxers interrupt my conversation.

I first saw Wham! in July 1983, at the launch of their debut LP Fantastic *(such confidence!), in a small suite of offices just behind Fulham Broadway tube station in London. While dozens of sneering music journalists and record company bigwigs stood about, working at being brilliant, the two nineteen-year-old soul boys, dressed in Hawaiian shirts, cutaway jeans and deck shoes, jived together on the dancefloor, jitterbugging along to their own version of the Miracles' 'Love Machine'. Rarely had I seen two men enjoying themselves so much. To be dancing to one of their own records! At their own party! In front of other people!*

For a while, we even shared a tailor, Wham! and me. From his shop in Kentish Town, an ex-boxer called Chris Ruocco (introduced to me by Chris Sullivan) would knock up the most delightful suits and stage costumes for the boys, and though it would be unusual to see George on the premises, you'd occasionally see Andrew trying on a new pair of trousers, his hot hatchback double-parked out front.

George was less homeboy than homely boy. If he was the suburban sonneteer, happy in his bedroom writing tear-jerkers, then Andrew was the quintessential party animal, the Liam Gallagher of his day, unable to leave a party without a bottle of Moët in one hand and a bottle blonde in the other. It was Andrew who realised George's pop ambitions, Andrew who acted the extrovert to George's shy loner. George might have written the songs (in four years Andrew gained only three co-writing credits: for 'Wham Rap!', 'Club Tropicana' (No. 4, July 1983) and 'Careless Whisper'), yet it was his partner who looked the part when they sang them. Andrew's image would crystallise on the twelve-inch version of 'I'm Your Man' (No. 1, November 1985): a racing car is heard careering through a plate-glass window, followed by the sound of its driver cackling with laughter as he asks, 'Where's the bar?'

The boys were managed for a time by sixties impresario Simon Napier-Bell, but it was always George who had the vision thing, even at school. There was nothing haphazard about this affair, and Wham!'s seemed organised with staggering efficiency. Their songs were hardly arch (unlike, say, the Pet Shop Boys), but even to the untrained ear one instinctively knew the people behind them weren't stupid. Not only were they perfect fodder for twelve-year-old girls, but they also had a superior ironic quality. Whether you were an art student or an estate agent, you knew they were cool.

Simon Napier-Bell: We were all very competitive with each other. I mean, I don't think they talked about it in competitive terms, but of course George and Andrew were looking at the others. Sometimes they liked them a lot, and sometimes they didn't. All of the groups were competitive. Don't you remember when Boy George made endless bitchy comments about Wham!? There was a moment when we went to America to film the 'Careless Whisper' video. They saw that Culture Club were playing, so they asked our tour manager if he could call them up and get a couple of seats left at the stage door so they could come and see the show. And a message came back saying, 'No, you can't.'

Elton John (*icon*): George [Michael] was always great fun to be with. He was never afraid to speak his mind. Like me, he'd often get himself into trouble by saying what he really thought. He was straightforward, which meant you always knew where you stood with him – rather than someone who will be nice in front of you and then horrible behind your back. So meeting up with George was always an event because he had such a definite opinion on everything, and when opinions clashed, it would make for an interesting evening. People genuinely adored George, and it wasn't just the music. They felt for him and they felt his struggles; he was completely authentic. He wasn't touring all the time or putting records out year after year. He was a true star. When you saw George perform, you were going to see someone who really could sing beautifully and move you with his music. It was a treat. With all his trials, tribulations and the publicity, people could relate to the imperfection. We're all imperfect and we all have our flaws. He had his fair share of pain in life, and this came out in his songs. He wrote unbelievable melodies and had an amazing voice. I never heard him sing a bad note. You can hear every emotion in his voice – pain, sorrow and joy – and that's the mark of a truly great singer. George could sing anybody's lyric and make it sound like his, and that's an extraordinary talent to have – to be able to interpret his own and other people's songs in different ways every time he performed them.

George Michael: We [Wham!] knocked Duran Duran from No. 1, then Frankie Goes to Hollywood knocked us off, then 'Careless Whisper' knocked them off. I really loved that. I never felt threatened. I must admit, I never thought the Frankies would be around for very long. All the English bands were dependent on other people for songwriting, production . . . you name it.

Elton John: One of my earliest memories with George is of him and I sitting in a car just off Hyde Park listening to 'Wake Me Up Before You Go-Go' on cassette, and I said, 'This is the nearest record I've heard to Motown.' It was – and still is – just such a brilliant record, and we went on to have a brilliant relationship. George was a very private man. He always had the mystique thing about him. He wanted to keep things private, had his own group of friends and didn't want people to know everything about him. Of course, he lived under massive scrutiny, and some artists would do anything for that level of publicity all the time. Not George, though. You can always tell a George Michael song from the intonation of his words and the way he breathes and the way he phrases. I will always remember him for his wonderful music, his kindness and his beautiful voice. Voices like that don't come along that often.

Simon Napier-Bell: Andrew had given George the courage to stand up and be a pop star – to be on stage, to be in the public eye – but, with that accomplished, his usefulness had become limited. George was working night and day to make an album, while Andrew was getting drunk and having a good time. Elton, on the other hand, provided the perfect model for George to follow in his new career as a solo artist: in charge of his own business and his own life, able to make every decision himself, good or bad. He was self-managed, self-sufficient and self-confident. Once George had seen it close up, it had to be what he aspired to from then on. Which left Andrew precisely nowhere. As soon as the second album had been recorded, released, promoted and sold to its maximum potential, it already seemed obvious – Wham! were due for deletion.

Fiona Dealey: I really don't remember people saying anything about their ambitions. It was just small talk. I just remember at any club you went to, somebody would come up and say, 'I'm gonna be a photographer,' or 'I'm gonna be a director' or 'a journalist', 'I want to be a singer,' and you just would think, 'Oh, OK.' Then it would happen. So [Boy] George wanted to have a band, and so George got Culture Club, George got a record deal. Sade was a backing singer for Pride, and then she became the lead. I made dresses for her, she got a really great record deal – it all seemed really easy. It seemed like anything we wanted to do came true. The ones who got lost were the fashion designers – us. We never really made the same sort of money as the pop singers or the journalists or the photographers . . . But even then, everything anybody said came true. I didn't question it. None of us did. I think we had the most amazing time. I didn't like being at St Martin's, I didn't enjoy being on the fashion course, but I look back now and realise how lucky we were. It was kind of like going to Oxford or Cambridge, but I'm afraid I took it for granted.

1984
THE PLEASUREDOME

'It was much more baroque. I think what happened is that as we became a successful touring band, we were no longer those kids in the street, we were no longer going to those clubs. Even though London is an exciting place, all of those poor Blitz Kids were becoming rich kids because they were becoming successful.'

GARY KEMP

Kim Bowen: I went to Australia in 1981, got married, and when that went wrong, I moved back to London in 1984. I'd started working for *Harper's Bazaar* in Australia, and came back and started working on *Blitz*. The thing that shocked me about moving back was how many people were on heroin. There were drugs literally everywhere. I thought it was odd that George O'Dowd and I always used to go on about bloody hippies and people smoking weed, and now everyone was on smack. It was funny, everyone at that time was either a stylist or on heroin. *Blitz* was a hovel. I had this tiny shithole of an office and an assistant who worked for free. She was on the dole, and that's how she got paid, but it was really fun, really exciting. Tim Hulse was my editor, who I always loved, and John Galliano was on the cover of the first issue I worked on. A lot of vulnerable people who had come through the clubs were now in positions of power, which created an incredibly diverse and creative environment. Some fell by the wayside and suffered through drugs, but others soared. Some did both. Someone like George – I remember when I met him, with that bright green face, just thinking, 'You were born to be a star.' And it was such a relief when he did make it. It was delightful, because there were so many people who didn't.

Boy George: I worked bloody hard for Culture Club at the beginning, because I was hungry. I worked much harder than anyone else in the band. Culture Club was my every breath, it was every minute of every day. I became besotted with Culture Club. I worked so fucking hard at making it work that I don't feel ashamed at being a celebrity. I used to run round to *i-D* and *The Face* with my band's pictures. The others never did any of that.

Malcolm McLaren: [Boy] George gave you visual imagery right between the eyes. If it hadn't been George, it would have been another guy from the Blitz. George was hungry and a bit more tenacious than the rest, plus he was incredibly hard working and he had talent. He was even more popular than I think he thought he'd be. He was very clever and took all the old Tamla Motown stuff and proved that you could *still* regurgitate it. I mean, Holland–Dozier–Holland don't just go away! All this androgynous stuff has always gone on, [but] England had this incredible craze at the time for homosexuals and lesbians. For some reason, it was decided that coming out of the closet was something everybody wanted to discuss, *and* it sold newspapers. I loved watching Marilyn on TV because, just like everyone else, I wanted to see what his dress looked like, how he was going to take off his jacket. Sade? Art-school nonsense. Nik Kershaw? Wimp rock. Duran Duran? More wimp rock. The Thompson Twins? I once said that if they went to Africa, they'd be stoned to death. I was being facetious. [However,] the Thompson Twins fed off ethnic culture without creating anything new.

Boy George: After Culture Club's first *Top of the Pops* performance, there was Wally of the Week in one of the papers. There was the whole is it a bird, is it a plane? I mean, it was just amazing. The press were quite horrible, but people in the street were really embracing and nice. Nobody had cameras then, but people would come up and get things signed or just talk to you. It was really exciting. But the tabloids, you could really work with them, although I didn't realise in the early days that it's a trade-off. When the papers got a whiff of the drug issue, they went into overdrive. People chasing me in cars, following me to people's houses – it was relentless. And then friends selling stories. It was quite a lot to deal with. When you're doing drugs, you're not exactly a rational human being; your reaction to it isn't helpful either. It was just an insane time; some of the things that happened were just so bonkers. I felt like a fox. I remember, I think it was David Hogan – it was quite a big paparazzo – he was following me one night, and I was driving a lime-green car I bought off my brother, and he was driving a Porsche, and I basically almost made him crash into the back of me on Hamilton Terrace. I got out of the car and said, 'If you keep following me, your car is going to be a write-off.' And he just took my picture and drove off. There wasn't much of a collegiate relationship with anyone else, either. Every other star was a threat, even other gay singers – like there was only room for one gay singer. It's a very British thing, this idea that somebody else's success is your own failure. I was really good friends with George Michael, but when he became famous he was kind of cagey with me. I guess I was seen as the queen bitch then, not somebody who kept their mouth shut. I like consistency. There were people that would speak to you one day, and then the next time they saw you they would ignore you. And I'm someone that likes certainty. If you don't like me, that's fine, but just keep it up. I've found that the really charming and consistent people are the real legends, who don't need to talk behind your back. Maybe when you're legendary, you're more confident.

Jon Moss: I got really frightened in Culture Club because it was my life, you know? I was touring all year, doing interviews, and it was *all* Culture Club. You start to get scared after a while. It's like being married, and you think, 'If anything goes wrong with the band, my whole life's going to hit rock bottom,' which is a terrible way to start thinking. I was quite pleased when 'The Medal Song' didn't do well. It was quite a masochistic thing, but it meant we would have to think about what we were doing and work harder. Having said that, *Waking Up with the House on Fire* [released in October 1984] sold about five million around the world. It was a big success, but it rode on the others to a certain extent. If you're in a very successful pop group – which most people aren't, that's why it's difficult to understand – you get to a stage where no matter how well you plan, the tidal wave sweeps over the top of you, and in the end you don't know what you're doing. [With fans] when you start you get a few real fanatics who are very sweet, and you tend to look after them, but you quickly realise if you're too nice to some of the more crazy ones, they start getting a bit funny and start having a one-sided relationship with you. Then you get the fans who go with you on your initial outburst for the first year or so, and then they'll go on to Frankie [Goes to Hollywood] or whoever. Then you've got the fans who are still there when you go through a trough and who write letters of encouragement. Then you get the people who go, 'Fucking Jon Moss . . . fucking Boy George . . . fucking queers.' Culture Club were always about the things that you could have if you really wanted them. We said it doesn't matter if you hadn't got a penny, go and get a dishcloth and look brilliant.

Boy George: To be good you've got to have a certain amount of evil in you, because if you don't know what evil is, you can't be good. You've got to have some perception of what is nasty in order to avoid it. Just look at the police – they're the most evil bastards in the world. You have to be criminally minded to understand the mind of a criminal. The police used me, they really used me. They had a real bumper Christmas package because of me. The whole operation was called 'Operation Culture', can you believe that? That's how fucking corny it was. And they were watching my family, all my friends. They wanted to get me so bad . . . and they went out of their way to get me. I remember when they were searching my house, I was sitting there being so rude to them. I was saying, 'You bunch of pigs, I hate you!' I wasn't in my Buddhist state at the time! I just couldn't believe their cheek, their whole fucking pathetic attitude. You should have heard the things they said to me. The second time I was arrested they beat me up in the cells of Harrow Road police station. The first thing this policewoman said to me was, 'Have you got Aids?' So I spat in her face and said, 'No, but you have.' What a fucking cheek. Basically, they made my life very, very difficult. But in the end they got what they wanted: they got me, and they also got all the publicity that went with it. To the public they looked like they were doing their job – *'We've arrested a famous pop star and saved society once again.'* They know that everybody involved in the music industry is dropping ecstasy; they just like making examples of people. They knew about me and they obviously had to do something . . . but they acted like complete fucking animals. They stopped my family everywhere they went. One of the worst things I remember from the heroin period was this journalist standing outside my house on Christmas Day, waiting for me to die. He actually said to my mother, 'Well, I can't go, he might drop dead.' What the fuck can you do with people like that? But I don't really care what people write about me any more. There was some old dragon who wrote a three-day extravaganza in the *Mirror* exposing all of Jon's flings and all the women he got off with. But so what? I knew all that, that's why our relationship ended. All this bitching was so silly.

Malcolm McLaren continued to pursue his portmanteau career by releasing Fans, *a semi-successful attempt at fusing opera and dance music, overlaying arias from* Madame Butterfly *and* Carmen *with rap. Ever the media provocateur, this was another project that came girded with ideology, although this didn't make it any less fun. He loved weaving stories around his projects. 'Elvira, the wife of Puccini, would spike his coffee with bromide to suppress his urges for their young dinner guests,' he said. 'And then Doria, their maid, died of poison, yes, after Elvira accused her of mounting Puccini while he lay ill.'* Fans *not only showed how eclectic McLaren could be, it also afforded him yet another opportunity to tamper with the architecture of tradition. Like his Sex Pistols cohort Jamie Reid, McLaren could be guaranteed to offer disruption whenever he was presented with an opportunity involving the Establishment. In fact, he seemed programmed to disrupt. One of his minor obsessions was the Union Jack. He was convinced that both Scotland and Wales would one day leave the union, and that once this had happened, the flag would need to be reinvented, or at the very least accessorised. He always felt that the Cross of Saint George looked too much like the Red Cross symbol, and thought that any new version of the English flag should include a pineapple – not because it was still recognised as the international symbol of hospitality and welcome, but as a way of acknowledging the importance of Caribbean immigration. McLaren's reluctance to do anything with this idea was simply due to the fact that he couldn't work out a way of making any money from it.*

Malcolm McLaren: The greatest thing is taking something that is so historic and marrying it with something as modern as R&B and putting it on the streets, away from the hoi polloi, and making Carmen a wonderful Times Square stripper and Cho-Cho-San that little, lost, innocent housewife living in St Albans. Carmen attracted me because she was the extreme opposite of the ardent, trustful and innocent Cho-Cho-San. She was a tough, anarchic, wild and free sort of woman who was almost admired by both sexes. She could have been a gang leader. With opera, you don't have to worry about what they're singing about, you feel it anyway. The emotion behind the lady's voice is such that once married with an interpretation such as the R&B singer's doing, you really know what she's singing about.

Jon Savage: Much of the bitterness surrounding the end of the Sex Pistols had hinged on the question of authorship. *The Great Rock'n'Roll Swindle* film had been McLaren's attempt to tell the whole story from this perspective – that he had originated and planned the whole thing.

It was the old, classic battle between manager and performer, which the artist is always bound to win, if only because he or she is in the public eye. So McLaren did the logical thing: he reinvented himself as a performer. 'Being a mercenary in the form of a manager centred me in a position which I didn't want any part of,' McLaren told me in 1983. 'I preferred, in the end, to opt out. My own inspiration, I couldn't secure that in Boy George or Bow Wow Wow. I never had the confidence at the time. Maybe I never saw myself as a presenter in terms of being the artist.'

Malcolm McLaren: When I worked with Vivienne in Worlds End, there was always a happy marriage between sound and vision, and I could harness it to a record. You could make a splash, even if it was on the catwalks of Paris for half an hour. After *Fans*, I had finished with Vivienne *and* the record business. Vivienne left me and went off and tried to market the clothes as best she could.

Vivienne Westwood: I hate the underground, always did. Just being in a corner or a tunnel, it's just a trap. You have to step out of it, you have to seduce people into revolt. The minority can't even move if the majority is all solid. Fashion is the most important thing in the whole media – visuals are clearer than words. I am a very political person, so I really think if you put my clothes on, you will be a force to be reckoned with. I thought this in 1977 as much as I thought it in 1984.

Malcolm McLaren: After I made the *Fans* videos with Terence Donovan, I realised I had sketches for things that could be taken a hell of a lot further. Something bigger, something braver, something louder . . . *movies*. I was always interested in telling a story, and [Vivienne] wasn't. Music was always important to those clothes. On her own I don't think she understands the politics of fashion. Looking back now, I don't think the clothes really delivered at the end of the day. There is no way that punk clothes would have happened without the music.

I went off willy-nilly to America, and I really wasn't sure where I was gonna park my butt. I found that a lot of people in the States had bought *Fans*, but not necessarily people involved in the music world – people like the theatre entrepreneur Joseph Papp. My reputation had gone before me and was already working on my behalf. I went to Hollywood with Chris Blackwell, on some misbegotten radio tour to promote *Fans*. I wanted to get into the film business, and I thought I could use *Fans* as an introduction to this world. The radio tour was a bit of a disaster, but it did introduce me to a few good people, and I didn't see any point in returning to Britain until I'd exploited that. And then, luckily, I landed a job at CBS Films – a very, very powerful job on an extremely healthy retainer – being an independent producer with the job of developing music-based movie, TV and theatre projects.

It was great. I had the whole of CBS at my disposal. I was given an office, a secretary and a phone. I went through the process of trying to make a movie just like any other Hollywood producer – my life was full of riders and contracts and phone calls and bureaucracy – playing footsie with guys who really didn't know what was in my mind at all. The biggest problem was I'd come up with an idea, and then they'd give it to some writer who had no empathy with the project at all. And that was a very difficult situation for me to be in, as I'd never been subject to anything like that before. It was the first proper job I'd had since I was a trainee wine taster after I left school. I was a bit like the crazy guy on the lot, and people would say to me, 'You'll soon calm down, Malcolm, you'll soon fit in. Just go home and play some tennis, and everything will work out.' Frankly, it wasn't a great experience, but I did meet a lot of people. Out of twelve [projects] I sold four: *Fashion Beast* [a biopic of Christian Dior] to boutique owners in New York; *Fans* to Steven Spielberg; the surfing movie I sold to Edward Pressman, who then sold it to Brian Grazer and Ron Howard; and *Rock'n'Roll Godfather* [the Peter Grant biopic] to Disney.

Robert Sandall (*journalist*): To those who had lived through the mayhem of punk and the righteous anger of 2-Tone, and who had convinced themselves that music had a duty to bring about radical social change (or failing that, to be as shouty and annoying as possible), the early eighties were a difficult time. Synth pop was all right but lacked conviction. The New Romantics, with their unhealthy preoccupation with hair, make-up and nightclub VIP lounges, were clearly suspect. But the advent of Sade in 1984 was seriously bad news. Not just bad, but baffling. Some rockist doctrines said soul music was OK, as long as it came raw and bleeding, like Aretha Franklin, or had some kind of socio-political agenda, as in Marvin Gaye's 'What's Going On'. The softer stuff could be justified, in extreme cases, in terms of its gospel roots or as a badge of historical authenticity. But as for this girl from Essex singing dreamily about a smooth operator, above an insolently schmaltzy sax line . . . nothing had prepared the post-punk generation for a No Future as bland as this one. The whole thing reeked of supper clubs, suburbs and boil-in-the-bag sophistication. The fact that it seemed to strike a chord with the country known as Thatcher's Britain made it even more difficult to come to terms with. The principal charge that 'rock'n'roll journalists' held against her at the time was that Sade had made an unholy pact with the devils of marketing and image manipulation. Her arrangements can be restrained to the point of half-empty, as though to deliberately remove all things distractingly flashy or pointlessly muso. This refreshing inversion of pop music's usual priorities is, contrary to what many critics think, a Good Thing. Instead of aiming for overkill and then turning up the heat a bit, Sade the underkiller always seems to be heading in the opposite direction: stripping things down to the absolute bare essentials of groove, rhythm and melody.

Sade Adu (*singer*): I was born in Nigeria, in somewhere called Ibadan, and my true Nigerian name is Folasade, which means 'crowning glory'. It was abbreviated, so I could actually have been called Fola, which is quite a common prefix. When we moved back from Nigeria, we didn't have anywhere to go, so first we lived with my grandparents, and then my mum got this job as a nurse. From the first day we moved into the house, I was making friends; no one ever brought up my colour. I think that children aren't naturally racist at all. It's more about society and culture and their parents. And the history as well. There was one kid who jumped out of the bushes once and insulted me, but I told my big brother, and the next day my brother jumped out at him. I used to read a lot back then as well, at least up until the age of fifteen. Whatever book I was reading, that would become my entire life. I was so engrossed in the process of reading.

Andrew Hale: Musically, we had common ground, because we all loved classic soul records. We were all obsessed by soul, but we also loved imperfections. All the singers that Sade liked – like Marvin Gaye, Roberta Flack, Donny Hathaway, Billie Holiday, Bill Withers – they weren't necessarily technically perfect, but you hear their life in their music. Equally, we were driven by punk because it was a sort of fuck-you, DIY attitude. With hindsight, you realise there was so much music that was an influence. We were listening to early hip hop and electro coming out of New York, like Schoolly D and Mantronix, which had a rawness and a similar energy to punk. But alongside that I was obsessed by Talking Heads and the Yellow Magic Orchestra and Steely Dan, so it was coming from all over. It was a combination of feeling that you could try anything, but you had a respect for musicianship and dogged perseverance at the same time.

Paul Spencer Denman (*musician*): If any kind of music was missing from the industry at the time, it was soul. Everything got a bit electronic, and we weren't into that at all. On our first *Top of the Pops*, we looked like we'd landed from Mars, all dressed in black, and we didn't smile! We were of our time but not in time with what was going on around us. Our producer, Robin Millar, recognised that we had something that was a bit different, if not special, and we needed someone to guide us as opposed to moulding us.

I had moved to London in about '79, '80, and I wanted to be part of that Blitz scene I'd seen in magazines. It was a lot more colourful than punk, but the attitude was just as gritty. The title of our first album, *Diamond Life*, wasn't meant to be about money and flash cars and upward mobility. It was a comment on living a hard life, but a life that shone bright like a diamond. The Blitz and, more importantly for me, Le Beat Route and the Dirtbox were filled with really interesting characters. I made a lot of friends, and we really came out of that scene. We played all the clubs, and it felt really important. All the 'cool' people seemed to like us, and it made you feel really special. We had Ollie O'Donnell and Chris Sullivan and Christos [Tolera] and Spandau and Steve Strange saying great things about us and what we were trying to do. They were a big help. I think they got it, whereas the labels really didn't. So much so that our first album was never scheduled for release in America. People buying the album on import forced the label to release it over there, and it went on to sell ten million.

Sade Adu: I went out one night to a Misty in Roots concert, and I met some guys who I had known from the town I grew up in, and they asked me to sing with them. They asked if I wanted to be the singer, but I told them, 'I'm not a singer, why do you want me?' I was black, and they assumed I could sing, which is not [always] necessarily so, but they persuaded me to help them out until they found a singer.

Andrew Hale: We were reflecting black American music that was quite polished in its delivery, whether it was Marvin Gaye or Maze. The sonics of our records had a smoothness, but a kind of Englishness too. And even though we obviously played our songs to the best of our abilities, none of us were virtuosos. There weren't any flashy solos because, frankly, we weren't probably capable or interested in doing them. It would have felt like showing off! Trying to approximate the soul records we loved helped create our sound. I think we were trying to make a coherent soul record that crossed over into pop. Our manager at the time, his reference point for *Diamond Life* was always *Rumours* by Fleetwood Mac. It is soulful music that could cross over, and I think that was inherent in the songs that Sade and the band were writing.

Sade Adu: I was there on the edge, but I wasn't that into [punk]. I love what punk did for the music industry, particularly since it gave everybody different ideas of what the music business could be. It liberated the industry and gave people a lot of opportunities. Everything changed around. As for me, I was always Mrs Soul Woman. [I liked] Donny Hathaway, Marvin Gaye and Sly Stone. I also liked the heavier stuff as well, like Gil Scott-Heron. I wasn't someone who had a lot of music around me when I was a child, really. I was quite deprived of music, because my mum wasn't particularly into it. My father is totally into music and surrounds himself with music, but I didn't grow up with him. When I got to be about thirteen, I started listening to pirate stations, and that really did change my life, because I wasn't that interested in the pop stations. There are more licensed stations now, but when I was growing up, there weren't many options. When I was ten, I remember quite liking 'Maggie May', but that was it. I loved that song; I can't remember liking anything else I heard on standard pop radio. I wasn't really a Rod Stewart fan, but that one song . . . Then, when I was thirteen, I discovered a pirate radio station that played all sorts of stuff: folk, rock, soul . . . everything. They played really good music, basically. So that got me interested, and I started collecting albums. At that time, not many girls bought records; they were just listening to the same records as their boyfriends. There was a station called Radio Caroline. The first time I listened to it, I heard 'The Revolution Will Not Be Televised', and I was like, 'Wow!' In fact, that's when I also heard 'Why Can't We Live Together' for the first time. I got into that slightly later. When I was fourteen or fifteen, I started listening to Billie Holiday and Miles Davis – *Kind of Blue* and *Sketches of Spain*.

Paul Spencer Denman: We had played a lot of shows with Sade before Andy joined and filled out the sound. After he auditioned, Stu [Matthewman] and Sade said to me, 'What do you think?' And I said, 'We don't need him!' How wrong I was. We were talented but raw. I'd been playing in bands since I was thirteen, and I think the same for Stu, so we had experience and we were hungry. Sade hadn't really been in bands before, but she had a massive work ethic and always wanted to be better, and that was infectious. It rubbed off on all of us. She's special, unique. Our sound is just us playing off and around each other. It's the sound of four people being honest with each other. For me, I just wanted to play bass from a young age. It's all I can ever remember wanting to do. My mother, Ethel, took me to see Tommy Steele and Freddie and the Dreamers in about 1962, when I was five, at Hull ABC, and I can remember dancing in the aisles, thinking, 'This is amazing!' Then, later, I saw Jimi Hendrix, and I thought, 'I'll never be that, but I could be that cool-looking bloke in the background with that four-stringed thing . . .' And of course Ziggy. Mick Ronson was from Greatfield Estate in Hull, which is where I'm from. I lived a couple of streets away from him. They lived on Dodswell Avenue, and I lived on Corbridge Close. I'd see him on the estate and in his other bands, and I knew his sister Maggi really well, so seeing him on the TV with Bowie draped around him really made me think, 'If he can do it, why can't I?' I saw Black Sabbath in '71 and just wanted to be up there doing it. Then the Pistols came along, and I just thought, 'If I don't go for it now, I'll never know.' So that's what I did. I got lucky. I met some stellar people who were really talented, and they liked me. If it wasn't for the Sex Pistols, I wouldn't have had the balls – or what you might call testicular fortitude – to do what I did. They were totally inspiring. When I saw them on *So It Goes* in 1976, and Rotten shouts, 'Get off your arse!' before they power into 'Anarchy', I swear to God I thought he was talking to me. So that's what I did. I quit my factory job, cut my hair, took in my flares, ripped up my T-shirt, got those plastic sandals I'd bought for Blackpool when I was a kid out of the closet, and BOOM! I bought a one-way ticket to London and lived in squats and derelict houses, trying to be in a band. It was a lot tougher than I expected and it fucking sucked at times, but I stuck at it, and with a lot of luck and determination it worked out in the end.

Sade Adu: I was pretty much one of the lads, but I was an old soul even when I was a child. I grew up on a council estate in a village [in Essex]. It was the epitome of the English village. Our family was accepted really well. I had an older brother who was always very protective of me. My mum was a single parent, which was pretty unusual back then. Even more unusual was that she had two black kids, and the village was pure white as the driven snow. But we were accepted and there were no problems, no questions or conflicts because we were different. We were no threat to anybody, but it might've been different if we had grown up in the city.

Andrew Hale: The smoothness of our sound was sometimes misunderstood as being too literal, I think. A record like 'Twilight' by Maze, for instance, with its mixture of programmed beats and playing, had a 'sheen' which felt quite modern, quite counter-intuitive. I loved the way Roxy Music sounded in the early eighties, songs like 'The Main Thing' and 'Avalon', which quite deliberately had that sonic veneer. The sheen of eighties aspiration! *Diamond Life* sounds timeless but also very much of its time – aspiring to the classic soul records which influenced it, but also with those early-eighties sonics embedded.

Sade Adu: When you're singing, when you're presenting yourself, you don't give everything away. You don't choose 'I'm going to show this, but I'm not going to show that,' but it happens that way. So the picture someone has of you is never completely true. I think people do think of me as this depressed person crying in my ivory tower. What I personally like when I listen to other people's music is when the music makes you feel something: sad, happy, makes you want to dance, makes you feel elated. Sadness in songs is positive because it brings it out of you, it brings the sadness out. It's not that the song makes you feel sad; the sadness is already there. The song just makes you recognise it. I don't think I've ever really known what romance is. I'm a mixture of being really idealistic and hopeful and really pessimistic about our future. I've always been like that. But, individually, as far as people are concerned I'm an optimist, because I believe there's a lot of good in people. When it comes to trusting people, I have quite good instincts. I'm a bit witchy – witchy woman. I think now I'm sometimes less open than I used to be, because I have to protect myself.

Andrew Hale: Success happened so quickly and I was still so young that I didn't often have time to stop and think about it. You know, one minute you're at college, the next minute you're making an album, signed to a record company, and a year later you're on *Top of the Pops*. These things happened so quickly that you just did them as they came. I remember, like a lot of people, I'm sure, feeling sick to my stomach as I walked on stage sometimes, because of the enormity of it. You didn't have anything to compare it to, so it wasn't something that you'd primed yourself for. I wasn't some musical prodigy, just waiting for that moment. I did think there was a sense of community, though, as so many people who became successful at the time had been in the same room at the Wag Club. That feeling did dissipate quite quickly, though, as the more sinister side of eighties capitalist entrepreneurialism reared its head. It's weird that to many people at the time Sade seemed to be this poster child for a kind of coffee-table, eighties Filofax aspiration, which was pretty much everything we were against. So, in that sense, we all felt slightly misrepresented.

Paul Spencer Denman: There wasn't really a plan, but there was desire, and we were ambitious. We had a manager at the time, Lee Barrett, who really believed in us and was really kind of inspiring in a way. He was really motivated and he pushed us on. Martin Kemp said that Spandau opened a lot of doors for people, and I think that's true. We played different music but we came from the same scene, and labels were looking for people from that scene who they could exploit. It's difficult to relate to now or imagine, but literally every new or about-to-happen pop star would be at Le Beat Route every week. It all just fell together. Sade, Stu and myself had been in another band called Pride, and we had done that for maybe two years, then Sade and Stu started writing songs that more suited Sade's voice. Originally, we just had sax, bass, drums and vocals, so it was really sparse, and we mostly did covers, like 'Cry Me a River' by Julie London and 'Why Can't We Live Together' by Timmy Thomas. And I really liked how open our music was. No one was doing anything like that at the time, and we were just trying to be the best that we could be.

Andrew Hale: The American press could be far more welcoming, as they took the music at face value. There was also some slight exoticism about the band, with it being British and Sade's Nigerian heritage. They appreciated the simple idea of music that was well crafted and had strength and meaning behind it, combined with what they perceived as an American work ethic. In America, you're an entertainer, and you're respected as such, despite your political leanings or any sense that you might be selling out. Americans don't care about that. If you look at those bastions of entertainment culture in America, like the late-night talk shows or *Saturday Night Live*, it didn't matter if you were Sade or David Byrne, there was this notion that you were entertainers. I think in Britain that felt a lot more politicised, it felt much more detrimental. Like, if you were on *Top of the Pops*, you were an arsehole; or if you weren't on *Top of the Pops*, you were an arsehole because you were up your own arse. You couldn't win. For us, the positivity of youth and the rich cultural scene we were part of in London resulted in some great music. There was a feeling of decadence, which emphasised freedom and discovery. An openness that, after the depressed atmosphere of the late seventies, was exciting and powerful.

Paul Spencer Denman: I remember after we finished recording *Diamond Life* in '84, I said to Sade, 'Shall we stop now?' I knew we had recorded something special, and I was happy to leave it at that. She thought about it but decided to carry on. When we made the album, we had no idea how successful it would become. I was getting eighteen quid a week on the dole at the time, so when we got the cheque from Sony for forty grand, we all felt like millionaires. I went round to Marco Pirroni's flat and told him we had signed and got the money, and he told me, 'Paul, it doesn't matter how much money you get, it will never be enough.'

By 1984, pop stars had been elevated from Neanderthals to sex symbols, their every word splashed across the gossip columns. It was a cultural melting pot, a visual melange. It was almost as if there were a blueprint for the interface between celebrity and fashion, one that determined that the best place to be at any given time was either propping up the bar in a nightclub or grinning your rictus grin at a shop opening.

At the start of the decade, the men's clothing industry in the UK was contained, to say the least. There was Paul Smith, a bit of Bond Street, and some activity on the high street. And that was just about it. Then, in the mid-eighties, along came Next, the fast emergence of a strong middle market, a generation of young men encouraged by youth culture and style magazines to start buying clothes with a vengeance, and you had the explosion of a money culture which encouraged men to consume in ways they had never done before. This was the age of the yuppie, when double-breasted suits became double-barrelled suits and making money suddenly became sexy. The generation of young men who began shopping like women in the eighties were egged on in their task by the emergence of i-D, The Face *and* Blitz, *journals that acknowledged the fact that men were as interested in designer suits as they were in Martin Scorsese or New Romantic nightclubs. They were the first generation of men to see images of themselves reflected back at them in magazine pages, and these reflections helped turn them into consumers. They stopped being defined solely by their jobs and started being defined by where and how they spent their money. Did they spend their wages in Marks & Spencer or Giorgio Armani? The lifestyle explosion was such that street style began morphing into its own designer reflection. Doc Martens were no longer the boots of the disenfranchised but were worn by everyone, from seventeen-year-old bricklayers to forty-five-year-old architects, from schoolgirls to ageing rock stars. Distressed leather jackets were just as likely to be found on the backs of advertising executives as they were on biker boys. People had done just about everything with their hair, with their clothes and with their bodies, piercing all the parts it is possible to skewer. As the American performer and comedian Sandra Bernhard said, there was not much more people could do to themselves, 'unless they start wearing lumber'. Recycled nostalgia was the thing, and in a postmodern age of arbitrary gesture and kitsch'n'sink subculture, urban tribes were ten a penny.*

By the mid-eighties, everyone was a trendy of some description, comparatively speaking. Everyone codified and hip to the modern world, while elitism was becoming increasingly fetishistic. Odd. Weird. Uncalled for. Why be wilfully different when you could consume with impunity? For many who came through the eighties unscathed and successfully negotiated the perilous contours of the new face of consumerism and the free-market economy, life was good. Very, very good indeed. And many people – those living in the right postcodes, at least – saw how easy it was to become the people they had pretended to be all those years ago.

The contextualisation of lifestyle – which is what good style journalism had always been about – suddenly became extremely important, so much so that Tom Wolfe's obsession with status (something that had propelled him through a career which, at the time, had lasted for a quarter of a century) began to be looked at with renewed interest. In his vignettes of contemporary life, Wolfe had always examined the sounds, the looks, the feel of whatever place he was writing about: brand names, tastes in clothes and furniture, manners, the way people treat children, servants or their superiors were important clues to an individual's expectations. This was something he had been endlessly criticised for, mocked for, ridiculed for, although he took some solace in the fact that the leading critic of Balzac's day, Charles Sainte-Beuve, used to say the same thing about Balzac's fixation on furniture. 'You can learn the names of more arcane pieces of furniture reading Balzac than you can reading a Sotheby's catalogue,' said Wolfe. 'Sainte-Beuve said, If this little man is so obsessed with furniture why doesn't he open up a shop and spare us these so-called novels of his? So I take solace in this. After all, we are in a brand-name culture.'

That may have been so, but even Wolfe was slightly bamboozled by the petit *hierarchies of our fair country. 'Britain has more tribes than any other place I've been, and I still don't profess to know anything about them,' he said to me once. 'So many insecurities, so many grand wizards, so much complexity.'*

If, in the nineties, the prefix of choice would become 'luxury' – luxury clothes, luxury hotels, luxury bath soap, luxury breakfast cereal, etc. – then it shouldn't have come as much of a surprise that it was swiftly followed in the noughties by 'bespoke', a word used by the marketing departments of luxury-goods houses to flatter those customers of theirs who had become rather alarmed at just how many people could now afford 'luxury'.

In the eighties, things were slightly more prosaic, as the prefix of choice back then was simply 'designer'. This was everyone's favourite retail tag, used in conjunction with everything from cars, double-barrelled suits and supermodels to personal organisers, kitchen fittings and vegetables, and it was one we were all encouraged to embrace with gusto. 'Designer' was originally used adjectivally to describe the notionally elitist jeans produced by Murjani, Gloria Vanderbilt Jeans, in the seventies. It is often said that the company had actually wanted Jackie Onassis to lend the brand her name (and thus enormous added value), but when it could not get the former First Lady, it called in the New York socialite. These garments were advertised on the sides of buses with the slogan, 'The end justifies the jeans,' alongside photos of a line-up of Vanderbilt-clad (signed) bottoms.

The idea soon caught on, though, and soon the word 'designer' was being stuck in front of everything, even pop groups.

Which is how Sade became the first designer pop group, a band who dared to whisper about the good life, the thread of the exotic. In various obvious ways, Sade were the quintessential eighties act, adored and vilified in equal measure because of it.

At the time, the very idea of Sade was anathema to the music press in the UK, principally because she was so different to pretty much everything that had gone before.

'The whole thing is extraordinarily composed, very civilised,' wrote a Melody Maker *journalist. 'Which makes her arrival as a bona fide pop star even more incongruous. Is this music for young marrieds? Songs for the Habitat generation? A voice for the discerning adult? Fact of the matter is there are no easy categorisations for Sade. One of the reasons she's so fascinating is that she conforms to nothing. She straddles all manner of age, creed and market, confounding the rules of the business at every turn, but doing it with such style and charm that after a while you just don't care any more. A woman for all seasons and the first lady of '84.'*

The way she looked was discussed almost as much as her music. In fact, for many journalists this was her biggest problem – her beauty, and the way in which she dressed. 'In England, 'twas ever thus,' wrote Charles Shaar Murray in Rolling Stone, *in an attempt to explain her to a potential American audience. 'Before the hit records, before the acclaim, before even the voice . . . there comes The Look. And what a look Sade has: the high forehead; the svelte shape; the luminous, almost Oriental eyes; the generous, sensual mouth. Without pastel cosmetics or a hedge-clipper haircut, Sade has a look that's both distinctive and unconventionally alluring.'*

The thing about Sade was the fact that she, and the band, were obsessed with less as opposed to more, a distaste for wildness and flash that was reflected in Sade's public persona. 'It's now so acceptable to be wacky and have hair that goes in 101 directions and has several colours, and trendy, wacky clothes have become so acceptable that they're . . . conventional,' she said at the time. 'From being at art college, I've always hated people that have the gall to think they're being incredibly different when they're doing something in a very acceptable way, something safe that they've seen someone else doing. I don't look particularly wacky. I don't like looking outrageous. I don't want to look like everybody else.'

What the cloth-eared, dog-eared music critics didn't understand was that the eighties generation wanted designer dreams just as much as their predecessors did – and what the market wants, the market tends to get. Or at least it did in the eighties. Which is probably why Sade became one of the biggest bands of the decade, 'designer' or not. People weren't kind about them in the early days, but then most of the criticism came from those critics who were championing the likes of the Birthday Party, The The and German avant-garde bands like Einstürzende Neubauten. Elsewhere, the band – and Sade were always a band, never just a gorgeous Nigerian-born singer called Helen Folasade Adu – were welcomed with open arms, cutting through class, culture, age, race and sex, while their first album, Diamond Life *('Smooth Operator', 'Your Love Is King', 'Hang on to Your Love', 'Why Can't We Live Together', etc.), sold six million copies in the UK and in the region of seventeen million in the US. One of the reasons they were so successful was because they slotted nicely into 'Quiet Storm' programming, the sexy, late-night radio format featuring soulful slow jams, smooth R&B and misty-eyed soul, pioneered in the mid-seventies by DJ Melvin Lindsey at WHUR-FM, in Washington, DC. The 'Quiet Storm' radio format reflected an emerging genre of smooth, romantic, contemporary, jazz-flavoured R&B. Named after the title track on Smokey Robinson's 1975 album* Quiet Storm, *it was a niche that turned into a substantial programming sector in the early eighties, as artists like Luther Vandross, Anita Baker,*

Al Jarreau, Loose Ends and Sade became popular. Political commentary was downplayed, while sex and lifestyle were pushed to the fore. Essentially a gentrification of soul, some critics found it emasculating, while others – many others – saw it as simply a reflection of the growing affluence of middle-class African Americans.

Andrew Hale: We were definitely aligned in the US with 'Quiet Storm' radio. It was a positive thing, although there was a slight crossover into smooth jazz, with Kenny G and all that, which was the opposite of what we were about. I think we became pigeonholed in Britain because we weren't overtly politicised. It was really about doing something you love. With Sade, you had two guys from Hull, a woman of English–Nigerian heritage and me coming together because of a love of music. Stuart would be listening to Black Sabbath, I would be listening to Funkadelic, Sade would be listening to Marvin Gaye, and between us we found some kind of cohesiveness.

The odd thing about Sade herself was her almost total ambivalence towards success, and no sooner had the band conquered the world, than she would encourage them to run back home again (to London, Cheltenham, New York or the Caribbean), only to emerge, sleepy-eyed, three or four years later, when it was time for another record (she appears in public so rarely that she goes by the nickname Howie, after Howard Hughes). Their initial appeal was that they didn't appear to have any 'issues': they were modern, they made contemporary-sounding soul music, yet they weren't in any way angry, thus appealing to the widest demographic. But at least Sade had their own sound, their own sonic world.

Much of the commercial music produced in the eighties was swathed in artificiality, driven by barely humanised software, as manifested by the Fairlight synthesizer, the Australian-manufactured machine used by the likes of Thomas Dolby, Peter Gabriel, Alan Parsons, Herbie Hancock and Miami Vice *producer Jan Hammer. If you wanted to sound futuristic, modern, then the Fairlight was your studio toy of choice. In the eighties, every established pop star, from Bob Dylan to the Rolling Stones, also began using entry-level drum machines, in the hope of being embraced by the new MTV generation, and grasping another lifeline. If you wandered through a Virgin Megastore in the eighties, you'd hear the time-capsule clank of over-produced synthesized drums.*

Gated reverb would also begin to define the sound of eighties pop. The accentuated drum sound was used by everyone from Phil Collins, Peter Gabriel, Sade, Kate Bush and XTC to Bruce Springsteen, Duran Duran, the Power Station and Prince, and for a while was as ubiquitous as the padded shoulder. Its discovery came in 1979, at Townhouse Studios in west London, where Steve Lillywhite and Hugh Padgham were recording Peter Gabriel's third album (often called Melt *because of its cover). Phil Collins was playing on the album, and when his drums were accidentally picked up by the microphone used by the engineers to talk to the musicians in the studio, they decided to try the effect on the record. The microphone was designed to amplify quiet noises – like talking – and the effect on this occasion was to make the drums sound huge. Padgham, who was engineering the record, also combined the happy accident with a 'noise gate', which immediately cut off the beats so they sounded metronomic as well as incredibly loud. 'One day Phil was playing in the studio, and I inadvertently pressed the talkback button,' says Padgham. 'Out came this ginormous sound, which everyone in the control room said sounded incredible. They all said, "Let's have a bit of that on something."' After finding a way to record it, 'We started recording, and almost for a laugh I switched on a noise gate. That's where the cut-off sound came from. So now we had something that sounded enormous but with no die away.' The sound became so popular that it was used by dozens of artists over the next eighteen months, but it really cut through when Collins used the effect on his massive global hit 'In the Air Tonight' in 1981.*

Another big drum sound of the eighties was the 'bathroom reverb' first used by Bob Clearmountain on the Rolling Stones' 'Start Me Up', released in August 1981. The song had originally been rehearsed during the Black and Blue *sessions as a reggae track called 'Never Stop', but was completely overhauled for its single release, a raunch-by-rote construction that would eventually become one of their most famous songs (it was licensed by Microsoft for the launch of Windows 95). The infectious 'thump' to the song was achieved using Clearmountain's soon-to-be-famous reverb, a process involving the recording of some of the song's vocal and drum tracks with a miked speaker in the bathroom of the Power Station recording studio in New York City. It was there that the final touches were added to the song, including Jagger's switch of the main lyrics from 'Start it up' to 'Start me up'. Keith Richards fretted that the riff was just 'Brown Sugar' in reverse, yet it soon became perhaps the signature Stones riff, in what was a sticky, hand-clap-fuelled romp.*

By 1984, most music was being produced with one eye – or, more accurately maybe, one ear – on the dancefloor.

'As clubs became workplaces and nightlife the essential engine of cultural evolution, they liberated music, design and, especially, ambition,' wrote the Guardian. *'In 1978, London offered only one hip club a week; by 1984,* Time Out *magazine was listing fifty, while the British Tourist Authority reported that dancing was a serious reason visitors gave for visiting the UK. London Transport rolled out a whole network of night buses.'*

After the raw emotion and unsullied rock of the seventies, the eighties were all about cold conformity, unabashed ambition and surface smarts, much of it standardised by a metronomic backbeat. Essentially, dance music had always been driven by fashion and technology, so it was no surprise that much of it concerned itself with the notion of perfection, and variations thereof. As soon as drum machines began taking over dance records in the mid-seventies, the art of the impossible became the only reason to make records: what exactly was the perfect beat? First we had click tracks and rhythm boxes (samba, mambo, bossa nova, etc.), and then in 1978 the £200 Wasp synth. The same year, Roland launched the CR-78, and a year after that Roger Linn unleashed the world's first mass-market drum machine. As soon as the LinnDrum appeared, it had a huge effect on the way records were put together, and for months afterwards the charts were full of songs underscored by the metallic thud of the Linn Mark I. Drummers liked to say the sound was reminiscent of damp cardboard being struck by a large fish, although this begs the question: how did they know? Roland then came up with the TR-808 (heard on Marvin Gaye's 'Sexual Healing'), then the 909, which was the drum box of Chicago house, and the TB-303, the sound of acid house.

As club culture became more sophisticated, or at least more homogeneous, the records started to get more uniform. DJs would alter the bpm in order to slide seamlessly from one track to another, so that in effect what you got was one long song with various highs and lows. And as art tends to imitate life, so records started to get longer and longer – first five minutes, then six, seven, eight, then ten, then – unbelievably – sixteen or seventeen. In DJ booths the world over, the question was: how long can you keep it up for? In the laser-beamed, mirrorballed, smoked-mirrored eighties, the twelve-inch remix wasn't so much king as an all-singing, all-dancing, insomniac emperor with a propensity for fast drugs and a libidinous streak as wide as the dancefloor at Studio 54. Remixes started off as simple repagination, reassembling the constituent parts in a novel but comprehensible manner. Soon, though, they were doubling in length, trebling, quadrupling. Patrick Cowley's 1982 remix of Donna Summer's 'I Feel Love' – quite probably the most architecturally sound dance record ever constructed – was over fifteen minutes long, and for a while became the benchmark for dance remixes.

As the eighties blossomed, it seemed as though most things could be remixed, remodelled, redesigned. Designers assumed god-like status, as young urban professionals surrounded themselves with the trappings of the upwardly mobile: the Tizio lamp, the Breuer chair, the Dualit toaster, the Alessi kettle, the Tag-Heuer watch, the Golf GTI convertible . . . and, of course, the Paul Smith Prince of Wales checked suit. Smith sold suits to managing directors, but also to art directors and plumbers, and became famous for clothes which screamed when you wanted them to, not when you least expected it. We were told that everyone could have a designer lifestyle, if they were so inclined. Money wasn't mentioned, but then how on earth could it be? That was the illusion: money was no object.

This was the decade when air-conditioning was suddenly a 'luxury good', when chilled air became a rarefied and objectified perk. All of a sudden we were surrounded by things previously denied to us. Bottled water, imported cheeses, twelve-inch remixes, designer clothes in all their finery. We could get money from a hole in the wall, and magazines were beginning to write about people in the lifestyle industry – club runners, photographers, restaurant managers, the designers of board games – as though they were heroes, as though they were all choosing careers in the same way that they might choose lifestyles – if they were given the opportunity, that is. The Pet Shop Boys sang, 'I've the brains, you've got the looks, let's make lots of money,' and they were only half joking. This was rare in itself, as jokes were thin on the ground in the eighties, as irony had to elevate itself in order to be taken seriously.

The eighties were reduced to a single word: cool. Everything was cool, or not. There was a complete anorexia of language. And Sade was accused of being complicit in this time and time again.

'I do care about clothes and glamour, but not because I'm a singer,' she said, in her defence. 'When you have a photograph taken of you, it's a permanent thing, so you make an effort. If someone comes up to you at a party with a camera, you don't then start scratching your ear unless it's for a joke. If I have a picture taken of me for the cover of a magazine, I don't want to look gruesome 'cause I have to look at it. The same way I don't want to look gruesome walking about the streets. I pay attention to detail 'cause it's a frozen image that reports you. I have to project myself. But I only do that because that's the way I want to be.

'I didn't want to be signed up because I was glamorous, because I might make glamorous records.'

For Sade, it was always about the music. 'When it comes to writing songs, I think I could be anywhere. Inspiration doesn't come from sitting on a beach somewhere and trying to write a song, it comes from moments than can arrive out of just about any situation you could ever find yourself in, from the most mundane to the most magical. If our music has to be labelled as anything, I would say it was soul, but we have our own feeling and our own sound, which have come from many things that have subconsciously influenced us. But soul is the common denominator.'

Like the designer decade it would soon become synonymous with, the CD was an emblem of burnished success – a smarter, more upmarket version of all that had gone before it. The CD was a designer accessory like no other, and heralded an era in which music became codified. Almost overnight, music became a lifestyle accessory, a muted background fizz to be played at designer dinner parties in designer lofts in designer postcodes. 'CD music' became pejorative, as did the likes of Sade, Anita Baker and Luther Vandross. Critics – the sweaty guys at the back with the bad teeth, the bad shoes and more opinions than money – said this was just music with the edges rubbed off, with the soul extracted. 'Sade?' they said, almost as one. 'Those guys are so boring their dreams have muzak. And barely audible muzak at that.' Aspirational in essence, if you didn't have the wherewithal to surround yourself with the occupational hazards of yuppiedom, then a few CDs left casually on the sub-Matthew Hilton coffee table would suffice.

The rise of Sade coincided with a short-lived jazz revival in London, driven by a DJ called Paul Murphy and a genuinely original working band called Working Week, led by a passionate left-wing advocate named Simon Booth. This was a revival based almost exclusively on the dancefloor, as Murphy, Booth and their acolytes looked for new ways to entertain the troops. As more nightclubs opened, so more customers poured into the marketplace, creating more appetite and causing club runners and DJs to become increasingly esoteric in their choice of theme nights. Working Week mixed intricate Latin beats with strident agitprop, most notably on their brilliant debut single 'Venceremos (We Will Win)', a tribute to the Chilean protest singer Victor Jara. The NME *lapped this kind of stuff up. As they were uncertain about endorsing the new pop bands, they latched on to anything they thought might catch the attention of their readers: one week it was the rockabilly revival, goth 'rock' the next, then socialist skinheads, 'industrial', alt-country, post-punk R&B, shoegazers, go-go, winsome bossa nova . . . anything and everything. Working Week were an extraordinary live proposition, they had terrific songs, used a variety of appealing singers (including Tracey Thorn, Julie Tippetts and Juliet Roberts), while espousing the kind of politics which played well with the largely student readership of the* NME. *But they couldn't catch a break. They neither looked nor sounded like Sade.*

Even though Sade tended to dress herself, she looked as though she had been styled by a team of industry heavyweights. As the decade progressed, having your photograph taken when you weren't looking at your very best became unthinkable; only by employing the talents of a stylist would it be possible. All over London, stylists were now working with photographers to form partnerships, through which they could forge a recognisable, and commercially viable, style.

One such partnership was Buffalo, although it was less a partnership and more of a collective. In the early eighties, a loose-knit gang began congregating in photographic studios in west London and in the nightclubs of deepest Soho. Primarily, they were friends, but friends with ambitions: there were singers (Neneh Cherry, Nick Kamen), photographers (Roger Charity, Cameron McVey, Marc Lebon, Jamie Morgan) and stylists (Mitzi Lorenz), and their mentor, a quiet man from Dundee called Ray Petri. Petri was also a stylist, but he had the kind of magnetism that drew people to him, specifically young creatives. A shy man with something of a stoic resolve (he didn't get frazzled, didn't shout), he possessed an uncanny coolness. The Clint Eastwood of trendy London, even Petri's voice was square-jawed.

Petri was slightly older than the rest of what became his gang. Born in Dundee in 1948, he left for Australia in 1963, where he formed and sang with an R&B group, the Chelsea Set. Back in England in 1970, he got involved in the antiques business, before becoming embroiled in photography – first as an assistant, then as an agent and finally as a stylist. It was here, in the early eighties, that he was to make his mark most deeply. Working with the likes of Charity, Lebon and Morgan, Petri began producing seriously iconic fashion photographs, creating a glamorised version of street style which, after initially appearing in Honey *magazine, began filling the pages of* i-D *and* The Face. *He mixed high fashion with streetwear, mixed vintage with ethnic, and was a keen advocate of black models.*

Petri had a very particular vision, one inspired by the photographs of Walker Evans, Richard Avedon and Bruce Weber, and by old black-and-white B-movies, Jamaican street style, classic rock'n'roll, the books of Hubert Selby Jr and by the London nightclubs they all went to – an American vision seen through strictly European eyes. There was always something insular about Petri's crowd, and it was this gang-like mentality which underpinned their creative energy. Rather enigmatically, he called this amorphous bunch of image-mongers Buffalo, and – very Petri, this – its pretensions had solid foundations. 'Buffalo was started as an umbrella,' he said, 'collecting different people with similar ideas all in one place. It was started as a whim, and we weren't really sure what would happen. I just knew that something would – we all seemed to be working towards the same ideal. What we wanted was a creative agency which would channel our work. If you work for other people, you soon become sucked into the mainstream, but with a corporate title suddenly everything takes on a different meaning.

'People tend to associate the word Buffalo with Bob Marley's "Buffalo Soldier",' he said at the time, 'but in fact it's a Caribbean expression to describe people who are rude-boys or rebels. Not

necessarily tough, but hard style taken from the street. It's the whole idea of boys – and girls – together, just like it was when you were a kid going around in a gang, looking cool. Buffalo can be anything – a movie, a car, a sound, whatever. But basically, Buffalo is a functional and stylish look; non-fashion with a hard attitude.'

Buffalo was also something of a code, as what Petri was doing was photographing far more black male models than anyone in the UK had before.

Nick Logan: It can be no surprise that Ray Petri showed up at our door. Other than *i-D*, where else would he have gone?

Neneh Cherry (*singer*): Buffalo was an attitude, a way of living. It stands for rebellious self-expression, friendship and a fearless creative spirit. It was about celebrating who you were and having a laugh. Buffalo clashed cultural and gender stereotypes. Tough mixed-race boys in skirts and a pair of DM boots. Utility sportswear mixed with high fashion. Casting girls as boys. Kids as men. Breaking down boundaries, creating iconic images . . . 'Buffalo Stance' was a tribute to the Buffalo crew. What they did in fashion, we did in music.

Jamie Morgan (*photographer*): It was experimental, and it had never been done before. There was no template or references; instead our references were American Indians and photographers from the thirties, so it was very different back then to how the industry is now. There was no Internet or mobile phones; people met in clubs, at parties, on the street, and it grew over quite a long period of time. It all happened live: you would turn up at the studio, put the music on, smoke a spliff, and people would just arrive throughout the day. We would transfer our lives to the studio and start working. There is power in that, because it is authentic. Also, you were shooting on film, so you didn't even know what you were shooting; it was just there, contained within the film, so you were living it as opposed to having an outside view. However, the key element of Buffalo is that a Buffalo image is styled by Ray Petri. That is what Buffalo is, and it was formed to support his vision.

I found Nick Kamen in the model agency under 'black models'. I said, 'This guy isn't black, he's half Burmese.' And they replied, 'That's as black as we go, I'm afraid.' There just weren't any black models back then, so we found them on the street, through friends and through word-of-mouth; we never used models from agencies. It was about the way they walked and stood, not just how they looked. It was about the attitude, mixing genres and the idea of gender and models, and turning it all around.

'We became a family,' says Neneh Cherry. 'We had real group intuition and really fed off each other's creativity. We were always aware of how valuable that was, but it was still funny when everything started rolling so fast.'

Juxtaposition is the stylist's currency, and back in the mid-eighties, few juxtaposed with greater aplomb than Petri. In the pages of The Face *and* i-D, *from 1983 until his death in 1989, his pictures became the cutting edge of fashion. He was at the epicentre of a so-called British street style that was starting to infiltrate the more corporate worlds of advertising and the global music industry. While his signature was a streamlined classicism, tough-edged and Brandoesque, he had a knack of producing iconic gay images which were somehow instantly appealing to heterosexual men. In the fashion pages created by Petri and the Buffalo team, credibility shone through, lifting the images off the page. 'I start outside of whatever I'm doing and try to look on it with a new perspective,' he once said.*

Models were almost always found through friends, and ideas were formed on the street, not in a fashion editor's office. The Buffalo look went beyond style into attitude. This, unlike the ideas, was beyond imitation, as it was all in the casting. 'If the face fits, then it's fixed,' Petri used to say, and you only had to look at his pictures to know what he meant. 'The important think in good styling is the people;

once you have the right face, it all fits into place.' He discovered Nick and Barry Kamen, used Naomi Campbell when she was just fourteen, and made glossy-paper stars out of a host of gorgeous-looking creatures whose Christian names became their monikers: Cameron, Tony, Simon, Felix et al. His pictures didn't have much respect for tradition. Here was the debut of ski and cycling wear as street chic, boxer shorts worn with Doctor Marten boots, dayglo dungarees and cashmere tops, muscle-rippling boys in jewellery, wild-eyed girls in Crombie coats. This seems silly written down, and yet these images became incredibly powerful symbols of a rejuvenated London. Heavily featured in Buffalo pictures were city cowboys, Olympic heroes, leather-clad biker boys, T-shirt De Niros – a hard, forthright mixture of mythical America and European street life. He could make a pork-pie hat, a white T-shirt and a pair of black Levi's look like a military uniform ('I think the strongest fashion statement that America has produced is denim,' he said. 'You have to go a long way back to look good in anything other than jeans'). He even famously put men in skirts, acknowledging the Blitz dressing-up box, but making the idea far more masculine in the process.

Perhaps Petri's most visible success was the surplus-store garment – the black nylon US Air Force flying jacket, the MA-1, which not only became the most ubiquitous fashion item of the decade, but also replaced the leather jacket as a symbol of rebellion as it traversed the global fashion underground. Unsurprisingly, it didn't take the rest of the world long to notice, and while the other members of Buffalo found sporadic fame and fortune, Petri was soon being courted from every area of the image business. Keen to acquire the force behind this new school of image, captains of advertising and publishing soon began knocking on the Buffalo door, asking Petri and his team to overhaul their corporate images, their ad campaigns, television commercials, promotional videos and editorial pages. He was hired to work on the Julien Temple promo video for the David Bowie single 'Day-In Day-Out' – a lamentable career low for the man who was largely responsible for the Blitz and much that came in its wake – but managed to fall out with him almost immediately. The first day on set, Bowie came out of his trailer and pointedly asked Petri just exactly what it was he was going to do to him. Petri, taken aback by Bowie's laddish and out-of-character demeanour, told him the first thing he needed to do was ditch his leather jacket and stop looking so old-fashioned. Bowie fired him on the spot, although he was persuaded to relent and let Petri stay for the rest of the three-day shoot.

Petri was also one of the main forces behind the launch of Nick Logan's Arena *in 1986, Britain's first general-interest magazine for men since the sixties. Often working with the American photographer Norman Watson, it was in the pages of the early issues of* Arena *that he would produce perhaps his finest work. In Petri's hands, androgyny took on a new form, a masculine image that was feminine around the edges, the counterbalance to a world awash with gender fluidity, at least in a visual sense.*

Debra Bourne (*PR*): I got lucky. When I secured an internship at Lynne Franks PR back in 1984, one of my first jobs was assisting a seventeen-year-old stylist called Mitzi Lorenz. Which is how I met Ray. I was nineteen. I have a special place in my heart for Ray, which is not something I'd say about all fashion folk. He was a beautiful man, charismatic, kind and effortlessly stylish. For whatever reason – maybe as a new mate of Mitzi's or the fact that I knew my fabrics – Ray and I connected. He was thirty-six, seventeen years older and super-cool. I was definitely in awe. He rarely gassed. When Ray spoke, it was in cryptic, poetic terms. In song titles, movie names and paradoxes. In two-word sentences. 'Cool, still.' 'OK, boss.' It was like he'd just left a Studio One all-nighter, and the slow, melodic reggae dub beat was still silently playing in his head. When he entered a room, he entered with that same slow, unspoken rhythm. Deliberate. Deep. Meditative. Always moving to his own tune. I never once saw the man run. That rhythm was ultimately expressed through Ray's styling and Buffalo imagery.

Whether in *The Face*, *Arena* or *i-D*, it felt like a finessing of the culture clash, gender-pushing swagger and multiracial diversity that we were all experiencing simultaneously on the club scene but never saw reflected in glossy fashion mags. By paying as much attention to the casting and model's stance as he did to the clothes, he managed to do that rare thing of creating groundbreaking iconic imagery without it being just about the surface. He gave them soul. There's always something going on behind the eyes.

In 1937, when George Orwell wrote that 'all of us owe the comparative decency of our lives to the poor drudges underground, blackened to the eyes', virtually all the energy consumed in Britain was produced by miners. By the early eighties, this was no longer the case – in their last full year of operation, British Coal made a loss of over £400 million, a figure that excluded the subsidy from the electric companies – which is why the government saw fit to try and dismantle the industry. As a coal strike in 1974 had brought down Ted Heath's government, this could have been a risky strategy, yet Thatcher knew she was made of stronger stuff than Heath. One of her economic policies was the privatisation of industries she didn't think should have been nationalised in the first place, not when they required such massive subsidies.

The first pit closure to be announced was Cortonwood, near Barnsley in Yorkshire, which was enough of a spark to ignite the wrath of the Marxist leader of the National Union of Mineworkers, Arthur Scargill, who used the 1981 NUM ballot (which legislated that strike action was permissible if any pit was threatened with closure, 'unless on grounds of exhaustion') as a call to arms. And what a call it was. In Britain, the miners' strike turned out to be the most bitter, fiercely fought industrial battle of the decade. This wasn't just eradication, this was ideological warfare. As Godfrey Hodgson wrote in the Independent, *'As we went into the eighties, the miner with his ravaged lungs and aching muscles was still as potent a symbol of division in British society as he had been for a hundred years, a black legend of pride and militancy for the working class and of middle-class guilt and fear.'*

It didn't matter how often the government emphasised that efficiency was the only reason that pits were being closed, didn't matter how many times they repeated their mantra of what they considered to be more than generous severance terms – no compulsory redundancies, early retirement on better terms than any other nationalised industry and larger redundancy payments to younger miners – Scargill was going to call a strike. And once it began, on 6 March 1984, parts of Britain became as dangerous and as confrontational as pockets of the Middle East. Scargill used the strike as a way to claim the soapbox as often as possible, but made a strategic error in not devising a strategy based on trying to win public support, rather than just using industrial muscle. Consequently, most of the country, and most of the press, turned against him. He may have been able to use television to exaggerate his personality, but it wasn't a personality it was easy to warm to. He was tireless, however. As Patrick Wintour said in the Guardian *the following year, 'His resilience and ingenuity in keeping the momentum of the strike going through twelve months was remarkable.'*

In July, having largely kept some judicious public distance from the National Coal Board's attempts to control the strike, Thatcher compounded what the Left saw as her party's audacity in trying to neuter one of the country's most inviolate national industries by making a speech so incendiary it galvanised those who had previously just been shouting from the sidelines. Like, for instance, many of the participants in, and organisers of, the left-wing pop collective Red Wedge. That month, she told the 1922 Committee of Conservative MPs that the striking miners and their violence were 'a scar across the face of the country . . . We had to fight an enemy without in the Falklands. We always have to be aware of the enemy within, which is more difficult to fight and more dangerous to liberty.' She continued, 'There is no week, no day, nor hour when tyranny may not enter upon this country, if the people lose their supreme confidence in themselves, and lose their roughness and spirit of defence. Tyranny may always enter – there is no charm or bar against it.'

While this infuriated the miners and gave them even more of a reason to keep on fighting, it also added an ideological top note to the government's rhetoric, which many on the Left took to be a declaration of class warfare. This more than anything made Thatcher the bogeywoman – more than her hard-line economic policies, more than her intransigent response to the riots or the way in which she had dealt with the Falklands. In a few short sentences she created a cultural divide as well as a political one. She had been railed against ever since she got into power, but these few words somehow sealed her legacy. She had informed a generational antipathy.

Not that it stopped her. Thatcher's myopic nature was not just one born of arrogance. Not only did she have little interest in what people said about her, most of the time she didn't actually know what people said about her, which probably came as a surprise to many of those journalists, leader writers and newspaper editors who perhaps thought she hung on every trenchant word. She certainly had no interest in pop culture, and was rather proud that she knew nothing about it. As Andy McSmith pointed out in No Such Thing as Society, *his history of Britain in the eighties, in Thatcher's memoirs she had nothing to say on Africa, Third World aid, Live Aid or Bob Geldof, subjects she just had no interest in. I had lunch with Thatcher's former gatekeeper, Sir Bernard Ingham, in July 2009, exactly twenty-five years after Thatcher's speech, and he confirmed that his former boss had little interest in the white noise of Fleet Street tittle-tattle. In his book* Kill the Messenger, *Ingham writes that Thatcher almost never read newspapers and would rely on him to cut out and photocopy the things she needed to see. He reiterated the point over lunch, stressing that she never read leader columns, and would only do so if Ingham shoved one under her nose. 'She didn't see the point,' he told me, as he nibbled on his fish. 'To her, it was a waste of time. Didn't watch much television either, maybe just [listened to] the headlines on the radio.'*

The IRA attempt on her life in Brighton that October, at the Tory Party conference, only strengthened Thatcher's resolve. Her battle with Scargill now took on a personal dimension (although she had always regarded him as a Marxist revolutionary rather than a normal trade union official), and as one minister said at the time, 'Our leader will not be satisfied until Scargill is seen trotting round Finchley tethered to the back of the prime minister's Jaguar.' In turn, Thatcher's intolerance served as an accelerant for Scargill's activities. Given their backgrounds, it was almost as if both of them had been preparing for the final battle all their lives.

In the end, there was no quarter given, although the government's tactics had to be altered, especially where it counted – outside the pits, in front of the television cameras. If it hadn't been for the riots, and in particular those in Toxteth, it's unlikely the government would have been so confident of defeating the miners. They knew industrial action would inevitably lead to violence, and it was their steep learning curve in terms of crowd control in the summer of 1981 that had forced them to encourage the police to seriously improve everything from weaponry to strategy, from body armour to on-the-ground communication.

Christmas 1984 was tough for families who hadn't seen any income for nine months, and men began heading back to the pits. On 3 March 1985, at a specially convened conference, NUM delegates voted by ninety-eight to ninety-one to call off the strike and go back to work. And so began the beginning of the end of the mining industry, as the pit-closure programme accelerated. Some saw this as collective punishment, but in reality it was simply part of the Conservatives' obsession with the privatisation of the energy sector.

It was a victory, but not much of one. As Hugo Young wrote in his remarkably deadpan biography of Mrs Thatcher, One of Us, *'Scargill's own imperishable extremism successfully placed him in the folk-memory alongside the Argentinian leader General Galtieri as an important accessory to the Tories' continuing political domination.'*

There were other legacies resulting from this victory. By 1991, trade union membership would be down by four million, or over 30 per cent. In 1979, for every thousand people in work, 1,274 working days were lost through strikes. By the end of the decade, the figure was down to 108 days. Thatcher would take this victory with her everywhere she went, and it gave her the confidence to do so much over the next five years. What she didn't do, however, was seriously look at the consequences of her actions, and while she had successfully started to dismantle the coalmining industry, she had paid little mind to the havoc that this would wreak, turning entire communities into ghettos, diminishing fathers in the eyes of their sons and helping to build an underclass that hadn't been seen on this scale since the nineteenth century.

Which was certainly enough to rebel against, if you were that way inclined, although there were predictable contradictions. Elvis Costello's 'Shipbuilding', for instance, had been released on Rough Trade, an independent label that was arguably a model of Thatcherite entrepreneurial flair; these inconsistencies were obviously not acknowledged by anyone involved.

While it was her dedication to the free market and to monetarism (protecting the economy) that had already polarised the media, it had been Thatcher's stand against Argentina over the Falkland Islands in 1982 that really proved divisive in the entertainment industry. While it was impossible to be ambivalent about the way she went to war with the Argentinians, it was the British victory in the Falklands, plus her own in the 1983 election, which gave her the confidence to be even more radical with her policies. And with scant regard for the communities she was shattering in the process, she continued her war against the miners.

George Michael: I must admit that when we did the [miners'] strike benefit [at the Royal Festival Hall in September], I was at a turning point. Not as to what I thought about the issue, because the issue was clear enough. But when I met Arthur Scargill, I got a terrible impression of him. He really did annoy me. He just seemed to be enjoying it all far too much. When I met him, I got the impression the only place he was leading the miners was further and further up their own arses. It was good that they were fighting, because nobody had been fighting for years, but I started to feel that by encouraging it, all they were doing was damaging their own industry and they were not going to make any ground. I was hoping that Scargill was going to become a realist and see that the government wanted to make an example of the miners. He didn't. I thought it was really sad when it came to an end because they really hadn't got anything out of it. When we did the benefit, I really thought there was some kind of hope.

Tony Parsons: Normality was a big thing with George. He was so normal. For someone who spent most of his time between the ages of seventeen and twenty-six trying to be the biggest act in the world, it was almost strange. There were no bodyguards. There was no cook, cleaner or trusty retainer to open his door. He drove himself around town in a Range Rover. He had been known to have too good a time, be dropped back at the pick-up point, only to realise he had forgotten where he had parked.

Andrew Ridgeley: For George, this period was a process of development in terms of writing, producing and performing, and I rather thought it was what was due to us! I was absolutely convinced from our first days in the Executive that we knew what we were doing and were going to be successful. It was a fairly limited ambition as far as I was concerned, as I wanted to be in a band, I wanted to write songs and I wanted to perform. I thought we were good at it, I thought we had potential and I thought we would make it. So our success was an affirmation of that belief. And life hadn't changed that dramatically, in the sense that while there was a lot of work, a lot of TV and press and travelling, aside from that, life wasn't that different. There were no fast cars, no swanky houses. George didn't buy a house until 1985. And regrettably, success meant there was a lot less time to do what we had initially gone into the business for, which was to make music. Most of the time you were doing promotion. That's why there are so many poor second albums in our business, as you've spent a lifetime making your first album and five minutes making the second one. Personally, I didn't take it all too seriously, and nor did George. Even when he achieved peak success, he made a very clear distinction between 'George Michael' and the person that he was, the artist and the person. And he kept those divisible.

George Michael: There is no such thing as a reluctant star. Stars are almost always people that want to make up for their own weaknesses by being loved by the public, and I was no exception to that. The whole business is built on ego, vanity, self-satisfaction, and it's total crap to pretend it's not.

Tony Parsons: I always liked Andrew. He was the smart, pretty friend who enabled George to do it. He wouldn't have had the nerve to do it without Andrew. They were a real band, and he gave George licence to do it. And Andrew never expected it to last a lifetime.

Andrew Ridgeley: George didn't allow success to define who he was, and if you do do that, therein lies a world of pain. I was always very clear about what I was in it for and what I saw as being the essence of Wham! And it wasn't skinny girls, it wasn't adulation, it wasn't great reviews. All that was a novelty. I think because we were such close friends there was always a levelling to what we did, and that friendship and growing up together helped us keep things in check. However, I think George wrestled with success from the off. As he evolved as an artist – in fact, as a person – he found it a strain. He said he created the image of George Michael in the image of a great friend, and so success was a far more complicated process for him because he was discovering who he was. I already had a fair idea of who I was. That was what distinguished us, even as kids. He wasn't comfortable as a youth. And his sexuality, latterly, had a big bearing on that discomfort and schism. There was a separation within. George was worried about his sexuality being a problem, but I never was. That may have been naivety, but I never thought it would be a problem. You can look back upon that period now and see a huge acceptance of homosexuality within the culture. George told me he was gay when I had just turned twenty and he was still nineteen, in '83. I suppose it had been a question mark, because he didn't have girlfriends and he had another social group of friends which I didn't really know about. It didn't make any difference to me, but it did to him. He understood – and he was probably right – that a certain part of the brand image could have been undermined had he admitted his homosexuality earlier. I'm not sure. It didn't do Marc Almond any harm, and he was a contemporary. Boy George. Steve Strange. There was a lot of androgyny about – just look at Phil Oakey. It was all becoming more mainstream. But it was more difficult for him than it was for me, at least in his eyes. He had an inner confidence, but he was still unsure about it. After all, there's a big difference between knowing you can do a job, and then telling everyone you can do the job.

Gary Farrow: I still think George was probably the smartest pop star I've ever met. He would say, 'Well, the record's going to come out in November and is going to be No. 1 for at least six weeks, and I don't think anybody else is going to want to come near us at that time.' His confidence level was so high, his strategy spot on. His judgement was better than anybody I've ever met. He was even smarter than Bowie, and you don't get much smarter than that. The most important thing was his understanding that he couldn't have done it without Andrew. They needed each other. Andrew was the stylish, good-looking guy. George was a bit uncomfortable on his own at that time. Andrew was great on photo shoots, incredibly well liked, well educated, loved his wine. You needed the two of them. It didn't work visually without the two of them. Andrew knew he was along for the ride.

I didn't get the gay thing. I missed it. George rang me from New York once and told me he was having dinner with Brooke Shields, and I went, 'Wow, you lucky sod. Let me know how you get on, and don't screw it up.' He told me, 'She's really charming and nice,' and said, 'I'm not interested in that.' I got an inkling then.

Simon Napier-Bell: You could be travelling with George and Andrew in a limo or a train or a band bus, they might be in the seats behind you, and you would hear this endless chattering, whispering and giggling. They would burst into hysterical laughter and bang each other on the knees, then go back to nattering like monkeys. They got off on everything about each other. Together they were in a world of their own, utterly private and intensely annoying. It was like travelling with a different species.

Andrew was the most delightful person ever, and I don't remember him showing signs of jealousy or upset. The image of Wham! was the real Andrew and the fake Andrew. I know from managing people that the image is the most important thing with groups. You can get someone to sing, you can get a songwriter, you can hire a producer and a stylist, but the fundamental image has to come from within the group, and that really came from Andrew. I absolutely love him. George couldn't have had a better partner. George was a very typical artist. He had pain and something uncomfortable inside him. All artists have it – it's what makes them artists. So you can't complain about that as you wouldn't have an artist to manage if they didn't have that, but Andrew didn't have that. The rubbish he had to put up with, people saying he couldn't play on stage. I don't know why people had it in for Andrew, as he was such a great guy, and George would never have become who he was without Andrew. George needed Andrew to get up there on stage, so Andrew was really the bridge between George being who he was before, when they were at school, and the superstar he became.

Gary Crowley: People forget this, but Wham! were really cool for a year and were actually on the cover of the *NME* and *Melody Maker*.

And then they didn't release anything for about a year, and when they came back with 'Wake Me Up Before You Go-Go', it was like they'd gone for the pop jugular. It was obviously daytime radio stuff, and I was in a bit of a dilemma as to whether I should play it or not. This was pop in twenty-foot-high capital letters. Then, when *Make It Big* came out, the hair started getting bigger and the shoulder pads got bigger, and then it did change. Pop was starting to get bloated.

Michael Bracewell: Having made a lot of money out of *Dare!*, there was the problem of how the Human League were going to follow it up. 'We spent ages making an album, *Hysteria*, that didn't sell,' Oakey recalls. Even as dance music was becoming the new official tempo of pop, the Human League were placed in the ironic position of having pioneered the idea of commercial British dance music, only to find themselves back on the sidelines.

George Michael: I created a man – in the image of a great friend – that the world could love if they chose to, someone who could realise my dreams and make me a star. I called him George Michael, and for almost a decade he worked his arse off for me and did as he was told. He was very good at his job, perhaps a little too good. My depression at the end of Wham! was because I was beginning to realise I was gay, not bi. I felt cornered by my own ambition. I didn't have the self-control to restrain my ego, but I knew it was leading me further and further towards an explosive end. I was becoming absolutely massively popular as a heterosexual male. It hadn't occurred to me, when I went solo, that I would get a whole new generation of thirteen-year-old girls [as fans] from *Faith*, but it happened. And in here, in here, I was gay. It takes so much strength to say to your ego, 'You know what? You're going to keep me lonely, so I have to ignore you.' I realised those things my ego needed – fame and success – were going to make me terribly unhappy. So I wrenched myself away from that. I had to. I had to walk away from America and say goodbye to the biggest part of my career, because I knew otherwise my demons would get the better of me. [It was] a very American form of blasphemy [to achieve success and choose to reject it]. They were like, 'You are making a $100 million, people love you – how can you quit?' But I knew that to develop as a gay adult – which I had never really been – I had to do it.

Gary Farrow: Every act had to have a killer emotional ballad: Duran, Spandau, George Michael, Culture Club. 'Victims' is one of the great records of the period, as is 'Save a Prayer', 'True' or, indeed, 'Careless Whisper'. That was the record that made everyone sit up and take notice of George.

Simon Napier-Bell: In July, 'Careless Whisper' came out as George's first solo record and went straight to No. 1. This was the beginning of the transition from Wham! to George Michael, but he still pretended to the press it was no such thing. 'Careless Whisper', he said, was only being issued as a solo record because it 'didn't fit' with the style of Wham! Then he spoilt it by telling them, 'Well, perhaps it *is* a sort of springboard for me.' He was testing the waters; edging things towards the result he wanted. With Wham!'s new album not yet recorded, he'd already told Jazz [Summers] and me to take him seriously about an eventual break-up. With 'Careless Whisper' he was telling Andrew too.

The video would give him an opportunity to create a new public persona. It was to be shot in Miami, and I went to watch, interested to see how he would approach the challenge of getting close to his real self.

I arrived at midday. The filming was being done around Coconut Grove, among hotels and marinas and outside cafes. George was out on a speedboat with the film crew, and since it was a blazing hot day, around ninety-five degrees, I went to the hotel bar. I found Andrew checking out its range of malt whiskies. 'Are you going to be in the video?' I asked. 'I thought it was going to be just George.' He laughed. 'I shall make a fleeting guest appearance. The time still hasn't come for me to be pushed aside completely.'

Later, George came back from his boat trip, happy with the day's filming. But the next morning, when he looked at the rushes, he flipped. 'It's my hair. It's dreadful. Too long. Too posey. Too poofy.'

His hair was as it had been for the last few photo sessions with Wham! For his first record as George Michael he now decided he should look different – more mature. Having his hair cut and the filming redone would add almost 50 per cent to the total budget of the video, but when George was firm, things were done. His sister Melanie was flown out to cut it, and the next morning – with his hair restyled and the speedboat re-rented – the first day's filming was reshot.

Mark Ellen: There was a time during the rise of Wham! when George Michael was so permanently orange that people thought he dyed his skin. 'Hence the old joke,' he would always say. 'Why hasn't George Michael got a girlfriend? Because you can only fit one on a sunbed.' George's intense self-consciousness about his appearance was obvious even then. He worried constantly about his looks and his weight – in fact, he originally saw himself as the band's songwriter and mastermind and never intended to appear on stage. At one *Smash Hits* photo shoot, we asked George and Andrew Ridgeley to pose in swimming trunks on a lilo (divinely eighties). When asked why he had one hand across his stomach in every shot, George replied sheepishly that he didn't want his fans to see his unsightly appendix scar. He wanted to look perfect. He loathed his right-side profile so much that he would only allow himself to be photographed from the left, he told me years later – 'I really should have therapy about it.'

Simon Napier-Bell: There was no doubt about it, he was no longer enamoured with the idea of being the biggest group in the world. The fame he'd so longed for was becoming a burden. The falseness of Wham!'s image was telling on him. It was meant to be two young guys being themselves, but the more successful Wham! became, the more difficult George found it to keep on playing the role of a second Andrew. His impatience was understandable. It wasn't simply a matter of ego; he felt he was wasting his creativity on something false. He was still unsure of his real nature, but to go solo and write for himself was the best way to find out. I could see that breaking up Wham! and becoming George Michael wasn't a petulant whim, it was necessary to his mental well-being.

After Wham! became famous, the boys still went out dancing, and it was not unusual to see Andrew on display at Do-Do's or George down at the Camden Palace. For about eighteen months in London, 'Everything She Wants' (No. 2, December 1984) was the hippest record to be seen dancing to, and George could often be seen doing just that, right in front of the DJ booth at the Wag Club, yet again dancing to one of his own records. Even at 3 a.m., in the bowels of some sweaty West End nightclub, he looked as though he'd just stepped off the plane from Ibiza: that tandoori tan, summer whites, designer stubble (something the singer invented) and perfect Princess Diana hair. He was always serious about his hair: 'Some days I made the covers of the tabloids. Some days Princess Di made the covers of the tabloids,' he said. 'Some days I think they just got mixed up.'

Neil Tennant: George Michael and Marc Almond were not openly gay at this point. The first people to say they were gay – apart from David Bowie, many years beforehand, even though he wasn't – were Frankie Goes to Hollywood. But they were like clubbing gays. Then you had Bronski Beat, who were clubbing gays with a political agenda. It was very impressive at the time, and they were on the front cover of *Smash Hits*, although, of course, in pop-music terms, remember that's also an angle [being gay].

Subtlety was a quality rarely invoked for anything to do with Frankie Goes to Hollywood. Spandau Ballet, Duran Duran and Ultravox all made music that is still synonymous with the times, yet whenever you see a television documentary about any aspect of the eighties, what you'll tend to hear is Frankie's 'Relax' or 'Two Tribes', perhaps juxtaposed with the unnaturally deep voice of Margaret Thatcher repeating one of her famous phrases, such as 'There is no such thing as society.' The effect is usually quite powerful, as it's hard to know which is more intimidating. Frankie emerged from the late-seventies post-punk scene in Liverpool, and took their name from a Guy Peellaert image of Frank Sinatra that appears in his book Rock Dreams. *Singer Holly Johnson had previously been in Big in Japan, while frontman Paul Rutherford had been in the Spitfire Boys. As Frankie, they started gigging and recording demos, before being asked in February 1983 to record a video for their song 'Relax' by the Channel 4 show* The Tube. *It was this performance that encouraged Trevor Horn to sign and record them for his new label, ZTT. Horn used Frankie as a vehicle for his extraordinarily maximalist productions, corralling former* NME *journalist Paul Morley into becoming ZTT's chief strategist, his very own Malcolm McLaren. Their single 'Relax' was released at the end of 1983, ever so slowly reaching No. 35 by January 1984. Eleven days into the new year, the Radio 1 DJ Mike Read branded the record 'obscene', and a few days later it was banned by the BBC, ensuring it instant notoriety. Because of this, and its equally incendiary follow-up 'Two Tribes', FGTH immediately became the biggest pop sensation of the decade so far. They would soon be overtaken by Madonna, but they owned most of 1984, at least in the UK. When you listened to Frankie Goes to Hollywood, you felt as though Holly Johnson had an almost insuperable urge to be naughty.*

Johnny Black (*journalist*): It started in jail. In the spring of 1982, Mark O'Toole, bassist of fast-emerging Liverpool band Frankie Goes to Hollywood, was jamming on a new bassline in The Cells, a disused police station which had become a popular rehearsal space. Simultaneously, the band's vocalist, Holly Johnson, was fast approaching The Cells along the central reservation of nearby Princess Avenue, with a saucy little rhyme going round his head that began, 'Relax, don't do it . . .'

Moments later, Holly was singing his rhyme along with Mark's bassline, and 'Relax' was born. The song would prove to be the cornerstone on which the Frankies' astounding run of success – three consecutive No. 1 hits with their first three singles – would be built. It was also the first track recorded for their multi-platinum debut album, *Welcome to the Pleasuredome*.

The Frankies were creating waves around Liverpool, but were having trouble breaking out of the city. The man who changed that was Trevor Horn. Already famed for his work with the Buggles, ABC and Yes, Horn first became aware of the Frankies when he saw them perform 'Relax' on influential TV show *The Tube* early in 1983. 'This video came on with these women chained to a wall and a load of other kinky stuff going on,' he remembers. 'Chris Squire [Horn's band mate in Yes] said, "This band looks really interesting. Why don't you sign them up for your new label?"' Horn and his wife, entrepreneur Jill Sinclair, had indeed just started a label named ZTT – an abbreviation of Zang Tumb Tumb, the title of a sound-poem by Italian Futurist poet Filippo Tommaso Marinetti.

Although intrigued by that *Tube* performance, Horn felt there were 'some obvious faults to the track'. By a happy coincidence, however, Horn was tuned in again on 15 March, when the band played a slightly amended version of the song on Radio 1's *Kid Jensen Show*. This time, Horn was bowled over. 'Hearing "Relax" on Jensen, I realised how fantastic the song was,' he says.

Unaware that the band, having already been turned down by several labels, was on the brink of splitting, Horn signed them to ZTT on what Johnson would subsequently describe as 'a very unfair £250 recording advance between the five of us'.

Asked what he saw in 'Relax', Horn says, 'It was a great combination of rock and Donna Summer dance music, with this Liverpool four-on-the-floor shagging beat that remained the root of the song right through. It was like a radio jingle or a chant, except Holly sang it like a wild animal.'

Nevertheless, Horn still harboured reservations. 'When I met them, I immediately liked them and they had great ideas, but I had doubts about their playing ability.' Horn's dilemma now became how to transform 'Relax' from a million pounds' worth of potential into a million pounds. 'I was pretty ruthless in those days,' he admits, 'so I brought in some better musicians – Ian Dury's band, the Blockheads – to show the Frankies another way to approach the song.'

The Blockheads' bass player, Norman Watt-Roy, came up with a descending three-note bass part that Horn loved, and decided to include. Then, ZTT engineer Steve Lipson delivered a guitar part which, says Horn, 'somehow caught the spirit of what the Frankies' guitarist, Nasher, had been doing and transformed it'.

The other ace up Horn's sleeve was the fact that he was one of only three people in the UK who owned a Fairlight computer synthesizer. At that time, the Fairlight was the state of the art in the cutting-edge technique of audio sampling. 'I remember playing Holly and Paul a sample on my Fairlight,' remembers Horn, 'where I'd synced the bass together with a LinnDrum beat, and I could see they were very interested in that.'

Many bands would have been outraged at the level of direct control Horn was taking of their signature song, but the Frankies were huge fans of New York dance music and well understood the potential of the Fairlight in that context. 'Trevor did kind of take control,' acknowledges the Frankies' second vocalist and dancer Paul Rutherford, 'but that's because he knows exactly where he wants to go. He stretches the material every which way, puts in everything but the kitchen sink.'

Once the backing track was nailed, Holly Johnson stepped up to the mic. 'By the time he sang the vocal, at 4 a.m., he was so hyped up, he was crazy, like a Doberman with a rabbit in its teeth,' remembers Horn.

At the end of the take, Horn felt the vocal was slightly out of tune, but Johnson put him straight. 'It was not out of tune,' he says. 'I was doing little slurs with my voice, using microtones. It was quite deliberate. That "Ow!" which I do is my Marc Bolan affectation, plus a bit of James Brown.'

Released on 24 October 1983, 'Relax' languished in the lower reaches of the chart for six weeks, before the band secured a *Top of the Pops* appearance at the start of the new year. The following day, 'Relax' shifted 54,000 copies, at which point Radio 1 breakfast show DJ Mike Read suddenly realised the lyric was virtually an audio guide to the finer techniques of oral intercourse. Deeply offended, he stopped playing it halfway through and declared it obscene. Days later, the BBC banned it, and before the end of the month 'Relax' was at No. 1, en route to an estimated 13 million sales worldwide.

ZTT now needed an album to capitalise on their runaway first hit and, fortunately, the band had no shortage of songs. 'As well as "Relax",' explains Rutherford, 'we'd already written "Two Tribes", "Welcome to the Pleasuredome", "The Only Star in Heaven" and "Krisco Kisses". "War" was something we decided to do in the studio, but we were already doing most of it live.'

With the album firmly in mind, Horn's first priority was to complete a follow-up to 'Relax', and the obvious candidate was 'Two Tribes'. 'The backbone of the track was a Linn 2 bass drum, with a sample of a slapped bass-guitar E string going across it,' remembers Horn. 'Bottom E is very sympathetic to a bass drum, and it sounded huge on the radio.'

Augmenting the Frankies this time around was arranger Anne Dudley, who would subsequently find chart success as a member of Art of Noise. 'I orchestrated the opening of "Two Tribes". Fairly straightforward,' she says. 'Trevor asked, "How many players would you like?" I said, "About twenty." He said, "Right, we'll have forty or fifty or sixty. We want to spend lots of money here." So there were clarinets and flutes and French horns and timps.'

With work moving ahead on the album, 'Two Tribes' followed 'Relax' into the UK's No. 1 single slot, aided and abetted by a string of carefully timed remixes, a barrage of slogan-bearing T-shirts and an eye-popping Godley and Creme-directed video.

The album's centrepiece, however, was its astonishing title track, with a lyric based on the Coleridge poem *Kubla Khan*. 'It started out as three and a half minutes,' says Horn, 'but we kept extending it until it was over sixteen minutes long.' Featuring Yes's Steve Howe on guitar, it became an audio epic which Rutherford accurately sums up as 'a Pink Floyd kind of thing but with a modern dance feel to it'.

The album also included their third No. 1, the big ballad 'The Power of Love', plus a muscular cover of Springsteen's 'Born to Run', not to mention Holly Johnson's Sinatra-like retake of Dionne Warwick's 'Do You Know the Way to San Jose', demonstrating that the band was capable of much more than dancefloor fillers.

Welcome to the Pleasuredome, a double album, was released on 28 October 1984, and entered the chart at No. 1. It quickly went triple platinum, eventually racking up an extraordinary sixty-six weeks on the chart, so that by the end of 1984, Frankie Goes to Hollywood was the most successful act in all of Europe.

Wyndham Wallace (*journalist*): One can't help but wonder whether such a debut, a sprawling, overambitious, sixty-five-minute grand folly, could ever hope to see the light of day in these times of lowest-common-denominator, marketing-led pop. And yet this oft-overlooked, barely remembered, rarely respected hour of preposterous indulgence stormed to the top of the UK charts upon release, with advance orders said to be in excess of a million. It inspired a nation to adopt uniform designer T-shirts, even now such an historic and iconic fashion statement that parodies like 'Frankie Say Xanax' or 'Frankie Say Chillax' remain available. It provoked controversy unseen since the days of punk (and arguably never since). And yet these days – singles aside – it's seen, by critics at least, as best forgotten, a moment of madness on the part of a British public fuelled by Thatcherite consumerism. If it's praised, it's only for Trevor Horn's production techniques. If it's referenced, it's normally in the context of discussions about the extravagance of eighties popular culture. And if its songs get played, it's rarely anything but the singles.

Undeniably far from faultless, *Welcome to the Pleasuredome* nonetheless challenged notions of authenticity, ridiculed the Establishment, confronted taboos, embraced artistic and cultural literacy and dissected contemporary paranoid society. Then, much as happened to the Stone Roses a decade later, the band fell apart in an ugly jumble of disappointment and legal wranglings so great that they rendered the band little more than a cautionary tale. Unlike the Stone Roses, though, Frankie's debut remains largely uncelebrated, excluded from the canon of great records established by the adult music media, a blot on the eighties landscape mapped out by revisionist historians who see the likes of ABC and Sparks as the great innovators worthy of praise. Hell, even Sade's been brought in from the cold.

They returned two years later with *Liverpool*, but it could only be an anticlimax. They could never compete with their debut, and in 1987 Johnson headed off towards a solo career inevitably overshadowed by Frankie's success. But the legacy of Frankie remains, unrecognised though it may be. Their harnessing of tabloid power, their acknowledgement that the studio is as important an instrument as the guitar, their 360° approach to their craft – music, image, T-shirts, performance, videos and personality – are now the goal of every band, whether they know it or not, and Frankie designed the template. These things, however, distract from the fact that, at its best, *Welcome to the Pleasuredome* is one hell of an album, its peaks made even mightier by its failures. We were 'living in a land where sex and horror are the new gods', but Frankie illustrated these with as much intensity as humour. Who cares who played the songs? Who really cares who wrote them? Frankie and *Welcome to the Pleasuredome* were a crucial pop experiment, messing with formulae and heads in equal measure.

Paul Morley: It was an unexpected combination of energies. You had a truly great producer – the best in the world, along with Quincy Jones – you had a slightly narcissistic journalist, you had this heterosexual

Scouse energy and this very exploratory gay energy, all mixed up in one place. It was a ridiculous formula, and you couldn't have planned it – it was too toxic.

Gary Farrow: With Frankie, it was a cauldron of sexual activity, heterosexual and homosexual. I can't think of many bands at that time who were doing the same. Frankie behaved as though it was the seventies.

Holly Johnson (*singer*): There have been artists who saw the controversial nature of 'Relax' as a blueprint. I think Madonna really wasn't very controversial on her first album particularly. We shared a management company in America, and she definitely plucked the power of sexual controversy. It became a blueprint for modern pop and dance, in a way.

Paul Rutherford (*singer*): We were a bunch of boys bent on getting pissed and having a laugh. We used to dress [the Lads, the straight members of the band] up in leather clothes and S&M stuff, and they loved it. It was meant to be fun: 'Let's drop a little acid and go nuts.' It was controlled mayhem. We were discovering our sexuality at the same time that the world was. We were at the forefront of that, making sense of gay rights.

David Bailey: I directed a promo for Frankie Goes to Hollywood, and I loved the singer, Holly Johnson, as he was like a working-class Noël Coward. There was also another guy, Paul Rutherford, who didn't appear to do anything at all! He was a nice chap, though.

Trevor Horn: The follow-up to 'Relax' was going to be 'Slave to the Rhythm', but it was shelved in the end. Grace Jones's version is a really great record, and of all the records I've done, it's definitely one of the best. And it has so much atmosphere.

Trevor Horn said that the reason he hired Paul Morley to work at ZTT was because he realised what journalists did: namely, taking normal things and romanticising them. There's no doubt that Morley caused waves: his original cover of the Frankie album Welcome to the Pleasuredome *contained depictions of thirty-two different sex acts between animals, but luckily Horn picked it up before it was sent to the printers.*

Peter Ashworth: I'd known Paul Morley, even though I didn't work for the *NME*, but when he started working with ZTT, he called me in for a meeting about taking some pictures of Frankie. He wanted a jungle of pleasure, pain and plenty. He had very extravagant ideas, which I loved, because it meant I could build an extravagant set: plants, animals, even children. There's a child in the foreground, right in the middle, on the floor, and Mary Whitehouse accused it of being a poster for paedophilia.

Paul Morley: I used to despair that others were getting all the space as spokesmen. I thought, 'Shit! I want to be there!' – on the radio, on the TV, and so on. But I wasn't conventionally stylish. I was a bit scruffy and I had a funny haircut and I didn't go to the right places. So I got elbowed from that trendy *Face* area of things. Is the art of propaganda simple? In one respect, yes, because pop music is a very soft and stupid area to work in. I liked the way Arista marketed the Thompson Twins. What you [had] there was NOTHING: a token black, a token woman and a token pretty boy, with some skilfully edited, bland pop music, yet it [got] to No. 1. With [Frankie], I wanted to compete with that kind of manipulation, but using something with more substance that was a little more provocative.

Trevor Horn: You could say that the Frankie Goes to Hollywood records were really Trevor Horn records. There was a lot of thought going into those records. The band would originate the idea, and then we would take the idea beyond their wildest dreams. 'Welcome to the Pleasuredome' was a three-and-a-half-minute song, and me and Lipo [Stephen Lipson] made it into an epic fifteen-minute thing. Looking back on it, we were crazy not to take writing credits on it, but we didn't, and that's our own silliness, because the whole middle bit is me. But, you know, that's the way it goes. There was Frankie, then there was the team behind them, and when it worked it was great. In the early days, they were a great band, because as they were all from Liverpool they all had a great sense of humour. The instantaneous success had a big effect on them, though, as it's quite difficult to handle when it happens so quickly. The phenomenal success of the record really affected me. I thought it was hair-raising. I was in one record shop, and there was this huge queue, and everybody had at least two or three Frankie records in their hands. When I got to the counter, the guy took my credit card and looked at me and said, 'Is it you?' They had just sold out of the ['Relax'] twelve-inch and had just ordered 2,000 more. I mean, everyone was listening to it, it was amazing. In the end, I was sick of doing so many remixes. By the end of 1984, I didn't want to mix a drink, never mind a record. You got a bit like that.

John Lydon: Frankie Goes to Hollywood were a glorious sham.

Peter Ashworth: For a while, money was no object, as record companies appeared to like spending it. Soon after Frankie, I went out to LA for three months to shoot an album cover for Eurythmics that never happened. I was actually put up in a hotel for three months, waiting for them to come back to LA, because Dave Stewart was doing something with Stevie Wonder.

To keep their ball in the air and not fall prey to the same criticisms that plagued Visage, Frankie needed not only to tour, but to be successful in the US, and while both 'Relax' and 'Two Tribes' were respectable hits in the States, they hadn't created the same kind of excitement that they had at home. So they tried to pump it up by touring, playing nineteen dates in the run-up to Christmas, centred around three gigs at the Ritz in New York, which is where most of the new pop Brit bands played. The city happened to be full of Brits, as dozens of them had flown over for an i-D *party at Danceteria, then one of the coolest clubs in New York. The excitement of seeing Frankie perform live for the first time was offset by a typically British curiosity regarding whether or not they could actually play. Knowing that their records had in large part been created in the studio by the wizardry of Trevor Horn, the British denizens in the Ritz on 15 November were suspicious, to say the least. If they had seen FGTH on* Saturday Night Live *the previous weekend, they would not have been impressed. In between sketches by George Carlin and Pamela Anderson, Frankie ambled meekly through 'Two Tribes' and Bruce Springsteen's 'Born to Run', while looking like they all wished they were somewhere else. They had already played Washington (on 6 November, the day of the US presidential election), after which a reporter from the US TV show* Entertainment Tonight *asked someone who saw the gig why they liked the boys from Liverpool.*

'Why have you come to see Frankie Goes to Hollywood tonight?'

'Because they are making an important political message with their song "Two Tribes".'

'What is that point?'

'Oh, I don't know.'

Perhaps sensing that their musical prowess was now under scrutiny, the band had reportedly been putting their all into their New York concerts, and on 15 November took to the stage as though they owned it, giving the crowd a fusillade of electronic rage – fast and furious, and designed to shock. The assault was so successful it soon ceased to matter how much of it was on tape. It was almost as though the music were in drag. Frankie exuded confidence, and their drama, sleight-of-hand and sense of self-importance seemed to be baked into their sound, a sound that had what can only be described as 'heft'. 'New York City, up the arse,' Holly Johnson announced, before the band plunged into 'Krisco Kisses'. Frankie also looked completely international, as though they were leaving the UK behind. As it was, they soon faded from view, releasing a disappointing second album and allowing Madonna to become the most controversial act of the late eighties.

Madonna (*icon*): I'm proud of the way I acted, because it set a precedent and gave women the freedom to be expressive. I'm happy to have been a pioneer. I wish people could understand me, but I guess unless you've had my experiences, you can't relate to them, or me. I think I am the most misunderstood person on the planet.

As a phenomenon, Madonna started attracting attention in 1983, the year of 'Holiday', 'Lucky Star' and 'Borderline'. Her influence would run through late-twentieth-century pop like a rogue hormone, yet while she would go on to have more self-administered make-overs than David Bowie, the popular perception is that without a pantechnicon full of costume changes, Madonna would have been just another jumped-up waitress with more mouth than was good for her. This was obviously unfair, but then the rules of pop have always been different when applied to girls. It is, after all, still an incredibly sexist industry. And it is for her music that she now wants to be remembered, not as a human tornado – the familiar cry of any celebrity who feels their intellect hasn't been fully appreciated. 'I want my music to be reviewed, not whether my ribcage is too small or not,' is a popular refrain of hers. 'You want to be thought of as attractive, but it's a very competitive world and there's always going to be another beautiful girl around the corner. Even though people don't admit it in the music business, people are very looks-conscious. And just like in the movie business, men are allowed to not meet the conventional standards of beauty and still be celebrated. It's much harder for women.'

The first time I met Madonna, she was a lot less predatory than she would later start to appear. This was early in 1984, and she was being photographed in Bow Street Studios in London's Covent Garden for her first British magazine cover. As the magazine in question was the style bible i-D, *where I was working, she was being asked by the photographer, Marc Lebon, to wink for the camera (all the magazine's cover stars are asked to wink – the logo is a winking face on its side). But the most famous non-famous person in the room couldn't wink with her right eye, so she winked with her left and the picture was flipped. The cover turned out well, coinciding with the release of 'Holiday' and 'Lucky Star', although the issue wasn't as successful as we'd hoped when it hit the stands – because of Madonna's recently acquired hair extensions, the readership assumed we'd photographed Boy George's boyfriend. Although she was dressed in raggedy-rawny club clothes and wore flat shoes, it was easy to see that she had a grasp on what her business was really about. The theme of this particular issue was, appropriately enough, sex, and when questioned after the photo session, Madonna was typically frank.*

Madonna: When I turned seventeen, I moved to New York because my father wouldn't let me date boys at home [in Detroit]. I never saw naked bodies when I was a kid. Gosh, when I was seventeen, I hadn't seen a penis! I was shocked when I saw my first one. I thought it was really gross. It was just the rules. There were so many rules, and I could never figure out what they all were. If somebody had given me an answer, I wouldn't have been so rebellious. But because no one did, I was constantly going, 'Well, fuck that and fuck that and fuck that,' you know? My father had all these rules and regulations: 'You can't wear make-up, you can't cut your hair, you can't, you can't . . .' So I just went to the extreme . . . and that just continued, because I was rebelling.

It would be easy to suggest that because she would prove to have such a wanton and seemingly insatiable appetite for reinvention, she has also applied this process to her past. However, since she burst into our lives with such irresistible force all those years ago, the memories have probably become as blurred for her as they have for us. 'I was really misunderstood.'

Prince often used to say the same thing.

Prince (*icon*): I ran away from home when I was twelve, and there was a great deal of loneliness. I grew up on the borderline. I had a bunch of white friends, and I had a bunch of black friends. I never grew up in any one particular culture. We basically got all the new music and dances three months late, so I just decided I was gonna do my own thing. Otherwise, when we did split Minneapolis, we were gonna be way behind and dated. The white radio stations were mostly country, and the one black radio station was really boring to me. For that matter, I didn't really have a record player when I was growing up, and I never got a chance to check out Hendrix and the rest of them because they were dead by the time I was really getting serious. I didn't even start playing guitar until 1974. I took a lot of heat all the time. People would say something about our clothes or the way we looked or who we were with, and we'd end up fighting. I was a very good fighter. I never lost.

Until he started throwing his toys out of the purple pram, rowing with his record company and embarking on a ludicrous strategy of flooding the market with product (most of which could be filed under Too Much Information), Prince was one of the biggest US stars of the decade. He started life at the end of the seventies, using sex as his calling card, writing explicit lyrics and becoming an unlikely sex symbol in the process.

Prince: When I brought *Dirty Mind* [in 1980] to the record company, it shocked a lot of people. But they didn't ask me to go back and change anything, and I'm real grateful. Anyway, I wasn't being deliberately provocative. I was being deliberately me.

Prince hit his stride in 1984, when he released Purple Rain*; at one point he had the top film, the top album and the No. 1 single in the US. The soundtrack was No. 1 for twenty-four weeks, while the accompanying film grossed $70 million – at the time, a phenomenal amount for this kind of music film.*

Prince: In some ways, *Purple Rain* was more detrimental than good. People's perception of me changed after that, and it pigeonholed me. I saw kids coming to concerts who screamed just because that's where the audience screamed in the movie. That's why I did [follow-up album] *Around the World in a Day* – to totally change that.

Sexual chameleon, James Brown clone, enigmatic imp and near-genius songwriter, Prince (who was once called 'the Joe Strummer of orgasms') treated his acclaim seriously, continually using his own success as a benchmark, striving to outdo himself with each subsequent album. And for a while it worked. He was the Todd Rundgren of his day, the Cobb salad of the studio, a funky little polymath, quixotic to the core. Some songs were down-home funky, some as stark and as minimal as a seventies video game, and others as extravagant as a Lacroix frock. He enjoyed his fame, but didn't feel the need to engage with his greater public, becoming a notorious recluse. He made a lot of records, but didn't like talking about them very much. The paradox is that for all his warts and insecurities, he was adored as much as the likes of Madonna, Bruce Springsteen and Michael Jackson – the other stadium giants of the eighties – who all had a far more urgent need to manipulate their audiences.

Prince: Michael [Jackson] and I both came along at a time when there was nothing. MTV didn't have anyone who was visual. Bowie, maybe. A lot of people made great records but dressed like they were going to the supermarket.

Daryl Hall (*singer*): I think one of the bad things about MTV is the way in which it de-regionalised all the nation's music, with everything geared towards the same formula. All the great bands from Tennessee, the south, Chicago blues bands or country, whatever . . . MTV diffused that by putting everything on the same level.

Hall & Oates were never cool. Not ever. Not at the start of their career in the early seventies, and not at the height of their success in the early eighties. And yet they were one of MTV's favoured children, and in 1984 it was impossible to turn on the television without seeing them. The 'cool' problem was a simple one. Even though they made some of the best blue-eyed soul ever recorded, they had an image problem, with Daryl Hall looking like a market-town hairdresser, and John Oates looking like Super Mario's smaller, uglier brother. They were a duo, but although it was more than plain what Hall did (sing, a lot, very well), it was never apparent what his partner did. In that respect, they were like an American Wham! Not only that, but whereas some people are born with a sense of how to clothe themselves, Oates always looked as if his clothes had been thrust upon him. And whenever he wore something expensive, it looked stolen. In essence, Hall was the tall, blond, good-looking one who sang all the songs, and he looked like the one who had all the fun.

Daryl Hall: The media were a bunch of fucking assholes, as far as I'm concerned. They always like a scapegoat. It's part of the journalistic attitude. And they decided, way back, in their infinite cynicism and ignorance, that me and John were going to be their goats. [*Rolling Stone*'s] Jann Wenner has a lot to do with it. It's a mindset that they basically created, and people fell for it. It was unbelievably angering and disappointing to me. But it happened, and I turned it around, and there it is.

Hall & Oates have a permanent home in the global jukebox hall of fame, and you could fill an entire streaming service with their greatest hits: 'She's Gone', 'Sara Smile', 'I Can't Go for That', 'Rich Girl', 'Every Time You Go Away', 'Wait for Me', 'Back Together Again', 'Private Eyes', 'Method of Modern Love' – songs that have become as ubiquitous on the radio as Motown standards or X Factor *cover versions. They are the most successful duo in the history of pop. Not that you're allowed to admit it, though. When I first worked at* The Face *in the mid-eighties, I remember one junior editor almost going into shock when I recommended one of their records. In her eyes, the only thing worse than admitting to liking a Hall & Oates record would have been to actually be Hall or Oates.*

Daryl Hall: I grew up with this music. It is not about being black or white. That is the most naive attitude I've ever heard in my life. That is so far in the past, I hope, for everyone's sake. It isn't even an issue to discuss. The music you listened to when you grew up is your music. It has nothing to do with 'cultural appropriation'. We live in America. That's our entire culture. Our culture is a blend. It isn't split up into groups. Anyone who says otherwise is a fool – worse than a fool, a dangerous fool.

Their records sounded great, especially in the nightclubs of Manhattan. On my first trip to New York, in 1984, Danceteria, Area, Limelight and all the other downtown hotspots reverberated to the thumping sounds of Afrika Bambaataa, Nuance, the SOS Band and Hall & Oates's 'Out of Touch', one of the great forgotten dance anthems of the decade.

Daryl Hall: I spent the summer of '84 in New York, so I really soaked up all the street and dance music. I'd met Arthur Baker through personal friends, loved his records, and we got him right in the beginning, instead of asking him at the end to do a dance mix.

John Oates (*musician*): It was a battle against the white stations, not the black ones. Adult-orientated rock was the scourge of the nation, but it was us who broke down a lot of those doors.

Daryl Hall: It was always a conscious thing to mix the black with the white. We were really battling in those days – it was really them and us. It was, like, people would hear our records and figure we were black, and it took a hell of a long time before we were accepted by the AOR stations, because it was only the black stations that were playing us.

Seven years after the launch of Studio 54, at the time the chicest nightclub in the world, 1984 was probably when New York nightlife was at its peak. Steve Rubell and Ian Schrager's hierarchical hotspot had reinvented the nightclub for the disco era, tantalisingly reinvigorating the after-hours experience as an exclusive will-I-won't-I-get-in 'members-only' citadel, mixing rich with poor(ish), white with black(ish) and uptown with downtown. Not only did it create a market, it created a sector, encouraging others to explore the idea that nightclubs could appeal to a wide demographic, as long as there were strict vetting processes.

And by 1984, that vetting process was being employed by dozens of clubs in Manhattan. The big three were Area, Danceteria and Limelight, all wildly different in tone, and all appealing to surprisingly diverse crowds. Area was the ultimate hipsters' paradise, a constantly evolving installation that had so many theme nights, it was almost impossible to second-guess how the club was going to be decorated from one week to the next. Danceteria mainly appealed to downtown rockers and the last vestiges of the seventies punk crowd, those gnarly, leather-jacketed subversives who previously might have been found in the back room of CBGBs. Limelight, which was housed in a deconsecrated church, was aimed at trendy Wall Street types who wanted to rub Armani shoulders with models, TV stars and people who looked like cocaine dealers.

All three clubs had the same binding agent: celebrity. In 1984, on any given night at Area, Danceteria and Limelight you might see Nile

Rodgers, Andy Warhol, David Bowie, Madonna, Deborah Harry, Daryl Hall, John Oates and Billy Idol; occasionally, you might even bump into Donald Trump.

New York at the time felt strangely boldface neutral, and if, for instance, you made it past the velvet rope that guarded the VIP room in Limelight, you could reasonably expect to see a smattering of Brat Pack actors, a literary sensation or two (namely Bret Easton Ellis, Jay McInerney and Tama Janowitz), an MTV-friendly pop star (Sting, say, Billy Idol or David Lee Roth), magazine editors (Tina Brown, probably), downtown gossip columnists, TV weather girls, fashion designers (LOTS of fashion designers), hip hop impresarios and minor politicians. You would no doubt also see some jet-lagged and extravagantly dressed renegades from London clubland, fresh from their economy trip on Virgin Atlantic and keen to see how the other half lived. Even if they were impressed, they never let on.

Alison Moyet: I didn't follow the scene very much, and that was my mistake. I never studied careers or made game plans. I didn't know you were expected to take a linear trajectory. Pick a team. Put on a face that you won't soon want to come off. When I signed a solo deal afterwards, I had never made a record before in that manner either. That's an interesting enough day for me. It's good to find out which instrument you truly are, what sounds your body can make, what you would never repeat. I took that lesson in the spotlight, and that's not the place to do it. *Alf* was massive. I sold a lot of records. Obviously, nothing less than a highly gratifying outcome, but when I immediately fancied sucking on something else, as I always would, the door was locked. You now have a blueprint you never knew existed. I couldn't live with that, and it confused everyone. Bloated, neither could my physical presence reflect a harder intent. I seemed manifestly soft. It denied me agency and energy. I got bored and disconnected and lazy. You can go left to right. You can't easily go right to left. It took me decades to be regarded again as something other than a singer, and it took a lot of turning down the wedge and saying, 'No.' I'd have known this had I read the music papers, had I wanted to make myself something in particular, but I was always fluid.

Andy Bell: When I went for the audition with Vince Clarke, I knew the songs off by heart. I was living in one of the last gay cooperatives in London and I used to sing along to Yazoo records, and when I went for the audition, my flatmate said, 'That will be you in a year's time.' I was the second-from-last person to audition for Erasure – I think the forty-third person – and over the weekend they said if they don't find anyone, they will review. And then they called and told me I'd got it. I think we got on because I was such a fan of Vince's, and when we first went into the studio, I was so shy it took me probably about six months before I even started talking to people. I was so intrigued by Vince I used to kind of stare at him, and he must have thought I was quite weird. When I think about it, it must have been pretty freaky for him. I knew I was employed as a singer in the first place, so I kind of behaved myself, but then after a while, after the first album, we just started co-writing. The first album was kind of a flop commercially, and I just thought Vince was so cool because he started from scratch, playing at universities and clubs. So it was as if he'd begun all over again, and I just thought it was such a humble thing for him to do, and for him to stick by me as well. So I just thought, 'Well, one good favour deserves another.' I did feel like we were never very fashionable. We weren't a hip band at all, and in some ways we were very much out of what was going on. But I think that's kind of what stood us in good stead for the future. I think quite soon we started to become known as a gay band. I remember we were doing TV shows, and I was going through my Madonna phase, wearing this dark black corset with leggings, and all these girls would be screaming at us. They'd say, 'Can we come with you?' And I'd tell them I was gay, and they'd say, 'We don't care.' When we were playing in North America, I was purposely as camp as I possibly could be on stage. I wanted to leave no one in any doubt. Obviously, there was a correlation between what the radio programmers would do if you were gay, as your airplay dropped off, but that was the climate in the US. However, the British sound was hugely influential. We felt like we were almost an experiment to see how successful we could be while being extremely camp, almost like a dare to the rest of the industry. I think we gave a lot of people the confidence to go out and be themselves and not be apologetic for who they were any more. But I think, in general, the music business is as homophobic now as it always was. It's based on machismo, the whole rock'n'roll thing.

Marc Almond: It started to end the minute we became successful. We were thrust together in hotel rooms, with PRs endlessly going round and round, and endlessly battling with the record company. We wanted to be reviewed in the *NME* instead of *Smash Hits*. We didn't want to repeat ourselves, and the record company just wanted another 'Tainted Love'. I love to perform, but Dave loves the studio, so we grew apart very, very quickly. Too much, too soon. Then, with the pressure, comes everything else – the excess of the early eighties, the drugs and the alcohol. I mean, both Dave and I have had our problems. I think we were sitting there recording an album, and we said we'd had enough. We'd been going for four years, and so we said, 'Let's split.' We had to do a bloody-minded American tour, where we refused to play any of the songs anyone wanted to hear. I think Michael Jackson came along to our LA show and was standing at the side of the stage. But we refused point blank to play 'Tainted Love'. That's how we felt at that time, and looking back on it now, it was stupid, but I suppose we were very confrontational and self-destructive.

Danny Eccleston: What Japan's atomisation opened was – for David Sylvian – one of the most interesting, and exasperating, solo careers of the eighties. It began almost perfectly, with an album that blazed a trail for art-pop, when its avatars – David Bowie and Roxy Music – had seemed to abandon it. Nineteen eighty-four's *Brilliant Trees* abounds with images of soil and growth – as if Sylvian were willing seeds into bloom. His team included Ryuichi Sakamoto, Can's Holger Czukay, Eno-associated trumpeter Jon Hassell, former Japan drummer Steve Jansen and ex-Japan keyboardist Richard Barbieri. Taking after *Low* and *'Heroes'*, side two was the more avant-garde. On the title track – an object lesson in ecstatic melancholy – and the hypnotic 'Weathered Wall', Hassell's treated trumpet is a shimmer of summer insects. The darker 'Backwater''s murky bass synth, discordant strings and metallic piano offer a portrait of the artist at bay, 'rushing to bite the hand that feeds me'. Sylvian seemed to regard *Brilliant Trees*' Top 10 success as proof that he wasn't being arty enough. 'I'm not going to repeat myself,' he once said. 'I'd rather stop making music than do that. You have to dive in the deep end and see what surfaces.' Maybe Sylvian thinks his pop music too shallow – perhaps he's embarrassed by it as he once was by Japan – but it's hard to think of music in any genre that dives deeper than *Brilliant Trees*, or that surfaces with more treasure.

The Police were another seventies band who made the most of the video decade, becoming bigger than ever in the first few years of the eighties. Their successful abstractions of pop-reggae made them largely inimitable, a success based on the increasingly robust songwriting ability of the band's singer, Sting. Their iconography centred on the trio's hair, their brooding good looks and Sting's physique. Their only acknowledgement of the enveloping electronic world around them was the cover of their 1981 album Ghost in the Machine *(a philosophical reference based on Gilbert Ryle's criticism of René Descartes*), on which Sting's, Stewart Copeland's and Andy Summer's faces (and haircuts) were represented*

* Ryle's work is one of the motifs of Arthur Koestler's *The Ghost in the Machine*. Sting had been an avid reader of Koestler, and the subsequent Police album, *Synchronicity*, was inspired by the author's *The Roots of Coincidence*, which mentions Jung's theory of synchronicity.

by seven-segment displays, the kind found on digital clocks. Like many of their peers, on this occasion the Police were acknowledging a worrying and increasing reliance on technology. Or at least their designer was. 'I wasn't their greatest fan,' says the sleeve's designer, Mick Haggerty. 'And their music always seemed a little cold. I kept putting it off, until one of my suppliers sent me a pocket calculator as a gift. The mailman folded the envelope in half, and when I undid the package, there on the [digital display] window was all this gobbledegook. I just immediately knew what I wanted to try.'

Sting (*singer, songwriter*): I have been perceived as an arrogant person, but I don't see that. I think I have a lot of self-esteem. I feel very happy with myself at the moment. I'm successful, I'm happy, I've got a good marriage, good children, and all that sustains me. I stand and fall on my own feet. I've always been confident, and even when I wasn't, I could pretend that I was. I have always been able to mask my fears, which is what I suppose was perceived as arrogance. I react to criticism pretty well. It used to annoy me, and I used to write back to the journalist involved, but not any more. Once you've done one interview, you've signed a pact with the devil, so you have to take what comes. Ideally, it would be better not to do any interviews ever, but you have to have relationships with the press; it's a cross I have to bear, I suppose. I've been called everything under the sun – God, they called me pretentious just because I read Proust. I don't think I'm a genius, but I also don't think I'm a shit; I'm somewhere in the middle. I feel pretty comfortable in that position, and I'm not looking for praise or blame. I think the critics have often overlooked the humour and the irony in my songs, but then I'm not supposed to have a sense of humour, am I? Criticism certainly toughens you up and gives you a thick skin. But you've got to remain sensitive to your art. If you stand up on stage and expose your innermost feelings, then you're really setting yourself up, especially if you are a confessional songwriter like I am. You're putting yourself in the stocks, so you need a certain amount of self-esteem and courage to carry on. I've never been the critics' darling, I've always been marginalised by them, so in a sense that has benefited me because I've got nothing to live up to. The press is cyclical, and when I was getting a lot of criticism, I figured it was my turn. Having said that, it did seem to be my turn for quite some time. It's certainly a price I've had to pay. The worst thing I remember is the *Village Voice* printing a caricature of my face that had been hacked with a knife – you know, 'Bring Me the Head of Gordon Sumner'. I was annoyed because it was New York, and things like that give people ideas. They read about it, and then they go and do it. I wouldn't have been the first British rock star to be assassinated in New York.

Nineteen eighty-four was not only the year that Duran Duran, Wham!, Spandau Ballet and Culture Club continued to conquer the world of MTV, it was also the year of the Band Aid single 'Do They Know It's Christmas?'. This charity record, organised by Bob Geldof and Midge Ure to raise funds for famine relief in Ethiopia, was not only a huge hit, it tapped into a new zeitgeist, one that initially appeared to be completely counter-intuitive compared to everything else that was happening in eighties Britain. In 1984, we were living in a world that was rapidly becoming obsessed by status, obsessed by the trappings of the designer lifestyle, full of newly empowered yuppies wrapping themselves in the spoils of style culture. In 1984, our new Swinging London had monetised itself and bought into (literally) a world of Italian espresso machines, lifestyle magazines, designer fashion, matt-black hardware, silver sports cars and lobotomised pop music. Nineteen eighty-four meant style over content, a Paul Smith suit, a Sade record (soon to be on CD!) and a European holiday.

The eighties was the decade of power dressing, concocted by the likes of Gianni Versace and Karl Lagerfeld, while the maxim of the moment was, 'If you've got it, flaunt it.' Hermès even produced a leather harness for carrying your bottle of Évian. The decade started with businessmen being knighted for go-getting, and then jailed when it was discovered how they had done it; it began with keeping your valuables in a vault, and ended with you pretending you used unleaded petrol.

Nineteen eighty-four wasn't meant to be the year that Britain remembered to celebrate the sixties. It wasn't meant to be the year of benevolence, charity or global empathy. We were living in the Reagan/Thatcher era, when intransigence was king, and when market forces determined everything – even what charity you donated to.

If the seventies had been the Me Decade, then, if anything, the eighties was the Media Decade, ten years in which cable TV took over the world, and when satellites gave us deep dish. VHS (and, for a while, Betamax) meant that we could now record everything, while CDs meant that the past was brought right up to date, remixed, burnished, and with a shiny, metallic, modern sheen (which a lot of people hated). Twenty-four-hour news meant that the world continued to shrink, and as the proliferation of newspapers and magazines continued exponentially, so lifestyles became content. It would be hyperbole to say that hype replaced art, but it appeared to replace just about everything else.

In this environment, Band Aid seemed positively contrary.

Which is possibly why it struck such a chord.

The idea for Band Aid started late on 24 October 1984, as Bob Geldof sat in his Chelsea home watching the BBC's Six O'Clock News *with his girlfriend, Paula Yates. This was in the days when the* Six O'Clock News *had an audience of around ten million, or roughly a sixth of the population. They were watching BBC reporter Michael Buerk's second film on the Ethiopian famine, and it was harrowing. In particular, it was the sight of a young English Red Cross worker that really shocked Geldof, as she had to decide which of the starving children she could try and help with her limited supplies. A long-term drought and secessionist wars in the Eritrea and Tigre regions had caused the failure of most food crops in Ethiopia and Sudan, and so a terrible famine struck the area. As the summer of 1984 dragged on and on, the fields withered and died, and the human tragedy grew worse. Western aid was organised immediately, but it was far too little to have any real impact. Geldof recalled the dignity of those condemned to death, hiding, almost cowering behind a low-lying wall.*

'I remember them staring over it,' he said. 'There was no rancour in their faces at all. That, more than anything, shocked me profoundly.'

Buerk's seven-minute report started with these two emotive sentences: 'Dawn, and as the sun breaks through the piercing chill of night on the plains outside Korem, it lights up a biblical famine, now, in the twentieth century. This place, say workers here, is the closest thing to hell on Earth.'

'I was based in Johannesburg at the time and was the BBC's correspondent in Africa,' said Buerk. 'The rains that should have come in around August to Ethiopia had failed again for the sixth season running, and it tipped over from being a crisis to a catastrophe. People suddenly realised they were going to die, and this huge mass migration started. It tipped very quickly.

'We flew and then drove up there, and the roads were just littered with dying people. It was extraordinary, it was just on such a huge scale. At Korem, there were 40,000–45,000 people, and in Makele there were another 80,000–90,000. They tended to congregate along the spinal road that led north from Addis, where they thought relief would get to them.

'It's difficult to express the inadequacy I felt. You take refuge in the technicalities of filming, finding sequences, working out the logistics and so on. There were two films, two pieces that finally aired. I knew they wanted about three minutes, but I cut eight and thought, "Fuck 'em." In those days, as a foreign correspondent, communications being what they were, I tended to work on the basis that they got what they were given. I knew it was a very powerful film.'

Geldof said, 'To die of want in a world of surplus is not only intellectually absurd, it is morally repulsive.

'It did not look like television,' he said. 'Vast . . . grey . . . these grey wraiths moving about this moonscape . . .'

The next day, Yates left a message for him on their kitchen noticeboard, encouraging them both to try and raise some money from their friends; but then Geldof decided that a better way to raise money would be to make a charity record. So he called Ultravox's Midge Ure, Sting and Duran Duran's Simon Le Bon, and proceeded to plan the Band Aid record. Geldof called every pop star he knew (and many he didn't) and persuaded them to record the single, under the title 'Band Aid', for free. So on Saturday 24 November, a star-studded group of musicians convened in a London studio to produce Geldof's folly: Duran Duran, Spandau Ballet, Wham!, Paul Weller, Phil Collins, Culture Club, the Police, Bananarama, Bono and many others.

Bob Geldof (*musician, activist*): 'Do They Know It's Christmas?' became, completely unwittingly, the focus for what must have been lurking about out there: a sense of impotence and compassion, a rejection of selfish values. I can't explain the song any other way. Musically, it wasn't the greatest thing ever written. Forget it. Three million sales in Britain alone cannot be explained, except as a social phenomenon. People must have tapped into this thing. What they'd seen on TV had appalled them, and they'd found no instrument to articulate that sentiment, and suddenly this silly piece of plastic came along, a fairly duff song, and that was it.

Midge Ure: I think the original tune for 'Do They Know It's Christmas?' had been turned down by the Boomtown Rats. But Bob didn't tell me that.

Gary Kemp: Band Aid was actually incredibly competitive, even people who came from the same club as us, like Boy George, Wham!, Duran . . . whoever it was. We hardly ever saw each other, but now we were all going to be in the same place at the same time. A few days after the Michael Buerk programme, I was in an antique shop on the King's Road, and I was in the window pointing at something I wanted to see, and Geldof pressed his face up against the window and said, 'Did you see Michael's programme?' And I hadn't. (I always find it hilarious, because there I was, an aspiring working-class kid, trying to buy old furniture. Alan Clarke would've been horrified.) And Bob said, 'Look, it was so moving, and I feel that we could all do something about this.' We all liked Geldof, as he was quite cool about hanging with the newer generation of kids. He and Paula came to some of those clubs [Blitz, Le Beat Route, Club for Heroes, etc.], and I think he was one of the few from that era who got what we were doing and wanted to kind of be part of it. And I always loved Paula. Even though he wasn't having hit records at that point, he was still a cool guy. When you're in a room with Bob . . . I mean, he's incredibly powerful. It's difficult to ignore him, you wanna be in his trench. He said, 'Do you fancy doing a single, making some music?' I thought, 'Dunno. It's a good idea,' but totally cynically thinking, 'Who the fuck's going to want to sing on that?'

Spandau were off to Japan that day, and I asked Bob to call if any more came of the idea, thinking that absolutely nothing would. But I got the call the very next day and was coerced into joining Geldof in his mission to get every major British pop star to sing on his charity record. We had to travel to Germany to do a TV show, before coming back to Britain to sing on the record, by which time Geldof had managed to co-opt most of the Top 30. While we were in Germany, we bumped into Duran Duran for the first time since they had come to see us play at the Botanical Gardens in Birmingham, when Spandau had just signed to Chrysalis Records. We decamped to the studio bar and proceeded to drink ourselves into a stupor. It was a big drinking match, and they were completely wrecked. I remember talking to Nick Rhodes, who said, 'Oh yeah, we've got a make-up artist meeting us at Heathrow so we can look half decent when we get out the other side.' I thought, 'Fuck me, we're going to be in trouble now.' So the actual day of recording became very competitive. We both got our private planes back, literally trying to beat each other to Heathrow. We were told that there were security guards waiting to meet us at Heathrow, but when we got there, the place was empty because all the press were down at Sarm Studios, waiting for everybody to arrive to record Band Aid.

We actually got our arrival at Sarm spectacularly wrong. We allowed cars to be organised for us, and when my brother Martin got out of his limo in front of the studio, he actually said, 'We're back.' Everyone knows how to be humble now, but not then. Sting got it perfectly right: he walked up the road with a copy of the *Guardian* under his arm. He probably got his driver to drop him off round the corner, but it looked as though he was completely on-message. He knew what to do immediately. Bollocks, he fucked us. But I'll never forget the day, because that was the best day, to have all those musicians in that studio, all trying to make it work and all getting on. U2 were there, and we were all thinking, 'Why the fuck are U2 here? They're nobody, they're punk wannabes.' And their bass player, Adam, said to Steve, our manager, 'Can I talk to you? What do you do about screaming girls, because we're starting to get them?' And Steve said, 'We love them.'

'Do They Know It's Christmas?' was released two days later, immediately going to No. 1 and becoming the fastest-selling single ever in Britain. The single raised £8 million worldwide (rather than the £50,000 or so that Geldof had originally envisaged), money that was used to buy and transport food, including 150 tons of high-energy biscuits, 1,335 tons of milk powder, 560 tons of cooking oil, 470 tons of sugar and 1,000 tons of grain. The Band Aid record immediately became part and parcel of the festive period, and that Christmas, and for most Christmases until the end of the decade, primary schools would sing the song as the finale of their carol service or Nativity play. Suddenly, everyone was channelling Sting, George Michael or Tony Hadley. Until Elton John's re-recording of 'Candle in the Wind', written for Princess Diana's funeral in 1997 (with all the proceeds going

to another charitable venture, the Diana, Princess of Wales Memorial Fund), it was the best-selling British single of them all.

Bob Geldof: When Midge and I did 'Do They Know It's Christmas?', I'd thought, '72,000 sales, give the money to Oxfam and Save the Children, and get the fuck out.' It was just a personal gesture, the only thing I could do at the time. I didn't have any money, we weren't successful, so I couldn't do the song myself – it would have been disastrous. The Rats wouldn't have sold anything.

Geldof already knew it was possible to change the world with a pop song, as he had seen the success of 'Free Nelson Mandela' by the Special AKA earlier in the year. Jerry Dammers was the creative genius behind the Specials, the man who gave them their political edge, who gave them their idiosyncratic musical tropes, and who set them apart from the likes of the Selecter, the Beat or Bad Manners. The Specials without Dammers were like the Doors without Jim Morrison, Queen without Freddie Mercury, Wham! without George Michael or Morecambe and Wise without Morecambe or, er, Wise. In 1981, he was left bereft when, after the huge success of 'Ghost Town', three members of the Specials left to form the Fun Boy Three – Terry Hall, Neville Staple and Lynval Golding – and so had to re-form the group, this time under the Special AKA banner. He then spent the next four years glacially recording an album – In the Studio *– and in the process released the epochal single 'Free Nelson Mandela'. It is difficult to imagine now, but back in the early eighties, there was not exactly a general awareness of Mandela's plight, and it took Dammers's heartfelt single (No. 9 in the UK charts in March 1984) to change that. 'I knew very little about Mandela, until I went to an anti-apartheid concert in London in 1983, which gave me the idea for "Nelson Mandela",' he said. 'I never knew how much impact the song would have; it was a hit around the world, and it got back into South Africa and was played at sporting events and ANC rallies – it became an anthem.'*

Its success eventually resulted in the Mandela Seventieth Birthday Tribute concert at Wembley Stadium in 1988, and helped add to the groundswell of support that led to Mandela's release from prison in February 1990. 'When "Nelson Mandela" came along, the band was falling to pieces,' said Dammers. 'But I had this idea that I knew was really important, like "Ghost Town", so there was that desperation to get it down on tape, before the thing disintegrated completely. I wrote the tune to "Nelson Mandela" before the lyrics. By that time, especially in London, rock music was dead. It was all electro-pop, hip hop, jazz or Latin. And also, Joe Hagan had this African club at Gossips [the Gold Coast Club]. I was inspired by the spirit and positivity of that African music. I was trying to get in a few Latin rhythms, but also township jazz. It was a very simple melody, three notes: C, A and E. That meant the public could sing it. And then I went to Nelson Mandela's sixty-fifth birthday party at Alexandra Palace. I'd never really heard of him, to be honest. Various bands sang about him, particularly Julian Bahula. And that's where I had the idea to put this message into this tune I had hanging around.' 'Ghost Town' is often considered to be Dammers's greatest achievement; however, considering the political impact of 'Free Nelson Mandela' – one of the most forthright pop records ever released – it is a wonder that its creation, and its creator, isn't more celebrated.

Gary Kemp: Band Aid was almost like a summit. It was so important, and it was weird to be part of it in a way, but then we were established by then. Spandau Ballet's records had become an important part of the evolution of British pop music. And I'm enormously proud of them. We were part of the golden age of pop. We were a gang who made records. It was madly competitive as we were all tribal. Duran Duran wanted to be more successful than us, we wanted to be more successful than ABC or Culture Club or Duran themselves. We spurred each other on. We went from playing electronica to funk and then blue-eyed soul, and then, like a lot of bands who suddenly find themselves selling out Wembley Arena for six nights in a row, music that sounds good in very large sheds. It was a fairly vertical take-off, and one we thought we might never come down from.

1985

LIKE PUNK NEVER HAPPENED

'It was never about philanthropy and charity; it was about politics and injustice. This poverty that was so hugely unnecessary and against our own self-interest. What I was saying then was, it's an asymmetric world. When you have half the world in poverty and half in wealth, things fall apart and the centre cannot hold.'

BOB GELDOF

Emboldened by the extraordinary success of 'Do They Know It's Christmas?' and frustrated by the way in which the aid agencies were distributing the money it was generating, Bob Geldof decided that there should be a concert too. He felt there was much more to do, and – Geldof being Geldof – he felt that he was the person to do it.

Midge Ure: Bob said we needed to break this trucking cartel in Ethiopia and buy a fleet of trucks and spares to deliver the aid. We didn't have the money, so Bob came in with this little drawing of the world with a knife and fork and the idea to do a concert. This mad, mad idea just grew.

Harvey Goldsmith: I didn't really get a chance to say no. Bob arrived in my office and basically said, 'We're doing this.' It started from there.

Bob Geldof: When I announced it, the only one who was dithering, as ever, was Bryan Ferry. So I just said, '. . . and Bryan Ferry.' And he rang to say, 'I didn't say "yeah".' I said, 'Well, say "no", then. You're the one who can announce it, though.'

Harvey Goldsmith: At one point, Bob and I sat in my boardroom, with David Bowie and Mick Jagger at the other end, trying to figure out how we could do a duet with one of them in America and the other one in the UK, and could we send one of them up in a rocket? It was just nuts.

Bob Geldof: For months, I'd been on an organisational continuum. I was full of fear: the great personal failure if it didn't work, that the bands wouldn't show up because we didn't have contracts, or that they would show up and be crap. But the primary fear was that we'd fail on behalf of those whom we were doing the whole thing for.

Harvey Goldsmith: The day before the concert, I went out and bought twenty or thirty very large clocks and just stuck them everywhere. I sent notes round to every single act, saying, 'I don't care what time you go on . . . I only care what time you come off.'

Bob Geldof: I was shitting myself. If the bands didn't show up, seventeen hours of the Boomtown Rats would have been a little too much for anybody. Paula put down white towels to sleep on that night because I had cold sweats.

One of the events of the eighties that never needed re-evaluating was the concert that took place on 13 July 1985 at Wembley Stadium, and later at the JFK Stadium in Philadelphia. The mother of all benefit gigs, Bob Geldof's Live Aid was one of the touchstones of the decade, a pinch point, an event that was deemed to have enormous relevance and a lasting legacy weeks, months before it actually happened. Live Aid was a global-village Woodstock with a mission. One of the reasons it caused such a stir was because of the environment in which it blossomed. An event such as Live Aid should have happened in the seventies, not the selfish, grasping eighties. On paper, a global charity concert featuring the likes of Bob Dylan, Elton John, the Rolling Stones and a Beatle should have happened in 1975, not 1985, surely. In the seventies, the benevolent gesture politics of the sixties were still being taken seriously, the shock waves still reverberating around the music industry. But by the midpoint of the eighties, we appeared to be far more interested in Boy George's make-up, the drum machines on the new Phil Collins record and the four-wheel drive option on the new Golf GTI.

Live Aid was organised in just twenty weeks, from scratch, immediately after a Boomtown Rats tour ended on 3 March. Not only did Bob Geldof want to put on a stadium show that would be televised worldwide, he wanted there to be two venues for the show: one in London and the other somewhere on the East Coast of the US (it had to be on the East Coast because of the time difference). The idea was to create a bill featuring the biggest contemporary acts in the world, mixed in with some heritage acts, and to use the concert as a massive fundraiser for the victims of the Ethiopian drought.

Live Aid was positively bipartisan, as it celebrated both the new guard and the old. It celebrated the new pop groups, the loose amalgam of New Romantic bands who had grown up out of punk, and who had all recently taken America by storm – Duran Duran, Spandau Ballet, Wham!, Sade, the Thompson Twins, etc. – while also celebrating the likes of Status Quo, Elton John and Paul McCartney, acts who were making records back when God was a boy. You could look at the Live Aid bill and think that punk had never happened, as though the social insurrection and class warfare of 1976 had been just a fantasy dreamed up by a couple of bored music journalists who had got sick of listening to their Iggy Pop and Lou Reed records.

Although Live Aid was a dual-venue concert held in London and Philadelphia, it is usually the London event that people think of whenever it is mentioned. Even though it was billed as the 'global jukebox', the event immediately became synonymous with London. That day, there were also concerts in Sydney, Cologne, Moscow and Holland, but it is the concert at Wembley Stadium that immediately became representative of a new kind of global celebrity culture, a concert which rubber-stamped the decade like no other. Not only that, it was also the largest-scale satellite link-up and television broadcast of all time: that day, an estimated global audience of 1.9 billion, across 150 nations, watched the live broadcast. Apart from Queen – who on 13 July would redefine what it meant to be a rock band – the other highlight of the day was the performance by U2. During 'Bad', Bono pulled a girl up from the audience and started to dance with her, something he had done before and would do again, but in the context of Live Aid, which was all about reaching out, touching, connecting, it was a magical moment. The girl he danced with later revealed that he actually saved her life. She was being crushed by the throngs of people pushing forwards; Bono saw this and gestured frantically at the ushers to help her. As they didn't understand what he was saying, he jumped down to help her himself.

Phil Collins famously performed at both Wembley Stadium and JFK, using Concorde to get from London to Philadelphia. Noel Edmonds piloted the helicopter that took Collins to Heathrow airport to catch his flight. Apart from his own performance at both venues, he also provided drums for Eric Clapton and (disastrously) Led Zeppelin at JFK.

The whole point of Live Aid was to raise money for Ethiopia, to extend the charitable efforts of Band Aid. Nearly seven hours into the Wembley concert, Bob Geldof enquired how much money had been raised. When he was told that so far they'd managed to raise £1.2 million, he marched to the BBC commentary box and gave the infamous interview in which he used the word 'fuck'. The BBC presenter David Hepworth, conducting the interview, had attempted to provide a list of addresses to which potential donations should be sent; Geldof interrupted him in mid-flow and shouted, 'Fuck the address, let's get the numbers!' After his outburst, giving increased to £300 per second.

Gary Kemp: It took an old punk who was also into pop music to recognise the power of MTV and the global pop video and say, 'We can change something here now by harnessing your success. And because we've got the new technology of wonderful TV satellites that can spread your image around the world, we can do something that will outplay the government.' And that's what Bob did with Live Aid. It was a bit like the first social media, and it made everyone feel more powerful than the government: you know, they weren't just putting a tick in a box every four years; now, they could go and put a postal order behind the counter, and the power of that pressure on the government would be so great they'd have to change their policies. And, of course, the power of that has never been forgotten.

Bob Geldof: Diana and Charles were hugely symbolic of the age, and it was a very big symbol that they came to Wembley. It was a huge endorsement of the entire project – of Band Aid, Live Aid, the whole project. And getting them to come was a major fucking thing, because I'm not sure Charles really wanted to be there. Diana certainly liked pop stars, and she was always flirting with them. Charles was saying, 'I don't really want to commit to something that isn't the Prince's Trust,' but I'd say, 'Hold on, Harvey Goldsmith organised the Prince's Trust. To all the rock guys, this is payback time.' I was so glad when they came. There were all these moments that came together on the day. You had this amazing galaxy of rock stars, and yet Diana was the most famous woman on the planet. Get her, and you've tuned in a whole section of American society. As soon as I knew she was going to come, I knew the Americans would tune in. I could hear them – 'Everyone, look at this.' That's literally what was in my fucking head. I really pushed this home in the States, as I knew it was the biggest button to push. To get all of these huge acts – which would one day become legacy acts – along with the biggest bands to have come out of the whole late-seventies, early-eighties New Romantic movement was a big deal for the show.

Midge Ure: Bob actually moved the Ultravox slot so that the Rats could play in front of Charles and Diana, the bastard!

Bob Geldof's big moment came halfway through the first song the Boomtown Rats played at Live Aid, 'I Don't Like Mondays', the song he had written as a knee-jerk response to the 1979 shooting spree of the sixteen-year-old Brenda Ann Spencer, who had fired at children in a school playground in San Diego, killing two adults and injuring eight children and one police officer. Spencer had showed no remorse, casually saying that 'I don't like Mondays. This livens up the day.' When Geldof got to the line 'And the lesson today is how to die . . .', the song was brought to a halt by the massive roar of the Wembley crowd. 'I let them shout, and then lifted my hand aloft with my fist clenched, and the audience fell into a massive breathing quietness.'

This moment lent a poignancy to the day that had so far been absent. The air was punched a lot after that, real 'fight-the-power punches', acknowledging the symbolism and shooting the sky for Geldof.

Gary Kemp, who was watching from the wings (they were on in an hour's time and were already dressed in their duster coats), said that the moment Geldof stopped the song and raised his fist in the air was evangelical. He says Geldof was statesman-like and had so much charisma he would have made a frightening politician. '[He was] a link between punk and the New Romantics and the eighties.'

Bob Geldof: When I stopped dead in the middle of 'I Don't Like Mondays', my brain was working ahead of me. Before I got to sing it, I thought, 'I'm going to sing that line out loud.' I'd done stadiums before, but this was different, and I had the feeling everyone I'd ever met in my life would be watching it. So I thought to myself, 'I'm going to stop and take that in.' It was a unique moment, and one I knew would never come again. Everything just pulled me up sharp. You can see me going from right to left, taking it in around the stadium. This is what I was in the middle of, and suddenly I understood another meaning to 'the lesson today is how to die', and I wanted that to impact anyway. Of course, it was one of the moments when the fucking floodgates just opened and cash poured in, because suddenly it hit home. I looked at the guys in the band, who were a bit freaked out that I'd stopped, as I'd never done that, and they all just looked at me and carried on. That was a big moment for me, the big romance of it. The emotion really grew after that. You could see the figures scale up as people got more involved and started competing with how much they could pledge. Then, when I was being interviewed by David Hepworth – who had started acting in this Smashie and Nicey way, even though he isn't like that – the money really started pouring in. I just couldn't be bothered with the formality of it all. You had Billy Connolly crying his eyes out, and all this BBC formality about the address. Fuck writing in. What the fuck are you talking about? Just give us the fucking money, OK? People aren't going to lick stamps and send it in. Do it now, over the phone. And don't go to the pub. So they didn't go to the pubs. That was it.

David Hepworth: My theory about Live Aid is that it suddenly sold the idea of huge great outdoor events to the general public. The sun was shining, there's Freddie Mercury, and you think, 'I like this.' And bands have been doing it ever since.

Jim Kerr: With Live Aid, apart from the politics of the charity behind it, it was the first time millions of people had looked at a so-called stadium gig and thought, 'I want to go to one of them' – that communal thing. And after Live Aid, everyone was in stadiums, or trying to be in stadiums. Who would've thought Depeche Mode, plink-plonking away, would play in stadiums? Things got very big, and when they do, there's a moment when you realise your band is no longer your band, that it's an industry itself.

Harvey Goldsmith: The night before, the biggest problem we had was the bloody turntable stage didn't work, and that was a real issue. There was quite low morale with all of the crew, and I had to go and pep them up. Then I got a phone call at about midnight from Tommy Mottola, from Sony. He said if we didn't make sure Hall & Oates were on the ABC two-hour special, as well as the MTV broadcast of the whole show, then he was pulling Mick Jagger. And I told him, 'It is what it is. It's too late now, and if you want to pull Mick Jagger, then pull him, but I don't actually think you're going to succeed on that one.' And then Bill Graham, who was organising the JFK show, phoned me up and said, 'I'm making this plea: if you want me to really get my head around this, you've got to put Black Sabbath on, because I've got a merchandising deal with them.' Love it! The crew had been working for thirty-six hours, so with all this going down, it was quite demoralising for all of us.

David Bailey: I loved it because I was one of only four people who had the magic pass, the pass where you could go everywhere. Bob Geldof had one, Midge Ure had one, Harvey Goldsmith had one, and I had the other. It was like Willy Wonka's Golden Ticket. I could even have gone on stage, if I'd wanted to.

Harvey Goldsmith: Status Quo were the only people who weren't nervous. Everyone was hanging around backstage, most of them in the Hard Rock Café at the back. Everyone was very aware of adhering to the schedule, of playing ball, so everyone was being mindful of the timings. And most people, believe it or not, were actually very nervous. David Bowie was nervous, Elton was nervous, Freddie Mercury was pacing around. The only people who weren't were Quo. As soon as we knew Charles and Diana were coming, we knew we had to alter the show, as we needed a big beginning, a grand opening. We knew the royals wouldn't stay all day, so we had to open big. That's when we decided that Status Quo were the right people to open the show. I had always assumed that Bob would open the show, but after a while, it made sense for Quo to do it, with 'Rockin' All Over the World'. They did it as a bit of a favour, believe it or not, but we kind of thought they would fit in somewhere in the show, an iconic British group. And it worked perfectly. Everybody remembers 'Rockin' All Over the World', *everybody.* It was like a stroke of genius. The atmosphere in the audience was fantastic, and it set the day up perfectly. At the end of the day, everyone kind of left it to me to sort out the running order, and I sort of did it using common sense, but primarily because of change-over times. So everybody accepted that because there was a logic to it.

Bernard Docherty (*publicist*): I remember being in the pit for Sade and thinking, 'What a goddess,' and thinking how great she looked. She was so anti-rock'n'roll, but she was one of the best performances of the day. The audience reaction was amazing – they loved her.

Bono (*singer, musician, activist*): People were very good to me. I was walking with [my wife] Ali, and Freddie Mercury pulled me aside and said, 'Oh, Bo-No . . . Is it Bo-No or Bon-O?' I told him, 'It's Bon-O.' He said, 'Come over here with me. We've all been talking, myself, Roger [Daltrey] and Pete [Townshend] and David [Bowie], and we all agree there's no singers any more. Everyone is shouting these days, but you're a singer.' I was up against a wall, and he put his hand on the wall and was talking to me like he was chatting up a chick. He had me laughing, but I was shifting nervously at the same time, with Ali and myself exchanging glances. I thought, 'Wow, this guy's really camp.' I was telling somebody later, and he said, 'You're surprised? They're called Queen!' But I was really amazed. It hadn't dawned on me.

The former New Yorker *writer Sasha Frere-Jones – who, unlike many of his peers, had a radar acquired from the very top shelf – has a word for it: 'squinting', the act of peering at a musician you fell in love with when you were much younger, trying to remind yourself why you found them so fascinating. 'The relationship grows through awkward phases,' he writes, '– nautical dress, orchestral arrangements, dodgy collections of poems. Along the way, you find yourself squinting to keep seeing what made you fall in love; you will need to pretend that the accordion and the Balkan song cycles are something else. (Fans of Bob Dylan have unusually deep creases). In pop music, which is a worse deal for the ageing than painting and fiction are, there can be a fair amount of effort involved.'*

And although the original version of Queen only really had a career that lasted twenty years, and whose oeuvre was crowded but not exactly perverse, their fans were always completely forgiving. As they started out as a rather orthodox (if flashy) rock band, this was even more unusual, but as the band pinballed between theatrical ballads, disco and high-camp pop, their legions of admirers blithely followed along (honestly, if you liked 'Seven Seas of Rye', you weren't programmed to enjoy 'Killer Queen'). The band got away with it as they wrote the sort of tunes that you couldn't shake off, even if you wanted to.

Their fans tended to be rather orthodox too, and for a while appeared to be in some sort of collective denial concerning Freddie Mercury's sexuality. I always think of Mercury in the same way as the Robert De Niro character in the 2007 movie Stardust. *De Niro plays a gay pirate called Captain Shakespeare, who tries to hide his sexuality from his crew. When he is eventually outed, his men give a collective shrug. 'We always knew you were a whoopsie,' says one.*

Queen's twenty-minute appearance at Live Aid at Wembley Stadium in the summer of 1985 was one of the most captivating performances of the decade (in 2005, Channel 4 voted it the greatest gig of all time). It was also great television. Seen by over two billion people, they stole the show and completely revitalised their career. In the weeks following the event, all of Queen's albums tumbled back into the charts.

Bryan Ferry: I have terrible memories of it all going wrong. I'd put together an all-star band, and the set was fraught with problems. We had David Gilmour on guitar and, poor David, his guitar wasn't working for the first couple of songs. With his first hit, the drummer put his stick through the drum skin. And then my microphone wasn't working, which for a singer is a bit of a handicap. A roadie ran on with another mic, so then I was holding two mics taped together, and I wasn't really sure which one to sing into. It was a great day, though.

What few talk about is the vast amount of cocaine that was backstage at Wembley that day. In truth, there had never been such a high-profile concert where there were so many Class A drugs. They were literally everywhere.

Harvey Goldsmith: Adam Ant didn't work at all. The audience hated it. I think there were a couple more in the middle of the day that probably didn't work as well as they might have, but overall everybody went that extra mile and rose to the occasion. Except Adam Ant. He looked out of sorts with the times and didn't fit in. He just wasn't 'Live Aid' enough, I suppose.

Marco Pirroni: I can't look back and say Live Aid was one of the greatest days in my life, but I was glad I was there.

Gary Kemp: God bless Adam. His career may have been faltering at the time, but he opened the door for so many people. What he was doing visually eased the way for acts like ourselves in a way.

At Live Aid, George Michael came on at the end of Elton John's set to sing 'Don't Let the Sun Go Down on Me', jumping around the stage like an animated glove puppet, the piano player's dummy, for tonight he was Elton's ami necessaire. *Live Aid was a big day for him, although Andrew Ridgeley wasn't really in the loop. He had raised funds backstage and sang backing vocals, but to all intents and purposes, this was a solo outing for George, the first of many.*

George Michael: The Live Aid thing was fantastic because the emotion behind it was genuine – at least on the English side of things. There was lots of talk about the squabbles that were going on over in Philadelphia, but over here the British bands were too nervous to push themselves up front, they didn't argue over their spots, and it went really well. I was aware that after Live Aid I was seen in some quarters as . . . a solo act. I was nervous as hell. It was the first time I had ever sung in front of an indifferent audience, because every one I had sung in front of before had been mine – or ours. The miners' benefit wasn't an indifferent audience – that was hostile. But that was OK. I did the miners' benefit because that was what I believed in, and I knew what we could expect from the audience. So I was angered by it, but I wasn't surprised. But with the Live Aid audience I knew I would be judged differently. More than anything, it showed that people wanted me – quite unfairly – to do stuff on my own, so they could admit to liking me. Everybody raved about my performance, which I honestly thought was very average. Everybody said, 'God, he showed he can really sing,' but I thought it was nothing special. The interpretation I did of 'Don't Let the Sun Go Down on Me' was very close to what Elton had done, and I was out of tune for the first couple of verses. I actually sing a lot better than that on my records, and I don't see why everyone should suddenly like me because I am up there with musicians twice my age and I am taking myself away from my friend. I didn't understand why that should be suddenly credible. Live Aid was good for me, but people's reaction kind of annoyed me. It irritated me.

Gary Farrow: George knew it wasn't the moment for a light-hearted band scenario, which is why Wham! didn't play Live Aid. He needed a big emotional song, which is what he did.

It would turn out to be a good year for George, and by Christmas his voice could be heard on four records in the Top 20: Wham!'s 'I'm Your Man', the re-released 'Last Christmas' and Band Aid's 'Do They Know It's Christmas?', as well as Elton John's 'Nikita'. Elton was on something of a roll too, and he hadn't been so popular since the mid-seventies. He had survived the hair transplants, the unlikely marriage to studio engineer Renate Blauel in 1984 – 'You may still be standing,' Rod Stewart's wedding telegram read, 'but we're all on the fucking floor!' – and appalling press intrusion. But by Live Aid he was well and truly back. The 'comeback' record, or at least the one that immediately made him relevant for an eighties audience, was 1983's Too Low for Zero, *which contained the mammoth hits 'I'm Still Standing' and 'I Guess That's Why They Call It the Blues'. This was his first album since 1976's* Blue Moves *to exclusively feature lyrics by his long-term partner Bernie Taupin, and it showed. He followed this with* Breaking Hearts, *in July 1984, which included 'Passengers' and 'Sad Songs (Say So Much)', and was the album he was still promoting throughout much of 1985. Four months after Live Aid, he released* Ice on Fire, *his nineteenth studio album, and again the first since* Blue Moves *to be produced by his old producer Gus Dudgeon (it included 'Nikita' and 'Wrap Her Up'). By the time of Live Aid, and at the age of thirty-eight, he was already a national institution and had already had enough careers for six people.*

Britain in the eighties had been called Fantasy Island by some, an age of bogusness, artifice and self-delusion, regardless of any liberal certitudes. 'In Britain, little remains that does not wear the cosmetic disguise of something else, considered happier, more desirable or glamorous,' said Philip Norman. Pastiche was ripe, as the emerging lifestyle culture determined that in order to be successful, entertainment had to be like stuff that had been before, but only slightly less. Elton may have worn some ridiculous outfits – coming on stage dressed as a duck or Minnie Mouse – but he was never a parody. Only Elton could do what Elton did, which is why he was a true original. You could maybe call Wham! a parody, but never Elton.

There was another true original in the stadium that day, a twenty-four-year-old Sloane from Sandringham: Diana Frances Spencer. Prince Charles, at the old-before-his-time age of thirty-six, may have worn a navy-blue suit to Live Aid and then referred to it as 'some pop concert jamboree my wife made me go to', but for Princess Diana, this was almost a coming-out party, four long years after their wedding. Here was a Sloane Ranger with a taste for pop – she adored George Michael and Duran Duran – and who wore John Galliano. A royal whose causes weren't typical of someone in her position – the victims of Aids and landmines. A royal who found a role by transforming herself into what Alastair Campbell would one day brand her, the People's Princess.

Geldof had buttonholed the pair at a Dire Straits concert ten days beforehand, corralling them and almost begging the royal couple to attend. 'I thought it would be important for them to come, because at that time it was glamorous, there was excitement around their relationship, and they represented the country,' said Geldof.

Mark Ellen: Live Aid sparked an appetite in people to want those communal moments again. They are very rare, and when they happen, they tend to mean a lot to people. When Princess Diana died, I was as fascinated as everyone else by the way it affected people. I wasn't a big admirer of hers, but I still went along to the funeral with my kids. There was a general desire to feel the same way at the same time as everyone else, and I know, on the face of it, Princess Diana and Live Aid don't have much in common, but they absolutely do. Diana's death had a very complicated political frame around it. I remember taking a photograph of the coffin going under the tree we were standing by, and all the people around me started tutting, because at that point everyone thought that she had been killed by photographers. And as I looked like a photographer, quite possibly a paparazzo, I was treated as one of the enemy, as one of them. That's how hot-headed people were at the time, as she meant so much to people.

Neil Tennant: Live Aid was the last thing I was asked to do for *Smash Hits*. Mark [Ellen] asked me to cover it, and for some completely childish reason I just sort of couldn't be bothered and said no. So I watched Live Aid sitting in my studio flat on the King's Road with

Jon Savage and [photographer] Eric Watson, all three of us slagging it off.

Nineteen eighty-five had already been a something of a tumultuous year, albeit one intertwined with entertainment-driven trivia. On the first day of January, the first British mobile-phone call was made (it was a stunt: the comedian Ernie Wise calling Vodafone), prompting British Telecom to announce it was going to phase out its famous red telephone boxes. On 20 January, US President Ronald Reagan was sworn in for a second term in office, while barely two months later, Mikhail Gorbachev became the General Secretary of the Soviet Communist Party and, therefore, de facto leader of the Soviet Union. At fifty-four the youngest member of the Politburo, he not only looked more youthful than any previous Soviet leader, but came armed with new ideas to boot. He eagerly wanted a dialogue with the West, and would seek internal reforms that were completely alien to previous regimes. He was driven by change, and by ambition: this was a man who had graduated from driving a harvester to a law degree from Moscow University.

In some respects, the world was a simpler place in 1985. At least it was mediated that way, with broadly defined ideas of good and evil. The Cold War was still raging, and a poll conducted in Britain in 1980 had found that 40 per cent of adults were convinced that a nuclear war was likely in the next ten years. The nuclear threat was referenced everywhere in pop culture, from Frankie Goes to Hollywood's 'Two Tribes' to Hollywood's own War Games *via Martin Amis's* Einstein's Monsters. *For many, the only sure-fire weapon against communism was Rocky Balboa, who managed to bring about world peace in* Rocky IV *by beating Russian boxing machine Ivan Drago. On 12 June 1982, over one million people had demonstrated in New York City's Central Park against nuclear weapons and for an end to the Cold War arms race.*

The third of March 1985 saw the end of the year-long miners' strike, although its place on the evening news was soon taken by the newly ascended football yoberati. Hooliganism was fast becoming one of England's worst exports. On 13 March, rioting broke out at the FA Cup quarter-final between Luton Town and Millwall at Kenilworth Road, Luton; hundreds of hooligans tore seats from the stands and threw them onto the pitch, before a proper pitch invasion took place, resulting in eighty-one people (thirty-one of them members of the police force) being injured. Two months later, an accidental fire engulfed a wooden stand at the Valley Parade stadium in Bradford, killing fifty-six people and injuring more than 200. On 29 May, at the European Cup final between Juventus and Liverpool at the Heysel Stadium in Brussels, thirty-nine spectators were killed in rioting on the terraces, casting an even larger shadow over English football. In response, on 2 June UEFA banned all English clubs from European competition indefinitely, and suggested that Liverpool be excluded for an extra three years.

Just three days before Live Aid, at the behest of President François Mitterrand French DGSE agents sank the Greenpeace vessel Rainbow Warrior *in Auckland harbour. Humbled by the outcry that followed, the French government decided to abandon nuclear testing for ten years.*

In April, worried about the continuing onslaught of Pepsi – who appeared to have decided that the eighties was going to be their decade – Coca-Cola had gone and done the unthinkable and announced a new formula, New Coke ('The best just got better . . .'). It had been such a disaster that three days before Live Aid, they had been forced to reintroduce Classic Coke. Pepsi couldn't believe they were gifted such a self-inflicted PR disaster by their fiercest rival. Coincidentally, on 13 July their logo was flying above the Wembley stage.

This was also the year the BBC launched its own soap opera, jumping ahead of the curve for once by using the increasingly popular conceit of abutting two words and inserting a medial capital letter, thus: EastEnders. *This was also called CamelCase, or bicapitalisation: compound words whose two components are joined without spaces – CinemaScope, FedEx, InterLink, PlayStation,*

HarperCollins, WordPad, SureStart, etc. This was what Tom Wolfe called the new, lean, mean fashion of jamming names together, 'as if that way you were creating some hyperhard alloy for the twenty-first century'. In the case of EastEnders, *it was curiously unnecessary, but it had the effect of making the BBC seem a little less stuffy than the competition. Not that the BBC needed to worry about being stuffy, as with Live Aid they would be the feeder broadcaster for the largest television event in history.*

Terry Waite, the Archbishop of Canterbury's special envoy, negotiated the release of four British hostages from Beirut, while the civil war in Lebanon continued. The Shias took over the city, and the Lebanese cabinet fell. The conflict then spread to a wider stage, as the Israelis bombed the Palestine Liberation Organisation's offices in Tunis. In June, just a month before Live Aid, a TWA jet was hijacked and diverted to Beirut and its thirty-nine American passengers held hostage by Shia terrorists for sixteen days, until 700 Lebanese Shia prisoners were released from Israel. Slightly less successful was the hijacking of the Italian cruise ship Achille Lauro *by a group of Palestinian pirates.*

Violence was also escalating in South Africa, with a broad pattern of racial strife spreading through the townships. While the ban on mixed marriages had ended, there was escalating pressure for international sanctions to be imposed. A state of emergency was declared, and press restrictions introduced.

Elsewhere, it was more than fitting that British Elle *launched in 1985, as this was the year that British fashion truly went global, with Vivienne Westwood, BodyMap, Scott Crolla, Rachel Auburn, John Galliano and a whole host of other, younger designers at the forefront of a movement that looked as if it were about to take over the world. Many of them had been born in the Blitz. Perhaps the most successful designer of the year was Katharine Hamnett, who briefly swapped places with Christo, as her shirts seemed to cover the planet like huge silk shrouds. She had become a household name the year before, when she had worn one of her protest T-shirts – '58% Don't Want Pershing', a reference to a poll showing public opposition to the basing of Pershing missiles in the UK – to Downing Street to meet Mrs Thatcher. Hamnett was another habitué of the Blitz.*

London was changing beyond recognition as new money swept into the city and we all tried to embrace the trappings of the upwardly mobile. We started defining ourselves in different ways too. At the start of the eighties, there were hardly any good restaurants in London, yet as the decade wore on, they appeared to arrive every hour, on the hour. Lindsey Bareham was a food writer for the London listings magazine Time Out *at the time: 'Suddenly we knew the names of top chefs in the same way we knew the names of the Beatles: the Roux brothers, Anton Mosimann, Nico Ladenis and Raymond Blanc. Rose Gray and Ruth Rogers tentatively launched The River Café as a works canteen for Richard Rogers' architectural practice next door; Alastair Little, Marco Pierre White and Simon Hopkinson, and the late Rowley Leigh at Kensington Place, all opened trend-setting restaurants within months of each other.'*

As Bareham and every other traditional recipe writer soon discovered, while these new chefs' coffee-table books inspired a new generation of newly confident home cooks, the meals they were making required unusual, esoteric ingredients, prompting the likes of Marks & Spencer to broaden its range of upmarket ready meals, bringing flat-leaf parsley, banoffee pie, rocket and plum tomatoes to the masses.

And we hoovered it up, thinking ourselves on the cusp of some great new foodie dawn. It wasn't just food that was being codified, though; it was everything – furniture, cars, the way your bank looked on the high street, the logos on your utility bills, the fanlights on your new docklands studio flat. It was the music too . . .

David Bowie: I went mainstream in a major way with *Let's Dance*. I pandered to that in my next few albums, and what I found I had done was put a box around myself. It was very hard for people to see me as anything other than the person in the suit who did 'Let's Dance', and it was driving me mad – because it took all my passion for experimenting away . . . Being shoved into the Top 40 scene was an unusual experience. It was great I'd become accessible to a huge audience, but not terribly fulfilling. It seemed so easy. It was cheers from the word go. You knew how to get a reaction – play 'Changes', 'Golden Years', and they'd be up on their feet. You get the reaction, take the money and run away. It seemed too easy. I didn't want to do that again.

By 1985, Bryan Ferry had already morphed from a tuft-hunter to a boulevardier dressed by Yohji Yamamoto and Savile Row. His records had gone from being almost indecently atmospheric to elegantly upholstered. While he had moved so far away from where he was that he was almost unrecognisable to some, surprisingly few held grudges against him. After all, we all figured this is where he had wanted to end up in the first place.

If, at the start of his career, the 'alpha male of highfalutin sleaze' occasionally came across as someone who – in the eyes of some – refused to accept he was in a rock band rather than at a dinner party, as he got older he would be criticised for performing as though he couldn't wait to get home to his wine cellar. In many ways Ferry had moved on, and yet in others he remained exactly the same. Certainly, his pre-1975 form was so well preserved in the imagination of the generation he inspired that his public obsessions from that time were still the way in which he was remembered and, yes, idolised. David Bowie might have continually moved on, reinventing himself in the time it took to imagine buying a new hat, and yet here was Bryan Ferry in 1985, much the same as he had been in 1975, or indeed in 1973.

And it is to 1973 where, I think, we need to return in order to understand the real motivations of the Sweet Dreams *decade, the reasons that so many from that period felt encouraged, persuaded maybe, to develop in the way they did.*

The crux, I feel, is the song 'Mother of Pearl', which is the third song on side two of Roxy Music's third – and best – album, Stranded, *released at the very beginning of November that year. The music arrived at two speeds: the first a rush into the night, a saraband, a snapshot of Swinging London, seventies style; and then a slow, protracted, piano-driven coda, a melancholy end to the evening. The lyrics mirrored the noise: cocaine and cocktails followed immediately by a deluxe ennui, a wistful meditation on a life lived too fast,, being up all night, and relentlessly party time wasting. For the listener, the spectator, the fan, this was the ambition template: the contemplative deconstruction of a world only imagined. Were we really that desperate to feel jaded? Apparently so.*

Peter York: Come the time, Bryan Ferry came back with a bang, but that had to wait, that had to wait quite a long time. I always thought he was an incredibly original, special person, and some of his music was the music of the spheres. I mean, he's absolutely magical. I loved [1982's] *Avalon*, I think it was marvellous. But, of course, it was in every way wrong. It was a hundred ways wrong, including sort of being England's dream, all that stuff. But I loved it. By 1985, he had come round again. By 1985, Bryan almost felt as important as he had been in 1972. Almost . . .

Keren Woodward: I went to see Roxy on their *Manifesto* tour, and I loved 'Dance Away' and *Avalon* and everything from the second period. I loved all that. They can do no wrong in my eyes. And all the stuff Bryan Ferry does on his own I love as well. The eighties were kinder to Bryan Ferry than people think.

Bryan Ferry: [To disband Roxy Music after *Avalon*], that was deliberate. It just felt so perfect; it was like, how can I follow that? The fact it was a high spot is the only thing that makes credible the idea of another Roxy album. It's interesting, this thing of group work. On the one hand, conflict is sometimes very good for creativity, and we certainly had plenty of that. The struggle for supremacy of ideas. I suppose it happens in every group.

The first Roxy period was especially good for that. Eno was a very good editor for me, a good sounding board. On the other hand, it's a knife-edge situation. It can also get so crazy with people that it does negative things. With Roxy, it felt like it was becoming a racket to see who could get in on the publishing. Really depressing. It seemed the only real interest they had was, 'Can I get a song on the album?' It was a drag, though occasionally good things would come out of it. Especially with Andy: 'Song for Europe' and 'Love Is the Drug', two really good ones. Still, the chemistry was never completely exhausted. It pulled interesting things out of me as well. Our audience knew it. We never had a hit single in the States, yet the audiences kept getting bigger every year. But after the *Avalon* tour, I was burned out. I didn't want the group any more, I didn't want to tour any more. My former manager and his partners had made a punishing schedule, sometimes five nights in a row in different countries, never mind different cities. I could hardly breathe, and I just said, 'That's enough.'

David Bowie: By 1985, I was something I never wanted to be: I was a well-accepted artist. I had started appealing to people who bought Phil Collins records. I suddenly didn't know my audience and, worse, I didn't care about them. I always looked OK in clothes – I was kind of a target for designers, always. They sort of made a beeline for me and tried to get me to wear their things. But I guess it was up to me to choose which ones I would wear. The thing is, I always wore clothes for a reason, not to be fashionable. I've never seen the point of being fashionable, as then you obviously just look like everyone else. Which is the one thing I have never, ever wanted to be. It doesn't matter in what context you're talking about, I never, ever wanted to be or look remotely like anyone else. Sometimes I was right in what I chose, sometimes I wasn't. I should never have touched the Culture Shock label in the early eighties.

Boy George: I remember going on my first Gay Pride march from Lewisham to the West End, and my brothers later told me they were there shouting out abuse. They didn't realise I was on it. There's so many things that went on in the seventies, but a lot of the forward thinking in culture came from Bowie and Roxy Music. It shaped us, people sort of trying to be who they wanted to be, whether it was gay, straight . . . whatever. We were outsiders, but by the mid-eighties we had been accepted. Growing up in south-east London, where there is a lot of racism, and, you know, being gay and obviously effeminate and obviously an outsider, I think I just really felt a kind of connection to anyone who was an outsider. The music would change – it would get better, then worse, then better again – but what I think the eighties encouraged was a wonderful sense of open-mindedness.

Andy Polaris: I think we really lived it large in those days. It was a really creative time, and so much of what happened then, you're still getting the ripples of influence now. It was amazing that so many successful people came out of that very central group of people. Even at the beginning of it, I can't say it was more than 100–150 people. It was a groundbreaking period too – just look at 'Smalltown Boy' by Bronski Beat, someone actually talking about homophobia and the danger there was in being a young gay person at that time. But even though people mention the androgyny, I actually knew quite a few people who were on the verge of transitioning. When you went to places like Sombrero, you would see many transvestites or transgender people. There was such a spectrum of gay life, which not many people understood. A lot of people at the time were navigating their sexuality in public.

Peter York: The gay emancipation was very important. There is a through line right back to Bowie, where a lot of games were being played with sexual identity. At the Blitz and everything that came after it, everyone was playing with gender. And the success of everyone just normalised it. I think it had an impact on girls, because girls responded to it, and it made its way back to their boyfriends in terms of their expectations and in a way sort of softened up the boys, in probably what was quite a civilising way. And this was global. The requirements of success change people. The requirements of America change people, and so after a while all the English groups started to know what you needed to do in order to get that big American recording contract. But for consumers, it went on being infinitely liberating.

Alison Moyet: I look back upon the eighties as a massive education. Some classes were exquisite and some I dropped very quickly because they offered nothing of substance. I am obviously lucky. I do what I do, and I do that as a result of what it taught me about myself and the world I work in. The difficult years have been most valuable. This period stunted me for a while. It killed my interest, it separated me from the lanes and people I would have found greater communion with, I suspect. It took extricating myself from the mainstream and accepting the loss of status that commercialisation affords, knowing you cannot just expect to find it renewed in the artistic sense without paying all your dues again. Which I have done. I am perfectly certain that my later work is superior, as well as I know that fewer seek it out. That's an acceptable enough exchange for me. It also gave me a platform. I can give a lot of sermons about how age can provide a valuable and slanted contribution to art. I can applaud my twenty-three-year-old self without wanting to still be her and without forgetting her reasons. I can also be glad she fucked off. I fought long and hard to exist beyond the eighties. Commercially, I was made in the eighties, but the eighties didn't make me. I'm not sorry I was there.

Grace Jones: There is some eighties music that is just timeless. The melodies, the lyrics . . . I called it church. Church in a club. You can shout and dance. The best of the eighties was club church.

Jim Kerr: The amazing thing about people in the eighties was their ambition. Not so much ambition for riches and fame – that was too far down the road – but ambition to do something glorious. And whether that was our band or spiky music like the Cure and Magazine or early Spandau Ballet and Duran. I mean, early Spandau wasn't Tony Hadley's chocolate box; from day one they were going to take over the world! And they did. And all of them were quite maverick. To me, it wasn't so much any movement; it was more like there weren't two or three bands like the Cure, there was the Cure. There weren't two or three bands like the Human League, like the Birthday Party, like the Smiths, there was one. A lot of real individualism and wonderful imagination, to such a level that it was almost overwhelming. It was an incredibly political decade – the Berlin Wall coming down, Mandela being freed, the miners' strikes, the poll tax, Tiananmen Square. It certainly wasn't all shoulder pads, *Rambo* and Filofaxes.

Mark Ellen: I've got tons of fond memories. Running into Gary Kemp in Soho as he was walking to a photo shoot wearing handmade shoes, a silk scarf and a striped suit and waistcoat with a gold watch-chain. No shirt. I remember being on a private plane to the San Remo pop festival with Duran, Spandau, Sade, Bronski Beat, Chaka Khan, Talk Talk and Frankie Goes to Hollywood and thinking how *huge* the whole thing had become. All those acts had evolved from the pop boom of the early eighties. My abiding memory is of being at a music awards in 1982, the week 'Do You Really Want to Hurt Me?' came out. All the Fleet Street press were there, Princess Margaret was making a speech. Virgin had brought the unknown Boy George along to try and cause a ripple – huge hat, dress, pendulous earrings, ribbons in his dreadlocks, vigorous application of make-up. Widow Twankey in biker boots. Towards the end he got up, strolled over to the two toilet doors and then trundled theatrically between them in a show of mock confusion. Ladies? Gents? *Decisions!* The whole room was watching. The press love a pantomime dame – camp, cheeky, harmless – and they all ran stories the next day. And that was the turning point. They'd found a widely appealing, deliciously quotable pop star who sold papers. From that moment the tabloids ran regular gossip pieces on pop musicians, and record sales went even further through the roof. Every broadsheet soon had a music column. They were a reaction to the punk and 2-Tone that had come before. Both those seemed very monochrome and rooted in the rigours of real life (and often politics), and being largely before video, they were a live event, so you had to be old enough to go to pubs and clubs to really feel part of it. But the New Romantics were a video/Radio 1/*Smash Hits* event, so you could be much younger but still feel fully connected. The potential audience was far bigger. And they were all about fantasy, glamour, romance, camp and colour – a broad canvas. They seemed like a high-vis bridge between the old rock world of amps and roadies and the MTV era of synthesized pop.

In August, Simon Le Bon experienced the kind of first world trauma that would have been unthinkable during the heady days of punk. In fact, it was the type of rock-star dilemma more suited to the likes of Rod Stewart, Mick Jagger or even Bryan Ferry himself. During the Fastnet Race, the biennial 608-mile round trip between the Isle of Wight and Plymouth, which Le Bon was using to prep for an attempt to sail around the world, his seventy-eight-foot yacht Drum *ran into difficulty off the Cornish coast when its keel broke and the vessel capsized, trapping six of the crew – including Le Bon, who was asleep – underneath. They were stuck there for forty minutes before being rescued by a Royal Navy helicopter. Tragedy averted, Le Bon inadvertently added a layer of slapstick to the story by tearing his long johns as he was hoisted to safety. 'I had to go down to come up,' he says. 'I dived in and started going up. As I came up the waistband got caught and pulled down. As I came up to the surface, I stopped about two feet away. I wanted to breathe, but if I did, I knew that would be the end of me. I managed to get them off my feet and came up with a big smile on my face. I got winched off into the helicopter, and one of the guys called, "Hey, Simon, where's your pants?" because I was just stood there in my knickers.' Paul Morley would have probably imagined him gurning, Alfred E. Neuman-like, as he said it too, but this is what rock stars did in 1985.*

Norman Jay: At the end of the eighties, we had what I call day dot. Acid house was born. It wasn't just about the music, it was a coming together of everything. The entire eighties period was everyone in their own way working towards that moment. Fashion, art, music, lifestyle, it was all coming towards that moment, and its social impact can't be overstated. It was that important. Acid house was really the end of something and the beginning of something, which movements often are. The eighties were so important because so many things happened. We are talking about the heyday of *i-D*, *The Face*, of style-watchers, innovators, great people coming to London to seek their fortunes. It was great. It was a great creative revolution.

Paul Spencer Denman: In retrospect, you can see how important it was and how the period had its own atmosphere and uniqueness. It's very hard to imagine anything like that will ever happen again. All those bands coming out of one scene, I don't see it happening again. It's a bit like the Man United Class of '92, really – not gonna happen again. Same for us. It was a vibrant and creative scene, and we all knew and supported each other and got wasted in the same places.

Gary Numan: After it had gone, I desperately tried to get back to being famous again. It was so soul-destroying. I was completely desperate, looking for new sounds and not caring really about whether I shot myself in the foot. Just desperate to try and do anything to get famous again. And it was absolutely pathetic, the most shameful, embarrassing period of my life by far. I'd run out of money, and they were trying to repossess my house. After a while, I realised that this desperate desire to get the success back again was completely the wrong way to be, and I went back to doing it as a hobby. I'd been totally corrupted by the whole thing and lost my way. I'd had enough, to be honest, as I was not a natural pop star. I did find it quite difficult. The attacks by the press really made their mark on me and spoiled my enjoyment of it to a large extent. I was also touring too much, doing two big tours a year. I thought by getting away from touring I could step away from the limelight, so to speak, and I could just become a studio act. I think it was actually quite a sound decision. What I did wrong was announcing it. I should've just done it, I should've just quietly drifted into the background and learnt the things that I felt I needed to learn and then come back when I was a bit more mature, with better music, and now with all this experience I would be able to handle it better when I had that second crack at it. This thing about me retiring, I think a lot of the fans saw it as an insult, and they just went away in their tens of thousands. I think I spent the next thirty-five years working my way back to where I was when I retired the first time. So it was a very sensible thing to do. On the one hand, I think it really was a big part of keeping me sane and not becoming a drug addict or drunk or whatever, you know? But on the other, it was extremely damaging to the career.

Martin Fry: *How to Be a . . . Zillionaire!* was our follow-up to *Beauty Stab*, and it was all electronic. It seems stupid to have to describe it as that now, but that's very much what we were trying to do. It was all about deconstructing what a successful pop group was at the time, leaving no trail. All the band members were animated, and this was decades before Gorillaz. But I don't know, would it have been better just to have been in Status Quo or something? I do look back upon those records we made in the eighties with some pride, though, because some of them have stood the test of time. It would have been better to go out in a blaze of glory early on, but instead we got longevity. What came afterwards I call the flatpack years, where I spent most of my life in IKEA. One minute I'm in Shoom dancing on a podium, and the next minute I've got kids and I'm in the queue on Tuesday morning, returning the flatpack furniture that I can't put together on Monday night. The Shoom and Haçienda membership cards had been replaced by

B&Q, and it's like that lovely Duran Duran song, 'Ordinary World': it's like suddenly, after ten years, there's a world out there, and that's what it was like for me.

Marc Almond: I think the eighties was a decade of two halves. The first half was a bit of a hangover from the seventies, with all the optimism and creativity that came with it. A lot of bands around that time, including Soft Cell, the Human League and Culture Club, were all influenced by glam rock, punk and disco – three huge seventies musical genres. I actually was an early starter and I started buying records in the sixties, so I was into rock as well. So a lot of bands were influenced by the blurred gender and fluidity of Bowie, [Marc] Bolan and Roxy Music, the sparkle and the optimism of seventies disco, and the kind of up-against-the-system of punk, so there was a melting pot. A lot came from gay culture as well. There was the *Rocky Horror Show*, we had films like *Cabaret*, Lindsay Kemp, and all kinds of decadence.

There was a naivety in the early eighties, a little bit of 'I'd Like to Teach the World to Sing', and you still felt very hopeful. I think 1985 was a pivotal year, as that was the last burst. Live Aid obviously reignited Queen, and some people successfully relaunched, while others didn't. But more importantly, there was the Aids realisation, and that was coming to the fore. It became a different decade after that. We had had the miners' strike, and you could tell society was changing, but Aids was a genuine crisis. That youthful optimism, that explosion of colours and the theatricality of the early eighties disappeared. When people talk about loving the eighties, they talk about the first half, that's what they love, as in the second half it became darker, and we became fearful. Suddenly gay culture was not a good thing, so it was kind of swept under the carpet. After that it became a very masculine culture, a very heterosexual culture, hence going into the nineties with Britpop and things like that. That's where I became very depressive. I kind of lost my way as a person, and it was all a reflection of that time, of that middle and latter part of the eighties. The eighties ended in 1985.

Gary Crowley: It all went a bit naff in the mid-eighties. There was an edge and a vitality in the early eighties. In the mid-eighties, the hair got big and the shoulder pads got bigger . . .

Wilma Johnson: I left London and moved abroad when people started dying. I just thought, 'I can't stand this any more.' Graveyards, coffins, real darkness. Aids.

Daniel Miller: I really think the eighties are very important in a cultural sense. I feel they are important because they gave a musical voice to people who wouldn't otherwise have had that chance, and it was very amateurish, in a very British kind of way. And if you think about Soft Cell, Depeche or Human League, these were people who didn't know what they were doing, there was no musicianship involved. There wasn't any training; it was people's ideas going straight down onto tape, without having to deal with all the niceties of being a good keyboard player, and it was this new whole new sound of electronic music. You can say this started with Kraftwerk, and we always referred to them as the grandfathers, even though they were only a few years older than us, but the thing turned into a completely new kind of teenage music. It wasn't like another retread of the Beatles or the Stones or some terrible prog-rock nonsense; this was a new, pure sound that was coming from the heart. It also encouraged so much music to come after it. I mean, what is electronic music? Hip hop is electronic music, but people don't think of it in that way necessarily. Some people when they talk about electronic music mean techno, which I love, but it's not the only electronic music. Everything these days is electronic music.

Economically, 1985 was an eventful year for the music industry. In both the UK and the US, record and cassette sales were up 14 per cent from the previous year, with cassettes outselling albums in Britain for the first time. The number of albums certified platinum in the US increased by 46 per cent over 1984, while compact discs accounted for twenty-one million of the 643 million total units sold, an astonishing increase of 250 per cent. In some respects, 1985 was the year of Madonna, who in twelve short months had become the most famous sex symbol since Marilyn Monroe. In Britain alone, she had seven zeitgeist-defining Top 5 hits: 'Material Girl', 'Crazy for You', 'Into the Groove', 'Holiday', 'Angel', 'Gambler' and 'Dress You Up'. However, it was the year that the second British invasion reached its zenith, with the likes of Duran Duran, Culture Club, Tears for Fears and Wham! crowding the US charts. It would soon begin a precipitous decline, as the sparkling video revolution helped spur a backlash. Perhaps sensing a shift in the zeitgeist, Wham! became the first Western pop group to perform in the People's Republic of China and release records there. Ironically, this was also the year in which heavy metal and hard rock began their renaissance: Kiss came back with a silver-tongued vengeance, W.A.S.P. reared their ugly codpiece, and Ratt's Out of the Cellar *and Mötley Crüe's* Shout at the Devil *both went double platinum. Whitney Houston also had a good year, as her eponymous first album became the best-selling debut album by a female act. Michael Jackson paid $40 million for the rights to the ATC Music catalogue, which included over 5,000 songs, including many written by Lennon and McCartney. A group of influential, if overly earnest, Washington housewives, including Tipper Gore, formed the Parents' Music Resource Center. The PMRC pressured the music industry to establish a rating system that would warn potential record buyers of sexually explicit and violent lyrics. Their purchases may as well have carried stickers emblazoned with 'THIS RECORD CONTAINS SEX AND DRUGS AND ROCK'N'ROLL!'*

Pop in the eighties developed like in no other decade before or since. During the eighties, it swept all before it. In the fifties, rock'n'roll defined itself by what it wasn't – and what it wasn't was anything that anyone was going to like. The fifties produced pop stars in the same way that Hollywood churned out celluloid idols, Elvis clones who had great hair and hooded eyes (when Elvis appeared for the third time on The Ed Sullivan Show *on 6 January 1957, he was shot from the waist up to protect the innocent from his libidinous hips; in reality, it made no difference whatsoever because the innocent could still see his hair). The sixties were all about gangs, groups that grew in stature as they experimented themselves to death (in the case of Jimi Hendrix, Janis Joplin, Brian Jones and Jim Morrison, quite literally). The seventies was the first decade where there were signs of splintering, particularly in the binary world of punk and what came after. The eighties, though, were when this splintering went mainstream, and the charts suddenly became full of the most diverse types of music: new wave, ska, synth pop, alternative, hair metal, yacht rock, house, acid house, stadium rock, R&B, go-go, Eurobeat, hi-energy, electro, techno, glam metal, hip hop, adult contemporary . . . you name it, it was in the charts. And that was the thing: this music – these musics – tended not to stay in the margins, which is why there is such variety in the type of records that became No. 1s in the UK during the decade. Synth pop, meanwhile, developed in such a way that the technology involved in producing the records started to seep into other genres. The eighties would continue to evolve, driven by ever more mutations of the LinnDrum, the Fairlight CMI, the 808 drum machine and various versions of the Roland synthesizer. If constant change is the breath of fashion, so the technological advances of the eighties gave the sound of the decade new life, even if in hindsight it would be described as brash and brassy.*

The second British invasion didn't last long, and while the US charts were still full of British acts, few of them had managed to turn themselves into successful live attractions. This meant the ability to play stadiums. The likes of Spandau Ballet and Duran Duran had always been disparaging about U2's relentless pursuit of the US market, and yet their dedication eventually paid off, and by 1985, Bono, the Edge, Adam Clayton and Larry Mullen Jr were on the verge of becoming the biggest band in America. Within two years they would be playing the biggest stadia in the country. The Irish behemoths had often been accused of being careerist by the British new pop groups, although individually they all had the same aspirations. It's just that U2's music was much better suited to the open-air-stadium experience: searing guitars, patriarchal vocals, anthemic songs. Depeche Mode would eventually break the US, and Sade continued to sell records in vast quantities there, but that was about it.

As the second half of the decade started to churn, it all began to fall apart: Spandau Ballet, Ultravox and Japan split up, Frankie Goes to Hollywood collapsed, Duran Duran fractured into the Power Station and Arcadia (two splinter groups that succeeded only in confusing their fans), Culture Club were destroyed by Boy George's heroin addiction, Visage appeared to lose the will to live, Martin Fry got cancer, Soft Cell outlived their welcome, George Michael went solo and OMD successfully alienated their fan base. Could anyone ever imagine the Human League or Heaven 17 playing in baseball stadiums or sports arenas in Des Moines, Denver or Dallas?

Martin Fry: I loved the eighties, loved *The Lexicon of Love*, loved working with Trevor Horn, and while a lot of people accused us of fiddling while Rome burned, I don't actually subscribe to that, as a lot was improving, a lot was opening up, a lot of things were becoming more liberal. Clubs were leading the way: when you went to Area in New York, it was like a utopia, a way of saying it doesn't matter if you're gay or straight or black or white for a couple of hours. These days you'd probably be accused of cultural appropriation, playing funk, playing R&B, but in the eighties that wasn't the case, as it felt as though people were becoming united. You know, George O'Dowd wearing dreadlocks, does that mean he's trying to become a Rastafarian? No, he was showing people what the future was about. Maybe that's an over-exaggeration, but that's what I felt.

Simon Napier-Bell: The most important thing I did for Wham! was taking them to China. George asked me how long it would take to break

America, and I said it would take five years, because traditionally that's how long it took. I mean, nobody ever does it in under four or five years, and even the Beatles had hits for three years before they broke America. The Wham! China trip was done deliberately for that reason, because George said, 'We don't want to wait.' He said he wanted to do it in a year. We were in the Bombay Brasserie, the first week we met them. They met me in my flat and we went to dinner to talk about it, and George said, 'Look, I've got to tell you, we want to be the biggest group in the world, and you've got a year to do it.' And when I said I couldn't, he said, 'That's the way it has to be.' So we had to think of something which maybe would do that. I suggested playing in China, as no Western group had ever done it. I said that if they managed to do that, they would be on every news broadcast in the world, every front page. So, a week later, I was sitting in a bleak hotel room in Beijing, in the middle of winter, freezing cold and wondering how I could meet the president of China, as he was the only person who could give permission. And the week they were in China they were on ABC, CBS and NBC News every hour on the hour, for twenty-four hours. Prior to going to China, they had had a hit in America, but there was no national press. MTV had only just started, and you couldn't really break something across America other than by going on tour and playing thirty cities and then going back six months later, moving from 600-seater auditoriums, then 1,000, then 2,000, and so on. It was a four- to five-year project. But by doing what Wham! did, they went immediately from China to America and did a stadium tour. George was looking at how the business works right from the beginning. Breaking a group is so much more fun than simply managing them. Managing is two things: either starting with an unknown group and breaking them, or looking after an established artist on a day-to-day basis, which, frankly, is boring. I've never stuck to it for very long, and once I break groups, I lose interest.

Harvey Goldsmith: I took Wham! to China, but George really didn't want to go. He hated the idea. He said, 'I don't like the food,

I don't like travelling and I don't want to meet a lot of government officials.' He hated touring and just didn't want to be involved at all. He had put up with the idea of going to China as he knew it was a good idea, but he didn't actually want to have anything to do with it. I could never work out George's motivation, as he had worked so hard for success, but almost the minute he achieved it, he wanted to stop it. He just wasn't interested. I remember I told the tour manager to stuff a couple of suitcases full of Wham! merchandise as I knew it would come in handy. I told him to get as many posters, programmes, baseball caps, T-shirts and CDs as he could. Which is just as well, because when we turned up in China, even though we obviously had an interpreter, they were dumbfounded when we arrived at the border. They just didn't know what we were talking about. I said, 'I am Wham!' as I pointed to the forty people behind me, but they didn't get it. So I had to empty the suitcases and start handing out the contraband, pointing at George and saying, 'Look, it's him, famous pop star.' There was no one to meet us, no one to take charge and ease our entry; it was all done on a wing and a prayer. When we finally got to our hotel, which was actually very nice, I got a call at 1.30 in the morning from the agency representative who was meant to be our contact. He just said, 'Good news. We've got the permits.' Which is when it dawned on me that we had organised this whole trip, this extraordinarily crazy enterprise, without having any work permits for the band. So I suppose that was actually quite a risky thing to do. And George was right: he hated it. I spent ages trying to get him to change his mind about performing, but he simply didn't like it. I even spent time with him at our house in Portugal, trying to see if there was a way we could persuade him to play more concerts. My son actually charged people to sit on our wall in order to see George sitting in our garden. He can't have been more than seven.

Andrew Ridgeley: To a degree, Wham! was built in my image, and George would certainly have said that. Because Wham! was a representation of our youth and our friendship, the decision to bring Wham! to a close was made quite early on. The decision to end it had been understood by both of us for a fair while before it was announced. George always thought it was going to impose limitations on him that would mean he couldn't fulfil his potential. And neither of us was going to stand in the way of that. But the image of Wham! was far closer to my character than it was to George's. He wasn't quite so comfortable in himself.

I think Wham! could have gone on for a while longer. There are elements of *Faith* that sound like Wham!, but by that point George had really discovered himself as an artist. He hadn't fulfilled it by any means, but he had changed. The irony is, his personal struggle regarding his sexuality was just beginning to give him real problems. When he did *Faith*, he was projecting this very strong, masculine, heterosexual image. It was certainly an image that was intended to convey his heterosexuality, and it did that very successfully. But he felt it was a real struggle to maintain that artifice. He had also started to realise how difficult it would be to live this by himself. I certainly think we should have toured *The Final*, just to honour the fans, as I think that was a betrayal. That was a poor decision. But, regrettably, that was that.

George Michael: There's a difference between people who are pop stars and people who are Fleet Street pop stars. Right up until our Christmas single, I could go on a train, in a store . . . I'd get a little hassle, but I could do it. Up until [then], I refused to stop doing things like that, because it worried me a lot, having to skirt round things, just as someone who writes and as someone who had a career to live out. You have to have some kind of relationship with what's going on. Before we were successful, I was going to vaguely underground clubs for a couple of years, and then when we became successful, I felt the resentment from those people, so I moved out of those clubs and started going to real shitholes, where the place would be full of real wallies but they still played decent music. Then it got to the stage where they would bother me, so I had to go back to the vaguely underground clubs. By that time, the people in them were so removed from us – and those people were so self-important that they wouldn't come up to you and hassle you.

Andrew Ridgeley: I look back upon those times, and upon George, with enormous fondness. To embark upon a career with your best friend, and to achieve success, it was a privilege, really. We saw a shining light and we went for it. It was a wonderful thing to have done, as friends, together. And I was right. I was always telling George we could do it. I knew we could do it. I couldn't see any reason why we shouldn't do what we wanted to. We didn't always have the proficiency. But we got there. The stars aligned. Four-track recording, drum machines . . . He wasn't as clear as I was, as he had too many insecurities and too much parental pressure. I had to badger him to do it, but we did it. His ambitions formed as we got more successful. But that wasn't how it was when we were kids. I was the one telling him we could do it. I wanted him to realise his potential, and mine. I always knew who I was, and George didn't [know who he was]. We were quite different in many ways, but we had enough shared characteristics and perspectives.

Simon Napier-Bell: Wham! invented this wonderful image, but the longer it went on, George thought more and more that he was being forced to project an image that wasn't his real character.

Andrew Ridgeley: It was an enormously rich period, quite an intoxicating one. It was so creative, and there were so many strands of style, design, art, music. Such extraordinary talent. It was a time like no other. You had disco, punk, post-punk, New Romantic, ska . . . the lot. It was rich, diverse, and George and I listened to it all. And I suppose you could really say it all goes back to Roxy Music. They were there right at the start.

Simon Napier-Bell: George never talked to me about being gay. I knew George was gay, but he never talked to me about it. And I figured he had to deal with it how he wanted to. He knew I was gay, so that was probably part of the attraction of having me as his manager, but he never discussed it with me, not directly. I don't think I really cared. I mean, I like problems and challenges, and almost everything which goes wrong in life makes life more interesting. If something happened, then we would have dealt with it. I think that was George's attitude too, as when it did happen, he dealt with it quickly. You deal with it, and you make out the dealing with it is more exciting than not having anything to do, and so I don't think it ever worried me at all. The one thing that would have changed was that we wouldn't have got into China, but I don't remember the tabloids being very pushy about it. It's a very strange thing how non-gay the music press has always been, because anyone gay in London gay society would have known that George was or might be gay.

Marco Pirroni: It all ended in 1985, because when the likes of Paul Young and Wham! became big, it was the end of freaks like us. It was suddenly all about the boys next door, and we were not the boys next door. Everything had suddenly moved back to the suburbs, which we had spent our adolescence trying to escape.

Robert Elms: I remember the opening of the Soho Brasserie, and I think it's the most important restaurant in London in the last fifty years. Suddenly you've got people looking like they did in Italy, you've got Tony Parsons having dinner with Nick Logan in the back, and you've got that bar at the front where you can see the street and they can see you, and it's got those green tiles they had in Paris. Then the Groucho Club opens about six months later, so suddenly Soho starts to change even more. You know you can go for lunch? I mean, whoever had lunch before the Soho Brasserie? I didn't even know lunch existed.

Gary Kemp: Do we see this as an exciting period of people power, of the working classes becoming mobile, of classes breaking down? Or do we see the eighties as something gross and dysfunctional and abusive? I think I'm more the former. I definitely think more working-class people joined the creative industries, and there was a shift culturally in all the media industries, where the pool was much wider. I think the record companies certainly were allowing us to do more. And I think it fostered a sense of bohemianism. Back in the seventies, sex was all hidden away. Gay men were terrified. We would dress up in our mad clothes and have to run home at night because there'd be other gangs chasing after us. If you were gay, you really ran a risk. What Blitz and Billy's did was all about flaunting, but those boys who flaunted it were flanked by heavy straight boys, who said, 'Yeah, well, you want to pick on them, then you're picking on us as well.' And it got louder and louder, and that became a roar. The first al fresco bar was Soho Brasserie, and I remember seeing people standing and eating outside, and that was illegal before. How wonderful! Then boys started to get braver and braver, and then the gay clubs started opening up and Soho started changing for the better. Inevitably, there was a backlash in the '90s, with all the laddishness and Britpop and all that parka mentality, but by then the genie was out of the bottle.

Nineteen eighty-five was a fitting time to look back at the decade of adventure that had begun in various dormitory-town nightclubs back in the mid-seventies, a convenient time to step back from the continuum, to take stock. Soho continued to be the fulcrum of so much activity in the creative industries, and this was helped in the spring by the opening of the Groucho Club. At the time, most of the members' clubs in London were the gentlemen's clubs in and around Pall Mall, which catered specifically for politicians, the legal fraternity, landed gentry or the theatrical community, and many of which had had to resort to trading on past glories by selling memberships to businessmen in the provinces. So, at the time, the Zanzibar, in Covent Garden, was unique, a club that catered largely for the advertising community, a club that felt eighties through and through, even though it had been around since 1976. Zanzibar regular Chris Jagger (Mick's brother) recalls, 'It had a great atmosphere. It was the first place to open late that did cocktails, which was revolutionary. Above all, it wasn't a wine bar with candles in Chianti bottles.'

In 1985, it was displaced, instantly, when one of its owners opened a rival: the Groucho Club, in Dean Street, a club which would inspire an entire generation of similar clubs in the city. The Groucho was conjured up by a group of fifteen writers, publishers and agents who were tired of having nowhere to meet in London, and who wanted somewhere that reflected the changing social attitudes of the city. It was famously named after a Groucho Marx quote: 'Please accept my resignation. I don't want to belong to any club that will accept people like me as a member.'

Lynne Franks (*PR guru*): I was one of the original members. London was buzzing in a way that it has hardly done since. You would go there and see your friends, and there would always be some amusing tale. I keep seeing Julie Burchill sitting in that corner with her little voice and those red lips. To me, that completely represents that time. You would sit down in the club, two or three of you, and then someone else would come along, and someone else, and you would end up with as many people as you could fit around a table, having an awful lot of fun and gossiping. There was a huge change going on in the UK at the time, and the Groucho Club was at the heart of that. Whatever was going on in politics, in the media, in fashion, you got to hear about it there.

I was in the Zanzibar when I first heard about the Groucho. It was late 1984, and I was having a drink with Peter York, discussing the pros and cons of this and that, and the ups and downs of the current ins and outs. As we were leaving, we stopped at the table of some high-flying advertising bods, who started discussing this brand-new media watering hole that was going to be opened up in Soho in a few months' time by the very same people who had started Zanzibar. What did we think? Who was going to join? Who would they let in? Who was already barred? Would it work? How long would it take for investors to get their money back? And, more importantly, for the high-flying advertising bods at least, would the Groucho Club (as this new designer den of iniquity was going to be called) kill off the Zanzibar?

Well, did it? You bet. Stone dead. The Groucho became legendary almost as soon as it opened its doors, which, in a decade that made a point of celebrating nightclubs, hotels and private members' clubs as though they were churches or palaces, maybe wasn't so surprising. A lavish watering hole catering for every Tom, Dick and Tarquin, a media-centric wet bar for every publishing wannabe, every aspiring film director, every copywriter and hack, the Groucho immediately became the centrepiece of trendy media London. Which meant from the off it was loathed as much as it was loved. And, boy, did some people hate it (including many of the original members).

The first time I went there was a hot Friday evening in the summer of 1985, to meet pop archaeologist Jon Savage. We were ostensibly there to discuss work – I wanted Savage to leave The Face and join i-D – but Jon spent the entire evening slagging off everyone in the bar. 'Hate him.' 'Hate her.' 'Talentless.' 'Fool!' 'What on earth is he doing here?' etc.

'Wow,' I thought to myself, as my head spun round like in a Hanna-Barbera cartoon, 'this is definitely the place for me.'

The Groucho quite quickly became the haunt of not just the new pop fraternity – Duran Duran, Ultravox, Spandau Ballet, etc. – but also an oasis for rock royalty. Pete Townshend would no longer have to carouse the night away at Club for Heroes or the Wag Club; in the Groucho he could do everything behind closed doors, away from the prying eyes of the public. It would not be unusual to pop in there on a Thursday night and find Mick Jagger, Freddie Mercury or Eric Clapton standing at the bar; they may only have been sipping sparkling water, but at least they were away from the throng. Instead *of propping up the bar at Dingwalls or the Marquee, Sting, Bono or David Bowie could curl up in one of the sofas and pore over the papers. Launch parties were held here, as were press conferences, private views and book signings. It became a popular place to conduct interviews, as no one would dream of disturbing you by walking up and asking for an autograph. Membership was cheaper than a hotel suite, and you didn't have to suffer the paparazzi stalking you in the lobby or the public spaces.*

It became an institution almost immediately. Many other members' clubs would come in the wake of the Groucho, but few of them would feel so lavishly louche. Once, when there was a power cut in Dean Street, those trapped inside numbered Jools Holland, who had just arrived with Tom Jones, and U2's manager Paul McGuinness, who was hosting a dinner in a private room. 'Tea lights were lit, and suddenly there was Jools on the piano, Tom Jones singing "Sex Bomb" and Bono duetting with Tom,' says one onlooker.

Many of the regulars at the Groucho had been regulars at the Blitz six years earlier, six years in which London, Britain and substantial parts of the US had been changed by a pop culture that felt truly international. For the rest of the eighties, the Groucho was like the Green Room at Live Aid, and it was not unusual to walk in and find one, two, sometimes three people who had been on the Wembley stage on 13 July. You'd see Midge Ure, Gary Kemp, Simon Le Bon, Nick Rhodes, Bryan Ferry, Daryl Hall, Bryan Adams, Sting, Ronnie Wood, David Gilmour, Madonna and, sometimes, when the stars were aligned, Bob Geldof himself.

Carey Labovitch: I think there were a lot of people who used play-acting as a way of actually expressing their inner self, which they had perhaps hidden from their families. I think it was the beginning of proper emancipation. It was a great opportunity for those [people], who were actually going to be able to express themselves without inhibitions. When you are living through a period, you don't think of it as a period. I suppose, looking back, I'm actually proud of what we did. I think magazines like *GQ* wouldn't have existed without the likes of *Blitz*, *The Face* and *i-D*, and what the three style magazines did in their formative years was to set a standard for the future. But, at the time, we were just having fun. I think of the eighties as being a time full of meeting fabulous new people, having offices teeming with creativity, parties all the time, freebies all the time.

Steve Dagger: Possibly one of the reasons the period has been demonised is because it did not stay in the avant-garde for very long and became overground very, very quickly. The longer things stay in the underground, the longer they can be mythologised.

In May, The Face *celebrated its fifth anniversary (Marlon Brando lookalike Mickey Rourke was on the cover, smoking); it seems almost inconsequential now, but in 1985, it felt like a lifetime. Rather conceitedly, the issue was branded 'Magazine of the Decade', and could you blame them?* i-D *would celebrate its own anniversary a few months later with a mammoth Nick Knight portrait gallery (he photographed one hundred people, and I should know, as I interviewed them all), but* The Face *put its ox-blood Bass Weejuns in the sand first. 'Take a look at the eighties and find that nothing succeeds like success,' blared the editorial. 'It's the credo of the decade. Scratch the surface and find, not the cynicism of the seventies, but a self-conviction that is the only faith left. The New Romantics hyped their way out of a recession. The government hypes self-help. Poke the decade a little deeper and find the despair of unemployment, the collapse of resources and ideals. Success and failure: these are the motors that drive the decade, the one powering riots, anger and violence in the streets, the other finding its outlets in cocktail bars, nightclubs and holidays in the sun. And between them a friction that will make or break the eighties.'*

As the decade hit its midpoint, so many things were changing, although some remained the same. The forgotten riot of the decade is the Brixton riot of 1985, which started on 28 September. It was sparked by the shooting of Dorothy 'Cherry' Groce by the police, while they were looking for her son Michael Groce, in relation to a suspected firearms offence; they thought Groce was hiding in his mother's home, raided it, and shot Mrs Groce, paralysing her below the waist in the process. As news of the attack spread, so hostilities began, with the police losing control of the area for over two days, during which time dozens of fires were started and shops looted. One photojournalist, David Hodge, died a few days later as a result of head injuries he received from a gang of looters he was trying to photograph.

The Broadwater Farm riot in Tottenham, north London, a week later was dominated by two deaths. During a police search of her home on 5 October, an Afro-Caribbean woman called Cynthia Jarrett died of heart failure, triggering a sequence of events that resulted in a full-scale riot on the Broadwater Farm council estate, involving youths throwing bricks, stones and Molotov cocktails, as well as using firearms. At 9.30 p.m. that night, police constable Keith Blakelock was trapped by a gang of balaclava-clad local boys, blowing whistles and ringing bells, who tried to decapitate him using knives and machetes. He was butchered to death. According to a man watching from his second-floor flat, the mob was relentless, like 'vultures tearing at his body'. When he was examined later, Blakelock had forty-two different wounds. Winston Silcott, Engin Raghip and Mark Braithwaite were convicted of murder and sentenced to life imprisonment, despite no witnesses and no forensic evidence, although all three were cleared by the Court of Appeal in 1991 (Silcott remained in prison for the separate murder of another man, Tony Smith, finally being released in 2003). By the decade's midpoint, politics had become more binary than ever.

By the end of 1985, pop was also becoming even more binary, ever more fractious. That year, Paul Weller, along with Labour leader Neil Kinnock, Billy Bragg and the Communards, helped launch Red Wedge, a pressure group that sought to engage young people with left-wing issues, and with the Labour Party in particular. The collective took its name from a 1919 poster by Russian constructivist artist El Lissitzky, Beat the Whites with the Red Wedge. *Despite echoes of the Russian Civil War, Red Wedge was not a communist organisation, although it was flagrantly socialist. With a logo designed by Neville Brody, the whizz-kid designer behind* The Face, City Limits *and soon* Arena, *Red Wedge was launched on 21 November at a reception at the House of Commons hosted by the Labour MP Robin Cook, alongside Weller, Bragg, Strawberry Switchblade and Kirsty MacColl. For a while, it became the cause* du jour, *and Red Wedge's first tour, in the first few months of 1986, featured appearances by Elvis Costello, Madness, Heaven 17, Spandau Ballet's Gary Kemp, Junior Giscombe, Jerry Dammers, Bananarama, Prefab Sprout, Sade, Tom Robinson, the Beat, Lloyd Cole, the Redskins (a hard-line Trotskyite trio from Yorkshire led by public-school revolutionary Chris Dean, the scourge of the bourgeoisie, who called Band Aid 'Egos for Ethiopia. Bob Geldof is the Third Division International Statesman of Pop, with the political perception of a dead slug') and even the Smiths. As if that weren't enough, there was a Red Wedge magazine,* Well Red, *and a Red Wedge comedy special starring Ben Elton ('Up the workers!'), Robbie Coltrane and Harry Enfield, who all appeared under the banner 'Move on Up and Vote for Labour'. The Blow Monkeys financed their own Red Wedge leaflet, which featured a cartoon of their singer, Dr Robert, and asked, 'How can you complain about the state of the nation; your vote to cast is your only salvation.' It rhymed. Because the proposition was so potentially drab, levity was the order of the day. When announcing his involvement, Kinnock tried a joke about how Red Wedge wasn't a reference to his haircut. He paused for the big laugh, but none came. On the campaign trail in Llandrindod Wells, a small spa town in Brecon, a tannoy system outside the Labour Party HQ blared out the following message: 'The Labour Party is the fun party, the good-time party. Come and enjoy yourselves.' Later that day, at a free concert organised by Billy*

Bragg, autograph-hunters approached the singer. 'And will you sign this one for Marie? asked one woman. 'She couldn't come because her mum votes Conservative.'

'I suppose the Wedge came about because we all kept meeting at benefit gigs for Nicaragua or whatever,' said Bragg, whose whole career appeared to be devoted to modern interpretations of the protest song. 'The same faces kept showing up, like Jimmy Somerville, Weller, Tom Robinson – and we all shared similar ideals. Those were the darkest days of the Thatcherite eighties, as well. There was a feeling that something had to be done.' Bragg had previously played benefit shows for striking miners, miners' wives support groups, CND, Amnesty International, the GLC, the Greenham Common women, the anti-apartheid movement, and rate-capping schemes in Liverpool and Sheffield.

What had to be done was an earnest jolly, a sort of dour Magical Mystery Tour, basically a loose collective going on tour like no bands had done since the Sex Pistols/Clash Anarchy *coach tour of 1976. The venture owed something to the Anti-Nazi League as well as to Rock Against Racism (RAR), an alliance between the Socialist Workers Party and various rock and reggae musicians that used local concerts and open-air festivals (the most famous of which was held in Victoria Park in Hackney in the summer of 1978, headlined by the Clash) to promote the fact that racism was unfashionable.*

The Red Wedge bands would roll into town, hook up with local community leaders, union leaders and Labour MPs, and attend rallies, shows and press conferences. Events were organised in key marginal seats across the country, with the aim of mobilising the normally apathetic youth vote. Pop stars signed autographs, while politicians kissed babies. It was as much of an eye-opener for the politicians as it was for the artists themselves, because while the bands were shocked by the way in which the politicians expected so much stage time, the MPs in turn were rather shocked by the attitude of the youngsters turning up for the events, most of whom weren't that interested in traditional

Labour Party policies but wanted instead to discuss gay rights, the environment, the marginalisation of minorities, etc. On a flying visit to Finchley, Billy Bragg offered to play a free victory show at a local school if Mrs Thatcher lost her seat. At one debate in south-east London with the Communards and a hopeful local Labour candidate, a trainee teacher asked about education policy and an art student asked about cuts, which a Labour supporter made a short speech about. Minutes after the Red Wedge crew moved on, the college administrators had put their Tory election posters back in the windows.

'The atmosphere on the bus was electric,' says the Red Wedge press officer and former NME *editor Neil Spencer. 'There had been nothing like this since the package tours of the sixties. Musicians in the eighties tended to live very segregated lives, but when they had a chance like this to collaborate, they really loved it. Everybody left their ego at the door and mucked in.'*

'The artists got along very well, but these politicians would turn up and want to go on stage,' says Tom Robinson, who also played at some of the Red Wedge gigs. 'The last thing we wanted was hard-line party blokes going out there and lecturing the crowd on the evils of capitalism. That's not how you change the minds of rock fans. We had to keep finding ways of keeping them off.'

The aspirations were to create some kind of common ground between the fans and Labour and to seed people into their local parties. But it was an uneasy mix, and although Red Wedge would continue for a year or so, there is little evidence that it made any difference. Youth support for Labour in the 1987 election (which the Conservatives won, for the third time in a row) was marginally higher than it was in 1983, although it would be difficult to attribute this to Red Wedge, as by then support for Margaret Thatcher was starting to slowly decline anyway. Red Wedge was a turn-off because not only was the proposition dull, but the politicians involved came across as self-serving and crass. While the Conservatives knew nothing about pop culture (the best they could get in terms of generating support in the entertainment industry was Gary Numan, the borderline racist comedian Jim Davidson and the Hot Chocolate singer Errol Brown), at least they didn't try to co-opt it.

Paul Weller (*icon*): The MPs we'd meet around the country were more showbiz than the groups. It was an eye-opener; it brought me full circle in how I feel about politics. It's a game.

Gary Kemp: The Style Council obviously topped the bill at all the Red Wedge gigs. One night when I was playing, I remember being in the dressing room with Billy Bragg and Johnny Marr, and one of Paul's roadies came in just before we were all going on to play and said, 'When you go on stage, don't play too loudly because Style Council fans don't like guitars.' And we're thinking, 'Hang on a minute, this isn't a Style Council gig, they're all here to see everybody, it's a Red Wedge gig. And in any case, what a prick.' When we went on stage – it was a bit like showing a red rag to a bull – I think Johnny and I played [Curtis Mayfield's] 'Move on Up'. Now, I'm never going to play it like it's heavy metal. I'm playing funk guitar. At one point, Weller came to the back and said, 'Turn that fucking thing down.' Honestly!

Red Wedge gave politicians a liking for this new kind of limelight. These days, they increasingly turn to pop culture to try and make themselves appear more relevant and credible, but obviously run the risk of making themselves look opportunist, irrelevant and behind the curve. At the time, the Tories were incapable of harnessing any serious cultural support, and so that left all channels open for the Labour Party to exploit (although Liberal leader David Steel did make an excruciating rap record – 'I feel Liberal, all right . . .'). Why else would Neil Kinnock, the leader of Her Majesty's Loyal Opposition, turn up on Swap Shop *in early 1987, sharing air time with the lead singer of Doctor and the Medics? He had already appeared in a cameo role in a Tracey Ullman video and been a guest presenter at the BPI Awards. Compared to Kinnock, Tony Blair would turn out to be a wallflower.*

Weller himself was soon off.

Paul Weller: We felt [the Labour Party] were totally out of touch. We wanted to find a way of closing the gap between youth and the party, but there were so many factions within the Wedge and so much red tape to go through within the party that it took ages to change anything.

Gary Kemp: Tony [Hadley] was very much a working-class Tory, and his dad was too, and that's what he'd grown up with. I was in a dilemma with politics because I didn't particularly love the Labour Party, but I knew I didn't like the methods of the Tory party either. It's really about who you want to be associated with. I mean, looking back on it now, there was good and bad on both sides. Bowie and Bryan [Ferry] always stayed very aloof from politics. They stayed right out of it because once they engaged with politics, they were real people, they were the same as us and they were just another person who voted. And I think to a certain extent I wanted Spandau to be like that, because it's a business as well – you want to sell to everybody. And I think I panicked a bit, maybe under pressure felt that too many people were saying, 'You're a bunch of Tories, aren't you? You're a bunch of fascists.' And so then I had to shout a bit louder, which ended up with me joining Red Wedge. Yes, I still voted Labour, but I still didn't feel I was understood on either side. I think that was what was so attractive about Blair in '97, offering a third way.

Bob Geldof: Red Wedge was a joke. It was so old hat they may as well have been in the 1920s, with no concept of what modern politics was about. The only one I've got a lot of respect for in this area is Billy Bragg, who has an idea of politics that he's utterly true to and maintains it with great integrity and makes fantastic music. He sees himself clearly in the Woody Guthrie vein, but for me it was very old hat.

It's like a Depression-era romanticism, with no basis in reality. Forget protesting. Forget marching around Trafalgar Square singing 'We Shall Overcome'. It fucking gets you nowhere! So get real. You want to stop something, then put your guitar down and engage. Otherwise, fuck off and make a hit record. You either stop and engage utterly or don't do it at all, because we can all write a nice little song like 'Give Peace a Chance'. Because music does not change things. As much as anything, the organisation was trying to quickly move pop from a world of image, escapism and conspicuous consumption into one of more overt political commitment. But this wasn't going to happen. Not with Red Wedge, anyway. Taking Live Aid as something of a template may have seemed like a good idea on paper (at least in terms of propaganda), but the failure of Red Wedge only highlighted the fact that activism can't be genuinely manufactured to any lasting effect.

If punk had drawn a line under extravagance, by the mid-eighties it was back again in a major way. There were the high-style music videos, shoulder pads for both boys and girls, and acres of postmodern architecture, with its pointless pediments and enormous arched windows. The eighties is often contextualised as a decade festooned with, and defined by, postmodernism, but actually a more appropriate aesthetic is maximalism, a cultural and design concept manifested by excess, redundancy and lots of 'more is more'. For instance, we were forever being told that Frankie Goes to Hollywood's records, videos – in fact, everything about them – were postmodern, but can you imagine a more maximalist group? The Pet Shop Boys and Sigue Sigue Sputnik may have been 'ironic' in a sense, but Frankie were just bold as brass – in the same way, actually, as David Bowie.

David Bowie: I was never actually a material person. Ideas always meant a lot more to me. I never bought a big car, [although] the company bought a big car for me to drive around in once. All the money I made was after 1980, as everything before that just went. *Let's Dance* helped, and 1983 for me was like manna from heaven. All that money I'd gone through in the seventies suddenly came back to me, in almost a year. My biggest mistake during the eighties was trying to anticipate what the audience wanted. On the one hand, I was trying to shed this skin, and on the other, I was second-guessing the future. I *hated* myself during that time. I probably hated myself more during the mid-seventies, during the drugs and what-have-you, but I suppose my depression and alienation were in keeping with the times. I had a very crystallised idea of where I was misguided and unfocused during both periods. I said to myself, 'I don't wish to live my life like this. I have to change or else I will do something stupid.' Strangely enough, my ambition tended to come in moments of depression. I think it was always this way, actually. Of course, it wasn't just the second-guessing of the audience that was a mistake during the eighties, as creatively I allowed myself to go in a direction I shouldn't have gone. I was trying to be predictable, but nobody wanted predictable. In terms of mistakes, there were a couple of albums that I rushed into, that I really should never have done. I was pressured by a record company, but not manipulated. I regret *Tonight* specifically, only because, taken individually, the tracks are quite good, but it doesn't stand up as a cohesive album. That was my fault because I didn't think about it before I went into the studio. Everyone takes notice of some kind of criticism. You wouldn't be human if you didn't respond to how your own work is received.

Midge Ure: This period is very important. I think every musical revolution has a style and a club and a place and a time and a leader associated with it. I suppose the new-wave thing would have been the Vortex or the 100 Club, the Beatles would have been the Cavern in Liverpool, and this time it was the Blitz in London, and that's what everything stemmed from. And it was important. You don't get the David Bowies of the world turning up to check you out at the Blitz, a little crappy club in Covent Garden, if it isn't important. I think it was an incredibly important period, not just for the music, although the music went hand in hand with the technological revolution. Home recording started as technology became readily available, as up until then the only people who could afford the Moog synthesizer were people like Rick Wakeman. It was a period of intense experimentation, which is why it is so durable and diverse. It was people sitting in their little studios going plink, plonk, plink, plonk on one track, and then putting a vocal on the other or making a bass drum sound out of a synthesizer. Plus, we all started to listen to Europe rather than America, as that was where all the electronic experimentation was coming from, from Kraftwerk to Jean-Michel Jarre, from Telex to Yello, even the Yellow Magic Orchestra from Japan.

I think by 1985 it had changed, and actually by the time 1983/4 came along, it was kind of hackneyed and had moved on. Spandau had reverted back to being the soul boys that they always were, writing 'True' and soul ballads, which is what they were in the first place, and they'll be the first people to admit it. Duran had moved on to almost stadium rock, and the idea of standing with a bank of synthesizers was kind of hackneyed. And I think that was the point where Ultravox certainly lost what we were doing. By 1985, we weren't sure what we were any more, and maybe if we'd stuck to our guns and carried on, it could have proved quite interesting, but it just deviated and meandered and turned into something that was nothing really. The last time Ultravox performed as that line-up was at Live Aid. Band Aid took me away from Ultravox for quite a while – nearly two years – and when you get back together again, you find it difficult to reintegrate yourself. When I came back to Ultravox, we weren't a band, we were four individuals. So Live Aid changed everything. It elevated U2 from being a college band to the biggest band in the world. It re-established Queen. It did a lot of things, but was that a good thing or not, I don't know. All of a sudden, we were looking at big screens, and stadium rock was well and truly established. You'd go and stand with 100,000 people and watch a TV screen, and we lost something there along the way. Everything had to be bigger and better and bolder, and everyone was trying to outdo each other.

But it was definitely a continuum. I hate the term 'New Romantic', but that whole period was instigated by punk: Steve Strange was a punk, Princess Julia, the Bromley Contingent and all of that stuff. But the people who instigated the punk scene were tired of it because it was now your third-generation punks appearing, with designer torn shirts and outrage for the sake of outrage, whereas two weeks ago they were playing in a pub somewhere, a perfectly normal band. So it really became watered down, became high-street fashion. You could buy torn T-shirts and sprayed bondage trousers or whatever in Topshop. So the instigators turned to something else, and what did they turn to? They turned to what they had heard when they were kids – to Bowie and Roxy. So when you went to Billy's, that's what you'd hear: you'd hear a lot of Roxy, Bowie, bits of whatever stuff already existed, in amongst this mix of things that had been found in Europe. So they are the ones who instigated this. It wasn't like they turned their back on it. It was a different look, a different design. It's that old thing of being one step ahead, and in the same way that no fifteen-year-old wants their thirteen-year-old brother or sister liking the same things as them, so the punk cognoscenti didn't want to be surrounded by a lot of followers. The instigators will instigate, and then they'll walk away from it the moment it becomes commonplace.

Gary Kemp: The handful of bands that came out of Britain reinvented pop music in a fresh, vibrant, exciting way, combining electronic sounds with something chic, an amalgam of what had gone before but also making something brand new that was our own. I still think some of the best-produced records came out of that period via the likes of Trevor Horn. Digital reverb was being invented and the capability to make glorious landscape sounds. Magazines became glossy. I don't know what inspired which or whether we kind of just inspired each other, or if it was just a coincidence, but we now had the ability to say, 'Fuck the *NME* and the inky press. *The Face* and *i-D* are the new bibles.' And that was key. MTV video was piped into people's rooms. All of this happened within two or three years.

Simon Napier-Bell: This period was as important as the original British invasion. If you really want to look back at pop culture, the first British invasion was during the first decade of the twentieth century, when every single musical on Broadway was British and Brits invaded Broadway. The second invasion was the one we call the first British invasion, which was the sixties. But the eighties one was equally relevant, and possibly more important, because the one in the sixties basically involved a lot of groups who sounded like the Beatles. There was much more variety in the eighties. The sixties were great because that was when we all discovered we could have sex every night, but the eighties were more creative.

Andy McCluskey: Were we important to the culture? That's a tricky question. That's kind of like, when did you stop beating your wife? I think we were arrogant enough to think we were doing something. Listen, standing on stage at *Top of the Pops*, about to be introduced by Peter Powell or Gary Davies going, 'And now in at No. 8 with "Maid of Orleans" . . .' which was a waltz with a bagpipe synth and thirty seconds of distortion, yes, we did feel we were being subversive. There's twenty million people out there going to cough on their sandwich at teatime, because they're going to go, 'What the fuck is that?' We did believe we were doing something special, and what's nice forty years later is that quite a few people seem to agree. Or singing 'Enola Gay', a song about the plane that dropped an atom bomb, or about Nikola Tesla, the inventor of alternating currents. 'You made us think, while entertaining us and dancing.' We did an interview on a cruise ship recently, and the guy interviewing us said, 'How do you put these things together? It's like dancing to architecture.' So yes, I'll take that as a compliment. Yes, we danced to architecture. The worrying thing is that the eighties are now in danger of being remembered as a fancy-dress-shop, neon version of 1987, not 1980, and that's the problem. There's a huge difference between all the shiny, empty rock pop of the late eighties compared to what we were doing. What we were actually trying to do was adopt art-school and Bauhaus principles to make beautiful designs for the masses. If you look at film of Liverpool or most of the northern industrial cities in the seventies, they still hadn't repaired the bomb damage from thirty years earlier. It was squalid and horrible and decaying, and punk had kicked it in the balls, and we came along out of art college with some new intellectual – not nihilistic – ideas for it. It was pop Bauhaus. It was shiny, modern beauty for the masses. It wasn't elitist. Why can't the working-class kids have something colourful and beautiful, instead of this shit we're all living in? And it shouldn't be mixed up with the self-indulgent, bright decadence of the second half of the decade. After 1985, it all soured.

Paul Humphreys: It was totally a golden age of pop, although the eighties are often demonised because people remember the big-hair rock and the big snare drums, and it all got a bit pompous towards the end of the decade. But up until '85, it was amazing. We were trying desperately to break America, and so we spent months and months touring there, and in the end America broke us. By the end of the decade, we had sold fifteen million albums, but we owed Richard Branson £1 million. The most important thing was that it was an era of music that was totally decentralised from London. There were people in the provinces, cut off from everyone else, just experimenting and doing their own things and learning their craft as songwriters. I mean, times were tough then, and in the late seventies, outside of London, there wasn't much money, but Liverpool produced us, Echo and the Bunnymen, Frankie, Wah!, Pink Military . . . There wasn't anything else to do really; it was a time when music was so important to everyone, and some saw it as an escape, a way to get out of their lives and a way to get out of the towns they were living in.

The other great thing about the period was the record companies. At the time, there were a lot of creative people at the record labels, rather than accountants. And because of the money available, they would bankroll bands who had raw talent, who weren't writing the right songs at that point. But they believed in them and they signed them, and they'd let them fail for two, three albums, until they had a hit. That was because of the vision of the people at the labels, and the industry was full of money and they could afford to lose on artists for years, until they paid them back. Doesn't happen now.

Personally, I think Kraftwerk are the route to pretty much everything. I mean, the dance-music scene came from Kraftwerk, early trance music, it's there in rap, R&B . . . it's everywhere. I love the early stuff more because it had more emotion, and by the time of their later recordings, they had become so robotic that they had almost done away with any human touch. All the humanity had gone. I love them, though. They came to see us play once in 1980. We looked up to see them all standing in a line on the balcony, and it was as though God had come to see us.

Kraftwerk, with their obdurate purity of voice, continued to have an influence that appeared to be exponential.

Liz Wendelbo (*artist, musician*): I grew up in Strasbourg, and I purchased *Radio-Activity* on vinyl at the local supermarket with my mother. I can still see the black rubber conveyor belt at the checkout slowly moving along with the black-and-white *Radio-Activity* cover artwork wrapped in cheap plastic, followed by a box of chocolates and a bottle of champagne. Surreal.

If there was anyone who really understood the magnitude of a 'European' music, it was Ralf Hütter's German Beatles. Decades before the existential threat of Brexit, years before the brutal reality of populism, and a generation before the Union Jack was starting to be sequestered because of its toxicity, the Düsseldorf four-piece had decided that inclusion was more important than excommunication.

Their masterpiece in this respect was 'Europe Endless', the beautiful first track on their 1977 album Trans-Europe Express, *a song that carefully expressed the apparently inexhaustible delights of the continent: parks, hotels and palaces, promenades and avenues, real life and postcard views. The robotic nature of the music was the most important aspect of the song, though, as at the time the band were keen to move themselves away from their German heritage towards a new sense of European identity. It has been described as an electronic pastoral, 'painting a picture of a unified, borderless Europe'. Since then, walls have come down, walls have gone up, although 'Europe Endless' exists in a state completely separate from all of this.*

There had been many ahead of them, and even more who came in their wake, yet it was Kraftwerk who made themselves seem truly European.

For some, the mock heroics of Ultravox's 'Vienna' were all they needed to hear in order to be transported to a mythical central European cake shop, while for others it was Lou Reed's 'Berlin', although for the generation of night owls who came to the fore in the late seventies and early eighties it was probably Roxy Music's 'A Song for Europe', the anguished warble of a continental sophisticate, wondering where his true love has gone, while possibly trying to attract the attention of his waiter.

The very idea of continental Europe is one that evokes melancholy, a wistful longing for a solitary existence, wandering the city streets while pulling on an unfiltered cigarette. In this instance, the most fulfilling record is probably David Bowie's nostalgic walking tour 'Where Are You Now?', an uncharacteristic look over the shoulder at a time and a place long gone, that period in the seventies when Bowie was inadvertently inspiring a generation that he had already culturally assaulted half a decade earlier. Bowie, in all his wondrous shapes, was – along with Bryan Ferry – one of the few entertainers of the seventies who celebrated Europe for its promise of escape, as well as its place in history. At the time, when music vaulted you around the world, it either dropped you in the bucolic British countryside or swept you along the coastal roads of southern California.

The electronic music which emerged from mainland Europe at the end of the seventies not only celebrated its provenance, but it also – fundamentally – sounded different. You could listen to it in one way and feel it was cold and dispassionate and codified, or you could let yourself be swayed by the smell of Gitanes and café crème *and allow yourself to drift across the rooftops all the way to the Caucasus. Europe's grand design was actually rather easy to sketch, which is why so many bands of the New Romantic period were determined to pull up the collars of their raincoats and look forlorn. If you needed an example of a song that had had all the meaning sucked out of it, then all you had to do was listen to Japan's 'European Son' (which sounds like a Duran Duran B-side, even though it pre-dates them by at least two years).*

There is one record from the period in particular that managed to escape the genre, creating something very special in the process. Under Chris Blackwell's direction, in 1981 Grace Jones recorded a reworked version of the Argentinian composer Astor Piazzolla's 'Libertango' as 'I've Seen that Face Before (Libertango)', with new lyrics written by Jones herself and Barry Reynolds. Driven by Sly and Robbie, and arranged by Blackwell and Alex Sadkin, it conjures something completely original, a mixture of soft reggae, tango and chanson, *as Jones recalls a man she sees in every street corner in Paris. In many ways, the song acts as a travelogue, taking us straight to a rainy night in Boulevard Haussmann, but in other, perhaps more sinister ways, Jones acts as a cipher, an androgynous one at that. All in all, it was a heady mix.*

In helping themselves to a particular part of history, namely the romantic and largely fictitious idea of a benign post-war Europe – from the nightclubs of Berlin and the cafes of Amsterdam to the airports of Scandinavia or the railway stations of Burgenland – the post-punk miserabalists and the synth-pop darlings of the period were clumsily putting stakes in the ground or, rather, plotting a meaningless journey on a pinboard. Some simply celebrated their internationalism, with a casual belief in the redemptive properties of global pop. So, in the same way that Sister Sledge (courtesy of Nile Rodgers and Bernard

Fowler) were espousing the liberating qualities of Halston, Gucci and Fiorucci, so Robin Scott's M were eulogising the giddy delights of London, New York, Paris and Munich. Escape rather than endurance, fantasy instead of reality.

By 1985, though, this illusion was becoming something of a reality, in terms of the way in which the new pop of the period was being mediated, as this coloratura was no longer ironic. When, in 1980, the Human League released their Travelogue *album, the cover featured a highly evocative photograph of a husky ski trek, similar to the way in which a post-punk band might have used a picture postcard as a way of contextualising luxury travel. As the eighties reached their midpoint, there had ceased to be anything ironic about the use, or the purpose, of 'international jet-set imagery'. In the worlds of Spandau Ballet, Duran Duran, Wham!, Frankie Goes to Hollywood, Madonna, Don Henley, David Bowie, Bryan Ferry, Sting or pretty much anyone else you cared to mention, luxury was a genuine desire.*

It was Kraftwerk, though, who truly shackled themselves to the egalitarian European project, albeit somewhat tangentially. Their Mitteleuropean iciness may have become something of a cliché over the years, but their unrelenting dedication to the European cause – a level playing field where one could rendezvous on the Champs-Élysées or go to a late-night cafe in Vienna – became a blueprint for romantic modernism. Who cared if you couldn't afford it, as long as you could feel it. Who cared if you weren't living the good life, as long as you could dance to it, as long as you could lose yourself in it. Kraftwerk perfected the illusory power of pop, and that's where it stayed – as a perfect illusion.

There was an appalling aftermath for many of those who were intrinsic to the Blitz scene, not least Steve Strange, who had a terribly volatile career after his heyday, involving dependency and insolvency. Even by

1985, Strange had started to lose his grip on London clubland. After the Playground, his Saturday-night extravaganza at the Lyceum ballroom on the Strand, his excursions became rather hit and miss. You would occasionally bump into him late at night, always the worse for wear and overly keen to tell you how well he was doing.

Others were ravaged by drugs, not least George O'Dowd, who had an extremely public evisceration at the height of his career due to his heroin addiction. Then there was Marilyn (né Peter Robinson), the Marilyn Monroe clone who was a mainstay of the original Blitz crowd, but who failed to successfully forge any kind of career. He spent years living an eremitic existence in his mother's house in Hertfordshire, taking crack and heroin and watching the Alien *films back to back. Others would die of Aids-related illnesses, including Ray Petri, singer Vaughn Toulouse and performance artist Leigh Bowery. As London clubland mainstay and creative director Jerry Stafford says, we should remember that the Blitz scene and the first wave of New Romanticism pre-dated Aids, and everyone was 'still innocently experimenting with everything in a rather fey, narcissistic way. By the time [Leigh Bowery's] Taboo opened [in 1985], we were disaffected and angry. Dressing up and performance were more about reclaiming the body and redressing a personal identity than simply fashion.'*

Leigh Bowery was the most recognisable – and genuinely iconic – figure of the second wave of New Romantics, an Australian (he was born and raised in Sunshine, a suburb of Melbourne) who moved to London in 1980, aged nineteen, with the express purpose of reinventing himself. What he created when he got there was little short of extraordinary, as he didn't so much dress up as turn himself into a living sculpture, accentuating his body to such extremes he almost created a new gender. In some respects, he was post-human, as his polymorphous creations looked more like 3D cartoon characters than the crazed fancy-dress imaginings of a benign, overweight drag queen. As the Guardian *critic Jonathan Jones said, Bowery had a complete lack of inhibition and took the greatest pleasure in his corpulence, regardless of how he was dressed.*

His transformations were surreal in the extreme: one moment he was a dayglo Nazi stormtrooper, the next his face would be entirely obscured by various 'pompom head' spheres, the next he looked almost as though a willing accomplice had dipped brightly coloured paint over his bald pate (actually, they probably had). For one long, debauched year he ran the most decadent nightclub in the city – Taboo, in Leicester Square – and found the time to form an art-rock group called Minty. His greatest transformation was becoming a performance artist, appearing to give birth to his friend and collaborator Nicola Bateman, who was so tiny she could hide in his skirts without being detected. I once saw him perform at the ICA, a display that seemed to largely consist of Bowery spinning around in circles, urinating wildly as he did so. He would go on to become a significant muse for Lucian Freud, who delighted in painting him naked.

I once bumped into Bowery in the daylight, in Cambridge Circus, and the sight of him without a costume, dressed only in what looked like a large white bedsheet, was positively disturbing. Bowery would die of an Aids-related illness at London's Middlesex Hospital on New Year's Eve 1994.

Michele Clapton: Sadly, some of the best didn't make it at all, and others' lives were blighted by drug addiction and they didn't achieve what I think they could have.

Fat Tony (*DJ*): The first drug I ever took was at Heaven, where I met Freddie Mercury. There was a party at his house, and so I went back, and they offered me a line of coke. I hated it at first, but then I was offered some more at the Playground, and it didn't take me long to develop a habit. Then I was put in charge of the VIP room at the Limelight, and I started taking a lot of cocaine and ecstasy. Was it a problem? Only when it ran out. I took drugs every day for the next twenty-five years, the last twenty with a full-blown addiction. My life suddenly was run by drugs, everything I did was based around drugs, and it just got progressively darker. The end started when I discovered crystal meth, as the psychosis that comes with that type of drug is so severe that I thought I had animals living in my mouth, and I pulled all my teeth out. Every single one. Because I used to bite my nails, my hands would always be in my mouth and I would kind of just dig at my gums, and when you had been up three or four nights and hadn't drunk water, your gums would start to burn, and I would dig at them and they would get infected. I would get toothpicks and I would dig and dig. I was obsessed. I would rock backwards and forwards digging at my teeth, pulling one out, then another, until they were all gone. By the end of it, I had a mouth of broken teeth and one tooth left. When I eventually went into recovery, all I had in the world was one tooth and one pair of trainers, and the trainers weren't mine because I had stolen them.

Rusty Egan: The Playground was 2,000 people lying on the floor on drugs. I didn't want everybody in my club on drugs – you know, 'Where's the party?' Suddenly everyone was on ecstasy. I started to go to Ibiza, but it was worse there. In London, Boy George was now in full heroin addiction, Steve was chasing the dragon. At one point a friend came up to me and said, 'Do you realise that you're the only person in this club not on drugs?' And so I started . . .

Steve Strange: George obviously got into heroin, but I remember him when he was so down on all drugs and used to tell us off. When he got into it, we were all so shocked, but things weren't going that well for him, what with his lover Jon Moss and his career, so he turned to that to sort his head out, but like a lot of us, he underestimated heroin. He once escaped from his house in St John's Wood, with hundreds of paparazzi outside, and came round to my house, where I let him meet my dealer. I cannot believe how mad I was to do that. But those were different days.

Ben Kelly: I knew Steve Strange quite well, and when he got some money when Visage were successful, he bought a house in Wales, near his mother. And he asked me to do it up. I found a local architect and got cracking. There was going to be a galvanised-steel spiral staircase – quite extravagant. I'd invoiced him for some fees, and the cheque he gave me bounced, and then the builder said he hadn't been paid, then the architect. And, of course, drugs had got the better of him. I've still got a cheque for £1,100 signed by S. Harrington. Heroin. Not all of those who scaled the dizzy heights survived.

Ollie O'Donnell: I went into treatment in Weston-super-Mare when I was thirty-two, and when I came out I started from scratch again. I was so broke I started fly-pitching. I sold disposable lighters I bought for five for a pound from the wholesaler's in Wembley, and then sold them outside Camden Town and Queensway tube stations. It was quite profitable. People would come out of Camden Town station who knew me from the club; they'd see me but would be so embarrassed for me they kind of swivelled around and went out the other exit, but I felt great because I was working. It actually felt really liberating because I'm a great believer in hard work. I couldn't go back to the club environment, couldn't go back to being a hairdresser, as that environment involved a lot of drugs too. So I kind of built myself back up again. Part of the thing when we were in treatment was we'd have to go shopping and budget for the week. I'd never done that. I didn't have a clue how to go shopping, as my previous existence had been similar to a rock star's. In fact, it was better, as at the Wag Club you had to do less: didn't have to go on tour, didn't have to rehearse; you just had to turn up and drink as much as you wanted, get loads of drugs and then have loads of sex. It was like real sex, drugs and rock'n'roll, and a load of money. It was crazy. It was a great life, but I became deeply unhappy as I had no motivation. I wish to God I had got out a few years earlier, but my life has been rich since.

Rob Hallett: Duran Duran's Andy Taylor is one of the most wasted talents ever. He was a great guitarist and responsible for co-writing a lot of Duran's early hits, but he wasn't one of them, from the start. He came from a *Melody Maker* ad ['live-wire guitarist wanted']. Andy's just one of those rock'n'roll casualties. He went to live in Ibiza and never came back.

Graham Ball: While everything had gone mainstream, there were now a hundred Leigh Bowerys, a hundred small, little clubs doing interesting things. There were more grass roots than ever, not just in London, but all over the country. What this period did was encourage people to do things on their own terms, in their own way. The decade from '75 to '85 was all about doing things for ourselves. It also removed a lot of sexual prejudices, somewhat subliminally. There was so much diverse sexual orientation going on, and it became legitimised. It was fluid and it became accepted. A lot of people experimented. And why not? No one ever judged them. You recognised each other as fellow travellers. It was the germ of a different type of egalitarianism. It's a period tainted by Thatcherism, as it was a period when you had to get out and do things, although not always from economic self-interest. We all looked out for each other, and we looked after our own. Maybe young people are always entrepreneurial, but this was definitely a break in the ice, just like the sixties. It was an opportunity, and we made the most of it. We ran through the hole in the wall.

Fiona Dealey: I don't think that I've ever really felt that it's over. I really don't.

Michele Clapton: I don't think I've ever really benefited professionally from my Blitz days directly, other than it gave me a chance to experiment with looks and styles at the time. It took me a while to find what I really wanted to do; if I had stayed in fashion, it might have had more impact. At the time, the dressing-up and showing off very much fed into my work, and in a funny way it still does. But I still care very much about not following others' style, for me personally and in my work. I am passionate about the story-telling and what the costume can say or hide, either knowingly or accidentally. I think for me it started off as a shyness, a lack of confidence in the way I looked, so I thought that if I didn't look like anyone else, then I wouldn't be compared [to anyone else], and if I didn't try to look pretty, then it acknowledged that I didn't think I was . . . I still think this way today to some extent. This pattern of thought also follows me into my design process: when working on characters' costumes for a film, I try to look at what they are trying to hide or say, to fill in the details that are unspoken and give them depth. I love working with actors to explore their character in this way. That period was important in the way that it exploded this sense of normality. It was across class and gender. It followed on from punk, which I'd also got into, and which was also hugely important. It was just this visual sense of the breaking down of barriers . . . which has continued. The period is still looked at as a time of change, questioning what is/was deemed beautiful, strange, acceptable . . . I think it was the catalyst for the more open views of most of society today, which I hope continues. Although right now I have worrying doubts.

By mid-decade, dozens of one-nighter clubs had been and gone, while many more were still in full swing, clubs that were wild and camp, clubs that were small and sticky, and clubs whose names were often their greatest achievement: Dial 9 for Dolphin, Wham! Live Tonight, Total Fashion Victim, Westworld, Jungle, Cabaret Futura, the Batcave, etc. There was now an expectation that nightclubs were there for the taking. Many were tactically frivolous, amiably aimless little clubs that reflected the egos of the organisers as much as the clientele. As the 1990s loomed, and as the world shrank, so clubs would begin to change, becoming industrialised, institutionalised, co-opting entire Balearic islands – along with most of the hen-party capitals of Eastern Europe – cruise ships and even, eventually, Las Vegas. All this lay in the future, but the generational groundswell of the eighties made it all possible. Indeed, made it all seem exciting, necessary, almost expected.

Princess Julia: The early Blitz scene was all about freedom, about expressing yourself and not caring, and it was the start of what could have been an incredibly emancipating period. It was a huge step forward and very important, but actually we now live in a time when it's regressing. Seriously, I thought we'd be living in a modern age by now. I really thought we would be living in some kind of utopia. I confess I live in a bubble, but outside of that bubble it's really dangerous. Back then, it was safe. It was maybe not real, but we felt weirdly protected by each other. There was an air of permissiveness, of living freely; if you wanted to flounce around and wear make-up, that was fine. I still like going to places in Manchester or Birmingham or cities in Europe and finding these little pockets of bohemia. I like that global family thing. As for us, well, I think we just had the fearlessness of youth. I think sometimes as you get older you tend to over-think things a bit, and that puts the fear in things. We didn't care what anyone thought. On a personal level, I felt very restrained and constrained by the way I was being brought up, and I remember consciously thinking, 'I don't want to have this life.' So I found another one.

Marco Pirroni: We were the kids who watched 'Starman' on *Top of the Pops* and who went on to become pop stars. Stephen Morris from New Order was doing a thing about his favourite albums, and one of them was *Ziggy Stardust*, and he said, 'It's a great album and all that, but I couldn't see me going down the pub in that get-up.' Well, thank you so much for your help, Stephen, in changing the culture. We hated all that stuff and the music papers who adored them. The whole 'Prince Charming' thing was done to annoy the likes of the *NME* – you know, what would they hate the most? We were like panto.

Stephen Jones: The seventies were all about being a nanny state, and there had been the oil crisis, the three-day week, piles of rubbish and rats in Leicester Square. So me opening a hat shop in the middle of all that just seemed like the most ridiculous and fabulous thing ever, and doing what we were doing was just so completely different to what had gone on ten years before. We were all incredibly entrepreneurial. *i-D*, *The Face*, new magazines, new shops, new clubs, new everything . . . And were we Thatcher's children? In a way we were, even though a lot of people would like to deny it and say they were not productive, but that entrepreneurial spirit was encouraged by her because it was somehow a fresh start. I'd always wanted to create my own world, and I certainly didn't want my parents' world, coming from a nice middle-class family in the Wirral, with my father playing golf. Ultimately, of course, you do realise you're genetically a product of your parents and you cannot escape, and there is nothing stronger. But we live in denial for as long as possible. The gay world was certainly a real engine for creativity. I mean, it's a real engine within the fashion world. It was a real engine for Vivienne and Malcolm. That's not to say they couldn't have done it without the gay world, but it would have been much more difficult, I'm sure. And where would David Bowie have been without that support? Where would Bryan Ferry have been without Antony Price? He wouldn't have thought of all of that by himself. But it's the mix that was the interesting thing. That's why we didn't like clubs like Heaven or the Coleherne, because we all thought they were too gay. What we were interested in was the combination of different things, because your straight friends couldn't go to those places, so therefore it was boring. But, you know, Steve Strange was gay, Rusty Egan was straight. Great combination. The Blitz scene wasn't an exclusively working-class scene either. Our value system was not about class. It wasn't that we wanted bread and dripping; we did want a cream cake as well. That, for some bizarre reason, is still considered to be the Achilles heel of this period: the fact that we all had some ambition. We all wanted you to get on. It was expected of you. Your peer group expected it of you, and you did it for yourself and for each other. This was the thing. Was it selfish ambition or was it an exploration? I think it was more of an exploration. Success was a by-product.

Andrew Hale: Our can-do attitude in Sade was more about being young, and when you're young, you're quite fearless. I think there is a misapprehension that somehow the success that came out of that creative group we were part of identified with a Thatcherite capitalist viewpoint, which we hated. We ended up helping to build a successful creative community in London, but then at that age you're not necessarily thinking about where things are going to lead. So, while the eighties made us wealthy – we all bought flats which doubled in value very quickly when we were making money – I'm not sure that is something we should be so thankful for thirty years later, when our kids can't afford a place to live and the discrepancy between rich and poor is ridiculous. There was such a great collective creative community in London in the early eighties, and we all scrambled together enough money for rent and we had a support system, but at the same time it's true we contributed to the gentrification of a city which has priced out the new young creatives. I think the opening of that free-market, deregulated world we all grew into in the eighties, followed by all the 'Cool Britannia' stuff with New Labour in the nineties, had ramifications that were far more damaging in the long term.

Paul Spencer Denman: I don't think Sade get the credit we deserve in England. No one has sold more records than us or plays to larger audiences, and we are massive in every territory in the world apart from England. Sade, Stu and Andy certainly don't get enough respect as songwriters, nor Sade as a lyricist. She is actually more like a poet. We endured because we evolved. ABC or Heaven 17 or Culture Club or Spandau, as amazing and brilliant as they were/are, split up or just fell apart. We didn't. We always stayed together and always tried to support each other through thick and thin. It's been a thirty-five-year journey, and we all matured and fell into our roles as a band. Listen to our albums – *Diamond Life* and then *Love Deluxe* and then *Soldier of Love.* They are all radically different, and you can see how maturity affected the songwriting and playing. In America, Sade is an icon, and we are seen as a band. In England, it's not quite like that: Sade is seen as a solo artist, and we're not relevant or seen as a band. Which is very, very annoying.

Peter York: In the future, people will blame the eighties for all societal ills, in the same way that people have previously blamed the sixties. The various Thatcherite Big Bangs – monetarism, deregulation, libertarianism – have been working their way through the culture ever since. Mrs Thatcher didn't really understand the sociological forces she was unleashing; she didn't grasp that deregulation would lead to a booming pornography industry, for instance. She was possibly too straitlaced to imagine such a thing. When we look at the profit-and-loss account of the '80s, we come to the conclusion that the economic agenda would have to have been done by almost any government of any colour that wished to survive. In other words, if the Labour Party had been in office, it would have had to invent Tony Blair and his agenda. But what they left out of the account was the cultural agenda. There was this fascinating combination of a radical economic agenda with an amazingly conservative social agenda. The radical economic agenda worked, and the conservative social agenda simply didn't. They were tearing in absolutely opposite directions. So to say, on the one hand, that we want 'the market will decide', and on the other 'warm beer and village greens', is completely impossible. And they didn't recognise the impossibility of those things. The poverty of the imagination was that they didn't begin to grapple with the social consequences of the agenda or plan in any way for them.

DRAMATIS PERSONAE

Sade Adu (born Helen Folasade Adu) is the singer with the band Sade. One of the most important artists to emerge from the Blitz scene, Sade has produced a series of monstrously successful albums, including *Diamond Life*, *Promise*, *Lovers Rock* and *Soldier of Love*. She is almost pathologically private, shunning celebrity almost as soon as she was presented with it as a career option. Plangent, mellifluous, potent, Sade's music is the acceptable face of modern soul, a hybrid for all seasons.

Viv Albertine was a member of the Slits.

Marc Almond (born Peter Mark Sinclair Almond) was the singer with Soft Cell, the archetypal synth duo. They formed in 1977, when Almond met David Ball at Leeds Polytechnic. Released in 1981, 'Tainted Love' was their second single and was a No. 1 in seventeen countries. The band lasted until 1984, although there have been various short-lived reunions since then.

Adam Ant (born Stuart Goddard) was a dandy highwayman, among many other things.

David Bailey is a world-renowned photographer, a legendary figure who has photographed everyone from the Kray twins to the Queen, from Mick Jagger to Jeff Koons.

David Ball was one half of Soft Cell.

Graham Ball was a seminal club runner of the early eighties.

Afrika Bambaataa (born Lance Taylor) is an American DJ, rapper, songwriter and producer from the South Bronx. He is notable for releasing a series of genre-defining electro tracks in the eighties that influenced the development of hip hop.

Andy Bell sings with Erasure.

Edward Bell studied art at Brighton College of Art, Chelsea School of Art and the Royal College of Art. He worked as a freelance photographer and illustrator for *Vogue*, *Tatler* and *Elle*, before being commissioned to provide illustrations for David Bowie's *Scary Monsters (and Super Creeps)*.

Christine Binnie is a ceramicist and one of the original Neo Naturists, who formed in 1980.

Jennifer Binnie is, like her sister Christine, one of the originators of the Neo Naturists, as well as being a painter.

Johnny Black is the founder of the website www.musicdayz.com.

Judy Blame (born Christopher Barnes) was a creative director, stylist, accessories designer and New Romantic iconoclast.

Bono (born Paul David Hewson) is the lead singer in U2, and one of the greatest rock stars of them all.

Debra Bourne is a highly sought-after communications expert, brand consultant and advocate for diversity in fashion. Before co-founding All Walks Beyond the Catwalk (with Caryn Franklin and Erin O'Connor), she was a director at Lynne Franks PR.

Kim Bowen is a highly respected stylist, costume designer and fashion editor. She has worked for *Harper's Bazaar* and *Blitz*, as well as for many performers, including Pink and George Michael. She was one of the original Blitz Kids.

David Bowie (born David Robert Jones) was largely responsible for the New Romantics, tangentially at least.

Boy George (born George Alan O'Dowd) was a teenage Bowie obsessive. The future Culture Club singer says Ziggy-period Bowie was the reason he started to dress extravagantly: 'He emboldened me, gave me the strength to look different.' He started borrowing clothes from family members and throwing things together. He also asked his auntie Jan to give him a Ziggy haircut, although after she was finished, 'I came off more like Dave Hill from Slade.' Exactly the same thing happened to me, as having seen Bowie's performance of 'Starman' on *Top of the Pops*, I decided I wanted to look like him and promptly started calling round the various unisex hair salons in my home town, Deal, in Kent. They didn't know what I was talking about, although one eventually took pity on me, intently studying the photograph of Bowie I brought in with me when I turned up at the salon ten days later. He took one look at my flat, thin hair and said it was impossible. So I too left the hairdresser's that Saturday afternoon looking like Dave Hill and feeling rather sorry for myself.

Michael Bracewell is a writer, novelist and cultural commentator whose first novel, *The Crypto-Amnesia Club*, was published in 1988. He has written extensively about Roxy Music, most notably in *Roxy: The Band that Invented an Era* (2008).

Louisa Buck is an art critic and columnist for *The Art Newspaper*.

Nell Campbell is best known for her portrayal of Columbia in *The Rocky Horror Show* and her song 'Do the Swim'.

Joanne Catherall is a singer with the Human League.

David Cavanagh was a hugely respected music journalist.

Robert Chalmers is a contributing editor of *GQ*.

Neneh Cherry (born Neneh Mariann Karlsson) had her breakthrough hit, 'Buffalo Stance', in 1988.

George Chesterton is the managing editor of *GQ*.

Michele Clapton is a British costume designer. She won a BAFTA for the four-part television series *The Devil's Whore* and won an Emmy for the costumes in the hit HBO show *Game of Thrones* in 2012. She went on to win again in 2014 and 2016.

Anita Corbin is a British photographer whose exhibitions include *Visible Girls* (1981) and *First Women UK* (2018).

Jason Cowley edits *The New Statesman*.

Mikey Craig is Culture Club's bass guitarist.

Gary Crowley is the ever-youthful broadcaster, television presenter and DJ.

John Cummins is a media corporate adviser who started as a researcher on *The Tube*, before ascending through the ranks at Channel 4.

Steve Dagger is, among many other things, the manager of Spandau Ballet.

Fiona Dealey is a highly successful costume designer who works on commercials, TV and film. She graduated from St Martin's in 1981, producing one of the most celebrated collections of the time. She was one of the queens of the Blitz.

Paul Spencer Denman is the bass guitarist with Sade.

Robin Derrick was the creative director of *The Face* and then *Arena*, before performing the same role at *Vogue* and then Spring Studios.

Bernard Docherty was the PR for Live Aid.

Keanan Duffty is an award-winning British fashion designer, musician and author.

Danny Eccleston is an accomplished music journalist.

Alan Edwards is the chairman of the Outside Organisation and, in a PR capacity, represented David Bowie for over thirty years, and continues to do so.

Rusty Egan was one of the original Blitz Kids, the DJ at Billy's and the Blitz, and a member of Visage.

Mark Ellen is the former editor of *Smash Hits*, *Q* and *The Word*, and one of the nicest music journalists you could ever hope to meet.

Robert Elms is a broadcaster and author and the original chronicler of the New Romantics.

Tracey Emin is one of the world's leading artists.

Gary Farrow was George Michael's PR.

Fat Tony (born Tony Marnach) is a superstar DJ.

Eve Ferret is a singer, actress and cabaret artist.

Bryan Ferry is one of the most important and influential figures in British post-war pop culture, notably as the force behind Roxy Music.

Kathryn Flett is a journalist and former editor of *Arena*.

Wolfgang Flür is one of the original members of Kraftwerk.

John Foxx (born Dennis Leigh) was one of the first electronic artists of the seventies.

Martin Fry created ABC.

Dave Gahan has been the singer with Depeche Mode since 1980. Towards the end of the nineties, they started to have a huge global impact, and *Violator* (released in March 1990) was a dark monster of an album. Gahan suffered protracted drug problems – he is a recovering heroin addict and has had four brushes with death – but the band remain a huge draw, being one of the most successful groups to have emerged from the whole New Romantic electro period.

Lee Gale is a journalist who works for *GQ*.

Kate Garner is a photographer and was once a member of Haysi Fantayzee.

Bob Geldof fronts the Boomtown Rats and famously initiated Live Aid.

Ricky Gervais is a comedian, actor, director and world-famous stand-up.

Harvey Goldsmith is a promoter and co-instigator of Live Aid. He has worked with everyone from Led Zeppelin, Pink Floyd, Queen, Elton John, Madonna, Muse, the Rolling Stones, Bruce Springsteen, Oasis and Paul Weller to Coldplay, Eric Clapton, Supergrass, the Black Eyed Peas, John Legend, the Who, Van Morrison, Iron Maiden, Bob Dylan, the Eagles and Sting.

Martin Gore is a member of Depeche Mode.

Andrew Hale plays keyboards with Sade and is much celebrated for his acuity and elegance.

Daryl Hall is one half of the staggeringly successful duo Hall & Oates. Their 246 weeks in the US charts made them the most popular act of the eighties, ahead of Michael Jackson, Bruce Springsteen and Madonna.

Jerry Hall is the iconic model.

Rob Hallett is CEO and founder of Robomagic. With more than thirty years' experience in the music industry, he is recognised as one of Europe's most successful music promoters.

Deborah Harry sings with Blondie, the architects of punk disco and creators of such classics as 'Heart of Glass', 'Rapture', 'Call Me', 'One Way or Another', 'Atomic', 'In the Flesh' and dozens more.

Nicky Haslam is a journalist, author and interior designer.

Hector Heathcote was born in Derby but became one of the Wag Club's most famous DJs. (Chris Sullivan says it was Heathcote who played the first house record at the club, 'Your Love', in 1985, after a record-buying trip to Chicago.)

David Hepworth is the author of a variety of terrific books on pop, most notably *1971: Never a Dull Moment* and *Uncommon People: The Rise and Fall* *of the Rock Stars 1955–1995*, two tremendously entertaining and trenchant music books that shed new light on old bones.

Trevor Horn is one of the most accomplished producers of the eighties, having worked with ABC, Dollar, Malcolm McLaren, Frankie Goes to Hollywood, Grace Jones and the Pet Shop Boys.

Matthew Horton is a music journalist who works for the *Guardian*, *NME* and *The Quietus*.

Paul Humphreys is 50 per cent of Orchestral Manoeuvres in the Dark.

Ralf Hütter is a member of Kraftwerk.

Chrissie Hynde has had a phenomenal career steering the Pretenders.

Norman Jay (born Norman Bernard Joseph) is a club, radio and sound system DJ who is credited with coining the phrase 'rare groove'.

Elton John (born Reg Dwight) is one of the biggest entertainers in the world, a genuine colossus, and was a very dear friend of George Michael.

David Johnson was one of the first journalists to write about the Blitz Kids.

Wilma Johnson was a founder member of the Neo Naturists.

Grace Jones is a Jamaican-American supermodel, singer, songwriter, record producer and actress.

Mick Jones was a singer, songwriter and guitarist with the Clash.

Stephen Jones is a world-renowned milliner and was one of the original Blitz Kids.

Terry Jones invented *i-D*, as well as being one of the most comprehensively influential creative directors and editors of his day.

Ben Kelly was the architect behind the Haçienda, among many other things.

Gary Kemp is an actor and the creative powerhouse behind Spandau Ballet.

Jim Kerr sings with Simple Minds.

Carey Labovitch created *Blitz*.

Simon Le Bon is the singer with Duran Duran.

Annie Lennox was one half of the Eurythmics.

Don Letts (born Donovan Letts) is a British film director, DJ and musician. He first came to prominence as the DJ at the Roxy, and then as the videographer for the Clash, directing several of their music videos, before becoming a member of Big Audio Dynamite.

Nick Logan invented *The Face*, *Arena* and *Smash Hits*.

Annabella Lwin (born Myant Myant Aye) was the singer with Bow Wow Wow.

John Lydon was one of the chief progenitors of punk and helped create both the Sex Pistols and PiL.

Madonna (born Madonna Louise Ciccone) has been calibrating her legacy since she first signed to Sire Records in 1982. Often referred to as the Queen of Pop, she has spent her career ruthlessly administering the David Bowie method of reinvention. Richard Goldstein once said that Bob Dylan's great achievement in the sixties was not wisdom, but dexterity. You could say the same about Bowie in the seventies and, of course, Madonna in the eighties.

Andy McCluskey is one half of Orchestral Manoeuvres in the Dark.

Malcolm McLaren was an impresario, performer, clothes designer and boutique owner who worked closely with his ex-partner, Vivienne Westwood. He was largely responsible for kick-starting punk and is obviously best known as the manager of the Sex Pistols. He died in 2010.

David Mallett directed the videos for Bowie's songs 'Boys Keep Swinging', 'DJ', 'Look Back in Anger', 'Ashes to Ashes', 'Fashion', 'Wild Is the Wind', 'Let's Dance', 'China Girl', 'Loving the Alien', 'Dancing in the Street' and 'Hallo Spaceboy'.

George Michael (born Georgios Kyriacos Panayiotou) was one half of Wham!, before launching himself as a solo performer. One of the most iconic and successful figures of the era, he blossomed into a singer and songwriter of great depth and maturity. He died in 2016.

Daniel Miller started Mute Records.

Jamie Morgan is a British photographer who worked extensively for *The Face* and *Arena* in the eighties.

Paul Morley wrote for the *NME* from 1977 to 1983 and was a co-founder of the record label ZTT and a member of the Art of Noise.

Jon Moss is Culture Club's original drummer.

Kate Mossman is a journalist who has worked for *The Word* and the *New Statesman*.

Alison Moyet (born Geneviève Alison Jane Moyet) came to prominence as half of the duo Yazoo, but has since worked mainly as a solo artist.

Simon Napier-Bell is something of a talismanic figure in pop management, having looked after the Yardbirds, Marc Bolan and Japan, before being asked to manage Wham!

Gary Numan (born Gary Anthony James Webb) first entered the music industry as the frontman of Tubeway Army.

John Oates is the other half of Hall & Oates. Much derided, damned with faint praise, they nevertheless recorded some of the most successful modern pop of the eighties. They were also unlikely MTV favourites.

Karen O'Connor was a regular club-goer in London during the late seventies and early eighties.

Ollie O'Donnell (born John O'Donnell) launched the Wag Club with Chris Sullivan, among many other ventures.

Betty Page (born Beverley Glick) is a former journalist who worked for *Sounds* and *Record Mirror*.

Jan Parker was a member of the punk band Security Risk.

Tony Parsons is a best-selling author and journalist who in his time has worked for the *NME*, *The Face*, *Arena*, the *Daily Telegraph*, *GQ* and the *Sun*.

Grayson Perry is an English contemporary artist known for his ceramic vases, tapestries and cross-dressing.

Oliver Peyton is a restaurateur, entrepreneur and television personality.

Marco Pirroni was the guitarist and co-songwriter in Adam and the Ants.

Andy Polaris was the lead singer with Animal Nightlife.

Antony Price is the legendary fashion designer who worked closely with both Roxy Music and Duran Duran.

Prince (born Prince Rogers Nelson) was an American singer, songwriter, musician, record producer, actor and film-maker. Often touched with genius, he was also something of a virtuoso; his guitar solo on 'While My Guitar Gently Weeps' at the 2004 Rock and Roll Hall of Fame inductions is proof he wasn't just a studio wizard. He died in 2016.

Princess Julia (born Julia Fodor) is an English DJ and music writer who was one of the faces of the Blitz scene.

Nick Rhodes (born Nicholas James Bates) is the keyboard player in Duran Duran.

Andrew Ridgeley was the other half of Wham! and the childhood friend who gave George Michael the confidence to pursue a career as a performer. He is considered to be one of the most charming people in the industry.

Dave Rimmer is a music journalist who wrote for *Smash Hits* and *The Face*, before writing *Like Punk Never Happened*.

Chris Salewicz is a distinguished music critic and author.

Robert Sandall was a music critic for *GQ* and the *Sunday Times*.

Jon Savage (born Jonathan Malcolm Sage) wrote for *Sounds* and *Melody Maker*, before joining *The Face*. He is probably best known for his history of the Sex Pistols and punk, *England's Dreaming*, which was published in 1991.

Alix Sharkey (born Alexander Campbell) is a journalist, performer and academic who was closely associated with *i-D*.

Paul Simonon was the bass player in the Clash.

Siouxsie Sioux (born Susan Janet Ballion) is the singer with the Banshees and was a member of the infamous Bromley Contingent, the proto-punk collective full of Bowie obsessives.

Sir Paul Smith is an internationally recognised fashion designer who has had a close association with many of the artists featured in *Sweet Dreams*.

Terry Smith is a freelance photographer who catalogued the original Blitz Kids.

Dave Stewart is a writer, producer, performer and one half of the phenomenally successful Eurythmics.

Sting (born Gordon Sumner) was the singer and principal songwriter with the Police, before successfully embarking on a solo career.

Steve Strange (born John Harrington) launched the Blitz with Rusty Egan, and then went on to have a short-lived career as the singer with Visage. He died in 2015.

David Stubbs is the author of, most notably, *Future Days: Krautrock and the Building of Modern Germany* (Faber & Faber, 2014).

Susan Ann Sulley sings with the Human League.

Chris Sullivan was one of the original Blitz Kids and went on to launch clubs, steer the jazz combo Blue Rondo à la Turk and work as a journalist. He is best known for launching the Wag Club in 1982.

Bernard Sumner is a founding member of both Joy Division and New Order.

Andy Taylor is a former member of Duran Duran.

John Taylor remains a member of Duran Duran. He was considered to be the principal pin-up of the New Romantic period.

Julien Temple directed *The Great Rock'n'Roll Swindle*, *Glastonbury*, *The Filth and the Fury*, *Jazzin' for Blue Jean*, *Absolute Beginners* and many other films, mainly documentaries.

Neil Tennant became notable as a journalist writing for *Smash Hits*, before launching the monumentally successful Pet Shop Boys, the synth-pop duo to end them all. Their song 'Being Boring' could be an allegory for the whole Blitz period.

Sue Tilley was a close friend of Leigh Bowery and Lucian Freud's muse.

Pete Townshend is one of the legendary four pillars of the Who.

Nicola Tyson is a highly successful British painter who lives in New York.

Midge Ure co-wrote 'Do They Know It's Christmas?', as well as being a member of Slik, the Rich Kids, Visage and Ultravox.

Diane Wagg owns Deluxxe Management and Ideal Music Productions. She is a board member and former chair of the Music Managers Forum (MMF UK). Her career spans A&R and artist, producer and studio management.

Wyndham Wallace writes for *The Quietus*.

Martyn Ware was a founding member of the Human League and Heaven 17, and produced data sonifications of Bowie's albums for the V&A exhibition *David Bowie Is . . .*

Iain R. Webb is a journalist, author, academic and fashion editor who was one of the influential forces behind *Blitz*. He was one of the original Blitz Kids.

Paul Weller is the Modfather, the man who started both the Jam and the Style Council, becoming a national institution in the process.

Liz Wendelbo is a Norwegian-born video artist and photographer, now resident in New York.

Vivienne Westwood is one of the most important fashion designers of her time, an extraordinary woman who was instrumental in the look, feel and sensibility of punk and much of what came in its wake.

Toyah Willcox is a four times Brit Award-nominated English musician, singer, songwriter, actress, producer and author.

Dencil Williams was a model and club-runner, before becoming an artist and therapist.

Keren Woodward is one-third (sometimes half) of Bananarama.

Alan Yentob is a hugely influential English television executive and presenter who has spent his entire career at the BBC, steering the groundbreaking documentary series *Arena* and latterly presenting *Imagine*.

Peter York (born Peter Wallis) is a British social commentator, author and management consultant probably best known for the classic *Style Wars* and *The Official Sloane Ranger Handbook*, which he wrote with Ann Barr. He has written for *GQ*, the *Independent* and the *Sunday Times*.

DISCOGRAPHY

(THEY DON'T MAKE THE FUTURE LIKE THEY USED TO)

I usually feel that if discographies aren't completely comprehensive, then they aren't doing their job properly, aren't telling the whole story (like – once upon a time – buying a greatest hits album and finding only the successful singles). The completist in me tends to want to see everything. But as anyone can be an expert now just by using their phone, subjectivity (taste, opinion, expertise) becomes even more important. *Sweet Dreams* covers the period from 1975 to 1985, a big fat decade that witnessed the birth of so many musical subgenres, from early punk to the new pop of the early eighties, via electronica, synth pop, modern funk and those records that could loosely be described as 'New Romantic'. Here, I've attempted to list the important records of the time that fit the narrative arc of the story, complemented by various records which help contextualise the period. Consequently, there are many great post-punk records you won't find here, as they don't fit the narrative; nor will you find a list of clubland's greatest hits. What you will find is a selection of records that give a very strong sense of the time – tunes you might have heard in bedrooms, nightclubs and cocktail bars, and songs you could still be singing in your head right now.

1975

'Moonlight Serenade', Glenn Miller
Resuscitated by the Goldmine's Chris Hill.

'Never Can Say Goodbye', Gloria Gaynor
A defining recording of the disco era.

'Do It Any Way You Wanna', People's Choice
Philadelphia comes to Canvey Island.

Down by the Jetty, Dr Feelgood
When pub rock was going to rule the world.

No Mystery, Return to Forever
No – when fusion was going to rule the world!

Young Americans, David Bowie
A musical deep dive, a complete style makeover.

Neu! 75, Neu!
Proto-punk, *kosmische Musik* (cosmic music), a pulse for the future.

Slow Dazzle, John Cale
At the time, any ex-Velvet Underground member was immune to criticism (apart from, strangely, Lou Reed).

'The Hustle', Van McCoy and the Soul City Symphony
An actual dance, born in the New York nightclub Adam's Apple.

Winter in America, Gil Scott-Heron and Brian Jackson
Rivalling Marvin Gaye for social commentary.

The Tubes, the Tubes
The Rocky Horror Show for US suburbanites.

Deluxe, Harmonia
Produced by the legendary Kraftwerk auteur Conny Plank.

'Cut the Cake', the Average White Band
Blue-eyed soul, made in Scotland, lauded in Essex, produced by Arif Mardin.

Another Green World, Brian Eno
The Roxy renegade defining his own margins.

Siren, Roxy Music
Bryan Ferry discovers the disco, arriving in a sports car rather than public transport.

Radio-Activity, Kraftwerk
One of the most genuinely influential records of its age.

'Lady Marmalade', Labelle
Saucy on the dancefloor: *'Voulez-vous coucher avec moi, ce soir?'*

'Fire', the Ohio Players
Classic soul-boy anthem.

'Love to Love You Baby', Donna Summer

One of the very first extended remixes, in which Summer (according to the ever-prurient BBC) 'produced twenty-three orgasms'.

Horses, Patti Smith
The first female proto-punk iconoclast, and her finest record.

1976

Station to Station, David Bowie
His best record, and the one that saw him pivot from West to East.

Satta Massagana, the Abyssinians
Classic roots reggae.

Silk Degrees, Boz Scaggs
Peak King's Road wine bar.

'I Want More', Can
When Can incongruously appeared on *Top of the Pops*, the presenter Noel Edmonds quipped, 'I wonder if Can will get into the Top Tin!' Such was the state of BBC light entertainment in the seventies.

'Movin'', Brass Construction
One of the great dancefloor chants.

'Love Hangover', Diana Ross
The producer Hal Davis asked the record's engineer, Russ Terrana, to install a strobe light in the recording studio, and the resultant 7'49" epic turned Ross into a bona fide disco diva.

I Want You, Marvin Gaye
The sexiest record of the year, the sexiest record of Gaye's career.

The Ramones, the Ramones
A statement of intent, and the first punk album.

'Police and Thieves', Junior Murvin
In the absence of any punk records, reggae was the soundtrack of the early punk clubs.

'Sun . . . Sun . . . Sun . . .', Ja-Kki
A generic disco record that would soon start to be mixed with Kraftwerk's 'Trans-Europe Express'.

Sowiesoso, Cluster
Conny Plank again.

'Shake Some Action', the Flamin' Groovies
One of those bridge records between what had gone and what was to come.

The Modern Lovers, the Modern Lovers
It's extraordinary how many nascent punks bought this record.

Car Wash, Rose Royce
A disco movie that worked.

'Cherchez la Femme', Dr Buzzard's Original Savannah Band
Soon to be a frequent performer at Studio 54, they spawned both Kid Creole and Coati Mundi.

Let's Stick Together, Bryan Ferry
It wasn't the best use of his talents, but he was still Bryan Ferry.

'Open Sesame', Kool and the Gang
One of the last great soul-boy anthems.

'I Love Music', the O'Jays
Gamble and Huff attack the dancefloor.

Blondie, Blondie
The sound of the Bowery goes global.

'Anarchy in the UK', the Sex Pistols
The Damned's 'New Rose' may have been the first British punk single, but this was the first one to make a difference.

1977

The Ramones Leave Home, the Ramones
Second verse, same as the first.

Low, David Bowie
The second side is a blueprint for much of the post-punk period between 1978 and 1981.

In Your Mind, Bryan Ferry
Still not the best use of his talents, but this was a Bryan Ferry record all the same.

Marquee Moon, Television
New York gentrification which ignored punk altogether.

Trans-Europe Express, Kraftwerk
The dawning of a new era.

The Idiot, Iggy Pop
A companion piece to *Low*, this created yet another sonic moonscape.

'Got to Give It Up', Marvin Gaye
Gaye's greatest club track started life as a disco parody.

The Clash, The Clash
West London concept album.

'Magic Fly', Space
Doctor Who meets 'Popcorn'.

'I Feel Love', Donna Summer
It's impossible to overemphasise just how influential this was, and still is.

Lust for Life, Iggy Pop
Proved that punks could smile.

'Psycho Killer', Talking Heads
As if on a loop, this snappy bass-to-the-fore twelve-inch pointed to where David Byrne and co. would go next.

Heart of the Congos, the Congos
Lee 'Scratch' Perry at his finest.

Portfolio, Grace Jones
Contains her first proper hit, 'La Vie en Rose'.

'Heroes', David Bowie
Stylistically at least, this was Bowie's nod to punk.

Chic, Chic
Proof that disco acts could make albums.

'(I Can't Get No) Satisfaction', Devo
An inspired cover version that deliberately ignores the world's most recognisable guitar riff.

Before and After Science, Brian Eno

Initially portrayed as a victim for being ousted from Roxy, Eno was increasingly framed as a future-facing genius.

Suicide, Suicide
Punk synth pop in dark glasses. Reviewing a remixed version of one of the album's singles, 'Cheree', in the *NME*, John Lydon described it as '"Je t'aime" with tape hiss'.

'Supernature', Cerrone
The epitome of uncool (and yet somehow cool).

1978

'TV-Glotzer', Nina Hagen
A German take on 'White Punks on Dope'.

'Broken Head', Eno, Roedelius, Moebius
Conny Plank. Flanging. Declaimed vocals.

'Stayin' Alive', the Bee Gees
Peak disco, recorded in France and based on a piece of journalism about Brooklyn nightlife that was actually based on experiences in London's Shepherd's Bush in the sixties.

Baltimore, Nina Simone
Heard most nights in the Ralph West Halls of Residence.

Ambient 1: Music for Airports, Brian Eno
'Ambient music must be as ignorable as it is interesting' – Brian Eno.

The Man-Machine, Kraftwerk
The Blitz boilerplate.

Real Life, Magazine
Post-punk pomp.

'Hong Kong Garden', Siouxsie and the Banshees
Keeping the punk dream alive.

'International', Thomas Leer
The author's favourite record from the period.

'Young Parisians', Adam and the Ants

When Adam used to perform this, he always looked as though he was practising for the Christmas panto.

'Hot Shot', Karen Young
Gay disco classic.

'The Chase', Giorgio Moroder
Suddenly we were all together in Electric Dreams.

'Viva', La Düsseldorf
A Blitz favourite.

'Hiroshima Mon Amour', Ultravox
Ditto.

Yellow Magic Orchestra, Yellow Magic Orchestra
Modern pop like we'd never heard before.

C'est Chic, Chic
Another collection of classic disco anthems.

'No G.D.M.', Gina X
Very German, very noir.

Wunderbar, Wolfgang Riechmann
Tragically, Riechmann didn't live to see his album released, as three weeks before the launch date he was the victim of a random knife attack.

'Warm Leatherette', the Normal
One of the most important records of the decade.

'You Make Me Feel (Mighty Real)', Sylvester
Possibly gay disco's finest eight minutes.

1979

'Off White', James White and the Blacks
Downtown punk jazz in a bow tie.

'Pop Muzik', M
Genius pop single from a friend of Malcolm McLaren.

Looking for Saint Tropez, Telex
Another Blitz classic.

'Nag Nag Nag', Cabaret Voltaire
Dada disco.

'Life in a Day', Simple Minds
Suddenly looking like world-beaters.

Manifesto, Roxy Music
Roxy return: six out of ten.

'Underwater', Harry Thumann
German space rock, built for the disco.

'Willie and the Hand Jive', Rinder and Lewis
Dancing to the space station and back.

The Bridge, Thomas Leer and Robert Rental
A beautiful, accomplished, albeit unsuccessful record.

'Are "Friends" Electric?', Tubeway Army
British synth pop arrives, world takes notice.

Lodger, David Bowie
The third, rather underwhelming, part of the Berlin trilogy.

'Electricity', Orchestral Manoeuvres in the Dark
Quickly followed by . . .

Risqué, Chic
Possibly their greatest achievement.

Off the Wall, Michael Jackson
Repudiating the past in style, with Quincy Jones at the helm.

'Cars', Gary Numan
And he does it again, this time under his own steam.

'Hot on the Heels of Love', Throbbing Gristle
As theatrical as it was organic.

'Spacer', Sheila and B. Devotion
At the time, Nile Rodgers had the Midas touch.

Solid State Survivor, Yellow Magic Orchestra
Containing 'Behind the Mask', later covered, somewhat incongruously, by Eric Clapton.

Reproduction, Human League
A radical, if subdued, direction.

'Deputy of Love', Don Armando
The very last US dance No. 1 of the seventies, and a taste of what was to come (diversity).

1980

'Funkytown', Lipps Inc.
Goosed by a killer ten-note synth riff.

Metamatic, John Foxx
Statement electronics.

The Correct Use of Soap, Magazine
If only for 'A Song from Under the Floorboards'.

'Car Trouble,' Adam and the Ants
Getting boisterous, although no less camp.

Warm Leatherette, Grace Jones
Success – finally – courtesy of Sly and Robbie.

'Atmosphere', Joy Division
Forever associated with the suicide of the band's singer, Ian Curtis.

Travelogue, Human League
Intriguing, full of potential.

Flesh and Blood, Roxy Music
Still back, and slightly dialling it up (although still without the great Paul Thompson).

Multiplies, Yellow Magic Orchestra
Classic cut: their version of Archie Bell and the Drells' 'Tighten Up'.

'Kings of the Wild Frontier', Adam and the Ants
The Adam Ant redux in full bloom.

Gentlemen Take Polaroids, Japan
Of course they do.

'I'm Coming Out', Diana Ross

The ultimate anthem for LGBT+.

Scary Monsters (and Super Creeps), David Bowie
Bookending the decade with an album that wore its references on its sleeve, while feeding into the Blitz Kids and creating a clutch bag of memorable, pertinent singles. Happy days.

'Enola Gay', Orchestral Manoeuvres in the Dark
One of the things that people tended to take for granted as far as OMD were concerned was their seemingly limitless ability to conjure beautiful melodies out of nowhere.

'Is That All There Is?', Cristina
Imagine a no-wave Jackie O working her way through a shopping list of disappointments.

'Shock', R.E.R.B.
Almost sounds as though John Barry had been involved.

Solid Pleasure, Yello
A yelled 'Hello'.

'To Cut a Long Story Short', Spandau Ballet
Such a brilliant statement of intent, and a complete validation of their hype.

'Vienna', Ultravox
Quintessential New Romantic tale, production and video. It remains one of the most evocative records of the period.

'Fade to Grey', Visage
And the same could be said about this.

1981

'Memorabilia', Soft Cell
Sleaze nation: the first in a series of untouchable singles.

'The Freeze', Spandau Ballet
Gary Kemp knew precisely what to do with his band, and their first few singles were testament to that.

'Planet Earth', Duran Duran
Urgent, modern electro-pop.

'Mind of a Toy', Visage
Steve Strange's apotheosis.

Nightclubbing, Grace Jones
Grace's imperial period.

Computer World, Kraftwerk
A different kind of noise – softer, slightly more sophisticated, but no less ingenious.

Was Not Was, Was Not Was
Art rock and Reagan-era social commentary defined Don Was's foray into club culture.

'New Life', Depeche Mode
And the synth-pop bands kept coming, bobbing about like *Thunderbirds* puppets in their costumes and schoolboy frowns.

'Chant No. 1 (I Don't Need This Pressure On)', Spandau Ballet
This is up there with 'Ghost Town' by the Specials as a portrait of urban paranoia.

'Girls on Film', Duran Duran
This time with a saucy video.

'Me No Pop I', Coati Mundi
When percussionists and kipper ties were going to save the dancefloor.

Dare!, Human League
Some say this is the best album of the whole New Romantic era; it certainly contains the most memorable singles.

Penthouse and Pavement, Heaven 17
Play-acting with pretty good tunes.

'You're No Good', ESG
An elliptical, broody and thoroughly sexy record.

'Einstein a Go-Go', Landscape
A novelty record by any other name, but with an infectious appeal.

'Going Back to My Roots', Odyssey
Written four years earlier by Motown legend Lamont Dozier, Odyssey turned it into an anthemic espousal of repatriation.

Non-Stop Erotic Cabaret, Soft Cell
Their imperial period too.

Architecture and Morality, Orchestral Manoeuvres in the Dark
An entire album of electronic wizardry.

'Genius of Love', Tom Tom Club
Near-genius playground post-disco.

'Go Wild in the Country', Bow Wow Wow
In which Malcom McLaren manages to magic up a version of feral Britain.

1982

'Love Plus One', Haircut 100
They were the future once.

'It Ain't What You Do (It's the Way That You Do It)', Fun Boy Three with Bananarama
A pop-up collab.

'Planet Rock', Afrika Bambaataa and the Soulsonic Force
A hip hop milestone that reimagines Kraftwerk for an even more contemporary world.

'I'm a Wonderful Thing, Baby', Kid Creole and the Coconuts
Zoot suits and Latin beats.

Rio, Duran Duran
Another classic, late-New Romantic album.

Avalon, Roxy Music
The *New Yorker* called it the 'deathless baby-making album'. It was their final album, and rightly so.

'Temptation', New Order
Where New Order discover their dance chops for the first time.

'Living on the Ceiling', Blancmange
Synth duos soon became a genre in their own right.

The Lexicon of Love, ABC
Lush, ironic pop with Rat Pack undertones.

Love and Dancing, Human League
A remix album, it was released under the name 'The League Unlimited Orchestra' as a nod to Barry White's disco-era Love Unlimited Orchestra. Essentially an instrumental 'dub' album, it was heavily influenced by the New York DJs of the time.

Upstairs at Eric's, Yazoo
'Part of the charm of that album is naivety,' says Vince Clarke. 'We just came together, and it was a bit of a mishmash.'

New Gold Dream, Simple Minds
Their crowning glory.

Kissing to Be Clever, Culture Club
There was no reason why George O'Dowd and his band should have been so adept at making modern, polished pop at this level – surely he had done his job just by turning up and looking so extraordinary – but this is what they achieved with this album.

'Young Guns (Go for It)', Wham!
We're all going on a summer holiday!

1999, Prince
An old-school revelation, during a period when it was still seen as a novelty to mix 'rock' with 'black' music.

Living My Life, Grace Jones
On the cover of which her then-partner, Jean-Paul Goude, gives Jones the most angular flat-top of all time. Sharp, remember!

'Love Is a Stranger', Eurythmics
Their very best record, when Dave and Annie still had some danger about them.

'Club Country', the Associates
Forever sleeping giants.

'How We Gonna Make the Black Nation Rise?', Brother 'D' with Collective Effort
Often called the first truly political rap record.

Thriller, Michael Jackson
Off the Wall + video.

1983

Duck Rock, Malcolm McLaren
Genuinely iconic pick-and-mix pop.

'Looking for the Perfect Beat', Afrika Bambaataa and the Soulsonic Force
When dancefloors were eclectic.

'Blue Monday', New Order
Changing the sound of alternative disco for good.

Let's Dance, David Bowie
Success as role play.

Dazzle Ships, Orchestral Manoeuvres in the Dark
Derided at the time, this departure now has a huge following.

The Luxury Gap, Heaven 17
The irony of wealth.

'True', Spandau Ballet
The torch song as a modern parable.

Excess, Yello
European eclecticism.

'The Reflex', Duran Duran
Surrealism as a pop single.

'Dancing with Tears in My Eyes', Ultravox
New Romanticism as a style.

Sweet Dreams, Eurythmics
The eighties incarnate.

'Cruel Summer', Bananarama
Somewhat shambolic, somewhat accidental, somewhat cool.

Fantastic, Wham!
Hello, everyone. We're here!

Madonna, Madonna
Suddenly, out of nowhere, a so-so singer and better-than-average dancer who really wanted to be really, really famous.

'Gold', Spandau Ballet
Gary Kemp's chariot of fire.

'Confusion', New Order
And again . . .

Rock 'n Soul Part 1, Daryl Hall and John Oates
Ignored or patronised by most of the music press, the dynamic duo became the most successful double act of the decade, creating masterful pop in the process.

Electro Vol. 1, Various Artists (Streetsounds)
Morgan Khan was an entrepreneur who made his name producing urban compilations, specialising in the electronic club cuts of the early eighties.

Touch, Eurythmics
Gentrified androgyny.

'Hyperactive', Thomas Dolby
The electronic tool kit as a new idiom.

1984

'It's My Life', Talk Talk
Mark Hollis's band took synth pop and turned it into an existential genre of its own.

'Thieves Like Us', New Order
Any song that can survive 'love is the air that supports the eagle' must be special, and this is, a haunting dance track that almost acts as a precursor to acid house.

Shango Funk Theology, Shango
A computerised Funkadelic.

'Only When You Leave', Spandau Ballet
When Spandau suddenly started making records that sounded like they were built for daytime radio.

Hysteria, Human League
The inevitably disappointing follow-up to *Dare!*

UK Electro, Various Artists (Streetsounds)
A true cult classic.

Diamond Life, Sade
The apotheosis of designer pop.

Fans, Malcolm McLaren
Another oddball excursion from the relentless showman.

'Master and Servant', Depeche Mode
Starting to explore the darker side of love and life.

'Together in Electric Dreams', Phil Oakey and Giorgio Moroder
More Kraftwerk derivations.

Purple Rain, Prince
A *Saturday Night Fever* for the eighties.

'This Is Mine', Heaven 17
Their finest song, their strangest hit.

'Loveride', Nuance
Proof that the dancefloor was still the place where metronomic transgression loomed large.

Welcome to the Pleasuredome, Frankie Goes to Hollywood
Maximalism's greatest hits, all held together with Trevor Horn's audio sticky tape.

Who's Afraid of the Art of Noise?, the Art of Noise
Now that's what we call postmodernism.

'Like a Virgin', Madonna
Retouched for the very first time.

'Out of Touch', Hall & Oates (Arthur Baker remix)
One of the very best pop extended remixes of the decade.

Make It Big, Wham!
Harvesting ambition and then adding a chorus or two.

The Age of Consent, Bronski Beat
Finally, overt gay politics.

'Do They Know It's Christmas?', Band Aid
No other record sums up the decade better; remembered less for its musical merit and far more for its unequivocal ambition.

1985

'Material Girl', Madonna
A song to be played whenever there are video montages of the eighties.

'Crockett's Theme', Jan Hammer
Naff TV with good sounds.

Songs from the Big Chair, Tears for Fears
Big pop with big tunes.

'Move Closer', Phyllis Nelson
A ballad that was played both on drive-time radio and in the Wag Club.

'Feel So Real', Steve Arrington
This shows the diversity there was in dance pop at the time.

'Hanging on a String', Loose Ends
Ditto . . .

Around the World in a Day, Prince
As exacting as James Brown and as prolific as Todd Rundgren.

'A View to a Kill', Duran Duran
'The name's Bon, Simon Le Bon.'

Boys and Girls, Bryan Ferry
And so Bryan picked up where Roxy left off, and all was seamless. Too seamless, in fact.

Cupid and Psyche, Scritti Politti
So contextualised, so thoughtful, so temporary.

'Opportunities (Let's Make Lots of Money)', Pet Shop Boys
With this . . .

'West End Girls', Pet Shop Boys
. . . and this, the last great synth-pop duo stride into town, with both tongues firmly in their cheeks.

'Oh Yeah', Yello
'Chicken tikka.'

'I'm Your Man', Wham!

Iconic, ironic and bringing a smile to the faces of millions.

'Loving the Alien', David Bowie
An often forgotten classic from a fairly dismal period.

'This Is Not America', David Bowie/Pat Metheny
Oh – and another!

'It's Called a Heart', Depeche Mode
Continuing their extraordinary winning streak . . .

'Who Needs Love Like That', Erasure
. . . And the start of another.

'Slave to the Rhythm', Grace Jones
Perhaps Trevor Horn's finest hour, and a high point of eighties pop.

Promise, Sade
Building a legacy through sheer hard work and talent.

ACKNOWLEDGEMENTS

First of all, I would like to thank the 153 people who appear in this book: those who agreed to be interviewed, those who contributed and those quoted by others. This book is their book, as it contains their testimonies, their own stories. I hope they feel I've done them all justice. Most of the interviews were conducted by myself between September 2018 and August 2019, either in person or (occasionally) on the phone; some of the people included here are my friends, others I hadn't spoken to for decades – some not since the eighties, in fact, and a few not since the late seventies – and others (such as the charming Martin Fry, Marc Almond and Daniel Miller, for instance) I'd never met before. I spoke to people all over the world, in London, Brighton, Canvey Island, Anglesey, Miami, New York, Los Angeles, Paris, Cornwall, Milan, St-Tropez, Barcelona, Thailand, Manchester . . . There are surprisingly few books about this period, and most are picture books (some of the best and most helpful are included in the Bibliography); given the huge visual sweep of the time, perhaps this is not so strange. It is, however, an incredibly important part of British pop culture, and one that still feels ill served; perhaps, as Jon Savage so eloquently admits, we were all experiencing a post-punk hangover. I've always felt that the period deserved more, and I've tried in this book to add as much context as possible.

As for myself, having dipped in and out of the Blitz to no great consequence, in 1979 I threw myself into London clubland with something of a vengeance. I like to think I was fairly dedicated, and I lasted until 1988, when, in the space of a few months, acid house suddenly turned a cult into a custom. I'd only recently started at *Arena*, and my double-breasted Jean Paul Gaultier jacket didn't seem to fit in among the T-shirts and bandanas at Shoom. During that time, I had many favourites: Chris Sullivan's first warehouse parties, Le Beat Route, Club for Heroes, White Trash, the Dirtbox, the Wag, Taboo – probably too many favourites, actually. One night in 1984, in the horseshoe bar in Do-Do's, I turned to Robin Derrick (who was working with Neville Brody at *The Face* at the time, and who was dressed – in the style of the summer – in a pair of patent leather shoes and a pale-pink zoot suit with windowpane checks that appeared to be bigger than the suit itself) and said, rather haughtily, 'You know, these are the good old days.' For some, and for many people in this book, they were.

As well as speaking to most of the principal characters, for this book I've also spoken to the raft of people who previously maybe hadn't had the opportunity to tell their stories with as much encouragement or fanfare, as well as those perhaps perceived to be on the periphery of all the commotion. As I attempted with my book on David Bowie, *A Life*, I hope the oral history form used here allows a broader picture to be built, an honest portrayal unencumbered by quite so much editorial subjectivity. Some of the testimonies have had to come from other sources, as some of the significant people who were around at the time have since passed on (David Bowie, Malcolm McLaren, George Michael, Steve Strange, etc., all of whom I interviewed at some point – McLaren at least five times), while there were others whom it was not possible for me to pin down. A few of the interviews were conducted for newspaper or magazine pieces, or for other projects, and in the case of Madonna, the Clash and Grace Jones, for instance, I have used quotes from interviews I conducted with them some time ago; none of them have been taken out of context, and whenever I was in two minds about the continued relevance of a quote, I didn't use it. Quotes have not been used in order to try and make a 'point', only to further the narrative. Small sections of the text have been rewritten from passages appearing in my book on Live Aid, *The Eighties: One Day, One Decade*. The other sources include *i-D*, *The Face*, British *GQ*, British *GQ Style*, the *Independent*, *The Times*, *Arena*, *New Sounds New Styles*, *Hi-Fi News & Record Review*, *Record Mirror*, *Smash Hits*, *Blitz*, *10*, the *Guardian*, *Uncut*, the *NME*, *The Quietus*, *The Electricity Club*, *Classic Pop*, *Direction*, the *Financial Times*, *Dangerous Minds*, BBC Radio 6 Music, *On: Yorkshire Magazine*, *UK Music Reviews*, *Rolling Stone*, the *Belfast Telegraph*, the *South Bank Show*, BBC TV News and *Vice*. A few of the quotes have an unknown provenance, although every effort was made to find their true source. I'd like to thank everyone who agreed to speak with me for this project and all of those who helped me along the way, deither by allowing me to use their material or by facilitating interviews. I would also like to thank Lee Brackstone (whose original idea the book is based on, and who commissioned *Sweet Dreams*), Jonny Geller (for his guidance and for brokering the deal), as well as Ian Bahrami, Paul Baillie-Lane, Angus Cargill, Sarah Walter, Edie Walter Jones and Georgia Sydney Jones. My immediate family's ability to feign enthusiasm whenever I would shout, 'I've just secured an interview with XXXXX!' was not only impressive, it was much needed (by me). I am particularly indebted to Sade Adu, Mel Agace, Viv Albertine, Adam Ant, Peter Ashworth, David Bailey, Graham Ball, Jason Barlow,

Thomas Barrie, Andy Bell, Edward Bell, Christine Binnie, Jennifer Binnie, Johnny Black (so kind!), Judy Blame, Debra Bourne, Kim Bowen, David Bowie, Michael Bracewell, Louisa Buck, Nell Campbell, Richard Campbell-Breeden, Samantha Campbell-Breeden, Joanne Catherall, Mark Cecil, Murray Chalmers, Neneh Cherry, George Chesterton, Andrew P. Childs, Michele Clapton, Angela Cliffe, Nicholas Coleridge, Anita Corbin, Jason Cowley, Gary Crowley, John Cummins, Stephen Dalton (not least for his help with Depeche Mode), Fiona Dealey, Martin Degville, Paul Spencer Denman, Robin Derrick, Bernard Docherty, Keanan Duffty, Danny Ecclestone, Alan Edwards, Rusty Egan, Mark Ellen, Robert Elms, Tracey Emin, Gary Farrow, Fat Tony, Eve Ferret, Bryan Ferry (coincidentally, the first time I ever interviewed Ferry was back in 1985, the year this book finishes, in his management's office in the King's Road; there are selections from three Ferry interviews included here), Kathryn Flett, Wolfgang Flür, Jus Forrest, John Foxx, David Furnish, Martin Fry, Carl Fysh, Lee Gale, Bob Geldof, Boy George, Ricky Gervais, Harvey Goldsmith, Andrew Hale, Jerry Hall, Rob Hallett, Sophie Hamblett, Deborah Harry, David Hepworth, Trevor Horn, Matthew Horton, Barney Hoskyns, Paul Humphreys, Ralf Hütter, Chrissie Hynde, Norman Jay, Elton John, David Johnson, Wilma Johnson, Grace Jones, Mick Jones, Stephen Jones, Terry Jones, Tricia Jones, Ben Kelly, Gary Kemp, Carey Labovitch, Jane Lawson, Simon Le Bon, Annie Lennox, Nick Logan, Annabella Lwin, John Lydon, Andy McCluskey, Paul McGuinness, Malcolm McLaren, Madonna, David Mallet, Glen Matlock, George Michael, Daniel Miller, Jamie Morgan, Paul Morley, Jon Moss, Kate Mossman, Alison Moyet, Simon Napier-Bell, Jonathan Newhouse, Gary Numan, Ollie O'Donnell, Alex Ogg, Betty Page, Dan Papps, Jan Parker, Sylvia Patterson (for helping with Toyah and Jim Kerr), Mike Penrose, Grayson Perry, Oliver Peyton, Antony Price, Bill Prince, Princess Julia, Albert Read, John Reid, Nick Rhodes, Andrew Ridgeley, Dave Rimmer, Mark Roland, Chris Salewicz, Robert Sandall, Jon Savage, Alix Sharkey, Paul Simonon, Siouxsie Sioux, Paul Smith, Terry Smith, Dave Stewart, Steve Strange, David Stubbs, Susan Ann Sulley, Chris Sullivan, Bernard Sumner, Andy Taylor, John Taylor, Julien Temple, Neil Tennant (nearly twice!), Graeme Thomson, Sue Tilley, Pete Townshend, Nicola Tyson, Midge Ure, Jo Vickers, Wyndham Wallace, Martyn Ware, Iain R. Webb, Paul Weller, Liz Wendelbo, Vivienne Westwood, Toyah Willcox, Dencil Williams, Jah Wobble, Keren Woodward, Alan Yentob and Peter York. Thank you also to Paul Gorman for interviewing Danny Kleinman for the *GQ* website, Dave Simpson for his help with the

Eurythmics material, and to Unicorn books for allowing me to reproduce the Edward Bell quote. Thank you to Professor Mark Banks, the head of CAMEo, the Research Institute for Cultural and Media Economies, at the University of Leicester. Finally, thank you to Robert Chalmers for allowing me to quote from his 1995 interview with Adam Ant, and to Tony Parsons for, among many other things, allowing me to quote so comprehensively from his George Michael interviews. I would especially like to pay my respects to David Cavanagh, whom I spoke to just a week before he took his own life at the very end of December 2018.

BIBLIOGRAPHY

Ant, Adam, *Stand & Deliver: The Autobiography* (Sidgwick & Jackson, 2006)

Baker, Danny, *Going to Sea in a Sieve* (Weidenfeld & Nicolson, 2012)

Bell, Edward, *Unmade Up . . . Recollections of a Friendship with David Bowie* (Unicorn, 2017)

Bracewell, Michael, *England Is Mine* (HarperCollins, 1997)

Bracewell, Michael, *When Surface Was Depth* (Da Capo, 2002)

Dunphy, Eamon, *Unforgettable Fire: The Story of U2* (Grand Central, 1988)

Geldof, Bob, *Is That It?* (Sidgwick & Jackson, 1986)

George, Boy, *Take It Like a Man* (Sidgwick & Jackson, 1995)

Hamilton-Paterson, James, *What We Have Lost: The Dismantling of Great Britain* (Head of Zeus, 2018)

Ingham, Bernard, *Kill the Messenger* (Fontana, 1991)

Jones, Jonathan, *Sensations: The Story of British Art from Hogarth to Banksy* (Lawrence King, 2019)

Jordan, *Defying Gravity: Jordan's Story* (Omnibus, 2019)

King, Richard, *How Soon Is Now?* (Faber & Faber, 2012)

Kureishi, Hanif, and Jon Savage (eds), *The Faber Book of Pop* (Faber & Faber, 1995)

Lydon, John, *No Irish, No Blacks, No Dogs* (Hodder & Stoughton, 1994)

McKeen, William, *Tom Wolfe* (Clemson University, 1995)

McSmith, Andy, *No Such Thing as Society: A History of Britain in the 1980s* (Constable & Robinson, 2010)

Majewski, Lori and Jonathan Bernstein, *Mad World* (Abrams Image, 2014)

Marko, Paul, *The Roxy London WC2: A Punk History* (Punk 77, 2007)

Michael, George, and Tony Parsons, *Bare* (Penguin, 1990)

Napier-Bell, Simon, *Black Vinyl White Powder* (Ebury Press, 2001)

Napier-Bell, Simon, *I'm Coming to Take You to Lunch* (Ebury Press, 2005)

Napier-Bell, Simon, *Ta-Ra-Ra-Boom-De-Ay* (Unbound, 2015)

Reynolds, Simon, *Rip It Up and Start Again: Post-Punk 1978–1984* (Faber & Faber, 2005)

Reynolds, Simon, *Totally Wired: Post-Punk Interviews and Overviews* (Faber & Faber, 2009)

Rimmer, Dave, *The New Romantics: The Look* (Omnibus, 2003)

Savage, Jon, *England's Dreaming* (Faber & Faber, 1991)
Scura, Dorothy (ed.), *Conversations with Tom Wolfe* (University Press of Mississippi, 1990)
Smith, Graham, *We Can Be Heroes* (Unbound, 2012)
Stanfill, Sonnet (ed.), *Eighties Fashion: From Club to Catwalk* (V&A, 2013)
Stubbs, David, *Mars by 1980* (Faber & Faber, 2018)
Sudjic, Deyan (ed.), *From Matt Black to Memphis and Back Again* (Architecture, Design & Technology Press, 1989)
Tannenbaum, Rob, and Craig Marks, *I Want My MTV: The Uncensored Story of the Music Video Revolution* (Dutton, 2011)
Taylor, John, *In the Pleasure Groove: Love, Death & Duran Duran* (Sphere, 2012)
Turner, Alwyn W., *Rejoice! Rejoice! Britain in the 1980s* (Aurum Press, 2013)
Ure, Midge, *If I Was . . .* (Virgin, 2004)
Weingarten, Marc, *Who's Afraid of Tom Wolfe: How New Journalism Rewrote the World* (Aurum Press, 2005)
York, Peter, *Modern Times* (Trafalgar Square, 1984)
York, Peter, *Style Wars* (Sidgewick & Jackson, 1980)
York, Peter, *The Eighties* (BBC Books, 1995)
Young, Hugo, *One of Us* (Macmillan, 1989/1991)

INDEX

2-Tone (music genre) 343, 357–58, 389; *See also* Madness; *The Selecter*; The Specials
100 Club 78, 79, 88, 117

ABC: beginnings 231–32; gig, Futurama festival 231; influences 231, 442–43; look 367–68; records ('All of My Heart' 367, 370; *Beauty Stab* 442–43, 585; *How to Be a . . . Zillionaire!* 585; *The Lexicon of Love* 367, 368, 369–70, 383, 590; 'The Look of Love' 367, 370; 'Poison Arrow' 367, 369, 370; 'Tears Are Not Enough' 367, 369; 'That Was Then but This Is Now' 443); in *Smash Hits* 377; sound 368, 369, 370, 442–43; UK critical reception 371, 443; *See also* Fry, Martin; Horn, Trevor; Temple, Julien
acid house, advent of 584
Acme Attractions (shop) 48, 49, 66, 77, 83, 138
Adam and the Ants: appear on *Top of the Pops* 11, 241, 253, 381; beginnings 111, 112; look 253, 255, 623; records ('Antmusic' 332; 'Beat My Guest' 112; 'Dirk Wears White Sox' 243; *Dirk Wears White Sox* 244–45; 'Dog Eat Dog' 332; 'Human Bondage Den' 112; *Kings of the Wild Frontier* 252, 253, 255; 'Prince Charming' 332, 396, 623; 'Rubber People' 112; 'Whip in My Valise' 112; 'Young Parisians' 243); in *Smash Hits* 377; sound 244, 251, 252; split in 1982 296; tour, *Ants Invasion* (1980) 253; video, 'Stand and Deliver' 314; *See also* Adam Ant (born Stuart Leslie Goddard); Pirroni, Marco
Adam Ant (born Stuart Leslie Goddard) 65, 627: early life and career 112; influences 245, 250–51; at Live Aid 569; look 111, 112–13, 242, 244, 245–46, 250, 251, 314, 569; personality 245, 253; quoted 112–13, 241, 244, 245, 246, 249, 250, 251–52, 254–55, 266; seeks help from Malcolm McLaren (who steals his band) 243, 245–46, 249, 251–52; *See also* Adam and the Ants; Bazooka Joe
Adu, Sade *See* Sade (born Helen Folasade Adu) (singer)
Afrika Bambaataa (born Lance Taylor) 627: early life 404; gig, Wag (1982) 397; look 404; 'Planet Rock' (with Soulsonic Force) 404; quoted 405
Aids 185, 485, 572, 586, 587, 617, 618
Albertine, Viv 79–80, 627
Almond, Marc (born Peter Mark Sinclair Almond) 627: DJs in Leeds 231; early life and career 33–34, 330–31; experience of fame 335, 336, 546; haunts 238, 446; influences 34, 330–31, 335–36; look 238, 332, 335–36; personality 333; quoted 33–34, 90–91, 238–39, 330–32, 333–36, 372–73, 546, 586; sexuality 373; *See also* Soft Cell
Ambrose, Dave 259
American charts, British acts in 291, 321–22, 346–47, 387, 438, 448–49, 472–73, 474, 491, 588, 589, 611
androgyny: 1976 86; 1977 104; 1978 136; 1980 300, 305; 1981 332–33; 1982 394–95; 1983 441, 459; 1984 513, 521; *See also* Bowie, David (born David Robert Jones); Boy George (born George Alan O'Dowd); Harry, Deborah; Jones, Grace; Lennox, Annie; Marilyn
Animal Nightlife 348; *See also* Polaris, Andy
Ant, Adam *See* Adam Ant (born Stuart Leslie Goddard)
The Ants *See* Adam and the Ants
Area (club) 543–44, 590
Arena (magazine) 513
art schools 191–94; *See also* St Martin's School of Art
Arthur, Neil 421; *See also* Blancmange
Ashworth, Peter: early life and career 87–88; quoted 87–88, 191, 253, 287–88, 336–37, 475, 534, 535
Axiom (shop) 214, 344

B-52's 154: look 132, 234; records ('53 Miles West of Venus' 132; 'Quiche Lorraine' 132; 'Rock Lobster' 132; 'There's a Moon in the Sky (Called the Moon)' 132); 'Wig' 132
Bailey, David 627: quoted 32–33, 171–73, 174, 378, 462–63, 533, 566; *See also Ritz* (magazine)
Baker, Danny 215, 383
Ball, David 238–39, 627: experience of fame 546; look 332; quoted 239, 332; *See also* Soft Cell
Ball, Graham 627: haunts 24–25, 81, 144, 191; quoted 24–25, 81, 107, 143–44, 621

Ballard, J. G., influence of 162, 200, 203–4, 226
Bananarama: appear on *Top of the Pops* 386; beginnings 195, 385, 386; gig, Whiskey-A-Go-Go 383; haunts 407; influences 385; look 386, 387; personalities 386–87; records ('Aie e Mwana' 385; Band Aid, 'Do They Know It's Christmas?' 549, 550–55, 556; 'Cruel Summer' 387; 'Really Saying Something' (with Fun Boy Three) 385); in *Smash Hits* 386; tour, Red Wedge (1986) 602; US success 387; *See also* Dallin, Sara; Woodward, Keren
Band Aid, 'Do They Know It's Christmas?' 549, 550–55, 556
Bandwagon (club) 22
Bang (club) 80, 82, 111
Banks, Mark and Oakley, Kate, 'The Dance Goes on Forever? Art Schools, Class and UK Higher Education' 192–93
Banshees *See* Siouxsie and the Banshees
Bareham, Lindsey 576
'bathroom reverb' 503–4; *See also* drum sounds
Bazooka Joe 63–64; *See also* Adam Ant (born Stuart Leslie Goddard); Kleinman, Danny
Beachcomber Bar, Mayfair Hotel 150–51, 197
Beat Instrumental (magazine) 281–82
Beatles: 'A Day in the Life' 39; 'Tomorrow Never Knows' 59; *See also* Lennon, John
The Bell (pub) 446
Bell, Andy: early life 445; haunts 446; look 545–46; quoted 445–46, 545–46; sexuality 445–46; *See also* Erasure
Bell, Edward 296–97, 627
Bentinck, Baron S. 168; *See also Boulevard* (magazine)
Berrow, Michael and Paul 257; *See also* Rum Runner (club)
Billy's (club) 138–39, 175, 176: ambience/décor 135, 136, 137, 139; clientele 133–35, 137, 140, 141–42, 143, 144, 145, 147, 148–49, 208, 214, 230–31, 238, 296; *See also* Egan, Rusty; Strange, Steve (born John Harrington)
Binnie, Christine and Jennifer 354, 628; *See also* Neo Naturists
Black, Johnny 628
Black, Pauline 358; *See also The Selecter*
black clubs (US) 401
black models 510, 511, 512
Blame, Judy (born Christopher Barnes) 140, 292, 628
Blancmange 363; *See also* Arthur, Neil
Blitz (club): ambience/décor 3, 175, 176, 181, 189, 196, 208, 289; Boy George works at 4, 180, 186, 304; clientele (*See* Blitz Kids); closes (1980) 305; David Bowie at 293–97; door policy 2, 5, 180, 182, 186–87, 190, 191, 196–97, 296, 304, 305–6 (Mick Jagger is turned away 178, 197, 294); *See also* Egan, Rusty; Strange, Steve (born John Harrington)
Blitz (magazine) 266–67, 282–87, 481; *See also* Labovitch, Carey; Tesler, Simon
Blitz Kids 2–6, 180–82, 185–89, 190–91, 196–97, 207, 210–11, 218: in 'Ashes to Ashes' video 290, 295, 296, 297, 299–300, 301; dressing up 3, 4, 133, 180, 185, 188–89, 197, 218, 291–92, 305–6, 307–8; gay element 187, 188, 196, 207, 208, 211, 289; in New York with Spandau Ballet 345; *See also* Blitz (club); Bowen, Kim; Dealey, Fiona; Egan, Rusty; Jones, Stephen; Princess Julia (born Julia Fodor); Sullivan, Chris; Webb, Iain R.
Blondie: 'Call Me' 309; influences 155, 308–9; in *Ritz* (magazine) 462; sound 156; UK success 308, 315; *See also* Harry, Deborah; Stein, Chris
'Bloody Saturday' 359–61, 362; *See also* riots
The Blow Monkeys, Red Wedge leaflet 602
Blue Rondo à la Turk (band): gig, Clerkenwell warehouse (1981) 344–45, 402; haunts 363, 385; 'Klactoveesedstein' 345; look 345; sound 345; UK critical reception 437; *See also* Sullivan, Chris
Bogart's (club) 386
Bolan, Marc 316
Bono (born Paul David Hewson): Band Aid, 'Do They Know It's Christmas?' 549, 550–55, 556; haunts 599; quoted 567, 628; *See also* U2
Boomtown Rats: at Live Aid 563–65; tour, UK (1985) 561; *See also* Geldof, Bob
Boulevard (magazine) 168–70, 269
Bourne, Debra 513–14, 628
Bow Wow Wow 243, 247, 254: records ('C-30 C-60 C-90 Go!' 248; 'Giant-Sized Baby Thing' 249; 'Hello, Hello Daddy' 249; 'Radio G-String' 249; 'Sexy Eiffel Tower' 249); *See also* Gorman, Leigh; Lwin, Annabella (born Myant Myant Aye); McLaren, Malcolm
Bowen, Kim 628: early life 50–51; haunts 5, 50–51, 80, 147, 186, 198, 296; look 198; quoted 50–51, 80, 147–48, 198, 481; *See also* Blitz Kids
Bowery, Leigh 617–18
Bowie, David (born David Robert Jones) 628: gigs (Meltdown festival (2002) 228; Wembley Empire Pool (1976) 76); goes to the Blitz 293–97; haunts 397, 406, 408, 409, 544, 599;

influence of 9, 25, 34, 49, 120, 151, 152, 179, 199, 219, 220, 231, 234, 256, 265, 300, 303, 316, 336, 429, 442–43, 464, 547; lifestyle 607–8; at Live Aid 566; look 20, 21, 25, 35, 290, 295, 299, 300, 467, 579; personality 220, 228–29, 293, 297, 408–9, 607–8; quoted 19, 20, 23, 25, 33, 110, 227, 228, 229, 298, 299, 300–301, 408, 576–77, 579, 607–8; records ('After All' 82; 'Ashes to Ashes' 300; 'Changes' 577; 'Golden Years' 577; *'Heroes'* 129, 130, 446; 'Let's Dance' 576–77; *Let's Dance* 576–77; 'The London Boys' 97; *Low* 121, 129, 130, 146, 228; 'The Man Who Sold the World' 220; *The Man Who Sold the World* 82; *Scary Monsters* 31, 298–99, 300–301; 'Space Oddity' 297, 300; 'Starman' 35, 623; 'Stay' 231; 'Suffragette City' 331; *Tonight* 608; 'Warszawa' 121; 'Where Are You Now?' 614; 'Young Americans' 20; *Young Americans* 9, 22, 23, 33, 51–52, 85; *Ziggy Stardust* 318, 623); sexuality 440; sound 20, 23; tours (*Diamond Dogs* (1974) 21; *Serious Moonlight* (1983) 433, 467; *Station to Station* (1976) 70, 151); turned away from Japan gig 419–20; TV appearances (*Extras* 466; *The Kenny Everett Show* 297; *Top of the Pops* 336, 623); videos 408, 409 ('Ashes to Ashes' 290, 295, 296, 297, 299–300, 301; 'Day-In Day-Out' 512–13; 'Jazzin' for Blue Jean' 409); *See also* Jones, Duncan
'Bowie twins' 85–86
Boy George (born George Alan O'Dowd): arrested by police ('Operation Culture') 484–85, 617; experience of fame 367, 444–45, 450; haunts 47–48, 78, 82, 133–34, 177, 186, 293, 397, 403, 407; influences 52; lifestyle 485, 617, 619; look 1, 82–83, 254, 289, 308, 438, 481, 582, 590; performs with Bow Wow Wow 254; personality 4, 373–74, 441, 445, 482, 483; quoted 1, 47–48, 82–83, 133–34, 186, 253–54, 339, 367, 373–74, 394, 439, 440, 444–45, 447, 482–83, 484–85, 579–80; relationship with Jon Moss 440, 441, 468, 485, 619; sexuality 440, 454, 579–80; works at Blitz 4, 180, 186, 304; works at Hell 186, 628; *See also* Culture Club
Boys Town Gang, 'I Can't Take My Eyes off You' 404
Bracewell, Michael 629: quoted 20, 159, 317–18, 319–20, 367, 523
Bragg, Billy 602–3: plays benefit shows 603; quoted 363, 603; *See also* Red Wedge (pressure group)
Brandon, Kirk 407
British Electric Foundation 323, 423: records (*Music for Stowaways* 424; *Music of Quality & Distinction* 423; 'Optimum Chant' 424); *See also* Heaven 17; Ware, Martyn
Brixton riots: 1981 359–61, 362, 600; 1985 600–601; *See also* riots
Brody, Neville 461, 461–62, 602
Bromley Contingent 36, 76, 78, 120, 188; *See also* Idol, Billy; Siouxsie Sioux (born Susan Janet Ballion); Soo Catwoman
Bronski Beat: 'Smalltown Boy' 580; in *Smash Hits* 526; *See also* Somerville, Jimmy
Browne, Tara 39
Buck, Louisa 354, 629
Buerk, Michael, report on Ethiopian famine 551, 553
Buffalo movement 508, 509–13; *See also* Cherry, Neneh (born Neneh Mariann Karlsson); Kamen, Nick; Morgan, Jamie; Petri, Ray
Buggles: influences 203–4; sound 203–4; 'Video Killed the Radio Star' 203–4, 311; *See also* Downes, Geoffrey; Horn, Trevor
Burchill, Julie 67, 97, 597
Burden, Ian 318; *See also* Human League
Burns, Ricci 39, 83
Buzzcocks 74, 75

Cabaret Voltaire 157, 198, 236
Callis, Jo 318, 321; *See also* Human League
Cambridge (pub) 101–2
Camden Palace (club) 415, 416: artists 394; clientele 388, 394; door policy 394; *See also* Egan, Rusty; Strange, Steve (born John Harrington)
CamelCase (bicapitalisation), trend for 574–75
Campbell, Naomi 512
Campbell, Nell 84, 629
Caplan, Melissa 137, 177, 191, 212
Catherall, Joanne 319, 320–21, 629; *See also* Human League
Catwoman, Soo: *See* Soo Catwoman
Cavanagh, David 157–58, 356, 629
CDs (compact discs) 507, 550, 587–88
A Certain Ratio 231
Chaguaramas (club) (later Roxy) 49, 66; *See also* Roxy (club) (previously Chaguaramas)
Chalmers, Robert 112, 629
Channel 4 470, 471; *See also The Tube* (TV show)
charity shop clothing 72, 183–84, 233
Charles, Prince of Wales: at Live Aid 563, 571–72; meets Duran Duran 451–52
Cherry, Neneh (born Neneh Mariann Karlsson)

629: 'Buffalo Stance' 510; haunts 397, 403; quoted 510, 511; *See also* Buffalo movement
Chesterton, George 629: quoted 225–26, 425
Chic: 'Good Times' 20, 132, 395; influence of 256; influences 20
Chicken (magazine) 247–48, 249, 251; *See also* McLaren, Malcolm
Christgau, Robert 130
Clapton, Eric 562, 598
Clapton, Michele 629: haunts 3, 187, 211, 621; look 187, 621–22; quoted 211, 618, 621–22
Clarke, Vince: early life 264, 328; leaves Depeche Mode 326–27, 423; personality 545; quoted 327; *See also* Composition of Sound; Depeche Mode; Erasure; Yazoo
The Clash: beginnings 71–73, 75; gigs (Lacy Lady 333; Victoria Park (1978) 603); influence of 264; look 72, 75, 101, 129; records ('1977' 128; *The Clash* 96; 'I'm So Bored with the USA' 101); tour, *Anarchy* (1976) 91; *See also* Jones, Mick; Simonon, Paul; Strummer, Joe
A Clockwork Orange (film) 78, 161, 201, 317
clothes and fashion (in general): British fashion goes global (1985) 575–76; charity shop clothing 72, 183–84, 233; men's clothing industry, changes in 1980s 497–98, 506, 610; power dressing 242, 549, 607; *See also* Buffalo movement; 'look' *under individuals/bands*
Club for Heroes (club) 355, 393, 407, 553, 598; *See also* Egan, Rusty; Strange, Steve (born John Harrington)
Coca-Cola introduces New Coke 574
Coffee, 'Casanova' 404
Cohn, Nik 131
Cold War 573
Coleridge, Nicholas 168, 169
Collins, Phil: records ('In the Air Tonight' 503; Band Aid, 'Do They Know It's Christmas?' 549, 550–55, 556); works with Peter Gabriel 503
colour bars 400, 402, 405–6
Composition of Sound 262; *See also* Clarke, Vince; Depeche Mode; Gahan, Dave
Cook, Paul 138, 194–95
Cook, Robin 602
Corbin, Anita 188–89, 629
Costello, Elvis: 'Shipbuilding' 430, 518; tour, Red Wedge (1986) 602
Cowley, Jason 629: haunts 178, 394; quoted 19, 178, 394
Cowley, Patrick, 'I Feel Love' (remix) 505
Crackers (club): ambience/décor 84–85; Bowie nights 66, 121; clientele 48, 49, 66, 77, 80, 81, 84, 85–86, 142, 143; Ferry nights 121
Craig, Mikey 441, 445, 468, 629; *See also* Culture Club
Crazy Daisy (club) 318, 320
Crisp, Quentin 52
Croc's (club) 41, 259–60, 332, 373
Crowley, Gary 629: haunts 383; live DJing 385–86; quoted 383–84, 385–86, 522–23, 587; works at Capital Radio 383–84, 385; *See also* *The Modern World* (fanzine)
Culture Club 296: appear on *Top of the Pops* 289, 374, 381, 441, 482; gigs (Croc's (1981) 373; Dominion Theatre (1983) 438; Heaven (1982) 373); haunts 363; influence of 469; influences 586; records (Band Aid, 'Do They Know It's Christmas?' 549, 550–55, 556; 'Do You Really Want to Hurt Me?' 289, 374, 384, 437–38, 582; 'Karma Chameleon' 445; 'The Medal Song' 483; 'Victims' 524; *Waking Up with the House on Fire* 484; 'White Boy' 373); in *Rolling Stone* 472; in *Smash Hits* 377; tour, America (1983) (refuse entry to Wham!) 478; UK tabloid coverage 482–83, 485; US success 291, 438, 440, 588; young female fans 438, 440, 445;*See also* Boy George (born George Alan O'Dowd); Craig, Mikey; Hay, Roy; Moss, Jon
Cummins, John 470–71, 629
Currie, Billy 205; *See also* Ultravox

Dagger, Steve 629: early life 19–20; haunts 3, 19, 120–21, 134–35, 136, 140, 143; influences 212–13; look 442; personality 214; quoted 19–20, 74, 119, 120–21, 134–35, 212–14, 218, 255, 600; *See also* Spandau Ballet
Dallin, Sara 194–95; *See also* Bananarama
Dalton, Stephen 262–63, 324, 325, 327–28, 446
Dammers, Jerry: influences 556; quoted 357, 555, 556; tour, Red Wedge (1986) 602; *See also* Special AKA; The Specials
The Damned 69
dance remixes: *See* remixes
Danceteria (club) 543–44
Darnell, August 407
de Graaf, Kasper 345
Dealey, Fiona 629: haunts 3, 40–41, 68–69, 70, 145, 177, 182, 190, 197, 348–49, 476; lifestyle 197–98; look 69, 70, 146, 147, 187, 197, 266; quoted 40–41, 50, 68–69, 70, 144–45, 190–91, 197–98, 207–8, 266, 348–49, 394, 476, 480, 621; *See also* Blitz Kids
Degville, Martin 66, 141, 232

Denman, Paul Spencer 629: haunts 491; influences 493; look 493–94; quoted 490–91, 493–94, 495–96, 497, 584, 625–26; *See also* Sade (band)
Depeche Mode: Alan Wilder joins 327–28; appear on *Top of the Pops* 325, 326; beginnings 259, 260–61, 262; gigs (Croc's (1981) 332; Sweeney's (1981) 329); haunts 41, 407; influences 199, 263, 300, 325; lifestyle 446; look 260, 328; records (*A Broken Frame* 446; *Construction Time Again* 446; 'Get the Balance Right' 260; 'Just Can't Get Enough' 260; 'Master and Servant' 446; 'New Life' 260, 325; *Speak & Spell* 325, 326, 329; *Violator* 630); signing with Mute Records 261, 325–26; in *Smash Hits* 377; sound 260, 324, 328, 446; tour, *Speak & Spell* (1981) 326; UK critical reception 328, 330; US success 291, 590; Vince Clarke leaves 326–27, 423; working-class roots 262, 328; *See also* Clarke, Vince; Fletcher, Andrew; Gahan, Dave; Gore, Martin; Wilder, Alan
Derrick, Robin 282, 630
'designer' (adjective and lifestyle) 12, 15, 499–500, 505–6, 507, 549
Devo 154–55
Diana, Princess of Wales: funeral 554–55, 572; at Live Aid 471–72, 563; look 379, 572; meets Duran Duran 451–52
Dire Straits, 'Money for Nothing' 313
Dirtbox (club) 394–95, 491
disco: 1975 20, 23, 60, 208; 1976 69, 80, 86; 1977 108; 1978 130–31, 132, 152, 153, 154, 160, 208; 1980 265; 1981 330, 346, 364; 1982 380, 385, 388, 401; 1983 454, 459; gay disco 208–9, 330, 401, 404; *See also Saturday Night Fever*
Docherty, Bernard 630quoted 567
Doig, Peter 102
Dollar: records ('Give Me Back My Heart' 368; 'Hand Held in Black and White' 368–69; 'Mirror Mirror' 368); *See also* Horn, Trevor
Downes, Geoffrey 204; *See also* Buggles
Dr Feelgood 35
drug addiction, prevalence of 481, 616–17, 618–20
drum machines 58, 109, 200, 203, 237, 335, 404, 502–3, 505: LinnDrum 417, 505, 529, 589 (Linn 2 530); Oberheim 457–58; Roland 235, 335, 404, 505; *See also* electronic music
drum sounds: 'bathroom reverb' 503–4; gated reverb ('noise gate') 237, 503; *See also* drum sounds
Dudley, Anne 530
Duffty, Keanan 230–31, 304, 304–5, 630
Duran Duran: beginnings 255–59, 339; female fans 433, 435, 453; gigs (Aston Villa (1983) 451; Birmingham Odeon 338; Dominion Theatre (1983) 451; Madison Square Garden (1984) 453); haunts 407, 598; influence of 420; influences 152, 256, 379; lifestyle 377–79, 433, 435–36, 452, 454; look 153–54, 256, 257–58, 337–38, 377–78, 379–80, 473; meet Prince and Princess of Wales 451–52; records (Band Aid, 'Do They Know It's Christmas?' 549, 550–55, 556; 'Girls on Film' 339, 420; 'Is There Something I Should Know?' 337; 'Ordinary World' 586; 'Planet Earth' 256; 'Rio' 288, 337; *Rio* 377; 'Save a Prayer' 337, 524); rivalry with Spandau Ballet 340, 371, 372, 375, 449–50, 556; signing with EMI 259; in *Smash Hits* 377; sound 256, 380, 609; split 590; tours (*Sing Blue Silver Tour* (1983–1984) 453; support David Bowie (1983) 433; support Hazel O'Connor (1980) 258–59); UK critical reception 337, 338–39, 378–80, 450–51; UK tabloid coverage ('Duranysty') 451, 452–53; US success 291, 448–49, 588; videos 378, 448–49, 473 ('Rio' 288, 377–78, 379); *See also* Edwards, Alan; Le Bon, Simon; Rhodes, Nick (born Nicholas James Bates); Taylor, Andy; Taylor, John; Taylor, Roger

Eccleston, Danny 419, 546–47, 630
Echo and the Bunnymen, Futurama festival (1979) 234
Edwards, Alan 258–59, 433–34, 630; *See also* Duran Duran
Egan, Rusty 630: early career 35; haunts 35; look 35, 138, 175; personality 140; quoted 35, 71–72, 97, 109, 137–39, 175–76, 205, 210, 214, 302–3, 414, 415, 619;*See also* Billy's (club); Blitz (club); Blitz Kids; Camden Palace (club); Club for Heroes (club); Hell (club); Rich Kids; Visage
Eldridge, Roy 403
electronic music: 1977 108; 1978 129, 136, 153, 154, 159, 162–64; 1979 184, 198–99, 204, 615; 1980 255, 300; 1981 325, 331, 334, 346, 364; 1982 388, 403; 1983 458; 1984 490; 1985 585, 587, 610; *See also* The Normal; Depeche Mode; drum machines; Kraftwerk; Numan, Gary (born Gary Anthony James Webb); Roxy Music; science fiction, influence of; synth duos/groups; synthesizers
Elle (magazine) 575

Ellen, Mark 630: quoted 339–40, 341–43, 344–45, 371–72, 525, 572, 582–83; *See also Smash Hits* (magazine)
Elliott, Tony 276
Elms, Robert 630: early life 22; haunts 3, 22, 187–88, 191, 211; look 22; quoted 22, 23–24, 48–49, 66, 74, 92, 142–43, 176–77, 187–88, 211–12, 286–87, 346, 406, 437, 463–64, 595; *See also* Le Kilt (club); St Moritz (club)
Elton John (born Reg Dwight) 632: lifestyle 435–36; at Live Aid 566, 569; personal life 571; quoted 478, 479; records (*Blue Moves* 571; *Breaking Hearts* 571; 'Candle in the Wind' 554–55; 'I Guess That's Why They Call It The Blues' 571; *Ice on Fire* 571; 'I'm Still Standing' 571; 'Nikita' 570, 571; 'Passengers' 571; 'Sad Songs (Say So Much)' 571; *Too Low for Zero* 571; 'Wrap Her Up' 571); video, 'I'm Still Standing' 435; works with George Michael 569–70
Embassy Club 150, 168, 209: clientele 49, 87, 137, 198, 446
Emin, Tracey 295–96, 397, 630
Eno, Brian 52, 59, 178; *See also* Roxy Music
Erasure 445, 545–46; *See also* Bell, Andy; Clarke, Vince
Eric's (club) 166
Ethiopian famine 550–52, 554; *See also* Band Aid, 'Do They Know It's Christmas?'; Live Aid
'European' music and imagery 613–16
Eurythmics: beginnings 82, 473–74; in *The Face* 475; influences 300; records ('Sweet Dreams (Are Made of This)' 474–75, 476; *Touch* 475–76); in *Smash Hits* 377; styling 42; US success 291, 474; video, 'Sweet Dreams (Are Made of This)' 474, 475; *See also* Lennox, Annie; Stewart, Dave
Extras (TV show) 466–67; *See also* Gervais, Ricky; Merchant, Stephen

The Face (magazine): 1980 241, 266, 267–68, 276, 277–82, 286, 287, 288, 292; 1981 332, 343–44; 1982 395; 1983 461–62; 1985 600; *See also* Logan, Nick
Fad Gadget (Frank Tovey) 163, 325
Fairlight synthesizer 502–3, 529, 589; *See also* synthesizers
Faith, Adam 38, 39
Falklands War 429–31, 460, 518
fanzines (in general) 167, 383–84; *See also specific fanzines*
Farrow, Gary 448, 521–22, 524, 533, 570, 630; *See also* Heaven 17
Fat Tony (born Tony Marnach) 397, 407, 618–19, 630
Ferret, Eve 181–82, 297, 378, 409, 630
Ferry, Bryan 630: early life 27; haunts 599; influence of 28–29, 37, 245, 265; lifestyle 28; at Live Aid 559, 568–69; look 20, 28–29, 37, 38, 50, 442, 577; personality 33, 37–38, 42; quoted 25–26, 27, 29–30, 568–69, 578–79; records (*The Bride Stripped Bare* 19; *These Foolish Things* 38); *See also* Roxy Music
Fletcher, Andrew: early life 261, 264, 328–29; quoted 264, 325–26, 327; *See also* Depeche Mode
Flett, Kathryn 407, 630
Flür, Wolfgang 54, 55–56, 630; *See also* Kraftwerk
food and restaurants (developments in 1985) 576, 595, 596
football hooliganism 128, 574
Foundry (shop) 293
Foxx, John (born Dennis Leigh) 630: goes solo 234, 235–37; influences 237; quoted 58–59, 122, 127–28, 234–37; records (*Metamatic* 236–37; 'Underpass' 237, 238, 320); *See also* Ultravox
Frankie Goes to Hollywood: beginnings 527; influence of 533; legacy 532; look 446; records ('Born to Run' 531, 536; 'Do You Know the Way to San Jose' 531; 'Krisco Kisses' 530; *Liverpool* 532; 'The Only Star in Heaven' 530; 'The Power of Love' 531; 'Relax' 527–30, 535; 'Two Tribes' 527, 530, 536, 573; 'War' 530; 'Welcome to the Pleasuredome' 531, 535; *Welcome to the Pleasuredome* 528, 530–32, 534); sexuality 526, 532–33; signing with ZTT 527, 528; in *Smash Hits* 377; sound 528–29, 536–37; tour, US (1984) 536–37; Trevor Horn's influence 528–29, 533–35; TV appearances (*Saturday Night Live* 536; *Top of the Pops* 530; *The Tube* 471, 527, 528); videos ('Relax' 527, 528; 'Two Tribes' 530); *See also* Johnson, Holly; Rutherford, Paul
Franks, Lynne 597
Frith, Simon and Horne, Howard, *Art into Pop* 192
Frostrup, Mariella 373
Fry, Martin 630: early career 97–98; 'flatpack years' 585–86; haunts 590; influences 89, 368, 370; *See also* ABC
Fun Boy Three 385, 555: 'Really Saying Something' (with Bananarama) 385; *See also* Hall, Terry

Funkadelic, 'One Nation Under a Groove' 52
Futurama festival (1979) 231, 233–34

Gabriel, Peter, Peter Gabriel ['Melt'] 503
Gahan, Dave 630–31: early life 261, 262, 263–64; influences 264; quoted 261, 263–64, 330; *See also* Composition of Sound; Depeche Mode
Gale, Lee 454–55, 631
Garner, Kate 384–85, 631; *See also* Haysi Fantayzee
Garrett, Malcolm 337–38, 345
gated reverb ('noise gate') 237, 503; *See also* drum sounds
gay anthems 208
gay bands/gay pop 10, 247, 332–33, 373, 545 *See also* Bronski Beat; Pet Shop Boys; Soft Cell
gay clubs 111, 149–50; *See also* Bang (club); Billy's (club); Chaguaramas (club) (later Roxy); Crackers (club); Louise's (club); Sombrero (club)
gay disco 208–9, 330, 401, 404
Geldof, Bob 631: haunts 349, 553, 599; infamous Live Aid interview 562, 565; personality 553; quoted 551–52, 553, 555, 559, 560, 564–65, 572, 606–7; *See also* Band Aid, 'Do They Know It's Christmas?'; Boomtown Rats; Live Aid
Generation X: gigs (Nag's Head (1976) 87; Roxy (1976) 92)
George, Boy *See* Boy George (born George Alan O'Dowd)
Gervais, Ricky 464, 465, 466, 467, 631; *See also* *Extras* (TV show); Seona Dancing
Global Village (club) (later Heaven) 47, 49, 70, 81; *See also* Heaven (club) (previously Global Village)
Godley and Creme 303, 530
Gold Coast Club 396
Goldmine (club) 40–41, 69, 81
Goldsmith, Harvey 259, 631: quoted 37–38, 117, 241, 559–60, 565–67, 569, 591–92; *See also* Live Aid
Goodman, Dave 115
Gore, Martin 631: early life 261, 263, 328–29; look 324–25; quoted 262, 263, 324–25, 327, 328; sexuality 446; *See also* Depeche Mode
Gorman, Leigh 247; *See also* Bow Wow Wow
goth 428
Goude, Jean-Paul 364
Grandmaster Flash: gig, Wag 397; records ('The Adventures of Grandmaster Flash on the Wheels of Steel' 403; 'The Message' 395, 403–4)
Grayling, A. C. 11
Gregory, Glenn 317: look 324; quoted 323–24, 424; works with Tina Turner 423, 424; *See also* Heaven 17
Grogan, Clare 350, 467
Groucho Club 595, 596, 597–99
Grundy, Bill 93

Haçienda (club) 409–13, 459; *See also* Kelly, Ben; New Order; Wilson, Tony
Hadley, Tony 211, 308; *See also* Spandau Ballet
Haggerty, Mick 548
Haines, Perry 275
hair styles: beehive 132, 148; bird's-nest 386; bleached hair 155, 188; Brian Ferry/Roxy Music (and fans) 38, 42; David Bowie (and fans) 20, 85; dreadlocks 289, 590; dyed hair 20, 48, 50, 79, 81, 85, 194, 361, 429; Mohikan (Mohawk) 128, 218, 404, 427; 'piste' 319; quiff 27, 38, 64, 66, 102, 134, 296; shaven heads (women) 189; short and lacquered 156; wedge 20, 22, 23–24, 25, 50, 135; *See also* 'look' *under individuals/bands*
Haircut 100 388
'haircut bands' 319
hairdressers' salons: Crimpers 50; Ricci Burns 39–40, 83; Smile 38, 39, 83–84, 88; Vidal Sassoon 24
Hale, Andrew 51–52, 631early life 51–52; experience of fame 495; haunts 406; influences 52; quoted 406, 490, 491–92, 494, 495, 496, 502, 625; *See also* Sade (band)
Hall, Daryl 631haunts 544, 599; look 541; quoted 541, 542, 543; *See also* Hall & Oates
Hall, Jerry 32–33, 631
Hall, Terry 385; *See also* Fun Boy Three; The Specials
Hall & Oates 439, 541: critical reception 541, 542; records ('Back Together Again' 542; 'Every Time You Go Away' 542; 'I Can't Go for That' 542; 'Method of Modern Love' 542; 'Out of Touch' 542; 'Rich Girl' 542; 'Sara Smile' 542; 'She's Gone' 542; 'Wait for Me' 542); sound 542–43; *See also* Hall, Daryl; Oates, John
Hallett, Rob 112, 241, 258, 259, 338–39, 434, 435, 620–21, 631
Hamilton, Richard 27
Hamnet, Katharine 575–76
Harpers & Queen (magazine) 22–23
Harrods, party 406–7
Harry, Deborah 458–59, 631: haunts 118, 544; look 155, 309; personality 308; quoted 155–56, 309, 315; *See also* Blondie

Haslam, Nicky 174, 631
Hay, Roy 469; *See also* Culture Club
Haysi Fantayzee 363, 384–85; *See also* Garner, Kate; Healy, Jeremy
Healy, Jeremy 33, 133, 141, 186, 384; *See also* Haysi Fantayzee
Heartbreakers: gig, Roxy (1977) 118; tour, *Anarchy* (1976) 91
Heathcote, Hector 402, 631
Heaven (club) (previously Global Village) 87, 373, 407, 446, 618; *See also* Global Village (club) (later Heaven)
Heaven 17: appear on *children's TV shows* 448; beginnings 201, 317, 323; haunts 407; influences 201; look 324; records ('Come Live with Me' 317; 'Crushed by the Wheels of Industry' 317; 'Let Me Go' 317; *The Luxury Gap* 424; *Penthouse and Pavement* 323, 324; 'Play to Win' 317; 'Temptation' 317; 'This is Mine' 317; '(We Don't Need This) Fascist Groove Thang' 317); rivalry with Human League 323–24; tour, Red Wedge (1986) 602; *See also* Farrow, Gary; Gregory, Glenn; Marsh, Ian Craig; Ware, Martyn
Hebdige, Dick 288
Hell (club) 186, 293, 305, 306; *See also* Strange, Steve (born John Harrington)
Hepworth, David 631–32: at Live Aid 562, 565; quoted 244, 292–93, 341, 342, 375–77, 383, 565; *See also Smash Hits* (magazine)
Hill, Chris 69
hip hop 397, 404, 405, 490, 587; *See also* Afrika Bambaataa (born Lance Taylor)
Hodgson, Godfrey 514–15
Hogan, David 483
Holland, Jools 470, 599; *See also The Tube* (TV show)
Holleran, Andrew, *Dancer from the Dance* 208–9
homophobia 182, 208, 306, 484–85, 580, 596
Horn, Trevor 632: quoted 60, 116–17, 203–4, 367, 368–69, 370–71, 443–44, 529, 533, 534–35; works with Malcolm McLaren 443–44; ZTT Records 527, 528, 529, 534; *See also* ABC; Buggles; Dollar; Frankie Goes to Hollywood; Spandau Ballet; Yes
Horton, Matthew 458–59, 632
Howe, Steve 531
Human League: appear on *Solid Gold* (US) 321–22; beginnings 97, 160–61, 201–2, 316; gigs (Fulham Greyhound (1978) 161–62; Marquee Club (1978) 161); influence of 331; influences 160, 161, 200, 586; look 318–20, 321; 'manifesto' 161; new line-up 317, 318, 320–21, 322, 323; records ('4JG' 200; 'Being Boiled' 159, 160–61, 164; *Dare!* 318, 321, 322, 323, 383; 'Don't You Want Me' 318, 322–23; *Hysteria* 523; '(Keep Feeling) Fascination' 424–25; 'Love Action (I Believe in Love) 318; 'Mirror Man' 321; *Reproduction* 200, 316, 324; 'The Sound of the Crowd' 318; 'Sound of the Crowd' 436; *Travelogue* 200, 316, 324, 616); rivalry with Heaven 17 323–24; in *Smash Hits* 376, 377; sound 200, 317, 323, 425; tours (1979-1980 201–2; nearly support Talking Heads (1980) 316–17); US success 291, 321–22, 425; videos ('Don't You Want Me' 319; '(Keep Feeling) Fascination' 424–25); *See also* Burden, Ian; Callis, Jo; Catherall, Joanne; Marsh, Ian Craig; Oakey, Phil; Rushent, Martin; Sulley, Susan Ann (previously Susanne); Ware, Martyn
Humphreys, Paul 57–58, 166–67, 199–200, 421–22, 612–13, 632; *See also* Orchestral Manoeuvres in the Dark
Hunter-Tilney, Ludovic 288, 289
Hütter, Ralf 53–56, 127, 632; *See also* Kraftwerk
Hynde, Chrissie 115–16, 632; *See also* Moors Murderers (band); Pretenders

i-D (magazine) 12–13, 90, 214, 266–67, 268–71, 272–77, 286, 287, 538, 600; *See also* Jones, Terry
Idol, Billy 70, 71, 78: gig, Roxy (1976) 92; haunts 49, 78, 93, 136, 182, 544; personality 123; *See also* Bromley Contingent
Iggy Pop, tour, *Soldier* (1980) 202
The Image (magazine) 170
Imagination, 'Just an Illusion' 436
Indeep, 'Last Night a DJ Saved My Life' 403–4
Interview (magazine) 269
Irish troubles: 1974 152; 1975 7; 1982 351; 1984 (IRA Brighton bombing) 517; peace process (later) 362

Jackson, Michael: attends Soft Cell show 546; and MTV 382–83; Neverland 381; records ('Beat It' 382; 'Billie Jean' 381, 382, 383; 'Don't Stop 'Til You Get Enough' 381; 'The Girl Is Mine' 382; 'Human Nature' 382; 'Off the Wall' 381; 'P.Y.T. (Pretty Young Thing)' 382; 'Rock With You' 381; 'Thriller' 382; *'Thriller'* 383; *Thriller* 382; 'Wanna Be Startin' Somethin'' 381, 382); videos 382 ('Thriller' 449)
Jagger, Bianca 39, 293

Jagger, Chris 597
Jagger, Mick 39: haunts 397, 598; lifestyle 401; in *Ritz* (magazine) 462
The Jam: disband in 1982 425–26; gigs (100 Club (1977) 95–96; Roxy (1977) 118; violence at 425–26); records 96 ('All Around the World' 96; 'Away from the Numbers' 96; 'A Bomb in Wardour Street' 97; 'In the City' 96; 'Down in the Tube Station at Midnight' 97; 'The Modern World' 96; 'Sounds from the Street' 97);*See also* Weller, Paul
James, Clive 173
Japan (band): gig, Hammersmith Odeon (1982) 419–20; Japanese fans 418–19; look 417, 418, 419; records (*Adolescent Sex* 418–19; 'Don't Rain on My Parade' 418; 'European Son' 615; 'Ghosts' 419; *Tin Drum* 419); sound 417, 419, 615; split 590; *See also* Sylvian, David
Jarman, Derek 17
Jay, Norman (born Norman Bernard Joseph) 632: haunts 81; quoted 81–82, 337, 401–2, 441, 584
John, Elton *See* Elton John (born Reg Dwight)
Johnson, David 632: haunts 180–81; quoted 180–81, 216–17, 218–20, 470
Johnson, Holly 529–30, 532, 533; *See also* Frankie Goes to Hollywood
Johnson, Wilma 351, 352–53, 354, 587, 632; *See also* Neo Naturists
Johnston, Steve 90, 125, 140
Jones, Duncan 408–9
Jones, Grace 632: haunts 349, 350, 397; look 363–64, 365; personality 364–65, 397; quoted 364, 365, 581; records ('I've Seen that Face Before (Libertango)' 615; *Nightclubbing* 364; 'Slave to the Rhythm' 533); sound 364, 365, 615
Jones, Jonathan 617
Jones, Mick 128, 632: quoted 72, 73; *See also* The Clash
Jones, Stephen 632: early life and career 25, 88; Endell Street shop 185, 624; haunts 3, 87, 177, 182, 185; lifestyle 91; look 86–87, 148; quoted 25, 65, 86–87, 177–78, 183, 185, 277, 293, 416, 623–25; swears on TV 93; *See also* Blitz Kids
Jones, Terry 267, 268, 270–71, 272, 273, 274, 434, 632quoted 90, 125, 140–41, 271, 272, 275–77; *See also i-D* (magazine)
Jones, Tom 45, 599
Jordan 79, 83, 86, 462
Joy Division: gig, Futurama festival (1979) 231, 234; influence of 370; records ('Love Will Tear Us Apart' 370; 'She's Lost Control' 455; *Unknown Pleasures* 456); UK critical reception 344; *See also* Morris, Stephen; New Order; Sumner, Bernard
Jubilee boat trip (1977) 104–7
Julia, Princess: *See* Princess Julia (born Julia Fodor)

Kamen, Barry 512
Kamen, Nick 511, 512; *See also* Buffalo movement
Keeble, John 448; *See also* Spandau Ballet
Kelly, Ben 632: Jubilee boat trip 107–8; quoted 61, 91, 106–7, 410–13, 619–20; *See also* Haçienda (club)
Kemp, Gary 632: haunts 120, 135–37, 140, 143, 599; look 119–20, 137, 582; personality 292; quoted 74–75, 92, 119–20, 135–37, 140, 214–15, 216, 218, 265, 314, 363, 378, 431, 467–68, 481, 552–54, 556–57, 562–63, 564, 569, 596, 605, 606, 610; tour, Red Wedge (1986) 602; *See also* Makers; Spandau Ballet
Kemp, Martin 216–17; *See also* Spandau Ballet
Kent, Nick 29, 95
Kerr, Jim 447, 565, 581–82, 632; *See also* Simple Minds
Kiedis, Anthony 400
Kinnock, Neil 601, 602, 605–6 ;*See also* Red Wedge (pressure group)
Klein + MBO, 'Dirty Talk' 458–59
Kleinman, Danny 63–64; *See also* Bazooka Joe
Korg synthesizers 163, 337; *See also* synthesizers
Kraftwerk: appear on *Tomorrow's World* 53; haunts 175–76; influence of 56–57, 157, 165, 193, 199, 203, 204, 404, 429, 459, 587, 613, 616; influences 300; look 53, 156; records ('Airwaves' 157; 'Autobahn' 56–57, 58, 157, 158; *Autobahn* 52, 53, 157, 158; 'Computer World' 157; *Computer World* 356; 'Europe Endless' 157, 613–14; 'Kometenmelodie 2' 157, 158; *Man-Machine* 130; *The Man-Machine* 156–57, 158; 'The Model' 158; 'Neon Lights' 157; *Radio-Activity* 157, 158, 613; 'Showroom Dummies' 157, 158; 'Spacelab' 157; *Trans-Europe Express* 129, 158, 356, 613–14; 'Uranium' 459); sound 53–54, 55–56, 157, 158, 176, 613; tour, 1975 56, 58; *See also* Flür, Wolfgang; Hütter, Ralf

Labovitch, Carey 267, 632: quoted 284–86, 599–600; *See also Blitz* (magazine)

Lacy Lady (club): artists (The Clash 333; The Damned 69); clientele 41, 47, 51, 68–70, 81, 120, 142
Lambert, Kit 135
Le Beat Route (club): clientele 349–50, 363, 392, 393, 406, 491, 496, 553; door policy 349–50
Le Bon, Simon 632: haunts 189, 599; look 257, 259; quoted 151–52, 338, 339, 433, 450–52, 583; yachting accident 583–84; *See also* Duran Duran
Le Kilt (club) 305
Leer, Thomas 164: records (*The Bridge* 164; 'Private Plane'/'International' 163–64, 235)
Lennon, John 309; *See also* Beatles
Lennox, Annie 475–76, 632; *See also* Eurythmics; Tourists
Letts, Don 97, 118, 633
Lime, 'You Love' 404
Limelight (club) 543–44
Linard, Stephen: haunts 147, 177, 187; lifestyle 147; look 187, 218; personality 211
LinnDrum 417, 505, 529, 589Linn 2 530; *See also* drum machines
Litchfield, David 167, 170, 173
Live Aid 559–73; *See also* Geldof, Bob; Goldsmith, Harvey
Logan, Andrew 4, 71, 176
Logan, Nick 266–67, 277, 278, 279, 280, 292, 633: haunts 595; influences 281; quoted 280–82, 287, 343–44, 416, 461–62, 510; *See also* NME (New Musical Express) (magazine); *The Face* (magazine)
London (band) 89–90: 'Everyone's a Winner' 89; *See also* Moss, Jon; Napier-Bell, Simon; Regan, Riff
Louise's (club) 77–78, 80–81: ambience/décor 120; clientele 77–81, 87, 92, 118, 120
Lowe, Chris 13; *See also* Pet Shop Boys
LSE (London School of Economics), students and alumni 142, 143, 191, 287
Lufthansa Terminal, 'Nice Video, Shame About the Song' 315
Lwin, Annabella (born Myant Myant Aye) 243, 247, 248, 633: quoted 251; *See also* Bow Wow Wow
Lydon, John (Johnny Rotten) 61, 633: haunts 78, 118; lifestyle 78, 128–29; look 63, 76; quoted 29, 69–70, 330, 444, 493, 535; *See also* Public Image Limited; Sex Pistols

M (band), 'Pop Muzik' 97
MacGowan, Shane 407
Mackay, Andy 27–28, 31, 38; *See also* Roxy Music
Macrae, Bill 464; *See also* Seona Dancing
Madness: tour, Red Wedge (1986) 602; *See also* 2-Tone (music genre)
Madonna (born Madonna Louise Ciccone) 633: early life 538; gigs, Camden Palace (1983) 394; haunts 407, 544, 599; in *i-D* 274, 538; look 537, 538; personality 537–38; quoted 537, 538; records ('Angel' 588; 'Borderline' 537; 'Crazy for You' 588; 'Dress You Up' 588; 'Gambler' 588; 'Into the Groove' 588; 'Holiday' 537, 538, 588; 'Lucky Star' 537, 538; 'Material Girl' 588)
Makers 92; *See also* Kemp, Gary
make-up: 1974 21; 1975 47; 1976 78, 83, 87; 1977 113; 1979 5, 350; 1980 247, 289, 305–6; 1982 382; 1983 467; Adam Ant 244, 246, 250; to age oneself 47, 50; Boy George (and fans) 47, 78, 83, 289, 440; David Bowie (and fans) 21, 299
Mallett, David 297–98, 633
Mandela, Nelson 555–56
Manilow, Barry, UK tour (1982) 403
Marcus, Greil 313
Marilyn 439: haunts 177, 293; lifestyle 617; look 482; quoted 293
Marsh, Ian Craig: *See also* British Electric Foundation; Heaven 17; Human League
Matlock, Glen 61, 63, 97, 127, 146; *See also* Rich Kids; Sex Pistols
maximalism 607
Mayhem Studios (Toyah Willcox) 305, 347
Maze, 'Twilight' 494
McCluskey, Andy 633: influences 56–57; quoted 56–57, 101, 164–65, 198–99, 348, 611–12; *See also* Orchestral Manoeuvres in the Dark
McDonald, Jock 306
McDowell, Al 140
McLaren, Malcolm 633: career 43–44, 46–47, 444, 488; early life and career 103, 249, 250; and 'French Soho' 45; *The Great Rock'n'Roll Swindle* (film) 486–87; haunts 6, 45, 78, 80, 92, 102; Jubilee boat trip 105, 106, 107; King's Road shop 40, 43–44, 47, 48, 50, 51, 60–61, 66, 71, 85, 86, 91, 112, 113, 114, 134, 138, 247, 255; look 6, 62; personality 45, 46, 102–3, 246, 248, 289, 444; quoted 42, 44, 45, 46–47, 50, 60, 61, 76, 103, 128, 175, 245–46, 247–48, 454, 482, 485–86, 487–88; records ('Buffalo Gals' (with the World Famous Supreme Team) 443–44; *Duck Rock* 443–44; *Fans* 485–86, 487–88); relationship with sex 246, 247–49, 250; Union Jack

obsession 486; works at CBS Films 488; works with Adam Ant (and steals his band) 243, 245–46, 249, 251–52; works with Sex Pistols 62, 76, 246, 247, 249; *See also* Bow Wow Wow; *Chicken* (magazine); Sex Pistols
Melody Maker (magazine): 1976 86; 1978 160; 1979 223; 1983 500, 522; 1984 522
Memphis style 312–13
Merchant, Stephen 466–67; *See also Extras* (TV show)
Mercury, Freddie 567, 568, 598, 618; *See also* Queen
Michael, George (born Georgios Kyriacos Panayiotou) 633: early life 388, 391–92, 393; experience of fame 520–21, 523–24, 525, 592, 593–94; goes solo 479, 524–26; haunts 349, 363, 397, 406, 407, 593–94; lifestyle 519; at Live Aid 569–70; look 391–92, 393, 525, 526, 593; personality 391, 477, 478, 479, 483, 519–21, 523–24, 592, 594; quoted 390–91, 393, 479, 518–19, 520, 523–24, 569–70, 591–92, 593–94; records ('Careless Whisper' 389, 477, 524; *Faith* 523, 593); sexuality 521, 522, 523–24, 593, 595; sound 478, 479; video, 'Careless Whisper' 524–25; works with Elton John 569–70; *See also* Wham!
Middle East (developments in 1985) 575
Midnight (magazine) 167, 269
Miller, Daniel 633: quoted 59–60, 89, 119, 162–63, 260–61, 325, 326–27, 328, 587; signs Depeche Mode with Mute Records 261, 325–26; *See also* The Normal; Silicon Teens
miners' strikes 378, 514–16, 517, 573
misogyny 79–80, 155, 201, 225, 309, 387, 475, 537; *See also* Neo Naturists
Modern Drugs (fanzine) 97
The Modern World (fanzine) 383; *See also* Crowley, Gary
money culture 288
Moog synthesizers 55–56, 109, 158, 226, 457, 609; *See also* synthesizers
Moors Murderers (band) 114–16, 138: 'Free Hindley' 115; *See also* Hynde, Chrissie; Soo Catwoman; Strange, Steve (born John Harrington)
Morgan, Jamie 510–11, 633; *See also* Buffalo movement
Morley, Paul 633: quoted 338, 378–81, 416, 532–33, 534; works at ZTT Records 527, 534; *See also Out There* (fanzine)
Moroder, Giorgio: 'The Chase' 436; personality 309; quoted 108, 109–10; *See also* Blondie; Summer, Donna
Morris, Stephen 457, 623; *See also* Joy Division; New Order
Morrissey (Steven Patrick Morrissey) 446
Moss, Jon 89–90, 441, 634: lifestyle 485; quoted 468, 483–84; relationship with Boy George 440, 441, 468, 485, 619; *See also* Culture Club; London (band)
Mossman, Kate 261–62, 634
Moyet, Alison (born Geneviève Alison Jane Moyet) 634: early life and career 98–100, 261–62, 327, 328–29; experience of fame 422, 423, 581; haunts 41, 329; influences 99; look 422; personality 327, 544–45, 581; quoted 98–100, 328–30, 422, 423, 544–45, 581; records (*Alf* 544; 'Love Resurrection' 436); UK critical reception 422, 423; *See also* Yazoo
MTV: 1981 311–14, 315, 449; 1983 439, 447–48, 472, 474, 476; 1984 540–41, 549
Mud Club (club) 406
Munn, Eric 381
Murray, Charles Shaar 405

Nag's Head (music venue) 87, 96
Napier-Bell, Simon 594, 634: quoted 89–90, 215–16, 339, 382–83, 390, 392–93, 417–19, 419–20, 441, 476, 478, 479–80, 522, 524–25, 525–26, 590–91, 595, 611; works with Japan 417–19; works with Wham! 391, 478, 522, 590–92; *See also* London (band)
Neo Naturists 351–54; *See also* Binnie, Christine and Jennifer; Johnson, Wilma; Perry, Grayson
Neu! 57, 193, 199, 204
New, Steve 122, 137–38; *See also* Rich Kids
New Order: beginnings (from Joy Division) 455; equipment (and problems with) 455–58, 459; gig, Toronto (1981) (with Simple Minds) 456; influences 458–59; lifestyle 434–35; look 457; records ('586' 459; 'Blue Monday' 457–59; 'Everything's Gone Green' 333, 459); sound 455, 457–58, 459; tour, America (1981) 455–56; *See also* Haçienda (club); Morris, Stephen; Sumner, Bernard
New Romantics: 1980 181, 242, 257, 260, 266, 283, 290–91, 300, 307; 1981 323, 333, 342, 343–44, 355; 1982 371–72, 380, 381; 1983 436–37, 467; 1984 489; artists 18; ethos 10, 242, 275, 290–91, 323, 352, 381, 441; origins 3, 10, 76, 78, 127, 128, 140, 141–42, 149, 292–93, 610
New Sounds New Styles (magazine) 345
New Style (magazine) 167, 169–70, 269
Newton, Helmut 414

NME (*New Musical Express*) (magazine): 1973 21; 1975 29, 35; 1976 71, 75, 86; 1977 96, 101, 106, 120; 1978 128, 129, 135, 162, 163–64, 167; 1979 212, 215, 221; 1980 282, 286, 290; 1981 324, 332, 337, 338–39, 341–42, 344; 1982 371, 386, 388, 402; 1984 508, 522, 546; 1985 610; *See also* Baker, Danny; Burchill, Julie; Crowley, Gary; Ellen, Mark; Kent, Nick; Logan, Nick; Morley, Paul; Murray, Charles Shaar; Parsons, Tony; Spencer, Neil
The Normal 129: influence of 203, 325; influences 162; 'T.V.O.D.'/'Warm Leatherette' 162–63, 164, 166, 235, 436; *See also* Miller, Daniel
Norman, Philip 571
northern soul 333–34, 402
nostalgie de la boue 395
nuclear threat 573, 574, 575–76
Numan, Gary (born Gary Anthony James Webb) 634: appears on *Swap Shop* 229–30; early life and career 59, 100–101; experience of fame 223–24, 301–2, 584–85; haunts 296; image 228; influence of 225, 420; influences 220, 227–28, 300; look 221, 226; personality 59, 223–24, 229–30; quoted 59, 100–101, 221–24, 227–28, 229, 301–2, 422–23, 584–85; records ('Cars' 223, 226, 228, 320; *I, Assassin* 422; 'M.E.' 226; 'Metal' 226; *The Pleasure Principle* 221; *The Pleasure Principle* 226); sees a ghost 228; in *Smash Hits* 377; sound 221–22, 226; *See also* Tubeway Army
Nuttall, Jeff 90–91

Oakey, Phil: early life and career 159–60; influences 316; look 159, 160, 311, 316, 319; quoted 162, 200, 201–2, 311, 316, 319, 322, 523; *See also* Human League
Oates, John 541, 543, 544, 634; *See also* Hall & Oates
Oberheim drum machines 457–58; *See also* drum machines
O'Connor, Hazel 258
O'Connor, Karen 634: look 93; quoted 92–93, 177
O'Donnell, Ollie 634
O'Donnell, Ollie (born John O'Donnell) 634: haunts 83, 84, 92, 137, 178, 179–80; look 49, 83; quoted 39–40, 47, 49, 83–85, 88–89, 92, 137, 179–80, 349–50, 400–401, 414, 620; *See also* Wag (club) (previously Whiskey-A-Go-Go)
O'Dowd, George 78, 141
Orchestral Manoeuvres in the Dark: appear on *Top of the Pops* 611; beginnings 57–58, 164–65, 166, 199–200; gig, Futurama festival (1979) 234; influence of 199; influences 58, 165, 193, 199; look 166–67; records (*Architecture & Morality* 421; *Dazzle Ships* 421; 'Electricity' 165, 166, 199; 'Enola Gay' 199, 611; 'Joan of Arc' 199; 'Maid or Orleans' 611; 'Messages' 199; 'Souvenir' 199); in *Smash Hits* 377; sound 165, 199, 348, 421, 590, 611; tour, US (1985) 612; *See also* Humphreys, Paul; McCluskey, Andy
O'Regan, Denis 453
Orzabal, Roland 420; *See also* Tears for Fears
Out There (fanzine) 98

Padgham, Hugh 503
Page, Betty (born Beverley Glick) 260, 634: quoted 257, 464, 464–65
Palmer, Robert, 'Addicted to Love' 314
Parker, Jan 69, 634
Parkin, Sophie 297
Parsons, Tony 634: haunts 97, 595; Jubilee boat trip 106; quoted 106, 128–29, 519, 520
payola system (US) 312
Perry, Grayson 354, 397; *See also* Neo Naturists
Pet Shop Boys: beginnings 337, 374–75; as a 'gay band' 373; haunts 407; records ('Being Boring' 636; 'Opportunities (Let's Make Lots of Money)' 506; 'Paninaro' 12–13); in *Smash Hits* 377; sound 374–75; *See also* Lowe, Chris; Tennant, Neil
Petri, Ray 508–10, 511–13, 617: quoted 509–10, 511–12, 513; works with *Arena* magazine 513; works with David Bowie 512–13; *See also* Buffalo movement
Peyton, Oliver 189, 634
Photons 137, 138; *See also* Strange, Steve (born John Harrington)
Pigbag 363
Pirroni, Marco 35, 634: early life 21; influences 28–29; look 21, 63; quoted 21, 29, 62–63, 250–51, 252, 253, 295, 396, 497, 569, 595, 623; *See also* Adam and the Ants
Playground (club) 618, 619
Plaza (shop) 255, 306–7; *See also* Price, Antony
Polaris, Andy 634: early life and career 41–42, 134; haunts 41, 134, 136, 141; influences 348; look 136, 347; quoted 41–42, 70, 134, 348, 580; *See also* Animal Nightlife
The Police: conspiracy theories 105; influences 547; look 547–48; records (Band Aid, 'Do They Know It's Christmas?' 549, 550–55, 556; *Ghost in the Machine* 547–48;

Synchronicity 547 (footnote)); sound 547; *See also* Sting (born Gordon Sumner)
political and social backdrop (UK): 1970s 1, 7–9, 13, 152, 161, 202, 216, 232, 347, 514, 623–24; 1980 202–3; 1980s (in general) 12–14, 15–18, 549–50, 626; 1981 356–57, 359–62; 1982 351, 395, 429–31; 1983 459–61; 1984 514–17; 1985 573–74, 576, 600–601; 1985-1987 601–6; *See also* 'designer' (adjective and lifestyle); miners' strikes; Thatcher, Margaret; Thatcherism; unemployment
Poly Styrene (born Marianne Joan Elliott-Said) 124, 348; *See also* X-Ray Spex
'poseurs' 123–24, 180, 224, 362
post-punk ideologies 225
Prefab Sprout, Red Wedge tour (1986) 602
Pretenders: 'Brass in Pocket' 241; *See also* Hynde, Chrissie
Price, Antony 29, 634: quoted 30–31, 32, 33, 42–43, 239, 255, 379; works with Bananarama 386; works with Duran Duran 256, 377, 379; works with Roxy Music 20, 29, 30–31, 32, 33, 37, 38, 42–43; *See also* Plaza (shop)
Price, Simon 358–59
Prince (born Prince Rogers Nelson) 634–35: appears on *The Tube* 471; early life 539; experience of fame 540; film, *Purple Rain* 540; haunts 397; look 540; personality 540; quoted 539, 540; records (*Around the World in a Day* 540; *Dirty Mind* 539; *Purple Rain* 540); sound 540
Prince Charles *See* Charles, Prince of Wales
Princess Diana *See* Diana, Princess of Wales
Princess Julia (born Julia Fodor) 635: early life 49; haunts 49, 118, 139–40; look 49–50, 140, 148; personality 86; quoted 49–50, 86, 118, 139–40, 623; works at Blitz 180; *See also* Blitz Kids
Public Image Limited 140–41, 234; *See also* Lydon, John (Johnny Rotten); Wobble, Jah
punk: 1976 70, 73, 76–77, 79, 81–82, 83, 86, 87, 89, 93–94; 1977 95–97, 99, 100, 101, 104, 108, 110, 112–13, 119, 120, 124; 1978 127–29, 133, 137; 1979 194; 1980 282, 309; 1981 341–42; androgyny 86, 104; demise 74, 93–94, 96, 109, 119, 127, 133, 140, 142, 152, 282–83, 289, 350, 610; ethos 45, 99, 103–4, 130, 148, 188, 224, 288; look 48, 51, 61, 65–66, 70, 76–77, 99, 103–4, 106, 112–13, 137, 148, 151; origins 9, 45, 65; and violence 73, 75–76, 99, 102, 107, 112–113, 116, 117, 120, 128–29; *See also* The Clash; Idol, Billy; London (band); Sex Pistols; Siouxsie Sioux (born Susan Janet Ballion); Soo Catwoman
Punk (magazine) 269
Pursey, Jimmy 376; *See also* Sham 69
PX (shop) 136–37, 139, 141, 142–43, 148, 180, 185

Queen: gig, Manchester Free Trade Hall (1975) 34; at Live Aid 566, 567–68, 609; records ('Bohemian Rhapsody' 7; 'Killer Queen' 34, 568; *A Night at the Opera* 34; 'Seven Seas of Rye' 568; *Sheer Heart Attack* 34); sound 568; *See also* Mercury, Freddie
'Quiet Storm' radio programming (US) 501–2

racism and racial tension 144, 208, 210, 276, 358, 360, 362, 382–83, 490, 494, 580: colour bars 400, 402, 405–6; *See also* black models
Rainbow Warrior, sinking of 574
Ralph West Halls of Residence 145–47
Red Hot Chili Peppers 400
Red Wedge (pressure group) 601–5, 606–7
The Redskins, Red Wedge (1986) 602
Reed, Lou, 'Berlin' 614
Regan, Riff 89–90; *See also* London (band)
Reid, Jamie 102
remixes 139, 370–71, 505, 530, 535
Rental, Robert 163: *The Bridge* 164
Reynolds, Simon 108, 192
Rhodes, Bernie 97, 289
Rhodes, Nick (born Nicholas James Bates) 635: haunts 189, 599; influences 151; look 151, 232, 257, 378; quoted 151, 152–54, 256, 259, 306, 379, 435, 447, 448, 452, 453, 454, 473, 553; *See also* Duran Duran
Rich Kids 122–23, 204–6: 'Rich Kids' 123; *See also* Egan, Rusty; Matlock, Glen; New, Steve; Ure, Midge
Richards, Keith 397
Ridgeley, Andrew 635: early life 388, 391–92; haunts 349, 407; lifestyle 479; at Live Aid 569; look 393; personality 391, 477, 519–20, 522, 594; quoted 232–33, 389–90, 392, 519–21, 592–93, 594; *See also* Wham!
Rimmer, Dave 52, 77–78, 113–14, 123, 355, 635
riots: 1981 338, 358, 359–61, 362, 600–601; 1985 600–601; *See also* violence
Ritz (club) 536
Ritz (magazine) 167, 169–70, 171–74, 269, 462–63; *See also* Bailey, David; Litchfield, David
Robinson, Tom 604
Rock Against Racism (RAR) 603
Rock America 346
The Rocky Horror Show 6, 83, 84, 167, 181, 586

Roland drum machines 235, 335, 404, 505; *See also* drum machines
Roland synthesizers 163, 421, 457, 589; *See also* synthesizers
Rolling Stone (magazine) 472
Rolling Stones: look 45; 'Start Me Up' 503–4
Ross, Diana, 'Love Hangover' 41, 78
Rotten, Johnny *See* Lydon, John (Johnny Rotten)
Roxy (club) (previously Chaguaramas): ambience/décor 92–93; artists 92, 118; opening 92, 97; *See also* Chaguaramas (club) (later Roxy)
Roxy Music: appear on *The Old Grey Whistle Test* 239; disband in 1983 578–79; influence of 9, 20, 23, 26, 40, 120, 199, 239, 250–51, 256, 385, 429, 494, 594; influences 27, 30; look 25–26, 27–28, 31, 32, 42–43; records ('2HB' 29, 200; 'Avalon' 494; *Avalon* 31, 578; 'Both Ends Burning' 9; *Country Life* 25–26; 'Dance Away' 578; 'Do the Strand' 28; *Flesh and Blood* 256; 'Ladytron' 239; 'Let's Stick Together' 31; 'Love Is the Drug' 579; 'Love is the Drug' 9, 20; 'The Main Thing' 494; 'Mother of Pearl' 577–78; 'Nightingale' 31; 'Pyjamarama' 28, 385; *Roxy Music* 26, 30; 'Same Old Scene' 256; 'Sentimental Fool' 31; 'She Sells' 31; 'Siren' 32; *Siren* 9, 20, 31–32; 'Song for Europe' 579; 'A Song for Europe' 614; *Stranded* 31, 34, 577–78; 'Street Life' 97; 'Virginia Plain' 28, 31, 37; *For Your Pleasure* 31); sound 20, 26–27, 31–32, 256, 494, 578; tours (*Avalon* (1982-1983) 579; *Country Life* (1974-75) 31; *Manifesto* (1979) 578; *Siren* (1975) 20, 31, 34–35, 42); *See also* Eno, Brian; Ferry, Bryan; Mackay, Andy
Rum Runner (club) 152, 153, 232: ambience/décor 257; clientele 186, 189, 257; *See also* Berrow, Michael and Paul
'rumour bands' 219, 265, 437
Ruocco, Chris 477
Rushent, Martin 321; *See also* Human League
Rutherford, Paul: personality 533; quoted 529, 530, 531, 533; *See also* Frankie Goes to Hollywood

Sade (band): appear on *Top of the Pops* 490; beginnings 406, 480, 491; as 'designer' pop group 500; haunts 363; influences 490, 491, 492, 502, 507; at Live Aid 567; look 490; records ('Cry Me a River' 496; *Diamond Life* 491, 492, 494, 497, 501, 626; 'Hang on to Your Love' 501; *Love Deluxe* 626; 'Smooth Operator' 501; *Soldier of Love* 626; 'Why Can't We Live Together' 496, 501; 'Your Love Is King' 501); sound 489, 491–92, 493, 494, 496, 507, 625–26; tour, Red Wedge (1986) 602; UK critical reception 500, 501, 507; US success 491, 496, 501–2, 590, 626; *See also* Denman, Paul Spencer; Hale, Andrew
Sade (born Helen Folasade Adu) (singer) 464, 627: early life 489–90, 492, 494; experience of fame 502; haunts 5; influences 490, 492; look 500–501, 506, 508; personality 493, 494–95, 500–501, 502; quoted 489–90, 491, 492, 494–95, 506–7; *See also* Sade (band)
Salewicz, Chris 244–45, 635
Sallon, Philip 80, 82, 134: haunts 78, 82, 118, 141; influences 52; look 75, 80, 141; 'Summer Dream' 439
sampling 404, 529, 530
Sandall, Robert 489, 635
Saturday Night Fever 130–31, 232
Savage, Jon (born Jonathan Malcolm Sage) 635: haunts 598; Jubilee boat trip 105; quoted 17, 67, 96, 109, 110, 129, 223, 264–65, 286, 299, 332–33, 436–37, 486–87
Scargill, Arthur 514, 515, 517, 518–19; *See also* miners' strikes
science fiction, influence of 161, 200, 201, 202, 203–4, 226, 227–28, 237, 411; *See also* electronic music; Futurama festival (1979)
Scott, Robin 97
scratching 397, 404, 443–44
Seditionaries (shop) *See* SEX (shop) (later Seditionaries)
The Selecter 357, 358; *See also* 2-Tone (music genre); Black, Pauline
Seona Dancing 464–65, 467: 'More to Lose' 464; *See also* Gervais, Ricky; Macrae, Bill
Sewel, Kerry 168
SEX (shop) (later Seditionaries) 40, 43-44, 47, 48, 50, 51, 60-61, 66, 71, 85, 86, 91, 112, 113, 114, 134, 138, 247, 255; *See also* Jordan; McLaren, Malcolm
Sex Pistols: beginnings 60, 61, 62, 64–65, 74, 81, 89; gigs (Lesser Free Trade Hall (1976) 89; Middlesbrough Town Hall (1976) 81; Nashville Rooms (1976) 75–76; Screen on the Green (1976) 74–75; St Martins (1975) 9, 63, 64–66; violence at 75–76); *The Great Rock'n'Roll Swindle* (film) 486–87; haunts 102; influence of 63, 66, 74, 75, 88, 89, 256, 264, 493; look 63, 75, 76; records ('Anarchy'

493; 'God Save the Queen' 108; *Never Mind the Bollocks, Here's the Sex Pistols* 85; 'Pretty Vacant' 116); tour, *Anarchy* (1976) 91; TV appearances (*So It Goes* 91, 493; *Today* 93–94); *See also* Lydon, John (Johnny Rotten); Matlock, Glen; McLaren, Malcolm
Sham 69 128, 129; *See also* Pursey, Jimmy
Sharkey, Alix (born Alexander Campbell) 635: quoted 397–99, 403, 405–6
Sheffield, Rob 420–21
Sheldrick, Lee 147
Silicon Teens 163, 325, 436; *See also* Miller, Daniel
Simonon, Paul 72–74, 635; *See also* The Clash
Simple Minds: gigs (Futurama festival (1979) 234; Toronto (1981) (with New Order) 456); 'Life in a Day' 205; *See also* Kerr, Jim
Siouxsie and the Banshees: are supportive of Human League 201–2; beginnings 78, 79; gig, Vortex (1978) 134; gigs (Futurama festival (1979) 231; Roxy (1977) 250); haunts 102; sound 428, 429; *See also* Siouxsie Sioux (born Susan Janet Ballion)
Siouxsie Sioux (born Susan Janet Ballion) 635: early life 35, 36; haunts 36, 49, 117, 180; influence of 428; influences 429; look 36, 78–79, 117, 428, 429; personality 36; sound 428; *See also* Bromley Contingent; Siouxsie and the Banshees
Slik 62, 308: appear on *Top of the Pops* 67, 68; changing fortunes 67–68; records ('Forever and Ever' 67–68; 'Requiem' 68); *See also* Ure, Midge
Smash Hits (magazine): 1981 339–43; 1982 371–73, 375–77, 386, 388; 1983 437; 1984 526; 1985 525; Neil Tennant works at 342, 372, 374, 375–76, 377, 452, 572–73; office culture 375–76; photo captions 372; *See also* Hepworth, David
Smith, Graham 143, 148, 191, 212; *See also* Le Kilt (club); St Moritz (club)
Smith, Paul 497, 506, 635Convent Garden shop 190; quoted 189–90
Smith, Terry 195–97, 635
The Smiths, Red Wedge tour (1986) 602
Soft Cell 627: appear on *Top of the Pops* 332, 335, 381; beginnings 238–39, 331–32; gigs (Croc's (1981) 332; Futurama festival (1979) 231, 234); influences 193, 331, 333–34, 586; lifestyle 546; records ('Bedsitter' 332, 335, 336–37, 437; 'Memorabilia' 331; 'Tainted Love' 332, 334, 335, 546; 'Torch' 436); rivalry with Spandau Ballet 372; sound 335; tour, US (1984) 546;*See also* Almond, Marc (born Peter Mark Sinclair Almond); Ball, David
Soho Brasserie 595, 596
Sombrero (club): ambience/décor 40, 120; clientele 40, 49, 80, 81, 118, 120, 134
Somerville, Jimmy 446; *See also* Bronski Beat; Red Wedge (pressure group)
Soo Catwoman 78, 114; *See also* Bromley Contingent; Moors Murderers (band)
Soulsonic Force, 'Planet Rock' (with Afrika Bambaataa) 404
Sounds (magazine): 1977 101, 115, 116, 129; 1978 162; 1980 257, 260; 1981 324, 331
South Africa, violence in 575
Spandau Ballet: beginnings 211, 212, 213, 217, 255; 'entrepreneurial zeal' 215, 217; gigs (Blitz (1979) 191, 213, 214; Scala cinema 219); haunts 178, 214, 259, 332, 385, 598; influence of 426, 495–96, 556; influences 265, 300; lifestyle 215, 362–63; look 135, 214, 216–17, 218, 362, 363, 467; records (Band Aid, 'Do They Know It's Christmas?' 549, 550–55, 556; 'Chant No. 1 (We Don't Need This Pressure On)' 362, 363, 426, 467; 'To Cut a Long Story Short' 214, 220; *Diamond* 370; 'The Freeze' 214; 'Instinction' 214, 370–71; *Journeys to Glory* 215–16; 'True' 467, 524, 609; *True* 467–68); rivalry with Duran Duran 340, 371, 372, 375, 449–50, 556; rivalry with Soft Cell 372; as 'rumour band' 219, 265; signing with Chrysalis 219–20; in *Smash Hits* 377; sound 216, 220, 467–68, 556–57, 609; split 590; TV appearances 219, 448; UK critical reception 362–63; US launch 346; US success 291, 346–47; video, 'Chant No. 1 (We Don't Need This Pressure On') 363; working-class roots 214–15, 216; *See also* Dagger, Steve; Hadley, Tony; Horn, Trevor; Keeble, John; Kemp, Gary; Kemp, Martin
Speakeasy (club) 93, 97, 120
Special AKA: 'Free Nelson Mandela' 555–56; *In the Studio* 555; *See also* Dammers, Jerry
The Specials: 'Gangsters' 357; 'Ghost Town' 356, 357, 359, 395, 555, 556; 'A Message to You, Rudy' 357; Rat Race' 357; 'Too Much Too Young' 359; *See also* 2-Tone (music genre); Dammers, Jerry; Hall, Terry
Spencer, Neil 604 *See also* Red Wedge (pressure group)
spitting 75, 76–77, 93, 123, 160, 255
Springsteen, Bruce: *Born to Run* 22; 'Dancing in the Dark' 314

'squinting' at musicians 567–68
St Martin's School of Art: Sex Pistols gig 9, 63, 64–66; students and alumni 43, 44, 46, 63, 65, 86, 87, 102, 138, 140, 143, 144, 145, 148, 168, 169, 185, 198, 207, 238, 268, 275, 351, 352, 480; *See also* art schools; Ralph West Halls of Residence
St Moritz (club) 305
Stafford, Jerry 617
Stanley, Bob 11–12
Status Quo, at Live Aid 566–67
Stein, Chris 155, 308 *See also* Blondie
Stevens, Lauren 476
Stewart, Dave 82, 473–74, 635 *See also* Eurythmics; Tourists
Stewart, Rod: influence of 316, 492; 'Maggie May' 492
Sting (born Gordon Sumner) 635: critical reception 548–49; experience of fame 548–49; haunts 544, 599; look 554; personality 548; quoted 548–49; *See also* The Police
Strange, Richard 81
Strange, Steve (born John Harrington) 636: haunts 78, 93, 118, 137; lifestyle 92, 113–14, 137–38, 415, 616–17, 619–20; look 2, 77, 114, 133, 148, 186, 206, 218, 302, 342, 413, 442; personality 178, 195, 355, 413, 414; quoted 2, 116, 137, 186–87, 197, 207, 294–95, 303–4, 413, 414–15, 619; rides a camel in New York 413–15; *See also* Billy's (club); Blitz (club); Camden Palace (club); Club for Heroes (club); Hell (club); Moors Murderers (band); Photons; Visage
Strummer, Joe 72–73, 146, 352, 384, 397; *See also* The Clash
Stubbs, David 156–57, 291, 323, 424, 636
Style Council: look 426, 427; 'My Ever Changing Moods' 427; sound 426; tour, Red Wedge (1986) 605; videos 426; *See also* Weller, Paul
style culture, criticisms 288
'style magazines' See specific magazines
stylists 508; *See also* Buffalo movement; Petri, Ray
Suicide 231
Sulley, Susan Ann (previously Susanne) 319, 321–22, 425, 636; *See also* Human League
Sullivan, Chris 636: early life 77; haunts 3, 47, 77, 78, 142, 144, 148, 182, 197; look 77, 144, 145, 197; quoted 47, 76–77, 148, 183, 197, 293–94, 305–6, 345, 397, 399–400, 402–3, 408–9, 463; *See also* Blitz Kids; Blue Rondo à la Turk (band); Hell (club); Le Kilt (club); St Moritz (club); Wag (club) (previously Whiskey-A-Go-Go)
Summer, Donna: 'Bad Girls; 209; 'I Feel Love' 108–10, 129, 130, 309; 'I Feel Love' (Patrick Cowley's remix) 505; 'Love to Love You Baby' 60; 'Our Love' 458
Sumner, Bernard 636: early life 454–55; haunts 455; quoted 412, 455–58; *See also* Joy Division; New Order
Sumner, Gordon *See* Sting (born Gordon Sumner)
Sweeney's (club) 329
Sweet, Matthew 364
Swing Out Sister 363
Sylvester: 'Rock the Box' 436; 'You Make Me Feel (Mighty Real)' 129, 208, 233, 459
Sylvian, David: influences 547; look 418, 419; personality 417, 419; quoted 417, 547; records ('Backwater' 547; 'Brilliant Trees' 547; *Brilliant Trees* 546–47; 'Weathered Wall' 547); *See also* Japan (band)
synth duos/groups 193, 224, 234, 260, 321, 326–27, 420–21; *See also* Blancmange; Buggles; Composition of Sound; Depeche Mode; Erasure; Eurythmics; Human League; Orchestral Manoeuvres in the Dark; Pet Shop Boys; Soft Cell; Spandau Ballet; Tears for Fears; Ultravox; Visage; Yazoo
synthesizers: capabilities 122, 221–22, 226, 262, 455; challenges 109, 200, 235; cost 58, 119, 163, 235, 260, 263, 504, 609; early 56; Fairlight 502–3, 529, 589; Korg 163, 337; Moog 55–56, 109, 158, 226, 457, 609; Musicians' Union calls on their banning 403; Roland 163, 421, 457, 589; Wasp (EDP) 263, 473, 504

Taboo (club) 617, 618
Tangerine Dream 35
Taylor, Andy 636: lifestyle 620–21; look 257; quoted 448–49; *See also* Duran Duran
Taylor, John 636: haunts 189; look 257, 375; quoted 256, 339, 453; *See also* Duran Duran
Taylor, Roger 153–54, 258; *See also* Duran Duran
Tears for Fears 420, 588: 'Mad World' 420; *See also* Orzabal, Roland
Temple, Julien 75, 369, 408, 636; *See also* ABC
Tennant, Neil 636: influences 130; quoted 22, 75–76, 106, 130, 220, 314, 335, 337, 374–75, 377, 420, 441–42, 526, 572–73; works at *Smash Hits* 342, 372, 374, 375–76, 377, 452, 572–73; *See also* Pet Shop Boys
Tesler, Simon 282–84, 285–86; *See also Blitz* (magazine)
Thatcher, Margaret: chosen as Conservative Party leader 8; leadership style 16, 203,

361–62, 460; as 'myopic' 460, 516; relationships with other heads of state 460; rhetoric 161, 362, 515–16, 527; as 'too straightlaced' 626; writing of 460; *See also* Falklands War; political and social backdrop (UK)
Thatcherism 16–17, 179, 203, 217, 288–89, 328, 333, 338, 363, 380, 405, 531, 625, 626; *See also* political and social backdrop (UK)
Thomas, David 29
Thompson Twins 482, 534
Thomson, Graeme 31–32
Throbbing Gristle: gig, Centro Iberico (1979) 238; *The Second Annual Report* 162
Tilley, Sue 636
Tony, Fat *See* Fat Tony (born Tony Marnach)
Top of the Pops 496: Adam and the Ants 11, 241, 253, 381; Bananarama 386; Culture Club 289, 374, 381, 441, 482; David Bowie 336, 623; Depeche Mode 325, 326; Frankie Goes to Hollywood 530; Orchestral Manoeuvres in the Dark 611; Sade 490; Slik 67, 68; Slik (1976) 67–68; Tubeway Army 222–23; Wham! 390; Yazoo 422
Tourists 473; *See also* Lennox, Annie; Stewart, Dave
Townshend, Pete 636: haunts 355, 407, 598; quoted 355
The Tube (TV show) 470–71, 527, 528; *See also* Channel 4; Holland, Jools; Yates, Paula
Tubeway Army: appear on *Top of the Pops* 222–23; records ('Are "Friends" Electric?' 220–21, 222–23, 226; *Replicas* 226); *See also* Numan, Gary (born Gary Anthony James Webb)
Turner, Alwyn W. 13–14
Turner, Tina: personality 424; records ('Ball of Confusion' 424; 'Let's Stay Together' 423, 424; *Private Dancer* 424
Tyson, Nicola 636: haunts 120, 141; look 104; quoted 104, 107, 120, 141–42

U2: Band Aid, 'Do They Know It's Christmas?' 554; gig, Greenbelt festival (1980) 264; at Live Aid 562, 609; US success 589–90; *See also* Bono (born Paul David Hewson)
UB40 258
Ultravox: beginnings 58–59; haunts 363, 598; at Live Aid 563, 609; look 416; Midge Ure joins 230, 302; records ('Sleepwalk' 315; *Systems of Romance* (1979) 234; 'Vienna' 302, 315, 614; *Vienna* 315); sound 302, 416, 417; split 590, 609; tour, *Systems of Romance* (1979) 234; UK critical reception 416; videos ('Love's Great Adventure' 450; 'Vienna' 311); *See also* Currie, Billy; Foxx, John (born Dennis Leigh); Ure, Midge
Undertones, 'My Perfect Cousin' 316
unemployment 13, 152, 159, 358, 362, 460, 470, 600 ; *See also* political and social backdrop (UK)
Ure, Midge 636: haunts 6, 136, 141, 599; look 61–62; quoted 61–62, 67–68, 122–23, 204–6, 230, 232, 295, 302, 303, 308, 311, 315, 413–14, 416–17, 449–50, 552, 559, 563, 608–10; *See also* Band Aid, 'Do They Know It's Christmas?'; Rich Kids; Slik; Ultravox; Visage
Usher, Martin 456–57

Valentine Brothers, 'Money's Too Tight to Mention' 395
Valentino, 'I Was Born This Way' 208
Venue (club) 353
Vidal, Gore 172
videos (in general) 313–14, 340; *See also* MTV; *under specific artists/bands*
Village Voice (magazine) 549
violence: clubs 182, 208, 306; gigs 64, 73, 75–76, 113, 117, 128, 129, 358; police 106–7, 485; and punks 73, 75–76, 99, 102, 107, 112–13, 116, 117, 120, 128–29; in South Africa 575; streets 99, 102, 107, 112–13, 128, 263, 361; *See also* football hooliganism; homophobia; Irish troubles; miners' strikes; riots
Visage: beginnings 205–6, 302–3; influences 204–5, 300, 303; look 206; Midge Ure leaves 413–14, 415; records (*The Anvil* 413; *The Anvil* 414–15; 'Fade to Grey' 206, 303; *Visage* 303–4; 'In the Year 2525' 207); sound 205; video, 'Fade to Grey' 206, 207, 303; *See also* Egan, Rusty; Strange, Steve (born John Harrington); Ure, Midge
Visconti, Tony 298–99
Viz (magazine) 167, 169–70, 269
Vogue (magazine) 267, 2761976 90; 1977 125, 268
'Vopping' 211–12

Wag (club) (previously Whiskey-A-Go-Go) 396–98: ambience/décor 397, 405–6, 408; artists 397; Black Market Friday-night slot 405–6; clientele 397, 400, 403, 405, 406, 407–8, 476, 526, 598, 620; door policy 397, 399–400, 400, 402, 405–6; Hector Heathcote DJs at 402; security 401; *See also* O'Donnell,

Ollie; Sullivan, Chris; Whiskey-A-Go-Go (club) (later Wag)
Wagg, Diane 298, 298–99, 636
Wallace, Wyndham 531–32, 636
Ware, Martyn 636–37: early life and career 159–60; quoted 121, 160, 161–62, 201, 323; *See also* British Electric Foundation; Heaven 17; Human League
Warhol, Andy 473
Wasp synthesizers (EDP) 263, 473, 504; *See also* synthesizers
Webb, Iain R. 637: haunts 148–49, 187; influences 149; look 148–49, 187, 305; quoted 110–11, 148–49, 187, 285, 299–300, 305, 306–7; *See also* Blitz Kids
Well Red (magazine) 602; *See also* Red Wedge (pressure group)
Weller, Paul 36, 637: Band Aid, 'Do They Know It's Christmas?' 549, 550–55, 556; influences 426, 427; personality 426–28; quoted 428, 605, 606; *See also* The Jam; Red Wedge (pressure group); Style Council
Wendelbo, Liz 613, 637
Westwood, Vivienne 575, 637: Pirate collection 355, 356, 395–96; quoted 45, 103–4, 113, 356, 395–96, 487; works with Malcolm McLaren 60, 61, 71, 76, 104, 113, 134, 487; works with Sex Pistols 76
Wham!: appear on *Top of the Pops* 390; gig, Royal Festival Hall (miner's strike benefit) (1984) 518, 570; haunts 233, 363, 385–86, 388, 392, 476–77, 526; influences 232–33, 388–89, 594; look 233, 388, 391, 392, 476–77, 523; in *Melody Maker* 522; in *NME* 522; records ('Bad Boys' 392; Band Aid, 'Do They Know It's Christmas?' 549, 550–55, 556; 'Club Tropicana' 363, 389, 392, 477; 'Everything She Wants' 407, 526; *Fantastic* 476; *The Final* 593; 'I'm Your Man' 477, 570; 'Last Christmas' 570; *Make It Big* 523; 'Wake Me Up Before You Go-Go' 523; 'Wham Rap!' 389, 392, 477; 'Young Guns (Go for It)' 389, 390, 392); in *Smash Hits* 377, 525; sound 389; tours (China (1985) 590–92, 595; US (1985) 591); US success 291, 588, 591; videos ('Bad Boys' 390–91; 'Careless Whisper' 478; 'Club Tropicana' 392); *See also* Michael, George (born Georgios Kyriacos Panayiotou); Napier-Bell, Simon; Ridgeley, Andrew
Whiskey-A-Go-Go (club) (later Wag): ambience/décor 398; artists 383, 399; clientele 383, 398–99; *See also* Wag (club) (previously Whiskey-A-Go-Go)
Wilder, Alan 327–28; *See also* Depeche Mode
Willcox, Toyah 637: gig, The Europa, Belfast (1982) 351; look 341, 350; quoted 350–51; in *Smash Hits* 341; *See also* Mayhem Studios (Toyah Willcox)
Williams, Dencil 207, 209–10, 637
Wilson, Tony 164–65, 410: *So It Goes* (TV show) 91; *See also* Haçienda (club)
Winter of Discontent and political aftermath 1, 202–3, 232; *See also* political and social backdrop (UK)
Wintour, Patrick 515
Withers, Simon 134, 135
Wobble, Jah 405
Wolfe, Tom 395, 498–99
Wonder, Stevie 397
Woodward, Keren 637: experience of fame 407; haunts 194–95, 407; look 194; quoted 37, 194–95, 385, 386–87, 407, 578; *See also* Bananarama
Working Week, 'Venceremos (We Will Win)' 508

X-Ray Spex: *Germfree Adolescents* 124; 'I Am a Poseur' 124; *See also* Poly Styrene (born Marianne Joan Elliott-Said)

Yates, Paula 470–71, 550, 552, 553; *See also The Tube* (TV show)
Yazoo 326: appear on *Top of the Pops* 422; records ('Don't Go' 99, 330; 'Only You' 327, 329–30; 'Situation' 330); UK critical reception 422; *See also* Clarke, Vince; Moyet, Alison (born Geneviève Alison Jane Moyet)
Yellow Magic Orchestra 5, 179, 404, 405, 490, 609
Yentob, Alan 102–3, 105, 248–49, 251, 444, 637
Yes 368; *See also* Horn, Trevor
York, Peter (born Peter Wallis) 637: haunts 4, 80, 176, 178, 597; and 'style journalism' 241–42
Young, Hugo 517
Young, Richard 4, 168, 174
yuppies (Young Urban Professionals) (etc.) 242

Zanzibar (club) 596–98
ZG (magazine) 266 (footnote)